THE ANNUAL REGISTER

Vol. 230

ANNUAL REGISTER ADVISORY BOARD

CHAIRMAN

H. V. HODSON

EDITOR

ALAN J. DAY

ASSISTANT EDITOR

VERENA HOFFMAN

JAMES BISHOP
Editor-in-Chief, The Illustrated London News

FRANK E. CLOSE, PhD
Distinguished Professor of Physics, The University of Tennessee

NOMINATED BY
THE BRITISH ASSOCIATION FOR THE ADVANCEMENT OF SCIENCE

M. R. D. FOOT
Formerly Professor of Modern History, University of Manchester

NOMINATED BY
THE ROYAL HISTORICAL SOCIETY

MICHAEL KASER
Fellow of St. Antony's College, Oxford

NOMINATED BY
THE ROYAL INSTITUTE OF INTERNATIONAL AFFAIRS

DEREK MORRIS
Fellow of Oriel College, Oxford

NOMINATED BY
THE ROYAL ECONOMIC SOCIETY

ALASTAIR NIVEN
Literature Director of the Arts Council of Great Britain

NOMINATED BY
THE ARTS COUNCIL OF GREAT BRITAIN

Rex Features

Homeward Bound

Afghanistan, 15 May 1988: Soviet forces begin their withdrawal from Afghanistan, in accordance with the agreements signed in Geneva on 14 April 1988.

Associated Press

Solidarity
Gdansk (Poland), 4 November 1988: UK Prime Minister Margaret Thatcher, on an official visit to Poland, shakes hands with Lech Walesa, leader of the still-banned Solidarity trade union movement.

THE ANNUAL REGISTER

A Record of World Events
1988

Edited by
ALAN J. DAY

assisted by
VERENA HOFFMAN

FIRST EDITED IN 1758
BY EDMUND BURKE

Longman

THE ANNUAL REGISTER 1988
Published by Longman Group UK Limited, Longman House,
Burnt Mill, Harlow, Essex, CM20 2JE, United Kingdom

Distributed exclusively in the United States and Canada by Gale Research Company,
Book Tower, Detroit, Michigan 48226, USA

ISBN 0–582–03829–4 (Longman)
　　　0-8103–4325–3 (Gale)

Library of Congress Catalog Card Number: 4–17979

© Longman Group UK Limited 1989
All rights reserved; no part of this publication may be reproduced,
stored in a retrieval system, or transmitted in any form or by any
means, electronic, mechanical, photocopying, recording or otherwise
without either the prior written permission of the Publishers or a licence
permitting restricted copying issued by the Copyright Licensing Agency Ltd,
33–34 Alfred Place, London, WC1E 7DP

British Library Cataloguing in Publication Data
The Annual Register—1988
　1. History—Periodicals
　909.82'8'05　　D410

ISBN 0–582–03829–4

Set in Times Roman by
QUORN SELECTIVE REPRO LIMITED, LOUGHBOROUGH
and printed and bound in Great Britain by
WILLIAM CLOWES LIMITED, BECCLES AND LONDON

CONTENTS

CONTRIBUTORS		ix
PREFACE TO 230th VOLUME		xv
EXTRACTS FROM 1778, 1838, 1888 and 1938 VOLUMES		xvi
EDITORIAL		1

I UNITED KINGDOM

1	Health and Wealth	8
2	Politics and the Economy	14
3	Legislative Controversies	19
4	The Opposition Parties—Future Obscure	26
5	The Final Quarter	33
6	International Affairs	39
7	Scotland	42
8	Wales	44
9	Northern Ireland	45

II THE AMERICAS AND CARIBBEAN

1	United States of America	48
2	Canada	68
3	Latin America: Argentina 72 Bolivia 74 Brazil 74 Chile 76 Colombia 77 Ecuador 78 Paraguay 80 Peru 80 Uruguay 82 Venezuela 82 Cuba 84 Dominican Republic and Haiti 84 Central America and Panama 86 Mexico 89	72
4	The Caribbean: Jamaica 91 Guyana 93 Trinidad & Tobago 95 Barbados 96 Belize 97 Grenada 98 The Bahamas 99 Windward & Leeward Islands 100 Suriname 102	91

III THE USSR AND EASTERN EUROPE

1	Union of Soviet Socialist Republics	103
2	German Democratic Republic 114 Poland 117 Czechoslovakia 120 Hungary 123 Romania 126 Bulgaria 128 Yugoslavia 131 Albania 136 Mongolia 138	114

IV WESTERN, CENTRAL AND SOUTHERN EUROPE

1	France 141 Federal Republic of Germany 147 Italy 153 Belgium 157 The Netherlands 159 Luxembourg 161 Republic of Ireland 162	141
2	Denmark 166 Iceland 169 Norway 170 Sweden 172 Finland 174 Austria 176 Switzerland 178	166
3	Spain 180 Portugal 184 Gibraltar 187 Malta 188 Greece 190 Cyprus 193 Turkey 195	180

V MIDDLE EAST AND NORTH AFRICA

1	Israel	199
2	The Arab World 203 Egypt 206 Jordan 208 Syria 211 Lebanon 213 Iraq 215	203

vi   CONTENTS

3   Saudi Arabia 218   Yemen Arab Republic 220   People's Democratic
       Republic of Yemen 222   Arab States of the Gulf 223   218
4   Sudan 230   Libya 232   Tunisia 235   Western Sahara 237
       Algeria 239   Morocco 242   230

VI   EQUATORIAL AFRICA
1   Ethiopia 245   Somalia 247   Djibouti 248   Kenya 249
       Tanzania 251   Uganda 253   245
2   Ghana 255   Nigeria 257   Sierra Leone 260   The Gambia 262
       Liberia 263   255
3   Senegal 264   Guinea 266   Mali 267   Mauritania 267
       Côte d'Ivoire 268   Burkina Faso 269   Niger 270   Togo and Benin 271
       Cameroon 272   Chad 272   Gabon and Central African Republic 273
       Congo 274   Equatorial Guinea 274   264

VII   CENTRAL AND SOUTHERN AFRICA
1   Zaïre 276   Rwanda and Burundi 277   Guinea-Bissau and Cape Verde 279
       São Tomé & Príncipe 280   Mozambique 280   Angola 283   276
2   Zambia 287   Malawi 288   Zimbabwe 289   Namibia 292
       Botswana 293   Lesotho 295   Swaziland 296   287
3   Republic of South Africa   297

VIII   SOUTH ASIA AND INDIAN OCEAN
1   Iran 302   Afghanistan 305   302
2   India 308   Pakistan 312   Bangladesh 316   Sri Lanka 318   Nepal 320   308
3   Seychelles 322   Mauritius 324   Madagascar and Comoros 326
       Maldives 327   322

IX   SOUTH-EAST AND EAST ASIA
1   Burma 328   Thailand 330   Malaysia 331   Brunei 333
       Singapore 334   Indonesia 336   Philippines 338   Vietnam 339
       Kampuchea 341   Laos 342   328
2   China 343   Taiwan 349   Hong Kong 351   Japan 352
       South Korea 357   North Korea 358   343

X   AUSTRALASIA AND SOUTH PACIFIC
1   Australia 360   Papua New Guinea 365   360
2   New Zealand   366
3   The South Pacific   371

XI   INTERNATIONAL ORGANIZATIONS
1   The United Nations and its Agencies   375
2   The Commonwealth   388
3   The European Community   391
4   Organization for Economic Cooperation and Development 397
       Council for Mutual Economic Assistance 400   Non-Aligned
       Movement 404   397
5   Council of Europe 406   Western European Union 409   European Free
       Trade Association 410   Nordic Council 412   406

CONTENTS vii

| 6 | African Conferences and Organizations 414 South Asian Association for Regional Cooperation 417 South-East Asian Organizations 418 South Pacific Regional Cooperation 419 Organization of American States 420 Caribbean Organizations 421 | 414 |

XII	DEFENCE AND ARMS CONTROL	
1	The Arms Trade	423
2	The Central Balance	427
3	Nato and the Warsaw Pact	429

| XIII | RELIGION | 435 |

XIV	THE SCIENCES	
1	Medical and Scientific Research	442
2	Technology	449
3	Environment	454

XV	THE LAW	
1	International Law 458 European Community Law 461	458
2	Law in the United Kingdom	465
3	Law in the United States of America	470

XVI	THE ARTS	
1	Opera 473 Music 475 Dance/Ballet 479 Theatre 482 Cinema 488 Television and Radio 492	473
2	Art 497 Architecture 501 Fashion 504	497
3	Literature	505

| XVII | SPORT | 515 |

XVIII	ECONOMIC AND SOCIAL AFFAIRS	
1	The International Debt Crisis	529
2	The International Economy	531
3	The Economy of the United States	534
4	The Economy of the United Kingdom	536
5	Economic and Social Data	540

XIX	DOCUMENTS AND REFERENCE	
	House of Lords 'Spycatcher' Judgment and the Law of Confidentiality	555
	Nato Summit Declaration	560
	Geneva Agreements on Afghanistan	563
	Declarations of Palestine National Council	567
	Mikhail Gorbachev's UN Address	571
	Namibian Independence Agreements	577
	The UK Conservative Cabinet	579
	The United States Cabinet	580

CONTENTS

OBITUARY 581

CHRONICLE OF PRINCIPAL EVENTS IN 1988 598

INDEX 617

MAPS
US Presidential and Congressional Elections 54
Soviet Armenia and Azerbaijan 109
Yugoslavia: Distribution of Nationalities 134

CONTRIBUTORS

EXTRACTS FROM PAST VOLUMES	**M. R. D. Foot**, Former Professor of Modern History, University of Manchester
PART I	
UNITED KINGDOM	**C. J. Bartlett**, PhD, FRHistS, Professor of International History, University of Dundee
SCOTLAND	**C. J. Bartlett** (see above)
WALES	**Gwyn Jenkins**, Assistant Keeper, Department of Manuscripts and Records, National Library of Wales, Aberystwyth
NORTHERN IRELAND	**Brian M. Walker**, MA, PhD, Lecturer in Political Science and Assistant Director of the Institute of Irish Studies. The Queen's University, Belfast
PART II	
USA	**James Bishop**, Editor-in-Chief, *The Illustrated London News*
CANADA	**David M. L. Farr**, Professor Emeritus of History, Carleton University, Ottawa
LATIN AMERICA	**Peter Calvert**, AM, MA, PhD, Professor of Comparative and International Politics, University of Southampton
THE CARIBBEAN	**J. C. J. Saurin**, Research Student, Department of Politics, University of Southampton
PART III	
USSR	**Stephen White**, Department of Politics, University of Glasgow
GERMAN DEMOCRATIC REPUBLIC	**Adrian G. V. Hyde-Price**, BSc(Econ), PhD, Research Fellow, International Security Programme, Royal Institute of International Affairs
POLAND	**Z. J. Blazynski**, Author and broadcaster on Polish and communist affairs
CZECHOSLOVAKIA	**Vladimir V. Kusin**, PhD, Deputy Director, Radio Free Europe research and analysis, Munich
HUNGARY	**George Schöpflin**, Joint Lecturer in East European Political Institutions, London School of Economics and School of Slavonic and East European Studies, University of London
ROMANIA	**Gabriel Partos**, BBC World Services
BULGARIA	**Stephen Ashley**, MA, DPhil, Research analyst, Radio Free Europe, Munich
YUGOSLAVIA	**J. B. Allcock**, MA, Head of Research Unit in Yugoslav Studies, University of Bradford
ALBANIA	**Anton Logoreci**, BSc(Econ), Writer on communist affairs
MONGOLIA	**Alan Sanders**, FIL, Soviet Regional Editor, BBC Monitoring, BBC World Services
PART IV	
FRANCE	**Martin Harrison**, Professor of Politics, University of Keele

CONTRIBUTORS

FEDERAL REPUBLIC OF GERMANY	**Gordon Smith**, BSc(Econ), PhD, Professor of Government, London School of Economics and Political Science
ITALY	**Muriel Grindrod**, OBE, Writer on Italian affairs; formerly Assistant Editor, *The Annual Register*
BELGIUM, NETHERLANDS, LUXEMBOURG	**J. D. McLachlan**, Managing Director, Marketing, FT Business Information Ltd
REPUBLIC OF IRELAND	**Louis McRedmond**, MA, BL, formerly Head of Information in Radio Telefis Eireann, the Irish broadcasting service
NORDIC COUNTRIES	**Hilary Allen**, BSc(Econ), DPhil, Writer on Nordic affairs
AUSTRIA	**Angela Gillon**, Researcher in West European affairs
SWITZERLAND	**Ulrich Sieber**, Editor, *Der Bund*, Berne
SPAIN, PORTUGAL	**G. A. M. Hills**, BA, DLit, Writer and broadcaster on Iberian current affairs and history
GIBRALTAR, MALTA	**D. G. Austin**, Emeritus Professor of Government, University of Manchester
GREECE	**Richard Clogg**, MA, University of London
CYPRUS	**Thomas O'Dwyer**, Director of the Levant Bureau; professional writer specializing in Cypriot and East Mediterranean affairs
TURKEY	**A. J. A. Mango**, BA, PhD, Orientalist and writer on current affairs in Turkey and the Near East

PART V

ISRAEL	**Noah Lucas**, PhD, Fellow in Israeli Studies, The Oxford Centre for Postgraduate Hebrew Studies
ARAB WORLD, EGYPT, JORDAN, SYRIA, LEBANON, IRAQ	**Christopher Gandy**, Formerly UK diplomatic service; writer on Middle Eastern affairs
SAUDI ARABIA, YEMEN ARAB REPUBLIC, PDRY	**R. M. Burrell**, Lecturer in the Contemporary History of the Near and Middle East, School of Oriental and African Studies, University of London
ARAB STATES OF THE GULF	**George Joffe**, Consultant Editor for Middle East and North Africa, Economist Intelligence Unit; journalist and broadcaster on North Africa and the Middle East
SUDAN	**Ahmed al-Shahi**, DPhil, Lecturer in Social Anthropology, Department of Social Policy, University of Newcastle-upon-Tyne
LIBYA, TUNISIA, WESTERN SAHARA ALGERIA, MOROCCO	**R. I. Lawless**, PhD, Chairman of Board of Studies, Centre for Middle Eastern and Islamic Studies, University of Durham

PART VI

ETHIOPIA, SOMALIA, DJIBOUTI	**Christopher Clapham**, MA, DPhil, Professor of Politics and International Relations, University of Lancaster
KENYA, TANZANIA, UGANDA	**William Tordoff**, MA, PhD, Professor of Government, University of Manchester
GHANA	**D. G. Austin**, (see GIBRALTAR)
NIGERIA	**Martin Dent**, Senior Lecturer, Department of Politics, University of Keele

SIERRA LEONE, THE GAMBIA LIBERIA	Arnold Hughes, BA, Lecturer in Political Science, Centre of West African Studies, University of Birmingham
CHAPTER 3 (SENEGAL to EQUATORIAL GUINEA)	Kaye Whiteman, Editor-in-Chief, *West Africa*

PART VII

CHAPTER 1 (ZAÏRE to ANGOLA)	Robin Hallett, MA, Writer and lecturer on African affairs
ZAMBIA, MALAWI	Robin Hallett (see above)
ZIMBABWE	R. W. Baldock, BA, PhD, Senior Editor, Yale University Press; writer on African affairs
NAMIBIA, BOTSWANA, LESOTHO, SWAZILAND, SOUTH AFRICA	Gerald Shaw, MA, Associate Editor, *The Cape Times*, Cape Town

PART VIII

IRAN	Keith McLachlan, BA, PhD, Senior Lecturer in Geography with reference to the Near and Middle East, School of Oriental and African Studies, University of London
AFGHANISTAN, INDIA, BANGLADESH, NEPAL	Peter Lyon, BSc(Econ), PhD, Reader in International Relations and Academic Secretary, Institute of Commonwealth Studies, University of London; Editor, *The Round Table*
PAKISTAN	David Taylor, Lecturer in Politics with reference to South Asia, School of Oriental and African Studies, University of London
SRI LANKA	James Jupp, MSc(Econ), PhD, Senior Research Fellow, Australian National University
SEYCHELLES, MAURITIUS	Jane Davis, Lecturer, Department of International Politics, The University College of Wales, Aberystwyth
MADAGASCAR AND COMOROS	Kaye Whiteman (see PART VI, CH. 3)

PART IX

BURMA, THAILAND, INDONESIA PHILIPPINES, VIETNAM, KAMPUCHEA, LAOS	A. S. B. Olver, MA, Specialist in South-East Asian affairs
MALAYSIA, BRUNEI, SINGAPORE	Michael Leifer, BA, PhD, Reader in International Relations, London School of Economics and Political Science
CHINA, TAIWAN	Brian Hook, Senior Lecturer in Chinese Studies, University of Leeds
HONG KONG	A. S. B. Olver (see above)
JAPAN	I. H. Nish, Professor of International History, London School of Economics and Political Science
SOUTH AND NORTH KOREA	Richard Sim, Consultant and political analyst on Far Eastern affairs

PART X

AUSTRALIA	Geoffrey Sawer, AO, LLD, DLitt, BA, LLM, Emeritus Professor of Law, Australian National University
PAPUA NEW GUINEA	Norman MacQueen, Senior Lecturer in International Relations, Department of Political and

xii   CONTRIBUTORS

                                           Administrative Studies, University of Papua New
                                           Guinea
NEW ZEALAND, SOUTH PACIFIC   **Roderic Alley**, PhD, School of Political Science
                                           and Public Administration, Victoria University of
                                           Wellington

PART XI
UNITED NATIONS   **Granville Fletcher**, Former Chef de Cabinet, UN
                                           European Headquarters, Geneva
COMMONWEALTH   **Derek Ingram**, Editor of *Gemini News Service* and
                                           author and writer on the Commonwealth
EUROPEAN COMMUNITY   **Michael Berendt**, Expert on affairs of the European
                                           Communities
OECD   **H. V. Hodson**, Formerly Editor, *The Annual Register*
COUNCIL FOR MUTUAL   **Michael Kaser**, MA, Reader in Economics, Oxford
  ECONOMIC ASSISTANCE   University and Professorial Fellow of St Antony's
                                           College, Oxford
NON-ALIGNED MOVEMENT   **Peter Willetts**, PhD, Lecturer in International
                                           Relations, The City University, London; author
                                           of *The Non-Aligned in Havana*
COUNCIL OF EUROPE   **Liam Laurence Smyth**, BA, Secretary to the UK
                                           delegation to the Parliamentary Assembly of the
                                           Council of Europe
WEU, EFTA   **H. V. Hodson** (see OECD)
NORDIC COUNCIL   **Hilary Allen** (see PART IV, Nordic Countries)
AFRICAN ORGANIZATIONS   **Kaye Whiteman** (see PART VI, CH. 3)
S. ASIAN ASSOCIATION FOR   **Peter Lyon** (see PART VIII, Afghanistan etc)
  REGIONAL COOPERATION
S.E. ASIAN ORGANIZATIONS   **A. S. B. Olver** (see PART IX, Burma etc)
OAS   **Peter Calvert** (see PART II, Latin America)
S. PACIFIC REGIONAL COOPERATION   **Roderic Alley** (see PART X, New Zealand etc)

PART XII
ARMAMENTS AND DEFENCE   **Phil Williams**, PhD, Senior Lecturer, Department
                                           of Politics, University of Southampton; Head,
                                           International Security Programme, Royal Institute
                                           of International Affairs

PART XIII
RELIGION   **Geoffrey Parrinder**, MA, PhD, DD, Emeritus
                                           Professor of the Comparative Study of Religions,
                                           University of London

PART XIV
MEDICAL AND SCIENTIFIC   **John Newell**, Editor, Science, Industry, Medicine
  RESEARCH   and Agriculture, BBC External Services
TECHNOLOGY   **Michael Cross**, Japan correspondent, *New Scientist*
ENVIRONMENT   **Lloyd Timberlake**, Director of External Affairs,
                                           International Institute for Environment and Devel-
                                           opment (IIED)

PART XV
INTERNATIONAL LAW   **Christine Gray**, Fellow in Law, St Hilda's College,
                                           Oxford

CONTRIBUTORS

EUROPEAN COMMUNITY LAW	**N. March Hunnings**, LLM, PhD, Editor, *Common Market Law Reports*
LAW IN THE UK	**David Ibbetson**, MA, PhD, Fellow and Tutor in Law, Magdalen College, Oxford
LAW IN THE USA	**Robert J. Spjut**, JD, LLM, member of the State Bars of California and Florida

PART XVI

OPERA	**Elizabeth Forbes**, Freelance journalist, critic and translator
DANCE-BALLET	**Mary Clarke**, Editor, *The Dancing Times*
THEATRE	**Charles Osborne**, Author; Chief Theatre Critic, *The Daily Telegraph*
MUSIC	**Francis Routh**, Composer and author; founder-director of the Redcliffe Concerts
CINEMA	**Derek Malcolm**, Film critic, *The Guardian*
TV & RADIO	**Raymond Snoddy**, Media correspondent, *The Financial Times*
ART	**Marina Vaizey**, MA, Art critic, *The Sunday Times*
ARCHITECTURE	**Jonathan Glancey**, Author and broadcaster on architecture; Editor, *World Architecture*
FASHION	**Bonny Spencer**, Freelance fashion writer; formerly fashion editor of *Fashion Weekly*
LITERATURE	**David Holloway**, Former Literary Editor, *The Daily Telegraph*

PART XVII

SPORT	**Tony Pawson**, OBE, Sports writer, *The Observer*; cricket, football and fly-fishing international

PART XVIII

CHAPTERS 1 to 4	**Victor Keegan**, Assistant Editor, *The Guardian*
STATISTICS	**Sue Cockerill**, Statistical Department, *The Financial Times*
OBITUARY	**H. V. Hodson** (see PART XI, OECD)
INDEX	**Beth Scott**, Professional indexer

ACKNOWLEDGEMENTS

The Advisory Board again gratefully acknowledges its debt to a number of institutions for their help with sources, references, documents, figures and maps: notably the Novosti Press Agency, the London office of the Palestine Liberation Organization and the South African embassy in London. Acknowledgement is also due, as the principal sources for the national data sections, to *Keesing's Record of World Events* (Longman), *People in Power* (Longman) and *World Development Report* (OUP for the World Bank). The Board, and the bodies which nominate its members, disclaim responsibility for any opinions expressed or the accuracy of any facts recorded in this volume.

ABBREVIATIONS

ACP	African, Caribbean and Pacific states associated with EEC
AfDB	African Development Bank
AID	Agency for International Development
AIDS	Acquired Immune Deficiency Syndrome
ANC	African National Congress
ANZUS	Australia-New Zealand-US Security Treaty
AR	Annual Register
ASEAN	Association of South-East Asian Nations
CAP	Common Agricultural Policy
CARICOM	Caribbean Common Market
CBI	Confederation of British Industry
CEEAC	Economic Community of Central African States
CIA	Central Intelligence Agency
COMECON	Council for Mutual Economic Assistance (CMEA)
Cwth.	Commonwealth
EC	European Communities
ECOSOC	Economic and Social Council (UN)
ECOWAS	Economic Community of West African States
ECUs (MECUs)	European Currency Units (Million)
EEC	European Economic Community (Common Market)
EFTA	European Free Trade Association
EMS	European Monetary System
ESCAP	Economic and Social Commission for Asia and the Pacific (UN)
FAO	Food and Agriculture Organization
FBI	Federal Bureau of Investigation
GATT	General Agreement on Tariffs and Trade
GCC	Gulf Cooperation Council
GDP/GNP	Gross Domestic/National Product
IAEA	International Atomic Energy Agency
IBRD	International Bank for Reconstruction and Development
ICBM	Inter-Continental Ballistic Missile
ICO	Islamic Conference Organization
IDA	International Development Association
ILO	International Labour Organization
IMF	International Monetary Fund
INF	Intermediate-range Nuclear Forces
IRA	Irish Republican Army
MBFR	Mutual and Balanced Force Reductions
NAM	Non-Aligned Movement
NATO	North Atlantic Treaty Organization
OAS	Organization of American States
OAU	Organization of African Unity
OECD	Organization for Economic Cooperation and Development
OPEC (OAPEC)	Organization of (Arab) Petroleum Exporting Countries
PLO	Palestine Liberation Organization
PTA	Preferential Trade Area (of Eastern and Southern Africa)
SAARC	South Asian Association for Regional Cooperation
SADCC	Southern African Development Coordination Conference
SALT	Strategic Arms Limitation Talks
SDI	Strategic Defense Initiative
START	Strategic Arms Reduction Talks
SWAPO	South-West Africa People's Organization
TUC	Trades Union Congress
UN	United Nations
UNCTAD	United Nations Conference on Trade and Development
UNDP	United Nations Development Programme
UNESCO	United Nations Educational, Scientific and Cultural Organization
UNHCR	United Nations High Commission for Refugees
UNRWA	United Nations Relief and Works Agency
VAT	Value Added Tax
WHO	World Health Organization

PREFACE

THE new hopes for a more peaceful world noted in the preface to the 1987 Annual Register were not confounded in 1988. Indeed, the year proved to be something of an *annus mirabilis* for the cause of peace and negotiation rather than war and confrontation. The INF Treaty between the superpowers was duly ratified and a start made on destroying US and Soviet intermediate-range nuclear missiles. Moreover, a number of seemingly intractable international conflicts were at last resolved or at least redirected into the sensible channels of negotiation and accommodation. The Geneva accords on Afghanistan, the Gulf War ceasefire and the Namibian independence agreements were prime cases in point. Elsewhere, there were significant moves towards the resolution of longstanding conflicts in Western Sahara, Ethiopia/Somalia and Kampuchea. In part, these hopeful developments reflected the new determination of the two superpowers to resolve regional conflicts in which their opposing strategic interests had previously been a key exacerbating factor. Also encouraging was the resurrection of the United Nations as an effective international peace-promoting body, a role for which it was of course originally intended.

All these positive developments are chronicled in the present volume. So too are the continuing festering sores on the international political landscape, where the writ of converging superpower interest does not run. These include, in the Middle East, the absence of any sign of accommodation between conflicting Palestinian and Jewish aspirations, highlighted by the brutalities of the *intifada* (Palestinian uprising), and the continuing lawlessness in Lebanon. Central America is another region where a key to unlock the door to peace has remained elusive. Also disturbing—and the subject of this volume's editorial—is the manifest inability of many countries around the globe to cope with ethnic and communal conflict within their borders. And overlaying such problems—and therefore also a theme of this volume—is the growing concern of the world community with environmental issues and with the rampant scourge of AIDS.

The present volume is the first under the new editorship of Alan J. Day, who has assumed the chair occupied with such distinction for 15 years by Harry Hodson. The latter remains closely associated with the Annual Register, as chairman of the Advisory Board and contributor. The Advisory Board welcomes Alastair Niven as the Arts Council's nominee in succession to Charles Osborne (who nevertheless continues as a distinguished contributor) and also several new contributors.

THE ANNUAL REGISTER

200 years ago

1788. *The grand vizir of the Ottoman Empire*. He perceived that the art of war had been long assiduously studied, as a science of the greatest difficulty as well as magnitude and importance, by the Europeans who had accordingly carried it to a height of perfection before unknown; that they had reduced their various theories into practice, and were continually improving upon and correcting them by experience, so that all the modes and practice of war had undergone a total revolution, even among themselves, within a century; while, on the contrary, his nation, without the smallest attempt at improvement, had during that time been continually declining from the severity and excellence of their own ancient discipline; so that their armies in the late war had fallen into the most abject contempt.

150 years ago

1838. *Lords debate Canadian unrest*. The Earl of Durham said, that it was impossible for words to express the reluctance with which he had undertaken the arduous task, and incurred the awful responsibility, which he knew must await him in his endeavours to execute the objects of his mission. Nothing but the most determined devotion to Her Majesty's service, and the welfare of his country, could have induced him to place himself in a situation, in which he much feared he should not answer either the expectation of his friends or of the nation.

100 years ago

1888. *Kaiser Wilhelm II*. On June 25 he opened the German Parliament with great pomp, and made a speech in which he repeatedly declared that he would continue the home and foreign policy of his late grandfather, but made no allusion to that of his father, and did not mention either England or France. A similar ceremony took place at the opening of the Prussian Diet on June 27. These preliminaries of the new Emperor's reign did not produce a very favourable impression of his character . . . . On Aug. 29 the *Official Gazette* announced the resignation of the post of Chief of the General Staff by the veteran Field-Marshal Moltke on the ground of his great age, which made him unable to mount a horse. The resignation was graciously accepted by the Emperor, who, however, appointed the Field-Marshal to the office of President of the National Defence Committee.

50 years ago

1938. *Munich settlement*. By the end of the year it was abundantly clear that the Munich settlement had not brought any nearer that "appeasement" and "relaxation of tension" which Mr Chamberlain had proclaimed to be the goal of his policy. Tension in fact had become more acute between Germany and England and between Italy and France; while the temporary friendship between Germany and France and between Italy and England rested on very shaky foundations. Similarly, in the country itself, while there was broadly speaking unanimity on the need for rearmament, the Munich settlement had served to accentuate the division of opinion on foreign policy which had existed since the resignation of Mr Eden, and the like of which had not been seen since before the war.

ANNUAL REGISTER

FOR THE YEAR 1988

EDITORIAL

ETHNIC AND COMMUNAL CONFLICT

IN the eye of history, 1988 may well appear as a year of grace for global peace. The longest international war of the twentieth century came to an end, instrumentally through the efforts of the United Nations, fundamentally through the exhaustion of the two combatants, Iraq and Iran: never was there a better example of 'The Great Illusion', as Norman Angell called it, the illusion that a nation could gain anything by war waged as an instrument of national policy. Also in 1988 truces were contrived in the undeclared but all too real wars waged in Angola and Namibia, on the borders between Ethiopia and Somalia, and in the Western Sahara. Large numbers of Russian forces in Afghanistan went home, under a pledge of complete withdrawal early in 1989. The Soviet-American INF disarmament treaty was ratified and began to be implemented. Late in the year, the whole world was cheered by President Gorbachev's speech at the United Nations, not only announcing a unilateral cut in Soviet troops and armaments deployed in Eastern Europe but, still more significantly, confirming a radical change in Soviet foreign policy away from conflict and confrontation towards compromise and common concerns.

These pacific dramas, however, could not hide from their audiences the violence of other scenes enacted elsewhere on the world stage. These were the internal wars, or warlike strife, which blazed or smouldered in many nations on all continents: in Central America, Lebanon, Iraq, Yugoslavia, Sudan, Ethiopia, Burundi, Indonesia, Sri Lanka, Kampuchea, New Caledonia and other countries. Violent regional or communal revolts plagued yet more states, from the Balkans to India, not least the uprising of Arab people in the Israeli-occupied lands. Even the Soviet Union, with its massive central authority, was shaken by the rebellion of Armenians against their Azerbaijani neighbours and the retaliatory massacres—events of a different order from the calls by the Baltic states for autonomy within the Soviet Union.

The common character of those internal conflicts and revolts was that, unlike the political upheavals in such countries as Burma, Haiti or Algeria, they were primarily racial or tribal; those who leagued together, and likewise those against whom they leagued, were linked by race, religion or culture, not by political or economic philosophies, save in so far as the political and economic establishment was seen by dissidents as racially or culturally oppressive. For that reason there could be no political *vade mecum* for their cure, nor economic calculation for their cause or proof of their unreason, though political structures might worsen or alleviate them, and economic conditions might heighten them or take away their sting.

To see them as a phenomenon particularly of our times would be an illusion of historical short sight. In whatever past decade or century we look, we see violent conflicts of religious or cultural communities within nation states: in England, France, Germany, Russia, the Holy Roman and Austro-Hungarian Empires, in the United States of America, in India, in the Islamic world, in pre-colonial Africa and Asia, in every colonial imperium. If they seem unusually rife in the contemporary world it may be only because modern communications expose them instantly and in detail to us all in the materially advanced nations. Those same swift communications, visual as well as verbal, may indeed have enhanced and inflamed the phenomenon itself. A dissident community, so aggrieved as to take to arms, can now address not merely its national rulers and compatriots but the whole world. External sympathy, always a coveted asset for revolt, can be more easily aroused.

Besides the communications revolution, two other revolutions that the world has undergone in our lifetimes have radically altered the scene of these bloody dramas of inter-communal strife. One is the almost total dissolution of the European empires and the consequent retreat of European nations from hegemonic power in Asia, Africa and the Pacific. In Sri Lanka, when it was called Ceylon, Tamils did not wage war on Sinhalese because both were subjects of British imperial rule, which in its own interests held the balance between them. When Kampuchea was part of French Indochina, the Pol Pots and Heng Samrins of the time led no more than factions which the power of France subdued. Whatever turbulence there was between classes and religions in the Philippines was the business of the over-riding American authority to suppress or appease. Inter-communal violence was perennial in India, but never matched the massacres that attended the withdrawal of the British

Raj. When imperial power is relinquished, it passes to someone—a democratic majority, a dominant community, a superior tribe, a ruling class, an entrenched party or an *arriviste* demagogue. Others become underlings, where all were once subjects of an alien empire. Rivalries are released, and instability may ensue, to be followed by violent action and reaction.

It is tempting but pointless to conclude that if the European and other widespread empires had not abandoned their self-appointed task of keeping order among their colonial subjects the world would be a more peaceful place today. That may or may not be true; for all we know, something much worse might have happened with the continuance of empires. Wistful sighs save no present lives, remedy no present grievances, lighten no present oppressions, moderate no present communal passions. Moreover, the liberal, evenhanded imperialism which we nostalgically idealize (though it was far from universal) was doomed to expire by its own nature. Its liberality unleashed the forces of nationalism and democracy which were bound eventually to win independence; its evenhandedness became harder and harder to sustain as democracy sharpened the conflicts of cultural and class divisions. Its spread of education and electoral practice sapped the authority of old indigenous systems—rajahs, chiefs, tribal structures, ruling castes or classes, some of which lingered in the political undergrowth, awaiting a more propitious hour. The better—in this context—that the former empires were, the more certain they were to dissolve, though of course other forces, including two world wars, determined the pace and actualities of the process.

In two other ways the decline of empires affected the number and shape of present inter-communal conflicts. First, especially in Africa, colonial frontiers had been drawn to suit the political, economic and administrative interests of the colonial powers, sometimes to implement treaty bargains between them. Consequently they often cut through tribal and cultural boundaries, or embraced in one state territory several hostile racial groups. When the imperial powers withdrew, their indigenous successors had no sensible option but to retain this colonial geography as the frame of independent nation states. Secondly, in earlier decades the economic interests of the European empires had led them to recruit workers from one dependent territory to man the industry or agriculture of another: for instance, Indian labour was brought to Fiji to work on the sugar plantations, and other workers from the Indian sub-continent migrated under the British Empire's protection to form significant minorities in the West Indies (a majority in Guyana), East African colonies and South Africa. North Africans who had been citizens of the metropolitan state became a large, permanent and indigestible minority in France itself. Puerto Ricans who have flooded into the United States have not yet dissolved in that great melting-pot of immigrant nationalities, and along with Mexicans and other Hispanics ally themselves more with the blacks than with the ex-European white majority.

The erasure of the European empires was part of a wave of change in common attitudes all over the world in the social and political sphere, a wave that has rolled on through the second half of this century and is still washing into the marshes, bays and inlets of the international landscape. It is a wave of discredit of former values—national loyalty, 'manifest destiny', missionary duty, socialism as an ideal goal, respect for order and discipline, for religious institutions and doctrine. As traditional structures and values lose their potency, other social impulses gain in attraction and prestige. Sectional groups become more ambitious and vociferous. War, once the clash of princes and potentates, then of nation states, is waged by religious, cultural and tribal communities, or ideological factions, by civil disorder, bellicose propaganda, assassinations, communal massacres and terrorism, including state terrorism in the name of national security.

The second revolution of the past half-century which is relevant to this matter is that which has fundamentally altered the world's power structure, the advent of the atomic bomb. The subsequent confrontation of the major powers has been like a gabled roof, whose stability is secured so long as the weights of both sides, in terms of nuclear arms, remain about equal. While this balance of forces has maintained a state of no war between those major powers, beneath the roof lesser conflicts have raged without risk of coercive intervention by the nuclear-armed nations, concerned above all not to endanger the stability of the whole system. The vision—bright for some minds at the birth of the United Nations—of a world forcefully policed by the permanent members of the Security Council has proved a mirage. UN 'peacekeeping', valuable though it has been, has done little more than stabilize boundary lines. The global power scene today embraces two worlds, one in which deterrence of war is wholly effective, the other in which such deterrence is weaker than it was in bygone days of authoritarian 'spheres of influence'.

So the phenomenon of bloody inter-communal war that we deplore because it mars a world scene which we would like to perceive as one of growing peace, and because it mocks the Whiggish interpretation of modern history as a progress, uneven but persistent, towards expanding liberty, democracy, good order and the rule of law, appears to be a constant in the political evolution of mankind, an ever-present virus sometimes dormant, sometimes virulent, incapable of being expunged from the body politic.

If there is no cure, maybe at least the worst symptoms can be mitigated. Partition has sometimes been an answer, during this century in Ireland, in India, *de facto* in Cyprus. But as the first and last of those examples demonstrate—and so does the twice redrawn map of the Balkans—such surgery is apt to leave behind traumas of the same kind as before, often inverted, perhaps on a smaller scale but no less bitter. Roman Catholic republicanism in Northern Ireland is the mirror image of the 'Ulster will fight, and Ulster will be right' syndrome which frustrated Irish home rule earlier in the century.

Nevertheless, 'the Irish problem' was radically changed by partition and the independence of the Irish Free State, now the Republic of Ireland. The ancient struggle of native Irish against British invaders, although still smouldering, is today expressed in a problem of terrorist crime, fought by Irish and British democratic governments alike against violent irreconcilables, minorities of their own communal tribes. Separatism is still the aim of militant Basques in Spain, Sikhs in the Punjab, Kurds in central Asia, and it may yet be the way out of black-white deadlock in South Africa, but it has no relevance to the rebellion of Armenians in the USSR, Polynesians in Fiji, or Islamic fundamentalists in the Middle East.

There can be less traumatic ways of taking bellicose heat out of the emotions of dissident communities: wider tolerance and liberty for different creeds, customs and tongues, improved political structures, devolution and power-sharing. Democracy—unitary or federal—on the pattern evolved by coherent nation states in the West is not necessarily the best solution in countries with different traditions and problems, where single-party systems may be the practical answer. An over-riding ideology, such as marxism-leninism, which subordinates all other group motives, is of course one way, if not to harmony, at least to cohesion; but ideologies are always prone to variants and challenges, and if these can harness communal emotions the forces of fission become doubly dangerous.

While in particular cases political and structural remedies may be available, they bear no guarantee of permanent cure. Man has certain traits and propensities which are part of his nature as a species: aggressiveness if provoked, family identity, combination in tribal groups. Through the millennia, his power of organization and his submission to leadership have controlled and sublimated those impulses in the various political structures that we see today—empires, nation states, federations, international communities, regional authorities, political parties, pressure groups and so on. But even in the strongest and most sophisticated of such structures the same impulses lurk beneath the surface, often concentrated by powerful emotive forces like ancestral glory, religion, language, love of land, which attract loyalties more dedicated and self-sacrificing than those accorded to political organs, however benign. The effect in the future will surely be as it has been in the past.

Nevertheless, the prospect is not without hope, nor is the liberal faith in progress altogether illusory. In Western Europe generally, or in the United States, we see political structures within which ancient communal groups, though still coherent and loud-voiced, have become subject to larger loyalties and democratic processes. They may demand attention, but only in a few cases, the exceptions that prove the rule, do they threaten national unity and general peace. Deep-seated tribal impulses have often been channelled into sporting loyalties; we hear much about football hooliganism, which is indeed a social blot, but rival fan gangs can be policed and contained, and their clashes normally produce few serious casualties.

A far more important example of alleviation of inter-communal conflict, once almost threatening civil war, is to be found in the USA. Only three decades span the contrast between Martin Luther King, protest leader and martyr, and Jesse Jackson, contender for candidature as President of the United States. The civil rights transformation in America has been one of the most profound events of our lifetimes, although in social *mores* and political emotion (as the 1988 presidential election showed) it still lags far behind institutional change.

The time-scale is significant. If, in a democratic, federal, multi-cultural and secular state it is a cause of congratulation that the relations of two racial communities should improve to that extent in as little as 30 years, how much longer may be needed for such a consummation in less favourable conditions, where, for instance, the rival communities are distinguished by different languages, religions and national aspirations? Tolerance and mutual respect are virtues that grow slowly in communities steeped in ancestral rivalry. Even if the will for reform is present, the process of persuading political factions and carrying through legal and constitutional changes which appease communal passion may take a long time. There is no swift, sure remedy for deep-seated communal strife. The specifics are slow-acting and hard to come by. Everywhere they remain the same: equality before the law, fair treatment for the less privileged, social and religious tolerance, protection of human rights, expressed in appropriate political structures and encouraged by other nations whose communal sympathies or national interests may be engaged.

More widely, the world community, mobilized through the United Nations and its agencies and other institutions, has a positive role to play as well as a negative one in identifying, condemning and penalizing communal or racial oppression and state crime wherever they abound. The United Nations is founded on the principle of exclusive national sovereignty, but that concept is weakening in a world more and more integrated by communications, commerce and international compacts. No nation, like no man, 'is an island, entire of itself'. The world is not yet ready for an international court applying principles of law to inter-communal disputes within nation states, but perhaps it is ready for a body concerned to investigate, conciliate and advise wherever such disputes threaten peace, order and basic human rights.

London, February 1989

I UNITED KINGDOM

CAPITAL: London AREA: 244,100 sq km POPULATION: 56,700,000 ('86)
OFFICIAL LANGUAGE: English, also Welsh (in Wales) POLITICAL SYSTEM: parliamentary democracy
HEAD OF STATE: Queen Elizabeth II (since Feb '52)
RULING PARTY: Conservative Party
HEAD OF GOVERNMENT: Margaret Thatcher, Prime Minister (since May '79)
PRINCIPAL MINISTERS: Sir Geoffrey Howe (foreign and Commonwealth affairs), Nigel Lawson (Exchequer), Lord Mackay of Clashfern (Lord Chancellor), Douglas Hurd (home affairs), George Younger (defence), Lord Young of Graffham (trade and industry) (*for full list see* DOCUMENTS)
INTERNATIONAL ALIGNMENT: Nato, OECD, EC, Cwth.
CURRENCY: pound sterling (end-'88 £1=US$1.81) GNP PER CAPITA: US$8,870 ('86)
MAIN EXPORTS: machinery and transport equipment, mineral fuels and lubricants, manufactured goods, chemicals

Chapter 1

HEALTH AND WEALTH

ON 3 January 1988 Mrs Thatcher became the longest-serving British Prime Minister of the twentieth century. Notable among the congratulatory messages was one from President Reagan. But this was also an opportunity for her critics to make themselves heard. One of the most interesting was her former Defence Secretary, Sir John Nott, who, while acknowledging her place among the greatest Premiers of the century, suggested that she was promoting 'a cult of personality', and was leading an increasingly 'centralist', even a 'slightly authoritarian' Government. Many commented upon the degree to which Mrs Thatcher differed from other postwar Conservative leaders. She lacked, it was said, their sense of upper class or 'bourgeois' guilt.

Certainly she placed greater emphasis upon individual responsibility and initiative by all who were not incapacitated, and looked to greater family and private charitable support for those who were unable to look after themselves. With other Ministers she demanded less criticism from the churches and more support for her reassertion of 'traditional' values. Opinion polls, however, showed that the public was not yet prepared for so great a diminution in state responsibilities, while dissenting Conservative MPs and peers caused the Government many problems. On the other hand, in the first part of the year Mrs Thatcher gained increasing popular applause for the success of her economic policies. Unemployment continued to fall and there was a widespread sense of prosperity.

The Government suffered an early setback on 10 January when Lord Whitelaw, Leader of the House of Lords and Deputy

Prime Minister, was obliged to resign from the Cabinet for reasons of ill-health. He was succeeded as Leader in the Lords by Lord Belstead. Lord Whitelaw was a noted elder statesman who had acquired a considerable reputation as a party manager during a period when the Conservative Party suffered many internal tensions as Ministers pushed through highly contentious legislation. He was described by Mr Norman Tebbit as the 'conscience of the Tory Party'. As a representative of the traditional Tories, his presence and influence in the Cabinet had been a source of reassurance to many.

Unease in some sections of the party over the Government's social policy was reflected in an amendment by Sir Brandon Rhys Williams to the Government's decision, announced in October 1987, to freeze child benefit at its current level. His motion was defeated in the Commons on 12 January by 288 votes to 241, but 14 Conservatives voted with the Opposition, and there were a number of abstentions.

Some Conservative MPs, and many Conservative voters, also shared the widespread concern over the state of the National Health Service (NHS). This was the most contentious political issue in the first part of the year. A leading article in the *British Medical Journal* of 2 January went so far as to claim that the NHS was moving towards 'terminal decline'. British per capita spending on health care was the lowest in northern Europe. The following day the Association of Community Health Councils asserted that some parts of the NHS were 'already on the brink of collapse' and would fall apart unless decisive action were soon forthcoming. Almost every day brought new reports of shortages of staff, equipment and funds, of delayed operations, empty beds, closed wards, long waiting lists, and of deaths which might have been prevented.

The Labour Party took advantage of the very first Prime Minister's Question Time of the New Year to go on to the offensive. In response Mrs Thatcher set out with an array of statistics to demonstrate how spending on the NHS had grown under the Conservatives. But with repetition this tactic began to seem arid and even insensitive. Given mounting evidence that the Chancellor would have ample funds to play with in his March Budget, a number of Conservative MPs began to speak out in favour of fewer tax cuts in order to increase spending on the NHS.

In a major debate in the Commons on 19 January Mr John Moore, then Secretary of State for both Health and Social Services, gave no promise of new initiatives or extra funds, stessing instead the need for greater efficiency in the service. The health authorities should try to generate more income by their own efforts. Spare capacity in one locality, for instance, might be used and paid for by others which were over-stretched. He also argued that comparisons with West Germany and France indicated that there was considerable scope for the expansion of the private sector. Private medicine in France absorbed five times as much of the gross domestic product (2.7 per cent) as in Britain (0.5 per cent). Labour still retorted that the NHS should have priority over tax cuts in the Budget, while on 21 January the presidents of the three royal medical colleges claimed that the Secretary of State had retreated from an earlier promise to provide more money in the not too distant future. At first the Government seemed unmoved, while the 'Thatcherite' 92 Group of MPs insisted that tax cuts should have priority. In addition many Tories in the centre of the party opposed the infusion of more money into the NHS until it had been reformed and restructured.

By the end of January there were signs that the Government was beginning to retreat from its original intention to leave serious reform of the NHS until the next Parliament. The scale and intensity of complaints, including warnings from the Royal College of Nursing and disquiet in certain Conservative quarters, were too strong to be ignored. On 3 February many nurses and health workers took part in a one-day strike, forcing the cancellation of numerous operations, especially in the London area. On 14 February much publicity was given to the tragic death of a four-year-old, Matthew Collier, whose parents had unsuccessfully applied for the intervention of the High Court after several postponements to a hole-in-the-heart operation. The operation had finally been carried out in January. Postponements of open heart surgery were also reported at the specialist Papworth Hospital in Cambridgeshire. Later in the month two all-party select committees, if with some qualifications, recommended increased funding for the NHS.

Labour were now demanding a £2,000 million increase for the NHS, and they launched a 'Make Budget Day NHS Day' campaign from 17 February. The party's leader, Mr Neil Kinnock, insisted at the Scottish Labour Party conference in Perth on 11 March that the future of the NHS was the most important issue facing Britain. Nevertheless he too admitted the need for a number of reforms, including improved training, greater efficiency and accountability. But the Chancellor, in his much anticipated speech of 15 March, offered no advance on the Government's earlier promise of at least an extra £1,100 million for the NHS in the financial year 1988–89. Indeed NHS funding formed little more than a footnote to a Budget which was both acclaimed and condemned as one of the most radical tax reform budgets of the century.

Mr Lawson's speech sparked off an uproar in the Commons, Mr Alex Salmond of the Scottish National Party being expelled from the House for five days for denouncing the tax cuts as an obscenity. A little later persistent chants of 'shame' from a number of Labour MPs led to a ten-minute suspension of the proceedings. Although the Budget was warmly applauded by much of the press, a leader in the *Financial Times* thought it 'one-sided', while *The Daily Mirror* bleakly rhymed 'It's tax cuts galore but not if you're poor'.

Buoyant tax revenues—as a result of high earnings and even higher consumer spending—turned out to be some £8,000 million in excess of Treasury expectations a year earlier. Mr Lawson was able not only to present a balanced Budget but to plan for a surplus in 1988–89 for the first time since the early 1950s. He declared that a zero public sector borrowing requirement would be the norm in the future, although tax would continue to absorb roughly the same proportion of the nation's income. Meanwhile he had a nest-egg of £4,250 million to distribute to the nation. He reduced the top rate of income tax from 60p to 40p, reduced the standard rate by 2p to his party's original target of 25p, and abolished all the intermediate tax bands. His aim for the future was a basic rate of 20p. From April 1990 married women would enjoy a large measure of independence in their tax affairs, a striking reform of a 180-year-old system whereby a husband had been responsible for his wife's tax liabilities. The capital gains tax was also reformed and simplified. From August 1988 tax relief on new mortgages (the limit remaining at £30,000) would apply to only one member of a household. The taxation scales on company cars were doubled, whereas the tax increases on petrol, cigarettes, beers and wines were broadly in line with inflation.

For the Opposition Mr Kinnock described the Chancellor's strategy as one of giving incentives to the rich to work harder while penalizing the poor to compel them to do the same. No less than £2,000 million of the tax cuts had been given to the wealthiest. Mr Kinnock claimed that even a married man earning £200 a week would be only £3.98 in pocket, whereas someone earning £1,000 a week would receive an extra £89. Some 15 million people would not benefit at all. A majority of the people would have preferred more spending on the NHS to tax cuts. Mr John Smith, the Shadow Chancellor, denounced the Budget on the following day as a demonstration of the 'Thatcherite' vision in all its vulgarity: it 'is immoral, it is wrong, it is foolish, it is divisive, it is corrupting'.

Criticism of the Chancellor on economic grounds came from various quarters. Sir Ian Gilmour (Conservative) feared that Mr Lawson was presiding over another example of 'the classic, authentic, British consumption-led boom, with imports rising far faster than exports'. Labour spokesmen argued that the boom was too dependent upon increasing household debts and a 'credit society', while long-term problems connected with industry and exports were being neglected. Government assistance and investment were required in many areas.

The Treasury admitted to some worries over the pace at which consumer credit was growing, and to a rate of inflation which was higher than that of several key competitors. The Chancellor himself made a plea for production costs to be kept under tight control. He also conceded that the balance of payments was expected to worsen markedly in the short term, but insisted that the strength of the British economy and the nation's vast overseas assets should suffice to maintain confidence until the imbalance was corrected. Some analysts were less impressed, and recalled the 'Barber boom' of 1972–73. Exporters were anxiously watching the value of the pound as it topped the sensitive DM 3 level. Some Conservatives were disturbed by the blatant manner in which the Budget favoured the rich while the Institute of Fiscal Studies asserted that there was little evidence to link improved economic performance with lower tax rates. Britain now had the lowest top rate tax in Europe: Japan had the highest rate among the leading seven industrial nations.

Critics also noted that National Insurance remained a regressive tax. In addition, it was estimated that from April some 60 per cent of all welfare recipients would be worse off as a result of government cuts in housing benefits, rent rebates and other forms of assistance. And the new 'poll tax' (see p. 19) was still to come. Mr John Rentoul in *The Rich Get Richer* had recently estimated that nearly a quarter of all adults were living on incomes at or below the level of supplementary benefit. It was noted in the *Financial Times* of 16 March that the 'welfare state' of tax advantages for the rich was still largely intact, while a leader in the same paper argued that the undoubted merits of the tax reforms had to be weighed against the undue generosity of the tax changes to the better-off. Mr Lawson, however, stood by his original contention that 'you don't make the poor richer by making the rich poor'. Britain, he insisted, enjoyed the highest growth rate of the leading European economies in the 1980s.

The ugly scenes which accompanied the Budget debate whetted the appetite of those who were looking forward to a six-month experiment in televising debates in the House of Commons. Would television, they wondered, encourage or discourage such behaviour? On 9 February in a free vote MPs had decided by 318 votes to 264, and against the wishes of Mrs Thatcher, to admit the cameras under conditions to be determined and monitored by a select committee of the House. A 20-year-old battle had swung for the time being against those such as Mr Tebbit who feared 'a success for the entertainment industry'.

Funding of the NHS and its employees continued to excite controversy, but not on the scale that had preceded the Budget. In

April the Government accepted the recommendations of a review body on pay increases for nurses and other medical staff. On 25 July Mrs Thatcher carried out an unexpected ministerial reshuffle, in which she split the huge Department of Health and Social Security. Mr Moore, whose parliamentary performance earlier in the year had been impaired by a severe illness, retained Social Security, but Health passed to Mr Kenneth Clarke, one of the Government's promising younger Ministers. At the end of July an all-party social services committee investigating the future of the NHS insisted that 'the strengths of the NHS should not be cast away in a short-term effort to remedy some of its weaknesses'. The committee rejected the more radical ideas already circulating on ways by which the private element in health care might be enhanced, notably with American-style health organizations. But it did accept the need for evolutionary change and the pursuit of more efficient and economical management.

In August the three nursing unions walked out of talks with the Department of Health amid rising fears that the pay award of April would not result in generous increases for as many nurses as had originally been expected. Local health authorities were regrading staff in accordance with government guidelines, so that many seemed unlikely to receive the anticipated average of 15.3 per cent. The Royal College of Nursing (RCN), which had delighted the Government in March with a 4 to 1 majority to preserve its no-strike policy, again drew attention to the exodus of experienced staff from the NHS to the private sector or to the United States. Although talks were resumed later in the month, and the Government announced the grant of an extra £98 million on 17 October to help fund the pay award, unrest over the issue of regrading speedily resurfaced.

Meanwhile the campaign continued for more funding of the NHS as a whole. The RCN at its national congress in Brighton in May, and the National Association of Health Authorities three months later, both supplied bleak assessments of the situation, especially in the hospitals. Mr Clarke himself admitted on 6 September that some ward closures were imminent, but he blamed these in part on managerial failings. A review of the NHS would result in 'fairly drastic steps' to transform what he believed was a 'ramshackle bureaucracy into a well run business–a business not of a commercial kind but a business delivering patient care and treatment'. The president of the Royal College of Physicians retorted that a policy of rewarding efficiency could result in inferior treatment.

At the beginning of November the Government announced an increase of £1,100 million in hospital spending for 1989–90, a figure which was in excess of the expectations—or fears—of the health authorities. They now thought that bed closures would be prevented, and new developments might be possible for the first time for several years. But Mr Clarke continued to underline the Government's preoccupation with efficiency.

Chapter 2

POLITICS AND THE ECONOMY

THE Government had the satisfaction of seeing unemployment fall rapidly in February to 9.1 per cent of the workforce, or, at just over 2 ½ million, to the lowest figure since February 1982. On the other hand, the middle of March brought to a head reported differences between the Prime Minister and the Chancellor of the Exchequer over the relative importance of controlling inflation and restraining the rise in value of the pound. Both represented a threat to British exports, yet to move interest rates upwards to check inflation carried the risk of an over-valued pound, whereas reduced interest rates were expected to encourage inflationary consumer expenditure over a period of time.

On 4 March the Government decided that the cost of intervention by the Bank of England to keep the pound below DM 3 was becoming unacceptable. But the continuing rise of sterling disturbed exporters, while even official sources were soon admitting the existence of a 'healthy argument' between Mrs Thatcher and Mr Lawson over the appropriate strategy. There were whispers of a resignation unless the Prime Minister took account of Mr Lawson's fears of an over-valued pound. The Chancellor, it seemed, was in the ascendant when interest rates were cut by half a per cent on 17 March to discourage foreign purchases of sterling.

The situation, however, soon became more complex as worsening monthly trade and current-account figures began to undermine Treasury predictions of a balance-of-payments deficit of around £4,000 million for the whole year—hardly a comforting figure in itself. There was other evidence that the economy was overheating as a result of the persisting consumer boom, the dramatic rise in personal debts, and soaring house prices in many parts of the country. Even so, the pound continued to edge upwards, to the dismay of exporters and the City of London. Confidence was further shaken when Mrs Thatcher, in response to repeated questioning in the Commons on 12 May, declined to speak out unequivocally in support of Mr Lawson's view that a rising pound was 'unsustainable and damaging' to the economy.

There were also indications that Sir Geoffrey Howe's sympathies lay with the Chancellor. He told Scottish Conservatives at a conference in Perth on 13 May that at an appropriate time Britain should join the European Monetary System (EMS), a step which was known to be opposed by the Prime Minister. Friends were on hand to explain that Sir Geoffrey had been upset by earlier comments by the Prime Minister which implied that she did not expect her successor to emerge from among the older generation of Ministers. There were more explicit signals from Mrs Thatcher later in the year which demonstrated her desire to serve for a fourth term as Prime Minister.

Although many Tory backbenchers were rallying strongly to the side of Mr Lawson, for the party as a whole the widely reported divisions between Nos 10 and 11 Downing Street were becoming too damaging politically for them to be tolerated much longer. A decision one way or the other had become a political imperative. The Chancellor and the Prime Minister met on the evening of 16 May. Enough was now said and agreed for Mrs Thatcher, on the following day, to make a statement to the Commons insisting that the Government would intervene as necessary to influence the level of the pound. The base rate was reduced to 7.5 per cent, while the Bank of England again intervened strongly to try to keep the pound below DM 3.20.

Even this gesture by Mrs Thatcher failed to dispel all doubts. The City of London continued to complain that the assumed divergence between Mrs Thatcher and Mr Lawson was undermining confidence in the Government's ability to handle the pound. The situation became more serious as sterling began to slip in response to disturbing evidence of a growing deficit on current account far in excess of earlier predictions. From 2 June interest rates began to creep up as a defensive measure. The trade figures for May showed that the Treasury estimate (announced in March) of a £4,000 million deficit for the whole year had already been exceeded. Pessimists observed that Britain was on course for a deficit which in relative terms was similar to that of the much criticized deficit of the United States. Imports of manufactures continued to rise much more quickly than their export counterparts.

Mr Lawson's response was to raise interest rates in small steps of half a per cent, in the hope of discouraging a sudden great inflow of foreign money to take advantage of higher returns. The rise in the base rate to 10.5 per cent on 18 July forced a sharp increase in mortgage rates from August, a rise which cancelled out much or all of the gains of the average taxpayer from the March Budget. The June trade figures added another £1,000 million to the deficit, yet the strength of sterling still required action from the Bank of England during July. Nor did it yet appear that Mrs Thatcher and Mr Lawson had resolved all their differences, especially when it was announced that the Prime Minister's former economic adviser, Sir Alan Walters, would be returning to Britain to assist her in 1989. Criticisms of the Chancellor's strategy by Sir Alan in line with the economic thinking of Mrs Thatcher—interest rates, in his view, should be used only to control the money supply and inflation—fuelled such speculation.

On the other hand, industrialists and the powerful 1922 Committee of Conservative MPs continued to favour Mr Lawson, and on 21 July the Prime Minister finally decided to speak out unequivocally in praise of her Chancellor. The Cabinet reshuffle four days later confirmed that both Mr Lawson and the Foreign Secretary were likely to enjoy security of tenure for the rest of 1988. Nevertheless, a point had been reached when the Government's claims concerning the success of its economic policies were beginning to be treated more sceptically, even by some of its erstwhile defenders.

As early as 28 June the worsening balance of payments had brought a sharp attack in *The Times* on the Chancellor's complacent claim of 30 March that the 'question of what level, within a wide range, the current account of the balance of payments may be in a particular year is really a very second-order matter'. Another remark was soon to return to haunt Mr Lawson. As City analysts became more alarmed during the summer, the Chancellor was reported as saying: 'I would not take too much notice of the teenage scribblers in the City who jump up and down in an effort to get press attention.' But even his critics were surprised as well as shocked by the July trade figures, which revealed a record deficit of no less than £2,150 million. This time there was a one point increase in the base rate to 12 per cent, the eighth increase since early June. The Chancellor conceded that this rate might be necessary for some time to reduce the over-heating in the economy.

Though themselves taken aback by the July figures, the City 'scribblers' felt entitled to claim that the Treasury had seriously misread the prospects of the economy in its preparations for the Budget, and that, while the tax cuts might not yet have had time to take full effect, they had helped to create the 'loadsamoney' euphoria of the spring and early summer (the reference being to a character created by a popular television comedian). The subsequent cuts in interest rates, though understandable in the battle to restrain the rise in the pound, had only made matters worse. But if the Chancellor was now forced to admit that the country had been enjoying rather too much of a good thing, he was still not prepared to bow to those critics in the City and within his own party who challenged his reliance on interest rates alone to control consumer demand.

The economy was growing at around 5 or more per cent per annum, and this was reflected in the fall in unemployment to 2.3 million in July, the lowest level since June 1981. But this growth, the fastest since 1973, was less than the rising spending power of consumers, aided by an abundance of credit and by a sharp drop in personal saving. Imports grew faster than exports. The Confederation of British Industry (CBI) was troubled by inflation, which reached 5.9 per cent in September, higher than that of any other leading industrial nation. But where exporters ideally needed a pound that was both stable and competitive, the Chancellor now agreed with the Prime Minister that any fall in its value to offset rising costs at home, or through declining foreign confidence, would only reinforce domestic inflationary pressures.

The Chief Secretary to the Treasury, Mr John Major, stated on 11 September that one of the purposes of higher interest rates was to slow the rise in house prices. He also insisted that apart from the balance of payments the economy was in good shape. The current account deficits proved much less horrendous in August and September, although there was still a deficit of £4,000 million for the third quarter. Mr Lawson himself admitted to some problems while attending the West Berlin meeting of the International Monetary Fund and World Bank on 28–29 September. But at the same time he accused his critics of being 'prisoners of the past'. They were failing to see that the British economy was now much better equipped to sustain a large deficit than it had been—that is, until 'self-correcting mechanisms' took effect.

The Government drew most comfort from its estimates of the dramatic improvement in industrial productivity which had taken place since 1979 and from tax revenues which were well in excess of public spending. The Ford motor company also provided a useful vote of confidence—in contrast to the unfortunate Dundee affair (see pp. 29–30)—when it chose South Wales in preference to West Germany or Spain as the location for new plant at which to build car engines. On the other hand there was mounting concern about rising prices and growing shortages of skilled labour. The returns from North Sea oil were also diminishing, and were temporarily further depressed by the effects of the North Sea *Piper Alpha* disaster (see p. 43). The British Engineering Employers' Federation and the *United Kingdom Productivity Survey* for 1988 provided further evidence of just how much leeway British manufacturing production and productivity had still to make up in order to draw level with Britain's leading competitors.

From October Labour tried to seize the initiative on the economy with their *Neglect into the Nineties* campaign. In particular they criticized the levels of government spending on roads, railways, schools and houses since 1979. Industry required more investment if it was to keep pace with foreign competitors and to reverse the decline in its share of the British market since 1979. The Chancellor himself spoke somewhat defensively at the Mansion House on 19

October when he suggested that a year or two of slower growth was likely as the nation caught its breath. He conceded that the current-account deficit might persist into 1990.

A week later in the Commons Mr Lawson made a further statement to sustain foreign confidence in sterling. A strong and stable pound, he affirmed, was vital in the battle against inflation, the latter being a graver threat to the economy than high interest rates. Businessmen were warned not to look to a falling pound to offset rising production costs. Labour members, meanwhile, were busy congratulating Mr Gordon Brown for his confident assault on government economic policy. At short notice he had become Labour's key spokesman when Mr John Smith was temporarily incapacitated by a mild heart attack. On 2 November his rapid rise in party esteem was confirmed when, at the age of 37 and after only five years in Parliament, he topped the poll for a place in the Shadow Cabinet.

The Chancellor delivered his autumn spending statement to the Commons on 1 November. The forecasts he had given in March on inflation, the money supply and the balance of payments had all gone badly wrong, but Mr Lawson was able to announce that public spending—despite the significant increases proposed for 1989–90—was falling in relation to the gross national product. It now represented less than 40 per cent of national income for the first time in 20 years. He intended to persist with the squeeze on consumers while warning of slower growth and a large balance of payments deficit in 1989.

The squeeze became even tighter on 25 November when base rates were raised by a further 1 per cent to 13 per cent in response to a record current-account deficit of over £2,400 million for the month of October. Mr Heath criticized the Chancellor on 29 November for playing—in golfing parlance—a 'one-club' game, while the Welsh Secretary, Mr Peter Walker (in a speech at a private dinner in the Carlton Club), was similarly critical of the reliance on interest rates. Nevertheless, Conservative MPs gave the Government a majority of 105 against an Opposition amendment which attacked current economic policies. At the same time, some economists with long memories unkindly recalled that a year earlier the Chancellor had been hoping to hold the pound at around DM 2.90 and $1.60, that is at more than 10 per cent below its current levels. Sir Donald MacDougall, in the Keynes Lecture to the British Academy on 8 December, criticized not only some aspects of Government policy but also some of the claims made relating to the economic achievements of the 1980s. CBI surveys at the end of the year suggested a deterioration in export order books (although domestic demand was strong) and reinforced worries lest sterling should remain 'uncompetitively strong'. Meanwhile inflation stood at around 6.4 per cent at the end of the year.

Chapter 3

LEGISLATIVE CONTROVERSIES

WIDELY described as the 'flagship' of Government legislation in Mrs Thatcher's third term, the Local Government Finance Bill to introduce the community charge or poll tax to replace rates in England and Wales had a stormy passage before it received the Royal Assent at the end of July. Its second reading in the Commons on 17 December 1987 had been opposed by 17 Conservatives, and there had been nearly as many abstentions. This unease in Tory ranks persisted in 1988, prompting Lord Jenkins to remark during a debate in the Lords on 8 May that of the present members of the Cabinet he believed its only convinced supporters to be Mrs Thatcher and Mr Nicholas Ridley (who, as Environment Secretary, was responsible for piloting the Bill through Parliament). At the beginning of April Mr Michael Mates led more than 40 Conservative backbenchers in a bid to establish a link between the poll tax and an ability to pay based on the highest rate at which an individual paid income tax. This move sufficiently alarmed the Government for Mr Ridley to meet numerous Tory backbenchers on 14 April in one of the largest such gatherings since 1979. The Minister agreed to increase the number eligible for relief by one million (to 9 million in all) and to increase the generosity of the levels of rebate in some other cases. Support for Mr Mates's amendment receded a little, but even so the Government secured a majority of only 25 after the crucial debate on 18 April. Mr Heath and Mr Heseltine were among the 38 Tory dissidents.

On the third reading of the Bill on 25 April the Government had a majority of 63, but 17 Tories still voted against and there were 10 or more abstentions. Sir Barney Hayhoe, a former Health Minister, went so far as to deny that the poll tax was a Conservative measure: it was a product of the imperatives of 'Thatcherism'. There were some further minor concessions by the Government. Thus pressure from three Conservative local councils led to a reversal of the decision that four London boroughs should phase in the poll tax—rates would now be ended entirely in April 1990. Mr Ridley also made concessions on the introduction of the uniform business rate.

Meanwhile, the Bill's treatment in the Lords was attracting intense interest. More was at stake than its detailed provisions. Given its financial character the right of the Lords to amend such a measure was in dispute. *The Times* of 20 April argued that, as the money in question was raised by the local authorities and was not subject to parliamentary approval, the Lords were constitutionally entitled to amend the Bill. Sir William Wade, a leading constitutional lawyer, cautiously commented that it seemed to be 'accepted' that amendments by the Lords to fiscal bills were not 'normally regarded outright as unconstitutional', but were considered on their merits by the Commons. These 'tolerant' rules suggested that their Lordships might feel entitled to 'have a go' and see what happened. The former Lord Chancellor, Lord Hailsham, however, insisted that the Lords would be exceeding their powers, while the Government itself left no one in any doubt of its determination to see off any challenge by the other House which, like the churches, had already earned itself no small reputation for its readiness to challenge Government policy.

Lord Chelwood, formerly Sir Tufton Beamish MP, introduced an amendment requiring that the community charge should be related to ability to pay. Lord Hailsham replied that this was a 'wrecking' and 'unconstitutional' amendment. But it was Lord Whitelaw who made the most influential speech in which he pleaded with his fellow peers not to damage the reputation of the revising chamber and precipitate a confrontation with the elected House. Amid whispers of a possible constitutional crisis, the Government busily mobilized support and even had recourse to a three-line whip (a rare occurrence in the Lords). The second reading of the Bill on 9 May drew the biggest attendance in the Lords since 1971 and one of the biggest of the century. The amendment was defeated by 317 to 183, with only 14 Conservative peers, including two former Cabinet Ministers, Lords Pym and Carr, supporting Lord Chelwood. Mr Kinnock commented bitterly on the appearance of so many (some 60 or 70 according to one Labour estimate) unfamiliar faces in the Palace of Westminster. 'Rarely', he said, 'has so much been taken away from so many by so few so unjustly.' Labour peers felt that the episode justified their earlier complaint that since 1982 their side of the House had suffered a net loss of seven peers compared with a Conservative gain of 18 as a result of Mrs Thatcher's selective creation of new peers.

The Government continued to take a firm line on the controversial Bill. Mr Ridley rejected such amendments as had been carried in the Lords on the ground that they represented a challenge to the 'financial privileges' of the Commons. On 26 July the Lords duly bowed to the Government's requirement that the disabled on low incomes should pay 20 per cent of the poll tax, and that there should be no discounts for student nurses. In the course of further debate on the constitutional position, Lord Tonypandy, a former Labour MP and Speaker of the Commons, was among those to uphold the

Government's claims that the Lords had been trying to overstep their powers.

On 11 April the Government's far-reaching changes to the social security system began to take effect. The *Observer* of 10 April protested that a new Poor Law had been established. There had been, it affirmed, a fundamental departure from the principles laid down in the Beveridge Report in the 1940s. *The Guardian* of 18 April protested, 'In the same month that the top 5 per cent of taxpayers were given £1,750 million in the budget, the poor have had their housing benefits cut, free school meals abolished and special emergency payments cancelled.'

There was also detailed criticism from the independent Social Security Advisory Committee. Although it welcomed the efforts to simplify the complex of rules and regulations which had accumulated over the last 40 years, and agreed that benefit should be concentrated upon those most in need without removing the incentives for personal effort, it drew attention to numerous examples of undeserved hardship.

The middle of April proved to be an unusually difficult time in Parliament for the Government as other issues excited controversy. In particular, the introduction of new charges for dental and eye tests provoked sufficient concern among a number of Conservative MPs for Mrs Thatcher to pay a visit to the House of Commons tea room to test the mood of Conservative backbenchers for herself. A Marplan poll at the same time highlighted popular dissatisfaction with the Government's handling of the NHS, while even Conservative voters appeared relatively unimpressed with its social policies. The Government, it seemed, was retaining its lead over Labour in the polls mainly because of fears of what might happen to the economy under a Labour Administration.

Mrs Thatcher's first reaction was to dig in her heels, and to reiterate her belief that the Government had funded social security on a generous scale—at some £46,000 million it represented one-third of Government spending. She claimed that five million would benefit from the new provisions, only one million would lose, while two million would be unaffected. But the unrest on the Tory backbenches persisted, some MPs claiming that they were receiving even more complaints from constituents than on the vexed subject of the community charge. A more damaging revolt than that on the poll tax was considered possible. The Government therefore finally granted a number of concessions, notably further transitional help for those who stood to lose more than £2.50 per week, while on the question of housing benefit the personal savings limit was raised from £6,000 to £8,000 before entitlement was lost. Many Conservative MPs had been particularly anxious not to be seen to penalize thrift.

Some former Conservative Ministers also continued to make comprehensive attacks on the Government. Mr Heath seized his opportunity when delivering the Harold Macmillan Memorial Lecture in Nottingham on 13 May to put the case for 'national', not 'divisive' policies. Mr Heseltine commanded even more attention as one who was still seen as a possible candidate for the Conservative leadership at some time in the future and especially in the event of a dramatic change in the fortunes of his party. On 11 April he offered his alternative to the Government's 'hands off' approach, and pleaded for direct intervention to channel resources from the south-east of England to the more depressed among the provincial areas. His speech came at a time when not a few Tory MPs with rural seats in the south were disturbed by Mr Ridley's readiness to permit more farmland to be transformed into housing estates, thus threatening the character of various parts of England's 'green and pleasant land'.

On 10 May Mr Ridley defended his deregulation of some green-field sites in southern England to the Bow Group. There was, he said, no threat to the Green Belt. The growing number of households necessitated more housing units if the housing cost spiral was to be checked and poorer families protected. He insisted that in time—and already he detected some movement in this direction—market forces would lead to economic expansion in the north with consequent relief in the south. But some 90 Tory MPs remained sceptical, to say the least, and agreed with Mr Kim Warren, the MP for Hastings, that a 'devastating attack' on the culture and lifestyle of people throughout the south-east was taking place. Elsewhere work on the Channel tunnel and on the M40 motorway added to the number of critics.

Meanwhile, the Government was not ruling out action on its own part on behalf of run-down areas. Mr Peter Walker, Secretary of State for Wales, announced a package of measures on 14 July which were designed to revitalize some of the valleys in South Wales. Through public expenditure of £500 million it was hoped to attract twice as much private investment, and so create some 25,000 jobs. It was acknowledged that some government help in the clearing of derelict land, in modernization of the infrastructure and in the improvement of housing was necessary. Meanwhile, an interesting and productive alliance was developing between the Labour-controlled city council of Newcastle and the CBI's inner-cities task force. This was very much in accord with the wishes of the Government. A number of southern businessmen were also beginning to discover that life north of Watford was not without its attractions.

Concern over the rise of violent crime and vandalism continued to mount in 1988, but there was additional evidence that these were not merely the by-products of poverty and unemployment. The Association of Chief Police Officers publicized the growth in crime among the young in small towns and rural areas. Reliance on mobile units rather than a few policemen on the spot when the pubs closed was one cause. But the outbreak of serious disorder in many parts of the country from Cornwall to Yorkshire during one weekend—that of 18–19 June—indicated something more serious. Senior policemen thought this a symptom of a 'national disease'. Many of the culprits were well-paid 'yuppies' from the affluent south. Although recorded crime in England and Wales in the year to June 1988 fell slightly (for the first time since 1983), violence against the person increased by 17 per cent, and sexual offences by 16 per cent.

The midsummer solstice at Stonehenge brought further disturbances, but more serious and disappointing was the behaviour of British football fans in West Germany during the European championships, also in the middle of June. This was frustrating after the time and money spent in the search for solutions to crowd violence. The Prime Minister gave vent to her anger when she met representatives of English football on 16 June. The Government warned on 6 July that it was preparing legislation to restrict entry to football matches to members who carried identity cards, and it was later announced that the new system would be introduced in 1990. A government source added: 'This sport is blackening the name of Britain [sic] across the world', and even stiffer penalties were under review, including England's non-participation in the 1990 World Cup.

The Prince of Wales addressed the theme of violence when opening the Museum of the Moving Image on London's South Bank on 15 September. He condemned the 'incessant menu of utterly gratuitous violence' on television and cinema screens. The Home Secretary, Mr Douglas Hurd, spoke in similar terms four days later, expanding upon remarks he had made during the Commons debate of 7 June on capital punishment (the motion for its restoration being defeated by 314 votes to 218). He had then insisted that preoccupation with the death penalty could deflect attention from the wider and more important issue of violence in British society. The rise in crime among the very young was also attracting attention. Children were turning to crime at the age of 11, with the peak of offences occurring at the age of 15. Teaching unions joined in the debate, reporting that it was now a serious problem even in primary schools.

Moral issues in politics were prominent in the first half of the year. It was argued that preoccupation with material success was leading to 'don't care' attitudes and to a disregard of means in the pursuit of individual rewards. Labour frequently claimed that Mrs Thatcher's legacy would be one of social disintegration and the blighting of individual lives. Churchmen were prominent among the critics, with the Bishops of Durham and Southwark differing only as to whether the Government's policy on social security was best described as 'verging on the wicked' or as only 'iniquitous' and 'insufficiently Christian'.

Mrs Thatcher struck back on 21 April. She addressed the General Assembly of the Church of Scotland, partly because of the criticisms directed against her policies by the Kirk, but also because of the depth of Scottish hostility to 'Thatcherism'. The Prime Minister set out the spiritual beliefs underlying her political philosophy. While acknowledging that the state had a duty to help the needy, she reaffirmed the importance of incentives and personal responsibility. From St Paul's Epistle to the Thessalonians she drew the text, 'If a man will not work he shall not eat'. Not surprisingly biblical quotations peppered the replies from the critics of 'St Margaret's First Epistle to the Caledonians', and there followed a particularly acerbic exchange between Mrs Thatcher and Mr Kinnock in the Commons on 24 May as they battled for the high moral ground of politics.

On 29 July the Education Reform Bill completed its passage through Parliament after some 370 hours of debate, a postwar record. Even so the Government was obliged to use a guillotine motion on 19 July to hasten the conclusion. Though subjected to a barrage of criticism from many quarters, the Secretary of State for Education, Mr Kenneth Baker, had achieved his main objectives (see AR 1987, pp. 27–9). It is true that he bowed a little to the worries of church leaders, offering reassurance on 24 March concerning the status of religious education within the national curriculum, while safeguards for other faiths were introduced alongside the provisions for regular Christian worship. Unease among some Conservatives, as well as the Opposition, over the procedure whereby schools would be allowed to opt out of local authority control reached a climax in the Lords on 12 May when an amendment was carried by 144 votes to 121 requiring a majority of *all* the parents with children in a particular school to vote in favour of receiving a grant direct from the Government. Here too Mr Baker yielded a little, agreeing that if less than half the parents took part in the vote a second vote would be necessary before a simple majority was allowed to prevail. The Act also provided for the abolition of the Inner London Education Authority from 1 April 1990, and redefined academic tenure and freedom in universities. Parents in Skegness became the first, on 2 November, to endorse plans for a school to opt out from local authority control.

A report by Her Majesty's Inspectors in July that one quarter of the nation's schools were unsatisfactory was seized upon by both Mr Baker and his critics. For Mr Baker it was further proof of the need for a national curriculum, the provision of greater choice and influence by parents, and the delegation of more financial autonomy to the schools themselves. He was confident that the Act would transform education over the next few years. But his critics continued to protest at the enhanced powers of the Secretary of State, and warned that 'opting out' would lead to the emergence of first and second class schools. The national curriculum itself remained a subject of controversy. Complaints about the under-funding of the new GCSE examination and other strains and shortages within the education system persisted.

Such worries reinforced interest in the outcome of the first GCSE examination held in the early summer. Her Majesty's Inspectors gave their first impressions in October. They thought it too early to judge whether standards had improved, but agreed that the GCSE was of major importance in the drive to improve the quality of secondary education. The examination was not yet properly serving either the least or the most able, nor were they so far convinced that it provided an adequate grounding for A level. Nevertheless, there was a widespread sense of relief at the overall results after the many difficulties which had attended the introduction of the new courses.

The Government continued its battle to control local authority spending with an announcement by Mr Ridley on 6 July that in future it would be looking very closely at the scale of local authority borrowing. Some councils had circumvented Government measures by recourse to various and often ingenious credit schemes, resulting in some £45,000 million of debt at a cost to the ratepayers of £6,000 million a year in interest. Permission was given for English local authority spending to rise by 4.7 per cent in the financial year 1989–90, but seven authorities, all in London, would continue to be rate-capped for a second year.

Meanwhile, the Local Government Bill had received the Royal Assent on 24 March, a measure which required local authorities to put more services out to competitive tender, and which was also designed to strengthen the private sector in the provision of rented accommodation.

Chapter 4

THE OPPOSITION PARTIES—FUTURE OBSCURE

THE Social Democrats (SDP) and Liberals offered their two big rivals a handsome New Year present when their first attempt to launch the new merged party ended, as one journalist put it, in 'a crash landing'. The policy document drawn up under the direction of the two party leaders, Mr Robert Maclennan and Mr David Steel, was promptly disowned by the Liberals on 13 January. It was surprisingly and provocatively detailed in its references to the retention of the Trident missile system and the extension of VAT to food, fuel and children's clothes. Mr Maclennan, it seemed, was more intent on thwarting any challenge from former SDP leader Dr David Owen and his followers than in reassuring and cultivating his intended partners. But Mr Steel's political judgment appeared equally suspect.

Neither Mr Steel nor Mr Maclennan was a member of the new two-party team which was set up to draft a fresh document. This was completed on 18 January and was altogether a more discreet affair. It avoided or postponed controversy with as much determination as the first attempt had courted it. On the question of Trident, for instance, it argued that the new party should be guided by circumstances. Even the proposed name of the party was changed—from New Liberal and Social Democratic Party, or Alliance for short, to Social and Liberal Democratic Party (SLDP).

Even so, the outcome of the special Liberal assembly to set its seal of approval on the merger was not regarded as a foregone conclusion. A week of uncertainty in Blackpool, however, ended on 23 January with a resounding vote for union by no less than 2,099 votes to 385. Mr Steel regained some lost ground with a skilful speech. A two-day Social Democrat meeting followed in Sheffield on 30–31 January. This, not surprisingly, turned out to be an acrimonious affair as the two factions from the old party battled to build new bases for the future. The final vote for union was overwhelming, but the Owenities claimed that only 57 per cent of those eligible to vote had in fact done so. They also insisted that they were the 'continuing SDP'. The extent of the rift and disillusionment in the ranks of the old SDP was apparent when a ballot of all members on union elicited returns from only 55 per cent of their number, and a vote of only 2 to 1 in favour of the SLDP. An even lower Liberal vote, in contrast, found support running at about 7 to 1 for the merger. The new party officially came into being on 3 March.

After a period of reflection Mr Steel finally ruled himself out as a candidate for the leadership of the SLDP. The contest was therefore between the contrasting personalities and political experience of two Liberal MPs, Mr Paddy Ashdown, the extrovert ex-marine officer who had been elected MP for Yeovil as recently as 1983, and the former Liberal chief whip and scholarly Mr Alan Beith. Although Mr Beith seemed closer to the mainstream currents in the Liberal Party, Mr Ashdown nevertheless won an impressive victory on 28 July, with some 70 per cent of the vote. His triumph probably owed much to the feeling of party members that they had lost much ground with the electorate in recent months and to their concern over the continuing challenge posed by the albeit much weakened Owenites. Forceful, eye-catching leadership—even a readiness to take risks—seemed imperative.

Apart from its performance in the local elections in May, the SLDP found little to boost its morale in 1988. The SDP and SLDP held their party conferences in quick succession in the second half of September. Dr Owen, who had hitherto appeared to lean towards the Conservatives rather than the left, was now moving back to the centre and even left of centre in British politics. At the conference in Torquay he accused Mrs Thatcher of creating 'an upstairs, downstairs' society. On 19 September he called on the other opposition parties to form a coalition to defeat the Conservatives. Not surprisingly there were no takers. Mr Roy Hattersley, the Labour deputy leader, dismissed Dr Owen as a man in search of a party, and some of his own supporters seemed doubtful of their leader's wisdom in placing so much emphasis on proportional representation in his programme for the future.

The SLDP in Blackpool were also striving to carve out a distinctive identity for themselves. Despite much soul-searching in the ranks of former Liberals, the short working title of Democrats was chosen for use when the party was working at national level. The name Liberal was not, however, to disappear from constituency and local politics. The new leader, Mr Ashdown, stamped his authority on the conference, and potentially controversial issues never really surfaced. He admitted that the party stood on the edge of a precipice, and that much had to be achieved in as short a space of time as possible. His ultimate aim was the displacement of Labour, but at the conference he concentrated on environmental problems and support for the EEC.

Meanwhile, neither the painful transformation of the Alliance into a new party nor the controversial legislation being pushed through Parliament by the Conservatives was working obviously to the advantage of Labour. Even when confidence in the state of the economy was disturbed in the summer, the Conservatives continued to retain a useful lead over Labour in the polls. Indeed, although the alliance of the soft left, centre and right under Mr Kinnock was being used to powerful effect to contain Mr Tony Benn and his allies on the national executive committee (Mr Kinnock could usually count on 22 votes against four for Mr Benn), and although the seven policy review groups were busily drafting the outlines of an updated programme, there was no reason to suppose that the position and influence of the so-called 'new realists' had been fully established. Mr Denis Healey, for instance, argued that the unions remained the party's biggest problem in view of the popular perception both of the unions in the workplace and of their influence over Labour.

In January a ballot for the executive in the Transport and General Workers Union resulted in a victory for the hard left, a setback for Mr Kinnock who now had to expect intermittent if not regular opposition from that powerful union. Meanwhile, many of the hard left launched a direct challenge to the 'new realists'. On 23 March Mr Benn announced that he would run against Mr Kinnock for the party leadership in October. Mr Eric Heffer agreed to stand against Mr Hattersley for the deputy leadership. It is true that this contest gave Mr Kinnock an opportunity to enhance his position as leader (Mr Benn's candidacy was opposed even by some on the far left of the party), but the ensuing months of highly charged debate provided the party's enemies with valuable propaganda openings, and hindered the efforts of the 'new realists' to project Labour as a united, forward-looking movement. Worse followed with the decision of Mr John Prescott, the shadow spokesman on energy, to join in the challenge to Mr Hattersley. Mr Prescott was a representative of the 'old Labourism', and those for whom Clause IV was still an essential part of the bible of the movement.

Labour's internal divisions deepened even as the party was celebrating its successes in the local elections of 5 May, Mr Kinnock claiming that Labour would have done still better had it not been for the leadership contest. Mr Benn retorted that it had helped the party's cause. Labour's pleasure in a net gain of 107 seats and a 4 per cent advantage in votes over the Conservatives was also tarnished a little by the fact that the SLDP vote (about 20 per cent of the poll) held up reasonably well, while it was only because of further setbacks in Scotland that the Conservatives emerged with a nationwide net loss of five seats. Psephologists concluded in the light of these results that there had been no fundamental change in political allegiances since the general election.

Meanwhile, the first reports of the policy review groups were completed and were approved by the NEC over the protests of Mr Benn and his allies, who now described themselves as the proponents of the only genuine alternative programme to 'Thatcherism'. They dismissed the work of the review committees as proof that Labour had become a party of Mark II Social Democrats—the groups had rejected wholesale nationalization, had acknowledged the importance of market forces, had accepted membership of the EEC, and had drawn up a general statement on defence which supported British membership of Nato. Mr Benn was determined to reverse party policy on all these issues. The party leaders fought back fiercely, with Mr Hattersley on 18 June accusing Mr Benn of 'giving comfort to our enemies', and of knowingly threatening Labour's chances at the next election. Mr Kinnock condemned the 'impossibilism' of the hard left.

The policy review process faced other problems within the party as a whole. The reports dealt with most problems only in broad terms, and many tough decisions had yet to be taken, notably on defence. Just how fragile the position could be was demonstrated by Mr Kinnock himself on 5 June when he commented on the future of Trident in the course of a television programme. He said: 'We want to get rid of Trident. But the fact is that it does not have to be something for nothing.' This was promptly interpreted by most people, though not by Mr Hattersley, as evidence that Mr Kinnock was moving away from unilateralism. Earlier remarks had contained hints of his acceptance of the facts that Britain was part of an alliance which was determined to resist and deter any potential threat, and that US membership of Nato meant that the nuclear dimension was bound to be present. On 20 June, after a surprising delay, Mr Kinnock offered a gloss on his remarks, claiming that under his leadership Britain's submarine missile fleet would be decommissioned irrespective of Soviet reactions. He added that it was now possible to forecast Soviet behaviour and to anticipate that the outcome would indeed be 'something for something', so deep was the Soviet commitment to disarmament.

In the interval, however, much damage had been done as people put their own interpretation on Mr Kinnock's words. There had been a storm of protest from the unilateralists. Mr Prescott insisted that the party leader could not depart from a conference decision. The Transport and General Workers' Union (TGWU), which sponsored Mr Kinnock as an MP and which would control more than 8 per cent of the votes to be cast in the October leadership elections, announced that it was not yet prepared to endorse the Kinnock-Hattersley 'dream ticket'. A representative of the soft left spoke of the 'confusion and general concern' which Mr Kinnock had caused with his remarks, and of the need for him to reaffirm his commitment to unilateralism. Finally, Labour's defence spokesman, Mr Denzil Davies, after several days of anguished reflection, announced his resignation from the post, complaining that he was 'fed up with being humiliated' and ignored by Neil Kinnock.

Earlier in the year the Labour Party was seriously embarrassed by an inter-union dispute which came to a head in the second half of March. This deprived Dundee of the prospect of perhaps 1,000 much-needed jobs. The Amalgamated Engineering Union (AEU) had negotiated a single-union deal with Ford to set up a £40 million high technology plant. The agreement, however, was resolutely opposed by the TGWU, which argued that this single-union arrangement would wreck its own 'blue book' agreement which governed union-management relations in other Ford plants. Various efforts were made by the TUC to devise a compromise, but overtures to Ford resulted in a blunt announcement on 25 March that the project could not go ahead when British unions could not guarantee the conditions which were needed to ensure the plant's competitiveness. At one point the AEU hinted that it might decide to leave the TUC, while the Labour Party was exposed to scathing Conservative attacks in Parliament. On 23 March Mr Malcolm Rifkind, the Secretary of State for Scotland, provoked pandemonium on the Opposition benches when he teased Labour with its 'deafening silence' on this issue. The *Observer* on 27 March noted that, although Mr Kinnock was in an awkward position as an MP sponsored by the TGWU, he had to make his position clear on the whole area of modern industrial relations if he was to convince the electors of his determination to meet the challenge of the hard left, and to justify his claims to be the leader of the 'realists'.

Mr Norman Willis, the TUC's general secretary, urged unions to be more flexible on the subject of single-union arrangements with management, and indeed the TGWU itself concluded two such deals which promised to generate 1,300 new jobs in Wales. In this instance the TUC's disputes committee had adjudicated between the unions competing for the agreement. But controversy continued. Thus Mr Clive Jenkins of the white-collar Manufacturing, Scientific and Finance Union rebuffed Mr Willis's advice and insisted that his union would not participate in 'bizarre auctions of the British people, selling them and their jobs for the lowest rates'. The TUC went on with its search for a code of practice to control single-union deals, but remained deeply divided over the question of no-strike agreements.

Meanwhile, Mr Eric Hammond and the electricians' union (EEPTU) provoked the angriest reactions from traditional trade unionists. On 22 June the TUC general council voted to suspend the EEPTU for its refusal to scrap two single-union no-strike deals in accord with the verdict of two disputes committees whose awards in inter-union conflicts had gone against the EEPTU. Mr Willis accused the union's leaders of 'wilfully refusing to accept their obligations'. But a ballot of EEPTU members in July produced a vote of over 80 per cent in favour of its executive (although less than half of the membership voted), while Mr Hammond on 19 July described the result as the first step towards an independent union organization.

With the approach of the TUC conference in Bournemouth there were last-minute efforts, notably by the TUC general secretary, to persuade the EEPTU to 'pull back from the precipice'. However, the vote for the expulsion of the 330,000 strong EEPTU was overwhelmingly carried, the most significant opposition coming from the AEU, whose leader, Mr Bill Jordan, warned that the movement now faced 'the most vicious membership war in its history'. Already a breakaway union, the Electrical Plumbing Industries Union led by Mr John Aitken, hoped to attract up to 30,000 from the EEPTU. Mr Hammond retorted that while members were free to leave his union, the door was 'also open for anyone to come in'. All trade unionists and potential trade unionists, he said, now had a choice between the future and past, and the opportunity to join a truly democratic forward-looking union.

The conference agreed that the decline in membership, despite the rising number of people in work, required positive action by the unions. But Mr Bill Jordan's enthusiasm for single-union deals was not seen as a solution by many of his comrades. They were not a panacea, said Mr John Edmonds of the General, Municipal, Boilermakers and Allied Trades Union (GMB), who, though leading a union which prided itself on meeting the needs of the home-owning, credit-card carrying employee, also warned against the acceptance of 'values handed down by multinational companies'. *The Times* of 5 September predicted, however, that the expulsion of the electricians would prove to be another example of the movement's tendency to dig 'elephant traps' for itself.

The fall in the membership of the National Union of Mineworkers (NUM) below 100,000—partly as a result of the general decline in the number of coal-miners but also of the continuing activities of the rival Union of Democratic Miners—meant that Mr Arthur Scargill was no longer automatically entitled to a place on the TUC's general council. His failure to be elected as a representative of one of the smaller unions marked the end of the mining union's continuous presence on the council since 1889. The TUC also drew back from supporting unlawful action to stop the implementation of the community charge, but promised its backing for every 'legal' endeavour to reverse the legislation.

The TUC discovered a new enthusiasm for the EEC, responding warmly to an address from M. Jacques Delors, President of the European Commission, on 8 September. M. Delors proposed European legislation to give all workers the right to be covered by collective agreements, and to enjoy other benefits. To the delight of the conference M. Delors insisted that 1992 meant more than the creation of a single market (see p. 40): it was also about workers' rights and social reform. Mr Ron Todd, the TGWU leader, argued that British unions must learn to use European languages and methods in the fight for the future of industrial democracy.

The TUC conference also provided a pointer to the Labour Party conference when it voted overwhelmingly in favour of unilateralism and rejected the Labour manifesto pledge to increase spending on conventional forces. An amendment that the unilateralist defence policy should be developed within 'the context of membership of Nato' was similarly turned down. Nevertheless, when the party met in Blackpool a month later those who favoured the introduction of a more flexible stance on defence were able to draw some comfort from the unusually small majority (only 1,244,000) which supported unilateralism in the vote at the end of the defence debate on 6 October. Unilateralism was seemingly weakening, and Mr Kinnock and his allies insisted that they did not regard the vote as 'conclusive'. The party required a defence policy which could 'secure the support of the people of our country'. This brought an angry retort from Mr Todd, whose union had done much to ensure a victory for the unilateralists. He warned that if an inch were conceded to those who wished to revise Labour policy they would take 'a mile, and another mile and another mile'. Mr Ken Livingstone MP predicted civil war within the party if Mr Kinnock tried to abandon unilateralism.

On the other hand the defence issue was exploited by those in the Labour movement who believed that the time had come to decrease the power of the unions which, it was estimated, controlled something like 90 per cent of the conference vote. The cause of 'one member, one vote' in the determination of party policy was very much alive, as action spearheaded by Mr Kinnock later in year demonstrated. The conference itself approved the introduction of national membership (as an alternative to membership of a constituency organization) as part of its campaign to quadruple party strength.

Mr Kinnock also had the satisfaction of seeing himself re-elected leader by 88.6 per cent of the vote. The 'dream ticket' was completed when Mr Hattersley fought off the challenge from Mr Eric Heffer and Mr John Prescott. There was an equally encouraging start for the 'realists' when the conference on 4 October voted by 5 to 1 in favour of the keynote document, *Aims and Values*, despite its emphasis on 'social ownership' in place of nationalization. A call from Mr Scargill for the renationalization of all industries privatized since 1979 was easily defeated, as was a left-wing proposal for a law-breaking campaign against the poll tax. But Mr Todd, whose union had belatedly confirmed its support for the 'dream ticket' and had voted for the *Aims and Values* document, warned the leadership not to think that it was being given a blank cheque. Where Mr Kinnock had urged the party to abandon sloganizing and to prove that it could run the market economy better than Mrs Thatcher, Mr Todd bitterly attacked this new 'sharp-suited, cordless telephone socialism'. *Aims and Values*, he insisted, would not win the battle of ideas for Labour. The conference reached its climax with a passionate call from Mr Kinnock for self-discipline and realism. There were no prizes for guessing which comrades he had in mind.

Chapter 5

THE FINAL QUARTER

THE Conservatives assembled in good heart for their party conference in Brighton on 11 October despite poignant memories of the IRA bomb blast at the Grand Hotel four years earlier (see AR 1984, pp. 27–8), and despite the intensive security precautions. Government Ministers left no one in any doubt of their determination to continue the fight against terrorism. The Energy Secretary, Mr Cecil Parkinson, on 12 October extended this mood of defiance to the campaign for further privatization, a campaign which, he insisted, would reject the presence of 'no-go' areas in any part of the economy. He delighted delegates with the prospect of the 'ultimate privatization'—that of the coal industry—after the next election. The following day the Transport Secretary, Mr Channon, promised that private sector investment would play a major role in future road and railway development—perhaps in the building of a high-speed London-Channel tunnel rail link. A study of the complete privatization of British Rail was also being undertaken.

The debate on Britain's relations with the EEC indicated that there was more support for the party chairman's view that the British people wanted neither socialism nor federalism in Europe than for the supra-national vision of Mr Heath. Lord Young joined in the attacks on M. Delors's corporatist proposals for Europe. Britain wanted free-market policies and did not intend to be forced backwards to the 1970s. While Mr Heseltine continued to put the case for more state involvement in economic and still more in social questions, enthusiasm for individual responsibility and the market generally dominated the conference.

These were the central themes of Mrs Thatcher's speech on 14 October. Speaking the day after her 63rd birthday, she announced that this was no time for the party to rest on its laurels. 'We are all too young to put our feet up. And I hope you will excuse me if I include myself.' Prosperity, she argued, meant that the majority had the means to help the poor, and the result was a 'generous' society, not the 'selfish' society invented by her critics.

It was generally agreed at the end of the party conference season that the political initiative still lay with the Conservatives. The SDP and the SLDP had lost a lot of ground compared with the Alliance a year earlier, while Labour was still struggling to put together a new programme and to convince voters that its divisions were no longer significant. Despite the fact that there was now much less popular optimism concerning Britain's economic prospects, and although much of the Conservative legislative programme had yet to win strong support among the public, opinion polls conducted in the last months of the year still gave the Conservatives a comfortable lead, founded in particular on the belief that the economy was safest in their hands.

But the autumn also witnessed growing interest in a longer time-span than the outcome of the next election as new and disturbing evidence appeared on a number of environmental problems, and especially on the hole in the ozone layer over the South Pole. This gave rise to varied estimates of the 'greenhouse effect', and possible climatic changes and rises in sea level in the twenty-first century. Mrs Thatcher in a speech to the Royal Society on 27 September described the protection of the balance of nature as 'one of the greatest challenges' to mankind in the next hundred years. On 21 December the Government announced its ratification of an international agreement intended to restrict the use of substances which were destroying the world's ozone layer. It had earlier agreed to participate in an international research investigation into the causes of the damage to the ozone layer. On the other hand, environmentalists were dismayed by its claim that more nuclear power stations were the only answer to the worsening 'greenhouse effect' caused by the atmospheric discharges from conventional power stations.

In the autumn the Government quickly ran into trouble in Parliament on a number of social and health issues. Many objected to the decision to freeze child benefit for a second year, despite the provision of an extra £70 million for parents on low incomes. Similarly on 1 November the Government had to be content with Commons majorities of only 8 and 16 in the votes on charges for eye and dental check-ups. At one time no fewer than 60 Tory backbenchers seemed prepared to defy the Government. Defeat was only averted by strenuous efforts by the Whips and by the Chancellors's promise of an extra £2,000 million for the NHS in 1989–90. Rebellious Tories in the Lords were also active. For the second time in the year the Government spoke of a possible constitutional crisis, and mobilized the support of rare attenders in the Lords to achieve a majority of 50 in favour of the charge for eye tests.

Meanwhile, the Government was already stumbling into another furore. A briefing to reporters by Mr Lawson on 4 November on pensioners' benefits ignited a fierce controversy with the Chancellor insisting that he had been misreported on the issue of future targeting of certain benefits. The 'misreporting' arose from a private briefing which he gave to journalists, although most of the latter were certain that they had conveyed his remarks accurately. On 7 November, in an effort to allay fears of what the Government might be contemplating with respect to pensioners, he announced that plans were afoot to provide more money for over a million of Britain's oldest and poorest pensioners. These increases would not be funded out of existing resources but by new funds from the Treasury. The Opposition, however, scented blood, encouraged by the uneasiness shown by some government supporters. On 8 November Mr Kinnock pressed Mrs Thatcher on Mr Lawson's thinking on the treatment of pensioners. To Labour protests—against what they considered to be evasive answers—the Prime Minister imperiously retorted: 'I will answer questions in my own way.' Details of a £200 million package to help the nation's 2½ million poorest pensioners were announced in the Commons on 24 November.

The Government was also embarrassed by a survey undertaken by the Citizens Advice Bureaux. This recorded that 80 per cent of claimants on income support interviewed by the bureaux were worse off as a result of the new social security scheme which had been introduced in April. Social fund payments were not reaching people who needed them, and the situation was being worsened by teething troubles in the new system.

But Labour, too, had its troubles when, in the biggest post-war swing, the Scottish Nationalists won the Govan by-election on 10 November. The collapse of a 19,000 majority had both Scottish and national implications. Labour could not hope to win the next election without a large number of Scottish MPs. Mr Kinnock continued to pledge that there would be no illegal action against the poll tax, a significant but not the only issue at Govan. Some Labour supporters feared that policies designed to recapture support in England might not be so effective in Scotland.

The Epping South by-election of 15 December proved equally disastrous for Labour, which failed to improve on its third place at the general election. The Conservative majority was drastically reduced in a low poll, and only the Democrats were able to draw some comfort from the result. Indeed, Mr Ashdown thought that the Tories might have been defeated had the centre vote not been split by the Owenite SDP candidate. In an interview on 18 December Mr Kinnock admitted that Labour's current standing was not good, but he rejected as defeatist those within his party who proposed electoral pacts with other opposition parties. He criticized, but did not absolutely reject, calls for proportional representation.

A Government White Paper, *Top-Up Loans for Students* (Cmnd. 520), appeared on 9 November. It announced proposals to freeze student grants from 1990. Thereafter loans would make up the difference as the real value of the grant declined in relation to student expenses.

The last legal word in the long-running *Spycatcher* affair (see AR 1987, pp. 8–9) was, it seemed, delivered by five Law Lords on 13 October (see DOCUMENTS). Newspapers were now free to comment on and publish extracts from this notorious work. The Government was also denied its request for a permanent ban on the sales of the book, but their Lordships agreed that members of the secret services owed a 'life-long obligation of confidence' to the Crown. Lord Keith described any breach as 'treachery', though Lord Scarman thought that the judiciary had also signalled the need for the law to strike a balance between national security and the public interest.

The Home Secretary on 30 November unveiled long-promised legislation to replace the 1911 Official Secrets Act, on the basis of a White Paper published on 29 June (Cmnd. 408). Among changes to the Government's original proposals was acceptance of the force of Mr Leon Brittan's argument earlier in the year that the disclosure of information released by foreign Governments and international organizations should not be an offence, unless national security was at stake. Other efforts had been made to improve on the White Paper by defining much more precisely what information should be described as vital to the nation's security. Legislation was also promised to regulate the operations of the Security Service to complement the attempt by the Government to safeguard its secrets from future Peter Wrights. It would also remain an automatic offence for members and former members of MI5 and MI6 to make any unauthorized disclosures about their work. Opposition spokesmen complained, however, that the courts were being given no opportunity to challenge the Government's definition of national security, while those who leaked information could no longer claim that they were acting in the public interest.

Government preoccupation with security had earlier led to action on 18 October against the 18 employees at General Communications Headquarters (GCHQ), Cheltenham, who remained union members in defiance of a government decision four years earlier (see AR 1984, p. 247). Social Security offices on 7 November were badly affected by protest strikes, while Mr Kinnock told a rally in London, with his eye on Mrs Thatcher's Polish visit (see p. 42), 'We just don't want freedom in Gdansk. We want it in GCHQ.'

The White Paper on the future of broadcasting in the 1990s (Cmnd. 517) was published on 7 November. This set out the Government's proposals for future television channels and radio services, how these might be financed, and details on means to control the quality of programmes. It evoked widespread criticism. The proliferation of channels and companies, it was said, would lead to declining standards. Lord Whitelaw, who had been Home Secretary at the time of the establishment of Channel 4, was among those who voiced their concern. Earlier in the year, such concern had led the Government to set up the non-statutory Broadcasting Standards Council under the chairmanship of Sir William Rees-Mogg (a former editor of *The Times*), whose brief (as announced on 16 May) was to regulate the portrayal of sex and violence on television.

A deeply critical report on the causes of the horrific King's Cross underground fire (see AR 1987, p. 36) was published on 10 November. But it was also apparent that only through vast capital investment could an over-stretched transport system be brought up to date. Furthermore, in company with the *Herald of Free Enterprise* (see AR 1987, pp. 35–6) and *Piper Alpha* disasters, questions continued to be asked about the adequacy of government supervision, and whether safety was suffering in the pursuit of profitability. Tragedy struck again on 12 December when over 30 commuters were killed in a train crash near Clapham Junction while the signalling system was in process of modernization.

The Queen's Speech on 22 November was followed by a bad-tempered start to the session in the Commons as backbenchers alternately barracked Mrs Thatcher and Mr Kinnock. Although the Government attempted to make its proposed privatization of the nation's ten water authorities more palatable by emphasizing the importance of a new National Rivers Authority to act as a watchdog against pollution, both Mr Kinnock and Mr Ashdown charged the Government with failing to produce a comprehensive bill for the protection of the environment. During the two-day debate (7–8 December) on the second reading of the Water Bill Dr John Cunningham announced that a future Labour Government would take the water companies back into public ownership. Some Conservatives were not satisfied with the provisions against pollution.

Concern for the environment also arose in connection with the privatization of the electricity industry as nuclear generating capacity would become directly associated with the pursuit of private profit. On 1 December Mr Cecil Parkinson, Secretary of State for

Energy, detailed the Government's plans for what was expected to be the largest-ever sell-off of state assets. Privatization was opposed by the current CEGB chairman, Lord Marshall of Goring, while Labour critics accused Ministers of inconsistency and confusion over the question of the expected costs for consumers. *The Times* of 2 December gave the proposals only a guarded welcome, and looked for effective protection for the consumer as well as for the promotion of genuine competition. It, too, recognized that the 'costs, problematic history, and political sensitivity of nuclear generation' all called for special measures. Even conventional power stations posed environmental problems which demanded expensive remedies.

The privatization of British Steel, however, made a good start at the beginning of December with ample small investor interest. In contrast, the Government announced on 7 December that it had failed to find a buyer for North East Shipbuilders, a subsidiary of British Shipbuilders which it was anxious to privatize. Closure would mean the loss of 2,000 jobs in Sunderland.

The second reading of the Government's Bill to renew anti-terrorist laws produced an internal revolt in the Labour Party on 6 December when two frontbenchers resigned rather than follow Mr Kinnock's instructions to abstain in the Commons vote. In all 44 MPs chose to vote against the Government.

On 3 December Mrs Edwina Currie, the forthright and energetic Under-Secretary of State for Health, uttered one fatal word when she remarked that 'most' British egg production was contaminated with salmonella. This provoked a storm of protest from egg-producers, as well as criticisms from the Ministry of Agriculture. Sales fell by over a half and many producers were reported to be facing bankruptcy. Mrs Currie was obliged to resign on 16 December, so ending (or interrupting) a brief but very public and controversial career as a junior Minister. Three days later the Government announced a £19 million relief scheme for the egg producers. Nevertheless, worries persisted over the extent of the salmonella problem despite efforts by the Government to reassure the public and to offer guidance on the safe use of eggs.

Britain suffered its worst-ever airline disaster on 21 December when a Pan American Boeing 747 airliner crashed on the Scottish border town of Lockerbie. All 259 people on the flight were killed, together with 11 inhabitants of Lockerbie. Official investigations quickly established that a bomb had exploded aboard the airliner, although as at the end of the year nothing definite was known about who had been responsible.

Chapter 6

INTERNATIONAL AFFAIRS

'THE European Community is on the move again', so Sir Geoffrey Howe assured Scottish Conservatives in Perth on 13 May. The single European market which was due to come into being in 1992 was ceasing to be an abstraction. Instead it was fast requiring detailed attention if businesses were to survive the removal of all trade barriers. A report by the European Commission of 9 May forecast an impending 'supply-side shock' to previously protected markets. The Government, while battling to limit change in the EEC in many fields, launched a £5 million publicity campaign on 18 April designed to awaken the insular-minded to the impending changes. At the same time, it continued its campaign in defence of VAT zero-rating for basic products such as food and clothes. Mr Lawson, speaking at an Anglo-German conference in Cambridge on 8 April, drew a distinction between the removal of restrictions on 'cross-border shopping' and the more profound question of 'fiscal harmonization'.

In general, during the year European Community Commissioners were frequently complaining that the Prime Minister was 'half-hearted about Europe at best'. They saw confirmation of their fears in July when the appointment of Lord Cockfield, Britain's senior EC Commissioner and an influential and passionate Europeanist, was not extended. Instead, Mrs Thatcher chose to replace him with Mr Leon Brittan, a former senior Conservative Minister who had resigned as Trade and Industry Secretary in January 1986 over the Westland Affair (see AR 1986, pp. 9–10).

Mrs Thatcher was even more blunt in her reaction to a West German call for the establishment of a European central bank. The Prime Minister declared in the Commons on 23 June that this 'would only come about with the dissolution of this House'. At the EEC summit in Hanover on 27–28 June Mrs Thatcher continued to resist French and West German proposals that Britain join the European Monetary System (EMS). She did, however, relent sufficiently to agree to a special EEC committee to study monetary union. Indeed, the mood in Hanover was relaxed compared with recent summits, and the Europeanists sought some consolation in the hope that British pragmatism would finally bend to the sheer weight of circumstances. There was a small step forward at the beginning of August when the Government began to issue a new type of Treasury bill which was denominated in European currency units (ECU). The European Commission approved, but added that it could not be regarded as substitute for membership of the European exchange mechanism. Later in the year the British agreed to continue to support the Centre Européen pour la Recherche Nucléaire (CERN) and to join the European Space Agency's 'Horizon 2000' space project.

Meanwhile Mrs Thatcher continued to insist that prosperity could only grow out of the creation of wealth, not the 'proliferation of regulations' and the growth of central bureaucracies. She responded with particular warmth on 27 July to the predictions of the President of the European Commission, M. Delors, on the extensive progress towards European unity which he expected to witness over the next ten years.

The tepid enthusiasm shown by the British people towards the EEC was not helped by a report from the National Consumer Council on 1 September which claimed that the common agricultural policy (CAP) was adding £13.50 to the weekly food bill of the average British family. The annual £18,000 million price-support system was said to be pushing up land and food prices, reducing the quality of food, and leading to damage to the environment. The Council thought the efforts of the British Government to effect changes in the agricultural policies of the Community had been too little and too late.

Mrs Thatcher's whirlwind tour of Europe later in September provided her with several opportunities to speak her mind on the future of the EEC, notably before the College of Europe in Bruges on 20 September. She spoke at length on the merits of free enterprise and warned the EEC against any drift towards socialism. So strident was her defence of national sovereignty that she rekindled memories of a French President of the 1960s and earned for herself the sobriquet of 'Lady de Gaulle'.

The Greek Prime Minister claimed that her attempts to qualify the abolition of frontiers by 1992 (on the ground that security was necessary against illegal immigrants, terrorists and drug traffickers) put her in breach of the Single European Act. She also opposed plans for the harmonization of taxes on capital, and for new regulations on company law and worker participation in industry. The nations of Europe, she protested in her Bruges speech, could not be fitted into 'some sort of identikit European personality'. During a visit to Italy on 21 October she emphatically rejected the idea of a United States of Europe. In the same week, however, five European Christian Democratic leaders, including the West German Chancellor, not only insisted that political union must accompany economic union, but also reaffirmed their support for a 'social Europe' which would protect workers' rights and standards of living.

Meanwhile, even in Britain there were critics who asked how the Prime Minister expected the country to benefit from the single market unless she was prepared to make concessions in return. Nor was there entire agreement that the abolition of frontier controls would be as damaging to British security as she suggested. But contrary to expectations the EEC summit on Rhodes at the beginning of December did not witness a showdown between Mrs Thatcher and those who favoured more political and economic integration. Differences remained, but it was agreed in November that it was time to see what a little patience and conciliation might achieve.

Nevertheless, the summit witnessed bitter exchanges between Mrs Thatcher and the Belgian and Irish Prime Ministers as a result of the frustration of British efforts to secure the extradition of Father Patrick Ryan, who was wanted in Britain as a suspected IRA paymaster and bomb-maker, from first one and then the other country (see pp. 187–8). The Rhodes communique did include a reference to the need for closer cooperation against terrorism, but Mrs Thatcher added that she was looking for early and effective action. Meanwhile, in November the European Court had ruled that Britain's anti-terrorist laws were in breach of the European Convention on Human Rights (see Pt. XV, Ch. 1). There was more unity between the leaders at the summit on the question of the environment, while Mrs Thatcher argued strongly that the Community should follow an open international trading policy and offer reassurances to other states concerning the implications of the single market.

Earlier in the year, at the end of July, Mrs Thatcher undertook a gruelling tour of the Middle and Far East. She was intent upon advertising her economic philosophy as well as British goods. The Prime Minister was also anxious to reassure the Australians concerning the creation of the single European market and to revitalize relations with a country which was a major participant in the rapidly expanding economy of the Pacific.

Government and Opposition continued to take contrary positions on the question of sanctions against South Africa, while in February a Commonwealth committee (with no British participants) began meetings in Lusaka to examine new forms of pressure to defeat apartheid. Even in the Conservative Party there was speculation as to how much longer Britain could follow its solitary course inside the Commonwealth. Mrs Thatcher toured parts of Africa at the beginning of the year, and was greeted in Nigeria on 7 January by protesters shouting 'Thatcher, mother of apartheid'. Despite strong criticism from the Presidents of Kenya and Nigeria, Mrs Thatcher reiterated her belief that sanctions were not the answer. But she did hint that she might try to visit South Africa if and when the time seemed ripe to try to ease apartheid.

The first week of November found Mrs Thatcher on a pioneering prime ministerial tour of Poland. The Polish Government was warned that it could not expect international aid to ease its heavy foreign debts unless there were radical changes to its economic policies. She called upon the Eastern bloc to assist in the creation of an open Europe freed from the Iron Curtain and Berlin Wall. The tour included a dramatic and emotion-laden visit to Gdansk, where she met Mr Lech Walesa. On the one hand, the Prime Minister recognized the importance of Solidarity as a political movement, but at the same time she warned of the difficult and unpleasant decisions which were needed to revive the Polish economy.

The Iran-Iraq ceasefire in August led to a slow improvement in Anglo-Iranian relations, and the two nations agreed to resume full diplomatic relations on 10 November. In December the British Government welcomed the renunciation of violence by the chairman of the Palestine Liberation Organization and his recognition of Israel's right to exist. Sir Geoffrey Howe urged Israel to make a positive response.

The British Government adopted a wary attitude to Soviet proposals for arms talks during the year, but it responded warmly to Mr Gorbachev's historic speech at the United Nations on 7 December (see DOCUMENTS). Sir Geoffrey Howe described it as 'remarkable by any standards', although he still warned of the many difficulties and differences which remained. Mr Gorbachev's intended visit to London following his trip to the United States had to be postponed as a result of the devastating earthquake in Armenia (see p. 113).

Chapter 7

SCOTLAND

SCOTTISH Conservatives made a determined effort in 1988 to reverse their disastrous performance of the previous year. Their pro-devolution advocates were decisively defeated at the party's conference in Perth on 12 May. Lord Mackay of Clashfern, the Lord Chancellor, warned that the effects of the establishment of a Scottish Assembly might lead to the dissolution of the Union. Two weeks earlier the pamphlet, *Devolution—Why Not*, published by Aims of Industry, argued that devolution would cause higher taxation and less investment in Scotland. The Government itself endeavoured, both through the Scottish Office and several visits to Scotland by the Prime Minister herself (including one to the

Scottish football cup final), to demonstrate the effectiveness and relevance of its policies.

The year started on a sour note when the future of what remained of the Scottish coal industry seemed in jeopardy as the South of Scotland Electricity Board and British Coal battled over coal prices. The SSEB absorbed about three-quarters of Scotland's coal output. A compromise settlement provided at least temporary relief, but Seafield Colliery in Fife closed with the loss of 700 jobs. On 24 February the Secretary of State, Mr Rifkind, revealed plans to privatize the SSEB and the North of Scotland Hydroboard.

In February there was a controversial takeover by British Petroleum of the Glasgow-based North Sea exploration group, Britoil. An increase in exploration in the North Sea created a more bullish mood in the oil industry in the first half of the year, but there was a tragic reminder of the perilous nature of such operations when an explosion on the *Piper Alpha* platform on 6 July caused the deaths of 166 workers—the world's worst oilfield disaster to date.

Despite Ford's decision not to establish a plant in Dundee (see p. 30), new growth was occurring in both the industrial and service sectors. The Scottish Secretary, Mr Rifkind, insisted that a new system of regional aid, with more emphasis on selectivity and enterprise, would not entail any less Government expenditure. Although he spoke regularly throughout the year of the need for more self-help and enterprise, a White Paper published on 6 December included proposals for more effective training schemes together with a government-funded development body, Scottish Enterprise. The Government also had the satisfaction of seeing unemployment fall during 1988 to 10.8 per cent, the lowest level for almost seven years. Scots noted, however, that only the north of England and Ulster had higher rates.

Although the Scottish National Party's (SNP) motion for an independent Scotland was predictably defeated by 206 votes to 5 in the House of Commons on 6 July, the party was encouraged by its net gain of 45 seats in the May local elections. At its annual conference in Inverness in September, and to the dismay of some of its own supporters, the SNP committed itself to independence within the European Community. By such means, the leaders argued, Scotland would be able to share those benefits already enjoyed by the smaller members of the Community, and would greatly enhance its influence in Europe.

In the Govan by-election on 10 November the party fielded a strong candidate in Mr Jim Sillars, formerly of the Labour Party and husband of Mrs Margo MacDonald, who had won a famous victory for the SNP in the same constituency 15 years before. Mr

Sillars, in addition to the new emphasis on the EEC, effectively exploited the discontent occasioned by the impending poll tax, the deep hostility to the Conservative Government, and doubts over the ability of Labour with its 50 'feeble' MPs (as they were dubbed by the SNP) to defend those who had voted for them in 1987. The Government retorted on 26 October that virtually every Scot had registered for the community charge, and reaffirmed its pledge to help the poorest through income-support payments. Mr Sillars, however, won a spectacular victory by 3,554 votes in what was effectively a two-horse race, overturning a Labour majority (1987) of 19,509. The SNP called upon the other opposition parties to combine with it in obstructing and finding alternatives to Conservative policies in Scotland.

The bid by the Australian Fosters lager group, Elders, to take over the Scottish and Newcastle breweries gave new vigour to complaints against the continuing erosion of Scottish influence over its own affairs. Rather belatedly, on 10 November, the Trade and Industry Secretary referred the bid to the Monopolies and Mergers Commission. Meanwhile the Educational Institute of Scotland was also protesting against the increasing efforts to 'Anglicize' Scottish education. (For the Lockerbie airliner disaster on 21 December, see p. 38.)

Chapter 8

WALES

NID yw Cymru Ar Werth—'Wales is not for sale'—was the emotive slogan used by the Welsh Language Society in its campaign against the substantial migration of English people into Wales which seemed to reach a peak during the summer. However, the Society's non-violent protests were overshadowed by the more sinister activities of *Meibion Glyndŵr* ('Sons of Glendower'), whose nine-year-old arson campaign against holiday homes spread into England for the first time. In February, May and October estate agents' offices known to advertise Welsh properties in border towns stretching from the Wirral to Bristol were firebombed and in November there were attacks on six offices in London.

An opinion poll showed some support for the aims if not the methods of the arsonists. There was considerable evidence that local people were being priced out of the housing market by wealthier English people moving into Wales. The damaging effect on the Welsh language was evident from the problems experienced by traditionally Welsh-speaking schools which found it increasingly difficult to assimilate non-Welsh-speaking children. The Secretary of State for Wales, Mr Peter Walker, claimed that economic regeneration was the only long-term solution to the problem. He rejected the calls for a new Welsh Language Act and instead set up a new Welsh Language Board.

An increasingly confident Mr Walker continued to pursue a vigorous regional policy which seemed at variance with the basic tenets of Thatcherism. In June he announced a £1,500 million package to bring new economic life to the Welsh valleys. The Ford Motor Company's £728 million plans for factories at Swansea and Bridgend were only the largest of a number of new investments attracted to Wales during the year. In contrast, the rationalization of the coal industry continued. The announcement in November that the Cynheidre and Marine collieries were to be closed added to the frustration of miners' leaders already troubled by the failure to reach a settlement over six-day working at the proposed Margam superpit.

Devolution returned to the political agenda at the end of November with the launching of the Campaign for a Welsh Assembly. Nearly ten years after the 1979 referendum had emphatically rejected devolution, opinion polls showed increasing support for an Assembly. One prominent promoter of the Campaign was Mr Denzil Davies, the MP for Llanelli, who had resigned as Labour's frontbench defence spokesman in June (see p. 29). Indeed Welsh Labour MPs were constantly in the news. Both Mr Roy Hughes and Ms Ann Clwyd were dismissed from Labour's frontbench and Mr Alan Williams was replaced as Shadow Welsh Secretary by his predecessor Mr Barry Jones. In December, Mr Brynmor John, MP for Pontypridd since 1970, died suddenly.

Chapter 9

NORTHERN IRELAND

HOPES raised at the end of 1987 were realized only in part during 1988. In spite of strong revulsion against the men of violence following the murder of ten civilians at the 1987 Remembrance Day service at Enniskillen (see AR 1987, p.44), political violence continued to be a major factor in Northern Ireland. No new political developments of significance were reported. On the economic front, however, the rate of unemployment continued to fall and a number of new major industrial developments were announced.

The number of murders due to political violence stood at 93, which was a similar total to that in the previous year. This figure consisted of 54 civilians and 39 members of the security forces. A new feature of the year was a rise in the number of army deaths. IRA attacks in England, the Netherlands and West Germany also led to deaths of members of the security forces. Three members of the IRA were killed by British security personnel during a bombing mission in Gibraltar on 6 March (see pp. 187–8). During their funeral at the Milltown cemetery in West Belfast on 16 March a man later identified as a Protestant militant threw grenades and shot at mourners, killing three people and injuring about 50. Three days later, at the funeral of one of the Milltown victims, two British soldiers in civilian clothes who had driven up to the cortege were pulled from their car, beaten and later shot dead, much of the incident being recorded by news cameramen.

During the year large quantities of guns and explosives were discovered in Northern Ireland. Hopes raised after the Enniskillen bombing that the men of violence would be isolated were not realized, but still the period witnessed many acts and gestures of reconciliation.

No developments of significance occurred in the contacts between the Government and Northern Ireland political parties or between the parties themselves. The Unionist parties remained opposed to the Anglo-Irish Agreement but the Irish and British Governments continued to hold meetings of the Anglo-Irish Conference. A series of meetings were also held between Sinn Féin and the SDLP but nothing concrete emerged from the contacts. A government Act forbade the broadcasting of interviews with members of paramilitary organizations or parties associated with them, such as Sinn Féin.

The year witnessed an improvement in the area of employment. The seasonally-adjusted figure of the number of people unemployed fell by 8,700 over the year to a total of 108,900 or 15.7 per cent of the workforce (10.6 per cent of females and 19.0 per cent of males). This figure was still well above the national average but the announcement towards the end of 1988 of plans for a number of major industrial developments augured better for the future. However, uncertainty over the future privatization of the shipbuilders Harland and Wolff and the plane-makers Shorts gave cause for concern.

Various issues caused controversy during the year. Proposals for changes in the Northern Ireland educational system were the subject of much debate. The question of extradition of persons charged with terrorist offences from the Republic of Ireland to Northern Ireland continued to be controversial, amidst Northern complaints about the Republic's failure to operate the existing system effectively. The conduct of the police and allegations of an earlier 'shoot to kill' policy remained as matters of public debate.

After long discussions the Government decided not to back

lignite mining and a new lignite power station. In May a White Paper on fair employment was introduced to attempt to ensure equality of employment for all sections. In November the European Court of Human Rights ruled that the Government had breached the European Convention of Human Rights by detaining suspects for over four days (see Pt. XV, Ch. 1).

In most parts of Northern Ireland standards of living continued to improve. New housing, both private and public, transformed areas throughout the region. New commercial developments in Belfast and many Ulster towns reflected growing prosperity. Ordinary crime was at a low level, compared to other parts of the UK. In spite of a rise in the mortgage rate in the last part of 1988, business remained buoyant thanks to low house prices and school fees.

II THE AMERICAS AND CARIBBEAN

Chapter 1

UNITED STATES OF AMERICA

CAPITAL: Washington, DC   AREA: 9,372,614 sq km   POPULATION: 241,600,000 ('86)
OFFICIAL LANGUAGE: English   POLITICAL SYSTEM: democratic federal republic
HEAD OF STATE AND GOVERNMENT: President Ronald Reagan (since Jan '81)
PRESIDENT-ELECT: George Bush (elected Nov '88)
RULING PARTY: Republicans hold presidency; Democrats control Congress
PRINCIPAL CABINET MEMBERS: George Bush (Vice-President), George Shultz (Secretary of State), Nicholas Brady (treasury), Frank Carlucci (defence), Donald P. Hodel (interior), Richard Thornburgh (Attorney General) (*for full list see* DOCUMENTS)
INTERNATIONAL ALIGNMENT: Nato, OECD, OAS, Anzus Pact
CURRENCY: dollar (end-'88 £1=US$1.81)   GNP PER CAPITA: US$17.480 ('86)
MAIN EXPORTS: machinery and transport equipment, agricultural products, chemicals, miscellaneous manufactures

IN an election year Americans tend to become introspective, brooding on the state of the union more intently than usual and anxiously considering the decision they are called upon to make once the long nine-month formal electoral process finally comes to an end. In 1988 there was little evidence to show that the voters were enjoying the responsibility. They were uninspired by the choice before them, with the result that on polling day the turnout was the lowest for more than 60 years. The fact that the majority voted for the Republican rather than the Democratic candidate probably reflected less on their individual characters and campaigns than on the general satisfaction with the way things had been going under the incumbent Republican President, Ronald Reagan. George Bush was the first sitting Vice-President to be elected President since 1836, and there seemed no doubt that his experience and share in the leadership of the nation in a time of peace and prosperity prompted his countrymen to vote in favour of more of the same. At home the economy continued to flourish throughout the year in spite of growing pressure on the dollar and continued fiscal and trade deficits, and abroad the policy of working for peace through strength seemed to be beginning to pay off.

For many Americans a more immediately compelling reason for introspection during the year was the intense heat and drought that oppressed large areas of the country for many months. The driest spring for more than 50 years was followed by a summer of intense heat, bringing water rationing to some parts and memories of the 1930s dust bowl to the Great Plains and Lakes and most of middle America. The corn harvest was down by some 37 per cent on the previous year, the soybean crop by 23 per cent and wheat by 13 per cent. New York and other big cities suffered an unprecedentedly long and relentlessly hot summer, and in Washington a scientist from the National Aeronautics and Space Administration told Congress that America was experiencing the 'greenhouse effect'. The fact that the Earth was warmer in 1988 than it had been in any comparable period since measurements began more than a century ago was not a natural variation, he said, but the result of an accumulation of carbon dioxide and other artificial gases.

HOME AFFAIRS. As Mr Reagan was constitutionally barred from offering himself again for re-election, there was no shortage of candidates seeking to succeed him. At the start of the year 13 had formally declared their candidacies—six Republicans and seven Democrats. The Republicans, in addition to Mr Bush, were Senator Robert Dole of Kansas, General Alexander Haig (former Secretary of State and Nato Supreme Commander), Pierre du Pont (former Governor of Delaware), Representative Jack Kemp of New York, and the Rev Pat Robertson (former head of a Christian television station). For the Democratic nomination the declared candidates were Bruce Babbitt (former Governor of Arizona), Governor Michael Dukakis of Massachusetts, Representative Richard Gephardt of Missouri, Senator Albert Gore of Tennessee, Gary Hart (former Senator from Colorado), the Rev Jesse Jackson of Chicago, and Senator Paul Simon from Illinois. Neither party's list was regarded as particularly impressive, but voters could not complain that there was lack of choice.

The first opportunity to choose came for the people of Iowa on 8 February, when the state held its party caucuses, each comprising some 110,000 votes from a total population of 2,800,000. On the Republican side the result was a considerable setback for Mr Bush, who had beaten Mr Reagan here in 1980 but who this time won only 19 per cent of the vote compared with Senator Dole's 37 per cent and Mr Robertson's 25 per cent. For the Democrats Mr Gephardt won 31 per cent, Senator Simon 27 per cent and Governor Dukakis 22 per cent. The main casualty in Iowa proved to be General Haig, who pulled out of the caucus vote and three days later withdrew from the presidential contest altogether, advising his Republican supporters to vote for Senator Dole. In the first primary election, in New Hampshire on 16 February, Mr Bush re-established his position by winning 38 per cent of the Republican vote compared with 29 per cent for Senator Dole, 13 per cent for Mr Kemp and 10 per cent each for Mr Robertson and Mr du Pont, who abandoned the contest two days later. On the Democratic side Governor Dukakis won 37 per cent of the vote, Mr Gephardt 20 per cent, Senator Simon 18 per cent, Mr Jackson 8 per cent, Senator Gore 7 per cent, Mr Babbitt 5 per cent and Mr Hart 4 per cent. Mr Babbitt withdrew his candidacy on 18 February.

The Republican nomination was virtually secured for Mr Bush on 8 March, called 'Super Tuesday' because 21 states voted in primaries or caucuses on that day. Mr Bush won 16 of the Republican primaries in all, losing only the caucus in Washington state, which gave him a total of 619 electoral delegates compared with 103 for Senator Dole, 10 for Mr Robertson and four for Mr Kemp, who resigned from the contest when the results became known. Senator Dole clung on for another round but was soundly beaten by Mr Bush in the primary in Illinois on 15 March and finally withdrew on 29 March. Mr Robertson did not formally withdraw, but abandoned campaigning and conceded victory to Mr Bush in early April by revealing that he had spent about all the $23 million permitted for campaigning, and by asking for his Secret Service protection to be withdrawn.

For Democrats the contest was less easily resolved. The results of 'Super Tuesday' gave each of the leading contenders some cause for hope: Mr Dukakis won the primaries in Florida, Maryland, Massachusetts, Rhode Island and Texas and the caucuses in Hawaii, Idaho, American Samoa and Washington state; Senator Gore won the primaries in Arkansas, Kentucky, North Carolina, Oklahoma and Tennessee and the caucus in Nevada; Mr Jackson won the primaries in Alabama, Georgia, Louisiana, Mississippi and Virginia; Mr Gephardt won the primary in Missouri. Mr Dukakis acquired 382 delegates, Mr Jackson 368, Senator Gore 325 and Mr Gephardt 95. Mr Hart, who won nothing, withdrew his candidacy on 11 March. Mr Gephardt followed on 28 March and Senator Simon, who also won nothing, stayed on to win his home state primary in Illinois before retiring after failing badly in the Wisconsin primary on 5 April. In Michigan the previous week Jesse Jackson had excited the political commentators by demonstrating that he could win outside the South, and for a few days he seemed to be presenting a real challenge for the nomination. But Wisconsin was a convincing victory for Mr Dukakis, who pulled further ahead of Mr Jackson on 19 April by winning the New York primary, taking 51 per cent of the vote compared with 37 per cent for Mr Jackson and 10 per cent for Senator Gore, who thereupon gave up his campaign. The New York result in effect set the seal on Mr Dukakis's nomination, which was confirmed in the final Democratic primaries on 7 June, in California, Montana, New Jersey and New Mexico, all of which he won to establish a margin of some 200 delegate votes above the 2,081 required to secure nomination on the first ballot in the Democratic convention.

Before going to Atlanta, where the convention was to be held, Mr Dukakis strove to settle differences with Mr Jackson, who was pointing out in his flamboyant style that, having finished first or second in 46 of 54 contests and won 7 million votes, he had earned the right to be considered for the vice-presidency or a Cabinet appointment. He also pressed for tough Democratic policies, including big defence cuts and tax increases on the wealthy and an overhaul of the party rules, which he said had deprived him of many delegate votes. After some weeks of negotiation the party managers drafted a platform for the convention that gave no specific commitments on Mr Jackson's demands, other than the reform of rules for the 1992 election. On 12 July Mr Dukakis announced that he had chosen as his vice-presidential running mate Senator Lloyd Bentsen of Texas, a 67-year-old conservative with more than 30 years' experience in Congress, most recently as chairman of the Senate finance committee.

The Democratic convention opened on 18 July amid much speculation that Mr Jackson and his crusading supporters might disrupt the proceedings and wreck the party's chances of uniting behind Mr Dukakis, without which victory at the polls was likely to be unattainable. In the event Mr Jackson contrived to dominate the convention, both with his rhetoric and with his tactical skill in exploiting the party's conscience, but failed to persuade the delegates to adopt any significant amendments of policy. Mr Dukakis, the 54-year-old son of Greek immigrants, was confirmed as the party's presidential candidate, and he retained firm control of the convention, emerging with an electoral platform that was one of the vaguest on record and with an undertaking from Mr Jackson of his full support in the campaign, regarded as an essential requirement for pulling in the black vote.

Opinion polls following the convention indicated that the Democrats were riding high. One showed Mr Dukakis leading Mr Bush by 17 percentage points, another reported that two out of every five voters viewed Mr Bush with active disfavour. All suggested that Mr Bush's campaign was in some disarray. Like his opponent he was not seen as an exciting candidate. 'Can't act', he said when asked during the campaign about his difficulty in communicating. 'Can't be as good as Ronald Reagan on conviction.' His struggle to take advantage of the President's popularity while distancing himself from some of the Administration's mistakes had at times during the primaries become painfully public, and it was generally conceded that he had not yet succeeded in establishing a clear identity for himself. His performance at the Republican convention, and his choice of a vice-presidential candidate, were thus seen as crucial to the attempt to recover lost ground.

In the circumstances his selection of Senator Dan Quayle of Indiana as Vice-President was to prove highly controversial.

Announced on 16 August by Mr Bush on his arrival in New Orleans for the convention, the choice of the 41-year-old relatively unknown Senator took the party by surprise. It was seen initially as a bold move to appeal to a younger generation, but this favourable response was overtaken by concern at the revelation that Mr Quayle had avoided combat duty in Vietnam by using family connections to get himself recruited to the National Guard instead. Though not a misdemeanour, it did not seem to reflect well on a Senator who was politically a hawk on military matters and a member of several defence sub-committees. His explanation, that he joined the National Guard in 1969 because he wanted to stay at home and go to law school, struck many delegates as worryingly inept. The issue nagged its way through the convention but was met head-on by Mr Bush, who made clear his determination to stand by his choice and delivered an impressive and confident acceptance speech, expressing pride in what had been achieved by the current Republican Administration and his ambition to create a 'kinder, gentler nation'.

The message got home, the media's Quayle hunt subsided and opinion polls put Mr Bush back in the lead. He did not lose it again during a campaign which one commentator described as lacklustre, another as being fought between two stuffed shirts (one from Harvard, the other from Yale), and which many characterized as unusually dirty (though not by those whose memories went back to the 1948 election and earlier). For most Americans the candidates could be most directly judged from their television debates. The first, watched by about 100 million people on the night of 25 September, was judged to have given an edge to Mr Dukakis, who appeared sharper and more in command of himself and his brief, putting Mr Bush on the defensive on doing business with 'drug-dealing dictators' (a reference to the Administration's problems with Panama—see pp. 65, 88–9) and on the Budget deficit. On 5 October it was the turn of the vice-presidential candidates to subject themselves to television debate, and again it was the Democratic nominee who was judged to have come out on top, not on matters of policy so much as on character and personal authority. The live audience watching the debate in Omaha particularly relished Senator Bentsen's snub when Senator Quayle suggested that he had as much congressional experience as Senator John Kennedy had had when he became President. 'I served with Jack Kennedy', said Mr Bentsen. 'I knew Jack Kennedy. Jack Kennedy was a friend of mine. Senator, you're no Jack Kennedy.'

In the final debate between the principals on 13 October, again watched by some 100 million Americans, Mr Bush was judged to have put on the most effective performance, repeating his pledge not to raise taxes and concentrating on arms control and defence, areas in which Mr Dukakis seemed vacillatory. Mr Bush reaped the benefit by a marked increase in his opinion poll lead, and in spite of a last-minute surge of adrenalin in the Dukakis campaign he kept in front. On 8 November, when the country finally went to the polls, Mr Bush won 47,662,777 votes, 54 per cent, compared with 40,817,438, or 46 per cent, for Mr Dukakis. Of greater significance, since American Presidents are formally chosen by state 'electors' (equal in number to its senators and congressmen), Mr Bush won 40 states to Mr Dukakis's 10 plus the District of Columbia, giving him 426 electoral college votes to 112.

The voters declined to extend their support of the Republican candidate into the congressional elections, the Democrats marginally strengthening their control of both Senate and House of Representatives. The composition of the new Congress, to take office in January 1989, was as follows:-

	Senate		House of Representatives	
	old	new	old	new
Democrats	54	55	257	262
Republicans	46	45	178	173

In the 12 gubernatorial elections the Democrats won five and the Republicans seven, giving the Democrats a total of 28 state governorships and the Republicans 22, an overall gain of one to the Democrats.

One of Mr Bush's first decisions as President-elect was the appointment of James Baker, his campaign manager and former White House Chief of Staff, as Secretary of State, and on 17 November he appointed John Sununu, the retiring Governor of New Hampshire, as White House Chief of Staff. Other nominations for Cabinet and Cabinet-rank posts quickly followed, so that by the end of the year the new Administration was virtually complete. Particular attention was paid to Mr Bush's appointments in the economic sphere, for it was here that he was expected to meet his most urgent problems. He seemed to recognize this by deciding to leave Nicholas Brady, a Reagan appointment, in charge of the Treasury and by putting the reliable Richard Darman, who had previously served as deputy both in the Treasury and in the White House, at the Budget Office.

Throughout his campaign Mr Bush had promised to get rid of the Budget deficit by 1993, and had repeatedly emphasized that he would not introduce new taxes. 'Read my lips: no new taxes' became a favoured catchphrase. During the election the American public did not seem too concerned about whether these two pledges could be reconciled, but as soon as it was over the questioning began: how could the deficit be reduced without an increase in taxes? Mr Bush's electoral formula of flexible controls on spending, pegged to inflation

THE AMERICAS AND CARIBBEAN

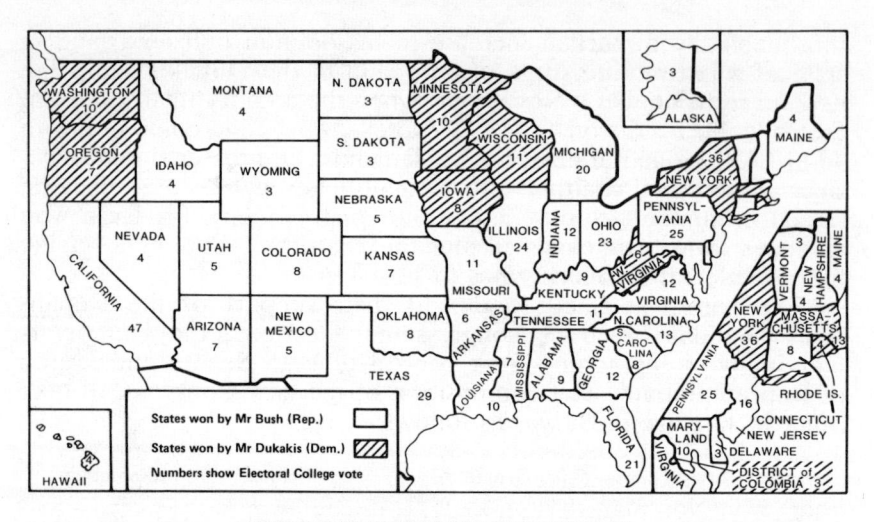

THE US PRESIDENTIAL ELECTION

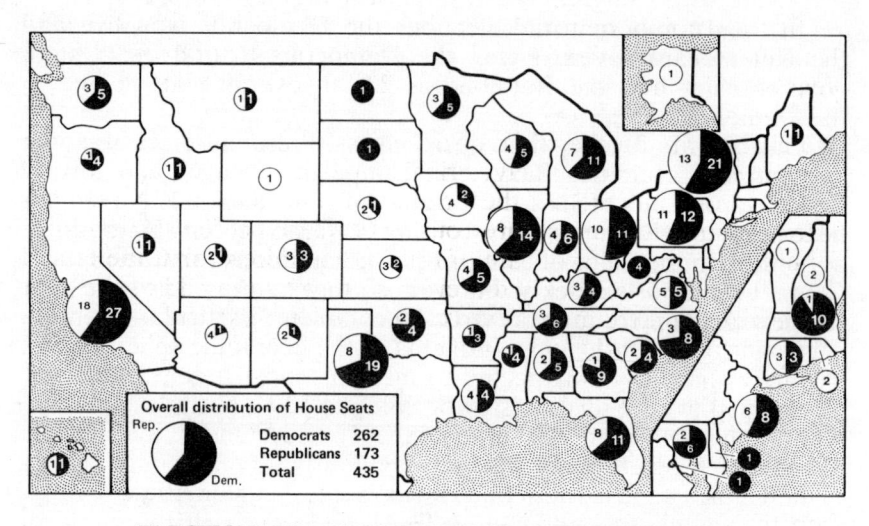

ELECTIONS TO THE US HOUSE OF REPRESENTATIVES

The maps illustrate the contrast between voting patterns in the presidential and congressional elections. Whereas the Republican candidate, Mr Bush, was elected President with 54 per cent of the popular vote and by majorities in 41 of the 50 states, the Democrats increased their majority in the House of Representatives to 262 of the 435 seats. As the map shows, all the big states returned more Democratic congressmen than Republicans.

and thus allowing the country to grow its way out of trouble, seemed rather too easy.

Overseas doubts were reflected in a substantial fall in the value of the dollar in the week following the election, while at home the Dow Jones industrial share index fell by 100 points in the same period. Alan Greenspan, chairman of the Federal Reserve Board, called for urgent action to reduce the deficit, as did the General Accounting Office, a bipartisan congressional agency, which published a report suggesting that higher taxes were 'probably an unavoidable part of any realistic strategy for ending the deficit'. On 21 November Mr Bush was confronted by two former Presidents, Jimmy Carter and Gerald Ford, who presented him with a programme called 'The American Agenda' calling for the levying of new taxes on petrol, cigarettes, drink and other consumer products. 'Americans are ready to do what has to be done', they said. 'All they want is leadership. Tell them the truth. Give them the facts, the good and the bad. Tell them what you plan to do and what they need to do.' Mr Bush was left in no doubt of what was expected, and before the year ended he promised that on his first day as President he would name a team to negotiate with Congress on ways of bringing down the deficit.

It was not a new problem for the United States. The twin Budget and trade deficits had worried Americans throughout the year, as they had in other recent years. In his State of the Union address to Congress on 25 January, President Reagan referred to the change in attitude towards deficits. 'At last there is agreement that we can't spend ourselves rich', he said, pointing out that the federal Government, for the first time in 14 years, had spent less in real terms than in the previous year. He repeated the diagnosis he had given in his first State of the Union address, that the federal Government was too big and spent too much money. 'The simple but frustrating problem of making expenses match revenues—something American families do and the federal Government can't—has caused crisis after crisis', he said. 'The Budget process has broken down: it needs a drastic overhaul. With each ensuing year the spectacle before the American people is the same. . . . Budget deadlines delayed or missed completely, monstrous continuing resolutions that pack hundreds of billions of dollars worth of spending onto one bill, and a federal Government on the brink of default.' He called for a Budget partnership between President and Congress, a joint agreement setting out spending priorities within available resources. His exasperation was no doubt partly stimulated by the experience of 1987, when the Budget had projected a deficit of $107,000 million, which was reduced by $30,000 million after negotiations between the White House and Congress, but which ended the year at nearly $150,000 million. Only in Washington, it was suggested, could you subtract 30,000 million from 107,000 million to end up with 150,000 million.

The Budget for fiscal 1989 (beginning 10 October 1988), presented to Congress by President Reagan on 18 February, totalled $1,094,000 million with a projected deficit of $129,500 million (compared with $146,700 million for 1988). In contrast to his previous Budgets the President called for no more than a minimal increase, amounting to about 2 per cent in real terms, in defence. Some domestic programmes were reduced but considerably more funds were allocated for education, science, AIDS research, drug prevention and for improving air traffic control. Because the broad elements had been agreed in advance, and because it was an election year, the Budget was not mauled beyond recognition in Congress. With the economy continuing to grow strongly throughout the year, the gross national product increasing at about 3 per cent, unemployment at not more than 5 per cent (the lowest for more than a decade) and inflation at 4.4 per cent, there was no disposition to find any cause for putting the seven-year period of economic growth in jeopardy. Business investment and exports increased, and even consumer spending seemed to have shrugged off the consequences of the Wall Street crash of the previous year.

After nearly three years' work both houses of Congress voted in favour of an omnibus Trade Bill in April. The Bill reflected American concern both at the country's huge trade deficit ($170,000 million at the start of the year but down to about $135,000 million by December) and at the increasing amount of foreign investment. It included provisions calling on the Administration to identify trade barriers in foreign countries, particularly those with large trade surpluses, and to seek to negotiate them away over three years. The Administration was also requested to retaliate when trade agreements were deemed to have been broken, to transfer authority for determining whether foreign practices were unfair to the US Trade Representative, to allow US concerns to file complaints when their position in Third World markets was damaged by dumping by foreign companies, to place a three-year ban on the Japanese Toshiba Machine Corporation and the Norwegian Kongsberg Vaapenfabrikk for violating export controls to the Soviet Union, to require companies with more than 100 workers to give 60 days' notice if they planned to close a plant, to repeal the windfall-profits tax on domestically-produced crude oil, and to restrict oil exports from Alaska to 70,000 barrels per day.

The Bill was passed by the House of Representatives on 21 April and by the Senate on 27 April, but was vetoed by the President on 24 May. On 13 July the House passed a revised Bill, omitting the provisions on plant closures and Alaskan oil exports, to which Mr Reagan had taken particular exception. The Bill was approved by the Senate on 3 August by 85 votes to 11, and signed into law by the President on 25 August.

Congress and President were also at odds during the year on two other significant measures. The first was on civil rights legislation and the second on plans for welfare reform. On 16 March the President vetoed the Civil Rights Restoration Bill, which had been passed by overwhelming majorities in both Senate and House of Representatives. The Bill aimed at expanding federal enforcement of civil rights laws by reversing the effects of a 1984 Supreme Court decision which had considerably limited the scope of the legislation. The Court had ruled that a federal law barring aid where schools practised sex discrimination applied only to the specific programme or activity receiving such aid, and did not debar aid for other programmes or for the institutions as a whole. The ruling had been interpreted by the Government as applying also to laws prohibiting discrimination on the grounds of race, age or desirability, and had been criticized as leading to a rising number of cases of discrimination. The Bill was vetoed by the President on the grounds that it extended far beyond educational institutions and would 'vastly and unjustifiably' expand the powers of the federal Government over private organizations. On 22 March the President's veto was overridden in both houses by substantially more than the two-thirds majority required.

During the summer both houses passed their own welfare Bills, designed to make the system fairer, but faced the threat of a presidential veto both because of the cost to the federal Government and because there was no requirement, as Mr Reagan was demanding, for some recipients to work in order to qualify for benefits. The Senate and the House of Representatives finally agreed, on 1 October, on a revised version of the Bill which reduced the amount of federal money required to $3,340 million spread over five years, and which extended help to poor families when both parents lived with their children so long as one of the adults worked for at least 16 hours a week for at least six months in the year. The Bill also provided state job opportunity and basic skill programmes to educate, train and help poor women with no children under the age of three to find jobs enabling them to support themselves and their children without state aid. The changes received the President's approval.

On 18 May Mr Reagan called for a bipartisan effort to wage war against drug abuse. He said the country faced a drug crisis and urged the creation of an executive-legislative task force to examine every aspect of the problem, from the interdiction of supplies and the eradication of demand to the adoption of more effective policies on treatment, education and prosecution. He announced also that he had ordered the Secretary of Defense to make proposals on using military resources and technology to detect and intercept drugs entering the US. The President's activity was widely interpreted as a political response to the Democratic election campaign, opinion polls showing at the time that illegal drug use was the single most important issue among the electorate and one on which Democratic candidates had been campaigning heavily and effectively, although in truth it was a national rather than a political problem. The National Institute on Drug Abuse published figures to show that the incidence of deaths from cocaine in major metropolitan areas had increased by more than 1,000 per cent in ten years. Both houses of Congress incorporated measures empowering the military to increase its role in the interdiction of drug trafficking in their defence authorization Bills for fiscal 1989. In the closing session of the year they were at work on a Bill which included new penalties for drug offenders including the death penalty for drug-related murders.

The Supreme Court upset many Congressmen and others by announcing, on 28 April, that it proposed to reconsider its 1976 decision prohibiting racial discrimination and giving blacks and other minorities the right to sue private citizens for violating the law. The Court, its numbers brought up to nine by the Senate's confirmation of the appointment of Judge Anthony Kennedy on 3 February, made its decision by a vote of 5–4 and was at once assailed by civil rights organizations, the American Bar Association, some 200 Senators and Congressmen, 47 state attorneys-general and many others who filed briefs urging the Court to let its past decision stand. The decision was also condemned by the four dissenting judges, who said it would undermine the confidence of minorities in the Supreme Court's commitment to the protection of their civil rights and would be seen as an unwarranted example of the 'activism of judges'.

The Administration no doubt took a similar view of another of the Court's judgments during the year, when it refused to overturn the law setting up special prosecutors to investigate the Iran-Contra affair and the finances of Edwin Meese, then Attorney-General. The inquiry by the special prosecutor, Lawrence Walsh, into the Iran-Contra affair followed those by the Tower Commission and the congressional committee (see AR 1987, pp. 47–51), and led on 11 March to four misdemeanour charges against Robert McFarlane, former National Security Adviser, to which he pleaded guilty after a plea bargaining agreement to appear as a prosecution witness in any subsequent trials. On 16 March grand jury indictments were brought against Rear-Admiral John Poindexter (another former National Security Adviser), Lieut.-Col. Oliver North of the US Marines and a former national security aide, Major-General Richard Secord and his business partner, Albert Hakim. The four were charged with conspiracy, fraud, obstruction and embezzlement. All pleaded not guilty, and trial was set for 20 September but later postponed until the New Year, much to the relief of Mr Bush and his election managers, to whom a trial conducted at the peak of the election campaign could have been an acute embarrassment. On 30 December both President Reagan and President-elect Bush were subpoenaed to provide testimony and 'certain personal records' in the forthcoming trial.

The investigations into the affairs of Edwin Meese brought much discomfort to the Administration in the early months of the year. Mr Meese was under investigation by a special prosecutor on three counts: his role in a planned oil pipeline in Iraq, his link with the Wedtech Corporation, which had been involved in defence contract scandals, and for his financial dealings. He had appeared before a grand jury on 15 occasions. In March six officials in the Justice Department resigned, including the Deputy Attorney-General, Arnold Burns, and the Assistant, William Weld, both of whom left because they believed the credibility of law enforcement was being tarnished by Mr Meese's legal problems. In April John Shepherd, the man chosen by Mr Meese to take Mr Burns's place as his deputy, withdrew because he said he was not prepared for the pressures involved. In May Charles Cooper, an Assistant Attorney-General, resigned, for reasons which he said were wholly unrelated to the controversy surrounding Mr Meese. In July Mr Meese announced his own resignation, following the delivery of the special prosecutor's report which said there was insufficient evidence for criminal prosecution. On 12 July Mr Reagan announced the nomination of Richard Thornburgh as new Attorney-General.

Americans returned successfully to space in 1988. All manned flights had stopped following the explosion of the *Challenger* space shuttle in 1986 (see AR 1986, pp. 48–9) and while intense research was carried out on making the space vehicle safer and more reliable. The commitment to the exploration of space remained, as President Reagan emphasized on 11 February when he declared the Administration's support for a permanently manned space station, due to be sent into orbit in the early 1990s, for strong commercial space programmes, and for the development of technology to put men on Mars. The actual re-entry into space took place on 29 September when the shuttle *Discovery* blasted off from the Kennedy Space Centre at Cape Canaveral, the 26th shuttle launch since the first flight in 1981. On board was a crew of five, all professionals, commanded by Captain Rick Hauck of the US Navy. A large communications satellite was deployed during the flight, but for the most part the programme was cautious and the only hitch was some discomfort to the crew caused by a faulty cooling system. After four days *Discovery* landed perfectly on a dry lake-bed in the Mohave Desert in California.

Earlier in the year the US launched a research satellite from Cape Canaveral for a test of the proposed 'Star Wars' space-based missile defence system. On 10 November the Pentagon released for the first time photographs of the F-117A 'Stealth' jet fighter, its revolutionary aircraft which had become operational in 1983 and which was designed to be 'invisible' to radar. On 22 November the Pentagon also showed for the first time the prototype of the B-2 'Stealth' bomber, which was shaped like a flying wing with four hidden engines and constructed of materials designed to absorb radar.

FOREIGN AFFAIRS. The improvement in communication between the United States and the Soviet Union was reflected on the first day of the New Year, when Mr Reagan and Mr Gorbachev exchanged television broadcasts in each other's country. Mr Reagan's message was surprisingly direct. He emphasized his commitment to the 'Star Wars' project, which the Soviet Government regarded as the main obstacle to a strategic arms reduction treaty, and he appealed for an end to the Soviet military presence in Afghanistan. 'We Americans are concerned, as I know you are', he said to some 100 million Soviet viewers, 'about senseless conflicts in a number of regions... too many mothers, including Soviet mothers, have wept over the graves of their fallen sons. True peace means not only preventing a big war but ending small ones as well. This is why we support efforts to find just, negotiated solutions acceptable to the people who are suffering in regional wars.' In his message, which was broadcast across the United States by the television networks, Mr Gorbachev said the signing of the INF treaty (in December 1987) was a good omen, marking a first step along the path of reducing nuclear arms. It had brought the Soviet and American peoples closer, he said.

The US tabled a draft treaty on space defence at Geneva on 23 January, embodying elements of the agreements reached by the two leaders at their Washington summit the previous month. The US draft committed both sides to observing the 1982 Anti-Ballistic Missile Treaty while conducting their research, development and testing of 'Star Wars' technology. Meanwhile, George Shultz, the Secretary of State, returned from a visit to Moscow to declare that both sides were hopeful that a treaty for halving strategic or long-range weaponry might be ready for signing at the next summit. He was also optimistic on prospects for Soviet troop withdrawal from Afghanistan and reported to Nato allies in Brussels in February that the Soviet Union had in fact already begun to pull out some of its troops when Mr Gorbachev announced on 8 February that the withdrawal would begin on 15 May. At US insistence it was agreed at Geneva in April that half the Soviet troops would leave by 15 August and the remainder by 15 February 1989 (see DOCUMENTS).

After tough bargaining sessions during a visit to Washington in March by Eduard Shevardnadze, the Soviet Foreign Minister, it was revealed that there had been little progress towards agreement on reducing strategic weapons and that a treaty was unlikely to be ready for the summit, whose date was fixed for the end of May. Mr Reagan's main formal act in Moscow was to hand over the documents ratifying the INF Treaty, although he knew he would be able to do so only on the eve of his arrival; for it was not until 27 May that the US Senate finally ratified the treaty (by 93 votes to 5), attaching to it a clause preventing any future Administration from reinterpreting the treaty without Senate approval.

Mr Reagan's meeting with Mr Gorbachev was his fourth in 30 months and his visit to Moscow the first by a US President for 14 years. There was a warm welcome for the President and Mrs Reagan on the streets of Moscow but a chillier one from the official Soviet reception party who had not appreciated a hard-hitting speech made by Mr Reagan in Helsinki on his way to the summit, during which he had been very critical of the Soviet Government's record on human rights. He pursued the theme at the first round of official talks in the Kremlin but the official Soviet spokesman, Gennady Gerasimov, said afterwards that Mr Reagan's remarks were based on outdated perceptions of what was now happening in the Soviet Union. 'We know our shortcomings', he said, 'but we don't like it much when somebody from outside tells us how we should live.'

The President continued his demands for increased human rights and greater religious freedom when he spoke at the Russian Orthodox Danilov monastery, to a gathering of dissidents and Jewish 'refuseniks' at the US ambassador's residence, and to a meeting of writers and intellectuals at the House of Writers. Mr Gorbachev responded at an unprecedented international press conference on 1 June, declaring that he had not admired Mr Reagan's 'propaganda gambits' on the subject. 'I can see that the US Administration does not have a real understanding of the real situation insofar as human rights are concerned', he said. 'They just don't know about the process of democracy and democratization in this country.' Nonetheless he thought progress had been made 'by one rung, maybe two', and the final communique was warmer and more positive than that of the Washington meeting, emphasizing the significance of the summit in laying the foundation of a realistic approach to reducing the risk of conflict. Minimum verification measures for a strategic arms reduction treaty were identified and listed, and it was noted that substantial additional common ground had been achieved during the meetings. On his way home from Moscow Mr Reagan stopped in London to brief the British Prime Minister, Mrs Thatcher, on the outcome of the summit, and to extend an invitation to her to visit Washington later in the year when his successor had been elected. In a speech at the Guildhall in London on 3 June, Mr Reagan said he thought that the barriers of the post-war era were quite possibly beginning to be broken down.

In November the US and the Soviet Union signed an agreement extending the existing pact for the purchase of American grain and soya beans for another two years, but more dramatic indications that long-established East-West attitudes were changing came in December, when Mr Gorbachev went to New York to address the General Assembly of the United Nations (see DOCUMENTS). His proclamation of the onset of a new era of peace and his announcement that his Government was cutting the size of its armed forces by half a million men and would withdraw 50,000 men, 10,000 tanks, 8,500 artillery systems and 800 aircraft from Eastern Europe took the US by surprise. Reaction was consequently cautious, though among politicians in Washington there was professional admiration of Mr Gorbachev's timing in making his announcement as the US was changing Administrations. Mr Reagan said that, if the Soviet Union carried out its unilateral cuts speedily and in full, history would regard it as important. Mr Bush applauded the planned reductions but told Mr Gorbachev that he needed time to complete his team, consult allies and make other preparations before working on the strategic relationship. Mr Shultz, after meeting Nato Foreign Ministers in Brussels, said he liked the notion that the cold war was dead but pointed out that there was still tension between East and West. 'The Berlin Wall is still there', he said. 'If there is any symbol of the cold war, that's it.'

The Gulf was once again a flashpoint of trouble for the US in 1988. The commitment to escort tankers continued to prove expensive and hazardous, US military commanders complaining that their sophisticated but hefty weaponry and ships were ill-suited to respond to the skirmishing of small, fast Iranian vessels. When the US frigate *Samuel Rogers* was holed by a mine on 14 April the US Navy launched what was described by the Secretary of Defense, Frank Carlucci, as a 'measured response' four days later. Two Iranian oil platforms were destroyed at Sirri and Sasson in the southern Gulf, and during the short engagement that followed an Iranian patrol boat was sunk and two frigates damaged. A British-flagged tanker, the *York Marine*, was slightly damaged by shells fired by Iranian gunboats. Iran complained to the UN and warned that it would retaliate, while President Reagan warned that Iran would continue to 'pay a price' if it threatened US interests in the Gulf.

On 3 July the US cruiser *Vincennes* mistakenly shot down an Iranian passenger airliner over the Strait of Hormuz, killing all 290 people on board. Mr Reagan immediately issued a statement expressing his deep regret at the incident, describing it as a terrible human tragedy. It was explained that the *Vincennes* was engaged with five Iranian patrol boats at the time when the aircraft was seen to be directly approaching. The aircraft was outside the commercial air corridor and apparently did not respond to warnings sent on both military and civilian frequencies. It was then assumed to be hostile and brought down with a surface-to-air missile. The captain of the *Vincennes*, Captain Will Rogers, admitted responsibility for the attack and said it was a burden he would carry for the rest of his life. 'I alone am responsible for any actions taken by the *Vincennes*', he said, while insisting that he was defending his ship from an apparent threat. A US military inquiry later suggested that crew error and inexperience resulted in false information being passed to the captain. Mr Reagan promised compensation for the families of those on board the aircraft but in Iran Ayatollah Khomeini called for an 'all-out war against America and its allies'. US embassies were alerted to brace themselves for retaliatory action, but were ultimately relieved to find that the response was mainly verbal. When the UN Security Council met in response to Iranian demands, Vice-President Bush defended the US against the charges of cold-blooded atrocity and the murder of innocent passengers, saying that the downing of the aircraft had been a legal right since Iran had allowed 'a civilian airliner loaded with passengers to proceed on a path over a warship engaged in battle. That was irresponsible and a tragic error'. Initial draft resolutions calling on outside powers to reassess their military presence in the Gulf and on the US to explain how reparation was to be made were dropped, leaving the resolution simply expressing deep distress and regret at the loss of innocent lives.

When the UN Secretary-General announced on 20 August that a ceasefire in the Gulf War had been agreed, Mr Reagan declared that it was news the world had waited for and the US had been pressing for. A month later the US began slowly to relax its escort duties, though emphasizing that withdrawal would not begin until a permanent settlement had been agreed between Iran and Iraq.

Elsewhere in the Middle East the US again found itself frustrated in its attempts to establish peace between Israel and its Arab neighbours. The US was concerned by Israel's harsh crackdown in the occupied territories and on 5 January expressed its displeasure by voting against Israel in the UN Security Council for the first time in six years. On 1 February the US vetoed a Security Council Resolution calling on Israel to stop violating the human rights of the Palestinians, maintaining that peace would be best served if the UN stood aside and allowed the US to organize a new initiative. The US was setting a hectic pace for this, aiming to set up direct negotiations between the parties concerned so that a permanent solution might be reached by December. The process would begin with an 'international opening' or conference which would enable Jordan to take part in the negotiations. Mr Shultz began the Secretary of State's familiar shuttle between Jerusalem and the Arab capitals at the end of February, but he failed to make progress and the US plan was rejected by King Husain of Jordan after a meeting with Mr Shultz in London in March. The plan, which was based on the US belief that a just and lasting peace could only be achieved if Israel was prepared to withdraw from occupied territories, was also rejected by Yitzhak Shamir, the Israeli Prime Minister. After further unproductive shuttling by Mr Shultz, Mr Shamir went to Washington, where he was urged by President Reagan to seize the opportunity of breaking the deadlock in the Middle East. But in an election year there was reluctance in Washington to push Israel too hard, so Mr Shamir left without yielding his ground. A further journey to the Middle East by Mr Shultz proved equally abortive, and the US peace plan was pigeon-holed until after the election.

The issue came dramatically to the fore again at the end of the year after the US had refused a visa to Yassir Arafat, leader of the Palestine Liberation Organization (PLO), who wanted to address the UN in New York. The US Government's decision was deplored by the General Assembly by a vote of 151–2, the two being the US and Israel, with Britain recording the only abstention. When the US refused to change its mind the UN decided to hold its debate on Palestine in Geneva instead of New York. In his address on 13 December Mr Arafat declared that the PLO recognized Israel's right to exist in peace and security, that it accepted UN Resolutions 242 and 338 as the basis for negotiations to end the Arab-Israeli conflict, and that it renounced terrorism in all its forms. At least, that is what he declared he had said, and meant, at a press conference on the following day—the message to the UN having been somewhat garbled in translation.

The US responded immediately. 'The US is prepared for a substantive dialogue with PLO representatives', said Mr Shultz, and on 16 December Mr Robert Pelletreau, the US ambassador in Tunis, met members of the PLO's executive committee there for what he said were 'very practical' talks. In Israel the US move was greeted with shock and dismay, a spokesman for the Prime Minister warning that it would not advance the cause of peace. In Washington Mr Arafat's timing was seen to be helpful. If there was to be a political backlash in the US it would fall on the outgoing Administration rather than the new, which would have the responsibility of pursuing a new chance for peace in the coming year.

Events in Central America proved equally frustrating for much of the year. Concern over events in Panama came to the boil in Washington early in the year when it was revealed that the Administration had bluntly informed General Manuel Antonio Noriega, the country's military ruler, that he should resign and allow free elections. The US also began investigating the General's involvement in drug trafficking, charges on which he was indicted by a grand jury in Florida at the end of January. An attempt by the Panamanian President, Eric Delvalle, to oust General Noriega on 25 February, with US connivance, failed, and Sr Delvalle was himself sacked by the General, although the US continued to recognize him as the legitimate President. On 1 March President Reagan formally declared that Panama was failing to cooperate with the US in fighting drug trafficking, which under American law meant that sanctions should be imposed. On the following day it was announced that these would take the form of the withholding of monthly payments for the operation of the Panama Canal. Some $50 million of Panamanian assets in US bank accounts were frozen and the US called on General Noriega to leave Panama immediately and live in exile.

Open talk in Washington about possible military intervention, an attempted coup or the kidnapping of General Noriega lost America much support in Latin American countries, who became critical of the intervention. A meeting of 22 Latin American Governments in April agreed to consider a Panamanian request for economic aid to offset the effect of American sanctions. On 9 April the US Administration ordered US companies and citizens in Panama to suspend tax payments, and one week later sent Marine reinforcements into the Canal Zone, although the President ruled out the possibility of military intervention unless the Panama Canal itself was threatened.

As General Noriega retained his control of Panama despite the damage that sanctions were doing to his country, the US in May offered him a deal which would have secured his resignation in August, after which he would leave the country until elections had taken place in 1989. Drugs charges against him in the US would be dropped. When General Noriega rejected the deal on 25 May, Mr Shultz announced that no further negotiations were contemplated. Economic sanctions remained in force, but the General was still in charge of Panama at the end of the year.

In January President Reagan declared that his final year in office would be 'the year that the US will strongly affirm that democracy, not communism, is the future of Central America'. He was referring specifically to Nicaragua, defending his Government's commitment to the Contras, the opponents of the Sandinista Government, and warning his countrymen of the danger of trusting Nicaraguan President Ortega's offer of negotiations for peace. 'It's time to realise that the Sandinista communists and their Soviet mentors are serious people with serious objectives', he said. 'It's time we got serious too.' He asked Congress for $36,250,000 in military aid for the Contras. This was rejected by the House of Representatives on 3 February by 219 votes to 211. On 17 March 3,150 US troops began arriving in Honduras after President Azcona had called for assistance to maintain the country's sovereignty and integrity, although it was generally believed that he had been persuaded to make the request in order to help the US display its commitment to the beleaguered Contras, who were being pursued close to, and sometimes across, the border. The Nicaraguan incursion encouraged the US Congress to approve legislation on 30–31 March to provide $47,900,000 in non-military humanitarian aid for the Contras. When, on 11 July, Richard Melton, the US ambassador in Managua, and seven other American diplomats were expelled from the country 'for fomenting political unrest' the US Government responded by expelling the ambassador and seven other Nicaraguan diplomats from Washington. Although peace talks between the Contras and the Sandinistas broke down during the year, the US tacitly conceded that the Contras no longer had a realistic chance of ousting the Sandinistas and that the eight-year guerrilla war had been lost.

The special relationship that Mr Reagan had fostered with the British Prime Minister during his presidency continued to flourish during 1988, and was put on public display in November when Mrs Thatcher visited Washington to meet Mr Reagan at the White House for the last time under his presidency. Mr Reagan told his guest that the United States acknowledged the special role which she and the people of Britain had played in achieving an extraordinary change in international relations, while Mrs Thatcher in reply said that Mr Reagan had restored faith in the American dream and, as a result, respect for America stood high in the world. Britain had been proud to be America's partner in that great adventure.

The partnership began to look less solid at the end of the year when the US drew up a list of European goods that were to be subjected to a tariff of 100 per cent from the start of 1989 in response to what Washington regarded as 'unfair trading practices' by the EEC. The proposed tariffs, which were to be applied to European beef, pork hams and shoulders (excluding those pre-cooked and packaged), canned tomatoes, soluble or instant coffee extracts, fruit juices and wine and soda mixtures, were in retaliation for the European ban on US beef imports containing growth hormones. The US Trade

Representative, Clayton Yeutter, said the EEC had not presented any evidence that proper use of hormones threatened human health. 'Therefore the decision to implement the ban constitutes an unfair trade practice', he said. The US also made it clear that it would take further countermeasures if the EEC retaliated to the new American tariffs, although Government officials were hopeful that a trade war with Europe might still be averted.

Agreements on overseas bases relieved some of the tension that had been growing up between the US and three other allies. On 15 January the US agreed, after nearly two years of difficult negotiations, to withdraw 72 F-16 fighters from Spain during the next three years. In October the US agreed in principle to a demand from the Greek Government to phase out the US Air Force base at Hellenikon, which shared some facilities with Athens airport. Later the same month an agreement was concluded with the Philippines for the continued use of US bases in that country to the end of 1991 in exchange for $481 million a year in economic assistance.

The United Nations was restored to the President's favour in 1988. In recent years he had insisted that the US, which normally paid about a quarter of the world organization's ordinary budget and nearly a third of its peacekeeping costs, should withhold its contribution in protest at the UN's profligacy. In September he instructed the State Department to find ways of paying the $520 million that had been held back in recognition, it was assumed, of the UN's recent efforts in Afghanistan, in securing the ceasefire in the Gulf War and the progress towards a settlement in Namibia. In his own valedictory address to the General Assembly on 26 September, Mr Reagan heralded the dawn of a new age of peace. 'A change that is cause for shaking of the head is upon us', he said. 'There is the prospect not only of a new era in Soviet-American relations, but a new age of world peace. The United Nations has the opportunity to live and breathe and work as never before.'

Chapter 2

CANADA

CAPITAL: Ottawa   AREA: 9,970,610 sq km   POPULATION: 25,600,000 ('86)
OFFICIAL LANGUAGES: English and French   POLITICAL SYSTEM: Confederal democracy
HEAD OF STATE: Queen Elizabeth II   GOVERNOR-GENERAL: Jeanne Sauvé
RULING PARTY: Progressive Conservative Party (since Sept '84)
HEAD OF GOVERNMENT: Brian Mulroney, Prime Minister (since Sept '84)
PRINCIPAL MINISTERS: Donald Mazankowski (deputy premier), Joe Clark (external affairs), Perrin Beatty (defence), Michael Wilson (finance), Marcel Masse (energy, mines and resources)
INTERNATIONAL ALIGNMENT: Nato, OECD, OAS, Francophonie, Cwth.
CURRENCY: Canadian dollar (end-'88 £1=Can$2,15, US$1=Can$1,19)
GNP PER CAPITAL: US$14,120 ('86)
MAIN EXPORTS: manufactured goods, fabricated and crude materials, agricultural products

CANADIANS took an historic decision in 1988 to enter into a comprehensive free trade agreement with the United States. The issue of freer US-Canadian trade had always been a sensitive one for Canadians, since many believed that to enter into closer economic relations with their neighbour would jeopardize Canada's independence. Others pointed out that Canada's trade was overwhelmingly with the USA and that 70 per cent of it was already free of duty. These conditions had not weakened Canada's ability to frame its own policies and to play a distinctive role in world affairs. Yet on three occasions, in 1891, 1911 and 1948, Canada had rejected the prospect of a free trade treaty with the USA.

The current free trade proposal was a principal objective of the Progressive Conservative (PC) Government of Brian Mulroney, elected in 1984 (see AR 1987, pp. 65–66). During 1988 Canadians engaged in a fierce debate on the issue—which, however, was not a primary concern in the USA. The free trade pact was easily approved in the House of Commons on 19 September, but the Canadian Senate, dominated by Liberal members appointed by former Prime Minister Pierre Trudeau, held up approval. It claimed that the Mulroney Government possessed no mandate to initiate such a sweeping change in Canada's trade orientation and insisted that the Canadian people should have a chance to express themselves on the issue through a general election. Mulroney finally accepted this position and on 1 October advised Governor-General Jeanne Sauvé to dissolve Parliament. The election was held on 21 November.

The campaign, dominated by free trade, represented the closest approach to a one-issue election in Canada's history. The Mulroney Government stressed the need for competitiveness in Canada's economy and pointed out that coping with US industry and services would help to prepare Canada for competition from across the seas and especially from the Pacific rim countries. The conditions of world trade were changing rapidly, the Government claimed. Canada needed to 'manage' its response to this change in a flexible and open manner. With a huge majority of 210 seats in the outgoing 282-seat House of Commons, the Mulroney Government entered the campaign in an advantageous position, although popular support for free trade ebbed away during the contest.

The two opposition parties, the Liberals under John Turner and the New Democratic Party (NDP) under Edward Broadbent, both emphasized the dangers for Canada's economic and social policies under free trade with the United States. They argued that the USA would claim that Canada's regional economic support programmes were a form of subsidy and, under the free trade agreement, would have to be phased out. Also forecast were US attempts to water down Canada's progressive legislation in unemployment insurance, social measures and health insurance, as well as the loss of thousands of jobs across the country. A better course for Canada to follow, the opposition parties claimed, was to pursue tariff reductions under the Uruguay round of GATT, a framework within which Canada had won important trading benefits in the past.

Two nationally-televised debates, one in French and one in English, proved to be high points in the campaign. Mr Turner rounded on Mr Mulroney with great passion, accusing him of 'selling out' the country in his desire to conclude a commercial arrangement with the USA. The Liberals had some success in convincing the electorate that they presented the most effective resistance to free trade, a tactic that drew support away from the third party, the NDP.

In the actual election the Mulroney Government obtained a solid vote of confidence and a majority which although not as massive as in 1984, was still comfortable. The PCs won 170 seats in a House increased to 295 members, against 82 for the Liberals (double their 1984 representation) and 43 for the NDP (31 in 1984). One seat was vacated by the sudden death of the newly-elected member. In terms of the popular vote, 43 per cent went to the PCs, 32 per cent to the Liberals, 20 per cent to the NDP and 5 per cent to fringe parties.

The most important aspect of the outcome was the PC triumph in Quebec, a Liberal stronghold under Mackenzie King, Louis St Laurent and Pierre Trudeau. A native son, Mr Mulroney had assiduously cultivated the province since 1984 with grants and economic support programmes. In return, Quebec elected 63 PC members, more than it had four years earlier. Premier Robert Bourassa who, although a Liberal, was a strong supporter of free trade, undoubtedly helped the Mulroney forces in the campaign.

The Liberals took the remaining 12 seats, most of which were concentrated on the island of Montreal.

Ontario, possessing 99 seats, was the key to the election. Here Liberal Premier David Peterson was a foe of free trade, but his influence did not prevent the PCs from winning 47 seats, compared with 42 for the Liberals and 10 for the NDP. On the prairies the Liberals, who had held only one seat before the election, captured five in Winnipeg (Manitoba), while the NDP won 10 of Saskatchewan's 14 seats; however, Alberta returned 25 PCs in its 26 seats. British Columbia, a favourable environment for the NDP, gave 19 of its 32 seats to the party, and Mr Turner (in Vancouver) was the only Liberal elected in the province. The Northwest Territories returned two Liberals and Yukon one NDP member.

Six members of Mulroney's Cabinet were defeated in the election, including Ray Hnatyshyn (Minister of Justice), Flora Macdonald (Minister of Communications) and Tom McMillan (Minister of the Environment).

Although more Canadians voted for parties opposing free trade than voted for the PCs, the latter party's parliamentary majority enabled it to move swiftly to enact the legislation necessary to put the deal into force. Parliament was recalled on 12 December to allow the Government to gain approval for legislation to implement the pact, which was intended to go into force on 1 January 1989.

While the free trade legislation was going through the House of Commons and the Senate in late December, the country was rocked by a language controversy. On 15 December the Supreme Court of Canada ruled that Quebec's language law, which prohibited the use of any language but French on exterior commercial signs in the province, violated both the federal Charter of Rights and Freedoms and Quebec's own human rights charter because it infringed the right of Quebec's Anglophone population (representing 12 per cent of the province's 6 ½ million people). The use of French-only signs had become a strong emotional symbol to the majority of Quebeckers and Premier Robert Bourassa found himself in an uncomfortable position. On 17 December he announced a compromise solution that failed to please either group. Using section 33 of the Charter of Rights and Freedoms, the 'notwithstanding clause', he introduced legislation exempting his language law from the rights guaranteed in the two charters. His law provided that exterior signs would continue to be permissible only in French but that signs inside stores could be bilingual, except that priority must be given to the French version. Nationalist Quebeckers denounced the compromise as permitting an unacceptable element of bilingualism in a French-speaking province surrounded by a sea of English-speakers. Three English-speaking members of Bourassa's Cabinet resigned over what they considered a betrayal of the rights of the English-speaking community in Quebec.

Premier Bourassa's action seemed to jeopardize the future of the Meech Lake Accord, the delicate constitutional agreement worked out in April and June 1987 setting out formal terms under which Quebec would accede to the 1982 constitution drawn up by Pierre Trudeau (see AR 1987, pp. 67–8). This document had been enthusiastically supported by Prime Minister Mulroney and premier Bourassa when it had been signed. The federal Parliament had approved it, as had the legislatures of eight of the ten provinces. (Unanimous agreement by all the provinces was required by June 1990 if the Meech Lake Accord was to go into effect.) Premier Gary Filmon of Manitoba, leading a government which had not yet approved the accord, announced on 19 December that he would not take action to endorse it until a new constitutional conference had been held. Premier Frank McKenna of New Brunswick, not in office when the accord was signed, also announced he would put off a decision until after a meeting of first ministers.

Two provincial elections were held in 1988. In Manitoba on 26 April the NDP government of Howard Pawley, in office since 1981, was defeated and replaced by a minority PC government under Gary Filmon, whose party won 25 of the 57 seats in the Assembly. The two opposition parties, the Liberals now with 20 seats and the NDP reduced to 12, did not combine against the Filmon administration during its first months in office. In Nova Scotia premier John Buchanan (PC) won his fourth consecutive majority term in an election held on 6 September. In spite of a number of ministerial scandals, Buchanan's personal popularity carried him to victory with 28 seats in the 52-seat legislature. The Liberals captured 21, the NDP was cut to two and there was a single independent member.

The Canadian economy performed strongly in 1988. An estimated 4 per cent growth rate brought its real domestic product, on an annual basis, to Can$590,900 million. Unemployment was at its lowest level for seven years but climbed slightly to 7.9 per cent of the labour force in October. The cost of living remained relatively stable, the year-on-year rise being 4.2 per cent in October. Inflationary pressures were held in check by the high interest-rate policy of the Bank of Canada.

Finance Minister Michael Wilson's fourth Budget, delivered on 10 February, provided for modest tax increases on gasoline and aviation fuel but generally held the line on taxes. Total spending for 1988–89 was predicted at Can$132,300 million, with revenues at Can$103,300 million. The resulting deficit was smaller in relation to GDP than had been the case when Wilson assumed the portfolio in 1984. Discussions continued with the provinces on the second stage of Wilson's tax reforms, introduced in 1987 with a simplified personal and corporate income tax structure. The second phase involved the imposition of a new national sales tax, planned to go into effect some time in 1989.

Prime Minister Mulroney hosted the 14th annual summit meeting of the leaders of the Group of Seven industrialized countries in Toronto on 19–21 June (see Pt. XVIII, Ch. 2). Canada engaged in two peacekeeping ventures in 1988: in May five officers were sent to Afghanistan to observe the Soviet troop withdrawal and in August about 500 military specialists set up a communications link along the Iraq-Iran border. Canada was also elected to one of the ten non-permanent seats on the UN Security Council in October.

Chapter 3

LATIN AMERICA

ARGENTINA—BOLIVIA—BRAZIL—CHILE—COLOMBIA—ECUADOR—
PARAGUAY—PERU—URUGUAY—VENEZUELA—CUBA—
DOMINICAN REPUBLIC AND HAITI—
CENTRAL AMERICA AND PANAMA—MEXICO

ARGENTINA

CAPITAL: Buenos Aires   AREA: 2,766,890 sq km   POPULATION: 31,000,000 ('86)
OFFICIAL LANGUAGE: Spanish   POLITICAL SYSTEM: federal presidential democracy
HEAD OF STATE AND GOVERNMENT: President Raúl Alfonsín (since Dec '83)
RULING PARTY: Radical Civic Union
PRINCIPAL MINISTERS: Víctor Martínez (Vice-President), Dante Caputo (foreign relations), José Horacio Jaunarena (defence), Juan Vital Sourrouille (economy), Enrique Nosiglia (interior)
INTERNATIONAL ALIGNMENT: NAM, OAS
CURRENCY: austral (end-'88 £1=A29.38, US$1=16.24)   GNP PER CAPITA: US$2,350 ('86)
MAIN EXPORTS: wheat, other agricultural produce, manufactures

WHILE the national currency, the austral, fell hour by hour even against the plummeting dollar, and the Government, faced with 176 per cent inflation, decreed New Year price rises of up to 20 per cent on food, petrol and other basic commodities, civilian minds, as a survey in the news weekly *Somos* showed, were preoccupied with the economic situation to the exclusion of all else. Meanwhile, Lieut.-Colonel Aldo Rico, focus of the Easter rebellion of 1987 (see AR 1987, p. 70), became the focus for continuing military discontent. At Christmas, while his supporters exchanged cryptic messages, he was allowed by the military command to be transferred to house arrest—a luxury denied to thousands of victims of the 'dirty war' who perished miserably and whose bodies have never been found. Worse still, while his supporters were escorting him home, one, a Lieut. Maguire, threatened a reporter with his service revolver and subsequently rammed his car.

These events caused a national sensation. A massive force, including tanks, was sent to recapture Rico, giving him adequate opportunity to escape. Rumours flew that there had been a shootout and that Rico had been wounded, but it soon emerged that a friend (subsequently arrested) had flown him in a light plane to the military base at Monte Caseros, in the north-eastern province of Corrientes, where he was supported in his defiance by 270 troops. Monte Caseros was an interesting place to choose. Symbolic as the scene of the last stand of the nineteenth-century dictator Rosas against the political opponents who drove him into exile in Southampton (UK), it was, more practically, very close to the borders of both Uruguay and Brazil. At the same time, there were sympathetic risings in many provincial garrison centres—Córdoba, Tucumán, Neuquén—and, a new and ominous factor, revolt spread to the Air Force, where a handful of officers tried to capture the capital's domestic airport, Jorge Newbery, known popularly as Aeroparque. But this time the hesitations of Easter 1987 were apparently not repeated. Caseros was surrounded, Rico recaptured by government forces, the townsfolk spat on his supporters as they were led away, and an official communique proclaimed that all units were now obeying their natural commanders. But once again it appeared that there had been deals behind the scenes for which the new Army Chief of Staff, General José Caridi, appointed after the Easter rebellion, took the blame.

At this moment the British Government presented the military opponents of the civilian rulers of Argentina with a heaven-sent opportunity to capitalize on the Falklands issue by announcing that 'Operation Fire Focus', large-scale reinforcement exercises, would be held in March. The response of the Foreign Minister, Dante Caputo, who had been elected President of the UN General Assembly, was judged firm enough and the Government turned its attention back to the economic crisis. It came as a further shock when, following the surprise victory of the orthodox faction in the Peronist Party (PJ), the charismatic Governor of La Rioja, Carlos Menem, was favoured over his 'renewal' rival, Antonio Cafiero, and was chosen as the Peronists' 1989 presidential candidate in the party primaries. For by this time support for the ruling Radicals was so low that the Peronists seemed bound to win. The President himself was booed at the annual Palermo Show after his Government had announced (in August) yet another stabilization plan, called the Primavera

(Spring) Plan, by which payment for agricultural exports was fixed at the commercial rate and not the financial rate. In replying, he lost his temper and said they would not have dared to do so under the military Government. Late in the year the IMF finally agreed to provide new loans to fund a pre-election boost to the economy.

BOLIVIA

CAPITAL: La Paz and Sucre AREA: 1,099,000 sq km POPULATION: 6,600,000 ('86)
OFFICIAL LANGUAGE: Spanish, Quechua and Aymará POLITICAL SYSTEM: presidential democracy
HEAD OF STATE AND GOVERNMENT: President Víctor Paz Estenssoro (since Aug '85)
RULING PARTY: Historic National Revolutionary Movement
PRINCIPAL MINISTERS: Julio Garrett Ayllón (Vice-President), Guillermo Bedregal Gutiérrez (foreign affairs), Juan Carlos Durán Saucedo (interior and justice), Alfonso Walter Revollo Thenier (defence), Ramiro Cabezas (finance)
INTERNATIONAL ALIGNMENT: NAM, OAS
CURRENCY: boliviano (end-'88 £1=Bs4.64, US$1=Bs2.57) GNP PER CAPITA: US$600 ('86)
MAIN EXPORTS: natural gas, tin

ACCUSATIONS that the party was associated with Bolivia's biggest drug dealer, Roberto Suárez Gómez, discredited the opposition Nationalist Democratic Action (ADN). With hydrocarbons now the main hope for the future of the legitimate Bolivian economy, particular interest attended the success of the Government of President Víctor Paz Estenssoro and the ruling Historic National Revolutionary Movement (MNRH) in finally concluding, after ten years of negotiation, a trade agreement giving Brazil preferential access to Bolivia's gas, hydrocarbon products and electricity, in return for lifting tariffs on Bolivian minerals, cotton, beer and food, some 700 items in all. Nevertheless, for the first time the Government benefited by issuing permits for the legal marketing of coca leaves, leading to the withdrawal of US technical and economic support for its armed forces. By the year's end the Government had won agreement from the Paris Club for the refinancing of up to $570 million of its $2,174 million debt, following agreement on its programme with the IMF.

BRAZIL

CAPITAL: Brasília AREA: 8,512,000 sq km POPULATION: 138,500,000 ('86)
OFFICIAL LANGUAGE: Portuguese POLITICAL SYSTEM: federal presidential democracy
HEAD OF STATE AND GOVERNMENT: President José Sarney (since March '85)
RULING PARTY: Liberal Front Party holds presidency; Party of the Brazilian Democratic Movement controls Congress
PRINCIPAL MINISTERS: Roberto Costa de Abreu Sodré (foreign affairs), Maílson Ferreira da Nóbrega (finance), Paulo Brossard de Souza Pinto (justice), João Alves (interior) João Batista de Abreu (head of planning secretariat)
INTERNATIONAL ALIGNMENT: OAS
CURRENCY: cruzado (end-'88 £1=Cz$1,364.45, US$1=Cz$1=754.26)
GNP PER CAPITA: US$1,810 ('86)
MAIN EXPORTS: coffee, iron ore, soyabeans

FOR President José Sarney the year began well when delegates to the constitutional convention failed to agree on proposals to reduce his presidential term and on 2 June it was confirmed by 328 votes to 222 at the current five years. The new constitution was finally agreed on 2 September after 578 days of debate and formally proclaimed in Brasilia on 5 October. Its limited checks on the power of the near-imperial presidency, however, reflected the waning position of the main Democratic Alliance (AD) power broker, Dr Ulysses Guimarães, president of the Party of the Brazilian Democratic Movement (PMDB), rather than the strength of the President, whose last-minute intervention against the new charter was not a success. A liberal document, it specifically rejected the so-called 'national security doctrine' and outlawed torture, though under Article 148 the armed forces formally retained the power to intervene whenever law and order were deemed to be under threat. But between 2 September and 5 October the President made a large number of dispositions by decree in defiance of his pledge to respect the constitution.

As elsewhere in the region, the economic crisis was the main issue facing the President and his handling of it in question. Inflation to the end of October reached an annualized rate of 714 per cent before Finance Minister Maílson Ferreira da Nóbrega, precluded by the fate of his predecessor from the sort of shock treatment he personally favoured, finally gained agreement on his much-heralded social pact at the beginning of November. It was then reported that interest payments on the country's commercial debt had been brought up to date for the first time for over a year. By then it was too late to improve a political climate characterized by growing radicalism amid widespread apathy.

The governing PMDB lost seats in the 15 November municipal elections to both right and left. Surprises included the victory of the left-wing Workers' Party (PT) in three state capitals. The PT elected Luiza Erundina, its candidate for the mayoralty of São Paulo (the largest city in the southern hemisphere), who beat ex-presidential candidate Paulo Maluf. The PT leader, Luis Inácio da Silva ('Lula'), emerged as a strong rival to Leonel Brízola, whose Democratic Labour Party (PDT) retained control of Rio de Janeiro and won in Curitiba and other provincial towns.

Measures announced in October to curb the destruction of the Amazon rain forest (including the withdrawal of tax exemptions, reduced subsidies for agriculture in the Amazon region, a ban on wood exports and strengthened environmental agencies) were welcomed but aroused only mild optimism because of important limitations. Some 77,000 square miles of forest had, it was estimated, been destroyed in 1987 alone, and in 1988 for the first time the contribution which the burning of the forests was making to the destruction of the Earth's ozone layer as well as to the 'greenhouse effect' was generally recognized by scientists. The bid of Brazil for $500 million from the World Bank to develop power resources in the Amazon, it was noted, looked much less desirable in that context.

The hostility in some circles to effective conservation measures was tragically demonstrated on 22 December when the Amazon ecologist Francisco Mendes (44), who from his position as local head of the Rubber Tree Tappers' Union had received UN commendation for his defence of the area against ranchers seeking to clear it for grazing land, was shot to death outside his home at Xapuri. Violence, however, was a general problem. On 28 March gunmen attacked members of Brazil's largest tribe of forest Indians, the Tikuna, adding one more to the total of some 1,000 killed over land conflicts since 1980. A journalist, Luis Otavio Monteiro, was shot on 30 December in Manaus after publishing investigations of death squad activities in the area.

CHILE

CAPITAL: Santiago   AREA: 756,600 sq km   POPULATION: 12,300,000 ('86)
OFFICIAL LANGUAGE: Spanish   POLITICAL SYSTEM: republic, under military rule
HEAD OF STATE AND GOVERNMENT: President (Gen.) Augusto Pinochet Ugarte (since '73)
MILITARY JUNTA: Gen. Santiago Sinclair (army), Gen. Rodolfo Stange Oelckers (police), Adml. José Toribio Merino Castro (navy), Maj.-Gen. Fernando Matthei Aubel (air force)
PRINCIPAL MINISTERS: Herman Felipe Errázuriz Correa (foreign affairs), Rear-Adml. Patricio Carvajal Prado (defence), Hernán Büchi Buc (finance), Carlos Caceres (interior), Hugo Rosende (justice)
INTERNATIONAL ALIGNMENT: OAS
CURRENCY: peso (end-'88 £1=Ch$453.30, US$1=Ch$250.58)   GNP PER CAPITA: US$1,320 ('86)
MAIN EXPORTS: copper, agricultural products

GENERAL Augusto Pinochet Ugarte, who had ruled Chile since the military seizure of power in September 1973, faced the first real test of his authoritarian regime's waning popularity on 5 October when under the imposed constitution a plebiscite was held to ratify the nomination by the junta of its choice of successor. Three out of the four service chiefs were known to favour a civilian candidate, but when the nomination was officially announced on 30 August it came as no surprise that they had chosen Pinochet himself, who had been campaigning for months ahead of the event. The decision, which if ratified would have enabled the President to serve a second eight-year term from 1989, was greeted by violent street demonstrations. In the capital alone, two died and at least six were seriously injured. However, in order to fulfil repeated promises of constitutional freedom of choice, the state of emergency was lifted, exiles permitted to return, censorship lifted and, despite intermittent harassment and the decision of the Supreme Court to sentence two labour leaders to 541 days internal exile for organizing strikes in 1987, opposition parties were permitted to campaign for a record registration and a 'No' vote.

Presidential optimism was based on the fact that the economy had grown at a steady 5 per cent for three years—although, following the sharp recession of 1982–83, this meant that production had in fact not yet even reached 1981 levels. Hence when the result of the poll was reluctantly released, it showed that the Chilean people had decisively rejected Pinochet, by 2,290,972 'Yes' votes (43 per cent) to 2,754,805 'No' votes (55 per cent). Afterwards the Cabinet was reshuffled, the former Finance Minister, Carlos Caceres, replacing the hard-line Interior Minister, Sergio Fernández, and so undertaking the delicate task of conducting discussions with the opposition parties.

In face of Pinochet's reluctance to concede that he had lost, Chile faced a further 17 months under a 'lame-duck dictatorship' before a democratically-elected President and Congress could take office in March 1990. By late December, however, it had been conceded that Pinochet himself would not be a candidate in the elections and some concessions on changes to the constitution had been made, though formal dialogue had not yet opened.

COLOMBIA

CAPITAL: Bogotá AREA: 1,141,750 sq km POPULATION: 29,000,000 ('86)
OFFICIAL LANGUAGE: Spanish POLITICAL SYSTEM: presidential democracy
HEAD OF STATE AND GOVERNMENT: President Virgilio Barco Vargas (since Aug '86)
RULING PARTY: Liberal Party
PRINCIPAL MINISTERS: Víctor Mosquera Chaux (Vice-President), Col. Julio Londoño Paredes (foreign affairs), César Gaviria Trujillo (interior), Gen. Manuel Jaime Guerrero Paz (defence), Luis Fernández Alarcon (finance), Carlos Arturo Marulanda (economic development), Guillermo Plazas (justice)
INTERNATIONAL ALIGNMENT: NAM, OAS
CURRENCY: peso (end-'88 £1=Col$610.18, US$1=Col$337.30) GNP PER CAPITA: US$1,230 ('86)
MAIN EXPORTS: coffee, oil and oil derivatives

THE struggle between the Cali and Medellin cartels for control of Colombia's highly lucrative cocaine traffic erupted into open violence in late 1987 and early 1988, resulting in at least 80 killings in Colombia itself, and dozens more in Miami and New York. The Government of Liberal President Virgilio Barco continued to enjoy relatively stable economic conditions, despite cuts in International Coffee Association (ICA) quotas and attacks by the National Liberation Army (ELN) on the Caño Limón-Covenas oil pipeline which cost export income and caused severe environmental damage, for some of which Colombia had to indemnify Venezuela. As the most conservatively managed economy in the region, and the only one so far not to have undertaken debt restructuring, Colombia took a strong line in its search for new credit, but with inflation over

30 per cent found funds scarce. A one-day general strike called by three main labour federations in October, in pursuit of pay rises, a price freeze and an end to repressive measures, was broken up by troops.

The Government came under colder scrutiny for the reported excesses of the armed forces in countering the endemic violence which in the previous 25 years had killed an estimated 75,000 people and had reached a level which the ILO described as 'beyond comprehension'. In May the kidnapping by M-19 guerrillas of the conservative editor of *El Siglo*, Alvara Gómez Hurtado, who was later released on Independence Day, not only converted him to dialogue but prompted the resignation of 13 members of the Cabinet. A new level of crisis came when on the night of 11 November some 30 gunmen drove in jeeps into the goldmining town of Segovia, in the department of Antioquia, threw grenades into the telephone exchange and then fired into houses and streets for more than two hours, leaving 43 dead. Initially blamed on guerrillas, it appeared later that the killings were the work of a local cocaine dealer, the so-called 'Rambo Criollo'. With some 15 per cent of the population involved in one way or another with the cocaine trade, the line between regular crime and insurgency had become totally blurred.

On 22 November the newly-appointed Defence Minister, General Manuel Guerrero Paz, was very nearly the victim of a car bomb attack outside the Ministry itself, responsibility for which was claimed by a splinter group of the Revolutionary Armed Forces of Colombia (FARC). Though General Paz restated his support for President Barco's policy of negotiation with the guerrillas, these incidents were followed by a further tightening of the 'Statute for the Defence of Democracy' decreed in January to prevent the intimidation of the judiciary and the raising of the maximum penalty for assassination to life imprisonment. Incidents of violence against foreign companies were a new feature, and there was concern that the nominal truce between the Government and the FARC might break up altogether.

ECUADOR

CAPITAL: Quito   AREA: 270,500 sq km   POPULATION: 9,650,000 ('86)
OFFICIAL LANGUAGE: Spanish   POLITICAL SYSTEM: presidential democracy
HEAD OF STATE AND GOVERNMENT: President Rodrigo Borja Cevallos (since Aug '88)
RULING PARTIES: Democratic Left, allied with Christian Democrats
PRINCIPAL MINISTERS: Luis Parodi (Vice-President), Diego Cordovez (foreign affairs), Jorge Gallardo (finance), Andrés Vallejo (interior), Juan José Pons (industry and trade), Gen. (rtd.) Jorge Félix (defence), Diego Tamariz (energy and mines)
INTERNATIONAL ALIGNMENT: NAM, OAS
CURRENCY: sucre (end-'88 £1=S/.915.20, US$1=S/.505.91)   GNP PER CAPITA: US$1,160 ('86)
MAIN EXPORTS: oil and oil derivatives, coffee, bananas

THE Minister of Government and Police, Luis Robles Plaza, was forced to resign on 28 January accused of human rights abuses which, it was alleged, had been overlooked abroad on account of President León Febres Cordero's free market policies. Elections on 31 January were inconclusive, so on 8 May a run-off election was held between the two leading presidential candidates, Abdala Bucaram Ortiz and Rodrigo Borja Cevallos, in which Dr Borja, of the opposition Democratic Left (ID) secured victory by 1,762,417 votes (46 per cent) to 1,572,651 (41 per cent) for Sr Bucaram. The candidate of the ruling Social Christian Party (PSC) of President Cordero, Sixto Durán Ballén, had come third in January with only 13 per cent of the vote. On 31 May the President decreed a national state of emergency in face of a one-day general strike, an action subsequently held by the Court of Constitutional Guarantees to have been *ultra vires.*

Dr Borja was sworn in as President on 10 August in the presence of an awkward mix of foreign dignitaries, which included President Fidel Castro Ruz of Cuba, visiting South America for the first time since 1971, and Secretary of State George Shultz of the United States, who refused to meet either him or President Daniel Ortega of Nicaragua. President Ortega's arrival, indeed, had to be postponed to the following day to give Dr Borja time to restore diplomatic relations with Nicaragua.

The outgoing President, León Febres Cordero, whose unthinking passion for free-market solutions had brought some revival to the oil industry but in the process had virtually crippled the economy—payments on the national debt having been suspended since January 1987—characteristically refused to hand the sash of office to his successor. Within hours President Borja had announced an emergency economic package, devaluing the sucre, placing sharp constraints on non-essential imports and doubling the price of petrol to the equivalent of US$0.50 a gallon. But the new social democratic Government faced the same problem as many of its predecessors, that of persuading Ecuador's traditionally turbulent Congress to make real economies. However, by November, with the aid of a bridging loan from Venezuela, prospects were good for the new Government to renegotiate its debt and secure fresh credits from the IMF.

PARAGUAY

CAPITAL: Asunción   AREA: 406,752 sq km   POPULATION: 3,800,000 ('86)
OFFICIAL LANGUAGE: Spanish   POLITICAL SYSTEM: republic, under quasi-military rule
HEAD OF STATE AND GOVERNMENT: President (Gen.) Alfredo Stroessner (since '54)
RULING PARTY: Colorado Party
PRINCIPAL MINISTERS: Elidio Acevedo (foreign affairs), Gen. Alonso Martino (finance), Delfin Ugarte Centurión (industry and trade), Sabino Augusto Montanaro (interior), José Eugenio Jacquet (justice and labour), Maj.-Gen. Gaspar Germán Martínez (defence)
INTERNATIONAL ALIGNMENT: OAS
CURRENCY: guaraní (end-'88 £1=G1,848.49, US$1=G1,021.83)
GNP PER CAPITA: US$1,000 ('86)
MAIN EXPORTS: cotton, soyabeans, meat

PARAGUAY, once under the theocratic rule of the Jesuits and now under the autocratic rule of General Alfredo Stroessner, showed its confused heritage when in May the visit of Pope John Paul II pointed up how far, in the absence of other effective opposition, the Church had become the vehicle of protest. As elsewhere on the continent, the Pope called for respect for human rights and political freedoms, but the crowd gathered outside Asunción cathedral were attacked by police with truncheons and many were injured. In response, Archbishop Ismael Rolón cancelled a ceremony to commemorate the 451st anniversary of the founding of the city, a date, not altogether coincidentally, chosen by General Stroessner for his inauguration to an eighth five-year term as President following his re-election on 14 February in a ballot in which he was said to have received 1,186,693 votes, or 88.6 per cent of those cast. The General was received coldly when, against advice, he visited New York in July to address the United Nations. During the visit 12 of his entourage attacked demonstrators so violently that one had to be taken to hospital.

PERU

CAPITAL: Lima   AREA: 1,285,000 sq km   POPULATION: 20,200,000 ('86)
OFFICIAL LANGUAGES: Spanish, Quechua and Aymará   POLITICAL SYSTEM: presidential democracy
HEAD OF STATE AND GOVERNMENT: President Alan García Pérez (since July '85)
RULING PARTY: Aprista Party
PRINCIPAL MINISTERS: Luis Alberto Sánchez Sánchez (Vice-President), Armando Villanueva del Campo (prime minister), Luis González Posada (foreign affairs), Gen. Enrique López Albujar (defence), Carlos Rivas Davila (economy and finance), Ivan García Cabrejos (industry and trade), Adml. Juan Soria Diáz (interior), César Delgado Barreto (justice)
INTERNATIONAL ALIGNMENT: NAM, OAS
CURRENCY: inti (end-'88 £1=I/.1,998.59, US$1=I/.1,104.80)   GNP PER CAPITA: US$1,090 ('86)
MAIN EXPORTS: copper, petroleum products

ON 26 July a Lima newspaper published an interview with Abimael Guzmán, 53-year-old leader of the maoist guerrilla movement Sendero Luminoso (SL), which was accepted to be the first public statement of the revolutionary leader's views in ten years. Omitting any reference to the capture by police of his deputy and military commander, Osman Morote, in early June, he called for a new stage in the struggle. 'Our process of the people's war has led us towards the apex', he claimed, adding: 'We have to prepare for insurrection, which will be the taking of the cities.' In May the discovery of five bodies in an unmarked grave confirmed the reported massacre by soldiers of 28 peasants in Cayará, but President Alan García, who had initially been critical of such excesses, indirectly defended the armed forces, who had been increasingly insistent that he should do so. Amnesty International confirmed that there had been a sharp increase in reported cases of torture and unlawful killing in the Andean emergency zone since 1987. Since the insurgency began, in 1980, Government sources said that between 11,500 and 15,000 people were known to have died, and since 1982 at least 3,200 people were said locally to have 'disappeared'. The Government, which had extended the state of emergency to cover six provinces and Lima itself, was also thought to be behind the emergence of a right-wing counter-terrorist group, the so-called Commando Rodrigo Franco.

On the economic front a February austerity package was a failure. In May the Prime Minister, Guillermo Largo Cox, who had held office since June 1987, resigned and was replaced by Armando Villanueva del Campo. In June a new stabilization plan was announced, but by July the rate of inflation had climbed over 400 per cent and looked set to reach 600 per cent by year end. On the eve of President Garcia's anniversary speech on 28 July guerrillas blacked out Lima and 180 miles of coastline. The President's refusal to deal with the international lending agencies and foreign bankers left him little room for manoeuvre, and his Government's moves to free up prices of more and more goods stemmed less from a belief in free market principles than from a desperate need to balance the books. A new austerity package in September was more drastic by far than anything yet demanded by the IMF.

On 11 October the commander of the first military district, General Victor Raúl Silva Tuesta, was dismissed amid rumours that he had been planning a coup. At the same time the ruling Aprista party expelled a deputy, Manuel Angel del Pomar, for suspected involvement in drug offences. In November Abel Salinas, the fourth Minister of the Economy to hold office in seven months, resigned because the latest package of austerity measures was watered down, even though, in face of a decree limiting wage increases, mines, public utilities, telecommunications, transport and many industries were brought to a standstill by a wave of strikes. At the end of the month 22 died when SL guerrillas ambushed a military patrol, while SL-backed strikes paralysed Ayacucho and insurgents again blacked out most of the country's electricity system.

URUGUAY

CAPITAL: Montevideo AREA: 176,200 sq km POPULATION: 3,000,000 ('86)
OFFICIAL LANGUAGE: Spanish POLITICAL SYSTEM: presidential democracy
HEAD OF STATE AND GOVERNMENT: President Julio Sanguinetti (since March '85)
RULING PARTY: Colorado Party
PRINCIPAL MINISTERS: Enrique Tarigo (Vice-President), Enrique Iglesias (foreign relations), Antonio Marchesano (interior), Ricardo Zerbino (economy and finance), Lt-Gen. (rtd) Hugo Medina (defence), Jorge Presno (industry and energy)
INTERNATIONAL ALIGNMENT: OAS
CURRENCY: new peso (end-'88 £1=NUr$813.01, US$1=NUr$449.42)
GNP PER CAPITA: US$1,900 ('86)
MAIN EXPORTS: wool, meat

URUGUAY benefited during the year from the general improvement in world trade. Delays meant that the promised referendum on the controversial 'Full Stop' law (see AR 1987, pp. 79–80) was postponed, so politically the most significant development was that the former guerrilla movement, the Tupamaros, abandoned the way of armed struggle to re-enter democratic politics by way of the 'third force' party, the Frente Amplio. The Frente itself, however, was in disarray following remarks by its leader, General Liber Seregni, accusing the ruling Colorados of governing unconstitutionally. At the end of October the country played host to the heads of state of Argentina, Brazil, Colombia, Mexico, Peru and Venezuela, when the seven countries agreed at Punta del Este on an agenda for talks with the next President of the United States. Their declaration that the debt situation threatened democracy in the region reflected a now widely accepted view, which saw prospects for progress on the debt issue under existing arrangements as minimal or even non-existent.

VENEZUELA

CAPITAL: Caracas AREA: 912,000 sq km POPULATION: 17,800,000 ('86)
OFFICIAL LANGUAGE: Spanish POLITICAL SYSTEM: presidential democracy
HEAD OF STATE AND GOVERNMENT: President Jaime Lusinchi (since Feb '84)
RULING PARTY: Democratic Action
PRINCIPAL MINISTERS: Germán Nava Carillo (foreign affairs), Simón Alberto Consalvi (interior), Héctor Hurtado Navarro (finance), Gen. Italo del Valle Alliegro (defence), Pedro Torres Agudo (justice), Arturo Hernández Grisanti (energy and mines)
INTERNATIONAL ALIGNMENT: OAS
CURRENCY: bolívar (end-'88 £1=Bs69.19, US$1=Bs38.25) GNP PER CAPITA: US$2,920 ('86)
MAIN EXPORTS: oil, aluminium

IN an election year, the state of the economy was the major talking-point. President Jaime Lusinchi of the ruling Acción Democrática (AD) party, faced with a soaring debt standing at some $30,200 million at year's end, sagging oil prices and a falling currency, sent a top-level team to Washington for talks with foreign bankers on the basis of a package of austerity measures such as might be recommended by the IMF. Venezuela, which unlike most other

Latin American states had been meeting its obligations on both capital repayments and interest in full, was unable to obtain a satisfactory arrangement with its creditors. Later, following the Finance Minister's presentation to Congress of a Budget based on absurdly over-optimistic assumptions, the Government turned to the much more risky course of seeking to raise US$1,000 million through discounting future receipts of the state oil corporation PDVSA.

With the President discredited by intra-party bickering, accusations of corruption against high-level appointees and the decision of the AD central committee to drop presidential secretary Blanca Ibáñez from its list of candidates, the party candidate, 66-year-old ex-President Carlos Andrés Pérez, ran well ahead of his party in the presidential elections of 4 December. In them he broke two decades of regular alternation between the two main parties by securing a decisive victory over his Christian Democratic (COPEI) rival, Eduardo Fernández (48), who was handicapped by divisions within his own party. Sr Pérez gained over 52 per cent of the vote as against 33 per cent for his rival, the remainder being divided between some 21 minor party candidates.

In his victory statement he promised to build on the work of President Lusinchi, to seek a 'social pact' and to 're-programme' payments on the country's foreign debt. Within days he had left for the Middle East for a 'study tour' and conversations with Opec heads of state, a sign that the would lend his considerable weight as a democratic socialist of international standing to the task of creating a common Latin American front on the debt issue. With the IMF as ever slow to respond, and the Baker Plan for Latin America (see AR 1985, p. 466) effectively dead (as its author prepared to become US Secretary of State), the prospects of confrontation seemed to have markedly increased.

Meanwhile, however, two incidents cast doubt on the longstanding stability of Venezuela's armed forces. Tanks surrounded the Miraflores presidential palace while President Lusinchi was attending a meeting of the Group of Eight in Uruguay, and a commander and a captain were arrested when they returned to barracks. A week later, troops who had in recent years established a number of bases in the border area fired on and killed 16 fishermen on the Colombian border who were mistaken for guerrillas. What was more difficult to explain was why they then published photographs of the bodies with guns and explosives next to them.

CUBA

CAPITAL: Havana   AREA: 115,000 sq km   POPULATION: 10,200,000 ('86)
OFFICIAL LANGUAGE: Spanish   POLITICAL SYSTEM: republic, one-party communist state
HEAD OF STATE AND GOVERNMENT: President Fidel Castro Ruz (since Jan '59)
RULING PARTY: Cuban Communist Party
PRINCIPAL MINISTERS: Gen. Raúl Castro Ruz (First Vice-President, defence), Isidoro Octavio Malmierca Peoli (foreign relations), Gen. José Abrantes Fernández (interior), Rodrigo García Leon (finance), José López Moreno (planning)
INTERNATIONAL ALIGNMENT: Comecon
CURRENCY: peso (end-'88 £1=Cub$1.38, US$1=Cub$0.76)   GNP PER CAPITA: n.a.
MAIN EXPORTS: sugar and sugar products

THE year began well with the ending of the drought that had afflicted agricultural production on the island for four years. The 1987–88 sugar crop was estimated to be at least 7.3 million tonnes, and tobacco and citrus fruit harvests were also expected to improve. Throughout the year it became increasingly clear that President Fidel Castro Ruz was determined to resist any attempt to extend the ideas of *perestroika* or *glasnost* to Cuban domestic politics. At the same time, relations with the Soviet Union, based as they were on mutual advantage, remained cordial. The Cuban Government, proclaiming its intention to free all but 44 of its 429 political prisoners, agreed to allow the first visit of the UN Commission on Human Rights, and was indeed elected to the 1989 Commission. Speeches by President Castro called for a substantial expansion of tourist facilities, and receipts were expected to rise by 14 per cent over 1987, to $115 million. Abroad the long-running negotiations between Angola, Cuba and South Africa (see DOCUMENTS) for a settlement that would permit the withdrawal of Cuban troops from southern Africa were successfully concluded, removing a major obstacle to a rapprochement between Cuba and the United States.

DOMINICAN REPUBLIC AND HAITI

Dominican Republic
CAPITAL: Santo Domingo   AREA: 48,400 sq km   POPULATION: 6,600,000 ('86)
OFFICIAL LANGUAGE: Spanish   POLITICAL SYSTEM: presidential democracy
HEAD OF STATE AND GOVERNMENT: President Joaquín Balaguer (since Aug '86)
RULING PARTY: Social Christian Revolutionary Party
CURRENCY: peso (end-'88 £1=RD$11.47, US$1=RD$6.34)   GNP PER CAPITA: US$710 ('86)
MAIN EXPORTS: sugar, metals

Haiti
CAPITAL: Port-au-Prince   AREA: 27,750 sq km   POPULATION: 6,100,000 ('86)
OFFICIAL LANGUAGE: French   POLITICAL SYSTEM: presidential republic
HEAD OF STATE AND GOVERNMENT: Brig.-Gen. Prosper Avril (since Sept '88)
CURRENCY: gourde (end-'88 £1=G9.03, US$1=G4.99)   GNP PER CAPITA: US$330 ('86)
MAIN EXPORTS: light manufactures, coffee

IN the DOMINICAN REPUBLIC, ex-President Salvador Jorge Blanco was sentenced in absentia to 20 years imprisonment for corruption, while the memoirs of his successor, Joaquín Balaguer (81, almost blind and still serving his fifth term), sold out at once. Corruption and inefficiency were blamed, too, for power cuts that had become endemic over the previous year. In July the Government instituted exchange controls and subsequently closed 36 finance companies that ran into difficulties by speculating on the exchange.

IN HAITI the civilian President, Leslie Manigat, was overthrown in a military coup on 20 June by his predecessor, General Henri Namphy, when he countermanded an order by the General dismissing the commander of the Dessalines batallion, Colonel Jean-Claude Paul. Death squads had already reappeared on the streets following the November 1987 election day massacre (see AR 1987, p. 83) and violence remained the theme of the rest of the year. Namphy's moves to strengthen his own position by retaining the Minister of the Interior, General Williams Regala, and bringing Duvalierists back into the Government backfired when he was in turn displaced in a sergeants' coup on 17 September by Duvalierist General Prosper Avril. The latter received cautious support from the United States when he appointed a civilian Cabinet, pledged to restore the constitution and hold elections and purged officers associated with drug smuggling. $15 million of US aid was thereupon released. Colonel Paul, who masterminded both the June and September military coups but was indicted in the United States on drug-running charges, was the most prominent of those dismissed in October. Shortly afterwards he collapsed at his villa and died after eating soup that was later shown to have been poisoned.

CENTRAL AMERICA AND PANAMA

Guatemala
CAPITAL: Guatemala City   AREA: 109,000 sq km   POPULATION: 8,300,000 ('86)
OFFICIAL LANGUAGE: Spanish   POLITICAL SYSTEM: presidential democracy
HEAD OF STATE AND GOVERNMENT: President Vinicio Cerezo Arévalo (since Jan '86)
RULING PARTY: Christian Democratic Party
CURRENCY: quetzal (end-'88 £1=Q4.92, US$1=Q2.72)   GNP PER CAPITA: US$930 ('86)
MAIN EXPORTS: coffee, sugar, cotton, petroleum, cardamom, bananas

El Salvador
CAPITAL: San Salvador   AREA: 21,400 sq km   POPULATION: 4,900,000 ('86)
OFFICIAL LANGUAGE: Spanish   POLITICAL SYSTEM: presidential democracy
HEAD OF STATE AND GOVERNMENT: President José Napoléon Duarte (since May '84)
RULING PARTY: Christian Democratic Party
CURRENCY: colón (end-'88 £1=C9.04, US$1=C4.99)   GNP PER CAPITA: US$820 ('86)
MAIN EXPORTS: coffee, cotton, sugar

Honduras
CAPITAL: Tegucigalpa   AREA: 112,000 sq km   POPULATION: 4,500,000 ('86)
OFFICIAL LANGUAGE: Spanish   POLITICAL SYSTEM: presidential democracy
HEAD OF STATE AND GOVERNMENT: President José Simeón Azcona del Hoyo (since Nov '85)
RULING PARTY: Liberal Party
CURRENCY: lempira (end-'88 £1=L3.62, US$1=L1.99)   GNP PER CAPITA: US$740 ('86)
MAIN EXPORTS: bananas, coffee

Nicaragua
CAPITAL: Managua   AREA: 120,000 sq km   POPULATION: 3,400,000 ('86)
OFFICIAL LANGUAGE: Spanish   POLITICAL SYSTEM: presidential democracy
HEAD OF STATE AND GOVERNMENT: President Daniel Ortega Saavedra
RULING PARTY: Sandinista National Liberation Front
CURRENCY: córdoba (end-'88 £1=C$578.78, US$1=C$319.94)   GNP PER CAPITA: US$790 ('86)
MAIN EXPORTS: coffee, cotton, sugar, bananas

Costa Rica
CAPITAL: San José   AREA: 51,000 sq km   POPULATION: 2,660,000 ('86)
OFFICIAL LANGUAGE: Spanish   POLITICAL SYSTEM: presidential democracy
HEAD OF STATE AND GOVERNMENT: President Oscar Arias Sánchez (since May '86)
RULING PARTY: National Liberation Party
CURRENCY: colón (end-'88 £1=C143.62, US$1=C79.39)   GNP PER CAPITA: US$1,480 ('86)
MAIN EXPORTS: coffee, bananas

Panama
CAPITAL: Panama City   AREA: 77,000 sq km   POPULATION: 2,200,000 ('86)
OFFICIAL LANGUAGE: Spanish   POLITICAL SYSTEM: presidential, under military tutelage
HEAD OF STATE: Manuel Solís Palma, Minister of the Presidency (since Feb '88)
COMMANDER OF DEFENCE FORCES: Gen. Manuel Antonio Noriega Moreno
RULING PARTY: Revolutionary Democratic Party
CURRENCY: balboa (end-'88 £1=B1.81, US$B1.00)   GNP PER CAPITA: US$2,330 ('86)
MAIN EXPORTS: bananas, shrimps, sugar

IN GUATEMALA President Vinicio Cerezo's civilian Government remained unpopular with businessmen over its tax reform package (see AR 1987, p. 86). It survived an abortive coup attempt on 11 May by military officers seeking a stronger hand in the counterinsurgency campaign. The Minister of the Interior, Juan José Rodil Peralta, was forced out but General Héctor Gramajo, the Defence Minister, also a target of rebel criticisms for his advocacy of political concessions and his belief in an apolitical army, remained in post. Subsequently the constitution was amended to strengthen security forces' powers of detention, police budgets were increased and civil defence patrols (PAC) introduced in the capital, but right-wing death squads stepped up their activities, although they remained below the level reached in 1987. At the end of May the Constitutional Court administered a further setback to democratization when it invalidated the October 1987 act setting up elected departmental and municipal councils, thus undercutting the ruling Christian Democrats' attempt to consolidate political support in the countryside. The rebel URNG, while accepting the principle of dialogue under the Equipulas II agreement, planned to double its strength and open four new fronts, two in the department of Quiché and two near the capital. The Government's long-term economic plan, 'Guatemala 2000', proclaimed in June, had a strong neo-liberal flavour. In view of the success of the voluntary austerity programme, at the end of October the IMF agreed a $98 million standby loan to support exports and enable the country to meet its debt service obligations.

President José Napoléon Duarte of EL SALVADOR, visibly wasting away from terminal liver cancer, remained in office but his power had effectively passed to the armed forces, within which the appointment of Colonel René Emilio Ponce as Chief of Staff marked the consolidation of La Tandona (the military class of 1966, which was double the normal size) in five of the six brigade commands and all major positions of influence. Veterans of several years of combat, the Tandona officers were known to hold views close to those of the right-wing National Republican Alliance (Arena) and to oppose the US strategy of low-intensity conflict. The US-backed candidate for the presidency in the 1989 elections, Fidel Chavez Mena, was defeated in the party convention for the nomination of the ruling Christian Democrats (PDC) by Adolfo Rey Prendes, but the leadership overturned the decision. Meanwhile, having won a decisive majority in Congress and in the municipal elections in March, Arena showed increased confidence in the prospects of victory for its presidential nominee, businessmen Alfredo Cristiani, by pushing through an act abolishing the state coffee-marketing monopoly, INCAFE, and giving its powers to a growers' organization, the Salvador Coffee Council. Coffee production, already affected by the long-running civil war, suffered further losses as a result of broca infestation.

In HONDURAS the US military presence had become effectively permanent, although at the year's end the future strategy of the Bush Administration towards the region remained uncertain. Meanwhile, death squad killings continued despite assurances from President José Azcona that abuses had been ended. At the end of April Congress ratified the agreement to set up a Central American Parliament, leaving only Costa Rica to agree. However, the armed forces objected to a proposed agreement with El Salvador, granting mutual transit rights for commercial exports destined for each other's ports.

NICARAGUA continued to be in serious economic difficulties despite the winding-down of Contra activities. In February measures were announced to tighten credit, end subsidies and cut Government expenditure, but after the annualized rate of inflation in May had exceeded 3,000 per cent on 14 June President Daniel Ortega Saavedra announced the severest austerity measures yet, including a wage freeze, although with guaranteed basic protection for lower-paid workers among whom hunger had become a serious problem. In July the Government nationalized the San Antonio plant of Nicaragua Sugar Estates because of poor productivity, but again guaranteed the retention of the mixed economy. Soon afterwards the US ambassador was expelled for alleged complicity in anti-Government demonstrations. US hostility to the coalition Government continued unabated and assistance was notably lacking when the country was devastated by hurricane 'Joan' at the end of October, its worst natural disaster since the Managua earthquake of 1972 (see AR 1972, pp. 82–3). The hurricane itself cost 137 dead, 185 wounded, 119 missing and 321,000 homeless. It destroyed all the rice crop, the third bean crop of the year, 40 per cent of the banana plantations, 80 per cent of palm oil and 80 per cent of coffee trees. The winds felled an estimated 15 per cent of the country's forests amounting to a million hectares, while 75 per cent of the fishing fleet was wrecked either at sea or in harbour.

COSTA RICA was lucky to escape the eye of the October hurricane. Although roads throughout the country were severely damaged by flooding, the coffee crop was relatively undamaged, and the IDB offered $200 million in emergency aid for reconstruction. In arrears with its creditors, the Government of President Oscar Arias had earlier been unsuccessful in talks with the Paris Club, but continued to receive substantial help through multilateral lending agencies, including a total of $125 million from US AID, $13 million from West Germany and some $76 million from other sources. But John Biehl, economic adviser to President Arias, charged that in setting up a network of private institutions to duplicate the work of Costa Rican state organizations, US AID had undermined the economy as well as the Costa Rican democratic tradition. Farmers strongly resisted the Government's own 'Agriculture for Change' programme, charging that by diverting land into export crops it would make the country dependent on expensive imported food.

It also appeared that the Costa Rican economy was gaining a great deal of help from the inflow of 'hot money' from the drug syndicates as a result of US sanctions against PANAMA, ostensibly intended to oust General Manuel Antonio Noriega from his post as Commander of the Defence Forces. General Noriega had been indicted for drug-related offences in February by US federal grand juries in Miami and Tampa (Florida), following which, on 25 February, President Eric Arturo Delvalle attempted to dismiss him. The following day the congressional majority, in the absence of the opposition, voted to oust both the President and Vice-President Esquivel. Sr Manuel Solis Palma, the Minister of Education, was appointed Minister in charge of the Presidency and President Delvalle went into hiding. On 4 March the United States froze all Panamanian assets, but as the pressure intensified and Panamanians suffered, a coup attempt on 16 March failed to dislodge General Noriega. The latter, his position consolidated, still held effective power in the country at the year's end, while the Government was still able to meet its internal obligations (although not payments on its foreign debt). Indeed, General Noriega looked likely to win the presidency in May 1989 on the nomination of the ruling Revolutionary Democratic Party, probably in alliance with the nationalist Authentic Panamanian Party, whose founder and leader, ex-President Arnulfo Arias Madrid, widely believed to have been the real winner of the 1984 elections, died in August at the age of 86 (see OBITUARY).

MEXICO

CAPITAL: Mexico City   AREA: 1,958,000 sq km   POPULATION: 80,200,000 ('86)
OFFICIAL LANGUAGE: Spanish   POLITICAL SYSTEM: federal presidential democracy
HEAD OF STATE AND GOVERNMENT: President Carlos Salinas de Gortari (since Dec '88)
RULING PARTY: Institutional Revolutionary Party (since '29)
PRINCIPAL MINISTERS: Fernando Solana Morales (foreign affairs), Pedro Aspe Armella (finance), Fernando Gutiérrez Barrios (interior), Gen. Antonio Riviello Bazán (defence), Ernesto Zedillo Ponce de Leon (planning and federal budget)
INTERNATIONAL ALIGNMENT: OAS
CURRENCY: peso (end-'88 £1=Mex$4,167.23, US$1=Mex$2,303.61)
GNP PER CAPITA: US$1,860 ('86)
MAIN EXPORTS: oil, motor machinery, coffee

SUSPICIOUS circumstances surrounding the announcement of the results of the presidential election on 6 July led immediately to accusations of fraud. Carlos Salinas de Gortari, 39-year old candidate of the ruling Institutional Revolutionary Party (PRI), who even before the poll had to admit that the 59-year-old domination of the PRI had come to an end, claimed victory shortly after the polls closed and reaffirmed his claim subsequently. According to official sources, however, the computer in the Electoral Commission had been so swamped by the incoming results which it had been especially programmed to handle that it broke down.

The most thorough independent survey of public opinion published before the election showed Sr Salinas leading with 56 per cent of registered voters, against 25 per cent for Cuauhtémoc Cárdenas Solórzano of the National Democratic Front (FDN), the left-wing electoral coalition specially formed from a number of smaller parties to back the son of Mexico's revered former President, General Lázaro Cárdenas. Manuel Clouthier of the main right-wing opposition party, the Party of National Action (PAN), was in third place with 19 per cent. The poll was conducted by the Gallup organization for the Spanish-language television network Eco, based in Los Angeles. Mexican polls had traditionally commanded little confidence as they were seldom independent and the results hardly in doubt; exit polls—a novelty in Mexican politics intended less to disclose trends than to make it more difficult for the authorities to tamper with the results—were hastily banned.

On 9 July, when the Electoral Commission had still failed to produce a final result, Sr Cárdenas claimed victory and declared that to deny him victory 'would be the equivalent of a coup d'état'. He said that he had, according to private sources, obtained a plurality of the votes cast, leading Sr Salinas by 38 to 32 per cent. It was clear that a major upset had occurred, since even the Commission's provisional figures suggested that only 48 per cent of the electorate had voted for Sr Salinas, against 29 per cent for Sr Cárdenas and 20 per cent for Sr Clouthier (100,000 of whose supporters met in the Zócalo and pledged themselves to oppose the alleged fraud).

When on 11 July incomplete results were finally announced, to no one's surprise they gave the victory to Sr Salinas. The final results were not announced until 14 July, and were barely bad enough, for the PRI, to be convincing. With only 50.36 per cent of the votes cast, Salinas' showing was far worse than that for any successful candidate for the presidency since 1917. Sr Cárdenas and the FDN established themselves in second place with 31.12 per cent, and Sr Clouthier, as expected, came third with 17 per cent.

The surprise decision of a fourth candidate, Herberto Castillo of the Mexican Socialist Party (PMS), to withdraw from the presidential contest a month before the election (8 June) and throw his support behind Sr Cárdenas had decisive consequences. As he intended, it united the left-wing vote behind Sr Cárdenas and so for the first time since the 1920s the formerly divided left were able to poll more votes than the traditional right opposition. But Sr Castillo's call to have his name removed from the ballot papers caused great Government embarrassment even before the election, when journalists found that 20,000 ballot papers for the northern state of Sonora, an area where electoral fraud had repeatedly been alleged in recent years, were being printed by a private firm in Mexico City. Contradictory explanations deepened the mystery: the Sonora Electoral Commission said that it knew nothing of the papers, while Manuel Bartlett Díaz, the Secretary of Government (Interior), claimed that they had been ordered legally.

Since 1929 the ruling PRI had never lost a state governorship nor a seat in the 66-member Senate. In 1982 it had officially polled only 71 per cent of the votes cast but had lost only one of the 300 directly-elected seats in the Chamber of Deputies; in 1985 it was credited with only 68 per cent and lost not a single seat. In 1988 the PAN won 32 of the 300 directly-elected seats in the Chamber and the FDN 20. The true figures should almost certainly be higher, but the allocation of the proportional seats nevertheless left the PRI in a minority. The FDN also won four seats in the Senate, suspiciously few but still a break in the PRI monopoly.

These results meant that for the first time since the 1920s the new Administration would have to deal with a Congress which would wish to show its independence and had some hope of being able to do so effectively. But omens were not good: at the inauguration of the new President on 1 December both FDN and PAN deputies walked out in full view not only of eight Latin American heads of state (including President Castro of Cuba) and the US Secretary of State, but also of the world's television cameras.

Chief among the causes of disillusion was the Government's financial policy. After five years of austerity, the Economic Solidarity Pact (PSE) announced in December 1987 had been extended in stages up to the election, and was subsequently further prolonged to the end of the year. But with oil revenues down, the Government was estimated to have spent $4,000 million in six months trying to keep the peso pegged at its new parity. Credit dried up, and despite a further US Treasury offer of a $3,500 million bridging loan, designed to exorcize the spectre of insurgency in Mexico, the debt burden remained crushing.

Chapter 4

THE CARIBBEAN

JAMAICA—GUYANA—TRINIDAD & TOBAGO—BARBADOS—
BELIZE—GRENADA—THE BAHAMAS—
WINDWARD & LEEWARD ISLANDS—SURINAME

JAMAICA

CAPITAL: Kingston   AREA: 11,000 sq km   POPULATION: 2,400,000 ('86)
OFFICIAL LANGUAGE: English   POLITICAL SYSTEM: parliamentary democracy
HEAD OF STATE: Queen Elizabeth II   GOVERNOR-GENERAL: Sir Florizel Glasspole
RULING PARTY: Jamaica Labour Party
HEAD OF GOVERNMENT: Edward Seaga, Prime Minister (since Oct '80)
PRINCIPAL MINISTERS: Hugh Lawson Shearer (deputy premier, foreign affairs and industry), Oswald Harding (justice), Errol Anderson (national security)
INTERNATIONAL ALIGNMENT: NAM, ACP, OAS, Caricom, Cwth.
CURRENCY: Jamaica dollar (end-'88 £1=J$9.75, US$1=J$5.39)   GNP PER CAPITA: US$840 ('86)
MAIN EXPORTS: bauxite/alumina, bananas, sugar

SPECULATION that this would be general election year in Jamaica continued incessantly until hurricane 'Gilbert' struck in September, leaving 20 per cent of houses badly damaged and 300,000 people temporarily without accommodation, with accumulated value of damages in the region of US$800–1,000 million. The post-hurricane reconstruction programme provided political capital which the incumbent Jamaica Labour Party (JLP), led by Prime Minister Edward Seaga, sorely needed to narrow the poll lead which Michael Manley's People's National Party (PNP) had held throughout the year. Carl Stone's polls, whose accuracy was legendary, indicated that a PNP–JLP margin of 49–34 per cent in June 1987 and 55–49 per cent in August had by October narrowed to 51–49 per cent. A variety of political and economic factors seemed to lend substance to election rumours, notably the terms of the 21 April Budget, Seaga-Manley negotiations to reduce pre-election political violence, and the Government's self-proclaimed success in complying with IMF conditions. However, despite the improved fortunes of the JLP, Mr Seaga had not set a general election date by year's end.

The Budget contrasted markedly with Mr Seaga's previous programmes by including increases in spending on health (123 per cent over 1987), on education (67 per cent), on poor relief and on basic food subsidies. The Prime Minister claimed that this expenditure was sustainable because of the 5 per cent growth rate, the widening of the tax base and projected external assistance. This was followed in May by an announcement that the national minimum wage would be raised from J$60 to J$80 in June and to J$100 in January 1989. The opposition PNP, which had boycotted the 1983 general elections (see AR 1983, p. 89), accused the Government of electioneering, a charge repeated in the aftermath of the hurricane when allegations of distributing aid on party lines were levelled, particularly building stamps and short-term employment relief for hurricane victims allocated via MPs. Mr Seaga said that hurricane relief pledged from all sources was valued at about US$515 million, although it was unclear how much of this was pre-arranged development aid, new loans or simply grants.

Despite bi-partisan agreements to minimize party political violence (there had been 600 politically-related deaths in 1987), disturbances continued and flared in July leading to the murder of a Kingston bus driver and related attacks. That the police were unable to solve the case brought shrill charges of political complicity, but more importantly damaged the necessary reconciliation process.

The Government complied with IMF adjustment terms at the end of one 15-month package in May and began to negotiate a further loan. Inflation had risen from 7 to 8 per cent but within prescribed limits, whilst the Government restricted wage rises to less than 10 per cent. Unemployment continued at 20.8 per cent, only marginally down, despite the increased capacity of the free zones. The terms and conditions of work in the zones led to strike action in March by the predominantly female workforce, who demanded the right to union membership and the right to strike action itself, which the Attorney-General later recognized and on which the PNP promised to legislate if elected. Textile production dominated the zones, whose production value increased from US$12 million in 1983 to US$174 million in 1987.

This increase, together with that in the garment sector (from US$97.8 million in 1986 to US$185.6 million in 1987), in the value of banana exports to Britain (almost doubling to J$161 million in 1987), and in sugar production (up 17.4 per cent in 1988) over 1987, all represented encouraging indicators of growth. They failed, however, to make much impact on the Jamaican debt of US$4,000 million, which represented 134 per cent of GDP. The debt service ratio at year's end stood at 48 per cent of export earnings.

Two major income earners experienced equivocal growths this year, namely tourism and bauxite production. The former, the country's largest foreign currency earner, bringing in gross receipts of US$600 million in 1987, was clearly hit by the lasting effects of the hurricane, especially for the main tourist season of December to March. However, the almost imperceptible rise in bauxite production masked the real achievement of the year, which was the Government's broad renegotiation with Alcan, Alcoa and Kaiser over output and the levy. The Government took on a 50 per cent share, with Alcoa, of the Clarendon aluminium plant, which had been run at 80 per cent capacity for two years but would increase to 100 per cent just as the Government was pushing other bauxite enterprises to do likewise. It was planned to increase production to 11 million tonnes by 1992 from the present 7.7 million tonnes. A standard bauxite levy (6 per cent of the average price of a primary aluminium ingot) was established along with a 33.3 per cent company profits tax.

GUYANA

CAPITAL: Georgetown   AREA: 215,000 sq km   POPULATION: 800,000 ('86)
OFFICIAL LANGUAGE: English   POLITICAL SYSTEM: co-operative presidential democracy
HEAD OF STATE AND GOVERNMENT: President Desmond Hoyte (since Aug '85)
RULING PARTY: People's National Congress (since '64)
PRINCIPAL MINISTERS: Hamilton Green (First Vice-President and prime minister), Mohamad Shahabuddeen (Vice-President, first deputy premier), Rashleigh Jackson (foreign affairs), Carl Greenidge (finance)
INTERNATIONAL ALIGNMENT: NAM, ACP, Caricom, Cwth
CURRENCY: Guyana dollar (end-'88 £1=G$16.25, US$1=G$8.99)   GNP PER CAPITA: US$500 ('86)
MAIN EXPORTS: bauxite, sugar, rice

NOTWITHSTANDING Guyana's admission into the Caribbean Basin Initiative (CBI), the Government's accommodation to IMF-type orthodoxy, and continuous negotiations by President Desmond Hoyte with aid and commercial agencies, the economic crisis had become a downward spiral. The base of the ruling People's National Congress (PNC) in the Trades Union Congress, upon whose cooperation the successful implementation of an IMF programme would depend, had been severely weakened by the setting up of a rival Federation of Independent Trades Unions.

The Budget presented by the Finance Minister, Carl Greenidge, on 28 March tended towards optimism: the reality was a finance gap of G$1,186 million, with an overall current-account deficit which had trebled from US$50 million in 1987 to US$187 million. Inflation was running at about 30 per cent. The current debt service ratio stood at 30 per cent of exports, with a US dollar exchange discrepancy of G$10 on the official market and between G$30 and G$42 on the parallel market. Mr Greenidge announced a plan to unify exchange rates, although not by devaluation unless agreed as part of an IMF package. Negotiations over a structural adjustment loan continued, but were hampered by Guyana's poor record in repayments (which had disqualified the country from new loans in 1985). President Hoyte estimated that recovery required a capital input of US$1,200 million; more realistically, an independent assessment by Prof. Clive Thomas put the figure much higher at US$3–4,000 million.

Guyana continued to experience comprehensive decay and mismanagement in all public utilities, including water shortages and contamination, electricity power cuts, and collapsing bridges and sea walls. Only 50 of the 300 buses of the state company were running due to lack of spares and fuel.

The profound economic crisis had long determined the political reaction of the Government to dissent. It took on a new harshness against the media and the unions when the National Assembly removed the right of the courts to require the Government to consult unions on labour legislation and to validate previously unconstitutional legislation, including retrospective legislation.

TRINIDAD & TOBAGO

CAPITAL: Port of Spain AREA: 5,128 sq km POPULATION: 1,200,000 ('86)
OFFICIAL LANGUAGE: English POLITICAL SYSTEM: parliamentary democracy
HEAD OF STATE: President Noor Mohammed Hassanali (since March '87)
RULING PARTY: National Alliance for Reconstruction
HEAD OF GOVERNMENT: Arthur Napoleon Raymond Robinson, Prime Minister (since Dec '86)
PRINCIPAL MINISTERS: Sahadeo Basdeo (external affairs and international trade), Lincoln Myers (food production), Herbert Atwell (national security), Kenneth Gordon (industry, enterprise and tourism), Selwyn Richardson (Attorney-General)
INTERNATIONAL ALIGNMENT: NAM, ACP, OAS, Caricom, Cwth.
CURRENCY: Trinidad and Tobago dollar (end-'88 £1=TT$7.68, US$1=TT$4.24)
GNP PER CAPITA: US$5,360 ('86)
MAIN EXPORTS: oil, chemicals

OF all the English-speaking states of the Caribbean, Trinidad & Tobago had lately experienced the deepest political and economic crises. The attempt by the National Alliance for Reconstruction (NAR) led by Prime Minister A.N.R Robinson to inaugurate a new era after the 30-year regime of the People's National Movement (PNM) appeared to have dramatically failed. The open split in the NAR, made public in November 1987 with the dismissal of four Ministers—Basdeo Panday (Deputy Prime Minister and external affairs), Kelvin Ramnath (energy), John Humphrey (works) and Trevor Sudama (junior finance)—was followed by their suspension from the party on 15 May by 100 votes to 78, and their expulsion on 25 September ostensibly on disciplinary grounds. The allegations included 'bringing the office of political leader into odium and/or contempt and/or disrepute; making racially and/or regionally divisive statements; and the unauthorized setting-up of a group known as 'Club '88, the Caucus of Love, Unity and Brotherhood'.

With the expulsions, those formerly associated with Club '88 and others critical of Mr Robinson's handling of this affair and economic matters formed a new party of the same name on 16 October. The widespread support for Club '88 appeared to be a reflection of the discontent with Mr Robinson's style of government in general, and the handling of the economy in particular. A further factor was the traditional constituency support for the leader of Club '88, Basdeo Panday, amongst those most affected by government spending cuts, i.e, sugar workers, public sector employees.

Prime Minister Robinson, as Minister of Finance and the Economy, presented a Budget on 8 January intended to attract private, including foreign, capital through tax relief, to reduce public expenditures, and to initiate the shift of the fiscal burden away from income to purchase taxation. The principal measures were the reduction of corporation tax (non-oil) from 45 to 40 per cent; reduction in the top rate of income tax from 70 to 50 per cent; reduction of supplemental petroleum tax from 55 to 20 per cent, with plans to remove it totally by 1992 and to replace it by a standard oil tax of 25 per cent; a 5–10 per cent increase on utility taxes; and a 5 per cent increase in purchase tax.

This package, with liberalized trade arrangements, resembled the type of requirements which the Government would have to fulfil were it to obtain IMF assistance. In the post-Budget debate Mr Robinson indicated his intention to negotiate for an IMF compensatory finance facility (confirmed at US$110 million in November) and then a stand-by arrangement (intended at US$75 million). In August the announcement of an 18 per cent currency devaluation, together with deeper public expenditure cuts, food price rises of between 20–30 per cent and unemployment in the region of 27 per cent, drew the admission from Mr Robinson that 'we are in a state of national economic emergency'.

Despite the Prime Minister's trip to the IMF, the World Bank, the EEC and the UK, as well as talks with commercial banks and businesses in September and October in search of aid and investment, no concrete plans could be discerned beyond the World Bank's regrading of Trinidad & Tobago to the status of a country eligible once again for concessionary loans. Mr Robinson's absence coincided with an increased level of dissent and public demonstration against Government policy from trade unions, civil servants and Club '88, combined with oft-repeated calls for a general election.

BARBADOS

CAPITAL: Bridgetown   AREA: 430 sq km   POPULATION: 254,000 ('86)
OFFICIAL LANGUAGE: English   POLITICAL SYSTEM: parliamentary democracy
HEAD OF STATE: Queen Elizabeth II   GOVERNOR-GENERAL: Sir Hugh Springer
RULING PARTY: Democratic Labour Party (since May '86)
HEAD OF GOVERNMENT: Erskine Sandiford, Prime Minister (since June '87)
PRINCIPAL MINISTERS: Philip Greaves (deputy premier), Sir J. Cameron Tudor (foreign affairs), Maurice King (attorney-general), Evelyn Greaves (trade, industry and commerce)
INTERNATIONAL ALIGNMENT: NAM, ACP, OAS, Cwth.
CURRENCY: dollar (end-'88 £1=BDS$3.63, US$1=BDS$2.01)   GNP PER CAPITA: US$5,150 ('86)
MAIN EXPORTS: sugar, light manufactures, chemicals

A general decline in economic performance from 1986 to a position in which GDP growth levelled off at 2 per cent in 1987 was beginning to be reversed in 1988, when growth in the region of 2.2–3 per cent was expected. The year started with unemployment down one point at 18.6 per cent and tourism revenue improving. The first half of 1988 registered manufacturing growth up 7 per cent (after a previous decline of some 25 per cent in 1987) and 1987 increases in tourism (13.9 per cent), construction (6 per cent) and non-sugar agriculture (9.1 per cent) were set to continue. Nevertheless, the 1987 trade deficit had increased by 16 per cent over 1986, since the value of exports had been halved from B$420 million to B$214 million. This reflected a drop in oil exports by 20.4 per cent to 331,768 bpd, a 6.5 per cent drop in mining, and a 6.6 per cent decline in sugar production. Two Barbados Sugar Industry refineries were closed in July, with the loss of 200 jobs. The Prime Minister, Erskine Sandiford of the Democratic Labour Party, pushed on with the reform of Barbados National Bank, Barbados Development Bank and the Insurance Corporation of Barbados, whose boards were dismissed in July as part of a comprehensive attempt at economic reconstruction.

BELIZE

CAPITAL: Belmopan   AREA: 23,000 sq km   POPULATION: 170,000 ('86)
OFFICIAL LANGUAGE: English   POLITICAL SYSTEM: parliamentary democracy
HEAD OF STATE: Queen Elizabeth II   GOVERNOR-GENERAL: Dame Minita Elvira Gordon
RULING PARTY: United Democratic Party (since Dec '84)
HEAD OF GOVERNMENT: Manuel Esquivel (Prime Minister since Dec '84)
PRINCIPAL MINISTERS: Curl Thompson (deputy premier, home affairs) Dean Barrow (foreign affairs, economic development, attorney-general), Edwardo Juan (commerce, industry and tourism)
INTERNATIONAL ALIGNMENT: NAM, ACP, Caricom, Cwth.
CURRENCY: dollar (end-'88 £1=BZ$3.61, US$1=BZ$1.99)   GNP PER CAPITA: US$1,170 ('86)
MAIN EXPORTS: sugar, citrus products, fish

FOLLOWING opposition to the Security Services Act (January 1987) and the December 1987 arson attack on the home of Deputy Prime Minister Curl Thompson, the ruling United Democratic Party under Prime Minister Manuel Esquivel sought to implicate leaders of the opposition People's United Party. The former Belize Defence Force second-in-command, Major Tom Greenwood (a PUP activist), was arrested, although he was acquitted with other arson defendants on 11 November. The detention of PUP leaders who became involved in 'unauthorized opposition activity', security-service surveillance of the opposition and strict control of media access by the PUP made Belizean politics reminiscent of its immediate neighbour (i.e. Guatemala). Despite such measures, or perhaps because of the unease thereby created, the PUP succeeded in securing control of four of the seven town councils in the 16 March local elections where the UDP had previously been strong. With a turnout of 70 per cent, the marked shift from the UDP indicated the level of discomfort with the Government.

Relations with Guatemala continued to improve, signalled by the creation in June of a permanent joint commission on territorial issues. Meetings were held in July and October in which a draft treaty and trade matters were discussed.

The March Budget, in which current expenditure was set at BZ$132 million and capital expenditure at BZ$47 million, was followed by a mini-Budget in September and increases in civil and military service salaries, partly from capital raised from the

Government's sale of Belize Telecommunications. Confidence in the Belizean banana industry by Fyffes, currently participating in a joint venture to improve port facilities at Big Creek, was justified as production for export increased from 1.1 million boxes in 1987 to 2 million in 1988.

GRENADA

CAPITAL: St George's   AREA: 344 sq km   POPULATION: 98,000 ('86)
OFFICIAL LANGUAGE: English   POLITICAL SYSTEM: parliamentary democracy
HEAD OF STATE: Queen Elizabeth II   GOVERNOR-GENERAL: Sir Paul Scoon
RULING PARTY: New National Party
HEAD OF GOVERNMENT: Herbert Blaize, Prime Minister (since Dec '84)
PRINCIPAL MINISTERS: Ben Jones (external affairs, agriculture), George McGuire (education, culture, local government, fisheries), Daniel Williams (attorney-general)
INTERNATIONAL ALIGNMENT: NAM, ACP, OAS, Caricom, Cwth.
CURRENCY: East Caribbean dollar (end-'88 £1=EC$4.88, US$1=EC$2.69)
GNP PER CAPITA: US$1,240 ('86)
MAIN EXPORTS: agricultural products

PRIME Minister Herbert Blaize of the New National Party presented an unremarkable Budget on 15 March, setting recurrent expenditure at EC$147.9 million with projected revenue at just EC$141 million, although it was to be doubted whether this amount would actually be collected given past performance. A 10 per cent surcharge on non-Caricom member imports was instituted, mirroring the direction in which other members were moving to encourage intra-Caricom trade. The Government also planned to reschedule the EC$300 million public debt with help from the IMF.

The constitutionality and the procedure of the trials of those convicted and sentenced to death for the murder of Maurice Bishop (see AR 1983, p. 92) continued to be criticized. Even the Organization of East Caribbean States refused to admit Grenada to its courts system until after the trial. Amnesty International were refused access to the defendants, who were reported to be subjected to beatings and to bread and water diets. At the year's end the death of the judge hearing the appeal meant that a new appeal hearing would have to be ordered.

THE BAHAMAS

CAPITAL: Nassau   AREA: 14,000 sq km   POPULATION: 236,000 ('86)
OFFICIAL LANGUAGE: English   POLITICAL SYSTEM: parliamentary democracy
HEAD OF STATE: Queen Elizabeth II   GOVERNOR-GENERAL: Sir Gerald C. Cash
RULING PARTY: Progressive Liberal Party
HEAD OF GOVERNMENT: Sir Lynden O. Pindling (Prime Minister since Jan '67)
PRINCIPAL MINISTERS: Clement T. Maynard (deputy premier, external affairs), Paul L. Adderley (attorney-general, education)
INTERNATIONAL ALIGNMENT: NAM, ACP, OAS, Cwth.
CURRENCY: dollar (end-'88 £1=B$1.81, US$1=B$1.00)   GNP PER CAPITA: US$7,190 ('86)
MAIN EXPORTS: petroleum products

THE planned increase of the islands' police drug squad from 18 officers to 270 reflected the heightened political profile of drug trafficking and its prevention in the Caribbean. Joint Caricom-US anti-trafficking exercises which took place in September followed requests from Sir Lynden Pindling's Government for the help of US frigates and coastguard cutters. Closer cooperation was set against a background of continued allegations in the United States that Sir Lynden and other Bahamian public figures had been paid large bribes by South American drug traffickers using the Bahamas as a staging-post for entry into the US market.

The construction of a new airport on Exuma and the expansion of Nassau harbour were primarily intended for the tourist market. By the end of 1987 external debt had dropped to $101 million, about 17 per cent less than at end-1986. GDP growth fell from 5 to 3.5 per cent over the same period, while inflation more than doubled from 5.8 to 12.2 per cent.

WINDWARD AND LEEWARD ISLANDS

St Kitts & Nevis
CAPITAL: Basseterre AREA: 260 sq km POPULATION: 43,000 ('86)
OFFICIAL LANGUAGE: English POLITICAL SYSTEM: parliamentary democracy
HEAD OF STATE: Queen Elizabeth II GOVERNOR-GENERAL: Clement Athelston Arrindell
RULING PARTY: People's Action Movement
HEAD OF GOVERNMENT: Kennedy A. Simmonds, Prime Minister (since Feb '80)
CURRENCY: East Caribbean dollar (end-'88 £1=EC$4.88, US$1=EC$2.69)
GNP PER CAPITA: US$1,700 ('86)
MAIN EXPORTS: sugar, agricultural produce

Antigua & Barbuda
CAPITAL: St John's AREA: 440 sq km POPULATION: 81,000 ('86)
OFFICIAL LANGUAGE: English POLITICAL SYSTEM: parliamentary democracy
HEAD OF STATE: Queen Elizabeth II GOVERNOR-GENERAL: Sir Wilfred Ebenezer Jacobs
RULING PARTY: Antiguan Labour Party
HEAD OF GOVERNMENT: C. Vere Bird Sr, Prime Minister (since Feb '76)
CURRENCY: East Caribbean dollar (end-'88 £1=EC4.88, US$1=EC$2.69)
GNP PER CAPITA: US$2,380 ('86)
MAIN EXPORTS: miscellaneous manufactures

Dominica
CAPITAL: Roseau AREA: 750 sq km POPULATION: 85,000 ('86)
OFFICIAL LANGUAGE: English POLITICAL SYSTEM: republican parliamentary democracy
HEAD OF STATE: President Sir Clarence Augustus Seignoret
RULING PARTY: Dominica Freedom Party
HEAD OF GOVERNMENT: Mary Eugenia Charles, Prime Minister (since July '80)
CURRENCY: East Caribbean dollar (end-'88 £1=EC$4.88, US$1=EC$2.69)
GNP PER CAPITA: US$1,210 ('86)
MAIN EXPORTS: bananas

St Lucia
CAPITAL: Castries AREA: 616 sq km POPULATION: 140,000 ('86)
OFFICIAL LANGUAGE: English POLITICAL SYSTEM: parliamentary democracy
HEAD OF STATE: Queen Elizabeth II GOVERNOR-GENERAL: Sir Vincent Floissac
RULING PARTY: United Workers' Party
HEAD OF GOVERNMENT: John Compton, Prime Minister (since '64)
CURRENCY: East Caribbean dollar (end-'88 £1=EC$4.88, US$1=EC$2.69)
GNP PER CAPITA: US$1,320 ('86)
MAIN EXPORTS: agricultural products

St Vincent & the Grenadines
CAPITAL: Kingstown AREA: 390 sq km POPULATION: 119,000 ('86)
OFFICIAL LANGUAGE: English POLITICAL SYSTEM: parliamentary democracy
HEAD OF STATE: Queen Elizabeth II GOVERNOR-GENERAL: Sir Joseph Lambert Eustace
RULING PARTY: New Democratic Party
HEAD OF GOVERNMENT: James F. Mitchell, Prime Minister (since '72)
CURRENCY: East Caribbean dollar (end-'88 £1=EC$4.88, US$1=EC$2.69)
GNP PER CAPITA: US$960 ('86)
MAIN EXPORTS: bananas, agricultural produce

THE Budget in ST KITTS & NEVIS reduced company tax from 50 to 45 per cent to create a more attractive investment climate. Tourism, the country's largest source of foreign exchange earnings, turned in gross receipts of EC$2.6m by the end of 1987, a rise of 22.5 per cent over 1986.

In ANTIGUA & BARBUDA the governing Antigua Labour party (ALP) was subject to continued charges both from inside the party and from the opposition that it had become a family business. Prime Minister Vere Bird's party held all 16 Antigua seats in the House of Assembly, and three of the family were Ministers, including Deputy Prime Minister Lester Bird. Allegations were made of assassination plots against the Trade and Education Ministers and the Antigua Trades and Labour Union leader in January, and of alleged misdealings by the Deputy Prime Minister in the Deep Bay Development Company in August. The Budget dramatized the current economic instability, in that utility charges, initially increased by anything from 45 to 67 per cent, were later partially rescinded. However, the Government still had to deal with an external debt which rose from US$63 million in 1986 to US$240 million in 1987, representing the highest per capita indebtedness in the eastern Caribbean. General elections were due in April 1989.

DOMINICA was one of the region's banana producers which succeeded in securing a large harvest in 1988, up 25 per cent over the first quarter, although stiff competition due to record harvests in Jamaica, Belize and Suriname was likely to diminish the benefits. In common with other eastern Caribbean states, Dominica under Prime Minister Eugenia Charles heightened its anti-drug-trafficking activities, with prompting and financial support from both the United States and United Kingdom. A new, UK-funded, coastguard base was opened in June. Investigative US journalist Bob Woodward alleged that Mrs Charles had received US$100,000 to support the 1983 US invasion of Grenada. The opposition Dominica Labour Party demanded an inquiry.

The tropical storm which hit ST LUCIA and later became hurricane 'Gilbert' caused damage to banana crops and roads estimated at not less than EC$3 million. A levy for the repair and upkeep of roads was to be placed on the banana-buying companies by the terms of the 29 March Budget presented by the Prime Minister, John Compton; however, this prompted severe criticism from the St Lucia Banana Growers' Association (SLBGA) and the opposition, with the result that it was reduced by 2.5 per cent in June. Additional disputes between the Government and the SLBGA developed over pricing policy and marketing strategy in the face of the 1992 single European market. This culminated in the suspension of the SLBGA, which was placed directly under Government control by a Bill passed on 25 October. Real GDP growth declined to less than 2 per cent in 1988, a problem compounded by intense competition in the banana market. The trade deficit increased from EC$195.4 million in 1986 to EC$272.2 million in 1987.

After complaints that the public had 'a poor image of the [police] force and the lack of public confidence', the Prime Minister ordered an inquiry; the result was the dismissal of the police commissioner and his deputy.

Prime Minister John Mitchell of ST VINCENT continued the

implementation of a major land reform programme through the extension of aid from the World Bank, the Caribbean Development Bank and the OECD to the tune of US$9 million. The Budget of 11 July increased the minimum income tax threshold from EC$5,000 to EC$10,000, taking two-thirds of current payers out of tax altogether.

SURINAME

CAPITAL: Paramaribo   AREA: 164,000 sq km   POPULATION: 402,000 ('86)
OFFICIAL LANGUAGE: Dutch   POLITICAL SYSTEM: republic, under military tutelage
HEAD OF STATE: President Ramsewak Shankar (since Jan '88)
MILITARY LEADER: Lt-Col. Désiré (Desi) Bouterse
PRINCIPAL MINISTERS: Henck Arron (Vice-President and Prime Minister), A. Sedoc (foreign affairs), Soebhes Chandra Mungra (finance and planning), Pretaapnarian Radhakishun (natural resources and energy), Evelyn Alexander-Vanenburg (home affairs), J. Adjodhia (justice and police)
INTERNATIONAL ALIGNMENT: NAM, ACP, OAS
CURRENCY: Suriname guilder (end-'88 £1=Sf3.22, US$1=Sf1.78)
GNP PER CAPITA: US$2,580 ('85)
MAIN EXPORTS: bauxite/alumina, aluminium, rice

THE rebel guerrilla Jungle Commando under Ronny Brunswijk, whose political support was predominantly among the *bosneger* of the east, continued to hold a grip on both the Suriname army and the country's politics. Despite year-long peace talks during ceasefires mediated by the Catholic Church, the Jungle Commando refused to concede until democracy was fully restored and army officers prosecuted for human rights offences. The same criteria had to be met for the Dutch Government to restore the vital 'independence' aid suspended in 1985; since then only emergency aid had been extended. The United Front for Democracy and Development, which had resoundingly defeated the army-backed National Democratic Party in the November 1987 elections (see AR 1987, pp. 99–100), advocated talks with Mr Brunswijk, as did the Dutch Parliament, which emphasized the importance of support for President Ramsewak Shankar if the fledgling democracy was to survive. Former military leader Desi Bouterse thus remained rather isolated domestically and internationally.

The greatest threat to stability in the country remained economic turmoil. With inflation running at 50 per cent and unemployment at least 33 per cent, Finance Minister Soebhas Mungra approached the IMF for a US$35 million loan and recognized the need to devalue the currency, since the parallel US dollar exchange rate stood at Sf10–12 compared to the official Sf1.75. Public sector debt stood at Sf1,900 million. But the ability to reconstruct the economy, particularly the bauxite industry, remained dependent upon a peace settlement which would halt the destruction of essential infrastructure, extraction plants and electricity generation and distribution systems.

III THE USSR AND EASTERN EUROPE

Chapter 1

UNION OF SOVIET SOCIALIST REPUBLICS

CAPITAL: Moscow AREA: 22,403,000 sq km POPULATION: 281,700,000 ('87)
PRINCIPAL OFFICIAL LANGUAGE: Russian
POLITICAL SYSTEM: federated republic under communist rule
RULING PARTY: Communist Party of the Soviet Union (CPSU)
HEAD OF STATE AND PARTY LEADER: Mikhail Gorbachev, Chairman of Presidium of Supreme Soviet (since Oct '88), CPSU General Secretary (since March '85)
PRINCIPAL MINISTERS: Nikolai Ryzhkov (prime minister), Yuri Maslyukov (first deputy premier, chairman of state planning committee), Vsevolod Murakhovsky (first deputy premier, chairman of state agro-industrial committee), Eduard Shevardnadze (foreign affairs), Gen. Dmitry Yazov (defence), Vadim Bakatin (internal affairs)
INTERNATIONAL ALIGNMENT: Warsaw Pact, Comecon
CURRENCY: rouble (end-'88 £1=R1.09 US$1=RO.63) GNP PER CAPITA: US$4,550 ('80)
MAIN EXPORTS: oil and oil products, machinery and equipment

THE year proved the most dramatic so far in the Gorbachev leadership's attempt to 'restructure' the society over which it ruled. Politically it saw the continued strengthening of the position of the CPSU General Secretary himself, first of all at the 19th Party conference in the summer and then again in the autumn, when a series of constitutional and personnel changes brought Mr Gorbachev the chairmanship of the USSR Supreme Soviet Presidium (i.e. the position of head of state) as well as the Party leadership. Domestically, however, there were continuing difficulties in economic performance, and most strikingly of all the national differences that had emerged publicly in 1987 (see AR 1987, p. 107) became still more widespread and violent. The Armenian earthquake in December, the most devastating in the USSR for at least 40 years, was a further major blow. The General Secretary had a more successful year in international relations, although there were relatively few formal achievements to show for it: the series of Soviet-US summits begun in Geneva continued in Moscow in the summer, and he paid several important foreign visits, most notably to the United Nations in December for a wide-ranging address on global cooperation and other matters (see DOCUMENTS). In his message to the Soviet people at the end of the year, however, it was upon the continuing difficulty of economic reform that the Soviet leader laid the greatest emphasis.

The 19th Party conference, the first since 1941, took place in Moscow from 28 June to 1 July, following a decision by the CPSU Central Committee in June 1987. The conference was preceded by an extensive and far-reaching debate on all aspects of Soviet society, but particularly on the 'democratization' of public life. Among the most notable contributions to this debate was a lengthy letter, entitled 'I cannot forego principles', by a Leningrad chemistry lecturer called Nina Andreeva. The letter, which appeared in the daily paper *Sovietskaya Rossiya* on 13 March, was widely regarded as an anti-*perestroika* manifesto and was published, according to Western press reports, at the behest of Yegor Ligachev, the second-ranking Party secretary and one of the more traditionally-minded members of the leadership. The Andreeva letter welcomed the new and more open atmosphere in which her students were discussing all kinds of issues, but deplored the way in which the Soviet past had come to be regarded as an unbroken catalogue of mistakes and failures. The complicated subject of political repression had been 'excessively magnified', the labour enthusiasm and genuine achievements of the 1930s had been overlooked, and all kinds of anti-socialist views and organizations had emerged which were in effect challenging the leading role of the Party.

The Andreeva letter was in turn attacked in a lengthy *Pravda* editorial on 5 April, after Mr Gorbachev had reportedly been able to obtain the agreement of the Politburo as a whole to a considered repudiation. The editorial, 'The principles of restructuring: the revolutionary nature of thinking and acting', insisted that there was 'no alternative to *perestroika*' and that even its postponement was fraught with 'very serious costs' both for the USSR itself and for socialism internationally. The Party's own response became known on 27 May when the Central Committee's 'Theses' were published in the central press. These argued that the country had gone through 'deep revolutionary transformations' since 1985, and called for the Party conference to give a 'new powerful impulse' to these changes and to make them irreversible. More specifically, the Theses called for the formation of a 'socialist law-based state', including a more independent judiciary; for democratic reform within the Party, including contested elections and limited tenure of Party posts; and for similar changes within the state, where full power must be returned to the elected Soviets.

Mr Gorbachev's report to the conference took three and a half hours to deliver and occupied the whole of the first morning session. The key question, he told the delegates, was how to deepen and make irreversible the process of *perestroika* which was taking place under the Party's guidance. The three previous years had been a turning-point in Soviet life: the whole social atmosphere had changed, and new ideas had begun to make themselves felt throughout the society. This did not, however, mean that improvements were taking place in all spheres or at the necessary speed. To be realistic about it, such a change had not yet occurred: resistance was still powerful, many Party organizations were not coping properly with the tasks that lay before them, and qualitative changes in Soviet society had still to take place. Many complicated questions stood before them in this connection, including the vital one of furthering economic reform. But the central issue, in the view of the Central Committee, was 'radical reform' of the political system.

Why was such a reform necessary? Partly, Mr Gorbachev suggested, because of the 'deformations' in Soviet political life which had occurred after the revolution, in particular the 'wave of repressive measures and lawlessness' of the Stalin period. This had led to a command system of political management which had resisted reform and which had led to the stagnation of the Brezhnev years. A massive ministerial bureaucracy had developed—about 100 at the national level and 800 more in the republics—which had begun to 'dictate its will' in political as well as economic matters. Public life had become unduly 'governmentalized', with central direction extending to every sphere of society. A wide gap had opened up between official rhetoric and everyday realities: government by the people was proclaimed, but what was actually practised was centralized authoritarianism. This had led to indifference and to the alienation of working people from public ownership and management, and it was this 'ossified system of government, with its command and pressure mechanism', that currently represented the greatest obstacle to *perestroika*.

How was this bureaucratic monolith to be demolished? In several ways, Mr Gorbachev suggested. One of them was an extension of political rights so as to ensure that matters of public concern were thoroughly debated and evaluated. Freedom of conscience must also be protected, a subject of particular topicality in the year of the millennium of Christianity in Russia (celebrated from 5 to 16 June—see also Pt. XIII—and preceded by a meeting between Mr Gorbachev and Patriarch Pimen on 29 April, the first such meeting since 1943). A further change was required in the local Soviets, which must be given full authority for the development of the areas for which they were responsible. This would in turn involve larger and more stable sources of revenue, and full-time activity on the part of at least some of the deputies. Leading positions in the Soviets should be filled by secret and competitive ballot, and the deputies themselves must be chosen through a 'lively and free expression of the will of the electorate'. At the national level a new representative body, the Congress of People's Deputies, should be established, which would elect a smaller working Supreme Soviet. The new post of Chairman of the USSR Supreme Soviet should also be established, and it should normally be combined with the Party leadership.

Summing up, Mr Gorbachev suggested that they were seeking

a socialism which 'renounced everything that deformed socialism in the 1930s and led to its stagnation in the 1970s', a socialism which would inherit the 'best elements' of the thinking of its founding fathers together with the experience of other periods and other societies. Although it was impossible to describe such a society in a detailed way, a socialism of this kind would be a system of 'true and tangible humanism in which man is really the measure of all things'. The purpose of all social development, from the economy to spiritual life, would be the satisfaction of popular needs. There would be a dynamic and advanced economy based upon a variety of forms of property and worker participation, combining a broad measure of central planning with a great degree of autonomy for individual enterprises. The basic needs of all would be provided, including health, education and housing, but individual talent would also be rewarded, where appropriate, in both moral and material terms. A society of this kind would have a high degree of culture and morality, and would be managed by a system of 'profound and consistent democracy'. This was the General Secretary's fullest exposition so far of the nature of the socialist society which he proposed to construct.

The debate that followed ranged over all areas of Soviet policy and did so with remarkable frankness. On the very first day, for instance, a rank-and-file delegate from Leningrad took it upon himself to disagree with the General Secretary's proposal that the existing Party membership be reaccredited. When, *Pravda* asked, had such a thing previously been known? Boris Yeltsin, the former Moscow Party leader, asked in an emotional speech for his political rehabilitation. There was a minor sensation when a speaker from the Komi republic, asked to identify some of the enemies of *perestroika*, reeled off a list of names including the editor of *Pravda*, the director of the USA and Canada Institute and the current Soviet head of state, Andrei Gromyko. There were slow handclaps for unduly orthodox speakers, but applause and laughter for many others. Again without precedent, at least since the earliest post-revolutionary years, was the spectacle of divided votes on issues such as the retrospective reckoning of limitations on tenure of office. Mr Gorbachev's concluding assessment, that nothing like it had been seen for 60 years, was hardly an exaggeration.

The reforms agreed by the conference were given legislative form at a session of the USSR Supreme Soviet in late November and early December. One of the major changes was an entirely new electoral law, which would apply to future elections at all levels of government and which was intended to ensure (though it did not formally specify) the nomination of a greater number of candidates than seats available. Candidates could in future be nominated by electors' meetings as well as by approved organizations, and would be required to present 'programmes of future activity' to the electorate and could appoint up to ten campaign staff to assist them. Voters, for their part, would have to pass through a screened-off booth before they reached the ballot box, and would have to mark the ballot paper in some way to record a valid preference even if (exceptionally) only a single candidate was standing. The Central Committee, at its meeting on 28 November, promised that the next national elections in the spring of 1989 would be 'unlike all those which have preceded them'.

A related series of constitutional amendments, also approved on 1 December, established the national representative body, the USSR Congress of People's Deputies, for which Mr Gorbachev had called in his speech to the Party conference. The Congress, which would meet annually, was to have a total membership of 2,250 drawn from population-based and territorially-based constituencies (750 each) and also from a wide range of public organizations, ranging from the Society of Philatelists with one seat to the CPSU and the trade unions with 100 seats each. The Congress would in turn elect a working Supreme Soviet of 542 members, which was to meet for spring and autumn sessions of three or four months each. It would also elect a new executive President, the Chairman of the USSR Supreme Soviet, who was given extensive powers including nomination of the Soviet Prime Minister and 'general guidance' of the work of the Congress and Supreme Soviet. Another entirely new body, the Committee of Constitutional Supervision, was to be elected by the Congress of People's Deputies with responsibility for ensuring the constitutionality of all government decisions. Mr Gorbachev, at the same session, assumed the chairmanship of the USSR Supreme Soviet Presidium on the retirement of the veteran former Foreign Minister, Andrei Gromyko.

If 1988 saw continued progress in implementing the General Secretary's policy of 'democratization', it also saw continuing and in some respects deepening difficulties in carrying forward the 'radical reform' of the Soviet economy that had been approved by the Central Committee in June 1987 (see AR 1987, pp. 104–5). The central measure of economic performance, the annual plan fulfilment report, was announced in January 1988; it showed that development had fallen short of the plan in almost every sector of the economy, this being attributed by the official news agency Tass to 'the failure to accomplish tasks for saving financial resources, lagging agricultural production and a decline in foreign trade revenues'. Soviet GNP was reported to have increased by 3.3 per cent over 1986, which was officially described as below the (unspecified) plan target. Industrial output was reported to have increased by 3.8 per cent, as compared with a plan target of 4.4 per cent; agricultural output rose by a still more modest 1.8 per cent, and labour productivity rose by 2.4 per cent as compared with the plan target of 4 per cent. Foreign trade showed an actual decline of 1.5 per cent, which was attributed in part to the depression in world prices for oil and gas. About two weeks after these results had been announced, Nikolai Talyzin was replaced by Yuri Maslyukov as chairman of the State Planning Committee (Gosplan).

Mr Gorbachev gave a particularly sharp assessment of the level of economic performance to date at a plenary meeting of the Central Committee on 17–18 February, whose main formal business was education reform. The economic situation in the USSR, he argued, already described as 'pre-crisis' in character, was in fact worse than he had previously suggested. Economic growth rates had not simply been declining, they had also been achieved on the basis of unhealthy and short-term factors such as the sale of oil at the high prices that prevailed during the 1970s and a 'totally unjustified increase in the sale of strong drink'. If these factors were removed from Soviet economic performance there had been no real increase in national income for four five-year plans in a row, and the early 1980s had seen an actual fall. The price of oil and energy had meanwhile fallen on world markets, and the production and sale of wines and vodka had been reduced in order to maintain public health standards. All of this required 'extraordinary' efforts by the country, both in implementing radical economic reform and in meeting current targets. Food, housing, consumer goods and services were particular priorities in this connection.

The difficulties being encountered by the strategy of radical reform emerged more fully at the session of the Supreme Soviet which took place in October, and which was concerned with the national economic plan and Budget. Mr Maslyukov, the Gosplan chairman, predicted a higher rate of economic growth in 1989 than in 1987, but this would still not be sufficient to cover the shortfall in economic growth that had occurred in 1986 and 1987. A series of particular difficulties, moreover, had not just continued but had become significantly worse: he instanced food, light industry and engineering. Boris Gostev, the Minister of Finance, added that rates of growth had been slower than expected, and that incomes were increasing faster than production. The fall in the price of oil on world markets had cost the state some 40,000 million roubles in lost revenue, and the measures that had been taken to reduce the sale of alcohol had led to a loss of 36,000 million roubles in duty. Apart from this, over 8,000 million roubles had to be allocated to deal with the damage caused by the Chernobyl nuclear explosion (see AR 1986, pp. 100–01). In 1988, state revenues were expected to fall short of state spending; and, for 1989, deputies were presented with a Budget in which, for the first time in Soviet post-war history, expenditure was expected to exceed revenue by a substantial margin (over 7 per cent). Mr Gostev concluded by arguing the need for 'severe economy' in state spending.

Still more serious was the outbreak, in several parts of the USSR, of the most significant nationalist disturbances in Soviet peacetime history. The most notable were in the Caucasus and in the Baltic. In the Caucasus a series of massive demonstrations, involving substantial loss of life and damage to property, centred upon the disputed autonomous region of Nagorno-Karabakh (see accompanying map). Located within the traditionally Muslim republic of Azerbaijan since 1921, the disputed region had a population that was overwhelmingly Armenian and Christian, and had complained for some time of economic and cultural discrimination against them. A constitutional crisis was precipitated when, on 20 February, an unprecedented vote was passed in the Nagorno-Karabakh regional Soviet calling for the region to be transferred from Azerbaijan to Armenia. Demonstrations in support of the Armenians in

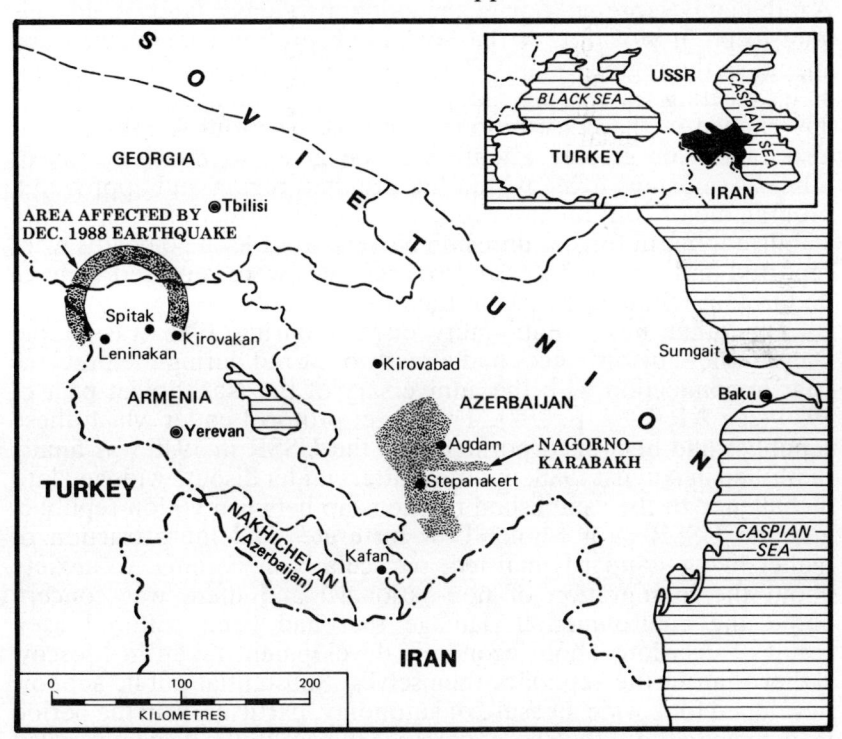

The map shows the disputed area of Nagorno-Karabakh (in Azerbaijan) and also the location of the December 1988 Armenian earthquake.

Nagorno-Karabakh had begun in Yerevan, the Armenian capital, on 15 February. By 22 February more than 100,000 people were reported to be demonstrating daily in the city's Opera Square. The demonstrations came temporarily to an end after a personal appeal by Mr Gorbachev on 26 February, but a report that two Azerbaijanis had been killed the previous week led to an anti-Armenian riot in the Azeri city of Sumgait on 28 and 29 February, in which 32 people (26 of them Armenians) were killed and 197 were injured, including more than 100 police officers.

Despite Mr Gorbachev's assurances to Armenian representatives that a 'just solution' would be found, statements by the central authorities made it clear that (as *Pravda* put it on 28 March) the transfer of Nagorno-Karabakh to Armenia would be a 'clearly anti-socialist solution' and that (as the Supreme Soviet Presidium put it on 23 March) 'all sorts of self-proclaimed groups' could not be allowed to call for the redrawing of state and administrative boundaries. On 15 June the Armenian Supreme Soviet voted for Nagorno-Karabakh to be transferred to their republic; the Azerbaijani Supreme Soviet, meeting two days later, held this vote to be in violation of the Soviet constitution and rejected any change in the region's status. The USSR Supreme Soviet Presidium, at its meeting on 18 July, adopted a formal ruling which rejected any change in the constitutional status of Nagorno-Karabakh, but also called for greater attention to be given to the concerns of ethnic Armenians living within the disputed region and approved a programme of cultural and economic aid. The situation temporarily stabilized, but in further unrest in November at least 30 deaths were reported and tens of thousands of refugees were reported to have fled to join fellow nationals in the other republic.

The other major nationality dispute during 1988 was in the Baltic, where disturbances had already occurred during the previous year in connection with the anniversary of the Nazi-Soviet pact of 1939 (see AR 1987, p. 107). The secret protocol under which these republics had been incorporated into the USSR in 1940 was finally published in August 1988, but the matters under dispute widened into a challenge to the established relationship between Union republics and the USSR as a whole. Low birthrates and the attraction of higher living standards had led, particularly in Estonia, to anxiety about the immigration of non-nationals; and there was concern about the environmental damage that had been suffered as a result of decisions about economic development taken in Moscow rather than in the republics themselves. Substantial public support developed for a wide measure of autonomy, particularly in the period leading up to the 19th Party conference (where Baltic delegates called for a far-reaching programme of devolution). Popular movements, ostensibly 'in support of *perestroika*' but in fact for the strengthening of local autonomy, came into formal existence in all three republics in October.

The publication of the draft constitutional amendments the same month led to widespread public protests; it was objected that the changes were centralizing in character and that the republics' (admittedly nominal) right of secession had been prejudiced. The Estonian Parliament, influenced by these concerns, adopted a constitutional amendment on 16 November providing for the right of veto over all national legislation. The decision was held to be unconstitutional by the USSR Supreme Soviet Presidium on 26 November and the Baltic republics generally came in for severe criticism by other delegates both at the Presidium meeting and at the Supreme Soviet session on 1 December which passed the constitutional amendments into law. Some changes were, however, made in the draft in order to satisfy those who had challenged it in this way: Union republics were given 11 rather than 7 seats each in the Council of Nationalities (one of the new-style Supreme Soviet's two chambers), and further changes of wording were made in order to remove what Mr Gorbachev described as the 'misunderstanding' that the rights of republics had been infringed. Further constitutional changes, he promised, would place the relationship between the USSR and its constituent republics on a new and more equitable basis.

The high point of the year in diplomatic terms was undoubtedly the Moscow summit with President Reagan, which began on 29 May and lasted until 2 June (see also p. 61). During the summit, talks were held on arms control, human rights, and regional and bilateral issues, with progress reported and agreements made in all these areas. The intermediate-range nuclear forces (INF) treaty, agreed upon in principle at the previous US-Soviet summit in Washington in December 1987 (see AR 1987, pp. 58–59, 108–9 and 558–66), was signed on 1 June by the two leaders, having been ratified by the US Senate and the USSR Supreme Soviet a few days beforehand. A joint statement issued by the two leaders described the meeting as an 'important step in the process of putting US-Soviet relations on a more productive and sustainable basis'; in particular, a draft treaty on the reduction and limitation of strategic nuclear arms had been discussed and a series of agreements had been made with regard to the verification of nuclear testing. Mr Gorbachev, at a press conference on 1 June, expressed the view that more could have been achieved, but politics was the 'art of the possible'. The Politburo, at its meeting on 6 June, described the summit as a 'major event in international life' whose 'main result' had been the 'deepening of the political dialogue between the Soviet Union and the USA'.

The Moscow summit followed shortly after the conclusion, at Geneva on 14 April, of a series of international agreements providing for the withdrawal of Soviet military forces from Afghanistan (see DOCUMENTS). What was described as a 'limited contingent', in fact about 100,000 men, had been based in that country since the end of 1979 following instability in its pro-Soviet Government. The agreements included bilateral accords between Afghanistan and Pakistan on non-interference and non-intervention, and on the voluntary return of refugees; a Soviet US declaration in support of these agreements; and a joint agreement on the settlement of the Afghan situation which provided for the 'phased withdrawal' of Soviet troops, half of them between 15 May and 15 August 1988, and the remainder within the following nine months. The Soviet Foreign Minister, Eduard Shevardnadze, gave a press conference following the signature of the agreements at which he drew particular attention to the role of the United Nations in facilitating and implementing the settlement, and to the need for a 'revived, neutral and non-aligned Afghanistan'. Soviet troop withdrawals began as scheduled on 15 May but were subsequently suspended in view of what the Soviet authorities claimed to be continued assistance to the mujahideen guerrillas by the Pakistani Government.

It was a busy year for the USSR in many other diplomatic contexts, and for the Soviet leader in particular. In March Mr Gorbachev paid an official visit to Yugoslavia, during which (on 16 March) he regretted the 'groundless accusations' which had led to the abrogation in 1948 of the 1945 friendship treaty between the two countries (see also p. 135). Since the reconciliation of 1955–56, however, the relationship had been placed on a different and more satisfactory footing, and Mr Gorbachev expressed the wish to take this process further so far as both states and parties were concerned. In an official visit to Poland in July (see also p. 120) the Soviet leader acknowledged that relations between the two countries had been marked by 'complicated turns and conflicts', but they shared a common fate and common interests. He called for intensified economic cooperation and for humanitarian measures, including closer cultural links and the elimination of 'blank spots' in the history of Polish-Soviet relations. Mr Gorbachev visited India in November, and important Western visitors during the year included Chancellor Kohl of West Germany in October and President Mitterrand of France in November.

The Soviet leader's most influential contribution to international affairs came in December, when he addressed the United Nations (see DOCUMENTS). In his speech, delivered on 7 December to the General Assembly, Mr Gorbachev expressed his personal support for the United Nations, which had 'increasingly manifested its ability to act as a unique international centre in the service of peace and security', and his belief that the most important issues that faced the world community were global rather than regional in character. This had been made clear by the development of nuclear weapons, by new popular movements and ideologies, and by scientific and technological developments. International communications were easier than ever before; the world economy was increasingly a 'single organism'. The French and Russian revolutions had made an enormous contribution in their time to human progress, but they lived today in a different world in which universal human values must have priority. This meant a common search for a new quality of international interaction, less reliant on military force and free of ideological prejudice.

In more practical terms Mr Gorbachev pointed to the need for a greater measure of agreement on the reduction of all forms of armaments and on the elimination of regional conflicts. There should be a 'more intense and open dialogue' between political leaders and their societies (he himself had already had more than 200 meetings with foreign government and political leaders). The United Nations should play a greater role, especially in problems such as Third World development, environmental assistance and the peaceful use of outer space. The UN could also play a greater role in regulating regional conflicts, as in Afghanistan. More work needed to be done to clarify and strengthen international law, particularly in relation to human rights.

Most spectacularly of all, the Soviet leader announced a reduction of 500,000 men in the Soviet armed forces together with reductions in conventional armaments. Helpful though such measures were likely to be in economic terms, the simultaneous resignation of the Soviet Chief of Staff suggested that not all powerful institutional interests in Soviet society had been persuaded of their necessity.

The massive earthquake in Armenia on 7 December caused Mr Gorbachev to cut short his stay in the United States (and to postpone scheduled visits to Cuba and Britain) in order to fly home to take charge of rescue and relief operations. The scale of the disaster, involving the destruction of whole towns, gave rise to a major international relief effort in which many countries offered assistance to the Soviet authorities. The eventual official estimate of the death toll, while lower than initially feared, was still a horrific 25,000.

At year's end the perceived iniquities of the Brezhnev era were further highlighted when the former leader's son-in-law, Yury Churbanov (52), was on 30 December sentenced to 12 years' imprisonment after being found guilty of extensive bribery and corruption as first Deputy Interior Minister in the early 1980s.

Six other defendants, all senior police officials from the central Asian republic of Uzbekistan, received prison sentences of from eight to ten years.

Chapter 2

GERMAN DEMOCRATIC REPUBLIC—POLAND—CZECHOSLOVAKIA—
HUNGARY—ROMANIA—BULGARIA—YUGOSLAVIA—ALBANIA—
MONGOLIA

GERMAN DEMOCRATIC REPUBLIC

CAPITAL: Berlin   AREA: 108,000 sq km   POPULATION: 16,600,000 ('86)
OFFICIAL LANGUAGE: German   POLITICAL SYSTEM: socialist republic under communist rule
RULING PARTY: Socialist Unity Party of German (SED)
HEAD OF STATE AND PARTY LEADER: Erich Honecker, Chairman of Council of state (since Oct '76), SED General Secretary (since May '71)
PRINCIPAL MINISTERS: Willi Stoph (prime minister), Gerhard Schürer (deputy premier, chairman of state planning commission), Oskar Fischer (foreign affairs), Gen. Heinz Kessler (defence), Ernst Höfner (finance), Gen. Friedrich Dickel (interior)
INTERNATIONAL ALIGNMENT: Warsaw Pact, Comecon
CURRENCY: ostmark (end-'88 £1=OM3.21, US$=OM1.77)   GNP PER CAPITA: US$7,180 ('80)
MAIN EXPORTS: machinery and transport equipment, consumer durables, raw materials

FOR the German Democratic Republic, 1988 was a year marked by positive international trends, contradictory domestic political developments, and indications of growing economic problems. In particular, as the Gorbachev revolution in the Soviet Union continued to gather momentum and to challenge the traditional icons of 'existing socialism', the waves it generated in the international communist movement were felt increasingly strongly by those on the bridge of the East German ship of state. Furthermore, it became more and more apparent that the ruling Party, the SED, was playing out the endgame of the Honecker era, and that domestic pressures for political and economic reform were growing.

As East-West relations continued to thaw and the international climate exhibited signs of overall improvement, the East German leadership made use of the greater room for manoeuvre afforded to it by the new Gorbachev leadership in order to pursue its active foreign policy. In January Erich Honecker paid an official state visit to Paris, where he was received with full honours as a head of state. This visit was significant because it was the first by an East German leader to the capital of one of the three Western powers with responsibility for Germany. Another first for Honecker was his visit to Spain in October. At the same time, the SED sought to maintain the momentum generated by the INF agreement for arms control and disarmament measures, firstly by publishing on 5 January a letter by Honecker to Chancellor Kohl of West Germany, calling for both Nato and the Warsaw Pact to forgo the modernization of their short-range nuclear forces, and secondly, by hosting a major international conference on nuclear-weapon-free zones in Berlin from 20–22 June.

Relations with the Soviet Union remained close, despite the obvious unease of the SED leadership with aspects of the Soviet reform process, particularly in the political and cultural spheres. This unease, if not hostility, was epitomized by the GDR's decision in November to ban the distribution of the Soviet journal *Sputnik* and five Soviet films. The Honecker leadership continued to maintain that, although it welcomed Mikhail Gorbachev's attempt to reform Soviet socialism, it did not regard such reforms as relevant to the GDR, and would consequently not seek to imitate them. Nevertheless, it was clear that many ordinary GDR citizens and SED members wished to see the reform of East German socialism, and looked to the Gorbachev reforms in the USSR with growing expectation and hope.

The domestic political calm of the GDR was shaken by a small demonstration of dissidents and regime critics at the annual commemorative rally for the murdered communist leaders Rosa Luxembourg and Karl Liebknecht on 17 January. Over a hundred demonstrators were initially detained, although only five were eventually tried and given mild sentences. Following a wave of special church services and public meetings held in support of the detainees, all were finally released and many allowed to emigrate to the West. Coming on top of the police raid on the unofficial environmental library at the Zionskirche in November 1987, this incident threatened to seriously disrupt Church-State relations. Furthermore, on 19 February, the Politburo member responsible for Church affairs, Werner Jarowinsky, met the chairman of the Evangelical Church Federation, Bishop Werner Leich, in order to warn the Church not to interfere in domestic political matters. However, in order to prevent a further deterioration, a high-level meeting was held on 3 March between Erich Honecker and Bishop Leich, and despite continued tensions over censorship of church publications and other human rights issues a major crisis was averted.

One religious minority which received very favourable treatment in 1988 was the small Jewish community. The GDR authorities agreed to fund the rebuilding of the former New Synagogue in Berlin and to the establishment of a Centre for Judaism, and organized an extensive programme of events to commemorate *Reichskristallnacht*, the anti-Jewish pogrom of 9 November 1938. Furthermore, they agreed to pay symbolic compensation to the Jewish victims of Nazism following a meeting with the Jewish Claims Committee. In May the American-born Rabbi of the Jewish communities in the GDR, Isaac Neumann, resigned amidst differences with his community, and was replaced by another American, Rabbi Ernest Lorge. In October Erich Honecker and the Foreign Minister, Oskar Fischer, met the President of the Jewish World Congress, Edgar Miles Bronfman, for talks in Berlin.

The GDR economy remained the most efficient in Comecon, although economic problems became increasingly apparent as the year progressed, particularly in the area of investments, labour productivity, raw material consumption, and energy savings. From the autumn onwards, the local press also gave increasing coverage to consumer shortages and deficiencies in the service sector. Nevertheless, Herr Honecker explicitly ruled out structural economic reforms, arguing that central planning and an extensive state sector were key features of socialism, and that they provided the guarantee for the 'unity of economic and social policy' which seeks to ensure full employment and comprehensive social welfare.

The political situation was highly contradictory. Repression of dissident activists, the banning of *Sputnik* and continuing censorship of church publications went hand-in-hand with a limited cultural *glasnost* and the beginnings of a debate on the GDR's own anti-fascist credentials. The SED rejected any substantial liberalization of the political system, but nevertheless strengthened the GDR's claim to be a *Rechtsstaat* by announcing new regulations governing foreign travel and emigration, and by proposing the establishment of a new court of appeal for administrative decisions. The Central Committee plenum in December brought the date of the next Party congress forward by a year to May 1990, and appointed Werner Krolikowski as the Secretariat member responsible for agriculture (following the death of Werner Felfe in September). However, there was still no clear successor to Herr Honecker.

Finally, the prodigious sporting prowess of the GDR was once again demonstrated at the Seoul Olympics, when the country's athletes won 102 medals, coming second only to the Soviet Union and clearly outperforming both the United States and the Federal Republic.

POLAND

CAPITAL: Warsaw AREA: 313,000 sq km POPULATION: 37,600,000 ('86)
OFFICIAL LANGUAGE: Polish POLITICAL SYSTEM: people's republic under communist rule
RULING PARTY: Polish United Workers' Party (PUWP)
HEAD OF STATE AND PARTY LEADER: Gen. Wojciech Jaruzelski (Chairman of Council of State since Nov '85, PUWP First Secretary since Oct '81)
PRINCIPAL MINISTERS: Mieczyslaw Rakowski (prime minister), Ireneusz Sekula (deputy premier, chairman of planning commission), Tadeusz Olechowski (foreign affairs), Andrzej Wroblewski (finance), Gen. Florian Siwicki (defence), Lt-Gen. Czeslaw Kiszczak (interior)
INTERNATIONAL ALIGNMENT: Warsaw Pact, Comecon
CURRENCY: zloty (end-'87 £1=Zl578,44, US$1=Zl315,78) GNP PER CAPITA: US$2,070 ('86)
MAIN EXPORTS: engineering equipment, coal, metals, agricultural produce

IN a climate of confusion and uncertainty Poland was still awaiting a breakthrough that could at least bring a partial solution to its growing economic and political crisis. Beneath the veneer of turmoil recent developments had already changed the stakes in Polish politics by focusing on the fundamental need to transform the very method of government. The authorities, unable to cope by themselves, were being reluctantly forced to seek accommodation with a genuinely pluralistic society demanding the right to participate in decision-making through its own organizations independent of Party control.

Two large-scale waves of strikes, mass demonstrations on various national and Solidarity anniversaries and an officially-announced 'round table' debate with opposition groups highlighted existing problems. The Government failed to implement fully economic reforms accompanied by genuine democratization (see AR 1987, p. 115). February price rises averaged 40 per cent for food and rose up to 200 per cent for fuel, gas and electricity while compensation in wages amounted to 20 per cent, producing a decline of 25 per cent in the standard of living. Inflation reached 56.7 per cent and was rising. The waiting period for state housing averaged 30 years with a two million queue. GNP growth of 2 per cent was much lower than in 1986 and agricultural production fell by 3 per cent.

Workers demanded better wages and working conditions, relegalization of Solidarity and reinstatement of workers dismissed for their Solidarity activities. Strikes spread spontaneously in April–May and then again in August–September, involving over 170,000 workers in key steelworks, shipyards in Gdansk and Szczecin, Silesian mines, public transport and students. Threats and intimidation predominated in official reactions. Curfew was imposed in some regions. Strikes were declared political and illegal, strikers were drafted into the army, opposition leaders detained, and occasionally riot police broke occupational strikes by force. The authorities refused to negotiate, but whenever possible defused strikes by pay increases of up to 15 per cent, promised no victimization but rejected the relegalization of Solidarity as an 'impossible demand'. Lech Walesa called for negotiations on all issues. The Church urged a 'dialogue' and pluralism.

In June the newly-elected Politburo member Wladyslaw Baka warned that no progress had been made in vital areas of the economic reform. The 1988 economic plan was amended because of a drop in productivity, shortages of basic commodities, decline in economic growth, and inflationary pressures. Investments were reduced by 15 per cent, 21 unprofitable enterprises were closed and 140 others considered for closure. Interest alone on Poland's Western debt of $39,200 million reached $3,000 million.

The strikes were organized by a young, determined, aggressive and radical generation which matured in the heyday of Solidarity and produced a new brand of leaders unwilling to accept defeat. Mr Walesa was recognized as their leader. On 26 August, in a remarkable political shift, the Interior Minister, General Czeslaw Kiszczak proposed a 'broad round-table discussion' between the Government and the strikers with no conditions attached excluding only 'persons rejecting the constitution' and turned to Walesa to stop the strikes. This he did.

Vilified and ridiculed for seven years, Mr Walesa re-emerged as a major political figure and after the first meeting (31 August) disclosed that reinstatement of Solidarity would be discussed. Four more meetings followed with Solidarity advisers and Church representatives present, but in these 'talks about talks' no substantive progress was made. General Jaruzelski was received by Cardinal Glemp in Gniezno. In Gdansk diverse opposition movements fully endorsed both Mr Walesa's leadership and his efforts to negotiate (11 September).

Events now moved quickly. According to Prime Minister Zbigniew Messner and Prof. Baka, speaking at the Party plenum, the reforms had failed because of conflicts within the establishment and the resistance of Party and state apparatus. The strikes were not a provocation by irresponsible extremists, said General Czeslaw Staszak, head of security service in the Interior Ministry, but 'an alarm bell stupidly ignored' by the authorities; he advocated 'a comprehensive dialogue.' The plenum called for a 'broad coalition of reformist forces'.

In an unprecedented move in Poland's post-war history, the Government, which Prof. Messner described as 'vulnerable to political pressure from one Party', resigned on 19 September. The new Prime Minister was Mieczyslaw Rakowski, a Politburo member and former editor of the influential weekly *Polityka*. Seen by opposition elements as anti-Solidarity and a tough political manipulator, he promised effective implementation of reformist policies while ruling with a strong hand to secure internal peace. He further promised a 'reasonable compromise' with any group prepared to strengthen the socialist system (13 October).

Mr Rakowski's political strategy, outlined in a report for the Party leadership, favoured far-reaching changes in the model of government. It accepted limited opposition provided that the ruling Party remained the driving force behind any reform and dictated its scope, speed and direction. Independent activities, including those by organized groups and open criticism of the system would be permissible but not attempts by forces independent of the Party to modify it.

Key political posts in the new Cabinet remained in old hands but administration of the economy was entrusted to new younger Party members. Mieczyslaw Wilczek, a private businessman and millionaire, became Industry Minister, and other key portfolios went to Dominik Jastrzebski (Foreign Economic Cooperation), Andrzej Wroblewski (Finance) and Kazimierz Oleksiak (Deputy Premier and Agriculture). Four opposition representatives declined Cabinet posts offered to them.

While the Walesa–Kiszczak talks continued, the Government took important decisions 'against the myth', as Mr Rakowski put it, 'that everything depends on Solidarity'. The 'consolidation plan' envisaged closing the Gdansk shipyard (Solidarity's birthplace) and 100 other unprofitable industrial giants, a 40 per cent cut in the coal and energy industries' labour force, and a transfer of resources from heavy and defence industries to agriculture and consumer goods production. Pensions and agricultural procurement prices were raised. To encourage private entrepreneurship and foreign investment, the Sejm (Diet) removed existing restrictions on private enterprise and permitted 100 per cent foreign ownership of joint stock companies, which could remit all profits in hard currency.

On 30 November some 20 million people watched a live television discussion between Mr Walesa and the leader of the official trade unions, Politburo member Alfred Miodowicz. The latter insisted that the solution to Poland's problems lay exclusively with the Party, while Mr Walesa argued fluently for pluralism, freedom, a final reckoning with the stalinist past and legalization of Solidarity, whereupon 'we will roll our sleeves up'. Reform was impossible, he said, while a monopoly existed in political and economic life.

Mr Walesa's first television appearance since 1981 was hailed, even by his critics, as a triumph for the banned union and for its leader. He then travelled to Paris for the 40th anniversary ceremonies of the UN Declaration on Human Rights and was received with full honours by President Mitterrand.

In two strong statements in November the Episcopate warned the authorities that no economic reforms were possible without political liberalization, accused them of creating an unfavourable atmosphere for round table talks and called for 'profound social and political reforms'. On 18 December in Gdansk a 128-strong Citizens' Committee headed by Mr Walesa was formed of mainstream opposition figures, uniting disparate elements from the new generation of strike leaders with farmers and Catholic intellectuals prepared to negotiate with the authorities. The country faced, the Committee stated, 'the prospect of political violence if the Government failed to reach a compromise with the opposition. . . . Without relegalization of Solidarity there is no adequate and credible structure for reform.'

Two days later the Party plenum ousted six Politburo members, including Prof. Messner and General Jozef Baryla (former associates of General Jaruzelski), and brought in eight new faces. But members clashed over whether to relegalize Solidarity, which some described as 'an enemy within'.

Among the many foreign visitors, two were particularly significant. In July the Soviet leader, Mikhail Gorbachev, came to Poland and spoke of transforming the socialist system to meet the challenge of the future, promising to 'use Polish experiences'. In November, during the first-ever visit by a British Prime Minister, Mrs Thatcher told the authorities that no centrally-planned economy could ever succeed, went to Gdansk to meet Mr Walesa and appealed for a 'real dialogue with all sections of society including Solidarity' as a condition for Western economic help (see also p. 42).

CZECHOSLOVAKIA

CAPITAL: Prague   AREA: 128,000 sq km   POPULATION: 15,600,000 ('86)
OFFICIAL LANGUAGES: Czech and Slovak   POLITICAL SYSTEM: federal socialist republic under communist rule
HEAD OF STATE: President Gustáv Husák (since May '75)
RULING PARTY: Communist Party of Czechoslovakia (CPCz)
PARTY LEADER: Miloš Jakeš, CPCz General Secretary (since Dec '87)
PRINCIPAL MINISTERS: Ladislav Adamec (prime minister), Bohumil Urban (deputy premier, chairman of state planning commission), Jaromír Johanes (foreign affairs), Gen. Milan Václavík (defence), František Kincl (interior)
INTERNATIONAL ALIGNMENT: Warsaw Pact, Comecon
CURRENCY: koruna (end-'88 £1=K9.50, US$1=K5.25)   GNP PER CAPITA: US$5,820 ('80)
MAIN EXPORTS: machinery, chemicals and fuels, manufactured goods

ECONOMIC performance continued to be lacklustre and in the latter part of the year it produced shortages in the shops such as the consumers had long not experienced. Growth barely touched the 3 per cent mark, according to official statistics, and the Government had once again to resort to emergency measures, including further cuts in the investment programme and a ban on individual exports of a number of items, mainly by tourists from the other socialist countries. Some reformist legislation came on the statute book, such as the new law on enterprises, but without visible effect other than the reorganization of industrial structures and a rather frantic scramble for positions in the new system. Government spokesmen said that they preferred a thought-out, albeit slow, reform and that results would begin showing in 1990. However, most Western observers regarded the Czechoslovak reformist exercise as lacking bite: too many central controls were being retained and too small a leeway was being given to private initiative, let alone to private enterprise.

Not supported by a stable economic situation, and evidently not quite ready to proceed with political reforms, the regime resorted to personnel changes in the leading agencies of the Party and the Government to demonstrate its adaptability to the Gorbachevian challenge. In three bouts of retirements, shuffles and cooptations (in April, October and December), several reputed reformers and hardliners as well as politically nondescript officials left the leadership, a few younger apparatchiks were elevated to higher positions, and a new federal Government was formed under the premiership of Ladislav Adamec. Among the more notable departures were the long-serving Prime Minister, Lubomír Štrougal, and the Party's chief ideologist and foreign political coordinator, Vasil Bilak. The highest profile among the newcomers belonged to Miroslav Štěphán, currently Party chief in the city of Prague, who many thought was destined for even higher honours. On the whole, supreme power remained vested in a hard core of five members of the old guard, all associated with the Soviet invasion which crushed the Prague Spring 20 years before, namely Miloš Jakeš, Gustáv Husák, Karel Hoffman, Alois Indra and Jan Fojtík.

It looked during the first part of the year as if the regime was not going to abate its repressive attitude to dissent, but the hard posture changed a little in the autumn, after Mr Gorbachev consolidated his domination over reformist liberalism in the USSR. A peaceful religious demonstration was dispersed by force in Bratislava at the end of March and the same happened with independent rallies in Prague to commemorate the 20th anniversary of the quashing of the Prague Spring in August and the 70th anniversary of the birth of independent Czechoslovakia in October. Two international seminars planned by Charter 77 and other independent groups were not permitted to happen. The regime did, however, seek to coopt national sentiments in connection with pre-war Czechoslovakia and its founder and first president, Thomas G. Masaryk, both anathemas until then. Alexander Dubček was permitted to collect an honorary doctorate from Bologna University in November. The authorities also allowed Youth Union patronage (and thus immunity from police interference) over a John Lennon commemoration and it issued the first-ever permission for an independent rally to mark

Human Rights Day on 10 December. In mid-December the regime stopped the jamming of Radio Free Europe which had been going on since 1951. After this surprising show of lenience, the posturing once again hardened in the last days of the year with warnings that independent activities, like the human rights rally, would not be tolerated in the future. It was also emphasized that political pluralism of the Hungarian kind and accommodation with the opposition as attempted by the Polish Government were out of the question in Czechoslovakia.

It was speculated that the temporary moderation might have been caused by Soviet pressure exerted during a five-day visit in November by CPSU Politburo member Aleksandr Yakovlev or by concern about Western opinion on the eve of a visit by President François Mitterrand of France in early December. Other important visitors included the West German Chancellor, Helmut Kohl, in January and the Austrian Chancellor, Franz Vranitzky, in June. The long-standing Czechoslovak Foreign Minister, Bohuslav Chňoupek, handed over his office to Jaromír Johanes in October. Czechoslovakia's image in the world remained poor because of the festering human rights and religious repression at home, but some improvements on the official level could be observed. An agreement was signed with the European Communities, but trade with both the West and within Comecon remained rather slack.

Public pressure on the regime increased considerably. A petition demanding religious freedom collected almost 600,000 signatures and hundreds of thousands took part in religious pilgrimages. Three new episcopal appointments in May were the first for 15 years but, with the subsequent death of a bishop, ten of the country's 13 dioceses still had no resident head at the end of the year. Further negotiations with the Vatican got bogged down in recalcitrance.

A number of new independent organizations came into being to promote a variety of causes, ranging from a study of Masaryk's heritage to a programme of transition to full-fledged democracy. Youth subculture became more political. Dissent moved to the streets as several demonstrations were held. Some 10,000 people rallied to recall and condemn the Soviet invasion of August 1968, several thousands demonstrated on Czechoslovakia's national day in October, and a few thousand attended the human rights meeting in December. Self-published *samizdat* leaflets, periodicals and books circulated in large numbers, including the first regular monthly newspaper titled *Lidové Noviny* (The People's News). The cultural scene became somewhat livelier, particularly the theatre, and there was greater *glasnost* in some cultural periodicals.

Alexander Dubček, long a pensioner in Bratislava, celebrated something of a comeback to the limelight with his long interview in the Italian Communist newspaper *L'Unità* in January, several other interviews for Western media in the course of the year, and his trip to Italy in November. Mr Dubček firmly proclaimed his support for Mr Gorbachev and stressed the similarity between the Prague Spring and current Soviet *perestroika*. The incumbent leaders in Prague rejected his overtures, however.

The mood of the public remained a combination of despair and anger, with a good deal of cynicism about the possible success of restructuring. A popular joke likened the Czechoslovak variety of *perestroika* to the rebuilding of a pig-sty into a modern apartment, with the swine continuing tenancy. Even so, more people were willing to stand up and be counted as followers of the independent movements, while the disaffection of others heightened over the short supply of goods in the shops.

HUNGARY

CAPITAL: Budapest   AREA: 93,000 sq km   POPULATION: 10,600,000 ('86)
OFFICIAL LANGUAGE: Hungarian   POLITICAL SYSTEM: people's republic under communist rule
HEAD OF STATE: President Károly Németh (since June '87)
RULING PARTY: Hungarian Socialist Workers' Party (HSWP)
PARTY LEADER: Károly Grósz, HSWP General Secretary (since May '88)
PRINCIPAL MINISTERS: Miklós Németh (prime minister) István Horváth (deputy premier, interior), Péter Várkonyi (foreign affairs), Péter Medgyessy (deputy premier, chairman of planning and economic commission), Miklós Villányi (finance), Lt-Gen. Ferenc Kárpáti (defence)
INTERNATIONAL ALIGNMENT: Warsaw Pact, Comecon
CURRENCY: forint (end-'88 £1=Ft94. US$1=Ft52.06)   GNP PER CAPITA: US$2,020 ('86)
MAIN EXPORTS: machinery and transport equipment, agricultural products, basic manufactures

THE year was a momentous one in Hungary, politically the most important since the 1956 revolution. It was the year that saw the disappearance of János Kádár, the country's leader for nearly 32 years—since 1956—from the political stage and his replacement by Károly Grósz, Prime Minister since 1987. But this was no more than the tip of the iceberg. What it concealed, though this concealment was increasingly thin, was a far-reaching crisis of the system, of public confidence in the authorities and of the economy. In effect, the Kádár system underwent an increasingly rapid disintegration as the year progressed, and by December it was clear that the emphasis of the public debate was over the shape and quality of the new system, rather than any question of shoring up the old.

The year began in an atmosphere of mounting concern about the deterioration of the economic situation and the evident inability of the political system and leadership to do anything effective about improving this. This came to a head during the Party conference in May, where the delegates assembled in a radical mood and removed not only Mr Kádár himself but eight other members of the Politburo closely associated with him. Many of them were removed from the Central Committee as well.

However, there was little to suggest that the Grósz team, which took over in May 1988, had any intention of launching the thoroughgoing programme of reform that critics were urging on it. The team itself was a coalition of committed reformers like Imre Pozsgay and Rezsö Nyers on the one hand and conservative modernizers like János Berecz on the other. Mr Grósz himself lacked the instincts of reformer, but was thought to be prepared to accept even radical measures if these would safeguard his power.

The origins of the crisis lay in the steady deterioration of the economy—in performance, in innovation, in output, in quality and in exports—during the 1980s. Hungary's foreign debt, the highest per capita in the communist world at $18,000 million, was the clearest indication of this. Although the country could maintain its creditworthiness for the coming two years, by 1990–91 the debt service ratio would jump from the existing 40 per cent to over 65 per cent. The only way in which this could be met was through refinancing; and refinancing was only likely if the leadership had embarked on genuine, as distinct from cosmetic, reform. This was the significance of the debate on political reform for the economy.

The crisis of the system had numerous symptoms. Perhaps most seriously for the regime, the combination of popular restiveness and dissatisfaction, coupled with intensifying expression of alternatives by widening sections of the intelligentsia, threatened to undermine the self-confidence of the rulers. As far as the intelligentsia was concerned, large sections of those who had accepted and supported the political order constructed by Mr Kádár over the years finally concluded in 1987 that it no longer deserved their backing.

This launched them on the path to overt criticism, with the result that by 1988 the atmosphere in Hungary was one of extraordinary political diversity, in which virtually nothing was taboo. Political regrouping led to the emergence or re-emergence of de facto political parties and dozens of semi-formal political groupings covering the entire spectrum. There was, notably, the Hungarian Democratic Forum, with a membership of around 10,000 by the end of 1988 and beginning to assume the shape of a national-radical party. The Alliance of Free Democrats (SZDSZ), the heir of the old democratic opposition, had embarked on a path that was taking it in a similar direction, although its membership was smaller and its ideas were liberal democratic. In addition, the Social Democrats and the Smallholders (the party that had won an absolute majority in the free elections of 1945) had also returned to the political stage.

The area most directly affected by the intellectual ferment

in Hungary was the press and other media. The spirit of *glasnost* had taken over with a vengeance, albeit the Hungarian press had been far more open than the Soviet when the process began, in the last year or so of Mr Kádár's power. Virtually no area was exempt from comment, except perhaps links with the Soviet Union.

Furthermore, there was a discernible shift in the location of power from the Party towards Parliament, as the Party leadership began tacitly to recognize its own inability to mobilize society and to move towards accepting a genuine coalition. By the end of the year, Parliament was emerging as the locus of genuine debates, around a quarter of the deputies were highly critical of the Government, and public opinion, alerted by the open press, was attentive to these debates. The pivotal issue thus became that of transition—would Hungary become the first communist country to move from a Soviet-type system to democracy and if so, how would it achieve this?

There were, however, serious obstacles to any smooth transformation of the political system. The Party and state bureaucracies, likeliest losers in any redistribution of power, would be reluctant to accept any change that did not offer them some security. And the population was largely inexperienced in day-to-day politics, having mostly known the Kádár years of depoliticization rather than being involved in the running of political institutions.

In addition, the strength of the pressure for change, its rapid pace and crucially the shift in the debate from whether a multi-party system should be introduced to when and how this should happen left Hungary in an exposed position in the communist bloc. Although there was evident satisfaction in Moscow at Hungarian developments (and benevolent neutrality in Poland), the other Warsaw Pact countries took a much more hostile attitude. There were fears that a new 'Holy Alliance' of antagonistic neighbours could emerge to exercise the maximum braking pressure on Hungary and to put heart in the conservative forces that were resisting change. It was an unprecedented state of affairs in the communist world.

ROMANIA

CAPITAL: Bucharest AREA: 237,500,000 sq km POPULATION: 23,000,000 ('86)
OFFICIAL LANGUAGE: Romanian POLITICAL SYSTEM: socialist republic under communist rule
RULING PARTY: Romanian Communist Party (RCP)
HEAD OF STATE AND PARTY LEADER: Nicolae Ceauşescu, President (since Dec '67), RCP General Secretary (since March '65)
PRINCIPAL MINISTERS: Constantin Dăscălescu (prime minister), Elena Ceauşescu (first deputy premier, chairman of science and technology council), Ioan Totu (foreign affairs), Col-Gen. Vasile Milea (defence), Tudor Postelnicu (interior), Radu Balan (chairman of state planning committee)
INTERNATIONAL ALIGNMENT: Warsaw Pact, Comecon
CURRENCY: leu (end-'88 £1=14.78 lei, US$1=8.17 lei) GNP PER CAPITA: US$2,540 ('81)
MAIN EXPORTS: oil, raw materials and metals, machinery and transport equipment, chemicals

THE year began ominously for many Romanians with the revival of President Ceauşescu's so-called 'systemization' programme for resettling large sections of the rural population in towns. This grandiose plan, outlined by the President in early March, envisaged the demolition of up to 8,000 of Romania's 13,000 villages by the year 2000. The official reason for systemization was to abolish the great inequalities between the living conditions of villagers and town-dwellers by transferring those living in the thousands of small unviable communities to large agro-industrial complexes. Opponents of the scheme around the world argued that the wholesale destruction of villages, together with many old churches, monuments and cemeteries, would put an end to many long-standing traditions of Romania's rural life and would do irreparable damage to Europe's cultural heritage.

Systemization apparently proceeded at a slow pace, perhaps under the impact of worldwide protests or because of a lack of funds. As with other developments in the country, reports remained scanty but they indicated that the programme got under way mostly in areas near Bucharest. Towards the end of the year Romanian officials dropped hints that systemization would be carried out in a less drastic way—without the demolition of villages which would simply be allowed to decay by being starved of funds. However, the main outlines of the policy were not reversed.

This grandiose project was matched by equally ambitious plans for economic development. The growth in national income for 1988 was set at 9–10 per cent and that for industrial output at 7–8 per cent. The paucity of information made available suggested that such targets remained hopelessly unrealistic. In any case, the benefits of any increase in production largely eluded the Romanian consumer because a very high proportion of output continued to be destined for export. This was designed to contribute to the crash repayment programme of Romania's foreign debt. To encourage this process new export incentives came into force in April, allowing enterprises to pay their workers up to 10 per cent of their profits from exports to the hard currency markets. A general pay rise of 10 per cent for all workers was also decreed, to be phased in from the second half of the year.

However, any additional income had little effect on the worsening living standards of Romania's population because the rationing of many foodstuffs, fuel and a range of other essential commodities continued without an end in sight. Strict limits on the use of energy also remained in force. However, in November electricity quotas available to households were raised by nearly a quarter compared with the previous winter. Although this measure did not alter the woefully inadequate state of energy supplies, it was probably designed to stave off any repetition of the Braşov demonstration of November 1987 (see AR 1987, p. 123).

On several occasions during the year President Ceauşescu demonstrated his absolute hold on power by reshuffling high-ranking officials at will. In June following revelations about the dumping of toxic waste at the Black Sea port of Sulina, three Government Ministers and several other officials were dismissed. They included the Chairman of the State Planning Committee, Ştefan Bîrlea, and the Minister of Foreign Trade, Ilie Văduva. At the same time formal admonitions were issued to some of the country's leading politicians, including Prime Minister Constantin Dăscălescu. Meanwhile, the President's wife, Elena Ceauşescu, herself accumulated more power and prestige. In 1988 for the first time it was Mrs Ceauşescu who delivered the festive speech on Romania's national day, 23 August.

Some of the excesses in the cult of personality surrounding the presidential couple caused further harm to Romania's image abroad. The fabrication of greetings from the British, Spanish and Swedish monarchs for President Ceauşescu's 70th birthday in January led to strong protests from the three countries concerned. However, the international impact of this incident was dwarfed by that of the systemization programme which cast a shadow over Romania's relations with the international community. The scheme was condemned by the United States, Britain, West Germany and by many other Governments and organizations around the world.

But nowhere in the world did systemization create as much hostility as in Hungary where it was seen as contributing to the forcible assimilation of Romania's Hungarian minority through the dispersal of compact Hungarian village communities to large settlements inhabited mostly by Romanians. Systemization also coincided with a flood of refugees fleeing Romania for Hungary. During 1988 over 12,000 of these refugees, mostly ethnic Hungarians, were granted residence permits in Hungary. As a result of these developments, relations between the two countries went from bad to worse. In June Romania closed down the Hungarian consulate-general in Cluj-Napoca following a protest demonstration in Budapest against systemization. A meeting between President Ceauşescu and the new Hungarian leader, Károly Grósz, in August—the first summit between the two countries in 11 years—failed to produce any positive results. Relations remained tense as Romania expelled a Hungarian diplomat in November and Hungary retaliated in kind.

The Hungarian-Romanian dispute, together with Romania's continued opposition to integration within Comecon, proved to be an increasing embarrassment for the Soviet leadership. President Gorbachev received the Romanian President in Moscow in October, but he appeared to make no headway in persuading the Romanian leader to adopt more flexible policies. President Ceauşescu persisted in his resistance to Soviet-style restructuring and ended the year with a veiled attack on his reformist allies when he criticized communist parties that were withdrawing from the day-to-day administration of government.

Relations with the West also deteriorated as a result of Romania's obstructionist attitude to the conclusion of a human rights accord at the Vienna Conference on Security and Cooperation in Europe. Romania lost its most-favoured-nation trading status with the United States in June after President Ceauşescu had declared that his country would no longer apply for its annual extension because the human rights conditions attached to it involved interference in Romania's affairs. Romania ended the year more isolated from the international community than ever before.

BULGARIA

CAPITAL: Sofia   AREA: 111,000 sq km   POPULATION: 9,000,000 ('86)
OFFICIAL LANGUAGE: Bulgarian   POLITICAL SYSTEM: people's republic under communist rule
RULING PARTY: Bulgarian Communist Party (BCP)
HEAD OF STATE AND PARTY LEADER: Todor Zhivkov, President of State Council (since July '71), BCP General Secretary (since March '54)
PRINCIPAL MINISTERS: Georgi Atanasov (prime minister), Petur Mladenov (foreign affairs), Gen. Dobri Dzhurov (defence), Stoyan Ovcharov (economics and planning), Georgi Tanev (internal affairs)
INTERNATIONAL ALIGNMENT: Warsaw Pact, Comecon
CURRENCY: lev (end-'88 £1=L1.49, US$1=L0.83)   GNP PER CAPITA: US$4,150 ('80)
MAIN EXPORTS: machinery and equipment, agricultural produce

THROUGHOUT 1988 it was admitted both in the press and at Party forums that Bulgaria's programme of economic and political restructuring—as set out at the July 1987 BCP Central Committee (CC) plenum (see AR 1987, p.126)—had serious shortcomings and was being implemented only haphazardly. In his report to the CC plenum on 13 December, veteran leader Todor Zhivkov blamed the middle-ranking bureaucracy for obstructing progress and called for a further reorganization of the economy, instituting bond-issuing firms as a new basic managerial unit.

Although in January the national Party conference had called for a gradual and realistic approach to reform, by the spring the sense of political drift had become so strong that foreign observers began to speculate about Mr Zhivkov's replacement as Party leader. It seemed that a possible successor had been approached by the Soviet leadership, when in May Politburo member and CC secretary Chudomir Aleksandrov travelled to Moscow to meet Georgi Razumovsky, the Soviet CC secretary for cadre affairs. At the Bulgarian CC plenum on 20 July, however, Mr Aleksandrov resigned from his posts, allegedly at his own request after the unearthing of a supposed family scandal.

The July plenum also accepted the resignation from the Politburo of National Assembly Chairman Stanko Todorov and dismissed CC secretary Stoyan Mikhaylov, who had been criticized for his liberalism towards the press and creative unions. At the December CC plenum the former economic supremo, Ognyan Doynov, 'tendered his resignation' from full Politburo membership. These purges of potential rivals to Mr Zhivkov reduced the Politburo to a tight clique of protegés and reliable former partisans. Mr Aleksandrov was replaced as CC secretary for cadre affairs by the former Minister of Internal Affairs, Dimitar Stoyanov, who won full Politburo membership at the December plenum. Also elected a full Politburo member was BCP first secretary in Sofia, Ivan Panev.

In spite of the incompleteness of the BCP's economic reform, the National Assembly was told in December that national income had grown by 6.2 per cent and labour productivity by 6.6 per cent in 1988. These figures, however, were hard to reconcile with other indices of economic performance. Bulgaria's indebtedness to Western banks rose by almost half to exceed $6,000 million, causing concern about the country's creditworthiness. Shortages of basic goods seemed to intensify, partly as a result of failures in agriculture. Against this background, Mr Zhivkov published a memorandum on agricultural reform on 28 September that promised a limited measure of privatization.

Moves towards a reform of the pricing system involved raising nearly a quarter of wholesale prices in January; but this encouraged unsanctioned increases, which were the subject of a State Council decree on 5 February. A Politburo document on the restructuring of internal trade was published on 1 March, but it was unclear to what extent it was implemented. It was also difficult to ascertain the fate of two of the central reforms of 1987: the transfer of property management rights to work collectives and municipalities, and the new system for quality standards. The Ministerial Council's Decree No. 35, promoting cooperative and private enterprise, enjoyed only a mixed success, largely because of the absence of legal guarantees.

The report to the national Party conference proposed that independent groups be allowed but those that did come into being were swiftly repressed. The Committee for the Protection of the Environment, which was founded in March by prominent cultural and sports figures to pressurize the Government to halve the pollution of Ruse, Bulgaria's fourth city, by chlorine from a chemical plant in Romania, was the first to suffer. In January dissidents founded the Independent Association for the Defence of Human Rights; the authorities' response was at first hesitant but in the autumn a number of the founding members were expelled from the country. The BCP also took immediate repressive action against a Club for the Support of *Perestroika* and *Glasnost* that was set up by over 100 leading intellectuals on 3 November.

A grassroots movement for openness in the press, which gathered strength in the early part of 1988, also met opposition. In March Damyan Obreshkov was replaced as editor of the trade union daily *Trud* after a series of reports on provincial corruption were denounced by a Party control committee. The editors of two cultural weeklies, Evtim Evtimov of *Literaturen Front* and Stefan Prodev of *Narodna Kultura*, were also dismissed for publishing on controversial historical and cultural topics.

Although the Bulgarian and Turkish Governments signed a protocol on 23 February shortly before the Balkan Foreign Ministers' conference in Belgrade, relations between the two states did not improve significantly. Further negotiations in May and July became stalemated over Bulgaria's refusal to make any concessions towards its ethnic Turkish minority.

YUGOSLAVIA

CAPITAL: Belgrade AREA: 255,804 sq km POPULATION: 23,270,000 ('86)
OFFICIAL LANGUAGES: Serbo-Croat, Macedonian, Slovene POLITICAL SYSTEM: socialist federal republic under communist rule
RULING PARTY: League of Communists of Yugoslavia
HEAD OF STATE: Raif Dizdarevic, President of collective Federal Presidency (from May '88)
PRINCIPAL MINISTERS: Branko Mikulic (prime minister), Budimir Loncar (foreign affairs), Veljko Kadijevic (defence), Dobroslav Culafic (interior) (*in caretaker government*)
INTERNATIONAL ALIGNMENT: NAM, Comecon (associate), OECD (observer)
CURRENCY: dinar (end-'88 £1=Din9.263.98, US$=Din5,121.05) GNP PER CAPITA US$2,235 ('86)
MAIN EXPORTS: transport equipment, metal manufactures, chemicals, textiles, agricultural produce

THE resignation of the Cabinet on 30 December provided a climactic end to a year marked by deepening political conflict and continuing economic difficulty. Warned at the end of 1987 by its international creditors (see AR 1987, p. 127), the Government was under pressure throughout the year to implement an array of economic and other reforms designed to ensure greater accountability and efficiency. In this respect it failed to achieve any of its central aims. A motion of no confidence was survived in the federal Assembly on 15 May; but the Assembly's rejection of the Budget for 1989 precipitated the resignations, unprecedented in post-war Yugoslavia.

Economic performance continued to be poor, with investment and productivity remaining low. The growth of exports to the hard currency countries by 15 per cent in the first ten months of the year constituted a great achievement, although trade with the Comecon countries remained sluggish and there was no significant improvement in trade with the non-aligned states. Agricultural exports were hampered by poor harvests caused by a combination of adverse weather and under-investment. There were significant reductions in the output of some important export crops with losses forecast for 1988 in the region of US$1,000 million. Nevertheless, the Government succeeded in rescheduling its foreign debt of some US$20,000 million.

Inflation was estimated by the respected monthly *Ekonomska Politika* to have exceded 250 per cent by the year's end, and remained Yugoslavia's most worrying problem. Domestic living standards continued to be depressed throughout the year, and were calculated to have fallen by 40 per cent over five years. In part these problems were related to the movement away from controlled towards more realistic prices and interest rates. The prices of some commodities were raised by up to 30 per cent in special measures introduced in May. Wage controls instituted at the same time were ineffective in limiting inflation, but did contribute to the wave of economic unrest and demonstrations which swept the country from June onwards. By October some 1,400 strikes had been reported, their main focus being the prospect of large-scale redundancies occasioned by the radical reorganization or threatened closure of economically unviable enterprises.

The economy of Bosnia remained shaken by the aftermath of the Agrokomerc scandal (see AR 1987, p. 128). In May the trials began in Bihac of Hakija Pozderac, Fikret Abdic and 23 others implicated in the affair. The Assembly of Bosnia-Hercegovina announced on 28 June the writing-off of nearly half of the US$261 million of fraudulent debt accumulated by Agrokomerc.

The familiar problems of domestic politics in Yugoslavia were refocused in 1988 by the reform programme. The more than 40 measures which made up the envisaged reform, including important amendments to the constitution, were designed to address the fundamental economic and political problems facing the country. The new measures included provisions for a stronger central banking system; limits on the powers of workers' councils; the strengthening of the voice of foreign management in joint economic ventures; and the expansion of private enterprise (farmers in the private sector, for example, would be able to expand their holdings from a maximum of ten to 30 hectares).

The reforms, accepted by the federal Assembly in December 1987, were then sent down to the republics for ratification. Enormous resistance was encountered, both from sections of the entrenched political bureaucracy and from the traditional buttress of the regime, organized labour. After the Mikulic Government survived its test in the Assembly in May, a Cabinet reshuffle followed in July, during which two new portfolios were created to strengthen the team dealing with economic affairs. However, these moves failed to secure for Mr Mikulic the political muscle he needed to push through his programme.

The problems of Yugoslavia's federal system had arisen in part from its great ethnic diversity (see accompanying map). In each of the six republics and two autonomous provinces one nationality made up a preponderant proportion of the population, with two major exceptions. In Bosnia-Hercegovina, where ethnic Muslims constituted roughly 40 per cent of the population, the republican framework reflected both the historical identity of the region and its religious diversity. Since 1974 the republic of Serbia had contained two autonomous provinces, namely the Vojvodina (with a large Magyar-speaking minority and strong historical links with Hungary) and overwhelmingly Albanophone Kosovo.

The status of the autonomous provinces created a serious constitutional anomaly, in that they were able effectively to veto developments at both the republican and federal levels of government, whereas the latter had no reciprocal rights of intervention in the provinces. This created acute resentment on the part of many

Serbs, who felt that their interests were least regarded in regions which were nominally components of the republic of Serbia. Anger and frustration grew as accusations circulated of the harrassment of the Serbo-Croat-speaking (and Orthodox) minorities in Kosovo by the rapidly growing Albanophone (and largely Islamic) majority. The inter-communal tensions which erupted in serious rioting in 1981 (see AR 1981, pp. 127–8) resulted in the steady emigration of Serbo-Croat-speaking inhabitants (at a rate estimated at 10,000 per annum). Taken together with the very high Albanian birth rate, this meant that by 1988 Albanian speakers probably made up 85 per cent of the population of the province.

Serbian Party chiefs, led by Slobodan Milosevic, took advantage of the process of constitutional change to seek to bring both of the provinces more directly under the control of the Serbian republic. The first stage of the struggle was won in 1987, when Mr Milosevic shot to prominence, and his adherents succeeded in displacing more conciliatory elements from the Serbian Party (see AR 1987, p. 129). During the summer of 1988 the Milosevic faction sought to mobilize massive popular backing. The front organization, the Socialist Alliance, organized a succession of demonstrations of Serbs during the summer months. These culminated in Nis on 24 September, where a crowd of 150,000 was reported, and the following day in Novi Sad, where between 70,000 and 100,000 assembled, demanding the unification of the republic.

In the Vojvodina these pressures, together with internal divisions within the Party leadership, led to the resignations of the veteran Bosko Krunic from the Presidium of the LCY on 1 October, and later of the entire Presidium of the LCY in the province. Serbian nationalist demonstrations also took place in Montenegro. The violence of the response by units of special police (the only serious political violence of the year) provoked such a public outcry in the republic that its Government also was compelled to resign.

Following the expulsions at the end of 1987 from the leadership of the LCY in Kosovo (for 'counter-revolutionary' views and actions in relation to the nationality question), Mustafa Pljakic (an ethnic Albanian) was also forced to resign as Federal Secretary for Transport and Communications. The LCY Central Committee meeting on 16–17 October was extremely acrimonious, and resulted in further resignations, although the Milosevic line was defeated there. In October further negotiations were instituted with the provincial leadership, while in November Kacusa Jasari and Azem Vlasi (both ethnic Albanians) resigned from the LCY Central Committee in Kosovo over their defence of provincial autonomy.

Under martial law since October 1987, Kosovo was shaken by a further succession of large demonstrations between 17 and

134   THE USSR AND EASTERN EUROPE

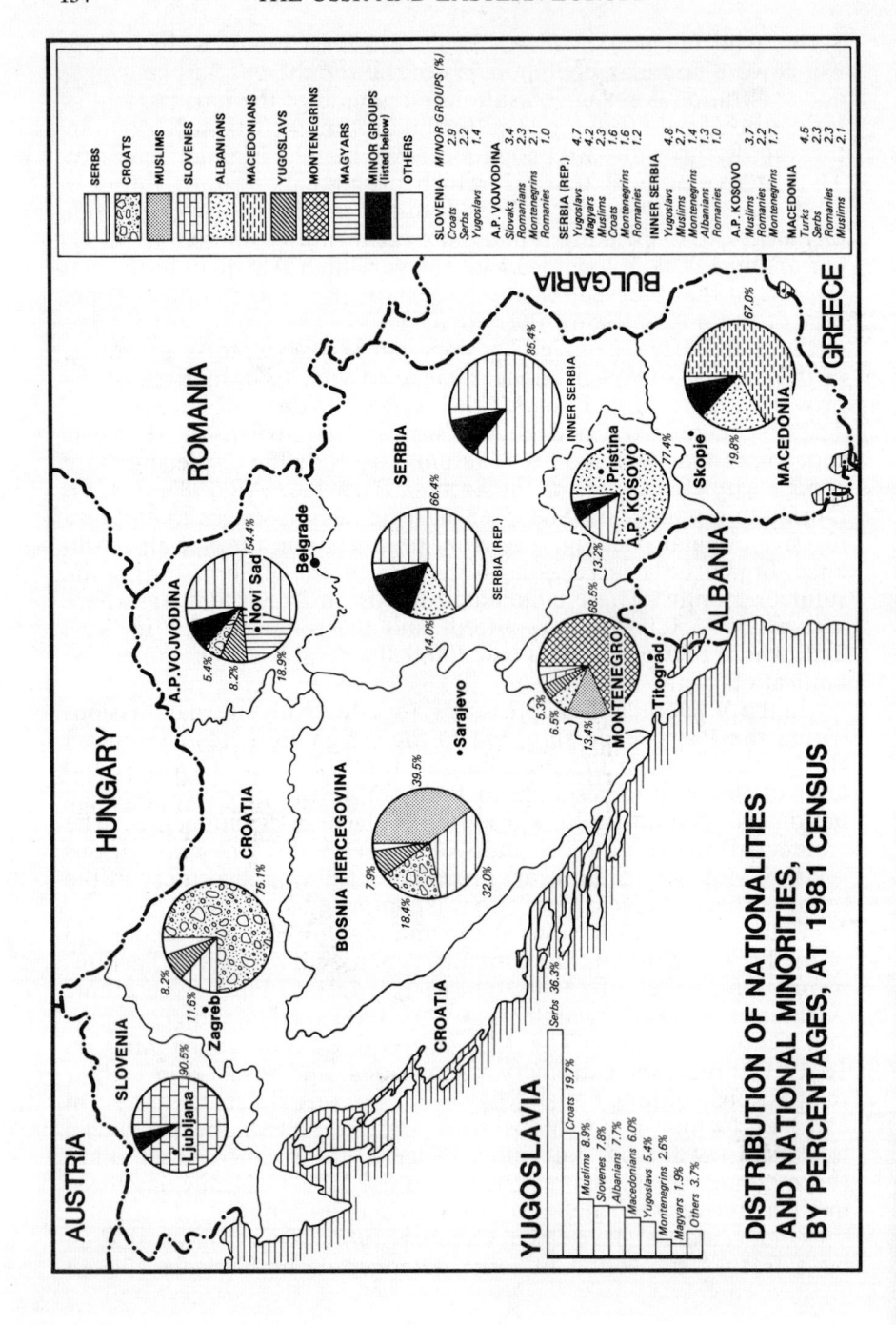

DISTRIBUTION OF NATIONALITIES AND NATIONAL MINORITIES, BY PERCENTAGES, AT 1981 CENSUS

Legend:
- SERBS
- CROATS
- MUSLIMS
- SLOVENES
- ALBANIANS
- MACEDONIANS
- YUGOSLAVS
- MONTENEGRINS
- MAGYARS
- MINOR GROUPS (listed below)
- OTHERS

MINOR GROUPS (%)

SLOVENIA
- Croats 2.9
- Serbs 2.2
- Yugoslavs 1.4

A.P. VOJVODINA
- Slovaks 3.4
- Romanians 2.3
- Montenegrins 2.1
- Romanies 1.0

SERBIA (REP.)
- Yugoslavs 4.7
- Magyars 4.2
- Muslims 2.3
- Croats 1.6
- Montenegrins 1.6
- Romanies 1.2

INNER SERBIA
- Yugoslavs 4.8
- Muslims 2.7
- Montenegrins 1.4
- Albanians 1.3
- Romanies 1.0

A.P. KOSOVO
- Muslims 3.7
- Romanies 2.2
- Montenegrins 1.7

MACEDONIA
- Turks 4.5
- Serbs 2.3
- Romanies 2.1
- Muslims 2.1

Republics (with pie chart percentages):

SLOVENIA — Ljubljana: 90.5%

CROATIA — Zagreb: 75.1%, 11.6%, 8.2%

A.P. VOJVODINA — Novi Sad: 54.4%, 18.9%, 8.2%, 5.4%

SERBIA (REP.) — Belgrade: 66.4%, 14.0%

INNER SERBIA: 85.4%

BOSNIA HERCEGOVINA — Sarajevo: 39.5%, 32.0%, 18.4%, 7.9%

MONTENEGRO — Titograd: 68.5%, 13.4%, 6.5%, 5.3%

A.P. KOSOVO — Pristina: 77.4%, 13.2%

MACEDONIA — Skopje: 67.0%, 19.8%

YUGOSLAVIA:
- Serbs 36.3%
- Croats 19.7%
- Muslims 8.9%
- Slovenes 7.8%
- Albanians 7.7%
- Macedonians 6.0%
- Yugoslavs 5.4%
- Montenegrins 2.6%
- Magyars 1.9%
- Others 3.7%

21 November. The largest of these were in the provincial capital, Pristina, led by a large force of Albanian miners from the neighbouring Stri Trg mines, whose protests about the falling standard of living were linked to demands for the defence of the 1974 constitution and the continuing autonomy of Kosovo's leadership.

In February Belgrade hosted a meeting of the Foreign Ministers of all six Balkan countries—the first since the 1930s. The event was especially noteworthy for Albania's abandonment of isolationism, and for its conciliatory stance on the position of the Albanophone minority in Yugoslavia. The optimism of the occasion was offset later by Yugoslavia's criticism in July of Romania's treatment of its 5,000-strong Serbian minority, and by controversy with Greece in August over the Yugoslav refusal to restore the flow of the Vardar. In drought conditions, the Yugoslavs had been diverting river water for the irrigation of their own land at the expense of the cultivators in the Salonika plain.

A landmark of the year was the visit on 14–18 March of Mikhail Gorbachev to Belgrade, where he addressed the Yugoslav federal Assembly. His speech affirmed that 'the strength of socialism lies in the diversity of its colours', and regretted the 'groundless accusations' which were the occasion of the bitter break between the two countries in 1948 (see also p. 112). The central issue of the talks between the Soviet leader and the Yugoslav Government was future economic cooperation between the two countries. Yugoslavia's trade surplus with the Soviet Union was expected to exceed US$2,000 million during the year (partly a product of the movement of oil prices).

On 27 November a crowd of about 1,500 supporters of an emigré organization demonstrated outside the Yugoslav consulate in Sydney, marking the 70th anniversary of the foundation of a united Yugoslav state. A part of the crowd broke into the compound, and in a scuffle with embassy staff shots were fired, resulting in the injury of one of the demonstrators. The Yugoslav mission in Sydney was closed on 4 December, and in retaliation three officers of the Australian embassy in Belgrade were asked to leave.

ALBANIA

CAPITAL: Tirana   AREA: 29,000 sq km   POPULATION: 3,000,000 ('86)
OFFICIAL LANGUAGE: Albanian   POLITICAL SYSTEM: socialist people's republic under communist rule
RULING PARTY: Party of Labour of Albania (PLA)
HEAD OF STATE AND PARTY LEADER: Ramiz Alia, President of the People's Assembly Presidium (since Nov '82), PLA First Secretary (since April '85)
PRINCIPAL MINISTERS: Adil Carcani (prime minister), Hekuran Isai (deputy premier, internal affairs), Reis Malile (foreign affairs), Prokop Murra (defence), Niko Gjyzari (chairman of state planning commission)
CURRENCY: lek (end-'88) £1=AL10,15, US$1=AL5,61)   GNP PER CAPITA: US$820 ('81)
MAIN EXPORTS: crude oil, minerals, agricultural products

THE year had two main features: a greater willingness on the part of the communist regime to admit serious economic, social, cultural and other failures; and some genuine attempts to reduce the country's long isolation from the outside world by cultivating new diplomatic and trading contacts. The country suffered an exceptional drought throughout most of the year, and the authorities urged people to save electricity. One of the consequences of the drought was to reduce the amount of electricity exported to neighbouring Yugoslavia, and hence the income derived from that source.

Official spokesmen and the press showed serious concern during the year about many shortcomings of Albanian society, such as inefficiency and low productivity in several fields, widespread corruption and crime, cultural mediocrity, bureaucratic incompetence and sluggishness. Complaints about poor performance in both agriculture and industry were rife. Several essential foodstuffs such as vegetables and fruit were said to be in short supply because of low productivity and inadequate methods of distribution. In July a meeting of the Politburo was wholly devoted to agriculture. It criticized, among other things, the fruit-growing industry, which was called the most backward branch of agriculture. Over many years plans for fruit production had only been fulfilled by 60 to 70 per cent. Apart from the usual exhortations to do better in fruit-growing and other branches of agriculture, there was no clear indication what measures the authorities intended to take to bring about a real improvement in efficiency and productivity.

What the country's highly centralized economic system needed more than anything else to meet the demands of a fast-growing and discontented population was radical reform as well as some modification of its Stalinist political structures. But apart from an ingrained reluctance to take any political risks, the Albanian regime was alarmed more than ever by the sweeping economic, social and political reforms in the Soviet Union. These were criticized by official sources as revisionist and capitalist, hence as a dangerous example for a country like Albania to follow.

Widespread crime was another thing that worried the authorities.

In March a Party official spoke about what he called certain 'alien manifestations' among young people, such as stealing state property, vandalism and unbecoming behaviour in public places. Yet at the same time it was admitted that young people had good reasons to feel frustrated, unhappy and rebellious. The blame for this was put on certain official conservative and dogmatic attitudes towards the young generation as well as on poor and inadequate information and entertainment provided by the country's television, radio and press.

But if on the domestic scene there was greater readiness to admit failures, although not the need for radical changes, the Government was more forthcoming in its efforts to break down the country's isolation from the outside world. Albania took part in the Balkan Foreign Ministers' conference which was held in Yugoslavia in February (see p. 135). In his address to the meeting, the Albanian Foreign Minister, Reis Malile, referred to the current crisis in Kosovo, the Yugoslav province with a large Albanian-speaking population, when he said: 'Albania had never raised the issue that national minority problems should be solved by changing state frontiers or by interfering in the internal affairs of other states. But, on the other hand, this did not rule out the legitimate interest of neighbours in their national minorities.'

There was a significant improvement in the country's relations with the Federal Republic of Germany. The first West German ambassador arrived in Albania in January. In June the two countries signed an agreement on economic, industrial and technical cooperation. This was followed by another agreement in September on the exchange of scientists, scholars and specialists as well as cooperation in literature, art, television, radio and sport.

The year also marked an important rapprochement between Albania and some of the communist states of Eastern Europe. Whereas relations between them had been badly disrupted when Albania was expelled from the Soviet bloc in 1961, 27 years later full diplomatic relations at ambassadorial level were restored with Bulgaria, Czechoslovakia and Hungary.

Diplomatic relations with Canada were established in April. In August the Japanese Deputy Foreign Minister, Takujiro Hamada, visited Tirana, where he signed a trade agreement with the Albanian Government. The Japanese side hoped thereby to increase its imports of chrome from Albania, which was the largest producer of the ore in Europe.

MONGOLIA

CAPITAL: Ulan Bator AREA: 1,565,000 sq km POPULATION: 2,100,000 ('88)
PRINCIPAL LANGUAGE: Khalkha Mongolian POLITICAL SYSTEM: people's republic under communist rule
RULING PARTY: Mongolian People's Revolutionary Party (MPRP)
HEAD OF STATE AND PARTY LEADER: Jambyn Batmönh, Chairman of Presidium of People's Great Hural (since Dec '84), MPRP General Secretary (since Aug '84)
PRINCIPAL MINISTERS: Dumaagiyn Sodnom (prime minister), Myatavyn Peljee (deputy premier, chairman of Comecon affairs committee), Puntsagiyn Jasray (deputy premier, chairman of state planning and economic committee), Tserenpiliyn Gombosüren (foreign affairs), Col.-Gen. Jamsrangiyn Yondon (defence)
INTERNATIONAL ALIGNMENT: Comecon
CURRENCY: tugrik (end-'88 £1=T6.06, US$1=T3.35) GNP PER CAPITA: US$2,140 ('86)
MAIN EXPORTS: livestock, agricultural products, copper ore

IN the most striking development since Jambyn Batmönh took over in 1984 as MPRP General Secretary and President of Mongolia, towards the end of 1988 the Party leadership raised the policy of *il tod (glasnost,* or greater openness) to new heights by initiating the first public criticism of Mr Batmönh's predecessor, Yumjaagiyn Tsedenbal, for the country's past and present economic and political difficulties. Admitting that the drive for economic reform under way for the past two years was bogged down in bureaucracy, it proposed a new programme for the restructuring of the country's political and social institutions, including reassessment of the role of past Mongolian leaders.

The new proposals—described as an 'urgent task'—were issued by the Politburo in November for public discussion in advance of a plenary meeting of the MPRP Central Committee. Economic reform without social renewal had been 'one-sided and incomplete', the proposals said. They made no direct reference by name to Mr Tsedenbal, although 'subjectivism' (a codeword for the former leader) was blamed for the 'stagnation' that had to be overcome. The proposals also ranged over such sensitive issues as the introduction of multi-candidate elections, limited terms of office for Party and Government officials and constitutional and legal reform, as well as Mongolian nationalism and the 'cult of personality' of Mongolia's stalinist dictator, Marshal Horloogiyn Choybalsan (who died in 1952). The proposals were published shortly after reports that Mr Tsedenbal had been allowed to return to Mongolia from exile in Moscow.

The Party and Government newspaper *Unen* printed a large number of readers' letters in response to the Politburo's proposals, culminating in mid-December in the first published references to Mr Tsedenbal by name in the four years and more since he had been removed from power. In view of the need to remove the 'blank spots' in Mongolian history covering the period of the Choybalsan dictatorship, *Unen* said that many people also wanted a clear evaluation of Mr Tsedenbal who, 'influenced by the veneration of Stalin', had 'concentrated all powers in his own hands'. One of the letters, from a pensioner, asked, for example: 'What did Tsedenbal really do for the 40 years that he was leader of the Party and the state?' Other letters called for 'Party judgment' of leaders who had been promoted by Mr Tsedenbal and were still in power.

Addressing the Central Committee plenum, held at the end of December to discuss and approve the Politburo's proposals, President Batmönh said: 'The truth is that our successes and achievements as well as our main shortcomings and omissions are in many ways linked with Tsedenbal's activities. . . . The greater the power that was concentrated in his hands, the more strongly the negative side of his character was displayed — lack of principle in matters of Party and state leadership and cadre policy, the belittling of collective leadership, wilfulness and disregard for the opinion of others and disparity between word and deed.' He added that for some 30 years there had been virtually no discussion of organizational and ideological work within the party; it had become 'vitally imperative' to end this 'unhealthy' state of affairs and renew the country's socio-political system in its entirety.

There had been much talk of 'stagnation' since the beginning of the year. In a seminar speech published in the Party journal *Namyn Amdral*, Kinayatyn Dzardyhan (head of a department at the Institute of Social Sciences of the MPRP Central Committee) put the blame for 'stagnation' in the economy on the 'dogmatic interpretation of socialism based on over-simplification'. Dr Adultashiyn Minis, first deputy director of the Institute of Social Sciences, said at the same seminar that the 'distortion of history' in Party documents and 'super-secrecy' had reached the point where 'today we have almost no idea which stage of the building of socialism Mongolia has reached'.

The restructuring of economic management begun in 1987 (see AR 1987, pp. 132–4) proceeded in early 1988 with the formation of a new State Planning and Economic Committee to replace the State Planning Commission and the state committees responsible for labour, social security and prices. A new Law on the State Enterprise was approved, giving individual enterprises greater autonomy in management, although there was some uncertainty about how effective this would be. There was more encouragement for the establishment of urban cooperatives producing consumer goods and providing services, and in the countryside family production contracts were on the increase. However, nearly 1 ½ million head of livestock were lost in the winter-spring period and surviving newborn stock reached only 8.4 million at mid-year, marking another year of decline in the animal husbandry sector. There were shortages of consumer goods and foodstuffs, and the Government was obliged to considerably reduce plans for state meat purchases and meat exports in 1988 and 1989.

Tserenpiliyn Gombosüren was appointed Foreign Minister in June, replacing Mangalyn Dügersüren, who had held the post in 1963–68 and again since 1976. The new Chairman (Speaker) of the People's Great Hural, Lodongiyn Rinchin (another former Foreign Minister), headed Mongolia's first parliamentary delegation to China in 28 years. Mr Gombosüren said in an interview for the Soviet paper *Sovietskaya Rossiya* that the process of restoring ties between the Mongolian and Chinese parties had begun. Following Soviet leader Mikhail Gorbachev's statement at the UN General Assembly in December (see DOCUMENTS), that a 'considerable part' of the Soviet troops in Mongolia would be returning home in the next two years, Mongolian First Deputy Foreign Minister Daramyn Yondon was reported to have said that all the Soviet troops could be withdrawn if relations with China continued to improve. He added that Mr Gombosüren would visit China in 1989 for the first high-level meeting there since the Sino-Soviet split.

IV WESTERN, CENTRAL AND SOUTHERN EUROPE

Chapter 1

FRANCE—FEDERAL REPUBLIC OF GERMANY—ITALY—
BELGIUM—THE NETHERLANDS—LUXEMBOURG—
REPUBLIC OF IRELAND

FRANCE

CAPITAL: Paris   AREA: 544,000 sq km   POPULATION: 55,400,000 ('86)
OFFICIAL LANGUAGE: French   POLITICAL SYSTEM: presidential and parliamentary democracy
HEAD OF STATE AND GOVERNMENT: President François Mitterrand (since May '81)
RULING PARTIES: Socialist Party (PS) holds presidency; Government is centre-left coalition of the PS, Left Radicals (MRG) and elements of the Union for French Democracy (UDF)
PRINCIPAL MINISTERS: Michel Rocard (PS/prime minister), Roland Dumas (PS/foreign affairs), Pierre Bérégovoy (PS/economy, finance and budget), Maurice Faure (MRG/equipment and housing), Pierre Arpaillange (non-party/justice), Jean-Pierre Chevènement (PS/defence), Pierre Joxe (PS/interior)
INTERNATIONAL ALIGNMENT: Nato (outside military structure), OECD, EC, Francophonie
CURRENCY: franc (end-'88 £1=F10.96, US$1=F6.06)   GNP PER CAPITA: US$10,720 ('86)
MAIN EXPORTS: machinery and transport equipment, manufactures, chemicals, food and beverages

TWO sets of national elections, as well as cantonal elections and a referendum, made 1988 a bumper year for politicians—although many ordinary Frenchmen and women found so rich a diet of politicking less congenial. The first and most important contest was for the presidency. There were nine candidates but the real battle lay between François Mitterrand, the Socialist incumbent, and two right-wingers, the Prime Minister, Jacques Chirac, and Raymond Barre, a former Premier. In 1981 M. Mitterrand had stood for radical social change. Now he presented himself reassuringly as the embodiment of continuity, consensus and the outstretched hand to centrist voters. It was the right that offered the uncertainties of change, whether in the form of the energetic, opportunist Chirac or the didactic, deliberate and anti-demagogic Barre. Initially M. Barre had the advantage, but once M. Chirac embarked on a whirlwind American-style campaign in January he overtook his rival, who stuck to a more traditional style.

Nevertheless, in the first ballot on 24 April M. Mitterrand handsomely outstripped the rest of the field. Though M. Barre thereafter threw his support behind M. Chirac, the right was badly divided, the key to the outcome lying with the surprisingly large number of voters who had supported the candidate of the extreme right, Jean-Marie Le Pen. M. Chirac faced the second ballot in an impossible situation: he could not win without M. Le Pen's voters, yet

PRESIDENTIAL ELECTIONS (FIRST ROUND)

	Votes	Per cent
Mitterrand (Socialist)	10,367,220	34.09
Chirac (neo-Gaullist)	6,063,514	19.94
Barre (UDF)	5,031,849	16.54
Le Pen (N. Front)	4,376,894	14.39
Lejoinie (Communist)	2,055,995	6.76
Waechter (Ecologist)	1,149,642	3.78
Juquin (Ind. Comm.)	639,084	2.10
Laguiller (Ext. Left)	606,017	1.99
Bousset (Ext. Left)	116,823	0.38

any deal to win them would throw many moderate conservatives into the arms of M. Mitterrand. (Historically as remarkable, though less immediately decisive, support for the Communist candidate slumped to the lowest level for over half a century.) In the run-off on 8 May M. Mitterrand scored a decisive victory. He won 16,704,279 votes (54.02 per cent) on a turnout of 84.06 per cent to Chirac's 14,218,970, attracting a majority of votes in 77 of the 96 departments.

M. Chirac immediately resigned the premiership, and President Mitterrand appointed a Socialist, Michel Rocard, to attempt to compose a Government reflecting his policy of 'opening' to the centre. But the opposition for the most part rebuffed M. Rocard's advances. His Government contained only two centrist Ministers from their ranks. President Mitterrand promptly dissolved the predominantly right-wing Assembly, calling elections for 5 and 12 June.

The Assembly results reflected both the extent to which M. Mitterrand's victory had been a personal one and uncertainty whether he really wanted clear-cut victory for the left. In the first ballot turnout was down to 66 per cent, and both the Socialists

NATIONAL ASSEMBLY ELECTIONS (FIRST ROUND)

	1986 Votes ('000)	1986 Per cent	1988 Votes ('000)	1988 Per cent	Seats
Communists	2,740	9.78	2,766	11.32	27
Soc. & Allies	8,810	31.42	9,178	37.55	277
UDF & RPR	11,490	41.98	9,207	37.75	{ 130 UDF / 129 RPR
National Front	2,706	9.65	2,360	9.65	
Other Right	1,094	3.90	697	2.85	13

and the hastily reassembled alliance of the centrist Union pour la Démocratie Française (UDF) and the neo-Gaullist Rassemblement pour la République (RPR) lost ground. The National Front vote plummetted; and the Communists experienced a modest revival compared with the presidential election. On 12 June the second ballot produced an Assembly in which the 275 Socialists and their allies were the largest grouping, although well short of an overall majority of the 577 seats, while the National Front was 'squeezed' by the electoral system and virtually wiped out.

The survival of the new Government formed by M. Rocard after the election was less difficult than the unpromising parliamentary arithmetic suggested. Not only did the French constitution bristle with devices to allow minority Governments to operate successfully, but the Communists were unlikely to join with the right to overturn the Government, and the right was deeply divided on tactics. Some 40 UDF deputies who were hostile to systematic confrontation with the Rocard Government broke away to form a separate parliamentary group, the UDC (Union du Centre). The 49-member Government, the largest under the Fifth Republic, included six Ministers from non-left parties and ten non-aligned 'technicians', although all the major posts were in Socialist hands, with Pierre Bérégovoy again in charge of the economy, Roland Dumas at the Quai d'Orsay, Pierre Joxe at the Interior and Jean-Pierre Chevènement at Defence.

To the frustration of some in his own party, M. Rocard declared his intention to promote a more common social purpose and follow the President's policy of 'opening' to the centre. He did so with some success. His role in achieving an apparently unattainable solution to the desperate and deteriorating situation in New Caledonia (see pp. 146-7) won widespread praise. His conciliatory approach also won backing beyond the Socialists' ranks for a modestly-scaled tax on capital and the introduction of a national minimum for people on very low incomes. Educational reforms drawing heavily on ideas circulating in the previous Government also received wide acceptance. Even the Budget was adopted more readily than might have been expected. Only at the end of the year was the Government forced back on its constitutional armoury, to carry a controversial audiovisual reform, replacing the regulatory body for broadcasting, the CNCL, with the High Audiovisual Council (CSA), the third such body in as many years. Opposition members feared it would be unduly politicized—i.e. dominated by the left.

Nevertheless, the main challenge to the Rocard Government, as so often in France, came from outside Parliament. Between October and December a succession of strikes for higher pay among prison officers, nurses, postal workers and transport employees caused widespread disruption in the public services, which was slow to end even after the Government had made concessions. M. Rocard warned of the possibility of legislation to require public sector workers to provide a minimum service during periods of industrial action.

The strikes reflected exasperation among many low-paid public workers that Socialist rule was not bringing better times—fanned, alleged the Government, by a Communist Party intent on demonstrating it was still a force to be reckoned with. Yet the economy remained much healthier than had been feared after the 1987 stock market crash. The Bourse rose 49 per cent, almost cancelling the 1987 losses. Defying earlier fears of recession GDP rose 3.5 per cent (the most since 1976), industrial production by 5.1 per cent and investment by over 10 per cent. Retail prices went up 3.1 per cent during the year, outstripped by earnings, which rose 3.4 per cent. Unemployment climbed in July to 2,613,000 (10.4 per cent of the registered labour force), but had fallen again by the end of the year. The main causes for concern were lack of international competivity and the continuing tendency for imports to outstrip exports. The deficit on visible trade for 1988 was about £2,900 million, compared with £3,000 million in 1987. 1988 was also noteworthy for company takeovers and mergers. Fuelled by increased company profits, takeovers ran at twice their 1987 level. While there was an obvious element of fashion in this, it was one of many indications that French firms were coming to terms with the 'challenge of 1992' (i.e. the creation of a single European market).

Nevertheless the strength of the economy eased M. Bérégovoy's budgetary task. Buoyant revenues meant that he could cut taxes by some £1,600 million on top of cuts amounting to around £800 million announced by the Chirac Government in the run-up to the election, while preserving financial orthodoxy. Reductions were shared between individuals and businesses, with taxes on reinvested profits cut from 42 to 39 per cent and reductions in VAT on travel, books, theatre and cinema tickets and cassettes. Expenditure was set to rise 4.68 per cent, slightly more than inflation, to £110,000 million, the favoured sectors being education, research, culture, housing and employment. However, with receipts of £100,000 million the deficit was expected to be down to £950 million—bettering the Chirac Government's target.

EXTERNAL AFFAIRS AND DEFENCE. The substantial consensus between the main contenders meant that foreign affairs featured only episodically in the election campaigns. M. Chirac's hopes of advantage from the release of hostages in Lebanon were twice disappointed. Attempts to improve relations with Ayatollah Khomeini by deporting Iranian dissidents (see AR 1987, p. 139) were humiliatingly frustrated when seven were returned to France from Gabon after worldwide protests and a six-week hunger strike, and nine had their deportations quashed. When three hostages were released on the eve of the second ballot in the presidential election M. Chirac furiously denied that there had been any deal. Nevertheless, it was understood that France had undertaken to curtail arms sales to Iraq and repay Iranian funds being held against compensation for sequestrated French assets. Attacked as a cynical bid to win votes the deal availed M. Chirac little. Despite its criticisms of the deal the Rocard Government agreed to honour it, informing Iraq that it could not count on delivery of 20 Mirage fighter bombers and withdrawing the aircraft-carrier *Clemenceau* from the Gulf.

Another troublesome legacy was of the *Rainbow Warrior* affair —although this had been launched by the Socialists themselves (see AR 1985, p. 130). During the presidential campaign the Chirac Government again breached its agreement with New Zealand by unilaterally repatriating a second agent on grounds of pregnancy. It was left to its successor to appease New Zealand anger. This it did with some success, partly as a result of its generally more conciliatory line in the South Pacific and the change of line in New Caledonia (see below), and partly by agreeing to an arbitration tribunal to decide the fate of the two officers.

With the election over, France took a more active international role. It successfully proposed a major international conference on the limiting of chemical weapons, announced the cancelling of one third of debts owed to France by the poorer countries and displayed greater interest in arms control. Following a visit to Paris by Herr Erich Honecker in January, the first ever by a head of the GDR, in the autumn President Mitterrand embarked on a series of visits to Eastern Europe, starting with the USSR, where he witnessed the launch of a Franco-Soviet space mission. Little concrete emerged but these visits served to restate French policy towards the area and stake a place for France in the new climate of East-West dialogue, recalling General de Gaulle's vision of a Europe extending beyond the boundaries of the European Community.

Political change had few immediate consequences for defence, where the problem remained of how to sustain a superpower's panoply of weapons without a superpower's budget. President Mitterrand's emphasis on the need for arms reductions rather than modernization of short-range nuclear weapons in some measure reflected these pressures. At the same time, he insisted that France would not deprive itself of any kind of weapon held by other powers, notably the neutron bomb, favouring modernization of the nuclear submarine force and land-based missile systems. However, the army had to cut its orders for Lerclerc tanks from 1,100 to 825, halve purchases of Gazelle helicopters and anti-tank missiles and defer the S-4 missile programme. The only major programme agreed during the year was for prototypes of the new Rafale aircraft, which was to form a force of 300–320 aircraft in naval and air force service during the 1990s. But unless the Rafale could be sold abroad in substantial quantities the cost of some £30 million each was making this programme appear rather over-ambitious. The strain showed in the defence budget for 1989. Expenditure was to rise 4.6 per cent, but the equipment estimates were up 7.9 per cent, leaving only 1.1 per cent more for operating costs—a cut in real terms. Some 8,000 military and civil posts would be lost in consequence. The new Defence Minister, Jean-Pierre Chevènement, also announced new forms of civil military service to include the 25–30,000 young men currently exempt from conscription.

OVERSEAS DEPARTMENTS AND TERRITORIES. In a quiet year marked mainly by electoral preoccupations the exception was again NEW CALEDONIA (see also Pt. X, Ch. 3). The situation became increasingly tense following the announcement by the Minister for Overseas Departments, Bernard Pons, that regional elections would be held to coincide with the presidential election. This was taken by the nationalists as an attempt to break their movement and impose the new statute for the island (see AR 1987, p. 140). Violent incidents increased. The security forces were substantially enlarged in March following an incident in which nine gendarmes were briefly held hostage. However, in April, four gendarmes were killed and 23 taken hostage at Ouvéa in the Loyalty Islands, ensuring that the island became a major cause for contention in the presidential election. M. Chirac accused the Socialists of encouraging the separatists; they in turn alleged that his provocative policies had polarized the European and Kanak communities. Just before the second ballot 19 Kanaks and two members of the security forces died in an assault to free the hostages and it was alleged that the leader of the Kanaks had been summarily executed.

With passions running high the new Government dispatched a peace mission, which was so successful in re-establishing dialogue that in June a settlement was announced in Paris. This entailed direct rule by the central Government for a year, suspending the previous statute, followed by the introduction of three provinces, a southerly one dominated by the Europeans, the north and the Loyalty Islands being predominantly Kanak. After ten years there would be a vote on self-determination. With both Kanak and European leaders adopting conciliatory positions, the New Caledonia Bill passed the Assembly with only one dissenting vote and the plan was then submitted to a national referendum in November. The National Front was the only sizeable group to oppose it, but much of the mainstream right found reasons to advocate abstention. The general public showed little interest in so apparently remote a problem at the end of a year which had already called them to the polls so often. The turnout of 37 per cent was the lowest in a national ballot under the Fifth Republic, though those who did vote gave the settlement massive approval by 9,859,557 votes (80 per cent) to 2,464,735. In New Caledonia itself the turnout was 63 per cent with a 57 per cent Yes vote. Subsequently 26 Kanaks who had been held in France after Ouvéa were released. Although neither community backed the new system wholeheartedly there seemed a chance that what M. Rocard termed 'decades of incomprehension and violence' might at last be over.

FEDERAL REPUBLIC OF GERMANY

CAPITAL: Bonn   AREA: 249,000 sq km   POPULATION: 61,000,000 ('86)
OFFICIAL LANGUAGE: German   POLITICAL SYSTEM: federal parliamentary democracy
HEAD OF STATE: President Richard von Weizsäcker (since July '84)
RULING PARTIES: Christian Democratic Union (CDU), Christian Social Union (CSU) and Free Democratic Party (FDP)
HEAD OF GOVERNMENT: Helmut Kohl (CDU), Federal Chancellor (since Oct '82)
PRINCIPAL MINISTERS: Hans-Dietrich Genscher (FDP/Vice-Chancellor, foreign affairs), Gerhard Stoltenberg (CDU/finance), Helmut Haussmann (FDP/economics), Friedrich Zimmermann (CSU/interior), Hans A. Engelhard (FDP/justice)
INTERNATIONAL ALIGNMENT: Nato, OECD, EC
CURRENCY: Deutschmark (end-'88 £1=DM3.21, US$=DM1.77)   GNP PER CAPITA: US$12,080 ('86)
MAIN EXPORTS: machinery and transport equipment, manufactures, chemicals

DURING the year the Government of Christian Democrats (CDU/CSU) and Free Democrats (FDP) failed to capitalize on its comfortable 1987 election victory (see AR 1987, pp. 141-3), although it was more successful in the international sphere. In particular, the German presidency of the European Communities (EC) was notable in achieving substantial progress towards the 1992 creation of a single EC internal market, advancing plans for monetary union and resolving problems of the common agricultural policy. Also important were the indications of improving relations with the Soviet Union. Chancellor Kohl's visit to Moscow in October was significant in this respect, especially in furthering West German financial and export interests. Herr Kohl also pressed claims for the eventual reunification of Germany and the inclusion of West Berlin in international treaties, but they were rejected from the Soviet side. Evidence of better relationships was also apparent in the fact that during 1988 no fewer than 200,000 ethnic Germans (mainly from Poland and the Soviet Union) were allowed to emigrate to the Federal Republic. However, this large influx placed increased burdens on the West German *Länder* (states) in the provision of housing and social security, and it also led to feelings of resentment, as shown by public opinion surveys, in some quarters. More generally, it appeared that the Federal Republic was taking the lead in initiatives towards the Eastern bloc countries and was showing a renewed interest in the concept of *Mitteleuropa*. Yet at the same time its Western presence was strengthened by the appointment of Manfred Wörner (formerly Defence Minister) to succeed Lord Carrington as Secretary-General of Nato.

Two events attracted international attention. One was the death in October of one of West Germany's best-known politicians, Franz Josef Strauss (see OBITUARY), Minister-President of Bavaria and leader of the Bavarian Christian Social Union (CSU), the sister party of the Christian Democratic Union (CDU). Herr Strauss had been a constant critic of Herr Kohl as Chancellor, and the relationships between the CDU and CSU were henceforth expected to improve. The other event was a speech given in November by Philipp Jenninger, the Speaker of the Bundestag (lower house), to mark the 50th anniversary of the Nazi pogrom against the Jews, the *Reichskristallnacht*. Although Herr Jenninger was factually accurate, it appeared that he was excusing Germans for following Hitler, and there was an immediate walk-out by several Bundestag members. It was conceded that Herr Jenninger had attempted an objective analysis of the popular outlook among Germans in the 1930s, but it was felt that the tone and content were inappropriate. Herr Jenninger resigned and was replaced by Rita Süssmuth (formerly Minister for Health, Family and Youth Affairs), one of the most respected of CDU politicians.

The fortunes of the CDU continued to be dogged by scandals. The May election in Schleswig-Holstein resulted in the CDU being forced out of the *Land* Government for the first time in 38 years, and the Social Democrats (SPD) won an absolute majority. The former CDU Minister-President, Uwe Barschel, had died in mysterious circumstances in 1987 (see AR 1987, p. 142), following a smear-campaign against his SPD opponent, Björn Engholm, who now headed the SPD Government. In December the ruling CDU in Lower Saxony was thought certain to be brought down by a vote of censure stemming from a casino scandal that had already led to the resignation of the CDU Interior Minister. In the event the CDU was saved—reportedly by an SPD deputy voting on the Government side. Loss of Lower Saxony would have been a severe embarrassment to the federal Government, since it would have deprived it of a majority in the federal upper house, the Bundesrat. In November the long-serving CDU leader in the Rhineland-Palatinate, Bernhard Vogel, was ousted by his own party and promptly resigned as Minister-President. The fact that Herr Vogel was strongly supported by Herr Kohl, himself once head of government in this *Land*, was an indication of the Chancellor's difficulties in leading the CDU.

The sole relief for the Christian Democrats was the result of the March election in Baden-Württemberg, where the incumbent CDU Government retained its parliamentary majority, although it lost its overall majority of votes. Lothar Späth, the capable Minister-President, was seen as a possible successor to Herr Kohl. The Free Democrats performed weakly in this election, as they did in Schleswig-Holstein, where they failed to gain representation. On a federal level, however, the FDP continued to have a prominent profile, largely due to the international stature of the Foreign Minister, Hans-Dietrich Genscher. The FDP was also strengthened by the election of Otto Graf Lambsdorff as its new leader in place of Martin Bangemann, who was appointed to the Commission of the EC. Helmut Haussmann, general secretary of the FDP, replaced Herr Bangemann as Economics Minister.

Coalition wrangling between the CDU and FDP harmed the Government's and Chancellor Kohl's standing. There were open differences between Herr Kohl and Herr Genscher on the question of European monetary union and ideas about the creation of a European central bank. There were also differences concerning proposed reform of the abortion law, the issue of political asylum, and over the controversial tax-reform package due to take effect in 1990. This complex measure would as one effect make income tax less progressive, and it would also reduce the standard rate of income tax to 19 per cent and the highest rate to 53 per cent. In the other direction, many tax allowances were to disappear, and the SPD appeared to benefit from its opposition, since the tax reform might, on balance, adversely affect lower-paid workers. Also the subject of public controversy were the new measures aimed at containing the escalating cost of health provision. Some benefits were reduced and the full costs of treatment for a range of services would no longer be met through the insurance system.

Despite the CDU-FDP coalition's difficulties, it did not seem likely that it would break up before the next federal election scheduled for 1990. Herr Lambsdorff, as the new leader of the FDP, was unlikely to favour a coalition with the SPD, since he strongly adhered to a free-market philosophy. For its part, the SPD enjoyed a revival of its fortunes during 1988, especially with its decisive win in Schleswig-Holstein, and towards the end of the year was running close to the Christian Democrats in the opinion polls. Although it narrowly failed to dismiss the CDU Government in Lower Saxony, the party was confident that it would succeed at the next *Land* election due in 1990. At the federal level, the Minister-President of the Saarland, Oskar Lafontaine, was emerging as the most likely person to be the SPD's Chancellor-candidate at the next federal election in preference to Johannes Rau (who had unsuccessfully contested the 1987 election) and Hans-Jochen Vogel, the federal leader of the SPD. Herr Lafontaine sought to combine ecological issues with the more traditional values of the party, although he encountered opposition from some trade union leaders because of his view that sacrifices might have to be made by better-paid workers in order to compensate for lower economic growth. These and other economic policy controversies raised the possibility that the work currently in progress on a revised long-term SPD programme might not be completed in time for the August 1989 party conference, where its adoption had been envisaged.

At the SPD party conference in August at Münster, a large majority of delegates voted in favour of a new quota system for women. In future they would have to occupy at least 40 per cent of elected party posts and form the same proportion of the SPD's elected representatives at communal, state and federal levels. As one among several moves to modernize the SPD, this reform was intended to recover some of the support lost to the Greens, who had made feminist issues a part of their appeal.

After their strong showing at the 1987 federal election, the Greens experienced a number of problems. One was the extent of the continuing factional dispute between the radical 'fundamentalists' and the more moderate 'realists'. Another was the realization that the SPD would be most unlikely to form an alliance with the Greens and that the latter could become marginalized in the future. Most serious of all were revelations of financial irregularities involving prominent figures in the party, which led to the resignation of the 11-member national executive at the Karlsruhe party conference in December. The scandal affected the Greens particularly because they had been in the forefront of criticism of the other parties for their alleged corrupt financial practices.

Although in the ten years of their existence the Greens had voiced many popular concerns, they appeared to lose momentum in 1988, as shown by their poor results in *Land* elections. However, the issues that had led to their formation in the first place—those relating to the environment and the quality of life—still attracted popular attention. One that caused widespread unease in 1988 was the outbreak of a virus infection affecting the seal population off Germany's North Sea and Baltic coasts, widely believed to result from industrial and household pollution, causing the number of seals to be reduced by half.

Germany's rivers, especially the Rhine and the Elbe, were still heavily polluted, and as far as the Elbe was concerned the federal Government sought to persuade the German Democratic Republic to reduce the level of effluents discharged into the river. In August some 65,000 head of livestock, mainly calves, were slaughtered in North Rhine-Westphalia on the orders of the food authorities after it was found that they contained traces of an illegal hormone preparation. The question of nuclear energy continued to arouse intense debate. In December an 'operational oversight' caused an incident at the Biblis nuclear power station in Hesse, which was temporarily shut down pending an inquiry; at first unreported, the incident led to renewed fears about the safety of such plants.

Of a rather different nature was the catastrophe at an air display at the US Ramstein base on 28 August, which led to the deaths of 70 people and more than 300 being injured. Although unconnected, the Ramstein tragedy came after a number of crashes of Nato aircraft engaged in low-flying training manoeuvres. In all there were 21 crashes of Nato aircraft in West Germany during the year, the worst occurring in December at Remscheid, near Düsseldorf, killing four people and destroying 20 houses. As a result there were demands that such low-flying exercises should be curtailed. But there was also resentment that Allied aircraft were not subject to German controls, and views were expressed that, given the better climate of relationships with the Warsaw Pact countries, such intense activity in face of a declining threat was unnecessary.

More fundamentally, there were various expressions of general anti-Nato sentiment on the grounds that German interests were not best served by what was perceived as the country's subordinate status in the alliance. The most significant of such statements was made in December by Admiral Elmar Schmäling, head of the armed forces' office for studies and exercises. He argued for the removal of all nuclear weapons from both parts of Germany, his comments applying especially to short-range, tactical nuclear weapons which would principally affect the two German states if they were ever used; pointing out that the Federal Republic had no say in the matter, he maintained that it was time to assert German national interests.

Economic forecasts for 1988, made in the shadow of the October 1987 stock market crash, proved to be unduly pessimistic. Especially in the second half of the year, growth in almost all sectors was higher than anticipated. For the year as a whole the level of gross national product rose by about 3.4 per cent. One reason for the marked recovery was the higher demand for capital goods consequent on the investment boom in Western Europe. This demand also accounted for a record export surplus, helped in part by a softening of the DM exchange rate. It was also notable that the export surplus was increasingly based on trade with Western Europe rather than the United States. A further sign of optimism was the

29.3 per cent rise in share prices. At least in comparison with most other countries, the level of consumer prices rose modestly, at under 2 per cent, but that was considerably higher than the previous year (0.2 per cent). The one statistic that was less favourable was that for unemployment, which fell only slightly to 7.6 per cent. One reason was the larger number of women entering the labour market. Since 1983 almost 900,000 new jobs had been created, of which 150,000 became available in 1988.

Traditional industries such as shipbuilding, coal and steel continued to decline. A further 8,500 jobs were lost in deep-coal mining, leaving only 150,000. Fears were expressed about the future of this industry, especially since its decline might mean an over-reliance on nuclear energy. The problems of the steel industry were highlighted by the planned run-down of the plants of Krupp and Mannesmann at Rheinhausen. After five months of protest action on the part of the work-force, a compromise was reached in May to keep one of the ovens working until 1990. In fact, there was a surprising upturn in the demand for steel during the year, so that the immediate crisis was overcome.

One of the most important company mergers in recent times was agreed in November, when Daimler-Benz acquired a 30 per cent stake, eventually to be a majority holding, in MBB, the aerospace group which embraced famous names such as Messerschmidt, Heinkel and Junkers. The new conglomerate thus constituted a significant part of the automobile and truck industry, owned the large electrical firm (AEG), had a stake in European Airbus, and would effectively have control over the West German armaments industry. The Mercedes-Benz trademark, the star, symbolized the new grouping. The merger was opposed in all political parties, since Daimler-Benz was already the largest industrial undertaking in the Federal Republic, it being feared that competition would be undermined.

These serious matters, however, did not concern the West German public too much. Attention was focused on the exploits of the tennis stars: the feat of Steffi Graf in winning the 'grand slam' of three major tournaments and the reinstated Olympic gold medal, and the German team taking the Davis Cup (see Pt. XVII). Tennis had become the most popular sport in the Federal Republic.

ITALY

CAPITAL: Rome AREA: 301,000 sq km POPULATION: 57,200,000 ('86)
OFFICIAL LANGUAGE: Italian POLITICAL SYSTEM: parliamentary democracy
HEAD OF STATE: President Francesco Cossiga (since June '85)
RULING PARTIES: Christian Democratic (DC), Socialist (PSI), Democratic Socialist (PSDI), Republican (PRI) and Liberal (PLI) parties
HEAD OF GOVERNMENT: Ciriaco De Mita (DC), Prime Minister (since April '88)
PRINCIPAL MINISTERS: Gianni De Michelis (PSI/deputy premier), Giulio Andreotti (DC/foreign affairs), Antonio Gava (DC/interior), Giuliano Vassalli (PSI/justice), Amintore Fanfani (DC/budget and economic planning), Emilio Colombo (DC/finance), Valerio Zanone (PLI/defence)
INTERNATIONAL ALIGNMENT: Nato, OECD, EC
CURRENCY: lira (end-'88 £1=Lit2,362, US$1=Lit1,306) GNP PER CAPITA: US$8,550 ('86)
MAIN EXPORTS: machinery and transport equipment, manufactures, chemicals, agricultural products

THE year opened with Giovanni Goria, Prime Minister since August 1987 (see AR 1987, pp. 147–8), already in considerable difficulties. A Christian Democrat, aged 44, he was Italy's youngest-ever Prime Minister. His premiership had followed that of Bettino Craxi (Socialist), whose rule had lasted nearly four years—the longest ever by comparison with normally short-lived Italian Governments. Signor Goria, like Signor Craxi, headed a five-party coalition. It consisted of his own Christian Democrats (still numerically the country's largest party), the Socialist Party (accounting for 14 per cent of the electorate) and three smaller democratic parties, the Democratic Socialists, Republicans and Liberals. Some such coalition had governed Italy throughout most of the post-war years, and seemed the most feasible combination given the country's unwillingness to admit the Communists—at 28.5 per cent the second largest party—into the Government.

Signor Goria's seemed likely to be yet another short-lived Government. He had already attempted to resign in the previous November owing to difficulties over the financing of the 1988 Budget, but President Cossiga had refused to accept his resignation. Problems in relation to the 1988 Budget continued to beset the Government, however. That Budget should in theory have been passed by the end of 1987 but, under cover of secret voting in Parliament, backbenchers siding with the Opposition contrived to throw out numerous items. By early February Signor Goria had been defeated 17 times during debate on the Bill. On 10 February he resigned again, citing political sabotage. But President Cossiga again refused to accept his resignation and told him to go back to Parliament and get the Bill through.

Parliament at last passed the Budget on 10 March, and next day Signor Goria tendered his resignation, as he had virtually undertaken to do once the Budget was out of the way. The ostensible reason for his resignation was the Socialists' opposition on nuclear policy.

President Cossiga on 16 March called on the Christian Democrat secretary, Ciriaco De Mita, to form the new Government. Obviously, much would depend on agreement between the Christian Democrats and the Socialists—which meant in effect between Signors De Mita and Craxi. Personally, they were at loggerheads and always had been. They did, however, share some views, particularly about the need for parliamentary reform to obviate the fiasco of secret voting. But a serious bone of contention was the development of nuclear energy, which the Socialists strongly opposed. A referendum held in November 1987 had come out in favour of limiting development (see AR 1987, p. 148), and in consequence work on Italy's third reactor, at Montalto de Castro, north of Rome, had been suspended.

Signor De Mita, aged 60, a southerner from Avellino, near Naples, had never before been Prime Minister but had served in several Cabinets; as Christian Democrat secretary since 1982 he had striven to steer his party away from its earlier factionalism. An enthusiastic European, he aimed to establish a stable Government that might last until 1992. He took nearly a month to form his Cabinet during which time Signor Craxi remained eminently correct but obviously had to be taken into consideration. So too had the Communists, whose apparent willingness to provide a 'constitutional opposition' and support the Government's programme for institutional reform could, in the more relaxed East-West climate arising from Mr Gorbachev's reforms, be regarded as acceptable. In the new Cabinet announced on 13 April, several Ministers remained unchanged, including the Prime Minister's great rival in his own party, Giulio Andreotti, as Foreign Minister. An innovation was to bring in a non-party technocrat, Antonio Meccanico, chairman of the Milan merchant bank Mediobanca, as Minister for Institutional Reform.

In his programme speech to Parliament on 19 April, Signor De Mita stressed the need for wholesale parliamentary and institutional reforms, mentioned that a revised nuclear policy might include the conversion of the Montalto station to non-nuclear fuel, and referred to the prospect of 'constructive opposition' from the Communists. On 21 April he secured a vote of confidence of 336 to 215 in the Chamber, and on 23 April the Senate did likewise by 177 to 106.

The Government's first test came with local elections on 29–30 May affecting councils in 1,204 towns. The Christian Democrats remained firm at 36.8 per cent of the electorate, whereas the Socialists improved their position, especially in the north, to secure 18.3 per cent. Socialist gains were largely at the expense of the Communists, whose vote fell to 21.9 per cent in a further closing of the gap between Socialist and Communist electoral support. The smaller democratic parties did quite well at around 5 per cent each, but the neo-fascist Italian Social Movement slumped from 6 to 3.9 per cent. Regional elections held a month later, on 26 June, in Venezia Giulia and the Val d'Aosta showed a similar decline for the Communists and improvement for the Socialists in Venezia Giulia and, less markedly, in Val d'Aosta, where the local Val d'Ôtaine party improved its position to secure 34.2 per cent of the total.

The Communists were in fact in a difficult situation, half-preparing to 'come in from the cold' but not yet quite ready to do so. A Communist delegation under the party's then general secretary, Alessandro Natta, had visited Moscow at the end of March and been welcomed by Mr Gorbachev in an atmosphere of reconciliation. But Signor Natta was a sick man, and following a heart attack he offered his resignation in June. The Communist Speaker of the Chamber, Nilde Jotti, in an interview with *The Guardian* (16 June) said that the party had lacked a charismatic leader since the death of Enrico Berlinguer in 1984, and it was in fact a Berlinguer follower, Achille Occhetto, who was appointed to succeed Signor Natta on 21 June. His hope was eventually to draw the Socialists into a left combination, but Signor Craxi preferred to wait until the Communists should be in a weak enough position to make it worth his while.

The most controversial of the Government's proposed institutional reforms, that on the abolition of secret voting in Parliament, reached safe harbour in October after three tense weeks of haggling during which Signor De Mita threatened to resign if open voting were rejected. On 13 October the Chamber—ironically enough in a secret vote—agreed by 323 votes to 58 to overturn the 140-year-old tradition of secret voting, which would henceforth be retained only on certain specified issues. All the opposition parties abstained in the vote, which needed 316 (i.e. half the Chamber plus one) to get through. Most of the 58 voters against came from recalcitrant Christian Democrat backbenchers unwilling to lose their nuisance value.

Roberto Ruffilli (51), a close adviser of Signor De Mita in formulating the plans for institutional reform, was gunned down in Forlì on 16 April, just three days before the Prime Minister laid those plans before Parliament. The Combatant Communist Union, successor of the Red Brigades, claimed responsibility. Most of the original Red Brigade leaders were now in prison, and terrorism was chiefly concentrated in Sicily, where in the last week in September alone it claimed 14 victims of inter-Mafia warfare related to competition for the heroin trade. On 12 January Giuseppe Insalco, an ex-mayor of Palermo, was shot dead in the city by two Mafiosi gunmen. He had been investigating links between politicians and the Mafia. The Anti-Mafia Commission, in suspense during the huge Mafia trial of 1987 (see AR 1987, p. 149), was revived and concentrated such investigations under the Chief Magistrate,

Giovanni Falcone. But on 31 July Signor Falcone asked to resign and to be transferred to the mainland. He had been investigating how the Mafia laundered its drug profits and had regularly come up against a brick wall. His successor, Dr Domenico Sica, was to be given enhanced powers under a package of anti-Mafia measures passed by Parliament in early October

On 11 July, after an 18-month trial, a Bologna court sentenced to life imprisonment four right-wing extremists accused of involvement in the bombing of Bologna station on 3 August 1980 when 85 persons were killed and over 200 injured (see AR 1980, p. 144). A prime mover behind the outrage, Licio Gelli, grand master of the now outlawed 'P-2' masonic lodge (see AR 1981, pp. 147–8), was cleared for lack of evidence of subversive conspiracy but got ten years for trying to mislead the investigators. This mysterious figure, also sought in connection with various financial scandals, had fled to Latin America in 1981 but surrendered in Switzerland in 1987. He was smuggled into Italy on 17 February and lodged in a high-security prison in Parma. He was now free thanks to the Swiss-Italian extradition agreement, which ruled out extradition for political offences (such as the Bologna affair), but would still have to face trial for his part in financial scandals such as the collapse of the Banco Ambrosiano in 1982 (see AR 1982, p. 146).

On the economic side, following the passage of the 1988 Budget, the main problems facing the new Government were the massive public spending deficit and the overweighted public sector. Signor De Mita's programme included immediate plans to cut the public spending deficit by 7,000,000 million lire and a balanced budget by 1992. In this always European-minded country the 1992 single European market looomed large. In some respects, despite the difficulties, Italy was reasonably well-qualified to meet it. Growth rates were high, the inflation rate was around 5 per cent, and tremendous strides had been made in technology, now permeating much of the traditional system, especially in the north, although the economic gap between the north and the more backward south still remained.

Pollution of the coastal waters by industrial and other effluents caused anxiety, and a related problem was the disposal of toxic waste, which some entrepreneurs unsuccessfully attempted to dump in Third World countries. Two freighters, the *Zenobia* and the *Karin B*, turned back from Nigeria and refused admission to Britain and other European countries, spent the year's latter months lying off Genoa and Livorno respectively awaiting unloading. Legislation was rushed through in mid-September banning exports of waste to Third World countries and forcing every region of Italy to accept its own industrial refuse for treatment.

In the external field, Signor De Mita represented Italy at the economic summit conference in Toronto in June and he and Foreign Minister Andreotti went on to Washington to see President Reagan. Italy welcomed the Gulf War ceasefire, Signor Andreotti being one of those who worked behind the scenes to secure acceptance of the truce. The Italian task force in the Gulf was reduced from three to two vessels in August and by the year's end the remaining ships had returned to Italy. The Prime Minister and Signor Andreotti paid a four-day official visit to Moscow from 14 October. They returned increasingly ready to put trust in Mr Gorbachev's reforms, as Signor De Mita made plain at a meeting with Mrs Thatcher in Pallanza on 21 October. Italy was among the countries sending aid to Armenia following the earthquake (see p. 113). President Cossiga paid an official visit to Australia from 10 to 17 October, going on for two days to New Zealand.

Alexander Dubček, former leader of Czechoslovakia, was in Italy from 12 to 25 November and on 14 November received an honorary degree from Bologna University (see also pp. 122–3).

BELGIUM

CAPITAL: Brussels   AREA: 30,500 sq km   POPULATION: 9,900,000 ('86)
OFFICIAL LANGUAGES: French and Flemish
POLITICAL SYSTEM: parliamentary democracy, devolved structure based on language communities
HEAD OF STATE: King Baudouin (since July '51)
RULING PARTIES: Christian People's Party (CVP/Flemish), Christian Social Party (PSC/Walloon), Socialist Party (SP/Flemish), Socialist Party (PS/Walloon), People's Union (VU/Flemish nationalist)
HEAD OF GOVERNMENT: Wilfried Martens (CVP), Prime Minister (since Dec '81)
PRINCIPAL MINISTERS: Philippe Moureaux (PS/deputy premier, Brussels, institutional reform), Willy Claes (SP/deputy premier, economic affairs), Jean-Luc Dehaene (CVP/deputy premier, communications, institutional reform), Melchior Wathelet (PSC/deputy premier, justice), Hugo Schiltz (VU/deputy premier, budget), Léo Tindemans (CVP/foreign affairs), Philippe Maystadt (PSC/finance), Guy Coëme (PS/defence), Louis Tobback (SP/interior)
INTERNATIONAL ALIGNMENT: Nato, OECD, EC, Benelux, Francophonie
CURRENCY: franc (end-'88 £1=BF67.55, US$1=BF37.34)   GNP PER CAPITA: US$9,230 ('86)
MAIN EXPORTS: machinery and transport equipment, chemicals, agricultural products

IN the first four months of the year, several attempts to create a new coalition Government ended in failure. Willy Claes, leader of the Flemish wing of the Socialist Party, whose parliamentary representation had been strengthened in the 1987 general election (see AR 1987, p. 151), sought to create a Socialist-led coalition, but was unable to muster the necessary support. However, he was at least successful in generating a dialogue with the Social Christians, still the largest single grouping and hence a necessary participant in any viable coalition. Then, for a much longer period lasting until early March, Jean-Luc Dehaene, a Social Christian and previously the Minister for Social Affairs, sought to build a framework for a Social Christian/Socialist/Volksunie coalition, but was unable to build a consensus on intercommunal issues, including the next phase of devolution and the problem of French-speaking communities located just inside Flanders. The most difficult problem in all these negotiations was to reconcile the aspirations of the French-speaking wing of the Socialists and the Flemish-speaking wing of the Social Christians.

Ultimately, a centre-left coalition took office in early May after Belgium had been without a Government for nearly 150 days, the country's longest political crisis since World War II. The coalition brought together five parties—the two linguistic wings of the Social Christian and Socialist parties, and the Volksunie (the Flemish nationalist party)—and was again headed by Mr Martens, who had also been Prime Minister of no fewer than seven previous coalitions.

Made possible by prior agreement among the participants on continuation of the existing austerity programme and on a far-reaching plan for regional devolution of political and economic responsibilities, the new Government in theory commanded 150 of the 212 seats in the Chamber. It was on this reckoning more firmly based than its predecessor, which had staggered from crisis to crisis. However, there were severe weaknesses which placed its longer-term survival in doubt: an estimated 40 per cent of Socialist deputies had not fully accepted the agreement; and the need to accommodate representatives of the main power groups meant that the new Cabinet was excessively large, with no fewer than 19 Ministers and 13 Secretaries of State.

In political terms, the commitment to a steady move towards a federal state was the most important distinguishing feature of the new Government. In summary, although central Government was to keep responsibility for foreign affairs, defence, justice, social security and monetary policy, directly-elected regional assemblies were to become responsible for education, culture, most public works and transport, and the environment. And, extremely important, around 30 per cent of total public funds were to be controlled at regional level compared with the 8 per cent of funds hitherto used in this way. The delicate issue of allocating regional shares of money was resolved on the basis of regional shares of national tax collection, but with the relatively poor Wallonia receiving a levelling-up payment from the national budget.

Also of great significance, Brussels was to have its own elected assembly and executive just like the other regions. And French speakers in Flanders were to receive increased local rights. In the Fourons area, where French speakers constituted the majority in a commune situated within Flanders, the boundary was not to be redrawn but people were to be able to vote across the language frontier in national and European elections.

The enormous size of the public debt meant that there was a very limited range of economic policy choices; the new centre-left policies were virtually indistinguishable from the austerity programme of the previous centre-right coalition. The main differences were the outcome of the compromises made necessary by the replacement of the right-wing Liberals by the Socialists. The key areas to be tackled by the new Government were job creation; reducing the fearsome public deficit; fiscal reform; economic restructuring, with the 1992 single European market in view; and democratization of the economy.

The Prime Minister soon persuaded the Socialists of the absolute necessity to curb public spending still further in order to allow the 1989 Budget deficit to be cut to no more than 7 per cent of GDP. For their part, the Socialists, seemingly desperate to avoid living up to their stereotype role of being 'irresponsible spenders', went along with the austerity programme with scarcely a protest. Their eyes were on their longer-term ambition to become the main ruling party, hence their emphasis on financial seriousness.

The financial situation of several major cities, most notably Liège, deteriorated to the point where urgent Government aid became imperative. Their borrowings being in effect guaranteed by the central Government, the cities had built up an enormous level of indebtedness, reaching the point where repayment of interest, let alone principal, was becoming impossible, and the Government risked having to take on over £1,000 million of liabilities for Liège and Brussels alone.

Despite the problems, 1988 was a year of stronger economic growth. Data for industrial production, business investment, construction, personal consumption and foreign trade all showed significant growth, while price rises and unemployment were falling.

THE NETHERLANDS

CAPITAL: Amsterdam   AREA: 34,000 sq km   POPULATION: 14,600,000 ('86)
OFFICIAL LANGUAGE: Dutch   POLITICAL SYSTEM: parliamentary democracy
HEAD OF STATE: Queen Beatrix (since April '80)
RULING PARTIES: Christian Democratic Appeal (CDA), People's Party for Freedom and Democracy (VVD)
HEAD OF GOVERNMENT: Ruud Lubbers (CDA), Prime Minister (since Nov '82)
PRINCIPAL MINISTERS: Rudolf de Korte (VVD/deputy premier, economic affairs), Hans van den Broek (CDA/foreign affairs), Frits Bolkestein (VVD/defence), Herman Ruding (CDA/finance), Cees van Dijk (CDA/interior), Frits Korthals Altes (VVD/justice)
INTERNATIONAL ALIGNMENT: Nato, OECD, EC, Benelux
CURRENCY: guilder (end-'88 £1=f3.62, US$1=f2.00)   GNP PER CAPITA: US$10.020 ('86)
MAIN EXPORTS: oil and gas, machinery and transport equipment, chemicals, agricultural products

WITH the Christian Democrat/Liberal coalition half-way through its term there was a tendency for bickering among members of the Cabinet to displace governmental action addressed towards the important political issues. Exemplifying this situation was the squabble over the design and introduction of a European Community passport to replace the traditional Dutch document. Minister for Defence Wim van Eekelen, who previously had been Deputy Foreign Minister and thus responsible for the new passport, was considered to have bungled its introduction. Such was the heat and emotion generated in the ensuing public debate, leading to the near collapse of the Government, that Mr van Eekelen resigned, together with the current junior Foreign Minister. An important side-effect of these resignations was that the threatened position of the incumbent Foreign Minister, Mr van den Broek, was safeguarded at a crucial moment for the Government.

Other, more important, issues on the political agenda were debated more calmly and included health care, education, unemployment and the environment. On this last issue, the Government defied the European Commission by deciding to pursue its plans to offer a tax credit for smaller and environmentally 'clean' cars, of the kind manufactured by Volvo Nederland, which was 70 per cent state-owned.

Partly in response to more complete European unification in 1992, the Government continued its efforts to introduce economic and social reforms, particularly in the areas of health care, housing, taxation and the deficit in public finances. By June disputes within the coalition about cuts in welfare spending had become extremely acrimonious. Most acutely, the Prime Minister's plans for health care reform were resisted by the right-wing Liberals, the junior partners in the Government, who were demanding higher flat-rate health insurance contributions in order to create scope for cuts in income tax. Mr Lubbers, the Prime Minister, demanded that the Liberals should accept income-linked insurance contributions in order to preserve the 'ability to pay' aspect of the welfare system. While not reaching the point at which the existence of the coalition was threatened, the dispute nevertheless impeded progress towards implementing the reforms which were a core element of the Government's programme.

The 1989 Budget, presented to Parliament on 20 September, set out to reduce taxation and welfare contributions and also ambitiously aimed to improve flagging economic growth, cut unemployment and curb inflation, yet still reduce the budget deficit. Both direct and indirect taxes, as well as corporation taxation, were to be reduced. However, most tax rates remained relatively much higher than the European Community average, and the Prime Minister was at pains to emphasize that the cuts were precursors of others intended to ensure that the Netherlands became more competitively aligned vis-à-vis other EC countries in terms of tax and wage rates, and costs of housing and health care.

General economic performance improved during the year, with industrial production, business investment and foreign trade on a better trend. But unemployment remained stubbornly high and real wages remained flat. Hardly surprisingly, the volume of consumer spending grew by no more than about 1 per cent.

At the beginning of April, a third television channel began operations, covering mainly the arts, information and sport, with an overall emphasis on Dutch culture from programming provided by the state broadcasting corporation and 16 cultural groups. A proposal, very radical by Dutch standards, to create a commercial television channel was rejected by the Government in the autumn, but the debate on opening up television broadcasting continued unabated.

LUXEMBOURG

CAPITAL: Luxembourg   AREA: 2,586 sq km   POPULATION: 367,000 ('86)
OFFICIAL LANGUAGE: Letzeburgish   POLITICAL SYSTEM: parliamentary democracy
HEAD OF STATE: Grand Duke Jean (since Nov '64)
RULING PARTIES: Christian Social People's Party (CSV) and Luxembourg Socialist Workers' Party (LSAP)
HEAD OF GOVERNMENT: Jacques Santer (CSV), Prime Minister (since July '84)
PRINCIPAL MINISTERS: Jacques Poos (LSAP/deputy premier, foreign affairs), Jean Spautz (CVS/interior), Robert Krieps (LSAP/justice and environment)
INTERNATIONAL ALIGNMENT: Nato, OECD, EC, Benelux, Francophonie
CURRENCY: franc (end-'88 £1=LF67.40, US$1=LF37.26)   GNP PER CAPITA: US$15,770 ('86)
MAIN EXPORTS: basic manufactures, machinery and transport equipment

GOVERNMENT policies emphasized stability and continuity. The 1988 Budget took a cautious approach, aiming at a larger surplus than in previous years as expenditure was reined back, but business benefited from a cut in corporation tax. The economy performed well overall, with the trend in most indicators clearly favourable. Industrial production, excluding steel, rose strongly, though the troubled steel industry itself made only limited progress as ECSC output quotas were ended during the second half of the year. It was clear that Luxembourg's steel industry still tended to have a secondary role compared with other EC producers, making it especially vulnerable to cyclical fluctuation in the main markets. Public investment increased sharply notwithstanding the slower expansion in overall government spending, but capital spending by business appeared to have weakened.

Although the aftermath of the October 1987 crash in financial markets affected Luxembourg, successful official efforts to create a favourable environment, in terms of taxation, banking secrecy and minimal restrictions on fund management, helped to sustain the Grand Duchy's competitive position and earnings vis-à-vis other international financial centres. The extreme flexibility of the authorities' approach to income generation was demonstrated by maturing plans to create a Luxembourg shipping register, intended to provide European shipowners with a respectable alternative, in a landlocked country, to the more usual convenience registers.

REPUBLIC OF IRELAND

CAPITAL: Dublin   AREA: 70,280 sq km   POPULATION: 3,600,000 ('86)
OFFICIAL LANGUAGES: Irish and English   POLITICAL SYSTEM: parliamentary democracy
HEAD OF STATE: President Patrick Hillery (since Dec '76)
RULING PARTY: Fianna Fáil
HEAD OF GOVERNMENT: Charles Haughey, Prime Minister (since March '87)
PRINCIPAL MINISTERS: Brian Lenihan (deputy premier, foreign affairs), Albert Reynolds (finance), Gerard Collins (justice), Ray Burke (communications, industry and commerce), Michael J. Noonan (defence)
INTERNATIONAL ALIGNMENT: neutral, OECD, EC
CURRENCY: punt (end-'88 £1=IR£1.20, US$1=IR£0.66)   GNP PER CAPITA: US$5,070 ('86)
MAIN EXPORTS: machinery and electronic equipment, agricultural products

IT was a remarkably successful year for the Irish economy, notably in that inflation was held at 2 per cent and Government borrowing kept down to 4 per cent of GNP as against the 8 per cent projected in the January Budget. Many other indices suggested that the country had begun at last to emerge from recession. Interest rates remained steady at 8 per cent. Exports increased by 10 per cent. Receipts from tourism went up by a similar figure, despite a fall in the number of trans-Atlantic visitors, and the value of domestic shares on the Dublin stock exchange rose by over 35 per cent.

Among the factors contributing to this outcome was the recovery of IR£500 million through an amnesty for tax defaulters who paid their arrears by a given date: only IR£30 million had been anticipated from this source. A self-assessment scheme for self-employed income-tax payers stimulated what promised to be a more permanent form of revenue buoyancy. Membership of the European Monetary System (EMS) protected the punt (the Irish pound) from the difficulties besetting sterling, as reflected in high British interest rates and a more sluggish increase in share values on the London stock exchange. While the volume of Irish economic activity was naturally very small by comparison with that of the United Kingdom, the escape from traditional thraldom to British interest rates and share movements brought a boost in business morale, consumer spending, investment and property prices.

The opposition Fine Gael and Progressive Democrat parties

supported the principal economic measures proposed by the minority Fianna Fail Government led by Charles Haughey. Without opposition approval, the Taoiseach (Prime Minister) and his Finance Minister, Ray MacSharry, could not have maintained their unyielding policy of spending cuts which exacerbated the existing deficiencies in the hospital services and education (see AR 1987, p. 155) and caused much sectional complaint. A more broadly-based criticism, growing louder as the year drew to its close, concerned the overall tendency of economic policy. As the favourable upturn became apparent, it was seen to favour investors, established businesses and trade unionists holding secure jobs. No corresponding improvement took place in the country's major problems of unemployment and emigration. Unemployment remained at the crisis level of 18 per cent. Emigration continued at the rate of 30,000 a year and consisted in large part of young professsional people whose expertise would be needed in a growth situation.

In a report on poverty in Ireland, based on a survey commissioned from the prestigious Economic and Social Research Institute, the state-appointed Combat Poverty Agency went far towards confirming the suspicion that the improvements in the economy effectively represented a better ordering of their affairs by the already wealthy or well-provided-for sections of the community rather than a genuine national recovery from recession. The Agency found that, by standard European measurements, about one-third of the Republic's population was living in poverty and that this was directly related to the numbers unemployed or working in low-paid jobs. Among its recommendations for coping with the problem, the Agency advised that economic policy should be restructured so that measures to reduce poverty and unemployment could receive equal priority with measures to reduce the national debt, that social welfare payments should be substantially increased and that, in order to facilitate such reforms, the extra resources now becoming available should be used to secure a more equitable distribution of wealth rather than to facilitate cuts in taxation.

These views had the support of disparate elements of opinion in the country, including the left-of-centre Labour and Workers' parties in Parliament, various voluntary agencies and, in particular, the Roman Catholic Church. Through statements by a number of bishops, the influential Conference of Major Religious Superiors and its own welfare organizations, the Church maintained a consistent critique of establishment economic theory throughout the year. By Christmas talk was being heard of the need to form a radical front of left-wing politicians, socially-concerned citizens and the Church to promote an 'option for the poor'. Given the pressure of high taxes on the not-very-wealthy middle and working classes, a dilemma could be seen looming for the Government in the coming year when, despite the improvement in its finances, it would be unable to satisfy all the mutually-contradictory demands to which it was being subjected.

Anglo-Irish relations came under severe strain in 1988. The news in January that the British Attorney-General, Sir Patrick Mayhew, had decided for reasons of national security that no prosecutions of police officers would be undertaken in Northern Ireland following the Stalker-Sampson inquiry into a 'shoot-to-kill' policy allegedly operated by the Royal Ulster Constabulary (see AR 1987, pp. 40–1, 47 and 148) was received with dismay in the Republic. The rejection in the same month of the appeal by the 'Birmingham Six' against their conviction in 1975 for bombing offences (see AR 1987, pp. 156–7) compounded the popular impression that the British system of justice could not be relied upon to deal fairly with cases related to the situation in Northern Ireland.

February brought an announcement that the Prevention of Terrorism Act, much criticized in Ireland, was to be made permanent in Britain. About the same time, Government sources in Dublin claimed that the British authorities were not conforming to Irish procedures in extradition cases. At an EC meeting in Brussels Mr Haughey told Mrs Thatcher that relations between Britain and Ireland were 'at an impasse', while at home he spoke about the difficulties of maintaining security co-operation with British forces in the prevailing circumstances. The release after little more than two years' imprisonment of a British soldier found guilty of murder in a Northern Ireland shooting incident made matters even worse, not because Irish public opinion objected to clemency for a young man who could be said to have made a serious error of judgment but because no such clemency was forthcoming for socially-deprived young people imprisoned in Northern Ireland for behaviour no more blameworthy.

Against this background it was inevitable that further tension should have followed the shooting of a civilian by a border-post sentry in County Tyrone and of three IRA members, thought to have been on a bombing mission, by the SAS in Gibraltar (see pp. 187–8). The atrocity during a subsequent funeral in Belfast, when two British soldiers were brutally killed, reawakened a sense of common purpose between Dublin and London for a time. Contacts between police chiefs were resumed, an emergency session of the ministerial Anglo-Irish Conference took place on security and Irish extradition procedures were complied with on the British side. Irish public opinion, however, again became disenchanted when a verdict of guilty was returned in the case of three young Irish persons accused at Winchester of conspiracy to murder Tom King, Secretary of State for Northern Ireland. It was popularly felt that the evidence presented at the trial justified neither the verdict nor the 25-year sentences imposed.

In November an Irish priest, Father Patrick Ryan, was returned to the country from Belgium following the rejection by the Belgian Cabinet of a British request for his extradition on charges related to terrorism. A similar request was sent to Ireland where, under Irish law, the warrants supporting the application were examined by the Attorney-General, John Murray. While this process was in train Mrs Thatcher, irked by the fact that Father Ryan had not been taken into custody in Ireland, made highly critical remarks in the House of Commons about the Irish commitment to combating terrorism, in which she was supported with varying degrees of vehemence by other MPs. Elements of the British press added their own condemnation of the Irish Government and of Father Ryan. Mr Murray decided that, in view of the comments in the UK Parliament and media, a fair trial could not be guaranteed in Britain and accordingly that the request for extradition should be refused. He added that some of the charges raised questions that called for an answer and he recommended that the British authorities should seek to have proceedings initiated in the Republic under the Criminal Law Jurisdiction Act of 1976, which permitted persons charged with certain offences in one jurisdiction to be tried in the other. At year's end no decision had been reported from London as to whether this advice would be accepted and implemented.

The episode blew apart whatever goodwill remained in official Anglo-Irish relations, especially when Mrs Thatcher described the Irish Attorney-General's decision as an insult to the British people and said that he had no powers under the most recent Irish legislation to refuse extradition because he believed the possibility of a fair trial had been prejudiced. Her attitude was widely regarded in Ireland as unacceptably intemperate. She also appeared to be ill-informed on Irish law regarding powers of arrest and the authority, independent of Government, enjoyed by the Attorney-General which is provided for in the constitution, in Supreme Court judgments and another Act of Parliament as well as the statute to which she referred.

Mr Haughey's public comments both at home and after he met Mrs Thatcher at an EC meeting in Rhodes were restrained. Other politicians of all parties as well as the Irish media were more outspoken. Although doubts were expressed whether the Attorney-General had been wise to make a quasi-judicial decision even if his right to do so could not be challenged, nobody doubted that the High Court would have refused extradition on the same grounds as Mr Murray: Irish judges had always adopted a stern line on public statements and press publicity which might prejudice a jury. Be that as it may, Mrs Thatcher's complaint that Irish extradition arrangements were faulty was answered before Christmas by a parliamentary resolution making these arrangements permanent.

The Minister for Finance, Ray MacSharry, was appointed to the Irish seat on the incoming EC Commission in November and given responsibility for agriculture and rural affairs. Despite tentative indications of interest on both sides and much encouragement by the media, no meeting took place during the year between Mr Haughey and James Molyneaux, leader of the Ulster Unionist party. After a succession of bids, counter-bids, court proceedings and applications to the European Commission, the French firm of Pernod-Ricard defeated the Grand Metropolitan group in its bid to secure control of Irish Distillers, the firm making all major brands of Irish whiskey. An Independent Broadcasting Commission was set up to supervise the establishment of local radio stations as well as national radio and television channels outside the public service system of Radio Telefis Eireann. The former Foreign Minister and winner of the Nobel and Lenin peace prizes, Sean MacBride, died in January (see OBITUARY).

Chapter 2

DENMARK—ICELAND—NORWAY—SWEDEN—FINLAND—
AUSTRIA—SWITZERLAND

DENMARK

CAPITAL: Copenhagen   AREA: 43,000 sq km   POPULATION: 5,116,000 ('86)
OFFICIAL LANGUAGE: Danish   POLITICAL SYSTEM: parliamentary democracy
HEAD OF STATE: Queen Margrethe II (since Jan '72)
RULING PARTIES: Conservative People's Party (KF), Venstre Liberals (V), Radical Liberals (RV)
HEAD OF GOVERNMENT: Poul Schlüter (KF), Prime Minister (since Sept '82)
PRINCIPAL MINISTERS: Uffe Ellemann-Jensen (V/foreign affairs), Palle Simonsen (KF/finance), Niels Helveg Petersen (RV/economic affairs), Erik Ninn-Hansen (KF/justice), Knud Enggard (V/defence), Thor Pedersen (V/interior, Nordic affairs)
INTERNATIONAL ALIGNMENT: NATO, OECD, EC, Nordic Council
CURRENCY: krone (end-'88 £1=DKr12.41, US$1=DKr6.86)   GNP PER CAPITA: US$12,600 ('86)
MAIN EXPORTS: agricultural produce, machinery and transport equipment, manufactures

BY January disagreements between Poul Schlüter's minority centre-right coalition and the opposition majority in the Folketing (Social Democrats, Radical Liberals, Socialist People's Party and Common Course) had led to an impasse in negotiations for a new four-year defence budget. While the Government proposed a real increase in defence spending, the opposition would agree only to compensation for inflation and wage rises. The defence budget impasse, coming on top of a series of parliamentary defeats for the Government on security issues, posed the question of how far Denmark's deviation from Nato policies could be taken without putting the country's continued alliance membership at risk.

For Mr Schlüter that point came on 14 April, when the opposition passed a resolution requiring the Government to inform all visiting naval vessels that Denmark did not accept nuclear weapons on its territory in peacetime. This broke with the previous practice of assuming that allied warships respected Denmark's restrictions and conflicted with the UK and US policy of refusing to confirm or deny that their vessels were carrying nuclear weapons. Mr Schlüter declared that the resolution jeopardized Denmark's Nato membership by threatening plans for seaborne reinforcements. The US and UK Governments postponed all planned naval visits to Danish waters and the US Secretary of State spoke of serious consequences for US-Danish relations.

On 19 April Mr Schlüter called an election for 10 May on the issue of Denmark's continued full participation in Nato. The election failed to produce a clear mandate for either the Government or the opposition. There were losses for both the pro-Nato Conservatives and anti-Nato Socialist People's Party and Common Course. The election's clear winner, the Progress Party, while recently supporting the Government's pro-Nato line, was principally concerned with domestic issues of lower taxation and immigration. The results were as follows, with September 1987 results in brackets:

	% of votes	seats
Conservatives	19.3 (20.8)	35 (38)
Liberals	11.9 (10.5)	22 (19)
Centre Democrats	4.7 (4.8)	9 (9)
Christian People's Party	2.0 (2.4)	4 (4)
Radical Liberals	5.6 (6.2)	10 (11)
Progress Party	9.0 (4.8)	16 (9)
Social Democrats	29.9 (29.3)	55 (54)
Socialist People's Party	13.0 (14.6)	24 (27)
Common Course	1.9 (2.2)	0 (4)
Others (Left Socialists, Communists, Greens)	2.7 (3.8)	0 (0)
Greenland and Faeroes	–	4 (4)
	100.0	179

Mr Schlüter's centre-right coalition still had 70 seats. The key to the negotiations lay with the Radical Liberals, holding the balance between the coalition parties and left-wing parties. They wanted a broad majority coalition but would not accept the new Social Democratic leader, Svend Auken, as Prime Minister. In the subsequent protracted negotiations, they supported first the Social Democratic Speaker of the Folketing, Svend Jacobsen, and then their own leader, Niels Helveg Pedersen, in their successive attempts to establish a viable coalition consensus. When both had failed to secure support for a majority coalition, the Radical Liberals transferred their support to Mr Schlüter. On 20 May he began negotiations with the aim of at last bringing the Radical Liberals into government and thereby breaking up the opposition majority on security policy.

On 3 June Mr Schlüter formed a new coalition of Conservatives, Liberals and Radical Liberals. Under the coalition agreement, the defence budget would be frozen until 1990, when a commission would report on future requirements. A compromise on allied warship visits, acceptable to Denmark's allies, provided that each time permission was granted for a warship to enter Danish waters the embassy in question would be sent a general reminder that the ship must respect Danish laws but containing no specific mention of nuclear weapons. The new coalition, with only 67 seats in Parliament, had to rely on shifting support to pass its legislation. Perhaps most significant for the future was its agreement with the Progress Party in June on the passage of measures to relieve Denmark's heavily indebted farmers. Mr Schlüter described their attitude as 'realistic' and as holding out hope of further cooperation in the future.

On 31 August the Government presented its draft Finance Bill. The top priority was to eliminate the current account deficit. Expenditure in 1989 was to be at the 1988 level, and cut by 1 per cent in 1990, without increasing the tax burden. This involved cutting various welfare payments, higher health charges, and cuts in the public sector workforce. Presenting the Government's programme on 4 October, Mr Schlüter warned that the only solution to Denmark's economic problems was a cutback in the public sector and welfare state, the encouragement of private enterprise and social flexibility, and a freeze on wage rises. He threatened resignation if the opposition vetoed his proposals for containing the welfare budget. The Finance Bill was passed in the Folketing on 15 December with the support of the Christian Democrats and Christian People's Party, the Social Democrats abstaining.

ICELAND

CAPITAL: Reykjavik AREA: 103,000 sq km POPULATION: 243,000 ('86)
OFFICIAL LANGUAGE: Icelandic POLITICAL SYSTEM: parliamentary democracy
HEAD OF STATE: President Vigdis Finnbogadóttir (since Aug '80)
RULING PARTIES: Progressive Party (PP), Social Democrats (SDP), People's Alliance (PA) and Equality and Social Justice Association
HEAD OF GOVERNMENT: Steingrimur Hermannsson (PP), Prime Minister (since Sept '88)
PRINCIPAL MINISTERS: Jón Baldvin Hannibalsson (SDP/foreign affairs and trade), Olafur Ragnar Grimsson (PA/finance), Halldór Asgrimsson (PP/justice and fisheries), Jón Sigurthsson (SDP/commerce, industry and Nordic cooperation)
INTERNATIONAL ALIGNMENT: Nato, OECD, Efta, Nordic Council
CURRENCY: króna (end-'88 £1=ISK83.19, US$1=ISK45.99) GNP PER CAPITA: US$13,410 ('86)
MAIN EXPORTS: fish and fish products

FACED by rising inflation and worsening terms of trade, Thorsteinn Pálsson's coalition of the Independence Party, Progressives and Social Democrats tried to maintain its anti-inflation policy based on a balanced budget and maintaining the value of the króna. However, with mounting losses for Iceland's vital fish exporters due to a falling US dollar and rising domestic costs, the Government was forced to undertake two devaluations (by 6 per cent on 29 February and 10 per cent on 16 May), accompanied each time by measures to help the hard-hit fishing industry.

During the summer it became clear that these measures had not solved the fish exporters' problems, while inflation worsened. On 27 August the Government introduced a one-month price and wage freeze while it decided on more long-term measures. Coalition disagreements worsened during September, reaching a head on 16 September when the Progressives and Social Democrats rejected the Prime Minister's proposals for further anti-inflation measures. On 17 September Mr Palsson handed in his Government's resignation. On 28 September the Progressive leader, Steingrimur Hermannsson, formed a coalition of his own party, the Social Democrats, People's Alliance and the Association of Equality and Social Justice, supported by 32 of the Althing's 63 members. On the day it took office the Government devalued the króna by a further 3 per cent, and issued a provisional law which extended the price and wage freeze until February 1989. It also announced a cut in interest rates, new taxes and subsidies for export industries.

On 25 June President Vigdis Finnbogadóttir was re-elected for a third four-year term of office. Backed by all the major parties, she won 92.7 per cent of the vote against 5.3 per cent for Mrs Sigrun Thorstensdóttir (Humanist Party), while 2 per cent of the ballots were blank or invalid.

NORWAY

CAPITAL: Oslo AREA: 324,000 sq km POPULATION: 4,200,000 ('86)
OFFICIAL LANGUAGE: Norwegian POLITICAL SYSTEM: parliamentary democracy
HEAD OF STATE: King Olav V (since Sept '57)
RULING PARTY: Labour Party (minority)
HEAD OF GOVERNMENT: Gro Harlem Brundtland, Prime Minister (since May '86)
PRINCIPAL MINISTERS: Thorvald Stoltenberg (foreign affairs), Gunnar Berge (finance), Johan Jørgen Holst (defence), Helen Bøsterud (justice), Arne Øien (petroleum)
INTERNATIONAL ALIGNMENT: Nato, OECD, Efta, Nordic Council
CURRENCY: krone (end-'88 £1=NKr11.88, US$1=NKr6.57) GNP PER CAPITA: US$15,400 ('86)
MAIN EXPORTS: oil and gas, machinery and transport equipment, manufactures, chemicals, fish

As 1988 opened the minority Labour Government of Gro Harlem Brundtland was still struggling with the effects of the 1986 oil price collapse and an overheated economy. Interest rates of 17 per cent had curbed consumer spending. The danger was of high wage settlements further pushing up inflation. On 29 February the Government, supported by the central blue-collar union organization, imposed a temporary freeze on wages and prices to allow time for legislation limiting wage rises to 5 per cent. The limit assumed price rises of no more than 5 per cent in 1988 and was accompanied by a package of improvements to pensions, maternity leave and mortgage rates. The legislation passed the Storting in April with the support of the Centre Party and Christian People's Party and would remain in force until March 1989.

The political impact was immediate. Labour's public opinion poll ratings fell sharply, from nearly 37 per cent in December 1987 to 27 per cent in April; support for Mrs Brundtland fell too. Yet this did not benefit the largest opposition party, the Conservatives, now under the leadership of Jan P. Syse, elected to replace Rolf Presthus following the latter's sudden death on New Year's Day. The main beneficiary of voter dissatisfaction was the right-wing Progress Party led by Carl I. Hagen. From 3.7 per cent of the national vote in September 1985 and 12.2 per cent in the September 1987 local elections, the party reached 24 per cent in an opinion poll taken immediately after its televised national conference in April. Advocating a policy of lower taxes, privatization and tighter immigration, Progress claimed to represent the 'small man' against the over-class of politicians and bureaucrats. With the Centre Party and Christian People's Party increasingly acting as unofficial supporters of Labour's economic policies, the prospect of renewed cooperation between these parties and the Conservatives was poor. The Conservatives no longer ruled out cooperation with Progress. Indeed, at the local level the parties were already working together despite significant policy differences at national level.

On 6 June the Government published its medium-term defence plan for 1989–93. This proposed a reduction in the annual real growth of defence expenditure from 3.5 per cent in the previous five year period to 2 per cent. Norway's dramatically altered economic outlook was given as the reason for the need to cut costs and to rationalize defence activity.

On 13 June Mrs Brundtland made the first major Cabinet changes since 1986. Three Ministers changed departments, three left the Government and three entered it. Over half of Mrs Brundtland's Ministers were still women. On 10 May the Storting passed a major reform of the electoral law, introducing for the next election in 1989 eight 'equalization' seats for which parties gaining over 4 per cent of the national vote were eligible. The number of Storting seats was thus raised from 157 to 165. On 5 June the Liberal Party and the Liberal People's Party agreed to re-unite under the former name after a split which had lasted 16 years caused by the referendum on European Community membership in 1972.

On 4 October the Government presented its 1989 Budget. This forecast a decline in the current-account deficit from an estimated NKr 17,500 million in 1988 to NKr 11,000 in 1989, and a small budget surplus despite the fall in oil revenue. It allowed for a real growth of Government spending of 3.5 per cent and no increase in direct taxation. The Government's 1988–89 programme called for a continuation of incomes policy, with a 4 per cent wage increase to compensate for a projected 4 per cent inflation rate. The budget projections were based on a forecast 1989 oil price of $14.30 a barrel.

The forecasts for the oil price and inflation were soon proved over-optimistic, however. In October oil prices dropped to $11–12 a barrel. Also in October came clear evidence that 1988 consumer prices would rise by more than 5 per cent, and the unions called for a reopening of wage negotiations. By mid-November low oil prices and a falling US dollar were putting pressure on the krone and keeping interest rates high.

Nevertheless, Mrs Brundtland's Government looked secure. The Conservatives and their former non-socialist allies were divided over the EC, taxation and incomes policy. In August the Conservatives' programme committee included a commitment to EC membership in the 1989 manifesto. The Centre and Christian People's party helped vote the Government's tax proposals through the Storting and maintained their backing for an incomes policy. By November the Progress Party's opinion poll ratings had fallen to 8 per cent, with both Labour and the Conservatives regaining support.

SWEDEN

CAPITAL: Stockholm   AREA: 450,000 sq km   POPULATION: 8,400,000 ('86)
OFFICIAL LANGUAGE: Swedish   POLITICAL SYSTEM: parliamentary democracy
HEAD OF STATE: King Carl XVI Gustav (since Sept. '73)
RULING PARTY: Social Democratic Party (minority)
HEAD OF GOVERNMENT: Ingvar Carlsson, Prime Minister (since March '86)
PRINCIPAL MINISTERS: Sten Andersson (foreign affairs), Roine Carlsson (defence), Kjell-Olof Feldt (finance), Laila Freivalds (justice), Ivar Nordberg (industry)
INTERNATIONAL ALIGNMENT: neutral, OECD, Efta, Nordic Council
CURRENCY: krona (end-'88 £1=SKr11.08, US$1=SKr6.12)   GNP PER CAPITA: US$13,160 ('86)
MAIN EXPORTS: machinery and transport equipment, timber and wood products, iron and steel

THE Swedish economy entered election year 1988 still performing well. But rising domestic costs were again undermining international competitiveness and labour shortages were putting pressure on wages and a brake on industrial production. The spring wage settlements averaged 7 per cent, while Sweden's export industries were hit by a three-week strike of clerical and technical staff in January and February. By May inflation was nearly 7 per cent.

On 26 January the Moderates (Conservatives), Liberals and Centre Party presented a joint family policy which proposed tax deductions for expenses incurred on child care as an alternative to the Social Democrats' policy of expanding public provision of nursery places. However, the electoral appeal of the bourgeois parties was undermined by unresolved differences over such important issues as nuclear energy, defence, tax reform and relations with the European Community.

According to public opinion polls, Swedish voters attached highest priority to environmental issues, highlighted by the Chernobyl disaster of 1986 and the fatal epidemic among seals along Sweden's western coast in the summer. The main beneficiary of this public concern was the Green Party, founded in 1981, which according to the spring polls was set to cross the 4 per cent threshold and enter the Riksdag with 30 to 40 seats. The minority Social Democratic Government of Ingvar Carlsson was also active on environmental issues. In March it announced plans to speed up the closure of Sweden's nuclear reactors and published plans for stricter anti-pollution controls. In May it announced funding for an international environmental institute based in Stockholm. With the economy performing well and the bourgeois parties divided, the main threats to its retaining power were the possibility that its Left Communist allies might poll below the 4 per cent threshold and the series of scandals associated with the unsuccessful investigation into the murder in 1986 of Olof Palme (see AR 1986, pp 154-5). In early June yet another one broke when it became known that the Justice Minister, Anna-Greta Leijon, had authorized a private investigation by a Social Democratic friend, Ebbe Carlsson, including contacts with foreign intelligence services. Mrs Leijon was forced to resign on 7 June. On 16 December a Swedish man appeared in court charged with the murder of Olof Palme.

The results of the general election (held on 18 September) were as follows, with changes from 1985 in brackets:

	% of votes	seats
Social Democrats	43.7 (−1.3)	156 (− 3)
Left Communists	5.9 (+0.5)	21 (+ 2)
Moderates	18.3 (−3.0)	66 (−10)
Liberals	12.2 (−2.1)	44 (− 7)
Centre	11.4 (+1.5)	42 (− 1)
Christian Democrats	3.0 (+0.4)	0 (− 1)
Greens	5.5 (+4.1)	20 (+20)
	100.0	349

The Social Democrats returned to office with three less seats but, with Left Communist support, a majority over all other opposition parties. The Greens entered the Riksdag as forecast but failed to obtain the balance between right and left. The Centre Party did well, the Moderates and Liberals badly, the cooperation between the three parties looked increasingly frayed as the Centre distanced itself from the other two, emphasizing its character as an environmentalist party. Indeed, observers were increasingly replacing the right-left analysis of Swedish politics by a three-block division into left (Social Democrats and Left Communists), Green (Left Communists again, Greens and Centre), and right (Moderates and Liberals).

On 4 October Mr Carlsson presented his Government's programme. Marginal income tax rates would be cut by 3 per cent in 1989 as the first step in a major tax reform, details of which would be published later. He also promised longer holidays and parental leave, higher energy taxes, and closer cooperation with the EC. On 23 October the Finance Minister, Mr Feldt, outlined proposals to encourage competition and personal enterprise and savings. These included tax incentives for small businesses and measures to alleviate labour shortages, for example by easing the entry of foreign workers. In early November the Government gave its support to the abolition of exchange controls over the years to 1991 and to the further deregulation of the financial system. On 23 November the Government published details of its tax reform. State income tax would be sharply reduced, freeing most Swedes from income tax after 1991, and reducing the top marginal rate to 60 per cent. However, local taxes would remain and indirect taxes extended.

The impact on Sweden of the EC's completion of its internal

market in 1992 was a major concern of the country's political and economic leaders. In May Mr Carlsson toured EC capitals. High-level committees were established to monitor EC developments and plan Sweden's response. The proposals to abolish exchange controls and open Sweden's labour market were steps in the strategy of moving in the same direction as the EC prior to 1992.

FINLAND

CAPITAL: Helsinki   AREA: 338,000 sq km   POPULATION: 4,900,000 ('86)
OFFICIAL LANGUAGES: Finnish and Swedish
POLITICAL SYSTEM: presidential and parliamentary democracy
HEAD OF STATE: President Mauno Koivisto (since Sept '81)
RULING PARTIES: National Coalition (KK), Social Democratic (SSDP), Swedish People's (SFP) and Rural (SMP) parties
HEAD OF GOVERNMENT: Harri Holkeri (KK), Prime Minister (since April '87)
PRINCIPAL MINISTERS: Kalevi Sorsa (SSDP/deputy premier, foreign affairs), Matti Louekoski (SSDP/justice), Jarmo Rantanen (SSDP/interior), Ole Norrback (SFP/defence), Erkki Liikanen (SSDP/finance)
INTERNATIONAL ALIGNMENT: neutral, OECD, Efta, Nordic Council
CURRENCY: markka (end- '88 £1=Fmk7.52, US$1=Fmk4.15)   GNP PER CAPITA: US$12.160 ('86)
MAIN EXPORTS: timber and wood products, manufactures, machinery and transport equipment

ON 31 January and 1 February Finland held its first presidential election under a new two-stage, semi-direct system. In the first stage voters cast two votes, one for a presidential candidate, the other for a member of the electoral college which would choose the President if no candidate obtained over 50 per cent of the first ballot. The results were as follows:

	% direct votes	Electors
Mauno Koivisto (Social Democrats)	47.9	144
Paavo Väyrynen (Centre)	20.2	68
Harri Holkeri (Conservatives)	18.1	63
Kalevi Kivistö (left alliance)	10.4	26
Jouko Kajanoja (minority Communists)	1.4	0
		301

In the second stage, on 15 February, the incumbent, President Mauno Koivisto, won on the second vote, when 45 of Prime Minister Holkeri's electors followed the party recommendation and transferred their support to him. The result was: Mr Koivisto 189, Mr Väyrynen 68, Mr Kivistö 26 and Mr Holkeri 18. President Koivisto began his second term of office on 1 March.

Mr Holkeri's coalition of Conservatives, Social Democrats, Swedish People's Party and Rural Party, in office since April 1987 (see AR 1987, pp. 168-9), continued to prepare its contentious reforms of Finland's tax system and employment legislation. In line with the trend in other Western economies, the proposed tax reform aimed to simplify the system and encourage enterprise by cutting the rates of income tax and corporation tax, while broadening the tax base through the progressive abolition of special allowances and exceptions. Agreement was reached on the broad principles of the reform in the spring. Implementation began with the 1989 budget, published in September, which cut the top rates of income tax from 51 per cent to 44 per cent. The employment law reforms, published on 18 March, gave employees a legal right to negotiations in any major changes affecting their companies and longer notice before dismissal. The Government's programme of partial privatization of some state-owned companies began in October with Valmet, followed by Outokumpu and Finnair. The Government retained its majority stake in each company.

The annual wage round was concluded in March without conflicts, but the relatively high rises increased inflationary pressures. Inflation at 6 per cent and a widening current-account deficit were forecast for 1989. On 3 May the Bank of Finland raised base interest rates by 1 per cent. On 23 August the Government reached a 'stabilization agreement' on wages with the employers' and unions' central organizations. This consisted of a package of measures which would provide a 2.5 per cent increase in real incomes in 1989 through tax concessions and a nominal wage increase of 1 per cent. The Bank of Finland promised to lower interest rates in January 1989 if all unions adhered to the recommended measures and the economic situation did not deteriorate further.

Also in September Finland and the USSR agreed on measures to reduce Finland's large bilateral trade surplus, a result of the declining value of Soviet oil exports. They agreed to modernize their trading relations, hitherto based on barter transactions, by introducing arrangements to correct structural imbalances and providing for the use of hard currencies and credit. In 1988 West Germany replaced the USSR as Finland's largest export market, trade with the USSR having declined from 26 per cent of Finland's external trade in 1983 to under 15 per cent.

The local elections on 16-18 October provided a vote of confidence in the coalition's performance. The Social Democrats won 25.3 per cent of the vote, improving on their performance in the last local and national elections. The Conservatives maintained their position with 22.9 per cent of the vote. The opposition Centre Party also did well, polling 21.2 per cent of the vote, but not well enough to encourage hopes of a return to power before the next election.

In April the Government decided to apply for full membership of the Council of Europe, in which Finland already enjoyed observer status. At the end of May President Reagan spent three days in Finland on his way to the Moscow summit. While there he met President Koivisto and addressed the Paasikivi Society.

AUSTRIA

CAPITAL: Vienna   AREA: 84,000 sq km   POPULATION: 7,600,000 ('86)
OFFICIAL LANGUAGE: German   POLITICAL SYSTEM: federal parliamentary democracy
HEAD OF STATE: President Kurt Waldheim (since July '86)
RULING PARTIES: Socialist (SPÖ) and People's (ÖVP) parties
HEAD OF GOVERNMENT: Franz Vranitzky (SPÖ), Federal Chancellor (since June '86)
PRINCIPAL MINISTERS: Alois Mock (ÖVP/Vice-Chancellor, foreign affairs), Ferninand Lacina (SPÖ/finance), Karl Blecha (SPÖ/interior), Robert Lichal (ÖVP/defence), Egmont Foregger (non-party/justice)
INTERNATIONAL ALIGNMENT: neutral, OECD, Efta
CURRENCY: schilling (end-'88 £1=Sch22.55, US$1=Sch12.47)   GNP PER CAPITA: US$9,990 ('86)
MAIN EXPORTS: basic manufactures, machinery and transport equipment, chemicals

THE year began with President Waldheim's war record still the subject of intense international speculation and with Austrian opinion deeply divided. The controversy reached its climax on 8 February when the international commission of historians presented its report to the Austrian Government. The commission found no evidence that the President had been personally involved in war crimes during his service with the German army in the Balkan campaigns of 1943–44, but went further than expected in attributing moral responsibility to him and was forthright in its criticism of his conduct both during and after World War II, particularly in attempting to conceal his war record. Much of the Austrian press and public nonetheless accepted the report as exonerating the President. His own announcement on 10 February that he would not resign his office was greeted with disapproval by the Federal Chancellor, Dr Franz Vranitzky, who implied that he himself might resign if the issue continued to detract from the efficient running of Government business; this precipitated a crisis in the ruling coalition between the Socialist Party (SPÖ) and the People's Party (ÖVP), which looked momentarily insecure when the latter, as the junior partner, made it clear that it would withdraw if President Waldheim's decision were not accepted.

After considerable debate and divisiveness over what part Dr Waldheim should play in the commemorations, the fiftieth anniversary of the 1938 *Anschluss* with Nazi Germany was commemorated on 11 March with dignity. International interest in Dr Waldheim seemed gradually to die away during the year, discouraged perhaps by the President's obduracy and the lack of conclusive evidence against him. Its corrosive effects on Austrian life continued to be felt, however, not least in occasional incidents and comments of a crudely intolerant or frankly xenophobic or anti-semitic kind.

In political terms 1988 was otherwise fairly uneventful, although there were a number of scandals involving senior members of the SPÖ, several of whom resigned their party offices during the year, including the former federal Chancellor, Dr Fred Sinowatz. Relations between the coalition partners were swiftly restored. In March they agreed an important and extensive tax reform, and further progress was made during the year on the controversial reorganization and part-privatization of the state-owned industrial sector (see AR 1987, p. 170). The Government's path was unexpectedly smoothed by an economic upturn, with growth among Austria's main trading partners giving renewed impetus to its industrial output and export performance. Real growth in GDP in 1988 was estimated at 4 per cent in December, with inflation up by only 1.9 per cent, unemployment down slightly at 5.4 per cent and further growth predicted for 1989. The Government was unable to avoid increasing state expenditure in the 1989 draft Budget presented to Parliament on 20 October, but achieved a small reduction of half a percentage point in the Budget deficit, to 4 per cent of GDP, as a result of rising revenues and some economy measures. Overall the Grand Coalition ended the year in better shape than could have been foreseen. Nonetheless, the FPÖ, as main opposition party, continued to gain support, picking up 5 seats and almost 10 per cent of the vote on 16 October in the one election of the year, for the provincial Assembly of Lower Austria.

Because of the Waldheim affair there were fewer distinguished Western visitors to Austria than usual, but Pope John Paul II paid his second visit in June and was welcomed by the President, who had himself just returned from a state visit to Saudi Arabia. The third review session of the Conference on Security and Cooperation in Europe (CSCE) continued its work in Vienna, and by the end of the year was close to agreement on a document involving progress on human rights and on security issues, as well as on a mandate for new negotiations on conventional arms control. The award of the Nobel Peace Prize to the UN Peacekeeping Forces in October was particularly gratifying to Austria, with 969 members of its armed forces seconded to UN duties and Austrians in command of the UN peacekeeping effort in Cyprus and on the Golan Heights.

However, the main topic of the year in foreign policy was Austria's decision, primarily on the initiative of the ÖVP and its leader, the Vice-Chancellor and Foreign Minister, Dr Alois Mock, to explore the possibility of applying for full membership of the European Community. This immediately raised the question of the compatibility of Austrian neutrality with the Treaty of Rome, and in September and October Dr Mock and Dr Vranitzky paid successive visits to Moscow in an attempt to forestall possible Soviet objections. On returning they professed themselves sufficiently encouraged by the Soviet response for the question in many Austrian minds at the end of the year to be not whether, but when? The year was therefore one of an Austrian *Drang nach Westen*; but also of a new warmth and intensification of contacts with Eastern Europe, particularly Hungary, which gave fresh impetus to talk of a revival of the old concept of *Mitteleuropa* in the wake of Mr Gorbachev's *perestroika*.

SWITZERLAND

CAPITAL: Berne   AREA: 41,300 sq km   POPULATION: 6,500,000 ('86)
OFFICIAL LANGUAGES: German, French and Italian
POLITICAL SYSTEM: federal democracy based on cantons
RULING PARTIES: Christian Democratic People's (CVP), Radical Democratic (FDP), Social Democratic (SPS) and Swiss People's (SVP) parties
HEAD OF STATE AND GOVERNMENT: Otto Stich (SPS), 1988 President of Federal Council and Finance Minister
OTHER MINISTERS: René Felber (SPS/foreign affairs), Jean-Pascal Delamuraz (FDP/economy), Adolf Ogi (SVP/communications and energy), Flavio Cotti (CVP/interior), Arnold Koller (CVP/defence)
INTERNATIONAL ALIGNMENT: neutral, OECD, Efta
CURRENCY: Swiss franc (end-'88 £1=SwF2.72, US$1=SwF1.50)   GNP PER CAPITA: US$17,680 ('86)
MAIN EXPORTS: metal products, chemicals

FOR public opinion it came as a shock when Elisabeth Kopp, Switzerland's most popular leader in a recent national poll, was forced to announce her resignation from the Federal Council (Government) on 12 December, only five days after she had been elected as its Vice-President. Mrs Kopp, then head of the Department of Justice and Police, had admitted on 9 December to having, on 27 October, urged her husband Hans W. to vacate his post as vice-president of the board of the Zürich-based firm Shakarchi Trading. A week after he had taken this advice, journalists had revealed that the firm was implicated in an investigation into a Lebanese-Turkish ring alleged to have laundered an estimated US$1,000 million of drug-related money through Swiss banks. Mrs Kopp proclaimed herself as 'not guilty, either legally or morally', but her political career came to an abrupt halt, even though her policy had in general proved successful.

Although Mrs Kopp was not the first Swiss Minister to resign under a cloud, such incidents had not occurred very often. The circumstances of the resignation (which was to take effect in January 1989) led to a passionate debate in the media. A graduate of Zürich law school and a member of the Radical Democratic Party, Mrs Kopp had been the first woman in the seven-member Federal Council. Women's organizations had enthusiastically welcomed her election in 1984 (see AR 1984, p. 166), so that her unexpected resignation left many women deeply disappointed.

In 1988 Switzerland remained split over energy policy, still one of the Confederation's hottest political issues. Switzerland had five nuclear power stations and 40 per cent of the electricity supply was based on nuclear energy. Although consumption per person in Switzerland was much lower than in most industrialized countries, demand was being boosted by the computerization of both industry and services. For more than 20 years a tense political debate had been waged over the construction of the sixth nuclear plant at Kaiseraugst, near Basle. At the beginning of March a group of 26 leading members of Parliament, all of them belonging to three bourgeois pro-nuclear parties, contrived a surprising political coup. They proposed that Kaiseraugst be abandoned, while at the same time identifying nuclear energy as an 'option' for the future. In October the two chambers of Parliament accepted the proposal after a long debate. The Kaiseraugst consortium had already spent SwF 1,200 million on the project; as compensation, the Socialist Finance Minister, Otto Stich, offered SwF 350 million from the federal Budget, which was accepted by the consortium.

During the year Switzerland showed a certain anxiety regarding the European Community's objective of completing its internal free market by 1992. As economic and trade cooperation with the EC was very important for both sides, many Swiss firms established themselves in the EC. One of the principal focuses was the increasing pressure on the Swiss weight-limit of 28 tonnes for road transport lorries, as against the Community limit of 40 tonnes. Because non-EC-member Switzerland played an important role in the exchange of goods between northern and southern Europe, the 28 tonnes debate tended to damage relations with the Community. Federal Councillor Adolf Ogi, head of the Department of Communications and Energy, said that Switzerland would never allow 40 tonnes on its motorways crossing the Alps. On the other hand, Switzerland was willing to build an expensive new railway-tunnel as a contribution towards support of the Community's free internal market.

In a referendum in June the electorate decided against the idea of more coordination between private and public transport. The Federal Council and the Parliament wanted a constitutional law, but this was rejected by 954,383 votes to 798,143. Also rejected were plans tabled by left-wing parties for a retirement age of 62 years (men) and 60 years (women), as against the current age of 65 years. A further referendum later in the year showed a similar result. Swiss voters also opposed a Socialist proposal for a 40-hour working week and plans for severe restrictions on the property business and for limited immigration.

In autumn the number of persons seeking asylum, especially from Turkey, reached a new record and overheated the political atmosphere for a while. The economy performed at a still very high level and was better than expected. Unemployment continued at 0.8 per cent. With an inflation rate of only 2 per cent, real standards of living rose again in 1988.

Jean-Pascal Delamuraz (52), the Radical Democratic head of the Economy Department, was nominated as President of the Federal Council for 1989.

Chapter 3

SPAIN—PORTUGAL—GIBRALTAR—MALTA—
GREECE—CYPRUS—TURKEY

SPAIN

CAPITAL: Madrid   AREA: 505,000 sq km   POPULATION: 39,000,000 ('86)
OFFICIAL LANGUAGE: Spanish   POLITICAL SYSTEM: parliamentary democracy
HEAD OF STATE: King Juan Carlos (since Nov '75)
RULING PARTY: Spanish Socialist Workers' Party
HEAD OF GOVERNMENT: Felipe González, Prime Minister (since Nov '82)
PRINCIPAL MINISTERS: Alfonso Guerra (deputy premier), Francisco Fernández Ordóñez (foreign affairs), Narcís Serra (defence), José Luis Corcuera (interior), Carlos Solchaga (economy and finance), Enrique Múgica Herzog (justice)
INTERNATIONAL ALIGNMENT: Nato (outside military structure), OECD, EC
CURRENCY: peseta (end-'88 £1=Ptas204.75, US$1=Ptas113.18)   GNP PER CAPITA: US$4,860 ('86)
MAIN EXPORTS: transport equipment, agricultural products, minerals and base metals

THROUGHOUT the early months of the year the socialist General Workers' Union (UGT) and the communist-led Workers' Committees (CC.OO.) kept up their verbal attacks on the Government's economic policy as anti-social as well as contrary to socialist principles. On several occasions, and particularly on 6 June, the Prime Minister, Felipe González, offered Nicolás Redondo, the UGT general secretary, the opportunity of discussions in depth with the Government on the conformity or otherwise of all or any of its policies with the election pledges of the ruling Socialist Workers' Party (PSOE). The Prime Minister declared himself willing to adopt any proposal from the UGT which could be shown to offer better prospects than the Government's plans for the betterment of the economic and social wellbeing of the country. Such matters as curbing inflation, or avoiding a trade deficit, he said, required a practical and not a doctrinaire approach.

Sr González reshuffled his Cabinet on 5 July. He kept Francisco Fernández Ordóñez as Foreign Minister and Narcís Serra as Minister of Defence, thereby indicating that there would be no change in his policy of gently integrating Spain more fully in Nato and the defence of Western Europe, and of correspondingly modernizing the Spanish armed services. He defied the left-wing critics of his economic and social policies not only by keeping as Minister of the Economy and

Finance Carlos Solchaga, whose industrial reconversion plan and wage restraint policy had caused the split between the Government and the UGT, but also by appointing as Minister of Industry a non-PSOE protegé of Sr Solchaga's. He rewarded two UGT members who had sided with him against Nicolás Redondo, giving one, José Luis Corcuera, the Ministry of the Interior, and placing the other, Matilde Fernández, at the head of a new Department of Social Welfare. He dismissed the leftist Ministers of Justice and of Education, and replaced them with men closer than they to his social democratic thinking.

Two days later the UGT's Institute of (Social) Studies published a lengthy analysis of the social situation in Spain during the previous decade. There were now one million fewer persons gainfully employed than in 1978. One in five of all workers were now on short-term contracts, and had therefore little or no job security. Whereas wage-earners were in real terms 6 per cent poorer, employers and self-employed professionals were considerably wealthier. No less than 23 per cent of Spanish families had incomes below the poverty level, a figure arrived at independently by Caritas, the Roman Catholic social aid organization. The decline in the situation, the Institute's analysts suggested, had been steeper under the Socialist Governments of the last six years of the decade than under the centre-right Governments of the first four.

The Government did not contest the findings but argued that higher wages would create more unemployment, and that increasing the national wealth had to have priority over its distribution. In October it announced a youth training and employment scheme, which offered subsidies to employers who took on youths in newly-created jobs. The labour unions denounced the subsidies as unnecessary, and as further proof that the Government favoured employers at the expense of the workers. They objected also to the issue of short-term contracts to young employees who, furthermore, were to be paid Ptas 390,000 annually, whereas the legal minimum for an unskilled worker was over Ptas 500,000. Employers, the unions affirmed, would find ways of dismissing adults and replacing them with youths.

The Government waved aside the objections, and the unions gave notice on 12 November of a nationwide stoppage of work for 24 hours on 14 December. Sr Redondo was careful to avoid calling the stoppage a *huelga general* (general strike), a term in Spanish socialist history reserved for attempts to overthrow a Government. This, he insisted, was not the objective; all that was wanted was a radical change in the Government's social policy. The CC.OO. were less concerned over semantics.

UGT local branch leaders who opposed the strike call were

replaced by men who backed it. The national leaders of both labour organizations, sensing that the youth employment scheme was not as unpopular as they had supposed, widened the appeal of the call. During the year the cost of living had risen 5 per cent, and there was deep resentment against the consequent fall in the purchasing power of wages and pensions and unemployment benefits. One of the new demands was for the relaxation of the limit on wage increases, and another for higher pensions and benefits. Unemployment had fallen by 1 per cent since January, with the creation of some 270,000 new jobs, but 19 per cent of the workforce was still unemployed. Therefore the unions demanded an all-embracing employment scheme, not one just for young persons. Yet another popular demand was for the grant to state-paid employees of the right to collective bargaining.

The theory began to be expounded not only by the strike leaders, but also by a prominent member of the PSOE executive, that if successful the strike would deprive the Government of its legitimacy and make necessary a general election. Sr González rejected the theory, on the authority of the president of the Socialist International, Willy Brandt, and stated that whatever the outcome of the strike he could not bring forward a general election.

On 14 December between 55 and 60 per cent of the employed were absent from work. The figure was higher than that expected by the Government. There were clashes between pickets and police protecting those who did not want to strike, but none was of major importance. A week later Sr González announced in the Cortes concessions on pensions and the salaries of state employees, offered to withdraw the youth scheme, and renewed his offer to the labour union leaders of discussions in depth on his policy. He invited them and the president of the Employers' Federation to meet him the following day and begin talks on a wages agreement. Sr Redondo and the CC.OO. secretary-general, Antonio Gutiérrez, ignored his invitation.

The Basque separatist ETA disturbed the peace intermittently throughout the year. On 18 January it offered a 60-day truce if the Government declared itself willing to negotiate a political settlement and suspended Franco-Spanish operations against the movement immediately. The Government replied that no discussions could take place until terrorist activity ceased; a bomb had been placed under a police car on the very day of the offer. However, on 19 February, since no incident had occurred in the meantime, the Government declared its willingness to talk. An emissary had barely arrived in Algiers to obtain details of the offer from Eugenio Etxebeste (see AR 1987, p. 175) when in Madrid, on 24 February, ETA kidnapped a financier, Emiliano Revilla, and demanded a ransom, it was learnt later, of £7 million.

Three weeks later ETA killed a Civil Guard, in March an 81-year-old retired General, Luis Azcárraga, great-uncle of a Basque politician who had obtained pardons for repentant terrorists, and in the months to the end of October another nine persons. Part payments by Revilla's family of the ransom were intercepted by the French police in Bayonne in April and in Paris in July, but, according to the family, they still managed to satisfy the kidnappers, and Sr Revilla was released unharmed on 30 October. On 2 November ETA renewed its conditional offer of a truce. All parties except the Basque Herri Batasuna (see AR 1986, p. 167) approved its rejection by the Government. ETA reacted spectacularly. Just before midnight on 22 November it exploded a bomb which blew a large hole in the wall of the Civil Guard general headquarters in Madrid, killing a man and a three-year-old child who were passing by, and injuring some 50 other persons

The following day Sr González and President Mitterrand of France met at Montpellier. The Spanish Government had reached the conclusion that the ETA top echelon was not to be found either among its 50 exiles in Algiers or among those extradited from France over the previous two years, but among 19 men protected from extradition because they had earlier been granted 'refugee status' by France. The French Government had promised to review their right to that status: Sr González sought immediate action. President Mitterrand would not go beyond stating that there was 'a will to end the turbulence [of terrorism] so dangerous to our two democracies'. The Spanish Government had just decided that Spain's economy would benefit from a high-speed train system. President Mitterrand pressed Sr González to choose the French system in preference to the German or Japanese; Sr González would not commit himself beyond the enigmatic statement that Spain favoured 'a European option'. However, he did agree to join France, Belgium and Italy in a new missile project; and he reassured the President that Spain's wishes on political and monetary developments in the European Community were similar to those of the French. On 23 December Spain finally decided to buy the French high-speed train system.

Spain's differences with Britain on EC matters were among the subjects of what was described as 'an enjoyable argument' between Sr González and Mrs Thatcher when they met in Madrid on 21 September. Another was Spain's application, submitted in April simultaneously with one from Portugal, to join the Western European Union (see Pt. XI, Ch. 5). France supported Spain's request; Britain had misgivings. One was over Spain's refusal to enter Nato's integrated command structure so long as the Gibraltar question remained unresolved; but in May Spain undertook to contribute to the defence of the eastern Atlantic, western Mediterranean and Strait of Gibraltar, to give Nato logistic support and to be involved in Nato planning procedures. It also joined Britain, West Germany and Italy in the European fighter aircraft project. Britain's other misgiving was over Spain's opposition to nuclear weapons on its territories. Following Mrs Thatcher's visit to Spain and a further one by Sir Geoffrey Howe, Spain accepted that nuclear as well as conventional weapons were necessary for Western defence. On 14 November Spain and Portugal were formally accepted into the WEU.

Apace with the greater involvement in Western defence, Spain negotiated a new treaty with the United States. The US conceded on 15 January the Spanish demand for the withdrawal of the fighter bombers from Torrejón (see AR 1987, p. 177). In April Spain tacitly agreed to renounce its right to inspect US ships for nuclear weapons. Sr González then had to overcome opposition within the PSOE to this concession. Negotiations over how many US personnel were to be stationed in Spain and over financial details further delayed the final drafting until September and its signature until December. The new treaty was to last for eight years.

In October Queen Elizabeth II paid the first-ever visit to Spain by a reigning British monarch. She was affectionately received by King Juan Carlos and Queen Sophia.

PORTUGAL

CAPITAL: Lisbon   AREA: 92,000 sq km   POPULATION: 10,200,000 ('86)
OFFICIAL LANGUAGE: Portuguese   POLITICAL SYSTEM: presidential and parliamentary democracy
HEAD OF STATE: President Mário Soares (since March '86)
RULING PARTY: Social Democratic Party
HEAD OF GOVERNMENT: Anibal Cavaco Silva, Prime Minister (since Nov '85)
PRINCIPAL MINISTERS: Enrico de Melo (deputy premier, defence), Joao de Deus Pinheiro (foreign affairs), Fernando Nogueira (justice), Miguel Ribeiro Cadilhe (finance), José Silveira Godinho (interior)
INTERNATIONAL ALIGNMENT: Nato, OECD, EC
CURRENCY: escudo (end-'88 £1=Esc264.50, US$1=Esc146.21)   GNP PER CAPITA: US$2,250 ('86)
MAIN EXPORTS: basic manufactures, textiles, agricultural products

THE final figure for the rise in the cost of living during 1987 turned out to be 9.4 per cent. Both the mostly socialist General Workers' Union (UGT) and the communist General Confederation of Portuguese Workers (CGTP) thereupon began calling out sections of their members on strikes with demands for wage increases of 9 and more per cent. The (centrist) Government instructed employers to agree to no more than 6 per cent, the figure to which it hoped to reduce the inflation rate during 1988. The Deputy Premier, Enrico de Melo, threatened that the Government would 'not hesitate to adopt Thatcher-like policies to deal with labour unrest if necessary'.

These partial strikes in January, February and the beginning of March were in fact rehearsals for a 24-hour general strike on 28 March, organized jointly by the two hitherto rival labour organizations. According to their estimates, 2 million of Portugal's 4.5 million labour force answered the call, and certainly the strike was almost total in the docks, nationalized heavy industries and public transport. Its immediate object was to demonstrate the strength of the opposition among workers to the Government's proposed amendments to the labour laws of the revolutionary Constituent Assembly in 1975.

These amendments, foreseen in the ruling Social Democratic Party (PSD) 1987 manifesto, had been put to the Assembly on 3 March. They were intended to simplify the legal procedures in the dismissal of employees, to authorize the employment of a greater number of workers under temporary contracts, and to enable employers to keep out known troublemakers. Notwithstanding the PSD's large majority in the Assembly, they were not approved till 15 April. The Prime Minister, Anibal Cavaco Silva, irritated his supporters by openly criticizing their slowness in getting the legislation through. He himself was angered when in May the Constitutional Court ruled that the amendments were incompatible with the articles in the constitution on job security and the right to work.

The Court also ruled unconstitutional other laws recently approved by the Assembly to allow the partial privatization of industrial and commercial enterprises (see AR 1987, p. 180). The Government therefore now took greater care in drafting what it called 'new bases for policy on agriculture', and presented them as necessary to bring Portuguese agriculture into line with EEC directives. They were, in effect, a law to turn the disastrously inefficient collectives in the Alentejo region into genuine cooperatives and others into privately-owned farms of various sizes. The pre-1976 owners of the lands now to become cooperatives were to be paid compensation and labourers surplus to requirements pensioned off. The law was put to the Assembly in June. The opposition Socialist spokesman on agriculture accepted that 'it did not violate the letter of the constitution', although it did in spirit. The Communists organized a march of a thousand or so labourers from the Alentejo to Lisbon. The law was approved on 28 June.

The removal from the constitution of its restraints on private enterprise and flexibility of labour had been among the declared aims of the PSD since its foundation. The 1987 election results (see AR 1987, p. 179) had left that party 19 seats short of the two-thirds majority required for it to be able to amend the constitution by itself. The only course open to the Government was therefore to seek a compromise with the Socialist Party (PSP). After lengthy negotiations, Manuel Vítor Constâncio, the PSP leader, agreed in principle to some of the changes proposed by the PSD, but he resigned the PSP leadership in October for personal reasons.

Heavy rains throughout the first six months of the year upset the Government's estimates on the amount which agriculture would contribute to Portugal's economy during 1988. In some regions the production of fruit, potatoes, olives and vines was less than half what had been expected, and Portugal had to apply to the EEC for emergency support. Such shortcomings, coupled with an increase in the demand for consumer goods, frustrated hopes that the rate of inflation would be reduced to 6.5 per cent. It proved to be little better than in 1987. During the debate in November on the 1989 Budget, the Communist Party (PCP) pressed for a 14 per cent increase in wages, arguing that even with such an increase wages in Portugal would be little more than half what they were in Spain. The Government replied that unemployment in Spain was proportionately more than twice as high as in Portugal, and refused to sanction wage rises in the public sector above 6 per cent, the figure to which it hoped the inflation rate would fall in the coming year.

The veteran leader of the PCP, Alvaro Cunhal, attempted in autumn to silence a debate begun in 1987 within the party on whether it should abandon its stalinist ideology in favour of *perestroika* and *glasnost* with the ruling that such notions were not applicable in Portugal. The party suffered a loss of active members, cash and popular support, and when its Congress assembled in December Cunhal was faced outside the building with banners challenging his ruling. Within, he presented, and the Congress approved, a party programme as stalinist in character as that of 1965 which it replaced, except in an equivocal affirmation that the party would keep to 'the democratic process' in its struggle for the abolition of capitalism, and accept the survival of limited private ownership.

At a meeting in Lisbon on 2-3 November, the Prime Ministers of Portugal and Spain agreed to cooperate in the development of the roads and railways, but a Spanish proposal to establish 'a unified Iberian market' in advance of 1992 alarmed Portugal. During the year Spain had become Portugal's top supplier and second largest investor. On 14 November both Portugal and Spain were accepted into membership of the Western European Union (see Pt. XI, Ch. 5).

GIBRALTAR

CAPITAL: Gibraltar   AREA: 6.5 sq km   POPULATION: 29,000 ('86)
OFFICIAL LANGUAGE: English   POLITICAL SYSTEM: UK dependency, parliamentary democracy
HEAD OF STATE: Queen Elizabeth II   GOVERNOR: Air Chief Marshal Sir Peter Terry
RULING PARTY: Socialist Labour Party
HEAD OF GOVERNMENT: Joe Bossano (Chief Minister since March '88)

IT was a year of crowded events and high drama. Elections brought a change of Government; the killing of three IRA terrorists aroused controversy; and the tortuous unfolding of inquiries into the collapse of the Barlow Clowes financial group linked investors in Britain to international funding in Gibraltar.

The elections took place on 24 March. Following Sir Joshua Hassan's resignation in December 1987 (see AR 1987, p.180), a new Independent Democratic Party (ILP) under Joe Pietaluga was formed by a breakaway group of the then ruling Labour Party-Association for the Advancement of Civil Rights (LP/AACR). The Socialist Labour Party (SLP) under Joe Bossano seized the opportunity of this split to capture eight of the 15 seats in the Assembly and 58 per cent of the popular vote. Adolfo Canepa, Sir Joshua's successor, tried to hold the LP/AACR together and won the remaining seven seats, but with a share of the vote much reduced to 29 per cent. The ILP won no seats but took 13 per cent of the vote.

Aged 47, Joe Bossano became Chief Minister and Economy Minister, ending 14 years of rule under Sir Joshua. Mr Bossano was a determined opponent of the airport agreement reached between Spain and Britain on 2 December 1987 (see AR 1987, p 180), but relations between the new Administration and London/Madrid were kept low-key in view of the visit of the Queen to Spain later in the year. Meanwhile, Mr Bossano began an active programme of public spending based on plans for renewed public ownership of the dockyards, the creation of a Gibraltar Investment Fund and proposals for a national bank.

The truly dramatic event of the year came on Sunday 6 March when Mairaed Farrell, Daniel McCann and Sean Savage—members of an IRA active service unit—were shot dead by soldiers of the SAS Regiment. The evidence suggested that the IRA intended to detonate a car bomb during the Changing of the Guard by the Royal Anglia Regiment below Government House. A white Renault car, parked overnight near the parade ground, was believed to contain explosives. In fact, a car containing false passports and bomb-making equipment was quickly discovered in Spain on 6 March, and a third car, with Semtex explosives, was found at Marbella two days later. The three IRA members were not armed and subsequent argument turned on whether they could have been arrested.

A 19-day inquest under the Gibraltar coroner, Felix Pizzarello, opened on 6 September and closed on 30 October before a jury which returned a majority verdict (10 to 2) of 'lawful killing'. Five members of the SAS Regiment gave evidence anonymously behind a screen as 'Soldier A', 'Soldier B', etc. They said on oath that they had no premeditated intention of killing the terrorists but that—echoing the words of Foreign Secretary Sir Geoffrey Howe in the House of Commons—movements by the three had led them to conclude that their own lives and the lives of others were under threat. 'Soldier A' said: 'He looked at me, his right elbow moved across the front of his body. At that stage I thought McCann was going to go for a button. For me the whole thing was the bomb in the band area.' Since bombs in Ulster were often exploded by remote control, and because the soldiers believed that the parked car held explosives, they were not prepared to venture an arrest.

Further controversy followed the broadcasting on 28 April by Independent Television of a programme, *Death on the Rock*, which purported to show, in particular, that two of the IRA members had raised their hands immediately before they were killed. One of the key witnesses, Carmen Proetta, was subsequently pilloried in the British press but was later (16 December) awarded 'substantial' though undisclosed damages in the High Court in London.

The inquiry into the Barlow Clowes collapse wound its way through the year. Investors in Britain who had entrusted their money to Barlow Clowes' holding companies in Gibraltar were said to be at a disadvantage in respect of compensation compared with those whose funds had been retained in the UK, but by the end of the year the fate neither of Mr Clowes nor of his luckless investors had been fully resolved.

The Duke of Gloucester visited Gibraltar on 23-26 May as president of the Gibraltar Heritage Society, an organization seeking to conserve the natural flora and fauna of the Rock and the records of its romantic past, including its military history.

MALTA

CAPITAL: Valletta   AREA: 316 sq km   POPULATION: 360,000 ('86)
OFFICIAL LANGUAGE: Maltese and English   POLITICAL SYSTEM: parliamentary democracy
HEAD OF STATE: Paul Xuereb, Acting President (since Feb '87)
RULING PARTY: Nationalist Party
HEAD OF GOVERNMENT: Edward Fenech Adami, Prime Minister (since May '87)
PRINCIPAL MINISTERS: Guido De Marco (deputy premier, interior, justice), Vincent (Censu) Tabone (foreign affairs), George Bonello Dupuis (finance)
INTERNATIONAL ALIGNMENT: Cwth.
CURRENCY: lira (end-'88 £1=Lm0.59, US$1=Lm0.33)   GNP PER CAPITA: US$3,450 ('86)
MAIN EXPORTS: manufactured goods, machinery

A year of political consolidation under Dr Eddie Fenech Adami produced few surprises. The familiar polarization of the island's politics saw a recrudescence of earlier disputes when the Royal Navy visited Malta on 25-27 June. The flotilla of four warships led by the aircraft-carrier *Ark Royal* was prevented from entering the Grand Harbour by the Labour Party and its dockyard followers, who seized control of the harbour entrance. The ships went instead to St Paul's Bay and were accorded an enthusiastic welcome by the Prime Minister and National Party supporters. The dispute mirrored old arguments between the Labour and National parties over the status of Malta as a 'non-aligned country'.

Despite such quarrels, Dr Adami continued to try to rescue Malta from its past without forfeiting earlier gains. An official visit to Libya on 4-6 January added a new protocol to existing agreements. The two Governments undertook (i) to abolish visa and passport requirements for travel between Malta and Libya: (ii) to establish a joint institute in Malta for technical training; and (iii) to fund a joint regional broadcasting station, also in Malta, as 'The Voice of the Mediterranean'. The agreement was implemented on 1 September.

An official visit to London on 13 September was used by Dr Adami to enlist British support for Malta's desire to draw closer to the EEC, which took 68 per cent of the island's exports. Membership was not an immediate issue and was likely to be linked with parallel bids by Cyprus and Turkey, but the visit gave long-term direction to Dr Adami's policy of strengthening Malta's links with the West. He made the point that 'the constitution provides that Malta cannot host any foreign military base and Malta cannot form part of a military alliance. It does not mean that Malta cannot take a stand for democracy and thereby be very much pro-West.'

Similar sentiments were voiced by John Dalli, Industries Minister, Michael Soler of the Development Corporation and George Bonello Dupuis, Finance Minister. The need was to shift the economy from its past dependence on state control (responsible for some 46 per cent of the working population) to the private sector and to new high technology industries in the hope of reducing the gap between exports (Lm 203 million) and imports (Lm 380 million). Tourism continued to be the mainstay of the economy, equal to almost a third of GDP. The total number of visitors reached 745,943, of whom 446,686 came from Britain. Dr Michael Rafalo, Tourist Minister, announced that he wished to shift the target from an increase in overall number to a more even distribution. Summer was overloaded, whereas the winter months had little more than a 30 per cent occupancy rate.

In January Andrew Bertie was elected Grand Master of the Sovereign Military Order of the Hospitallers of St John of Jerusalem

—the Knights of St John—following the death of Fra Angelo de Mojana. The Order has the distinction of being the only sovereign state without a country.

GREECE

CAPITAL Athens   AREA: 132,000 sq km   POPULATION: 10,000,000 ('86)
OFFICIAL LANGUAGE: Greek   POLITICAL SYSTEM: parliamentary democracy
HEAD OF STATE: President Khristos Sartzetakis (since March '85)
RULING PARTY: Pan-Hellenic Socialist Movement (Pasok)
HEAD OF GOVERNMENT: Andreas Papandreou, Prime Minister (since Oct '81)
PRINCIPAL MINISTERS: Karolos Papoulias (foreign affairs), Yiannis Kharalambopoulos (defence), Apostolos Tsokhatsopoulos (interior), Panayotis Roumeliotis (national economy), Dimitris Tsovolas (finance), Vasilios Rotis (justice), Agamemnon Koutsogiorgas (minister to prime minister)
INTERNATIONAL ALIGNMENT: Nato, OECD, EC
CURRENCY: drachma (end-'88 £1=Dr266.40, US$1=Dr147.26)   GNP PER CAPITA: US$3,680 ('86)
MAIN EXPORTS: textiles, agricultural products

EARLY in an unusually eventful year there was a significant breakthrough, in rhetoric if not necessarily in substance, in Greek-Turkish relations, while latterly the seriously-ill Prime Minister, Andreas Papandreou, spent the best part of two months in a London hospital. His illness coincided with highly-publicized difficulties in his domestic life, and on his return to Greece the country was rocked by the worst financial scandal in its history, the ramifications of which threatened the survival of the Pasok Government.

Talks between Mr Papandreou and his Turkish counterpart, Turgut Özal, at the World Economic Forum in Davos resulted in a joint communique on 31 January which appeared to presage an important breakthrough in Greek-Turkish relations. The 'no war agreement', as the Pasok Government referred to it, reflected the anxiety of both countries to avoid a recurrence of the March 1987 confrontation in the Aegean which for a time threatened open hostilities (see AR 1987, pp. 183–4). The two leaders agreed to establish a 'hot line' between Athens and Ankara, undertook to meet at least once a year and to visit each other's countries and called for the intensification of contacts at all levels, with particular emphasis on the encouragement of tourism and cultural exchanges. To this end, two joint committees were established to discuss the development of closer political and economic relations and these, and their sub-committees, met periodically throughout the year. Significantly, however, Mr Özal rejected Greek proposals that the Aegean continental shelf dispute be referred to the International Court of Justice at The Hague and that Cyprus be demilitarized.

In a gesture of goodwill the Turkish Government rescinded

a 1964 decree restricting the property rights of Greek nationals in Turkey. In return Greece, while continuing to complain of the Turkish occupation of northern Cyprus and of human rights abuses in Turkey, lifted objections to the reactivation of the Association Agreement between Turkey and the European Community which had been 'frozen' since the 1980 Turkish military coup. Reciprocal visits by, among others, the mayors of Athens and Istanbul and the Greek and Turkish Foreign Ministers were followed by an official visit by Mr Özal to Greece in June. This was the first such visit by a Turkish Prime Minister for 36 years and was accompanied by vociferous demonstrations. Mr Papandreou accepted an invitation to pay a return visit but deferred its timing until after the conclusion of the Greek presidency of the EC during the second half of the year.

However, despite these significant indications of an improved climate in Greek-Turkish relations, Greece repeatedly complained of Turkish (and US) violations of its airspace (ten rather than six miles offshore). Towards the end of the year, moreover, there were indications that 'the spirit of Davos' had lost momentum. The Turkish Foreign Ministry spokesman, Inal Batu, in November contested the statement of the Greek Government spokesman, Sotiris Kostopoulos, that the only dispute outstanding between the two countries was the delineation of the continental shelf in the Aegean. Mr Batu insisted that the extent of Greece's airspace, the militarization of the Aegean islands and the status of the Turkish minority in western Thrace were also at issue.

Greece participated in the conference of Foreign Ministers of the Balkan countries held in Belgrade on 24–26 February. This produced the usual platitudes about the need for increased regional cooperation and was noteworthy principally for the presence of the Albanian Foreign Minister and for the rejection of a Romanian proposal to hold a Balkan summit in Bucharest. Greek relations with the United States were coloured by protracted and inconclusive negotiations over the future of the US bases. In July the Government gave formal notice of the termination, with effect from December, of the 1983 Defence and Economic Cooperation Agreement and in October the US side accepted in principle the Greek intention to close the US base at Hellenikon airport in Athens in due course. Negotiations about the renewal of the agreement continued, however, albeit without substantive result by the year's end.

Further strain in relations with the United States was occasioned by the murder on 28 June of the US naval attaché (one of a number of terrorist incidents during the year), and by the continuing inability of the Greek authorities to bring to justice the 'November 17' group responsible for this and other assassinations. On 11 July, 11 tourists on a day cruise from Piraeus were killed, and 52 injured, by terrorists apparently hoping to hold the vessel hostage in an attempt to secure the release of Palestinians held by the Greek authorities.

Significant developments in the field of foreign policy, however, were to be overshadowed by the revelation at the end of August that the Prime Minister had a serious heart complaint and his departure for treatment in London, where he was in hospital or convalescing between 25 August and 22 October. In London Mr Papandreou had a continuous stream of ministerial visitors but his failure formally to delegate power to a deputy provoked opposition complaints of 'government by fax' and of the creation of a power vacuum. Confusion as to the true state of Mr Papandreou's health was compounded by the 69-year-old Prime Minister's announcement from his bed in Harefield Hospital that he was seeking a divorce from his American wife of 37 years, Margaret, herself a political figure of some standing, in order to marry Dimitra Liani, a 34-year-old former Olympic Airways stewardess, herself married and latterly an influential figure in the Prime Minister's personal entourage. Mr Papandreou's public appearances in the company of Ms Liani provoked massive press publicity and led to bitter exchanges.

What was intended as the Prime Minister's triumphal return to Greece on the seemingly successful completion of his treatment was overshadowed by the unfolding of a financial scandal, with strong political overtones, of enormous proportions. This centred on the activities of George Koskotas, a Greek-American who, in recent years, had built up a large press empire, which included the influential daily *Kathimerini*, formerly owned by Mrs Helen Vlachos, and had, in 1984, acquired the Bank of Crete. Mr Koskotas was placed under 24-hour police surveillance pending charges of embezzlement, illegal currency transactions and forgery. From this he escaped during the weekend of 5 November, precipitating the resignation of the Minister of Public Order, Tassos Sechiotis. Mr Koskotas fled first to Brazil and then to the United States, where he had been wanted for tax fraud. A commissioner was appointed by the Bank of Greece to oversee the affairs of the Bank of Crete, where a shortfall equivalent to at least £120 million was discovered.

Following vigorous opposition criticism, Mr Papandreou announced a second major Government reshuffle on 16 November (in the first, on 21 June, his son George had become Minister of Education). In the November reshuffle, Agamemnon Koutsogiorgas, one of two deputy prime ministers, who had been accused of delaying investigation of the Koskotas affair, stood down as Minister of Justice but remained in the Government in the important office of Minister to the Prime Minister. In the following weeks two junior Ministers were dismissed, and the Deputy Minister of Defence, a junior Finance Minister and the Government's legal adviser resigned.

Amid an almost daily litany of new allegations of scandal, including claims of wrongdoing in the Government-controlled armaments industry, and with the Government's standing in the opinion polls at its lowest ebb since 1981, Dr Papandreou sought to counter the slump in morale in his party by arguing at a 30 November meeting of the central committee of Pasok that the crisis had been engineered by sinister forces at home and abroad who were trying to destabilize his Government. He rejected unanimous calls by the opposition parties—the conservative New Democracy (ND), the small conservative splinter group Democratic Renewal (DA), the Communist Party (KKE) and the small left-wing party Greek Left (EA)—for the holding of elections before the expiry of the Government's present term of office in June 1989 as the only way out of the impasse. Dr Papandreou turned the vote on the 1989 Budget on 18 December into a vote of confidence and secured the support of the entire 156-strong Pasok contingent in the 300-seat Parliament. The Prime Minister's medical, personal and political problems tended to overshadow the Greek presidency of the EC during the latter half of the year, but the Rhodes summit of Prime Ministers, held on 2–3 December, was generally adjudged to have been a success.

On 19 November, Christina Onassis, the heiress of the multi-millionaire shipowner Aristotle Onassis and herself an astute businesswoman, died in Buenos Aires, the family fortune passing to her three-year-old daughter (see OBITUARY).

CYPRUS

CAPITAL: Nicosia   AREA: 9,250 sq km   POPULATION: 672,000 ('86)
POLITICAL SYSTEM: separate parliamentary democracies in Greek area and in Turkish Republic of Northern Cyprus (recognized only by Turkey)
HEADS OF STATE AND GOVERNMENT: President Georgios Vassiliou (since Feb '88); Rauf Denktash has been President of Turkish area since Feb '75
PRINCIPAL MINISTERS: (Greek Cyprus) Georgios Iacovou (foreign affairs), Georgios Syrimis (finance), Christodoulos Veniamin (interior), Andreas Aloneftis (defence), Christodoulos Chrysanthou (justice)
INTERNATIONAL ALIGNMENT: (Greek Cyprus) NAM, Cwth.
CURRENCY: Cyprus pound (end-'88 £1=£C0.84, $1=£C0.46)   GNP PER CAPITA: US$4,360 ('86)
MAIN EXPORTS: textiles, agricultural products

THE winds of compromise blowing through intractable problems in the Gulf, Afghanistan, Namibia and Kampuchea in 1988 did not leave Cyprus and its 25-year problem of Greek and Turkish Cypriot enmity untouched. The most important change was the election of Georgios Vassiliou, a 57-year-old self-made millionaire, as President. A political unknown, the Hungarian-educated businessman won the backing of the island's powerful AKEL communist party to sweep Spyros Kyprianou from power in the first round of the February election. President Kyprianou's 11 years in power had been marked by his total failure to reach a settlement with the Turkish Cypriots in their unrecognized breakaway republic in the northern third of the island. Mr Vassiliou went on to defeat veteran right-wing politician Glafkos Clerides in the second round on 21 February. Despite his East European background and AKEL's support, Mr Vassiliou was known as a practical man who had created one of the biggest marketing research organizations in the Middle East.

'The Cyprus problem is simple', Mr Vassiliou declared, and promptly called on Turkish Prime Minister, Turgut Özal, to meet him to discuss pulling Ankara's 29,000 troops out of Northern Cyprus. He pledged to dismantle all Greek Cypriot military forces if the troops went. But Turkish Cypriot leader Rauf Denktash reacted with suspicion and insisted President Vassiliou should meet him—not Mr Özal—as an equal, a ploy for recognition which Greek Cypriots could only reject. Mr Denktash later softened his stand and suggested informal talks and ad hoc contacts between the two communities. The prompting came from Ankara after Mr Özal and Greek Prime Minister Andreas Papandreou met in Davos, Switzerland, to begin a historic rapprochement (see p. 190). President Vassiliou readily admitted to the media in June, after he had met world leaders in Europe and at the United Nations, that if he refused to meet Mr Denktash, Cyprus could expect no international support.

Domestically President Vassiliou retained only highly-regarded Foreign Minister George Iacovou from the Kyprianou Cabinet. He revived the all-party policy-making National Council, which President Kyprianou had long abandoned. He also promised to remove anomalies from the island's democracy and ordered the secret service KYP to destroy all files on Cypriots' political opinions.

The United Nations responded with new interest in Cyprus and appointed Argentine diplomat Oscar Camilion to the long-vacant resident post of Special UN Representative. UN Secretary-General Pérez de Cuellar managed to combine opening the Gulf war peace talks in Geneva in August with getting President Vassiliou and Mr Denktash together informally. The two men struck up an instant rapport and agreed to open inter-communal talks in Nicosia the following month. They set themselves a startling objective—to reach agreement on a federal solution for Cyprus by June 1989. The Geneva meeting was followed by one in Nicosia under a glare of publicity before secrecy descended on a series of talks between the two Cypriot leaders.

The new climate was clouded by rare shooting incidents on

the Green Line dividing Cyprus. A Turkish Cypriot with a criminal record shot an Austrian UN soldier dead before another killed him. Six days later Greek Cypriot troops killed a Turkish deserter who broke into a house in the south. In December a Turkish Cypriot border-guard was shot in the buffer zone.

Apart from its own troubles, Cyprus continued to suffer from its proximity to the troubled Middle East. In February three senior Palestinians were killed by a car bomb in Limassol. A day later a ship the Palestinians were planning to use to sail deportees back to Israel was holed by a mine in Limassol harbour. In April two Kuwaitis were shot dead and dumped from a hijacked Kuwait Airways Boeing 747 which landed in Larnaca and later flew on to Algiers. In the worst act of terrorism, a huge car bomb intended for the Israeli embassy in Nicosia exploded in one of Nicosia's busiest streets, killing two people and injuring 19. The Greek Cypriot Government reacted angrily by deporting nearly 70 Arabs and refusing entry to another 140 in a week. A Lebanese caught with a pistol at Larnaca airport was gaoled for four years.

Economically, the Greek Cypriots continued their 13-year-old success story and President Vassiliou promised more dramatic changes after the first phase of a customs union with the European Community went into effect in January. Tourism continued to boom with a 16 per cent increase in visitors during the first six months. In 1987 tourists brought Cyprus a record $706 million in foreign exchange. But isolated Northern Cyprus continued to stagnate, with per capita Turkish Cypriot incomes a third of the $7,000 a year recorded in the south. The Muslim North's bid to win recognition from Islamic states at a summit meeting in Amman fizzled out, being no match for the superior diplomatic influence of the Greek Cypriots in the Third World, which was highlighted by their hosting a Non-Aligned Movement Foreign Ministers' meeting in Nicosia in September (see Pt. XI, Ch. 4).

TURKEY

CAPITAL: Ankara   AREA: 781,000 sq km   POPULATION: 52,000,000 ('87)
OFFICIAL LANGUAGE: Turkish   POLITICAL SYSTEM: parliamentary democracy
HEAD OF STATE: President (Gen.) Kenan Evren (since '80 military coup)
RULING PARTY: Motherland Party
HEAD OF GOVERNMENT: Turgut Özal, Prime Minister (since Dec '83)
PRINCIPAL MINISTERS: Mesut Yilmaz (foreign affairs), Ercan Vuralhan (defence), Mustafa Kalemli (interior), Ahmet Kurtçebe Alptemoçin (finance), Mehmet Tpoac (justice)
INTERNATIONAL ALIGNMENT: Nato, OECD, ICO
CURRENCY: lira (end-88 £1=LT3,279.41, US$1=LT1,814.84)   GNP PER CAPITA: US$1,110 ('86)
MAIN EXPORTS: textiles, agricultural products

THE first year of Turgut Özal's second term of office as Prime Minister was marked by an active foreign policy and the elimination of the deficit in Turkey's external current account. But at home his popularity suffered from a relentless rise in consumer prices, which reached an annual rate of 75 per cent at the end of the year.

The country's integration in the Western community and in the world free-market economy remained the main goal of Turkish foreign policy. This policy was promoted by President Kenan Evren, who made state visits to Western countries for the first time since his election in 1982. The President's visit to the United States in June was preceded by the Turkish decision to implement the extension of the Defence and Economic Cooperation Agreement, negotiated during the previous year in order to allow the continued use for Nato purposes of US military facilities in Turkey. Mr Özal travelled to the United States soon after the US presidential elections and held talks with the Administration before undergoing a medical check-up.

The progress of Turkey's application for full membership of the European Community was discussed during the President's state visits to Britain in July and to West Germany in October; and the same subject figured also in the discussions which Mr Özal held with Mrs Thatcher in Ankara in April, and with President Mitterrand and Prime Minister Michel Rocard in Paris and Chancellor Helmut Kohl of West Germany in Strasbourg in December. However, as the European Commission's preliminary report on the application was awaited, no European leader was willing to promise, as requested by Turkey, that substantive negotiations would start before the creation of the single European market in 1992. In the meantime, the European Parliament agreed to the reconstitution of a joint parliamentary commission with Turkey under the terms of the existing Association Agreement.

Turkey's relations with the European Community were affected by the agreement reached between Mr Özal and the Greek Prime Minister, Andreas Papandreou, on 31 January in the Swiss mountain resort of Davos, where they both attended the World Management Forum. The two Prime Ministers proclaimed their determination to avoid a repetition of the crisis in the Aegean Sea which had brought the two countries to the brink of war in March 1987 (see AR 1987, pp. 183-4, 187), and to work for the establishment of peaceful relations. This basic decision was reaffirmed when Mr Özal and Mr Papandreou met again in Brussels in March, and when Mr Özal visited Athens in June. Progress on the solution of mutual problems was, however, slow. On 20 April, Greece finally became a party to the agreements between Turkey and the European Community, in exchange for the withdrawal of the decree freezing the property of Greek nationals who had left Istanbul. But on 25 April Turkey cancelled the scheduled meeting of its Association Council with the Community, when the West German presidency gave satisfaction to Greece by including a reference to the Cyprus problem in the statement of the joint European position. There were many Greek-Turkish meetings: the political and cooperation committees, set up in Davos, both met twice, but the task of listing areas of disagreement had not even begun by the end of the year.

Turkey continued to insist that the quest for a solution to the Cyprus problem should be kept out of its current negotiations with Europe and Greece, and should be left to the two communities on the island. It consequently welcomed the decision, reached under UN auspices in Geneva on 24 August by the Greek Cypriot President of Cyprus, Georgios Vassiliou, and by the Turkish Cypriot leader, Rauf Denktash (recognized by Turkey as 'President of the Turkish Republic of Northern Cyprus'), to start another round of intercommunal talks in order to arrive at an agreement by June 1989.

Turkey did not ask for a reciprocal recognition of the Turkish Republic of Northern Cyprus, when it (and the TRNC) immediately recognized the newly-declared independent state of Palestine on 15 November (see DOCUMENTS). This decision was part of efforts to widen relations with Muslim countries, efforts promoted by President Evren during visits to Algeria and Kuwait, and by Prime Minister Özal, who went to Libya, Egypt, Saudi Arabia and Iran. Turkey continued to represent Iranian interests in Baghdad and Iraqi interests in Tehran. It welcomed the cessation of hostilities in the Gulf War. But while the re-establishment of Iraqi control over the Kurdish areas south of the Turkish border helped Turkish efforts to put an end to Kurdish separatist terrorism in its own territory, it created a new problem when some 60,000 Iraqi Kurds fled to Turkey. Turkey opened its borders to the refugees, but its willingness to allow (or encourage) some of them to move on to Iran created tension between Ankara and Tehran. Relations between the two countries were further strained when Iranian embassy officials in Turkey were caught trying to kidnap an Iranian dissident. By the end of the year, some 40,000 Iraqi Kurds remained in Turkey.

The improvement in Turkish-Soviet relations was symbolized by the opening of a crossing on the border between the two countries on the coast of the Black Sea. Soviet natural gas reached Ankara (where British engineers were given the work of converting installations), promising an increase in Turkish-Soviet trade. Turkey participated in the Balkan Foreign Ministers' conference in Belgrade in February, and discussed bilaterally with Bulgaria the problem posed by that country's attempt at the forcible assimilation of close on one million ethnic Turks. However, the Bulgarian gesture in releasing the family of the Bulgarian-born Turkish Olympic gold-medallist, Naim Süleymanoglu, was not followed by any general alleviation of the plight of ethnic Turks remaining in Bulgaria.

Mr Süleymanoglu's success as a weight-lifter was celebrated as a national victory by the Turkish public, which, otherwise, remained preoccupied by the rapid rise in the cost of living and the social effects of inflation. By gradually devaluing the Turkish lira (by 78 per cent against the US dollar and 73 per cent against the pound sterling over the course of the year), the Turkish Government succeeded nevertheless in improving the country's trading position, to the point where the external current account yielded a surplus of some US$740 million in the first 11 months of the year. Tourist revenue helped: the number of foreign tourists increased (in the first ten months) by nearly 50 per cent to 3.8 million (including 360,000 Greeks encouraged by the spirit of Davos, as well as by a favourable exchange rate). Turkey consequently had little difficulty in paying off and also refinancing its external debt (estimated at US$38,000 million, plus another US$10,000 million in undisbursed commitments), and in attracting fresh foreign credits and investments.

At home, however, there were constant complaints that government over-spending and the devaluation of the currency were increasing the burden of inflation. On 25 September the Prime Minister was supported by only 35 per cent of the electorate in a referendum on a proposal to bring forward the date of local elections. Although Mr Özal had threatened to resign if the results were unsatisfactory, he decided to stay in office on the grounds that the referendum figures differed little from the outcome of the general elections in November 1987, when the support of 36 per cent of the electorate allowed him to win an absolute majority in Parliament against a divided opposition. On 18 June Mr Özal survived an assassination attempt by a right-wing extremist.

The ratification by Turkey of both the European and the UN conventions banning the use of torture did not put an end to accusations (documented by Amnesty International) that human rights violations were still widespread in the country. Turkey continued to insist, on the other hand, that officials guilty of abuses were punished.

A second bridge linking the European and Asian shores of the Bosphorus in Istanbul was completed on 3 July. It was built by a consortium of Japanese, Italian and Turkish companies. On 7 December the earthquake which devastated Soviet Armenia (see p. 113) caused five deaths and damage in the eastern border area of Turkey (see also map on p. 109).

V MIDDLE EAST AND NORTH AFRICA

Chapter 1

ISRAEL

CAPITAL: Jerusalem AREA: 22,000 sq km POPULATION: 4,300,000 ('86)
OFFICIAL LANGUAGES: Hebrew and Arabic POLITICAL SYSTEM: parliamentary democracy
HEAD OF STATE: President Chaim Herzog (since May '83)
RULING PARTIES: national unity coalition led by Likud and Labour Party
HEAD OF GOVERNMENT: Yitzhak Shamir (Likud), Prime Minister (since Oct '86)
PRINCIPAL MINISTERS: Shimon Peres (Labour/deputy premier, finance), Moshe Arens (Likud/foreign affairs), Yitzhak Rabin (Labour/defence), Dan Meridor (Likud/justice), Yitzhak Modai (Likud/economics and planning)
INTERNATIONAL ALIGNMENT: backed by US
CURRENCY: new shekel (end-'88 £1=NIS3.03, US$1=NIS1.67) GNP PER CAPITA: US$6,210 ('86)
MAIN EXPORTS: diamonds, machinery, agricultural produce

ISRAEL'S new Government was formally installed on 22 December, after seven weeks of strenuous bargaining by party leaders in the aftermath of the inconclusive general election held on 1 November. Likud retained the premiership, and Yitzhak Shamir succeeded in forming a broad-based coalition uniting Likud and Labour, as in the previous four years. But the new coalition agreement reflected some shift in the balance of policy in favour of Likud. Moshe Arens, a hard-line nationalist of the Herut wing of the party, and Mr Shamir's own choice for eventual succession to the Likud leadership, became Foreign Minister in place of Shimon Peres, who accepted the Finance portfolio. In effect Labour renounced its pretensions in matters of foreign policy and relations with the Arabs, and also agreed to the establishment of eight new settlements in the West Bank, in return for control of the economy. Labour hoped thereby to be in a position to rescue the labour-owned sector of the economy from impending bankruptcy. Yitzhak Rabin retained the Defence Ministry, enabling Mr Shamir to foil the ambitions of his own rival, Ariel Sharon. The coalition agreement was entrenched by a novel formula precluding any attempt by either major party to bring down the Government without paying the penalty of holding a new general election.

The electoral deadlock between Likud and Labour, the former obtaining 40 and the latter 39 seats in the 120-seat Knesset, was not unexpected. The surprise of the election was a gain of six seats by the ultra-orthodox religious parties, to bring their total weight to 18 in the new Parliament. In previous elections the religious parties had lost ground to the nationalist parties. Now they restored and even surpassed their customary position of influence, not by dint of any religious revival so much as by mustering the maximum participation of their adherents. Abandoning their traditional ambivalence if not downright apathy in regard to secular politics, the religious leaders campaigned most energetically, galvanized by the intervention of the Lubavitch Rabbi of New York in support of the Agudah party. A feature of the campaign was the use of curses and blessings to rally the faithful. The intense rivalry between the four religious parties enhanced mobilization, with the unexpected effect that their total share of votes relative to the secularist majority was significantly increased.

If observers were surprised by the strength of the religious vote it was because they focused throughout the campaign, as did the media and the major political leaders, on the issues presented by the Palestinian uprising and changes in Arab diplomacy. A neutral observer could have been forgiven for thinking that the main debate of the campaign was about alternative approaches to peace with the Arabs. But in the weeks immediately following the election, coalition bargaining between Likud and the religious parties ignored these questions and concentrated instead on the delicate law of personal status involving the perennial question, 'Who is a Jew?'

As the price of their support for a Government of the right, the orthodox insisted on legislation to restrict recognition of conversions to Judaism to those conducted by Orthodox authorities, denying the validity of conversions performed under Conservative or Reform auspices. Probably no more than a dozen or so immigrants in any year would be affected by such legislation, being required to undergo an Orthodox conversion if they wished to qualify for automatic citizenship of the state upon immigrating, or for any of the ritual perquisites of Jewish status. However, the amendment of the law of status along these lines would have the effect of challenging the legitimacy of pluralistic Judaism, especially in the United States, where the great majority of Jews were of the Conservative or Reform persuasion (approximately equivalent in Britain to Reform and Liberal respectively). In fact, it appeared that the intervention of the Lubavitch Rabbi in the Israeli election was intended to achieve this very effect, and if he failed, at least for the time being, this was in part due to the vigorous response of US and British Jewish leaders who sought to persuade Prime Minister Shamir that such Israeli legislation would create a profound rift in Jewry and undermine support for Israel.

Although there was some doubt that Mr Shamir grasped the importance of the issue for foreign Jewry, it is certain that he was not keen on fielding heavy complaints from Jewish leaders abroad at the very time when he sought their support for hard-line Israeli policies that went against the grain of US diplomacy. Be that as it may, the Likud leader switched his main energies to securing a deal with the Labour Party that would enable him to form a Government not dependent on the religious formations. Indeed, it is probable that Mr Shamir only negotiated with the religious parties in order to demonstrate that he could form a Government without Labour, thereby giving him the leverage he needed to coerce Mr Peres to relinquish the Foreign Affairs portfolio. In any case, after a year in which the differences between Likud and Labour, and particularly between the Prime Minister and the Foreign Minister, provided the daily substance of political drama, the US recognition of the PLO for dialogue purposes in early December made it possible for Likud and Labour to unite on a stonewalling approach to foreign issues.

The simmering Palestinian uprising on the West Bank and the Gaza Strip had all year exposed the incapacity of the Government to cope with the Arabs under its rule. King Husain's initiative at the end of July, renouncing a Jordanian role in the occupied territories, left the Government diplomatically stranded, since both the Likud and Labour, in different ways, depended on Jordanian participation for the consummation of their respective approaches to a settlement. (Labour paid the heavier price in lost votes since its 'Jordan option' was more thoroughly discredited by Husain's *démarche*.) King Husain also sucked the PLO into the vacuum with a more active diplomacy of moderation, culminating in US acceptance of the PLO as an interlocutor for peace. Mr Arafat's acceptance of US conditions for dialogue with the PLO, followed by official US contact after some initial hesitation (see p. 205), staggered the Israelis and left them diplomatically isolated.

The Government's negative response revealed the extent to which both the Likud and Labour were trapped in fixed habits of thought. As Abba Eban put it, 'Israel won't take yes for an answer'. The worldwide support for a test, at the very least, of Mr Arafat's ability to enter the 'peace process' was shared by a majority of the Israeli public, according to an opinion poll conducted by the daily *Yediot Aharonot* in late December. The new Israeli Government went back to the drawing board with a promise to present a new peace plan within weeks. At the year's end it did not appear that Foreign Minister Arens and his colleagues were likely to come up with anything momentous, given the commitment of Likud, on the one hand, to holding the West Bank in perpetuity, and that of both Labour and Likud, on the other, to refuse to deal with PLO or to entertain the establishment of a new state for the Palestinians. The posture of the Government was studiously rigid in consensus, without a trace of the tension that had previously characterized relations between the partners on questions of foreign policy.

If King Husain at a stroke transformed the political equilibrium of the region, it was the uprising in Gaza and the West Bank that prompted his move. After a year of continuous turmoil under its military rule, Israel appeared no better able than at first to quell and contain the challenge. With over 300 fatalities and thousands of injured in the year, the Palestinians' nationalist sentiment was strengthened rather than daunted by the regime's iron fist. Considerable economic damage was sustained by the Arabs in the West Bank, resulting in enhanced stoicism rather than defeat.

On Israel's side the economic damage was considerable. Largely as a direct result of the uprising, economic growth was reduced to about 1 per cent gross compared with some 5 per cent in the previous year. Tourism declined, agriculture and manufacturing were hurt through the loss of markets in the West Bank, the wages bill increased as a result of the replacement of Arabs from the occupied territories by Israeli workers. The scrapping of the Lavi fighter plane in 1987 (see AR 1987, p. 195) was having an effect in reduced manufacturing orders. Apart from military procurement, the external trade deficit grew during the year by over $3,000 million. A recurrence of general economic crisis was feared. Inflation was successfully held down to around 17 per cent for the year, not much more than in the previous year, but the trend was in the wrong direction.

Shimon Peres lost no time, upon receiving his new portfolio, in announcing a 5 per cent devaluation as an emergency measure to deter a flight from the shekel. Draconian cuts in public expenditure and subsidies were forecast. The labour-owned sector of the economy, from the kibbutzim to the large manufacturing and holding companies, teetered on the brink of collapse. One member of the Knesset pointed out that there were 3,700 companies in the country in dire distress. The recovery that had been so laboriously crafted under Mr Peres' premiership in 1984–86 was threatened, and it appeared inevitable that once again the public would be required to accept a reduction in living standards.

The tempo of events towards the end of the year, as determined by the general election and the diplomatic initiatives outside Israel, reduced the salience of happenings earlier in the year. President Chaim Herzog was re-elected in the spring to a second five-year term, while Abba Eban in summer was dropped from the Labour leadership. In the autumn an international arbitration panel awarded the disputed territory of Taba on the Gulf of Aqaba to Egypt (see also Pt. XV, Ch. 1, INTERNATIONAL LAW).

Chapter 2

THE ARAB WORLD—EGYPT—JORDAN—SYRIA—LEBANON—IRAQ

THE ARAB WORLD

TWO developments dominated 1988 and transformed Arab politics. The Gulf ceasefire halted the eight-year-old conflict between Iraq and Iran; and the *intifada*, the Palestinian uprising in the Israeli-occupied territories, unified the Arabs behind the call for Israel's withdrawal. It was clear that the latter would be obtainable only by unambiguous recognition of, and negotiation with, Israel. Gradually this new line, symbolized by acceptance of the hitherto rejected UN Resolution 242, became PLO policy—ironically just as the Israeli elections (see p. 199) strengthened the other side's intransigence. At first the Americans, whose own inadequate initiative petered out, belittled the PLO's change of heart but in December they unexpectedly opened discussions with it.

PALESTINIAN AFFAIRS AND THE PEACE PROCESS. The *intifada* (see AR 1987, p. 197) continued daily in the occupied territories, despite Israel's unhesitating use of firearms against unarmed Palestinians, curfews, deportations and other measures in breach of international law. On 22 March Israel's Minister of Defence reported that 3,000 Palestinians were in detention; by December over 300 had been shot dead. In the West these Arab casualties aroused but a fraction of the outcry which would have erupted had the victims been Israeli. Ministers in Jerusalem blamed an activist Palestinian minority, declaring that force and beatings would continue. The violence seemed as intense in December as in January.

This dead-end, in which Israel retained Arab territories without either fully absorbing their inhabitants into the Israeli state or alternatively negotiating their return to Arab rule, could not last. On 22 January the UN Secretary-General appealed for 'an urgent effort' to negotiate peace. The US responded in late February by sending Secretary of State George Shultz to the area with a new peace plan, envisaging six months of Israeli-Jordanian negotiations, then three years of Palestinian autonomy in the occupied territories, with Israel retaining defence and Jordan providing policing; direct talks for a permanent settlement would begin in December 1988. The plan was thus a version of the 1978 Camp David framework agreement, in that a transitional period would precede the final settlement. The latter would not include an independent Palestinian state, nor, it seemed, would Israel have to surrender *all* the territory it had occupied in 1967, and there was no role for the PLO. However, the new plan did include an international conference, which the US had long resisted.

US envoys were in the Middle East, on and off, during February and March; however, as their discussions in the Arab and Israeli capitals proceeded, their reception grew cooler everywhere. In Israel Prime Minister Shamir, unlike Foreign Minister Peres, refused to exchange territory for peace and called the US proposals impractical. Mr Shultz made further visits in April and June but the *intifada*, Jordan's severance of links with the occupied territories and the Israeli elections were undermining his efforts.

The murder in April of Yassir Arafat's confidant, Abu Jihad (see below), brought warring Arab factions together. Syria's President Asad had to receive Mr Arafat but they had no genuine reconciliation and President Asad opposed the PLO's developing pragmatism.

The Arab summit in Algiers (6–9 June), besides promising total support, including money, for the *intifada*, advocated an international peace conference. This already implied acceptance of Israel's existence and tacitly abandoned the notorious clause of the Palestine Charter declaring illegal the partition of Palestine, Israel's easy answer to every Palestinian olive branch.

On 16 June Bassam Abu Sharif, Mr Arafat's information adviser, affirmed the PLO's acceptance of UN Resolutions 242 and 338; advocated Israel-PLO negotiations in the framework of an international conference; and proposed meeting Israel's security needs by backing the peace with international guarantees and stationing a UN force on its frontiers. He even suggested that the UN might administer the territories transitionally. This angered the PLO's hard-liners: Abu Nidal issued a death threat against Bassam Abu Sharif, who escaped an attempt on his life in Tunis in November. One of his critics, the PLO's second in command, Abu Iyad, later suggested that the Palestine Charter was out of date and spoke of mutual recognition by Palestine and Israel.

On 31 July King Husain announced his momentous decision to cut Jordan's links with the West Bank (see p. 209). This closed the so-called Jordanian option and brought nearer the declaration of a Palestinian state, which the Palestinian hard-liners opposed.

The peace caravan was now moving. On 13 September Mr Arafat reaffirmed to European parliamentarians the PLO's acceptance of UN Resolutions on Palestine without specifying which. In mid-November, after reportedly waiting for the end of the US and Israeli elections, the Palestine National Council (PNC) met in Algiers. With the hard-liners in muted disagreement (the voting was 253 in favour and 42 against) the PNC explicitly accepted Resolution 242, rejected terrorism and proclaimed an independent Palestinian state with Jerusalem as its capital (see DOCUMENTS). This new state was immediately recognized by over 30 Governments, including all the Arabs except Syria and Oman, China and Turkey and various Third World states including India and Pakistan. The USSR approved the declaration without recognizing the state.

The PNC's decisions were welcomed as a major advance by many non-Arab Governments, including Britain, but made no impression on the Israelis and not much, as it seemed, in Washington. Having already tried and failed to keep the PLO's New York office closed, on 26 November the US Government refused Mr Arafat a visa to attend the UN General Assembly's Palestine debate. The Assembly promptly voted to move it to Geneva. Meanwhile, Mr Arafat had met a group of Jewish Americans in Stockholm; according to their joint communique of 7 December the PNC had established the independent state of Palestine, accepted the existence of Israel and declared its rejection of terrorism in all its forms. On 13 December the PLO leader addressed the Assembly in Geneva and proposed a peace conference under UN auspices, a UN force to supervise Israeli withdrawal from occupied territory and a comprehensive settlement based on Resolutions 242 and 338. He also repeated his condemnation of terrorism. Immediate US reactions were cool, but next day Mr Arafat reiterated his position in less windy and less ambiguous terms. Within hours Mr Shultz had authorized the US ambassador in Tunis to start discussions with PLO representatives. A log-jam of many years had broken; only some maverick Palestinian action could reinstate it.

TERRORISM. Apart from one major hijack in Kuwait (see p. 224), several incidents in Israel proper, reciprocal killings between Arab and Israeli agents in Cyprus (see p. 195) and random outrages by an unidentified Arab lunatic fringe, the general terrorist level was lower than usual. Had it been otherwise, the political progress recorded above might have been impossible.

One sensational terrorist act, never acknowledged by its perpetrators, was the murder by Mossad (the Israeli secret service) in Tunis on 16 April of Khalil al Wazir (Abu Jihad), Mr Arafat's closest confidant. It also emerged that Mossad was responsible for the attempt on the life of Bassam Abu Sharif (see above).

THE ROLE OF THE SUPERPOWERS. The USSR of Mr Gorbachev no longer tried automatically to sabotage US peace efforts, which made the US readier than before to accept superpower collaboration. In the Gulf both powers had a strong common interest in preventing the spread of Iran's Islamic revolution, and their joint influence was largely responsible for the ceasefire. The USSR also impelled the

Arabs, and especially the PLO, towards acceptance of Israel and this helped on the Palestinian concessions and the US change of heart.

EGYPT

CAPITAL: Cairo   AREA: 998,000 sq km   POPULATION: 49,700,000 ('86)
OFFICIAL LANGUAGE: Arabic   POLITICAL SYSTEM: presidential
HEAD OF STATE AND GOVERNMENT: President Mohammed Husni Mubarak (since Oct '81)
RULING PARTY: National Democratic Party
PRINCIPAL MINISTERS: Atif Sidqi (prime minister), Field-Marshal Mohammed Abdel-Karim Abu Ghazalah (deputy premier, defence), Ahmed Esmat Abdel Meguid (deputy premier, foreign affairs), Kamal Ahmed Ganzouri (deputy premier, economy and planning), Yusuf Amin Wali (deputy premier, agriculture), Maj.-Gen. Zaki Badr (interior), Mohammed Ahmed al-Razaz (finance), Farouk Seif al-Nasr (justice)
INTERNATIONAL ALIGNMENT: NAM, Arab League, Oapec, OAU, ICO, Francophonie
CURRENCY: Egyptian pound (end-'88 £1=LE4.26, US$1=LE2.36)   GNP PER CAPITA: US$760 ('86)
MAIN EXPORTS: oil and gas, cotton

EGYPT'S search for a peaceful resolution of the Palestine conflict and its own reintegration into the Arab world continued in 1988, but the *intifada*—the Palestinian uprising in the Israeli-occupied territories—increased its difficulties at home. Promises made in 1987 to the IMF (see AR 1987, p. 199) remained unfulfilled and the resulting deadlock threatened Egypt's ability to remain financially afloat. Abundant Nile floods raised the Aswan High Dam above danger point.

President Husni Mubarak was constantly travelling in America, Europe and the Arab world to promote an international peace conference and to seek help in his economic difficulties. In January he found US political support half-hearted but Mrs Thatcher and other West European leaders were more sympathetic. Egypt's diplomatic isolation had nearly ended by December, only Syria, Libya and Lebanon still refusing to restore relations. On 21 November Egypt followed the Arab majority in recognizing the newly-declared Palestinian state (see DOCUMENTS).

The *intifada* and Israel's repression of it precipitated disorders in Cairo and soured relations with Israel, which were not improved by Shimon Peres' failure to win the Israeli election. *Agrément* for a new Israeli ambassador was held up. On 20 September the Taba arbitrators in Geneva (see AR 1986, p. 180), after an apparent US attempt to persuade Egypt to accept an out-of-court settlement, announced an unequivocal finding in Egypt's favour.

There was a flurry of exchanges with Israel after the US Government's talks with the PLO. In an interview on 25 December President Mubarak said that he would, like his predecessor, be ready to go to Israel if that would produce concrete results in advancing the peace process. This was so eagerly seized on by Israel that the

Egyptian leader had to add that he would go only if Israel started talking to the PLO.

The Libyan leader, Colonel Qadafi, somewhat lowered his anti-Egyptian rhetoric and the defection to Egypt of four Libyan pilots was quickly settled; anti-Qadafi Libyans were prevented from broadcasting to Libya. Visits were exchanged with the Sudanese Government and President Mubarak spent a day in Khartoum in early March; Egypt was mediating between Sudan and Ethiopia and the shortage of Nile water concerned both countries.

Internally, besides the anti-Israel agitation, there was anti-Coptic violence in Cairo and Upper Egypt. In July convicted members of the Jihad group which had murdered President Sadat in 1981 escaped from prison, and on 12 August police clashed in a Cairo suburb with Jihad sympathisers; three people were killed. Another two such were killed in Shubra on 19 December. The alleged involvement of President Nasser's son and nephew with the subversive Nasserists of 'Egypt's Revolution' (see AR 1987, p. 200) embarrassed the Government. Their trial was repeatedly postponed or adjourned.

The economic crisis remained unresolved. The IMF's 1987 stand-by had presupposed a gradual disinflation by means of that organization's favourite 'restructuring' remedies, with their attendant political disadvantages. Egypt could not implement them fully, so the Fund withheld the loan's later tranches. Egypt's creditors would not reschedule its 1988–89 debts until Egypt reached full agreement with the Fund; even the 1987–88 debts were not all rescheduled until December. Lack of agreement with the IMF also delayed the release of $800 million of IBRD loans already agreed but not paid out.

The IMF's anxieties concerned the size of the Budget deficit as a proportion of GNP; energy subsidies (Egyptian petrol prices being well below world averages); an interest rate less than inflation; and the use for food imports of an official exchange rate only one third of the rate on the free market. In March the central bank could not find enough foreign exchange to pay for cargoes of cooking oil and sugar; a ship loaded with sugar and already waiting outside Alexandria sailed away. In May the Prime Minister publicly explained these difficulties and said that Egypt simply could not meet all the IMF's targets at once. After several false starts and interruptions in talks with the Fund, President Mubarak on 10 September angrily compared the IMF to a quack doctor killing his patient by administering all his pills in one dose. Agreement with the IMF was at that stage unlikely for another six months. The 1988 balance-of-payments deficit would be at least $1,500 million. In the background lurked the danger that if Egypt fell for a year or more into arrears on its military debts the US Government would be legally obliged to withhold all further aid, on which Egypt now depended.

Already in the spring there had been protests at the interruption in supplies of essential foods (see above); in September strikers at the industrial centre of Mahalla al Kubra demonstrated against rising prices and the withdrawal of a traditional schooling allowance. The Government thought that it had already done enough to satisfy the IMF by devaluation and steeply raising the prices of electricity and petrol and that to go further down the deflationary path would be political suicide. It saw no option but direct administrative action, and on 24 October a meeting chaired by President Mubarak discussed controls to reduce imports and increase exports.

The so-called Islamic investment companies also posed economic problems. In accordance with the Koranic ban on usury, these aimed to give depositors, who flooded in, a share of profits. To invest all this money profitably enough to meet their high expectations, but also soundly, was difficult if not impossible. Some companies were reportedly simply accepting fresh deposits and using the money to pay 'profits' to the earlier depositors. In June the largest company froze all withdrawals and the Government legislated, against the opposition of Muslim Brotherhood deputies, to compel publication of accounts and the conversion of deposits into tradeable shares. Much of the money deposited had gone abroad, often into risky operations.

In September the theologians of Al Azhar ruled that birth control was not contrary to Islam; and in October the great novelist, Naguib Mahfouz, was awarded the Nobel Prize for Literature.

JORDAN

CAPITAL: Amman   AREA: 97,700 sq km   POPULATION: 3,600,000 ('86)
OFFICIAL LANGUAGE: Arabic   POLITICAL SYSTEM: monarchy
HEAD OF STATE AND GOVERNMENT: King Husain ibn Talal (since Aug '52)
PRINCIPAL MINISTERS: Zaid Rifai (prime minister, defence), Marwan al-Qasim (deputy premier, foreign affairs), Dhouqan al-Hindawi (deputy premier, education), Hanna Awdah (finance), Rajai Dajani (interior), Riyadh al-Shaker (justice)
INTERNATIONAL ALIGNMENT: NAM, Arab League, ICO
CURRENCY: dinar (end-'88 £1=JD0.86, US$1=JD0.47)   GNP PER CAPITA: US$1,540 ('86)
MAIN EXPORTS: phosphates, chemicals, cement

THE *intifada*, or Palestinian uprising in the Israeli-occupied territories, and the absence of progress towards a Middle East peace conference caused King Husain, at the end of July, to sever his links with the West Bank. Whatever its political advantages in clearing away ambiguities and illusions, this step was liable to have considerable economic consequences.

As 1988 opened the *intifada* continued. The US Secretary of State, hunting round the Middle East for some end to an untenable situation, could not persuade King Husain to support his new peace proposals (see p. 64). Based on the Camp David formula, Mr Shultz's plan envisaged temporary and limited autonomy for the West Bank under some degree of revived Jordanian control, pending a final settlement from which both Israel and the US persistently excluded Palestinian independence. King Husain moved steadily towards acceptance of the latter concept and could not, politically, contemplate substituting Jordanian for Israeli policing of the occupied territories. He could not help Mr Shultz.

A coolness with the US was also evident in King Husain's arms purchasing policy. On 4 April a deal with France gave Jordan 20 Mirages (Israeli pressure having prevented their being adapted for Exocet missiles). A parallel deal for Tornadoes, reportedly clinched with Mrs Thatcher in March, began to unravel in November for lack of funds.

That King Husain had a plan to revise Jordan's relations with the occupied territories became clear in advance of its execution. On 15 April he reiterated that Jordan could not negotiate on the Palestinians' behalf. On 20 April the newspaper *Al Quds* (published in east Jerusalem and immune from Jordanian censorship) began forecasting that Jordan would stop the salaries of officials in the occupied territories and proceed against Palestinian deputies in Amman.

On 28 July the Cabinet cancelled the development plan for the West Bank (see AR 1986, p. 188) and then dissolved the lower house of Parliament, thus unseating its Palestinian deputies; fresh elections were postponed pending a new electoral law. On 31 July Husain himself broadcast the Government's decision to cut Jordan's legal and administrative links with the occupied territories. Several thousand officials and teachers lost their Jordanian salaries. In September it was announced that Jordanian passports issued to residents of the occupied territories would not in future confer Jordanian citizenship. Palestinian affairs were transferred to the Ministry of Foreign Affairs. It later transpired that students from the territories would no longer enjoy a special quota in Jordanian universities, where they would be on the same footing as those from other Arab countries.

The King explained that he was merely doing as the Palestinians asked and obeying the 1974 decision of the Arab League that responsibility for their affairs lay with the PLO not with Jordan. Some suggested that he meant to confront the PLO with its incapacity to support the Palestinians as Jordan had done and thus force it back on to the Jordanian-Palestinian federal solution. No such reaction appeared in the occupied territories or the Palestinian diaspora. In any case, the federal solution looked by now impracticable. Neither the Palestinians nor the dominant Israeli Likud politicians would have it, in the latter case because it would involve the principle of exchanging territory for peace.

The ambiguous relations between Jordan and the territories had also been a potential security risk for Jordan. In January over 20 Palestinian militants were arrested and in April similar elements (under the code name 'Black September', referring to the September 1970 expulsion of the PLO from Jordan) staged bombings and demonstrations in Amman. In June a British correspondent referred to Jordanian resentment caused by anti-Jordanian manifestations in the occupied territories, which Amman viewers had seen on Israeli television. The King himself reacted to this and to the snub administered to him at the June Algiers summit (which failed to acknowledge his help to the Palestinians) by, as an Arab journalist put it, 'closing the shutters' and concentrating on the East Bank; what mattered now was 'loyalty to Jordan'. In September the Government appointed new boards to the Jordanian newspapers, clearly intended to increase control over the press and promote 'loyalty'.

However, this closing of the shutters did not imply a break with the Palestinians or the Arab states or a loss of interest in a solution of the Arab-Israel conflict. King Husain was seen on US television in October expressing a hope that the Labour Party would win the Israeli elections. On 21 October he had his first meeting with Yassir Arafat since the separation from the West Bank, and on 28 November he criticized the US refusal of a visa to Mr Arafat. Jordan had already recognized the independent Palestinian state when it was proclaimed by the PNC in Algiers in November (see DOCUMENTS).

By the autumn Jordan had economic as well as political preoccupations. These were increased by the break with the West Bank. Jordan's large visible deficit had traditionally been met from expatriates' remittances and subventions from the Gulf states. The former had fallen with the oil slump and the latter had seldom lived up to Arab commitments. Jordan was borrowing heavily, its debts of $6,000 million now costing $900 million annually to service. The crisis began in a row with Iraq, which had been hugely overspending credits granted exclusively for Jordanian goods but used for foreign products re-labelled Jordanian. The practice represented another drain on Jordan's already falling reserves, which had sunk from $243 million in July 1987 to $28 million by April 1988.

The break with the West Bank affected Jordan's economy by causing Palestinians, who held in Jordanian banks the dinar equivalent of $600–800 million, to change dinars into dollars, to the tune of $200–300 million; and by further reducing the flow of remittances from the Gulf. As a consequence the dinar fell by at least 60 per cent over the year. A total ban on luxury imports was imposed. Attempts to control prices in an economy so dependent on imports had little hope of success. On 8 November King Husain began a sudden tour of the Gulf which looked like a fund-raising trip.

SYRIA

CAPITAL: Damascus   AREA: 185,000 sq km   POPULATION: 10,800,000 ('86)
OFFICIAL LANGUAGE: Arabic   POLITICAL SYSTEM: presidential
HEAD OF STATE AND GOVERNMENT: President Hafiz al-Asad (since March '71)
RULING PARTY: Baath Arab Socialist Party
VICE-PRESIDENTS: Abdul Halim Khaddam (political and foreign affairs), Zuheir Masharqa (internal affairs)
PRINCIPAL MINISTERS: Mahmud Zuabi (prime minister), Gen. Mustafa Tlas (deputy premier, defence), Salim Yassin (deputy premier, economic affairs), Faruq al-Shara (foreign affairs), Khaled al-Mahayni (finance), Khalid Ansari (justice)
INTERNATIONAL ALIGNMENT: NAM, Arab League, Oapec, ICO
CURRENCY: Syrian pound (end-'88 £1=LS37.34, US$1=LS20.97)   GNP PER CAPITA: US$1,570 ('86)
MAIN EXPORTS: oil, cotton, textiles

PRESIDENT Hafiz al-Asad had always concentrated on foreign and defence affairs. 1988 brought him reverses in this field. In Lebanon Syria's large forces and unremitting activity could not get its candidate elected in the all-important presidential elections (see p. 213). The President's feud with Iraq's leaders had led him, against the Arab consensus, to back Iran in the Gulf war; at the ceasefire his horse had clearly not won. On the Palestinian question Syria had long been the most determined 'rejectionist', refusing any compromise with Israel, even to recover territory lost in 1967; he now could not halt the historic change to flexibility in Palestinian attitudes (see pp. 205–7).

These failures had cost Syria money, manpower and prestige, as had its vain pursuit of strategic parity with Israel; and the ceasefire which ended the Gulf war also ended Syria's unique opportunity to extract money from both sides at the same time. The country was paying for the Government's foreign adventures and dirigiste economic management. Nevertheless, President Asad could still keep several games going at the same time; if he could no longer count on unqualified Soviet support, his ability to help rescue Western hostages from Lebanon gave him contact and leverage with the USA.

In January Syrian diplomacy was pursuing a reconciliation between Iran and the Gulf Cooperation Council (GCC) states but not surprisingly, given the bitter Saudi quarrel with Tehran, nothing came of it. With the US again searching for an Arab-Israeli settlement (see p. 64), Secretary of State Shultz and his officials repeatedly visited Damascus. But the new US plan had even less chance with Syria than with Jordan and Egypt. Nevertheless, the US-Syrian dialogue continued and culminated in a joint but unsuccessful effort to fix the Lebanese presidential election. Syria had pleased the US by preventing a hijacked Kuwaiti airbus landing in Beirut (see p. 224).

Syrian forces still exercised much control in Lebanon. Having pacified west Beirut (see AR 1987, p. 206), they now moved, after much hesitation, into south Beirut and kept the Shia militants there in check. But in September hopes of establishing an effective all-Lebanese Government which might relieve Syria of some of these burdens proved vain. Two Syrian-backed presidential candidates failed and partition seemed inevitable. The Amal militia which Syria supported fell out with others financed, but not wholly controlled, by Syria's Iranian ally. Damascus made repeated efforts to frustrate them by using its influence in Tehran, but there were limits to what the latter could or would do. In April a new agreement with Iran provided Syria with one million tons of free oil; Syria still owed for previous deliveries. Damascus continued to support anti-Iraqi Kurds. Jallal Talabani, one of the two main Kurdish leaders, was in Syria in May and announced a joint Kurdish-communist front against Iraq.

President Asad looked particularly isolated in his relations with the Palestinians. In the outburst of Arab solidarity which followed the murder of Abu Jihad (see p. 205) he could not refuse a visit by PLO leader Yassir Arafat on 24 April, but this brought no sincere reconciliation and was immediately denounced by all of Syria's Palestinian clients. These followed Syria's lead in standing aside from the *perestroika* with which Arafat and the moderates were preparing for November's meeting of the Palestine National Council (PNC) in Algiers. Syria condemned its decisions and would not recognize the independent Palestinian state it had proclaimed. Nor, naturally, did Syria express pleasure at December's rapprochement between the US and Mr Arafat.

Little change was reported in internal politics, although it was rumoured that the ruling Alawi clique had increased its control over the Government machine, that a prominent Alawi officer sacked from his intelligence post after the Hindawi fiasco (see AR 1987, p. 203) was still close to the President and that another powerful figure, Ali Duba, had increased his influence. President Asad's black sheep brother Rifa'at was reported in April to have resigned all his posts and to be living, rather turbulently, in Spain.

New finds of lighter crude oil near Deir al-Zor yielded 100,000 bpd and reduced Syria's need for oil imports, whose cost had underlain Syria's shortage of foreign exchange. A modest surplus in visible trade was achieved largely by reducing imports of things needed for Syrian industry. Poor storage meant that much of the above-average grain harvest was lost and heavy food imports continued.

LEBANON

CAPITAL: Beirut   AREA: 10,500 sq km   POPULATION: 2,670,000 ('85)
OFFICIAL LANGUAGE: Arabic
POLITICAL SYSTEM: presidential democracy, based on power-sharing by religious groups
HEAD OF STATE AND GOVERNMENT: vacant (since Sept '88). Outgoing President Amin Gemayel appointed a transitional military Government under Gen. Michel Aoun (Maronite Christian), but the existing Cabinet headed by acting Prime Minister Salim al-Hoss (Sunni Muslim) claimed to be the constitutional Government.
INTERNATIONAL ALIGNMENT: NAM, Arab League, ICO, Francophonie
CURRENCY: Lebanese pound (end-'88 £1=LL954.80, US$1=LL527.80)   GNP PER CAPITA: n.a.
MAIN EXPORTS: agricultural products, precious metals and jewels

BY December fragmentation seemed irreversible. Beirut held two separate Governments. There were armed conflicts between and inside the Muslim and Maronite communities. The constant foreign interventions—from Syria, Israel, Iran, Iraq, USA, Libya and probably others—reflected the disappearance of any Lebanese authority able to control the country and Syria's failure, even with its large military deployment in Lebanon, to replace it in the face of unrelenting Maronite hostility and Iranian intrigue.

The Syrian-Lebanese Muslim search for constitutional changes which would readjust the confessional balance of power in Government to conform to that in the population was resisted by the Maronites, especially by the intransigent and anti-Syrian Samir Geagea, who commanded their militia, Forces Libanaises (FL). A new President was due in September and his election by Parliament became Lebanon's dominant concern. The Syrians backed their traditional ally, ex-President Sulaiman Franjieh, who was unacceptable to most of his fellow Maronites. The FL prevented a quorum for the first election by stopping deputies reaching the Parliament building. Syria and the US then agreed on a less controversial candidate, parliamentary deputy Michel Daher, whom President Amin Gemayel was ready to support; but Mr Geagea and the FL rejected him and again there was no quorum.

Before Amin Gemayel's presidency expired on 22 September he nominated as Prime Minister, traditionally a Sunni Muslim post, the Maronite army commander Michel Aoun, regarded previously as a presidential candidate acceptable to Syria and so suspect to the FL. Syria and the Muslims would recognize only the existing Muslim Prime Minister, Salim al-Hoss, so east Beirut now held one Government, west Beirut another. No Muslim would serve under

General Aoun and all Christian Ministers resigned from the Hoss Government. In east Beirut Mr Geagea's FL absorbed the lesser militias loyal to the Gemayel family and he began to overshadow General Aoun. Bitterly hostile to Syria, the dominant Maronites courted Syria's enemies in Baghdad, who sent them arms. Soon the Lebanese army and civil service were duplicated; only the central bank, with its Maronite governor and gold reserves, tried to remain a unifying factor.

Continued bloody conflicts among Muslims reflected the objectives, and depended on the support, of foreign Governments. The Syrians wanted to prevent the PLO chairman, Yassir Arafat, regaining influence and raised against him the secular Shia militia, Amal, as well as the Damascus-based Palestinians under Abu Musa. They also feared Iran's influence among the fundamentalist Shia force, Hizbullah, with its aim of establishing an Islamic state.

In January conflict between Amal and Mr Arafat's supporters seemed resolved by their common wish to avoid divisions during the *intifada* in occupied Palestine. Amal raised its siege of the Palestinian camps, but Syrian troops occupied the positions they had vacated. On 30 April Abu Musa's men, with Syrian artillery support, attacked Mr Arafat's supporters in the camps, the last one falling to Abu Musa on 8 July. The Arafatists were evacuated to Sidon.

Meanwhile, a deeper conflict involved the two Shia militias, Amal and Hizbullah, and their patrons Syria and Iran. On 17 February a US officer of the UN Truce Force was kidnapped near Tyre by Hizbullah supporters. Amal condemned this action and by April had forced Hizbullah out of south Lebanon. Encouraged by Syria, Amal next tried on 6 May to evict Hizbullah from south Beirut, but Hizbullah, reportedly reinforced by Iranian revolutionary guards, fought back and drove Amal from the Shia slums. Syria was finally compelled on 27 May to enter south Beirut in force. Its control there was less complete than in west Beirut, since the militias kept their weapons. On 3 June Nabih Berri, Amal's leader, disbanded his militia and asked its men to join the regular army.

Iran was watching all this closely. In mid-April it sent a mission to deplore Amal's campaign in south Lebanon; in May came another to dissuade Syria from occupying south Beirut.

The events of May and June were not the end of the confrontation between Amal and Hizbullah, which in August resumed activity in south Lebanon. There followed an exchange of assassinations. Amal lost three key figures when, on 22 September in west Beirut, they were assassinated, probably by Hizbullah. Clashes broke out again in south Beirut in November and the Syrians intervened to stop them. In the Israeli-controlled zone in southern Lebanon desperate Arab elements made suicidal incursions, regularly followed by massive

Israeli air and ground attacks on unoccupied Lebanon, which was invaded on 2–4 May by 2,000 Israeli troops.

Uncontrolled and uncontrollable, Lebanon remained the ideal base for international terrorist operations, whose origin lay usually in the Iran-Iraq conflict. Other minor, murky terrorist groups included that of Sabri al-Banna (Abu Nidal). Few new hostages were both taken and kept; of those held, Syria's genuine efforts could not free more than a few. The three remaining French hostages owed their release to Franco-Iranian negotiations. Iranian-inspired elements organized, doubtless from Lebanon, their most spectacular operation, the hijack of a Kuwaiti aircraft (see p. 224). Syrian vigilance prevented it from landing in Beirut.

The economy appeared crippled by destruction and disorder. Customs and income tax were levied by the militias, not the Government. What Government survived was financed by borrowing. Inflation was rampant and Lebanese currency volatile; 80 per cent of bank deposits were in foreign currency. Visible trade was $500 million in deficit. Yet the overall balance of payments was positive, manufactured exports and foreign exchange reserves had risen and the central bank still had 9.2 million ounces of gold. Over 1,000 travellers daily used Beirut airport and other airfields operated in the Christian zone. Visitors returning from Christian east Beirut reported an extravagant social life with champagne flowing. The Lebanese were still astute, determined and industrious, with sources of income quite beyond statistics—principally foreign subventions to the militias, Iran's being the biggest. According to the US State Department, Lebanon was now a major source of heroin, traded by, and usually to the profit of, the militias.

IRAQ

CAPITAL: Baghdad   AREA: 438,000 sq km   POPULATION: 16,500,000 ('86)
OFFICIAL LANGUAGE: Arabic   POLITICAL SYSTEM: presidential
HEAD OF STATE AND GOVERNMENT: President Saddam Husain (since July '79), also Chairman of Revolutionary Command Council and Prime Minister
RULING PARTY: Baath Arab Socialist Party
PRINCIPAL MINISTERS: Taha Yasin Ramadan (first deputy premier), Tariq Aziz (deputy premier, foreign affairs), Gen. Adnan Khairalla (deputy premier, defence), Hikmat Omar Mekhailef (finance), Samir Muhammad Abdul Wahhab (interior), Issam Abdel Rahim al-Chalabi (oil), Akram Abdel-Qader Ali (justice)
INTERNATIONAL ALIGNMENT: NAM, Arab League, Opec, Oapec, ICO
CURRENCY: dinar (end-'88 £1=ID0.56, US$1=ID0.31)   GNP PER CAPITA: US$3,020 ('80)
MAIN EXPORTS: oil and gas

THE eight years' war with Iran ended in August with a ceasefire, but not peace; for that, Iran lacked a Talleyrand, Iraq a Wellington.

Iraq continued attacking the Kurds who had supported the enemy. Brutality in the use of chemical weapons and inflexibility in negotiation lost Iraq the sympathy which the Khomeini regime, though busy polishing off its domestic opponents, was gaining.

Even a ceasefire was hardly foreseeable in January when Iran, with Kurdish support, attacked on the central and northern fronts. In March Iran took the Kurdish town of Halabja, whereupon Iraq bombarded its population with chemical weapons. Air warfare ebbed and flowed. Iran's airforce had reportedly re-equipped and could occasionally fight back. Iraqi aircraft twice narrowly missed US naval units; the latter inhibited their subsequent attacks on shipping. On 29 February Iraq resumed the 'war of the cities' (mainly Tehran and Baghdad), which continued at intervals with air-raids and missile attacks, despite international pleas to halt it.

By April Iraq was gaining ground. Disunity and war-weariness grew in Iran. The Soviet Government would no longer help Iran by delaying action on UN Resolution 598 (see AR 1987, pp. 208, 548). Iran's mining on 14 April of an American warship led the US on 18 April to attack Iran's radar platforms at sea and to eliminate much of its fleet. On 18 April, moreover, Iraq's forces drove Iran's back across the Shatt al-Arab from Fao. On 25 May they retook Iraqi territory opposite Basra and on 25–28 June the Majnoun oilfield. Iraqi aircraft were effectively raiding Iran's tanker terminals down the Gulf, with especial success at Kharg on 19 March and Larak on 14 May, and seriously reducing Iran's oil revenue.

On 18 July Iran notified the Security Council that it fully accepted Resolution 598, tacitly abandoning its objective of overthrowing Iraq's Government. Iraq responded with conditions it would never have dared to make in 1987. Resolution 598's main aims were an immediate ceasefire and withdrawal to international boundaries. Both were frustrated by Iraq's stand. On 20 July Foreign Minister Tariq Aziz made demands of substance and procedure which were not based on Resolution 598 and delayed the ceasefire by a month. They included (i) clearing of the Shatt by the UN, (ii) recognition of Iraq's freedom of navigation, and (iii) peace negotiations, direct and not through the UN, to *precede* the ceasefire. Iraq also rejected the existing Iran-Iraq frontier (as being based on the 1975 Algiers agreement which Iraq had in 1980 purported to abrogate) and refused to withdraw its forces to that frontier.

The ceasefire, which was supervised by UN observers as Resolution 598 provided, did not appear to cover auxiliaries. These included anti-Khomeini mujahideen who, from Iraqi bases, invaded Iran in June–July, losing many men. More significant were the pro-Iranian Kurdish irregulars, whom Iraq continued to attack after the ceasefire, using chemical weapons as it had done against

Iran since 1984. Already at Halabja in March 5,000 civilians were reported to have died from this cause; now, as Iraqi forces re-entered Kurdistan, thousands of refugees fled to Turkey after chemical attacks. Their fate aroused international concern. Iraq was condemned for its behaviour by the UN and also the US Congress, which threatened sanctions. On 6 September Baghdad announced an amnesty for Kurds and claimed that over 6,000 had returned to Iraq.

The ceasefire inaugurated an elaborate ballet of simulated negotiation, danced now in Geneva, the Iraqis' preferred theatre, now in New York, where Iran got more sympathy. These performances had achieved nothing by year's end. *Le Monde* commented: 'The two sides continue pointedly to ignore each other; no glances, no civil greetings are exchanged.' The main sufferers were the prisoners of war—according to the International Red Cross 19,000 Iranians and 50,000 Iraqis—who were not returned. Resolution 598 urged their release and repatriation immediately hostilities ended, but only a few sick and wounded were exchanged. Baghdad evidently feared that Tehran would insist on numerically equal exchanges, leaving many Iraqis unreleased; and also that Iran was training Iraqi prisoners to oppose the Baath regime. Iraq had already exploited the delayed ceasefire for brief raids to capture more Iranians as bargaining counters. But Iran-Iraq hostilities did not resume after 20 August and there were indications of Iraqi demobilization.

President Saddam Husain missed the Algiers Arab summit in June because of other preoccupations. Diplomatic relations with Egypt were resumed in February. Enmity intensified with Syria, which took various anti-Iraqi initiatives, encouraging the Kurds and the Iraqi communists. In August President Saddam demanded that Syria be expelled from the Arab League and deprived of Arab subsidies; next, he armed the Maronite militias in Lebanon against the Syrian-protected Muslims.

The Baath regime maintained its steely grip at home and was usually able to stifle any awkward news—but not the disgrace of the President's son and possible successor, Uday. His father announced on 21 November that he was to be tried for the murder of one of the presidential bodyguard who had disobeyed, when drunk, an order from Uday.

The ceasefire seemed unlikely soon to bring quick relief to Iraq's overburdened economy. The war had been costing an estimated $5,000 million yearly, and apart from huge debts to the Gulf states Iraq had by December over $25,000 million of commercial debt outstanding with annual service costs of $4–5,000 million. But higher oil prices had lifted oil income to $11,000 million from $7,000 million in 1986 and Opec's November agreement in Vienna granted Iraq's demand for production parity with Iran, both receiving a quota of 2.6 million bpd.

Ostensibly the drive begun in 1987 to liberalize the economy continued. Many government businesses, including the tourist industry, were offered on lease or sale to the private sector, although given the general uncertainty the extent of such purchases remained doubtful.

Chapter 3

SAUDI ARABIA—YEMEN ARAB REPUBLIC—PEOPLE'S DEMOCRATIC REPUBLIC OF YEMEN—ARAB STATES OF THE GULF

SAUDI ARABIA

CAPITAL: Riyadh   AREA: 2,200,000 sq km   POPULATION: 12,000,000 ('86 est)
OFFICIAL LANGUAGE: Arabic   POLITICAL SYSTEM: monarchy
HEAD OF STATE AND GOVERNMENT: King Fahd ibn Abdul Aziz (since June '82), also Prime Minister
PRINCIPAL MINISTERS: Crown Prince Abdullah (first deputy premier), Prince Sultan (second deputy premier, defence), Prince Nayef (interior), Prince Saud al-Faisal (foreign affairs), Muhammad Ali Aba al-Khail (finance and national economy), Hisham Nazer (petroleum), Shaikh Ibrahim ibn Muhammad ibn Ibrahim al-Shaikh (justice)
INTERNATIONAL ALIGNMENT: NAM, Arab League, Opec, Oapec, ICO
CURRENCY: riyal (end-'88 £1=SR1s6.68, US$1=SR1s3.69)   GNP PER CAPITA: US$6,950 ('86)
MAIN EXPORTS: oil and gas

THOUGH the year was by no means a calm and uneventful one for the kingdom, it was a little less difficult than the immediately preceding ones had been. Uncertainty about the level of oil prices continued to be a source of concern and apprehension for the Government, but the achievement of a ceasefire in the Iran-Iraq war during the summer was widely welcomed. The Government recognized, however, that it would be no easy task to bring about a lasting peace agreement between Tehran and Baghdad, and many diplomatic efforts were made to that end. At the same time, Riyadh continued to be involved in the task of trying to establish a minimum degree of security in Lebanon, while new efforts to break the deadlock in the Palestine dispute also attracted the active support of the Government. Contacts with Afghan resistance leaders were also maintained and a notable success was achieved in arranging for those representatives to meet senior Soviet officials in Saudi Arabia during December. This prompted widespread and renewed speculation that diplomatic relations between Riyadh and Moscow might be re-established after a break of 50 years.

The violent events in Mecca during the pilgrimage in July 1987 (see AR 1987, p. 210) had caused great concern to the Government, which expressed its rigorous determination to prevent their repetition.

One way to achieve this was believed to be a reduction in the number of Iranian pilgrims, and in March the kingdom announced that it was to introduce a quota system. In general, countries would be allowed to send one thousand pilgrims to Saudi Arabia for every million Muslims in their population. This would have meant that Iran's quota would have been approximately 45,000—less than one third of the previous total. Tehran reacted angrily to the new proposal and threatened to send the same number of pilgrims as it had done in the past. Saudi efforts to reach an accommodation failed and on 26 April Riyadh severed diplomatic relations with Tehran. As a result, it was difficult for many Iranians to obtain the necessary visa and the pilgrimage season in July was peaceful.

The year had begun on a note of some confusion as the Government declared, on 3 January, its intention to impose an income tax on expatriate workers in the country. An immediate outcry followed and many observers predicted a mass exodus of vital skilled personnel. Within three days the announcement was cancelled and the scheme was quietly abandoned. But when the new draft five-year economic plan was published at the end of October one of its stated aims was a gradual reduction in dependence upon expatriate labour. The plan also envisaged greater encouragement of the private sector, and a continuing emphasis on economic growth in different regions of the kingdom.

The prolonged weakness in international oil prices forced the kingdom to produce another deficit Budget. Government expenditures were again cut, largely by restrictions on recruitment in the public sector. Renewed attempts were also made to reduce the level of price support offered to producers of wheat, but output continued to grow and customers for the highly-subsidized harvest again included the USSR and China. Defence expenditures continued at a substantial level. In March the Government announced that it had purchased some intermediate range surface-to-surface missiles from China. Israel reacted angrily to this news and the decision also caused critical comment in Washington. This in turn annoyed the Saudi Government, and diplomatic relations with the USA were strained for some time. In June the Government announced an arms deal with France for the purchase of helicopters, missiles and coastal patrol boats. A much larger defence agreement was reached with Britain in early July. Full details were not made public, but it was believed that the contract envisaged the supply of further Tornado aircraft (see AR 1986, p. 197), as well as helicopters, training aircraft, minesweepers and the construction of two new air bases in the kingdom. The new agreement was again to be financed out of designated oil sales.

During the year the Government began to implement its decision to issue domestic treasury bonds to a total value of $8,000 million (see AR 1987, p. 212), but no details were given about the success of the venture, which had provoked some criticism in religious circles over the vexed question of interest payments. During the year there were renewed signs of Government interest in oil refining and marketing ventures overseas, and in November an agreement was signed with the Texaco Company for the joint ownership of a number of refineries and service stations in the USA.

In November Prince Muhammad, the eldest surviving son of the founder of the kingdom, the late King Abdul Aziz ibn Saud, died in Riyadh at the age of 78 (see OBITUARY). On 25 October a Saudi diplomat was murdered by terrorists in Ankara, and on 20 December another was shot and seriously wounded in Karachi.

YEMEN ARAB REPUBLIC

CAPITAL: Sanaa   AREA: 200,000 sq km   POPULATION: 9,275,000 ('86 est)
OFFICIAL LANGUAGE: Arabic   POLITICAL SYSTEM: presidential
HEAD OF STATE AND GOVERNMENT: President (Col.) Ali Abdullah Saleh (since July '78)
PRINCIPAL MINISTERS: Abdul Aziz Abdul Ghani (prime minister), Abdul Karim al-Iryani (deputy premier, foreign affairs), Mohammed Said al-Attar (deputy premier, development and planning), Alwi Salih al-Salami (finance), Abdullah Hussain Barakat (interior), Lt.-Col. Muhsin Ali al-Hamadani (justice)
INTERNATIONAL ALIGNMENT: NAM, Arab League, ICO
CURRENCY: rial (end-'88 £1=YRls17.76, US$1=YRls9.82)   GNP PER CAPITA: US$550 ('86)

THE most remarkable political event of the year occurred on 5 July when the country's first-ever general election was held, thus giving the YAR the only elected assembly in the Arabian peninsula. The new Consultative Council contained 159 members, of whom 31 were presidential appointees. The remaining 128 seats were actively contested by over 1,200 candidates, and while formal political parties were forbidden to campaign it was clear that a quite broad spectrum of opinion existed within the country. The turnout among the country's million or so registered electors was reported to be high, and there were no suggestions of widespread manipulation of the vote. In many areas local tribal leaders and political notables were, not surprisingly, successful; but in the capital, Sanaa, there was considerable support for candidates whose political views had strong Islamic overtones.

On 17 July the Council voted overwhelmingly to renew President Ali Abdullah Saleh's tenure of office for a further five years. This had, technically, expired on 22 May, but a 90-day extension had been declared to allow the election process to be completed. On 31 July the President reappointed Major Abdul Aziz Abdul Ghani as Prime Minister and a number of minor ministerial changes were subsequently announced. In addition, a new portfolio of Legal and Parliamentary Affairs was created to conduct relations between the Government and the Council. The new Parliament had no powers to initiate legislation, but by the end of the year it had begun to show some signs of a willingness to criticize and amend Government proposals. The new political experiment was observed closely by the YAR's neighbours.

The economy benefited from the first full year of oil exports, Italy, Japan, and South Korea being the main customers. This new source of revenue did not, however, prompt the Government to abandon its prevailing cautious economic policies. Income from overseas remittances and from foreign aid remained at relatively low levels. Some external assistance was received, notably from Saudi Arabia, the Arab Monetary Fund and Abu Dhabi. The latter was to finance the second stage of the Marib dam project. After reviewing its current developmental policy, the Government decided that greater priority should be given to the agricultural sector, as the YAR continued to remain heavily dependent on food imports.

Relations with the country's southern neighbour became a little easier during the year (see below), but the former PDRY President Ali Nasser Muhammad continued to live in exile in the YAR and his comments on the regime in Aden remained hostile. According to UN figures some 80,000 refugees from the 1986 civil war in the PDRY (see AR 1986, p. 199) also continued to resist Aden's appeals for them to return home.

In May President Mubarak visited Sanaa, thus signalling a full return to normal diplomatic relations with Egypt. In early August President Saleh visited Baghdad, where he expressed his Government's support for Iraq, and its welcome for the new ceasefire agreement with Iran. The YAR was also involved in the fresh round of diplomatic negotiations over the question of Palestine, and King Husain of Jordan and PLO leader Yassir Arafat both visited Sanaa twice during the year. On 10 May the US embassy in the capital was hit by a single anti-tank shell. No one was injured and no organization claimed responsibility for the attack.

PEOPLE'S DEMOCRATIC REPUBLIC OF YEMEN

CAPITAL: Aden AREA: 337,000 sq km POPULATION: 2,300,000 ('86 est)
OFFICIAL LANGUAGE: Arabic POLITICAL SYSTEM: one-party socialist state
HEAD OF STATE: Haidar Abu Bakr al-Attas, Chairman of Presidium of Supreme People's Council (since Jan '86)
RULING PARTY: Yemen Socialist Party (YSP)
PARTY LEADER: Ali Salim al-Bid (YSP Secretary-General)
PRINCIPAL MINISTERS: Yassin Said Numan (prime minister), Salih Munassar as-Siyayli (deputy premier, internal affairs), Saleh Abu Bakr bin Husain (deputy premier, energy and minerals), Abdul Aziz ad-Dali (foreign affairs), Salih Ubayd Ahmed (defence), Abdel Wasi Ahmed Sallam (justice)
INTERNATIONAL ALIGNMENT: NAM, Arab League, ICO, Comecon (observer)
CURRENCY: dinar (end-'88 £1=YD0.62, US$1=YD0.34) GNP PER CAPITA: US$470 ('86)
MAIN EXPORTS: agricultural products

THE year was a relatively tranquil one for the PDRY, whose political relations with several Middle Eastern states showed a measure of improvement. Those with Sanaa continued to be strained by the refusal of former President Ali Nasser Muhammad and many other refugees to return to Aden. Nevertheless, a series of discussions were held between the two states and in May it was announced that they would cooperate over the economic development of a sensitive border region which was believed to contain oil reserves. Arrangements were then made to improve trade and communication links between the two countries. An agreement was also signed which spoke of the need to devise a draft constitution for the possible future unification of the two Yemens, but there were few signs of any sustained progress towards that goal.

Diplomatic relations with Cairo were restored in February, and later that month talks were held with the Kuwaiti Government with the aim of securing technical assistance for the development of petroleum resources in the PDRY. An economic cooperation agreement was ratified with Saudi Arabia in July. President Haidar Abu Bakr al-Attas visited Oman in November and signed a cooperation agreement with that country. Aden continued to give great emphasis to its relations with the Kremlin and a series of protocols were signed with the USSR concerning the expansion of health care, electricity services and maritime trade. The most significant agreement, however, involved the provision of Soviet technical assistance for the exploration and development of the oil fields in the Shabwa province. This included the construction of a pipeline to an oil export terminal at Bir Ali on the coast. Work began during the autumn and it was hoped that the project would be completed by the end of 1989. At the same time the Government continued to secure greater participation by Western European companies in oil exploration ventures.

The PDRY's economy, however, remained weak and the country received external aid from several sources, including the International Fund for Agricultural Development, the Arab Monetary Fund and, perhaps surprisingly for a marxist regime, from the Islamic Development Bank (IDB). The IDB's loan of $15 million was to be used to pay for the importation of petroleum products.

ARAB STATES OF THE GULF

United Arab Emirates
CONSTITUENTS: Abu Dhabi, Dubai, Sharjah, Ras al-Khaimah, Fujairah, Umm al-Qaiwain, Ajmam
FEDERAL CAPITAL: Abu Dhabi   AREA: 77,700 sq km   POPULATION: 1,600,000 ('86)
OFFICIAL LANGUAGE: Arabic   POLITICAL SYSTEM: federation of monarchies
HEAD OF STATE AND GOVERNMENT: Shaikh Zayad bin Sultan al-Nahayyan (Ruler of Abu Dhabi), President of UAE (since Dec '71)
INTERNATIONAL ALIGNMENT: NAM, Arab League, ICO, Opec, Oapec, GCC
CURRENCY: dirham (end-'88 £1=DH6.64, US$1=DH3.67)   GNP PER CAPITA: US$14,680 ('86)
MAIN EXPORTS: oil and gas

Kuwait
CAPITAL: Kuwait   AREA: 18,000 sq km   POPULATION: 1,800,000 ('86)
OFFICIAL LANGUAGE: Arabic   POLITICAL SYSTEM: monarchy
HEAD OF STATE AND GOVERNMENT: Shaikh Jabir al-Ahmad al-Jabir as-Sabah (Emir since Dec '77)
INTERNATIONAL ALIGNMENT: NAM, Arab League, ICO, Opec, Oapec, GCC
CURRENCY: dinar (end-'88 £1=KD0.51, US$1=KD0.28)   GNP PER CAPITA: US$13,890 ('86)
MAIN EXPORTS: oil and gas

Oman
CAPITAL: Muscat   AREA: 300,000 sq km   POPULATION: 1,300,000 ('86)
OFFICIAL LANGUAGE: Arabic   POLITICAL SYSTEM: monarchy
HEAD OF STATE AND GOVERNMENT: Sultan Qaboos bin Said (since July '70)
INTERNATIONAL ALIGNMENT: NAM, Arab League, ICO, GCC
CURRENCY: rial (end-'88 £1=RO0.69, US$1=RO0.38)   GNP PER CAPITA: US$4,980 ('86)
MAIN EXPORTS: oil and gas

Qatar
CAPITAL: Doha   AREA: 11,400 sq km   POPULATION: 389,000 ('86)
OFFICIAL LANGUAGE: Arabic   POLITICAL SYSTEM: monarchy
HEAD OF STATE AND GOVERNMENT: Shaikh Khalifah bin Hamad al-Thani (Emir since Feb '72)
INTERNATIONAL ALIGNMENT: NAM, Arab League, ICO, Opec, Oapec, GCC
CURRENCY: riyal (end-'88 £1=QR6.54, US$1=QR3.61)   GNP PER CAPITA: US$13,200 ('86)
MAIN EXPORTS: oil and gas

Bahrain
CAPITAL: Manama   AREA: 685 sq km   POPULATION: 434,000 ('86)
OFFICIAL LANGUAGE: Arabic   POLITICAL SYSTEM: monarchy
HEAD OF STATE AND GOVERNMENT: Shaikh Isa bin Sulman al-Khalifa (Emir since Nov '61)
INTERNATIONAL ALIGNMENT: NAM, Arab League, ICO, Oapec, GCC
CURRENCY: dinar (end-'88 £1=BD0.68, US$1=BD0.37)   GNP PER CAPITA: US$8,510 ('86)
MAIN EXPORTS: oil and gas, aluminium

THE issue of the Gulf War between Iran and Iraq once again dominated the concerns of the Arab Gulf states during 1988, although, for the first time in eight years, Gulf leaders were able to anticipate the future with some optimism. Iran's surprise decision to accept UN Resolution 598 in July and the subsequent ceasefire agreement on 20 August meant that conditions in the Gulf would slowly return to normal. In the second half of the year, this development was increasingly reflected in the foreign policy decisions of individual states in the region.

In Kuwait, the Arab Gulf state most acutely affected by the conflict, the declaration of the ceasefire was greeted with quiet relief. The Emirate offered to finance the UN monitoring force, UNIIMOG, and restored air links with Iran by the end of August. At the end of September the Kuwaiti embassy in Tehran reopened and, in early November, Iran's Deputy Foreign Minister, Ali Mohammed Beheshti, paid a visit to Kuwait in a gesture that symbolized the restoration of normality.

The rapidity of the restoration of normal relations was particularly surprising in view of the tensions that had persisted earlier in the year. Fears of the conflict extending to Kuwait had subsided at the start of 1988 as a result of the US presence in the Gulf, the Iranian failure before Basra and the apparent suspension of the tanker war against Kuwait (after which Saudi Arabia appeared to become the favoured Iranian target instead). However, tensions rose again in April, after an incident on 30 March in which three Iranian patrol boats fired on Kuwaiti coastguards on Bubiyan island, killing two of them.

This was followed by the hijack of a Kuwaiti Airways Boeing 747 by pro-Iranian Shia terrorists on 5 April. The aircraft landed first at Mashhad and then flew to Nicosia before finally landing at Algiers, where negotiations led to the release of the passengers and the disappearance of those responsible for the hijack. Before this occurred, however, two Kuwaitis were murdered and threats were made against three relatives of the Emir who were on the plane. The terrorists had demanded the release of 17 Shia prisoners held responsible for attacks on US and French embassy property in December 1983, something which the Emirate had always refused to do. However, by the end of April the Iranian retreat from the Fao peninsula had relieved Kuwaiti anxieties, even though a Scud-B missile was fired at the Emirate in a last outburst of Iranian rancour.

The other Gulf states had not waited for the formal ceasefire to improve their relations with Iran. The UAE, indeed, even persuaded the Gulf Cooperation Council (GCC) summit meeting in December 1987 to act as an intermediary with Iran, both in maintaining contacts with the GCC and in restoring links with Saudi Arabia, although the latter was reluctant to permit this until the Gulf War ceasefire was signed in July. This conciliating role reflected the UAE anxiety to preserve its commercial links with Iran but did not protect it from suffering from the consequences of the US-Iran confrontation in April. As a result of US naval attacks on the Sirri offshore oil field on 18 April, Iranian naval units attacked Sharjah's Mubarak offshore field the following day. The UAE decided to evacuate all offshore personnel in the wake of the attack.

The crisis was, however, of short duration and by May Iran was anxious to rebuild relations with both the UAE and Oman. Both countries received a visit from Iranian Deputy Foreign Minister Beheshti, while the UAE President, Shaikh Zayad bin Sultan al-Nahayyan, called for better regional cooperation. He also reiterated the UAE's belief that a superpower or UN presence in the Gulf was unnecessary. It was a view echoed by Oman where, despite tensions further north in the Gulf, full diplomatic relations were maintained with Tehran. Oman also opposed calls for an arms embargo against Iran and, like the UAE, played a mediating role between the GCC and Iran.

As the memory of the Gulf War faded, so relations with the superpowers began to resume a more normal mode. By the end of September, Kuwait had accepted that the US naval guard for its reflagged tankers was no longer necessary. The decision freed the Emirate from at least one of the constraints that had tempered its irritation earlier in the year when Congress had attempted to hinder an Administration recommendation that it be granted a $9,000 million arms package including F-18 aircraft. Kuwait had brought pressure to bear by concluding another arms deal with the USSR for 245 armoured personnel carriers at the start of July and one with Egypt for an air defence system and armoured equipment.

Indeed, the year was one in which the USSR reinforced its position in the region at US expense, largely because of local resentment at the high-handedness of US policy. Soviet relations were strengthened with the UAE, where diplomatic relations had been opened the previous year, while Qatar opened formal diplomatic relations with both the USSR and China in August. The Qatari ruler, Shaikh Khalifah bin Hamad al-Thani, denied that the Qatari decision had been occasioned by bitter US complaint over Qatar's acquisition of two Stinger missiles from undisclosed sources, claiming instead that it was the result of two years of negotiations.

In Oman it was announced that the USSR was to open an embassy during the year. Only in Bahrain was there a determined effort to reinforce relations with the USA. This was in large part the consequence of Bahraini fears over Iranian intentions towards the island and of the fact that Bahrain had been the major repair centre for US ships during the Gulf conflict. One Bahraini ship was reflagged under the US ensign and Bahrain was promised Stinger missiles for defence purposes.

Within the region, the most notable development was the reopening of relations with Egypt in the wake of the Amman Arab summit in November 1987. In January the Egyptian President,

Husni Mubarak, visited the Gulf offering Egyptian technical military aid if the Gulf conflict should spread. He also sought to encourage Gulf leaders to renew support for Egypt's arms industry, which had originally been funded through Gulf finance. The UAE President visited Egypt at the end of March, as did the Omani Foreign Minister in September, thus finally ending the estrangement caused by the Egypt-Israel peace treaty almost a decade earlier.

A major regional event during the year was that Bahrain and Qatar—under Saudi pressure—decided to place their border dispute over the Hawwar islands before the International Court of Justice at The Hague. In a similar vein, Oman and South Yemen decided to settle their land border dispute after the first-ever visit by a South Yemeni President to Oman at the end of October. It was also announced that the combined population of GCC states at the end of 1986 had reached 15.71 million, of whom 6.9 million were expatriates. Bahrain had a population of 434,000, with 32 per cent expatriates, while Qatar's population of 389,000—the lowest in the GCC—contained 73 per cent of expatriates.

Significant domestic problems emerged only in Kuwait and Bahrain during the year. On 26 January the Emir of Kuwait reshuffled his Government, bringing in three new faces and reallocating four other portfolios, all to members of the ruling as-Sabah family. Later in the year a new Cabinet dispute surfaced as a result of the embarrassment caused by the Kuwait Investment Office's purchase of over 20 per cent of the shares of British Petroleum in 1987 and by British Government opposition to the move (see below). The Oil Minister, Shaikh Ali Khalifah as-Sabah, together with the Prime Minister, Shaikh Saad Abdullah al-Salam as-Sabah, had supported the move, despite the opposition of the Finance Minister, Jassim al-Khurafi, and the Deputy Premier and Foreign Minister, Shaikh Subah al-Ahmad as-Sabah. The dispute re-opened the long-standing dispute between the Salam and Ahmad branches of the ruling family.

More serious, however, was the continued evidence of Shia hostility to the Emir's Government in Kuwait. In April and May three bomb attacks shook Kuwait City. Three persons were arrested, while two of the bombers were destroyed by their own device in late May. Five other persons, Kuwaiti Shia citizens with links to Lebanon, were also arrested at the same time. A Shia teacher was sentenced to ten years in prison in July for plotting against the security forces, while new deportation regulations were introduced in June. Finally, in late November, three more persons were arrested in connection with a car bomb which exploded in July 1987.

In Bahrain, at the start of the year, three persons were arrested for an attempted bombing of the Bapco refinery, while in February the Government claimed to have foiled a coup attempt. The plotters had apparently intended to free prisoners held after a coup attempt in 1981 and to bomb economic and administrative targets. Equally grave, perhaps, even if less dramatic, was the news, published towards the end of the year, that a serious water shortage had developed in the Emirate as a result of salinity in the underground water supply. Urgent desalination plans were drawn up as a result.

A major event for the regional economy during the year was the successful negotiation by the GCC of the first stage of a tariff agreement with the EEC. This was signed in June, providing for a standstill in trade levels and tariffs and clearing the way for a second-stage agreement on trade liberalization between the two groupings. The Gulf had become a major market for EEC exports, which were worth $15,000 million in 1985, compared with $7,600 million from Japan and $5,900 million from the USA. Exports to the Gulf represented 15 per cent of total EEC exports and 34 per cent of Gulf imports, with Saudi Arabia taking 55 per cent of the total, the UAE 16.5 per cent and Kuwait 13 per cent.

In the face of continuing economic sluggishness in the Gulf, calls began to emerge for a degree of economic rationalization and for reductions in the role of the public sector in local economies. At the start of the year the Emirates Industrial Bank argued that the proliferation of iron and steel plants, as well as aluminium smelters and processing plants, required urgent rationalization. In a parallel move, other commentators began to argue that many of the industries created by public sector investment should now be privatized. The proposals were stimulated by the decision, at the December GCC summit, to permit cross-boundary share ownership amongst GCC nationals. Proposals were also put forward at the summit for a joint security system, a common GCC currency and unified regional stock markets. These matters, however, were far less likely to be put into effect in the near future, although the summit did renew the GCC's Unified Economic Agreement, first signed in 1983 and providing for tariff reductions on intra-GCC trade, for a further five years.

Individual Gulf economies began to show slight recovery throughout the year, assisted by an expansion in regional trade. In Kuwait, the GDP growth rate, which had reached 5 per cent in 1987, was expected to fall slightly to a still respectable 3.5 per cent in 1988. Caution continued to rule, however, and the 1988-89 Budget allowed for Government borrowing to cover an expected deficit of up to KD 1,400 million, compared with an actual deficit in 1987-88 of KD 554 million, only half the level forecast originally. The 1987-88 outturn resulted from Government underspending of 56 per cent and increased oil revenues, which were 42 per cent above the forecast level. However, since the central bank insisted on making treasury bill issues to finance the deficit, the Kuwaiti economy began to suffer from excess liquidity towards the end of the year. This in turn translated into fluctuations in interest rates, which annoyed the commercial banking sector, and a reduction in foreign currency holdings which fell in August to half their usual level of KD 1,300 million. In September, in an attempt to counter the problem, the Kuwaiti currency was devalued by 0.6 per cent.

In the UAE the usual bureaucratic delays clogged the Budget process. Since the 1987 federal Budget was not approved until December 1987, during 1988 the Government was obliged to base its expenditure on a monthly basis at a level equivalent to one-twelfth of the allocation for 1987, when expenditure cuts and buoyant oil revenues had reduced the deficit to Dh 3,350 million. Estimates of oil revenues in 1988, however, suggested that there would be a 20 per cent fall and thus a large budget deficit, which would have to be financed by a bond issue given the existing ban on government borrowing from the central bank. Outside the issue of government expenditure, the general economic climate for the UAE was quite good. Inflation was expected to be limited to between 2 and 3 per cent while in 1987 nominal GDP growth rate was 8.5 per cent, the trade surplus rose by 32 per cent and commercial bank activity rose by 7 per cent, with loans rising by 10 per cent.

In Qatar, anxieties over the economic situation meant that the 1987-88 Budget was heavily underspent. The 1988-89 Budget was set at expenditure of $3,420 million, a 2 per cent rise; revenues at $1,740 million, a 6 per cent fall; and the deficit at $1,700 million, a 12 per cent rise but easily covered from Qatar's foreign assets, currently estimated to be around $12,000 million. The general health of the Qatari economy was confirmed by the rise of 10.5 per cent in commercial bank assets during 1987. Nonetheless, official anxieties about the future provoked some careful thought about how to diversify the economy away from oil towards gas, while the private sector was to be encouraged to expand its activities in the light industrial sector. 'Qatarization' was also to be promoted.

In Bahrain as well, 1988 saw a general consensus that a greater degree of privatization and 'Bahrainization' of the economy was desirable. At the same time, an increase in foreign investment and in joint venture operations was encouraged. The Bahraini Budget deficit was estimated to be BD 50-60 million for the year, against oil revenues of around BD 220-230 million, and the current account was expected to be in surplus, with a GDP growth rate of around 1 to 1.5 per cent for the year, compared with 2 per cent in 1987.

Oman continued to suffer from the problems of the international oil market throughout the year. Its attempts to negotiate a restraining deal between Opec and non-Opec ('Nopec') oil-producing countries proved to be unsuccessful and its Budget deficit grew as oil prices fell in the second half of the year. With the projected Budget deficit of OR 252 million (already 169 per cent up on 1987) clearly running in excess, the Omani Government had to go to the international capital markets sooner than expected for a Euroloan. The $100 million loan raised in August was, however, smaller than had been anticipated. The consequent budgetary restraint was expected to hamper the third five-year plan (1986-90), which was finally published—two years late—early in the year.

The most important event of the year for the Arab Gulf states' individual economies was the Opec decision, in November, to compromise over quotas in order to bring Iraq into line. The overall Opec production ceiling was raised from 16.3 to 18.5 million bpd and Iran agreed to accept production parity with Iraq at 2.64 million bpd. The agreement brought to an end a calamitous period of over-production by virtually all Opec members which had led to a combined Opec production level of nearly 23 million bpd just before the decisive meeting took place in Vienna. The result had been a decline in prices to as little as $10 per barrel at one point in the latter part of the year. The major over-producer was, of course, Saudi Arabia which had been using its massive production potential to force Iran to concede production parity with Iraq and to persuade Iraq to eventually reduce its actual production level of over 3 million bpd. However, the other major Gulf producers had also been exceeding their Opec quotas for most of the year. Both Kuwait and the UAE supported the Saudi moves, although the UAE also had to cope with the chronic conflict between Abu Dhabi and Dubai over the division of the UAE quota between them and the other minor producers in the Federation.

Nearly every Gulf state was forced to discount on its prices during the year. In the UAE, despite attempts to maintain the official Opec price, Japanese consumers—accounting for half of UAE crude exports and all of its LNG exports—forced the Federation to accept discounts on its prices in April. A major reason for the UAE accepting demands for discounting was that Saudi Arabia had already agreed to discounts, while Kuwait, Qatar and Oman were charging market-related prices. Partly because of the continuing downward pressure on prices, there was a general interest during the year in downstream petroleum activities.

The commercial banking sector improved generally throughout the Gulf, with offshore banking sector profits in Bahrain gradually recovering and interest rates being reduced. In Kuwait, the aftermath of the Souk al-Manakh crisis continued to dog the KFTCIC, where an injection of KD 42 million was necessary during 1988 to cover 1987 loan losses. In an attempt to tighten banking practices, 13 moneylenders had their financial licences revoked in September by the central bank. Problems also attended the activities of the Kuwait Investment Office (KIO), which caused a crisis in relations with the UK through its purchase of 21.7 per cent of the share capital of British Petroleum (BP). The UK Government insisted that this should be reduced over a five-year period to below 10 per cent and, at the end of the year, BP offered to buy back the excess share capital.

Chapter 4

SUDAN—LIBYA—TUNISIA—WESTERN SAHARA—ALGERIA—MOROCCO

SUDAN

CAPITAL: Khartoum AREA: 2,500,000 sq km POPULATION: 22,600,000 ('86)
OFFICIAL LANGUAGE: Arabic POLITICAL SYSTEM: democracy under Supreme Council
RULING PARTIES: coalition headed by National Umma Party (NUP) and including National Islamic Front (NIF)
HEAD OF STATE: Ahmed al-Mirghani, Chairman of five-member Supreme Council (since May '86)
HEAD OF GOVERNMENT: Sayyid Sadiq al-Mahdi (NUP), Prime Minister (since May '86)
PRINCIPAL MINISTERS: Hasan al-Turabi (NIF/deputy premier, foreign affairs, justice), Gen. (rtd.) Abd al-Majid Hamid Khalil (NUP/defence), Omer Nour al-Daim (NUP/finance, economic planning, agriculture), Abbas Abu Shamah al-Mahmud (interior)
INTERNATIONAL ALIGNMENT: NAM, Arab League, OAU, ACP, ICO
CURRENCY: Sudanese pound (end-'88 £1=LSd8.13, US$1=LSd4.49)
GNP PER CAPITA: US$320 ('86) MAIN EXPORTS: cotton, agricultural products

FLOODING, famine, threat of locusts and civil war in the south were the dominant features of 1988. The continuing political stalemate and military operations in the south intensified the plight of thousands of southern refugees fleeing to the main towns of the south as well as to the north and to Ethiopia. Relief organizations highlighted the spread of famine, disease and high rate of mortality among the refugees. The problem of distributing aid to the famine-stricken people remained acute despite airlifts of supplies to Juba. Government troops recaptured the town of Gisan on the Ethiopian border from the Sudan People's Liberation Army (SPLA) and lifted a two-and-a-half year siege of the town of Bor. The SPLA captured Kayala and Kapoeta towns. The 480 Sudanese troops who fled to Uganda after the fall of Kapoeta were repatriated.

A hopeful step towards reconciliation and ending the civil war took place on 16 November when Sayyid Muhammed Osman al-Mirghani, president of the Democratic Unionist Party (DUP), and Colonel John Garang, leader of the SPLA, signed an accord in Addis Ababa which called for a ceasefire, a freeze on the implementation of the Shari'a laws and the holding of a constitutional conference. This accord was welcomed by the Sudanese and the international community but supporters of the National Islamic Front (NIF) regarded it as a surrender to the SPLA. Clashes in Khartoum between NIF supporters and supporters of the accord, mainly the southerners and the DUP, resulted in many casualties. The Cabinet provisionally approved the accord and a meeting to work out a new constitution was scheduled between Col. John Garang and the Prime Minister, Sayyid Sadiq al-Mahdi, and Sudan's political parties. Nevertheless, reports indicated that the Prime Minister and Dr Hasan al-Turabi, leader of the NIF, were not in support of the accord and blamed the continuation of the civil war on Ethiopia's support for the SPLA. The DUP accordingly resigned from the Government.

Earlier in the year internal political instability had been manifest partly in strikes by trade unions and demonstrations about the shortages and price increases of basic commodities. The Government increased wages but had to freeze price increases of commodities as a result of the general strike by the Sudan Workers' Trade Union in December. The draft for the reimposition of the Shari'a laws, the cause of the civil war, prompted a walkout by the southern politicians from Parliament and a threat that they would withdraw their support from the Government of National Unity. Internal squabbles among the coalition partners led to the resignation of the Prime Minister in April. On his re-election he formed another Government of National Unity, allocating five ministerial posts to the NIF. Continual criticism of the army's military performance in the south led to the dismissal of the Chief of Staff and his replacement by Major-General Mahdi Babu Nimr.

Two states of emergency were declared. The first was prompted by disastrous floods in August and the second by an attempted coup by senior army officers in December. It was reported that nine officers, including one of the leaders of the coup, were arrested, together with seven former government officials.

There were several politically embarrassing incidents. A prominent Iraqi dissident Shia cleric, Sayyid Mahdi al-Hakim, visiting Khartoum to attend an Islamic conference, was assassinated and this murder was attributed to Iraqi politics. Armed attacks at the Acropole Hotel and Sudan Club in Khartoum on 15 May killed five Britons and two others. Christopher Rolfe, who worked for the Ockenden Venture, his wife and two children were among those killed. Five Palestinians were sentenced to hang for their attack on the Acropole Hotel.

Heavy rain fell in Khartoum on 4–5 August, causing flooding and subsequent destruction to houses and crops. An estimated 1.5 million people were left homeless and many vital services were affected. Relief organizations, Arab and Western countries provided relief supplies and aid but the Government was criticized for its handling of their distribution. Subsequent flooding in the Blue Nile, Nile and Northern provinces caused extensive damage to crops and settlements. In response to the Government's appeal for assistance to rectify damage estimated in billions of dollars, European and Arab countries and other sources had provided some $125 million by year's end.

Famine and drought in Kordofan and Darfur continued and the Government claimed that crops had been halved by drought. Egypt, Sudan, Uganda and Zaïre agreed to set up an international committee to advise on the use of the Nile waters to combat drought. The refugees in eastern Sudan continued to be a burden. The influx of displaced southerners seeking refuge in southern Kordofan and Khartoum was seen as likely to continue until the civil war was solved. A hopeful move towards repatriating refugees from neighbouring countries took place when Uganda and Sudan signed a memorandum for the return of up to 60,000 Ugandan refugees.

Sudan continued to be beset with economic problems. A huge international debt made it difficult to alleviate the endemic shortages of basic commodities. However, Sudan received nearly $600 million in loans, aid and grants from the USA, European and Arab countries, as well as various international financial institutions.

LIBYA

CAPITAL: Jaffra (formerly Tripoli) AREA: 1,775,000 sq km POPULATION: 3,900,000 ('86)
OFFICIAL LANGUAGE: Arabic POLITICAL SYSTEM: socialist 'state of the masses'
HEAD OF STATE: Col. Muammar Qadafi, 'Leader of the Revolution' (since Sept '69)
GOVERNMENT LEADERS: Maj. Abdul Salem Jalloud ('Libyan number two'), Miftah al-Usta Umar (sec.-gen. of General People's Congress), Omar Mustafa al-Muntassir (sec.-gen. of General People's Committee), Jadallah Azouz al-Talhi (sec. for foreign liaison), Ammar al-Taif (sec. of people's supervisory apparatus), Farhat Sharnanah (sec. for economy and trade)
INTERNATIONAL ALIGNMENT: NAM, Arab League, Opec, Oapec, OAU, ICO
CURRENCY: dinar (end-'88 £1=LD0.52, US$1=LD0.29) GNP PER CAPITA: US$7,170 ('85)
MAIN EXPORTS: oil and gas

THE year witnessed a remarkable improvement in relations between Libya and its North African neighbours. Following the restoration of diplomatic relations with Tunisia at the end of 1987 (see AR 1987, p. 229), Colonel Qadafi visited Tunisia in February. In May he met President Ben Ali on the island of Djerba and reached an agreement for joint oil exploration on the disputed continental shelf in the Gulf of Gabes. When crossing into Tunisia Colonel Qadafi called for the dismantling of the Ras Djedin border post, since bilateral visa requirements had been scrapped on 15 February. On his return the customs and immigration buildings had been demolished. President Ben Ali visited Libya on 6 August. The reopening of the border and the agreement on free movement of nationals between the two countries resulted in a massive influx of Libyan visitors to Tunisia. It also provided many opportunities for Tunisian traders who were active selling imported consumer goods in Libya.

Although Colonel Qadafi's proposals for a union with Algeria had been rejected by the Algerian leader in November 1987, relations between the two countries continued to improve during 1988. In mid-January President Bendjedid Chadli paid a two-day official visit to Tripoli and Major Jalloud led a Libyan delegation to Algeria at the end of June. There were moves towards closer cooperation involving the abolition of customs dues and free movement of citizens of both countries. Further discussions took place about a union between the two countries, but while Libya insisted on a political union Algeria favoured a more gradual process of economic integration.

The ceasefire agreed in September 1987 with Libya's southern neighbour Chad was broadly maintained in spite of accusations about alleged violations by both sides in this long and bitter conflict. In May 1988 Colonel Qadafi surprised the diplomatic corps in Tripoli by announcing Libya's recognition of President Habré's Government in Chad. In June Libya arrested Acheikh Ibn Oumar, leader of the anti-Habré Conseil Démocratique Révolutionnaire. In July the Foreign Ministers of the two countries held talks in Gabon. In an interview with Algerian television in September Colonel Qadafi admitted that Libya's military intervention in Chad had been a mistake. On 3 October Libya and Chad announced that they would resume diplomatic relations, exchange ambassadors and abide by the ceasefire. Both states agreed to solve their territorial dispute over the Aozou Strip by peaceful means.

In March Libya announced that it was reopening the frontier with Egypt. In response, Egypt closed down the the broadcasts of 'The Voice of the Libyan People' run by the Libyan opposition in Cairo. Libya for its part stopped broadcasts by 'The Voice of Free Egypt' from Tripoli. Relations between the two countries remained tense, however, with Libya insisting that Egypt must sever relations with Israel before normal bilateral relations could be restored.

The United States remained the main target of Colonel Qadafi's verbal attacks. In April 1988, on the second anniversary of the US raids on Tripoli and Benghazi, the Libyan leader accused the US of state terrorism and aggression. The USA countered by maintaining that Libya had been involved in terrorist activities directed against US personnel. US policy towards Libya appeared to be no longer one of direct confrontation but of isolating it politically and economically in the Maghreb. In late December, after confirmation that a bomb was responsible for the destruction of a Pan Am airliner over Lockerbie, Scotland (see p. 38), the US extended trade and economic sanctions against Libya. Powerful demands for revenge in the US prompted new calls for a military strike against Libya, even though there was no evidence that Libyan-backed groups had planted the bomb.

On the domestic scene, the Libyan leader called for major policy changes in key areas. Following a major increase in some imports to dispel rising discontent over shortages of food and other basic commodities, Colonel Qadafi attacked the well-known abuses of the country's security services and revolutionary committees, announced the freeing of large numbers of political prisoners and called for the abolition of the death penalty. The ban that had prevented thousands of Libyans from travelling abroad was lifted and Libyan exiles were encouraged to return to a 'country of safety, a country of freedom'. The theatrical demolition of the walls of Tripoli prison in March appeared to have inaugurated the removal of at least some of the more repressive features of the regime.

In August Colonel Qadafi announced the dissolution of the conventional army and police forces. Defence would become the responsibility of 'people's committees for defence'. He also called for an immediate increase in the participation of Libyan women in the country's political and economic structures. Women were to be issued with identity cards (previously only issued to men) giving them freedom to travel within Libya and to neighbouring countries.

On economic matters Qadafi criticized the role of state agencies, accusing them of inefficiency and corruption. He called for greater freedom for private enterprise, presumably to stimulate more local output and improve the quality of services. This represented a major change of direction: for almost a decade the regime had aimed to eliminate private ownership.

In March a new General People's Committee was apppointed by the General People's Congress. Three new Ministries were created, to deal with marine wealth, vocational training, and mass mobilization and revolutionary guidance. Ammar al-Taif, a member of the inner revolutionary circle, was appointed to head a new people's committee of the People's Supervisory Apparatus charged with supervising the implementation of Government decisions. Major Jalloud, long regarded as Colonel Qadafi's deputy, assumed a new role in foreign affairs, taking responsibility for negotiations with Algeria and Tunisia on Maghreb unity.

The Government's decentralization plans continued with the transfer of most of the Secretariats and Ministries from Tripoli to provincial centres, the majority to Sirte, 400 miles east of the capital. In December Colonel Qadafi ordered the closure of Tripoli international airport and the transfer of all civilian operations to Mu'atiga military air base, formerly the US Wheelus base, in Tripoli's eastern suburbs.

TUNISIA

CAPITAL: Tunis   AREA: 164,000 sq km   POPULATION: 7,300,000 ('86)
OFFICIAL LANGUAGE: Arabic   POLITICAL SYSTEM: presidential
HEAD OF STATE AND GOVERNMENT: Gen. Zayn al-Abdin Ben Ali (since Nov. '87)
RULING PARTY: Constitutional Democratic Rally
PRINCIPAL MINISTERS: Hédi Bakkouche (prime minister), Abdelhamid Escheikh (foreign affairs), Hamed Karoui (justice), Abdallah Kallal (defence), Chedli Neffati (interior), Nouri Zorgati (finance)
INTERNATIONAL ALIGNMENT: NAM, Arab League, Oapec, OAU, ICO
CURRENCY: dinar (end-'88 £1=D1.61, US$1=D0.89)   GNP PER CAPITA: US$1,140 ('86)
MAIN EXPORTS: oil and gas, phosphates, olive oil

AFTER the palace coup in November 1987 during which the Prime Minister, General Zayn al-Abdin Ben Ali, seized the presidency from President-for-life Habib Bourguiba (see AR 1987, p. 228), the country's new leader moved swiftly to promote reforms and seek reconciliation with opposition groups. Political liberalization became the central platform of the new regime. A new press code placed the media under the jurisdiction of the courts rather than the Executive. The Chamber of Deputies adopted amendments to the constitution to promote a multi-party system. At a meeting of the central committee of the ruling Parti Socialiste Destourien in late February the party's name was changed to Rassemblement Constitutionnel Démocratique (RCD), demonstrating the President's intention to broaden its base and encourage more young Tunisians to join. On 11 April the President announced a Cabinet reshuffle, removing two Ministers from the Bourguiba era, Mohamed Salah Ayari and Mohamed Ghédira.

A number of prominent former Ministers living in exile were pardoned, notably Ahmed Ben Salah, the architect of the socialist planning programmes in the 1960s. Rachid Ghanouchi, leader of the banned Mouvement de Tendance Islamique (MTI), was pardoned from his life sentence but remained under house arrest. In early April the President held discussions with leaders of two of the legal opposition parties, Ahmed Mestiri of the Mouvement des Démocrates Socialistes (MDSA) and Mohamed Harmel of the Parti Communiste Tunisien (PCT), and made peace within the Union Générale des Travailleurs Tunisiens. In a public interview, MTI leader Rachid Ghanouchi expressed his confidence in President Ben Ali and his party's support for the Government's democratic policies.

In the run-up to an extraordinary congress of the ruling RCD held in Tunis in late July, the National Assembly approved constitutional amendments which abolished the presidency-for-life and the rule whereby the Prime Minister automatically succeeded the President. In order to encourage more young people to enter politics the minimum age for candidates to the National Assembly was reduced to 25. All Ministers were now required to resign their parliamentary seats when taking up office and the director of the RCD no longer had a seat in the Cabinet. At the same time, the President kept firm control over the ruling party and clearly aimed to maintain its dominant political role while broadening its base. He was re-elected president of the RCD with the Prime Minister, Hedi Bakkouche, as vice-president.

In a thorough Cabinet reshuffle on 26 July most members of the Government from the Bourguiba era were dismissed. Abdelhamid Escheikh, a close ally of President Ben Ali, was promoted to the Ministry of Foreign Affairs. Sadok Rabah became Minister of Energy and Mines and Habib Boulares Minister of Culture. For the first time a Minister was appointed who was not a member of the ruling party: Saadadine Zmerli, president of the Tunisian Human Rights League became Minister of Health. At the RCD congress President Ben Ali proclaimed his commitment to promoting democracy, asserting that this could be achieved only through party pluralism, freedom of speech and fair elections. Opposition leaders were invited to address the congress and confirmed their support for the President's political liberalization measures.

On 7 November President Ben Ali celebrated his first year in office by announcing that presidential and parliamentary elections would be held in April 1989. The announcement was welcomed by all opposition parties. In addition a national pact was signed by the President and members of the country's six legal parliamentary parties, the MTI and the trade unions. According to the pact, 'the state must guarantee basic freedoms', including freedom of opinion and association and the right to form political parties.

In foreign affairs the new President turned first to the Arab world and particularly to Tunisia's Maghreb neighbours. Diplomatic relations with Libya having been restored on 28 December 1987, Colonel Qadafi visited Tunis on 4–6 February. The reopening of the border on 15 February encouraged the return of Tunisian workers to Libya, a valuable source of foreign exchange for Tunisia. President Ben Ali met Colonel Qadafi on the island of Djerba in May, when the two leaders signed a number of conventions to encourage freedom of movement of goods and people. President Ben Ali paid his first visit to Libya on 6 August and an agreement was signed giving Tunisia 10 per cent of oil produced from the disputed offshore fields in the Gulf of Gabes.

Relations with Algeria were strengthened. President Ben Ali met President Chadli on 5 February at Sakiet-Sidi-Youssef, the Tunisian village bombed by the French air force during the Algerian war of independence. Several joint economic projects were agreed. Following the June summit of Maghreb leaders a

Maghreb Commission held its first meeting in July to examine practical steps towards achieving unity, with Tunisia actively involved. Tunisia continued to remain neutral on the question of the Western Sahara and maintained contacts with both sides in the dispute. President Ben Ali met the President of the Saharan Arab Democratic Republic (SADR), Muhammad Abd al-Aziz, at the Organization of African Unity meeting held in Addis Ababa in May. Diplomatic relations were restored with Egypt on 23 January and President Ben Ali made a state visit to Saudi Arabia on 8–11 March. His much publicized pilgrimage to Mecca served to reaffirm Tunisia's Arab and Islamic identity.

Relations with France, the former colonial power and Tunisia's main trading partner, which had remained strained after President Bourguiba's overthrow, improved as the year progressed. President Ben Ali led a delegation of Ministers to France on 12–14 September and held talks with President Mitterrand and senior officials on political and economic issues. The USA expressed its support for President Ben Ali's Government. The Tunisian Foreign Minister visited Washington in March for talks on bilateral military cooperation and several high-ranking US officials visited Tunis. Relations were strained when the US refused to support Tunisia's request for a UN resolution condemning the assassination of PLO second-in-command Abu Jihad in Tunisia on 16 April as an act of aggression, although Tunisia succeeded in securing the USA's abstention.

WESTERN SAHARA

CAPITAL: El Aaiun   AREA: 252,000 sq km   POPULATION: 164,000 ('82)
STATUS: regarded as under its sovereignty by Morocco, whereas independent Saharan Arab Democratic Republic was declared by Polisario Front in 1976

THE year brought a note of cautious optimism to the Western Sahara conflict. Peace moves launched by UN Secretary-General Pérez de Cuellar made some progress, encouraged by a growing rapprochement between the Maghreb states. The moves followed a visit by a UN peace mission to the area in late 1987 and the adoption by the UN General Assembly on 10 December (by 93 votes to none, with 50 abstentions) of a resolution calling for direct negotiations between Morocco and Polisario on a ceasefire and referendum. The mission's report was intended to assist a joint peace initiative by the UN Secretary-General and President Kenneth Kaunda of Zambia, current chairman of the Organization of African Unity. However, the role of the OAU in peace moves was compromised when President Kaunda expressed his open support for Polisario's position in the conflict during a visit to Lusaka, the Zambian capital, by a Polisario official.

As part of an active diplomatic campaign, Muhammad Abd al-Aziz, Polisario's secretary-general and President of the Saharan Arab Democratic Republic (SADR), met Colonel Qadafi of Libya and President Chadli of Algeria in February to reaffirm the SADR's support for Algerian efforts to promote Maghreb unity. Although the SADR was recognized by 71 states, mainly from the Third World, few Western states had given their diplomatic support. Spain continued to oppose the reopening of the Polisario Front's office in Madrid, and France ignored Polisario's protests about its decision to hold the Franco-African summit in Morocco.

The UN Secretary-General announced his peace plan for the Western Sahara in August. The plan called for a ceasefire followed by a referendum to determine the status of the disputed territory, the choice offered being either complete independence for the territory or its integration into Morocco. King Hassan also promoted a third option involving Saharan autonomy under Moroccan sovereignty, but this was rejected by Polisario. The UN suggested that voting in the referendum should be based on the 1974 Spanish census updated by detailed investigations by disinterested parties, and should be overseen by a UN representative with wide powers, assisted by a 2,000-strong UN monitoring force. Morocco would be instructed to reduce its troops in the Western Sahara from 100,000 to 25,000 and confine them to barracks. Polisario forces (estimated at 8,000) would remain in their bases under UN supervision. Morocco and Polisario formally accepted the UN peace plan on 30 August. On 20 September the UN Security Council authorized the Secretary-General to appoint a special envoy on the Western Sahara issue. A Uruguayan diplomat, Hector Gros Espiell, was appointed to the post in October. Several difficulties remained, however, notably King Hassan's refusal to accept Polisario's demands for direct negotiations. In early September Polisario declared that a ceasefire could be arranged before the end of the year, but claimed that Morocco's refusal to hold direct negotiations prevented progress. In October Bechir Mustapha Sayed, Polisario's foreign relations representative, met the UN Secretary-General and again pointed to the importance of direct negotiations with Morocco. He also requested a UN-Polisario-Moroccan administration during the six-month transition period to allow the return of those Sahrawis who fled during the Moroccan invasion in 1975-76.

In mid-September Polisario launched a heavy attack on Moroccan troops in the Oum Dreiga sector of the defensive wall and claimed 200 Moroccan casualties. There was speculation that the attack was organized to demonstrate that Polisario retained considerable military potential. Polisario shot down a US DC7 aircraft over the Western Sahara on 8 December, killing all five crew members. A second plane was also hit but managed to land safely at Sidi Ifni. The aircraft were chartered by the US Agency for International Development for work in their anti-locust campaign.

Hopes for peace improved in December when King Hassan announced that he was ready to 'discuss' but not negotiate with Polisario. On 24 December Polisario leaders issued a communique accepting the King's formula.

ALGERIA

CAPITAL: Algiers   AREA: 2,400,000 sq km   POPULATION: 22,500,000 ('86)
OFFICIAL LANGUAGE: Arabic   POLITICAL SYSTEM: presidential, one-party state
HEAD OF STATE AND GOVERNMENT: President Bendjedid Chadli (since Feb '79)
RULING PARTY: National Liberation Front
PRINCIPAL MINISTERS: Col. Kasdi Merbah (prime minister), Col. Boualem Bessaieh (foreign affairs), Aboubakr Belkaid (interior), Ali Benflis (justice), Sid-Ahmed Ghozali (finance), Sadok Bousena (energy and petrochemical industries)
INTERNATIONAL ALIGNMENT: NAM, Arab League, Opec, Oapec, OAU, ICO
CURRENCY: dinar (end-'88 £1=DA11.47, US$1=DA6.34)   GNP PER CAPITA: US$2,590 ('86)
MAIN EXPORTS: oil and gas

THE year opened with the Government strongly committed to pushing ahead with major structural changes in the dominant state sector, a process which dominated Algerian politics until the latter part of the year. As adopted by the Algerian Parliament on 29 December 1987, the reform measures aimed at reducing bureaucratic controls over state companies and giving managers greater freedom over decision-making. State firms were to be removed from direct control of their relevant Ministry and given full control over their resources and budgets. The Government retained responsibility for medium-term planning but the management of individual firms became responsible for making day-to-day decisions.

In a Cabinet reshuffle in February 1988 Kasdi Merbah moved to the Ministry of Public Health and was replaced as Agriculture Minister by Mohamed Rouighi. Ahmed Benfreha replaced Mohamed Rouighi at the Ministry of Hydraulics, Fishing and Forestry. These changes placed experienced technocrats in charge of key areas of government concern.

During the Algerian Parliament's summer session in June legislation was approved to complement the law on company autonomy by the creation of eight state-sponsored trust companies; these would hold shares in public companies on behalf of the state and public company managers would be accountable to them. The Parliament also passed a revised commercial law under which, although the state retained a monopoly over foreign trade, certain public companies obtained direct access to foreign markets. Moroever, private firms with access to foreign exchange now had permission to import on their own behalf or through the revised national Chamber of Commerce. Other legislation gave further incentives to stimulate the private sector in priority areas such as tourism.

In September, against a background of rising discontent among organized labour, President Chadli made a much-publicized speech to party officials. He emphasized his strong commitment to further reform measures in order to strengthen the economy and launched a sharp attack on those workers and officials who 'exploited the revolution'. The speech distressed many Algerians who had suffered years of austerity. Post and telecommunications workers went on strike on 2 October, demanding special treatment under the national salary scales, and it was rumoured that a general strike would be held on 5 October. However, the strike movement was overtaken by events which plunged Algeria into its most serious political crisis since independence.

On 4 October Algerian youths, most of them under 20, began attacking shops and party buildings in various parts of the capital. The violence spread rapidly, affecting not only Algiers but also the northern towns of Oran, Annaba and Blida. On 6 October President Chadli declared a state of siege in the Algiers region and the army was called in. The rioting was suppressed with unprecedented ferocity, the army's conduct being strongly criticized in the European press. The state of siege was not lifted until 11 October. Official sources said that the riots left 159 dead and 154 wounded, whereas estimates from news agencies for the number killed ranged from 200 to 600. Some 3,743 Algerians were arrested. The then Interior Minister, El-Hadi Khediri, told a press conference on 20 October that damage caused by the troubles amounted to $250 million.

Islamic fundamentalists played a highly visible role in the riots, and the most active resistance and the heaviest casualties were reported from strongholds of radical Islam such as Kouba, Bab el-Oued and Belcourt. A radical Islamic opposition had been re-establishing itself as a force in local politics in recent years, a trend acknowledged by President Chadli when he met leading opposition imams Ali Belhadj, Shaikh Sahnoun and Shaikh Mahfoud on 10 October. But there was little evidence that the rioters were motivated by the desire for an Islamic state. According to some observers, rising social tensions resulting from the Government's recent reform measures and moves to restructure the economy on market-oriented lines were the main cause of the riots. These reforms, it was argued, favoured the managerial elite and young technocrats but challenged the traditional privileges of administrators and party members and put lower-paid workers at a disadvantage. Others suggested that the riots might have been organized by conservative elements in the Algerian establishment who remained faithful to a radical socialist policy and opposed to the reforms promoted by the President and his supporters. Whatever the cause of the uprising, the events of early October strengthened the position of President Chadli and the reformers.

On 10 October President Chadli addressed the nation. He accepted responsibility for the crisis, promised swift political reforms and announced a referendum on 3 November to approve amendments to the constitution. In this plebiscite, 92.2 per cent of the votes were cast in favour of constitutional changes transferring power away from the presidency to a Government responsible to elected representatives of the people. Shortly before the referendum, Mohamed Cherif Messaadia, seen as the most prominent member of the 'old guard', was replaced as head of the FLN's permanent secretariat by Abdelhamid Mehri. General Lakhad Ayat, head of the Délégation Général à la Prévention et à la Sécurité was, also replaced. In a conciliatory gesture to mobilize public opinion in favour of the reforms, the President announced the release of those arrested in the riots and material assistance for the families of those killed.

As required by the amended constitution, Kasdi Merbah was named head of government by President Chadli on 5 November. Four days later Colonel Merbah appointed a 22-member Government composed largely of technocrats, including Sid-Ahmed Ghozali as Minister of Finance, Boualem Bessaieh as Minister of Foreign Affairs and Sadok Bousena as Minister of Energy and Petrochemicals. Changes in the party were to be the subject of a second referendum, in which, it was believed, the election of non-party members to the Algerian Parliament would be authorized. On 14 November Prime Minister Merbah presented a programme of emergency measures to Parliament covering the economy, youth employment, education, judicial and health reforms. President Chadli announced on 16 November that Major-General Abdallah Belhouchet had been replaced as army Chief of Staff. Further changes were made in early December in eight of the top eleven military posts, completing a major reshuffle of Algeria's military command.

In foreign affairs Algeria was active in promoting close relations with Tunisia and Libya as part of its efforts to achieve Maghreb unity. In January President Chadli visited Tunis for his first meeting with the new Tunisian leader, President Ben Ali, and then went on to Tripoli. The Libyan leader, Colonel Qadafi, met President Chadli in Annaba on 7 February and the next day they were joined by President Ben Ali to celebrate the 30th anniversary of the French bombing of Sakiet-Sidi-Youcef. Differences in approach to unity continued to divide Algeria and Tunisia from Libya, Colonel

Qadafi insisting on a common political unit whereas Presidents Chadli and Ben Ali favoured building economic ties. Nevertheless, during 1988 Libya agreed to a number of joint economic projects which strengthened relations with Algeria. Proposals for political union with Libya published in early October appeared to be the work of the FLN radical wing. Following the October riots which strengthened President Chadli and the reformers it was unlikely that these proposals would be implemented.

After months of quiet diplomacy, diplomatic relations with Morocco, broken in 1976, were restored on 16 May and the Algerian-Moroccan border was reopened in June. This move paved the way for the first joint meeting of the leaders of Algeria, Libya, Mauritania, Morocco and Tunisia on 10 June. The first Maghreb Commission meeting was held in July and agreed to examine new measures for economic integration. But the Western Sahara conflict (see pp. 238–40) remained a major obstacle to improved relations between Algeria and Morocco and to further progress toward Maghreb unity.

In April a hijacked Kuwaiti jumbo jet arrived in Algiers. After a week of difficult negotiations involving leading Algerian politicians, the remaining hostages were released without further bloodshed. Algeria's role was praised by many states but the USA and UK criticized the Algerian authorities for not detaining the hijackers, who were reportedly linked with pro-Iranian Shia Muslim groups in Lebanon. The substantial vote of the right-wing Front National in the French presidential elections caused deep concern in Algeria, where French racial feeling was seen as a potential threat to the million-strong Algerian community living in France.

MOROCCO

CAPITAL: Rabat   AREA: 460,000 sq km   POPULATION: 22,500,000 ('86)
OFFICIAL LANGUAGE: Arabic   POLITICAL SYSTEM: monarchy
HEAD OF STATE AND GOVERNMENT: King Hassan II (since March '61)
RULING PARTIES: Constitutional Union heads seven-party coalition
PRINCIPAL MINISTERS: Azzedine Laraki (prime minister), Abdel Latif Filali (foreign affairs), Mohammed Berrada (finance), Driss Basri (interior), Moulay Mustapha Ben Larbi Alaiou (justice)
INTERNATIONAL ALIGNMENT: NAM, Arab League, ICO
CURRENCY: dirham (end-'88 £1=DH14.63, US$1=DH8.09)   GNP PER CAPITA: US$590 ('86)
MAIN EXPORTS: phosphates, agricultural products

DURING 1988 the Western Sahara issue (see pp. 238–40) continued to dominate Moroccan political life. Although Morocco consistently refused direct negotiations with Polisario until after a referendum had been held, secret talks between Morocco and Polisario reportedly took place in Algiers and also Jeddah. On 30 August Moroccan Foreign Minister Abdel Latif Filali and Bechir Mustapha Sayed of Polisario met UN Secretary-General Pérez de Cuellar in Geneva and both accepted in principle the UN peace plan for the disputed territory. The UN initiative called for a ceasefire followed by a UN peacekeeping operation and a referendum in which the Sahrawi people would vote for independence or integration into Morocco. During September the president of the Moroccan Chamber of Representatives visited Beijing and Moscow to put the Moroccan point of view on the UN peace proposals.

The year began with relations between Morocco and its neighbour and rival Algeria at a low ebb. In response to an article in *L'Opinion* by M'hamed Boucetta, secretary-general of the Istaqlal party, stating Morocco's claim to the Algerian provinces of Tindouf, Knadsa and Touat, the Algerian press warned Morocco about taking any steps towards reclaiming the provinces by force. Yet despite these exchanges and continuing tension over the Western Sahara, contacts between the two countries increased, reflecting Algerian efforts to built a united Maghreb. Diplomatic relations between the two countries, broken by Morocco in 1976, were restored on 16 May. King Hassan visited Algiers on 7 June for the Arab summit.

A special effort was made to maintain good relations with Tunisia following the fall of President Bourguiba. In early February Moroccan Prime Minister Azzedine Laraki visited Tunis and the new Tunisian Prime Minister, Hédi Bakkouche, visited Rabat. Morocco began to participate more actively in discussions about Maghreb unity. King Hassan in August stressed that his country's participation in moves towards a united Maghreb did not conflict with Morocco's continued desire to seek membership of the European Community, with which a fishing agreement was concluded in February following months of negotiations. The agreement did not refer specifically to the waters off Western Sahara, merely to 'those waters under Moroccan sovereignty or jurisdiction'. Nevertheless, Polisario accused Morocco of trying to secure EC recognition of its claims to the disputed waters. Mohamed Seqat, Morocco's Secretary of State for European Affairs, denied this but affirmed that the Moroccan fishing zone included the waters off Western Sahara.

An official visit to Spain by King Hassan, his first since the death of General Franco in 1975, was to have taken place on 8 November but was cancelled on 28 October. Although relations between the two countries were cordial, Morocco was displeased by Spanish voting on Western Sahara at the UN Commission for Decolonization on 25 October. Another area of dispute concerned the Spanish enclaves of Ceuta and Melilla in Morocco. Notwithstanding the Moroccan claim to the enclaves, in August the Spanish Prime Minister declared that he was preparing legislation to ensure that the towns became 'integral parts of Spain' with some administrative autonomy.

Frank Carlucci, the US Defense Secretary, visited Morocco in April and was received by King Hassan. American sources revealed that US military aid to Morocco during 1988 totalled some $26 million, including $15 million for AGM-65D missiles and $11 million for M48-A5 tanks.

King Hassan used his annual speech in March on the occasion of the anniversary of his accession to the throne to reaffirm his commitment to liberalizing the economy and encouraging private enterprise and investment. Addressing Parliament in April, the King announced that some public enterprises would be transferred to the private sector and criticized the public sector for poor management and low efficiency. Legislation to privatize all but the most strategically important public companies was presented to Parliament on 19 October. Some 400 public companies were affected, but six key companies were exempt, namely Office Nationale des Chemins de Fer, Office National de l'Eau Potable, Office National de l'Electricité, Office Chérifien des Phosphates, Royal Air Maroc, and Office National des Postes et Télécommunications.

Mohamed Berrada, the Finance Minister, outlined other elements of the Government's liberalization policy. These included Government encouragement of private enterprise, cuts in state spending and a reduction in taxes. The opposition attacked the economic reforms, particularly the privatization programme, arguing that it could lead to job losses. They called instead for an increase in public expenditure, the maintenance of subsidies on basic goods and salary increases. The Government argued that its commitment to a liberal economy would encourage local and foreign investment which would in turn stimulate job creation.

Unemployment remained high and real wages and incomes declined for important sectors of the labour force. Concern was expressed that any attempt to reduce overstaffing in the public sector could destroy the fragile social peace. The IMF expressed its general support for Morocco's liberalization programme.

VI EQUATORIAL AFRICA

Chapter 1

ETHIOPIA—SOMALIA—DJIBOUTI—KENYA—TANZANIA—UGANDA

ETHIOPIA

CAPITAL: Addis Ababa   AREA: 1,200,000 sq km   POPULATION: 43,500,000 ('86)
OFFICIAL LANGUAGE: Amharic   POLITICAL SYSTEM: people's republic, one-party state
RULING PARTY: Workers' Party of Ethiopia
HEAD OF STATE AND PARTY LEADER: President (Lt.-Col.) Mengistu Haile-Maryam (since Feb '77)
PRINCIPAL MINISTERS: Lt.-Col. Fisseha Desta (Vice-President), Capt. Fikre-Selassie Wogderes (prime minister), Lt.-Col. Berhanu Bayeh (foreign affairs), Col. Tesfaye Wolde Selassie (internal affairs), Maj.-Gen. Haile Giorgis Habte-Maryam (defence), Wole Chekol (finance), Wondayen Mehretu (justice)
INTERNATIONAL ALIGNMENT: NAM, OAU, ACP, Comecon (observer)
CURRENCY: birr (end-'88 £1=Br3.72, US$1=Br2.06)   GNP PER CAPITA: US$120 ('86)
MAIN EXPORTS: coffee, agricultural produce

FAMINE did not reach the levels predicted in late 1987, and heavy main rains in July-September helped to produce a good grain crop; but the Government's position in the civil wars in Eritrea and Tigré deteriorated badly, with repercussions for famine relief, as well as for domestic and foreign policies.

The key event of the year was the capture by the Eritrean People's Liberation Front (EPLF) in March of the Ethiopian army base at Afabet in northern Eritrea. In the process, the EPLF routed a three-division Ethiopian force of some 18,000 men and captured three Soviet advisers and a huge amount of military equipment, including some 50 tanks. The defeat revealed severe problems of Ethiopian military morale, and was reportedly followed by the execution of several senior commanders. The Government pulled in outlying garrisons, abandoning much of the region to EPLF control, in order to consolidate its hold over central and southern Eritrea while moving in reinforcements.

In a broadcast on 31 March President Mengistu Haile-Maryam mobilized national resources to deal with the crisis, under the slogan 'everything to the war front'. A state of emergency was declared in May in Eritrea and the neighbouring Tigré region, where the Tigré People's Liberation Front (TPLF) had captured several strategic towns in March and April. The TPLF also re-established working relations with the EPLF after a four-year break, thus easing its supply problems from Sudan. By July the military situation had been stabilized, with Government forces recapturing much of the territory lost to the opposition movements, but still holding a weaker position than at the start of the year.

The fighting greatly disrupted famine relief operations. Early in the year, both the EPLF and TPLF continued their attacks on relief convoys, despite strong international condemnation. After the loss of Afabet, the Government ordered foreign relief agencies to cease operations in Eritrea and Tigré, which had been especially badly hit by drought the previous year. To the surprise of many observers, however, large-scale famine did not recur. The early-warning system established after the 1984-85 famine worked well. Substantial quantities of relief grain reached the country, including a 250,000 tonne donation from the Soviet Union, purchased on international markets, which contrasted with the low level of Soviet aid in 1984-85. Both Government and EPLF/TPLF relief distribution had improved since 1984-85, and peasants had evidently retained larger than expected grain stocks. Heavy rains washed out some crops, and helped contribute to a locust plague which threatened crisis proportions by the end of the year, but at the same time helped to produce perhaps the best annual grain crop of recent years. Huge influxes of refugees from fighting and famine in neighbouring countries—about 350,000 from Sudan and 400,000 from Somalia—also posed a major challenge to relief services.

In January, the Government announced its acceptance of agricultural policy reforms required by external donors (notably the World Bank and European Community) for the release of a $400 million agricultural aid package; these notably included a 10 per cent increase in grain prices paid to farmers, and a relaxation of restrictions on private grain traders. Further reforms, including an increase in producer coffee prices, were promised in October. At the same time, the authorities continued to pursue resettlement and villagization policies which were generally regarded with scepticism by Western aid agencies. In February, about 20 people were reportedly shot while resisting resettlement in Wollo region. By September, according to official figures, some 12.2 million people (about a third of the total rural population) had been grouped into villages, with numbers planned to rise to about 15 million in 1988-89. The economy as a whole continued to perform poorly. In a major speech in November, President Mengistu drew attention to the stagnation of export earnings (intensified by low world prices for coffee, the country's major export), accompanied by a failure to improve production or diversify foreign trade. He reported that defence costs absorbed 15 per cent of GNP, and 50 per cent of the national Budget.

Both Government and opposition movements sought to improve their international standing after the EPLF capture of Afabet. The Government immediately reached an agreement with the Somali Republic, abandoning an earlier insistence on prior Somali recognition of the existing frontier between the two countries; each side undertook to withdraw troops from the border, and to cease supporting opposition movements directed against the other. This released Ethiopian forces which were immediately moved to Eritrea. An exchange of prisoners from the 1977-78 war later took place, and President Mengistu welcomed President Siyad Barre of Somalia to the June OAU summit in Addis Ababa. Relations with Sudan were more ambivalent: Ethiopia both aided the Sudan People's Liberation Movement (SPLM) and hosted peace talks between it and the Sudanese Government late in the year.

In a gesture to appease Western opinion, seven women members of the former imperial family, imprisoned since 1974, were released in May. President Mengistu visited the USSR in July, and while he gained some Soviet military aid to help stabilize the position in Eritrea, the Soviet Government was increasingly overtly pressing for a negotiated settlement to the conflict. The EPLF leader, Isayas Afewerki, paid his first visit to Western Europe and the United States in October and November; while playing down his movement's longstanding marxist-leninist commitments in a bid for Western support, he also acknowledged the potential role of the USSR in reaching a settlement. In keeping with its close relationship with North Korea, Ethiopia was one of the small group of states which boycotted the Seoul Olympic Games.

SOMALIA

CAPITAL: Mogadishu AREA: 638,000 sq km POPULATION: 5,500,000 ('86)
OFFICIAL LANGUAGES: Somali and Arabic
POLITICAL SYSTEM: presidential, one-party state
RULING PARTY: Somali Revolutionary Socialist Party
HEAD OF STATE AND PARTY LEADER: President (Maj.-Gen.) Mohammed Siyad Barre (since Oct '69)
PRINCIPAL MINISTERS: Lt.-Gen. Mohammed Ali Samatar (prime minster), Maj.-Gen. Hussein Kulmiye Afrah (deputy premier, economic affairs), Ahmed Suleiman Abdalla (deputy premier, security affairs), Ahmed Mohammud Farah (deputy premier, political affairs), Mohammed Ali Hamud (foreign affairs), Maj.-Gen. Adan Abdullahi Nur (defence), Abdurahman Jama Barre (finance), Hassan Abdullahi Farah (justice)
INTERNATIONAL ALIGNMENT: NAM, OAU, ACP, Arab League, ICO
CURRENCY: Shilling (end-'88 £1=SoSh440.79, US$1=SoSh243.66)
GNP PER CAPITA: US$=280 ('86)
MAIN EXPORTS: livestock, agricultural produce

FIGHTING between Government forces and Somali National Movement (SNM) opponents in northern Somalia broke out into full-scale civil war between May and August. Following an agreement with Ethiopia in April, the Ethiopians withdrew their support from the SNM; its radio station (Radio Halgan) went off the air, and its training camps were closed. In late May and early June, however, SNM forces expelled from Ethiopia attempted to seize the two northern cities of Hargeisa and Burao, and also attacked the port of Berbera. Foreign aid workers were evacuated, and Government aircraft bombed densely inhabited urban areas occupied by the SNM. Large areas were destroyed, and the Somali commander estimated deaths at 20,000 in Hargeisa alone. Estimates of total casualties ranged up to 50,000. Government troops regained control of both towns by August. Amnesty International published detailed allegations of torture, and about 400,000 refugees fled to Ethiopia.

Factional conflict continued within the Government over the succession to the ageing President Siyad Barre. His eldest son, General Maslah Siyad Barre, was made military commander of the Mogadishu area, while his son-in-law, General Morgan, was commander of the northern region. Dissension within the armed forces was indicated by the arrest of several senior officers from the normally loyal Marehan and Ogaden clans. Eight people, including a former Vice-President and Foreign Minister, were condemned to death for treason in February, although the sentences were commuted to imprisonment.

Following unilateral suspension of an economic restructuring agreement with the IMF in September 1987, the Government introduced exchange controls in December 1987 and January 1988, and price controls on essential foodstuffs in February. The black market value of the Somali shilling fell to $1=SoSh300 in March, against an official rate of $1=SoSh100. The IMF declared Somalia ineligible for further borrowing in May, but talks were resumed following a 44 per cent devaluation in late June.

In April a Soviet Deputy Foreign Minister became the highest-ranking Soviet official to visit Somalia since the 1977 breach of the formerly close relationship between the two countries. A visit by a Kenyan military delegation in May was the first since the independence of the two countries.

DJIBOUTI

CAPITAL: Djibouti AREA: 23,000 sq km POPULATION: 362,000 ('86)
OFFICIAL LANGUAGES: Arabic and French POLITICAL SYSTEM: presidential, one-party state
RULING PARTY: Popular Rally for Progress
HEAD OF STATE AND PARTY LEADER: President Hassan Gouled Aptidon (since June '77)
PRINCIPAL MINISTERS: Barkat Gourad Hamadou (prime minister, planning), Moumin Bahdon Farah (foreign affairs), Hussein Barkad Siraj (defence), Mohammed Djama Elabe (finance and economy), Khayreh Alaeh Hared (interior), Elaf Orbis Ali (justice)
INTERNATONAL ALIGNMENT: NAM, OAU, ACP, Arab League, ICO, Francophonie
CURRENCY: Djibouti franc (end-'88 £1=DF313.00, US$1=DF173.02)
GNP PER CAPITA: US$480 ('81)
MAIN EXPORTS: agricultural products

DJIBOUTI concluded a border agreement with Ethiopia in February, designed to control movements in both directions, and President Gouled visited Addis Ababa in March. At the time of the fighting in northern Somalia in June (see pp. 247–8), he announced that Djibouti would not allow its territory to be used by the SNM, while allowing the Somali Government forces some use of local facilities. A military exercise in March indicated continuing French commitment to the country's defence, and this was strengthened with the addition of a Mirage squadron to the resident French garrison in June.

KENYA

CAPITAL: Nairobi AREA: 580,000 sq km POPULATION: 21,200,000 ('86)
OFFICIAL LANGUAGE: Kiswahili POLITICAL SYSTEM: presidential, one-party state
RULING PARTY: Kenya African National Union
HEAD OF STATE AND PARTY LEADER: President Daniel Arap Moi (since Oct '78)
PRINCIPAL MINISTERS: Josephat Karanja (Vice-President, home affairs), Robert J. Ouko (foreign affairs), George Saitoti (finance), Zachary Onyonka (planning and national development)
INTERNATIONAL ALIGNMENT: NAM, OAU, ACP, Cwth.
CURRENCY: shilling (end-'88 £1=KSh33.13, US$1=KSh18.31) GNP PER CAPITA: US$300 ('86)
MAIN EXPORTS: coffee, tea, petroleum products

ON 22 February the ruling Kenya African National Union (KANU) selected its candidates for the forthcoming general election by requiring party members to queue behind election agents displaying photographs of the contenders; about 43 per cent of the 4.3 million party members participated. Daniel Arap Moi, who had already been declared President for a third five-year term, and 11 other candidates were returned unopposed. This fact, and the rule which allowed any candidate who received more than 70 per cent of the party vote to enter Parliament unopposed, meant that only about two-thirds of the 188 parliamentary seats were contested by secret ballot on 21 March. The dominant issues were local, not national, and revolved round the voters' assessment of the candidate's ability to provide them with benefits. The President favoured amending the constitution in order to replace the secret ballot with the queuing system used by KANU.

Four Ministers were defeated in the elections and three others were dropped in a Cabinet reshuffle. President Moi increased the number of ministerial posts from 27 to 32 and introduced new Ministries of Manpower Development and Employment and of National Guidance and Political Affairs. The long-serving Vice-President, Mwai Kibaki, was demoted to Minister of Health and replaced as Vice-President by Dr Josephat Karanja, a fellow Kikuyu and wealthy businessman who had served as high commissioner in London before being made an Assistant Minister. In September Dr Karanja was elected unopposed as Vice-President of KANU;

Mr Kibaki did not seek re-election but won the important KANU branch chairmanship in his home district of Nyeri.

The voting at the 3,400-strong party delegates' conference in Nairobi further consolidated the President's power; in October he celebrated the tenth anniversary of his accession. He appointed a number of fellow Kalenjin to key positions, relied more on bureaucrats than elected politicians, and gave land in Government settlement schemes to army officers. His style of government was autocratic and critics of the regime were treated harshly. Religious organizations were not immune: *Beyond*, the magazine of the National Council of Churches of Kenya, was banned for condemning the administration of the queuing process used to select KANU parliamentary candidates; the President (in July) warned missionaries and church aid workers not to conspire against the Government and accused World Vision, an American evangelical organization based in Los Angeles, of doing so. Government charges that the Anglican Church was under foreign influence were repudiated in October by Archbishop Manasses Kuria. The local press increasingly covered only 'safe' subjects and parliamentary debate was stifled; the President charged foreign journalists, and the BBC especially, of anti-Kenya reporting.

In August Parliament unanimously passed a Bill to amend the constitution, giving the President and police more powers. To the dismay of the Law Society of Kenya, the new legislation authorized the President to sack High Court and Court of Appeal judges and members of the Public Service Commission without prior investigation by an independent tribunal; it also allowed the police to detain those arrested on suspicion of having committed capital offences for up to 14 days before bringing them to court.

International expressions of concern over police interrogation methods and detention without trial possibly helped to secure the release of ten political detainees in February. Among those released was Raila Odinga, the country's longest-standing political detainee and son of the former Vice-President and opposition leader Oginga Odinga; however, he was rearrested in August and charged with subversive activities. In March the chief magistrate found that Peter Karanja, a businessman who had died in police custody in 1987, had been tortured by his interrogators; the use of torture in detention was confirmed by Gibson Kamau Kuria, a leading Nairobi lawyer, upon his release in December. In September 5,000 students at Kenyatta university staged an angry demonstration when Nairobi Radio falsely reported that students' loans were to be abolished. One student leader was sentenced to five years' imprisonment and 43 students were not readmitted when the university reopened early in December.

On the economic front Professor George Saitoti, the Finance Minister, emphasized the need to achieve 'economic growth through financial discipline and efficiency' in introducing the 1988-89 Budget on 16 June. Development spending was to rise by 25 per cent and recurrent spending was roughly to match the 9.3 per cent inflation rate. Recurrent revenues were to benefit from the doubling of airport tax (to US$20) and higher levies on cigarettes, beer, soft drinks and petrol, but those increases were offset by substantial cuts in duties on bicycles, buses, passenger cars, television sets and radios—cuts that were designed to make local manufacturing more competitive. Price decontrol remained official policy. Additional incentives were provided for new investors. The Government wrote off KSh 5,000 million in bad loans to state corporations, underlining the need for tighter financial control if industrial performance was to be significantly improved. The agricultural outlook was regarded as encouraging and the price of coffee moved upwards towards the end of the year. Levels of poverty and unemployment remained high, however.

During her visit to Kenya in January—the first by a serving British Prime Minister—Mrs Thatcher announced a new aid package worth £20 million in balance-of-payments support, linked to the country's IMF programme. President Moi made state visits to Egypt in April and to Tanzania in July. In June the Government denied giving armed support to the Sudanese Liberation Army; cattle rustlers, thought to be from southern Sudan, operated periodically along the border with Sudan and Ethiopia. The poaching of ivory and rhino horn by heavily-armed professional gangs continued; the President instituted a shoot-to-kill policy against poachers.

TANZANIA

CAPITAL: Dar es Salaam/Dodoma   AREA: 945,000 sq km   POPULATION: 23,000,000 ('86)
OFFICIAL LANGUAGE: Swahili and English   POLITICAL SYSTEM: presidential, one-party state
RULING PARTY: Chama cha Mapinduzi
HEAD OF STATE AND GOVERNMENT: President Ali Hassan Mwinyi (since Nov '85)
PARTY LEADER: Julius Nyerere (former President)
VICE-PRESIDENTS: Joseph Warioba (prime minister), Idris Abdul Wakil (President of Zanzibar)
PRINCIPAL MINISTERS: Salim Ahmed Salim (deputy premier, defence), Benjamin Mkapa (foreign affairs), Cleopa David Msuya (finance, economic affairs and planning), Brig. Muhiddin Kimario (home affairs), Damian Lubuva (justice)
INTERNATIONAL ALIGNMENT: NAM, OAU, ACP, Cwth.
CURRENCY: shilling (end-'88 £1=TSh222.00, US$1=TSh122.72)   GNP PER CAPITA: US$250 ('86)
MAIN EXPORTS: coffee, cotton, tropical foodstuffs

THE 1988-89 Budget, covering the last year of the three-year economic recovery programme (ERP), was introduced on 16 June by Cleopa Msuya, the Finance, Economic Affairs and Planning Minister. It contained few major surprises. Revenue and expenditure (especially on development) rose sharply in absolute terms, though not in real terms in view of the shilling's 70 per cent depreciation against the US dollar and an inflation rate of some 30 per cent. The Government continued to rely heavily on foreign aid. Measures to alleviate the ERP's effects, particularly on urban dwellers, included raising the minimum wage, introducing rent assistance, reducing income tax, and increasing civil service salaries. On the other hand, the taxes on cigarettes, beer, soft drinks and wine were up by 15-25 per cent; the airport charge was increased (to TSh 300); and a new tax of TSh 20 was applied to video rentals. The price of petrol was not increased, but duty on spare parts was maintained. In pursuit of its continuing liberalization policy, which was not to the liking of radical elements within the ruling party, the Government again reduced the number of items subject to price control. Cash crop prices were increased and rural cooperatives took over many of the functions previously performed by crop marketing authorities. In these various ways, the Government met IMF conditions, but it did so at its own pace in order to reduce inflationary pressures and minimize social discontent.

In September General Ernest Mwita Kiaro, the 62-year-old former commander of the 20th division, was made head of the United Republic's defence forces and Major-General Tumainieli N. Kiwelu was appointed Chief of Staff with the rank of lieutenant-general. General Kiaro was from the Kuria ethnic group in north-west Tanzania. Ex-President Julius Nyerere, who was still chairman of the ruling party, Chama cha Mapinduzi (CCM), and Prime Minister Joseph Warioba also came from the area to the east of Lake Victoria (Nyerere himself was the son of a Zanak chief) and the predominance in the army of people from this area was said to be resented by a number of army officers. General Kiaro's appointment, and the appointment of people from the same ethnic group to head the central bank and the courts, was interpreted by *Indian Ocean Newsletter* as confirmation of the influence exercized on President Ali Hassan Mwinyi by Dr Nyerere and his entourage.

The Prime Minister paid a five-day official visit to Mozambique in March; satisfaction was expressed at the progress made in economic and commercial co-operation between the two countries. However, in November the Government, probably for financial reasons, withdrew its troops from Mozambique, where they had been helping since 1987 to defend the northern province of Zambezia against rebels of the South African-backed National Resistance Movement (MNR). Co-operation with land-locked Burundi was to be strengthened following President Pierre Bugoya's four-day visit to Tanzania in April.

Zanzibar was the focus of much attention. A power struggle within the islands' Government came to a head on 23 January when President Idris Abdul Wakil suspended the 18-man Cabinet and the advisory Revolutionary Council; he subsequently assumed direct control of the army. The struggle was believed to centre on Pemba dissatisfaction with the economic and social imbalance between the two islands, which were dependent economically on Pemba's production of 90 per cent of clove exports. The influential and liberal Chief Minister, Seif Shariff Hamad, who was of Pemba origin, was replaced by Dr Omar Ali Juma, a senior official in the Agriculture and Livestock Ministry; he was also dropped, with two former Ministers, from the reconstituted Revolutionary Council. On 14 May CCM's national executive committee (NEC) expelled Shariff Hamad and six other party officials for 'sabotaging the party and disrupting the unity of Tanzania'. The NEC also dismissed Rashid Hamad from his post of CCM chairman in Pemba South region for failing to prevent such sabotage.

Riots in Zanzibar on 13 May resulted in two deaths and injuries to several other people. They were possibly sparked off by disparaging remarks about certain Islamic laws on marriage and inheritance made by Mrs Sophia Kawawa, head of the Tanzania Women's Organization. However, the Chief Minister claimed that the riots were instigated by anti-government agents based in Dubai. President Wakil appointed a seven-man commission of community and religious leaders and civil servants to investigate their cause. In June, 15 of those arrested during the riots were released for lack of evidence, but 28 others were remanded in custody.

An issue underlying the tension in Zanzibar was the extent of the islands' autonomy within the United Republic, whose 24th anniversary was celebrated in April. Decisions which directly affected Zanzibaris, such as the choice of their leaders, were being arrogated by Dar es Salaam and this fact, coupled with a sharp downturn in the economy and rising unemployment, caused widespread frustration. In September the Zanzibari Government introduced legislation to curb the press. The runway at Zanzibar's airport was being extended to accommodate international jets and its main port, and harbour facilities on Pemba, were being rehabilitated.

UGANDA

CAPITAL: Kampala   AREA: 240,000 sq km   POPULATION: 15,200,000 ('86)
OFFICIAL LANGUAGE: English   POLITICAL SYSTEM: presidential
HEAD OF STATE AND GOVERNMENT: President Yoweri Museveni (since Jan '86)
PRINCIPAL MINISTERS: Samson Kisekka (prime minister), Paul Semogerere (deputy premier, foreign affairs), Crispus Kiyonga (finance), Ibrahim Mukiibi (internal affairs), Yoweri Kyesimira (planning and economic development), George Kanyeihamba (justice)
INTERNATIONAL ALIGNMENT: NAM, OAU, ACP, Cwth.
CURRENCY: shilling (end-'88 £1=USh297.84, US$1=USh164.64)   GNP PER CAPITA: US$230 ('86)
MAIN EXPORTS: coffee, cotton

IN a ministerial reshuffle in March, President Yoweri Museveni appointed three Deputy Prime Ministers to back up the 75-year-old Prime Minister, Dr Samson Kisekka; the latter and his three deputies were all Baganda. The Second Deputy Prime Minister was Paul Semogerere, leader of the former Democratic Party and previously Minister of the Interior; he was made Foreign Minister. The President retained the Defence portfolio. Dr Crispus Kiyonga stayed on as Minister of Finance and introduced the 1988-89 Budget on 1 July. Budgetary measures adopted to meet World Bank and IMF conditions included the devaluation of the Uganda shilling by a further 60 per cent (it was devalued by 72 per cent the previous year), 100-150 per cent increases in producer prices, steep rises in petrol, kerosene, and sugar prices, and higher taxation designed to curb the budget deficit of USh 38.9 million or nearly one-third of total spending. Public sector wages were raised by 120 per cent in line with the official estimate of inflation (the real level was believed to be much higher). GDP, which increased by an estimated 6 per cent in 1987, was expected to reach 8 to 9 per cent, with agriculture contributing over half, although low international prices for most cash crops had led to a decline in output in recent years. Most of the manufacturing sector, which accounted for approximately 4 per cent of GDP, was operating substantially below capacity, mainly because of shortages of imported materials, spare parts and fuel.

President Museveni continued his policy of pacifying the north and east, where anti-government rebel groups operated. Some 3,000 members of the north-eastern based Uganda People's Army surrendered to government forces at the end of April. At Gulu in northern Uganda in June the President signed a peace agreement with the military commander of the 5,000-strong Uganda People's Democratic Army (UPDA), whose guerrillas were either to be integrated into the Government's National Resistance Army (NRA) or helped to resettle into civilian life. The NRA also opened peace talks with the Holy Spirit Movement whose leader, Alice Lakwena, was imprisoned in Kenya for four months for entering the country illegally in late December 1987 (see AR 1987, p. 244); after serving her sentence, she was repatriated to Uganda. On 13 July the Army Council gave all rebels 30 days to surrender and said that special courts would be set up to deal with those who continued fighting the Government after 12 August. The civil war left almost half a million people destitute; in September an Oxfam report described malnutrition in the former war zones as comparable in intensity to the famine in Mozambique (see p. 282).

The text of the peace agreement with the UPDA provided a blueprint for the country's political future. It promised that local council elections and elections to the National Resistance Council (NRC), Uganda's interim Parliament, would be held in the north and east before the end of the year. Since its establishment in 1986, the NRC had been dominated by President Museveni's own supporters, mainly from the south. The agreement said that the interim Assembly's term would expire at the beginning of 1990 and that it would then be succeeded by an Assembly chosen in 'free and fair elections'. A national referendum would be held to determine what party system the people favoured. In October, the President renewed his pledge to restore constitutional government in 1990 and appointed a 15-member constitutional commission.

Relations with Kenya, although not cordial, were better than in 1987 and attempts were made to strengthen border security and restore transport links with the Kenyan coast at Mombasa. Border talks with Sudan at Arua, north-west Uganda, led to the signing in March of a memorandum providing for the return of up to 60,000 Ugandan refugees who had settled in southern Sudan following the fall of ex-President Amin in 1979. A Libyan diplomat was killed and several people were injured when two grenades exploded in Kampala in January; an unknown group opposed to the Government's Libyan links claimed responsibility. A fearless critic of the Idi Amin regime—Festo Kivengere, Bishop of Kigezi since 1972—died in May. Twenty-four people, including an army captain, were arrested in September and accused of plotting to overthrow the Government. Sir Geoffrey Howe, the British Foreign Secretary, on a visit to Uganda in September, announced an additional grant of £10 million but said that Britain would not extend export credit guarantees until outstanding debts had been paid; Uganda had therefore to pay cash in advance for all British imports. The President declared his preference for a mixed economy and improved terms of trade rather than aid.

Chapter 2

GHANA—NIGERIA—SIERRA LEONE—THE GAMBIA—LIBERIA

GHANA

CAPITAL: Accra   AREA: 240,000 sq km   POPULATION: 14,000,000 ('86)
OFFICIAL LANGUAGE: English   POLITICAL SYSTEM: military regime with civilian participation
HEAD OF STATE: Flt.-Lt. Jerry Rawlings, Chairman of Provisional National Defence Council (since Dec '81)
PRINCIPAL MINISTERS: P.V. Obeng (chairman of committee of secretaries),
   Obed Y. Asamoah (foreign affairs), Kwesi Botchway (finance and economic planning),
   Mohamad Idrisu (defence), G.E.K. Aikins (justice)
INTERNATIONAL ALIGNMENT: NAM, OAU, ACP, Cwth.
CURRENCY: cedi, (end-'88 £1=C419.68, US$1=C231.99)   GNP PER CAPITA: US$469 ('87)
MAIN EXPORTS: cocoa, gold, minerals, timber

THE country's hybrid of military-civilian rule underwent further transformation during the year. On 10 May the Ghanaian equivalent of a Cabinet—a combination of national and regional secretaries — was again reshuffled. Flight-Lieut. Rawlings remained the dominant figure, but only two of the 10 regional secretaries—Lieut.-Colonel Thompson for Greater Accra and Colonel (rtd.) Osei Owusu for Ashanti—were from the armed services. Similarly, within the Ministries, only two of the Secretaries were now military men — Commodore Obimpeh (Agriculture) and Lieut.-Colonel Mensah Gbedemah (Roads). Continuity of policy was ensured by the retention of Kwesi Botchway (Finance and Economic Planning) and Dr Obed Y. Asamoah (Foreign Affairs).

At local level, the announcement on 1 July that elections would take place for 110 district councils was made good in December. Registration was completed between 18-25 April and elections were held on 8 December. The turnout was estimated to be 60 per cent of what was said to be a registration figure of almost 90 per cent.

Democracy was returning at snail's pace, although the good was offset by the bad. Detention orders remained in force against members of a New Democratic Movement, including its leader Kwame Karikari, former head of Ghana Broadcasting. Corruption too was widespread within the public and private sector. Workers and management alike were accused by Flight-Lieut. Rawlings of 'having been corrupted . . . creaming off factory products, becoming thieves'. Criticism of the military was also voiced. The J.B. Danquah memorial lectures were given in January by Professor Adu Boahen, who argued that only fear kept the regime in power; there was the need for a full return to democracy. A right of reply was claimed by the Government and Lieut.-General Arnold Quainoo defended the military: its task had been that of 'surgeon who cuts off a cancerous finger to save the whole hand'. Meanwhile, all three universities were closed in July when students protested against the abysmally low level of their 'food allowance'. The military had yielded office, but not control, to civilians.

The economy continued its slow recovery. The Budget introduced by Mr Botchway on 16 January reflected the now settled policy of accepting IMF advice on restructuring. Government revenue increased by 28 per cent, its expenditure by almost as much. Inflation, having reached triple figures at the end of the 1970s, was now down to 35 per cent and, under IMF direction, was planned to reach 8 per cent in 1990. The price paid by ordinary Ghanaians was high—a huge increase in fuel costs, a higher sales tax, substantial unemployment and a devaluation of the cedi to little more than 2 per cent of its 1982 value.

The Government's 'programme of action to mitigate the social costs of adjustment' (Pamscad) secured international backing at a meeting in Geneva on 15 February of its donor-creditors, help being promised for housing, roads, water supplies and rural infrastructure. A parallel 'cocoa rehabilitation project' was also started in July, co-funded by several international agencies. Low international prices meant a falling-off of cocoa revenue, made worse by smuggling across the western border with the Ivory Coast. Output was some 200,000 tonnes, well above that for the early 1980s when production dropped to 160,000 tonnes, but still far behind the figure of 500,000 tonnes in the early 1960s. On the favourable side, gold production at Obuasi increased following renewed investment by the Ashanti Gold Fields Corporation. Figures released in February showed that the population was growing at 3.3 per cent per annum, (total mid-1986 = 14 million), that indebtedness was over $1,637 million, and GDP per capita was US$469.

On 14-16 April, Flight-Lieut. Rawlings visited Nigeria for talks with General Ibrahim Babangida in an attempt to heal the wounds following the expulsions of each other's citizens in 1983 and 1985 (see AR 1985, p.226).

NIGERIA

CAPITAL: Lagos/Abuja   AREA: 924,000 sq km   POPULATION: 103,100,000 ('86)
OFFICIAL LANGUAGE: English   POLITICAL SYSTEM: military regime
HEAD OF STATE AND GOVERNMENT: Gen. Ibrahim Babangida, President of Armed Forces Ruling Council (since Aug '85)
PRINCIPAL MINISTERS: Maj.-Gen. Ike Nwachukwu (external affairs), Lt.-Gen. Domkat Yah Bali (defence), S.E. Okongwu (finance and economic planning), Rilwanu Lukman (petroleum resources) Lt.-Col. John Shagaya (internal affairs), Prince Bola Ajibola (justice)
INTERNATIONAL ALIGNMENT: NAM, OAU, Opec, ICO, ACP, Cwth.
CURRENCY: naira (end-'88 £1=N9.57, US$1=N5.29)   GNP PER CAPITA: US$500 ('87)
MAIN EXPORTS: oil and gas

THE year was a time of continuing hardship for Nigeria, but also of considerable effort in the improvement of the economy and the continued process of return to civilian rule. The constitutional review committee presented its report in March, and the Constituent Assembly of 567 people, the majority elected from the elected local government councils and the remainder appointed by the military Government, was sworn in on 11 May at Abuja. It sat for the remainder of the year to consider the draft constitution, presided over by Justice Anthony Anyagolu, and divided itself into 23 sub-committees to consider specific aspects of the constitution. All of these made good progress except for that dealing with the so-called 'Sharia' issue of Muslim law. This sub-committee descended into such a slanging match between Muslim and Christian that the Government suspended consideration of the matter and declared that the position of Muslim law would be the same as under the 1979 constitution. The advisory council on religious affairs was boycotted by the Christian members for many of its meetings at the instigation of the Christian Association of Nigeria, on the grounds of excessive government interference with its work. Government did its utmost to restrain religious extremism and managed to avoid any recurrence of the disastrous riots of 1987 (see AR 1987, p. 248).

The Federal Electoral Commission successfully carried out the rescheduled local government elections in the many constituencies where they had been found unsatisfactory in 1987 (ibid.). There was, however, considerable friction between the Commission and the transition to civilian rule tribunal as to the procedure for assessing the eligibility of candidates.

Preparatory to the return to civilian rule the Armed Forces Ruling Council announced a 'change of gear' to make administration more accountable and more efficient. The office of permanent secretary was abolished and replaced by that of director-general, which was to be filled on a political basis. Even though the incumbent might still be a former civil servant, he would leave office at the end of the term of the Government which appointed him. Ministers would themselves become 'accounting officers' subject to audit query, and the powers of Director of Audit were to be greatly increased. Most of the state corporations were either totally or partially privatized, or 'commercialized', and the economy became considerably 'deregulated'.

The military Government sought to make a reality of the doctrine that elected local government was the 'third arm of federalism' by ordering state governments to dissolve their ministries of local government. As yet, however, the state military governors exercised a paternalistic tutelage over local administration, forbidding local government chairmen to leave their areas without permission, while in the case of the chairman of Enugu local government council the state governor of Anambra exercised a summary right of dismissal after a policy disagreement.

Nigeria's economic plight was recognized by the World Bank, which admitted Nigeria to the category of poor nations eligible for IDA assistance, since its GNP per head had sunk below US$500. Goods were in short supply and prices continued to rise despite the Government's efforts to control inflation. Nigeria continued to pay some 30 per cent of its foreign exchange for debt servicing, yet the debt had to be rescheduled and remained at the same figure of some $20,000 million. The Nigerian Government successfully exchanged a considerable proportion of it for equity.

The partial removal of the subsidy on oil provoked a major strike in April, to which the Government responded by detaining many trade union leaders. Total confrontation was avoided by a timely conference between Ministers and the union leaders in May, resulting in both a return to work and the release of the detained trade unionists. The universities continued, however, to be centres of periodic disturbance; almost all of them were closed for six weeks, in April–May and the Universities Academic Staff Union, was banned in early July following a strike by lecturers over pay.

A report from the Director of Prisons showed that 27,000 prisoners—half those in custody—had not yet been tried. The condemning to death of 12 youths who were under 18 for taking part in an armed robbery produced a national outcry led by Wole Soyinka, the poet and Nobel Prize winner and at least produced a stay of execution. Wole Soyinka made a general criticism of the Government for ruling 'by proscription' in an authoritarian manner.

In February the Government dissolved the Nigerian Labour Congress (NLC) and appointed a sole administrator, Michael Ogunkoya, who ran NLC affairs until December. The unions were then able to conduct a proper election, which resulted in the choice of Paschal Bafyau of the Railway Workers' Union as the new NLC president.

The Government showed its desire for national reconciliation by releasing all the remaining political leaders who had been imprisoned for corruption, and by removing all restrictions from former President Shehu Shagari and his Vice-President, Alex Ekuemme. Generals Mohammadu Buhari and Tunde Idiagbon and ambassador Rafindadi, the leaders of the previous military regime, were also released at the end of the year.

The dumping of poisonous waste by an Italian firm at Koko in Bendel state was brought to light through the vigilance of Nigerian students in Italy and resulted in a very firm Nigerian response, which induced the Italian Government to remove the waste and 2,000 tonnes of contaminated soil on the freighter *Karin B* (see p. 156). Nevertheless, on 8 November Nigeria announced that it was placing the issue before the International Court of Justice.

Nigeria continued to pursue a vigorous foreign policy. Mrs Thatcher paid a somewhat ad hoc visit to Nigeria on her return from Kenya in January. Despite initial hesitation on the Nigerian side, and a moderate level of public protest against Britain's failure to support all-out sanctions against South Africa, the visit was remarkably successful. Mrs Thatcher enjoyed a vigorous argument with General Babangida over South Africa. A conference at Foreign Minister and technical level was subsequently held in March at Chevening (the official country residence of the UK Foreign and Commonwealth Secretary, Sir Geoffrey Howe), after which Brigadier Ike Nwachukwu said that UK–Nigerian relations were 'back to normal' and that 'Britain is one country that Nigeria takes very seriously'. Britain's aid offer to Nigeria of £6 million was, however, dismissed as 'insignificant' by the Nigerian Minister of Works and Housing, Brigadier Moman Kontagora.

Nigeria enjoyed a state visit from Richard von Weizsäcker, President of the Federal Republic of Germany, who took the opportunity to declare that the West German Government would stop all private investment in South Africa. Brigadier Ike Nwachukwu paid a visit to the front-line state of Zimbabwe to offer any assistance that might be needed in confronting South Africa. Nigeria became involved in a confrontation with Equatorial Guinea over the presence of South African technicians whom Nigeria accused of being part of some military plan.

Early in the year Professor Ransome-Kuti, the Minister of Health, launched a new population policy aimed at voluntarily reducing the average number of children per mother to four from the present level of six. The policy was to be promoted in an 'intensive public enlightenment campaign' stressing that without such restraint the country's population would double in about 20 years. Nevertheless, some Muslim leaders complained that population control was un-Islamic, while Christian spokesmen said it discriminated against those practising monogamy.

The Sultan of Sokoto, Alhaji Sir Sadiq Abubakar III, died on 1 November after a reign of 30 years (see OBITUARY). An initial announcement was made that the kingship selectors had chosen his eldest son, Sarkin Kudu, to succeed, but this was soon contradicted as incorrect and the succession was given to Ibrahim Dasuki, the Baraden of Sokoto, a former federal permanent secretary and a rich businessman well known in Lagos. Many people in Sokoto thought that the selectors' choice had been altered by the military Government, with the result that the city erupted in riots which cost 10 lives.

SIERRA LEONE

CAPITAL: Freetown   AREA: 72,000 sq km   POPULATION: 3,800,000 ('86)
OFFICIAL LANGUAGE: English   POLITICAL SYSTEM: presidential, one-party state
RULING PARTY: All-People's Congress
HEAD OF STATE AND GOVERNMENT: President Joseph Saidu Momoh (since Nov '85)
PRINCIPAL MINISTERS: Abu Bakar Kamara (First Vice-President), Salia Jusu-Sheriff (Second Vice-President), Abdul Karim Koroma (foreign affairs), Hassan Gbassay Kanu (finance), Sheka Kanu (planning and development), Ahmed Sesay (internal affairs), Abdulai Conteh (justice)
INTERNATIONAL ALIGNMENT: NAM, OAU, ACP, ICO, Cwth.
CURRENCY: leone (end-'88 £1=Le66.82, US$=Le36.94)   GNP PER CAPITA: US$310 ('86)
MAIN EXPORTS: diamonds, cocoa, coffee

THE inability of President Joseph Momoh's 'New Order' Administration to eliminate corruption or to improve living conditions continued to give rise to expressions of dissatisfaction among the general public. Dissension was also detected within the Government and ruling All-People's Congress (APC) and these factors possibly explained the President's decision to downgrade the powers of the two Vice-Presidents and replace three middle-rank Ministers in November. Former President Siaka Stevens, who remained APC chairman after his retirement in 1985, died on 29 May (see OBITUARY). The appeal court rejected appeals against the death sentences imposed on ex-First Vice-President Francis Minah and 11 others for their part in the 1987 plot against the Government. Further appeals were made to the Supreme Court and Amnesty International also pleaded for clemency.

The economy suffered a continuation of problems dating back to the Stevens years. In spite of tough measures against public sector corruption and mismanagement, and policies aimed at stimulating agriculture and industry and stabilizing the currency, the Government met with only limited success. A chronic lack of foreign exchange led to shortages, inflation and breakdowns in infrastructure; increasing loss of foreign exchange resulted from gold, diamond and produce smuggling; corruption and indiscipline among civil servants persisted; and a failure to resolve its dispute with the IMF cost the Administration much-needed foreign aid. The July Budget statement anticipated increased revenues from a more effective tax up-take and tighter financial control over spending, but the trade balance worsened and total external debt was estimated at $787 million. Mining exports continued to suffer from depressed markets and depletion of alluvial diamond deposits, but an early start to kimberlite (diamond) mining was anticipated following encouraging talks with overseas backers.

President Momoh visited the USA in September and addressed the UN General Assembly. The Nigerian head of state, General Babangida, paid a state visit to Sierra Leone in November and a number of technical and educational agreements were signed. General Babangida was one of four ECOWAS leaders who helped improve relations between Freetown and Monrovia, which had deteriorated as a result of Liberian accusations of Sierra Leonian complicity in the 1985 coup attempt, compounded by Sierra Leonian counter-charges of the ill-treatment and explusion of their nationals from Monrovia in July.

THE GAMBIA

CAPITAL: Banjul   AREA: 11,300 sq km   POPULATION: 773,000 ('86)
OFFICIAL LANGUAGE: English   POLITICAL SYSTEM: presidential democracy
HEAD OF STATE AND GOVERNMENT: President Sir Dawda Kairaba Jawara (since April '70)
RULING PARTY: Progressive People's Party
PRINCIPAL MINISTERS: Bakary Bunja Darbo (Vice-President), Omar Sey (external affairs), Sherif Saikula Sisay (finance and trade), Mbemba Jatta (planning and development), Lamin Kiti Jabang (interior), Hassan Jallow (justice)
INTERNATIONAL ALIGNMENT: NAM, OAU, ACP, ICO, Cwth.
CURRENCY: dalasi (end-'88 £1=D12.22, US$1=D6.76)   GNP PER CAPITA: US$230 ('86)
MAIN EXPORTS: groundnuts and groundnut products

SEVERAL Gambians and Senegalese were arrested at the beginning of the year and charged with plotting against the Government in conjunction with Libya and the exiled leader of the abortive Gambian coup in 1981, Kukoi Samba Sanyang. Initial claims that Abdoulaye Wade, a prominent Senegalese opposition leader, was also implicated were subsequently rejected at the trial in May of the four accused Senegalese. All admitted to being members of the Casamance regional separatist movement, MFDC, but denied the charges. Three were found guilty: two, Musah Sanneh and Amadou Badjie, received 30-year gaol sentences. An additional source of political excitement during the year was allegations of corruption among prominent civil servants and several Cabinet Ministers. Twelve senior officials in the parastatal sector were placed under investigation, while separate inquiries took place into alleged irregularities in the customs and excise department. In November a presidential inquiry was ordered into the activities of the Ministers of Public Works and Communications, and Information and Tourism. Press accusations of corruption were also made against the Ministers of Lands and Local Government, and Agriculture.

The economy, after years of stagnation, was said to be picking up, according to Finance Minister Sherif Sisay in his June Budget address. GDP was reported to have increased by some 5 per cent in real terms during the past two years and the IMF reported favourably once again on the Government's economic recovery programme. Foreign aid in support of restructuring policies continued to flow in at a satisfactory rate, although difficulty was encountered in trying to raise the much larger funding needed to construct the bridge-barrage project at Balingho. President Jawara in addition to a busy international schedule during the year, was elected Chairman of ECOWAS.

LIBERIA

CAPITAL: Monrovia   AREA: 97,750 sq km   POPULATION: 2,300,000 ('86)
OFFICIAL LANGUAGE: English   POLITICAL SYSTEM: presidential democracy
HEAD OF STATE AND GOVERNMENT: President (Gen.) Samuel K. Doe (since April '80)
RULING PARTY: National Democratic Party
PRINCIPAL MINISTERS: Harry Moniba (Vice-President), J. Rudolph Johnson (foreign affairs), Maj.-Gen. Gray D. Allison (defence), David Fahrat (finance), Elijah Taylor (planning and economic affairs), Edward K. Sackor (internal affairs), Jenkins Scott (justice)
INTERNATIONAL ALIGNMENT: NAM, OAU, ACP
CURRENCY: Liberian dollar (end-'88 £1=L$1.81, US$1=L$1.00)   GNP PER CAPITA: US$460 ('86)
MAIN EXPORTS: iron ore, rubber, coffee

PRESIDENT Samuel Doe survived another two attempts to overthrow him during the year, although it was difficult to determine how far these incidents were fabricated by the President himself in order to justify authoritarian measures or eliminate rivals. In March Gabriel Kpolle, leader of the disbanded opposition Liberian Unification Party, and 18 others were arrested for allegedly plotting a coup. The purported ringleader, Joseph Kaipayi was stated to have committed suicide during interrogation. Mr Kpolle and several others were subsequently sentenced to death but pardoned by President Doe in November. In July Nicholas Podier, a former general and one-time 'vice-head of state' but in exile in Abidjan since 1986, was killed in questionable circumstances following his alleged 'invasion' of Liberia. Three others prominent in the 1980 military coup that brought President Doe to power were also arrested. The authorities continued to curb university students and legal action was taken against opposition newspapers. Parliament, dominated by President Doe's National Democratic Party, approved a constitutional amendment to allow him to serve as President beyond two terms, while elements in the NDP called for a one-party state.

As in previous years President Doe combined repression with appeals for reconciliation. He paid a conciliatory visit in January to Nimba county, a major seat of resistance. He also continued to recruit former members of the now fragmented and demoralized opposition to his Government. His new Finance Minister, David Fahrat, was formerly in the Liberian Action Party; a nephew of his murdered predecessor was made Minister of Commerce and Industry; and former President William Tubman's son was appointed an ambassador. In external affairs relations improved with Libya and neighbouring Sierra Leone and the 'special relationship' with Washington survived attempts by Liberian exiles to mobilize Congress against the Doe regime.

The economic situation worsened, with neither a turn-around in demand for the country's exports nor any convincing evidence of effective reform of financial management by the Government. Periodic action against incompetent or corrupt Ministers and officials, including the sacking of Finance Minister John Bestman, was negated by the unwillingness of the President and senior political figures to accept financial scrutiny by a team of US advisers ('operational experts') brought in at Washington's insistence. The latter returned home in frustration in December. External indebtedness was estimated at $1,500 million and a dispute with the IMF curtailed further overseas borrowing.

Chapter 3

SENEGAL—GUINEA—MALI—MAURITANIA—CÔTE D'IVOIRE— BURKINA FASO—NIGER—TOGO—BENIN—CAMEROON—CHAD— GABON—CENTRAL AFRICAN REPUBLIC—CONGO— EQUATORIAL GUINEA

SENEGAL

CAPITAL: Dakar   AREA: 196,000 sq km   POPULATION: 6,800,000 ('86)
OFFICIAL LANGUAGE: French   POLITICAL SYSTEM: presidential democracy
HEAD OF STATE AND GOVERNMENT: President Abdou Diouf (since Jan '81)
RULING PARTY: Socialist Party
PRINCIPAL MINISTERS: Ibrahima Fall (foreign affairs), Medoune Fall (defence), André Sonko (interior), Serigne Lamine Diop (finance and economic affairs), Seydou Madani Sy (justice)
INTERNATIONAL ALIGNMENT: NAM, OAU, ACP, ICO, Francophonie
CURRENCY: CFA franc (end-'88 £1=CFAF547.88, US$1=CFAF302.86)
GNP PER CAPITA: US$420 ('86)
MAIN EXPORTS: agricultural products and fish, chemicals

THE year proved to be a critical juncture in Senegalese politics. The 2½-month crisis which followed the presidential and parliamentary elections of 28 February proved the most serious crisis in the seven-year-old presidency of Abdou Diouf, and was arguably one of the most serious challenges to Senegal's democracy in the 28 years of independence. Although the election campaign officially opened on 6 February, forms of campaigning had been going on for much of 1987, and the poll was approached in a mood of high tension.

The two main candidates were President Diouf, representing the ruling Parti Socialiste (PS), and Maître Abdoulaye Wade, leader of the principal opposition Parti Démocratique Sénégalaise (PDS). They had already contested the elections of 1983, when Diouf won a decisive victory, albeit marred by charges of vote-rigging. Calls from the 16 opposition parties for reform in the electoral law had been ignored by the Government, although the election was organized by the Supreme Court, and not, as in the past, by the Ministry of the Interior, thought to be less impartial.

When first unofficial results were announced on the radio giving President Diouf a clear lead, the youthful supporters of the PDS in Dakar and the urban centre of Thiés went on a rampage of protest at alleged election-rigging, and the security forces were obliged to intervene. The day after the election a state of emergency was declared and Maître Wade, several of his supporters and two other opposition party leaders were detained on charges of incitement.

The results officially announced on 4 March gave President Diouf 73.2 per cent of the votes against 25.8 per cent for Maître Wade, with two other candidates, Babacar Niang and Landing Savané, getting 0.75 and 0.25 per cent respectively. In the parliamentary elections the PS obtained 71.43 per cent and the PDS 24.75 per cent, with four smaller parties sharing the remainder. These figures showed both President and party getting a lower percentage than in 1983, and most observers felt that there was less fixing of the vote than before. The crisis was, even so, more dramatic because of the emergency, and the loss of prestige for both President Diouf and Senegalese democracy in the detention of the opposition leader just after the election. Tension continued high, with sporadic outbreaks of violence until Maître Wade and others were put on trial at the end of April. This took place in a state security court, with a cooperative of more than 40 lawyers, including some from the Paris Bar, defending the opposition leader. Although the Government asked for heavy sentences, the court passed a suspended sentence on Maître Wade, who was immediately released, and much lighter sentences than expected on the other accused.

This caused a considerable relaxation of political tension, and was followed by the lifting of the state of emergency, and an amnesty from which Maître Wade and his lieutenants benefited. After a meeting with President Diouf, Maître Wade withdrew his claim that he was in fact the elected President and agreed to the establishment of a political round-table on the future of the country. This subsequently foundered because of exaggerated demands made by the PDS, but it soon appeared clear that, in agreeing to meet the President, Maître Wade had lost the initiative.

Against this background it was possible for the Government to tackle the underlying crisis in the educational system which had accompanied the political crisis: the *année blanche* experienced in secondary schools and higher education institutions which were on strike for several months after the election. The police had raided Dakar university on two occasions, and it was agreed that the return to school in October was crucial. That this occurred peacefully was due only to costly concessions to student demands for better conditions, rendered possible with extra financial assistance from France.

The social background to the crisis—the extreme hardship being experienced under the Government's structural adjustment programme—had not changed. The support of young people for *sopi* ('change' in the Wolof language) sprang from their numeric weight (over half the population being under 21) and the bleak lack of prospects once the education process was completed. One element in the relaxing of tension was President Diouf's May Day speech announcing reductions in the prices of key commodities for the urban population—rice, sugar and cooking oil. But, although there had been some economic growth, Senegal's fragile finances could not permit further relaxation. Only a little more time was thus bought.

GUINEA

CAPITAL: Conakry   AREA: 246,000 sq km   POPULATION: 6,300,000 ('86)
OFFICIAL LANGUAGE: French   POLITICAL SYSTEM: military regime
HEAD OF STATE AND GOVERNMENT: Brig.-Gen. Lansana Conté, Chairman of Military Committee for National Salvation (since April '84)
PRINCIPAL MINISTERS: Maj. Jean Traoré (foreign affairs), Kemoko Keita (economic and financial control), Maj. Babacar N'Diaye (defence), Maj. Ali Sofani (interior), Lamine Bolivogui (economy and finance), Bassirou Barry (justice)
INTERNATIONAL ALIGNMENT: NAM, OAU, ACP, ICO, Francophonie
CURRENCY: Guinean franc (end-'88 £1=GF541.95, US$1=GF229.58)
GNP PER CAPITA: US$320 ('85)
MAIN EXPORTS: bauxite, oilseeds

FOLLOWING reports at the end of December 1987 of unrest in the army, Conakry was shaken at the beginning of the year by demonstrations by ordinary people and students against price rises of essential goods and transport, following a Government decision to raise civil service wages and the price of fuel. In the wake of these, President Lansana Conté extensively reshuffled his Government, notably by demoting the man thought to have been the regime's 'number two', Commander Kerfalla Camara. The latter lost the key job of Permanent Secretary to the Military Committee of National Salvation (CMRN) and was sent to be resident Minister in Upper Guinea. The army was propitiated, however, with a number of promotions, and the military in the Government were increased in number from 12 to 15. The administration was also significantly restructured, paving the way for further retrenchment of the civil service establishment under pressure from the IMF and the World Bank, which were now extensively advising on Guinea's conduct of its economy. The Government having heavily devalued and then floated the Guinea franc in 1986, the Washington institutions had become an important source of aid, which continued in 1988. Economic indicators continued largely favourable, 6 per cent growth being recorded in 1987, and a similar figure being likely in 1988. In October, amid new rumours of military discontent, President Conté announced the establishment of a commission to draw up a draft constitution which could envisage an eventual return to civilian rule, although the military were not expected to leave power for at least another two years.

MALI

CAPITAL: Bamako   AREA: 1,240,000 sq km   POPULATION: 7,600,000 ('86)
OFFICIAL LANGUAGE: French   POLITICAL SYSTEM: presidential, one-party state
RULING PARTY: Mali People's Democratic Union
HEAD OF STATE AND PARTY LEADER: President (Gen.) Moussa Traoré (since Nov '68)
PRINCIPAL MINISTERS: Mamadou Dembelé (prime minister), Modibo Keita (foreign affairs), Tiena Coulibaly (finance and trade), Anthioumane N'Diaye (planning), Oumar Issaka Ba (justice)
INTERNATIONAL ALIGNMENT: NAM, OAU, ACP, ICO, Francophonie
CURRENCY: CFA franc (end-87 £1=CFAF547.88, US$1=CFAF302.86)
GNP PER CAPITA: US$180 ('86)
MAIN EXPORTS: cotton, agricultural products

LIKE other Sahel countries, Mali experienced the best rainfall for some years, only to be troubled by the threat of invasion by locusts, against which considerable international efforts were deployed. Politically it was a quiet year in spite of general elections from the single party for the National Assembly. The year also saw the 20th anniversary of the coup which brought President Moussa Traoré to power, and his earlier election as presiding chairman of the OAU for the year 1988-89. By the end of the year he had already made several journeys as chairman, notably concerned with the campaign against apartheid in South Africa, and peace between Chad and Libya.

MAURITANIA

CAPITAL: Nouakchott   AREA: 1,000,000 sq km   POPULATION: 1,800,000 ('86)
OFFICIAL LANGUAGE: French and Arabic   POLITICAL SYSTEM: military regime
HEAD OF STATE AND GOVERNMENT: Col. Moaouia Ould Sidi Mohamed Taya, Chairman of Military Council of National Salvation (since Dec '84)
PRINCIPAL MINISTERS: Col. Mohamed Sidina Ould Sidya (foreign affairs), Lt.-Col. Djibril Ould Abdullah (interior), Mohamed Ould Nany (economy and finance), Mohamed Salem Ould Mohamed Lamine (justice)
INTERNATIONAL ALIGNMENT: NAM, Arab League, ICO, OAU, ACP, Francophonie
CURRENCY: ouguiya (end-'88 £1=UM142.64, US$1=UM78.85)   GNP PER CAPITA: US$420 ('86)
MAIN EXPORTS: iron ore, fish

ALTHOUGH the serious drought which had affected Mauritania for most of the 1980s was eased by copious rainfall (followed by a locust invasion), the country continued to be victim of serious instability because of racial tensions between the Moorish Arab (Beydane) majority and the black African minority. Shock waves from the October 1987 coup attempt involving most of the senior black army officers were still being felt, and in May President Ould Taya (himself Beydane) received leaders of the black Peulh community in an attempt to defuse tension.

Earlier a school strike had taken place in April in protest against progressive replacement of French by Arabic in schools. In September there was an international outcry after the revelation that a noted black writer, Tené Youssouf Gueye, had died in the notorious Oualata prison. He had been detained since 1986 for having allegedly written a document entitled 'Manifesto for the Oppressed Black Mauritanians'. Opposition groups based in Senegal said that another black had died, and 40 others were gravely ill. Although the Government later announced the closure of Oualata and the removal of prisoners to another prison, concern continued to be expressed.

Fears of the blacks centred on the likelihood of Mauritania joining a 'Greater Maghreb' grouping, which would leave them further marginalized, and on the population census conducted in 1988, whose figures were expected to show a 'tilt' against the blacks. There was one major question-mark—the political allegiance of the Haratine, the racially-mixed, culturally Arab, former slaves, notionally given rights with the formal ending of slavery in 1980. To complicate matters, the regime was shaken by another coup attempt, this time, bizarrely, by pro-Iraqi Baathist army officers.

CÔTE D'IVOIRE

CAPITAL: Abidjan   AREA: 322,000 sq km   POPULATION: 10,700,000 ('86)
OFFICIAL LANGUAGE: French   POLITICAL SYSTEM: presidential, one-party state
RULING PARTY: Democratic Party
HEAD OF STATE AND PARTY LEADER: President Félix Houphouët-Boigny (since Nov '60)
PRINCIPAL MINISTERS: Siméon Aké (foreign affairs), Jean Konan Banny (defence), Abdoulaye Koné (economy and finance), Léon Konan Koffi (interior), Noël Némin (justice)
INTERNATIONAL ALIGNMENT: NAM, OAU, ACP, Francophonie
CURRENCY: CFA franc (end-'88 £1=CFAF547.88, US$1=CFAF302.86)
GNP PER CAPITA: US$730 ('86)
MAIN EXPORTS: cocoa, coffee, timber

REPORTS were confirmed in January that there had been some kind of destabilization attempt in December, involving the Navy Minister, Lamine Fadika, who was dismissed, and arms shipments in Abidjan port. The head of the armed forces, General Zézé Barouan, was also sent off to the embassy in Brazil. There was thus a period of uncertainty, also fuelled by the ill-health of the octogenarian President Félix Houphouët-Boigny, who had an operation for cataracts.

By March, however, the President had made a remarkable recovery. He told visitors that he was being rejuvenated by his major battle with the international commodity marketing system, which was, he felt strongly, cheating Côte d'Ivoire of a 'just price' for its products. Waged for most of the year, the battle focused especially on cocoa, which had been experiencing exceptionally low market prices. Côte d'Ivoire, as the world's leading cocoa producer, was feeling the brunt of this financially, a squeeze made worse by the fact that a large portion of Ivoirian cocoa exports were withheld in an unsuccessful effort to stimulate price levels. Thus, although a successful rescheduling of the commercial debt took place in April, by May Côte d'Ivoire was failing once more, as in 1987, to service the debt.

At the same time as trying to buck the market, the Ivoirians were resisting substantial international pressure from creditors/donors in Europe and North America, as well as the Washington financial institutions, to reduce the price paid to cocoa farmers because of the state of the markets. This the President resolutely refused to do, preferring to put severe pressure on the French to agree a deal whereby 400,000 tonnes of cocoa—two-thirds of the 1988-89 crop—was purchased by a French trader, aided by a subsidy from the French Government. Half of this amount would be stockpiled in Europe. This unprecedented agreement was announced at the end of 1988, but it was still not clear whether any more strings were attached other than an Ivoirian commitment to return to the debt-servicing fold as soon as possible.

The cocoa deal was complicated by the personal coolness that had developed between President Houphouët-Boigny and President Mitterrand of France from 1987 onwards. Although this was said to have been eased by mid-1988, the Ivoirian leader did not spend his normal August holiday in France. He eventually met President Mitterrand at the Franco-African summit in Casablanca. Part of his reproaches against the French—and, indeed, against the 'Anglo-Saxons' (the British and the Americans)—related to press criticism of a project dear to his heart, a £60 million basilica being built in his home town, Yamoussoukro.

BURKINA FASO

CAPITAL: Ouagadougou AREA: 275,000 sq km POPULATION: 8,100,000 ('86)
OFFICIAL LANGUAGE: French POLITICAL SYSTEM: military regime
HEAD OF STATE AND GOVERNMENT: Capt. Blaise Compaoré, Chairman of
    Popular Front (since Oct '87)
PRINCIPAL MINISTERS: Jean Marc Palm (external relations), Maj. Jean-Baptiste Boukary Lingani
    (defence), Capt. Henri Zongo (economic promotion), Bintou Sanogo (finance), Youssouf
    Ouedraogo (planning), Salif Sampegbo (justice)
INTERNATIONAL ALIGNMENT: NAM, OAU, ACP, ICO, Francophonie
CURRENCY: CFA franc (end-'88 £1=CFAF547.88, US$=CFAF302.86)
GNP PER CAPITA: US$150 ('86)
MAIN EXPORTS: cotton, agricultural produce

AFTER the turbulence of 1987, which saw the assassination of the charismatic Captain Sankara in a military coup (see AR 1987, pp. 256-7), this was a quiet year in which the successor regime, led by Captain Blaise Compaoré, tried to consolidate its power internally, and win friends and influence people overseas. Although in the former respect Captain Compaoré was largely successful, there was still some resistance to him from quarters sympathetic to Captain Sankara. On a visit to Lagos the new leader was bitterly criticized by the Nigerian press, and, although a reconciliation meeting was held with Flight-Lieut. Jerry Rawlings of Ghana, relations still seemed cool. It was only in Togo, where Captain Sankara had been disliked, that Captain Compaoré received a warm welcome. After various pleas on her behalf, Captain Sankara's widow Mariam was allowed to leave for Gabon. Later in the year an army officer prominent in the 1987 coup was killed by an anonymous commando in mysterious circumstances.

NIGER

CAPITAL: Niamey   AREA: 1,267,000 sq km   POPULATION: 6,600,000 ('86)
OFFICIAL LANGUAGE: French   POLITICAL SYSTEM: military regime
RULING PARTY: National Movement for a Developing Society
HEAD OF STATE AND GOVERNMENT: Col. Ali Saibou, President of Supreme Military Council (since Nov '87)
PRINCIPAL MINISTERS: Mamane Oumarou (prime minister), Allele Habibou (foreign affairs), Wassalke Boukary (finance), Yahaya Tounkara (planning and regional development), Soli Abdourahamane (justice)
INTERNATIONAL ALIGNMENT: NAM, OAU, ACP, ICO, Francophonie
CURRENCY: CFA franc (end-'88 £1=CFAF547.88, US$1=CFAF302.86)
GNP PER CAPITA: US$260 ('86)
MAIN EXPORTS: uranium, metal ores, agricultural products

COLONEL Ali Saibou, who had succeeded to the presidency in November 1987 after the death of his predecessor (see AR 1987, p. 258), spent the year successfully consolidating his power. He had already created a more relaxed political climate by the release of detained political leaders, and had promised a return to constitutional rule; however, it soon emerged that the change was more one of style (sociable as against austere) than substance. Colonel Saibou indicated that he believed that there would always be a military component to government, and that he favoured single-party rule. In June the National Development Council was given the task of drafting a new constitution, and in October he announced the setting up of a new political party, the National Movement for a Developing Society (MNSD). Behind the cheery smile he showed himself to be a tough operator. In the year he staged two major reshuffles in which potential rivals were effectively sidelined. In July Prime Minister Hamid Algabid became secretary-general of the Islamic Conference Organization, and was replaced by his predecessor, Mamane Oumarou.

TOGO AND BENIN

Togo
CAPITAL: Lomé   AREA: 57,000 sq km   POPULATION: 3,100,000 ('86)
OFFICIAL LANGUAGE: French, Kabiye and Ewe   POLITICAL SYSTEM: presidential, one-party state
RULING PARTY: Assembly of the Togolese People
HEAD OF STATE AND PARTY LEADER: President (Gen.) Gnassingbe Eyadema (since Jan '67)
INTERNATIONAL ALIGNMENT: NAM, OAU, ACP, Francophonie
CURRENCY: CFA franc (end-'88 £1=CFAF547.88, US$1=CFAF302.86)
GNP PER CAPITA: US$250 ('86)
MAIN EXPORTS: phospates, cocoa

Benin
CAPITAL: Porto Nova   AREA: 113,000 sq km   POPULATION: 4,200,000 ('86)
OFFICIAL LANGUAGE: French   POLITICAL SYSTEM: marxist-leninist one-party state
RULING PARTY: People's Revolutionary Party
HEAD OF STATE AND PARTY LEADER: President (Brig.-Gen.) Mathieu Kérékou (since Oct '72)
INTERNATIONAL ALIGNMENT: NAM, OAU, ACP, Francophonie
CURRENCY: CFA franc (end-'87 £1=CFAF547.88, US$1=CFAF302.86)
GNP PER CAPITA: US$270 ('86)
MAIN EXPORTS: cotton, palm products

IN TOGO it was an uneventful year, apart from the staging of the ECOWAS summit in the capital in June. The country concentrated on keeping its house in order economically, and in December earned praise from the IMF for its adherence to its structural adjustment programme.

The year was more troubled in BENIN, where continuing reports of discontent and coup plots were accompanied by international charges of deaths in detention and of deals to take in toxic waste. The coup plot was never officially admitted by the Government, although reports said that at the end of March nearly 150 soldiers, including officers, had been arrested following an attempt to overthrow the Government. Among those detained were Lieut.-Colonels François Kouyami and Hilaire Badjogoumé, both former Ministers. Another detained plotter, Captain Hountounji, allegedly the brain behind the plot, was subsequently said to have died in detention.

The economy of the People's Republic continued to drift downwards. Although there was an extensive reshuffle of economic Ministries, with a change at the Finance Ministry, by the end of the year an appeal had to go to France for aid to the recurrent Budget because the Government was unable to pay civil servants. It was reported that an agreement with the IMF, to include retrenchment and privatization in the state sector, was on the brink of being finalized.

CAMEROON

CAPITAL: Yaoundé AREA: 475,000 sq km POPULATION: 10,500,000 ('86)
OFFICIAL LANGUAGE: French and English POLITICAL SYSTEM: presidential, one-party state
RULING PARTY: Democratic Assembly of the Cameroonian People
HEAD OF STATE AND PARTY LEADER: President Paul Biya (since Nov '82)
PRINCIPAL MINISTERS: Jacques-Roger Booh-Booh (foreign affairs), Michel Neva M'Eboutou (defence), Sadou Hayatou (finance), Elizabeth Tankeu (planning), Benjamin Itoe (justice)
INTERNATIONAL ALIGNMENT: NAM, OAU, ACP, ICO, Francophonie
CURRENCY: CFA franc (end-'87 £1=CFAF547.88, US$1=CFAF302.86)
GNP PER CAPITA: US$810 ('86)
MAIN EXPORTS: oil, cocoa, coffee, aluminium

ALTHOUGH presidential and parliamentary elections were held in April, producing predictable results, the major political event of the year was in fact an economic one, the Government's decision to swallow its pride and seek assistance from the IMF. This was necessitated by the combined effect of the fall in the oil price, depressed agricultural commodity prices and the decline in the value of the dollar. This entailed the adoption of an 'in-depth' structural adjustment programme, in return for which the IMF provided a loan of $150 million and other donors such as the World Bank, France and West Germany rallied round with substantial assistance.

The elections were seen very much as a way of obtaining a mandate for such an important policy change. President Paul Biya received 98.75 per cent of votes cast, and the parliamentary elections were fiercely contested within the framework of the single party, the Democratic Assembly of the Cameroonian People (RDPC), so that 85 per cent of the new National Assembly were newcomers. There was also a significant post-election reshuffle, involving sweeping changes on the President's staff, as well as several new Ministers. The year also saw continued concern over human rights abuses.

CHAD

CAPITAL: Ndjaména AREA: 1,284,000 sq km POPULATION: 5,100,000 ('86)
OFFICIAL LANGUAGES: French and Arabic POLITICAL SYSTEM: presidential, one-party state
RULING PARTY: National Union for Independence and the Revolution
HEAD OF STATE AND PARTY LEADER: President Hissène Habré (since Oct '82)
PRINCIPAL MINISTERS: Capt. Gouara Lassou (foreign affairs), Mbailem Bana Ngarnayal (finance), Brahim Mahamat Itno (Interior), Kassire Delwa Coumakoye (justice)
INTERNATIONAL ALIGNMENT: NAM, OAU, ACP, ICO, Francophonie
CURRENCY: CFA franc (end-'88 £1=CFAF547.88, US$1=CFAF302.86)
GNP PER CAPITA: US$80 ('82)
MAIN EXPORTS: cotton, agricultural products

IF 1987 had been the year of the recovery of 'territorial integrity' (see AR 1987, pp. 260-1), 1988 was the year in which serious moves were made towards peace with Libya, even if it came no nearer to solving the vexed question of the Aozou Strip, a piece of territory lying between the two countries which both claimed, and which Libya still occupied. Although a further meeting of the OAU Chad committee scheduled for Dakar failed to take place, during the OAU summit in May Colonel Qadafi offered a substantial olive branch to President Hissène Habré, saying that Libya was prepared to recognize the Habré regime, and inviting him to Tripoli to meet former Chadian leader Goukouni Oueddeye. Although by the end of the year the visit had still not taken place, the 1987 Chad-Libyan ceasefire still more or less held. In October Libya and Chad resumed diplomatic relations, and further peace moves were in the air.

There was much confusion as to what was really going on in Darfur province in Sudan, where occasional skirmishes took place, possibly involving supporters of Acheikh Ibn Oumar, another opponent of Habré, and/or members of the shadowy 'Islamic Legion', said to consist of West Africans recruited by Colonel Qadafi. At the end of November, following Iraqi mediation, Acheikh Ibn Oumar returned to Ndjaména, and some of his supporters were said also to have returned.

GABON AND CENTRAL AFRICAN REPUBLIC

Gabon
CAPITAL: Libreville   AREA: 268,000 sq km   POPULATION: 1,100,000 ('86)
OFFICIAL LANGUAGE: French   POLITICIAL SYSTEM: presidential, one-party state
RULING PARTY: Democratic Party
HEAD OF STATE AND PARTY LEADER: President Omar Bongo (since Dec '67)
INTERNATIONAL ALIGNMENT: NAM, OAU, ACP, Opec, ICO, Francophonie
CURRENCY: CFA franc (end-'88 £1=CFAF547.88, US$1=CFAF302.86)
GNP PER CAPITA: US$3,080 ('86)
MAIN EXPORTS: oil and gas, manganese
Central African Republic
CAPITAL: Bangui   AREA: 623,000 sq km   POPULATION: 2,700,000 ('86)
OFFICIAL LANGUAGE: French   POLITICAL SYSTEM: presidential, one-party state
RULING PARTY: Democratic Assembly
HEAD OF STATE AND PARTY LEADER: President (Gen.) André Kolingba (since Sept '81)
INTERNATIONAL ALIGNMENT: NAM, OAU, ACP, Francophonie
CURRENCY: CFA franc (end-'88 £1=CFAF547.88, US$1=CFAF302.86)
GNP PER CAPITA: US$290 ('86)
MAIN EXPORTS: coffee, diamonds, timber

BOTH countries had uneventful years politically, and, like many other African countries, the struggle for economic survival was all. GABON, in particular was grappling with continued low oil prices, while nonetheless seeking to expand its production by signing new offshore exploration deals. President Omar Bongo was involved internationally early in the year when he briefly accommodated Iranian terrorists to help France in a difficult situation. He continued to be involved in peace-making in Chad.

The CENTRAL AFRICAN REPUBLIC agreed to a structural adjustment plan in May, receiving IMF and World Bank assistance, and later in the year was able to reschedule its official debt. The new plan involved a reduction of the number of civil servants, as well as a privatization programme.

CONGO

CAPITAL: Brazzaville   AREA: 342,000 sq km   POPULATION: 2,000,000 ('86)
OFFICIAL LANGUAGE: French   POLITICAL SYSTEM: presidential, one-party state
RULING PARTY: Party of Labour
HEAD OF STATE AND PARTY LEADER: President (Col.) Denis Sassou-Nguesso (since Feb '79)
PRINCIPAL MINISTERS: Ange Edouard Poungui (prime minister), Antoine Ndinga Oba (foreign affairs), Pierre Moussa (planning and finance), Dieudonné Kimbembe (justice)
INTERNATIONAL ALIGNMENT: NAM, OAU, ACP, Francophonie
CURRENCY: CFA franc (end-'88 £1=CFAF547.88, US$1=CFAF302.86)
GNP PER CAPITA: US$990 ('86)
MAIN EXPORTS: oil and gas, timber

FOR Congo, one of the main victims of the fall in the oil price, the year was dominated by the economy and the rigours of IMF-controlled policies, but it was not without political incident. In July the year-long armed rebellion of Captain Pierre Anga ended when he was killed by security forces in the bush near the northern town of Owando. In August the 25th anniversary of the revolution was celebrated, but most observers found that the poor state of the economy and increased dependence on Western assistance had dampened much of the revolutionary ardour. Following a toxic waste scandal two Ministers lost their jobs. President Denis Sassou Nguesso gained some international credit for the role he played in helping to facilitate the peace agreement on Namibia (see DOCUMENTS).

EQUATORIAL GUINEA

CAPITAL: Malabo   AREA: 28,000 sq km   POPULATION: 381,000 ('86)
OFFICIAL LANGUAGE: Spanish   POLITICAL SYSTEM: military regime
HEAD OF STATE AND GOVERNMENT: Col. Teodoro Obiang Nguema Mbasogo, President of Supreme Military Council (since Aug '79)
PRINCIPAL MINISTERS: Capt. Cristino Seriche Bioko (prime minister), Isidoro Eyi Monsuy Andeme (deputy premier, security), Marcelino Nguema Ongueme (foreign affairs), Antonio Fernando Nve (economy and finance), Angel Ndong Micha (justice)
INTERNATIONAL ALIGNMENT: NAM, OAU, ACP, Francophonie
CURRENCY: CFA franc (end-'88 £1=CFAF547.88, US$1=CFAF302.86)
GNP PER CAPITA: US$180 ('81)
MAIN EXPORTS: cocoa, timber, coffee

THE 20th anniversary of independence was celebrated in October amid expectations that the country was further on the road to recovery from the serious decline experienced in the first 11 years under the chaotic dictatorship of Macias Nguema. Before the end of the year the economy had received a double boost. A donors' meeting in Geneva in November agreed to provide $58 million over the next three years for development projects, including the renewal of the equatorial forest and the revival of cocoa plantations. Secondly, in December the IMF approved a structural adjustment loan of $16 million, a substantial amount for a country of 380,000 people. First steps were also being taken for a rescheduling of the country's $160 million debt.

VII CENTRAL AND SOUTHERN AFRICA

Chapter 1

ZAÏRE—RWANDA AND BURUNDI—GUINEA-BISSAU AND CAPE VERDE—SÃO TOMÉ AND PRÍNCIPE—MOZAMBIQUE—ANGOLA

ZAÏRE

CAPITAL: Kinshasa   AREA: 2,345,000 sq km   POPULATION: 31,700.000 ('86)
OFFICIAL LANGUAGE: French   POLITICAL SYSTEM: presidential, one-party state
RULING PARTY: Popular Movement of the Revolution
HEAD OF STATE AND PARTY LEADER: President (Marshal) Mobutu Sese Seko (since Nov '65)
PRINCIPAL MINISTERS: Kengo Wa Dondo (first state commissioner), (deputy first state commissioner, economic, financial and monetary affairs), Mozagba Ngbuka (deputy first state commissioner, interior), Nguza Karl I Bond (foreign affairs), Katanga Mukumadi ya Mutumba (finance), Biene Ngalisame (planning), Okuka wa Katako (mines and energy), Nsinga Udjuu Ongwakebi Untube (justice)
INTERNATIONAL ALIGNMENT: NAM, OAU, ACP, Francophonie
CURRENCY: zaïre (end-'88 £1=Z484.20, US$1=Z267.66)   GNP PER CAPITA: US$160 ('86)
MAIN EXPORTS: copper, other minerals, oil

'MR Mobutu presides over a nation in which there is thought to be no serious threat to his power', wrote a *Washington Post* correspondent at the end of 1987. 'More than any leader in Africa he has perfected the art of using power and money to keep the lid on.' Throughout 1988 there was no evidence of any diminution in the President's astonishing powers of manipulation.

On 17 January Kinshasa witnessed the first major demonstration organized by the opposition Union for Democracy and Social Progress (UDSP). It was followed by hundreds of arrests and some deaths. Tshisekedi wa Malumba, the leader of the UDSP, was arrested on the same day and was later reported to be receiving treatment in a psychiatric institution. He and other leading members of the UDSP were released after several months in detention. Another opposition group, the National Congolese Movement-Lumumba (MNC-L), was reported to have launched an attack on an army barracks in Kisangani in February. The MNC-L claimed to have 1,500 combatants at its disposal, some of whom had received training in Libya.

A more serious threat to President Mobutu's position came from a move by a number of US Congressmen, led by Ronald V. Dellums, to introduce a Bill that would cut off all US aid to Zaïre—set for 1988 at $60 million in economic aid and $3 million in military aid—unless the Government of Zaïre could show a substantial improvement on human rights. Another move against President Mobutu was launched by Senator Edward Kennedy when he asked the US State Department to prepare a report on corruption in Zaïre. During a visit to Washington in June President Mobutu denounced any criticism of his regime as 'an interference in Zaïre's internal affairs'.

President Mobutu's ambivalent attitude towards Angola was a matter of international concern. It was widely believed that he had allowed the US Government to pass supplies to Unita rebels through the base at Kamina in western Zaïre. At a meeting with the leaders of the front-line states held in Zambia in August President Mobutu was reported to have been 'grilled' on this issue by his fellow Presidents. Considerable concern was expressed in a number of African capitals after the visit to Zaïre on 1 October of an imposing South African delegation headed by President P.W. Botha. President Mobutu chose to receive the South African President, for the first meeting ever held between the leaders of the two countries, at his palace, 'the Versailles of the jungle', at Gbadolite in eastern Zaïre. The South African visit was seen as a move by Pretoria to drive a wedge between the front-line states, but there was no evidence to show that either side derived any tangible benefits from the encounter.

At the end of November President Mobutu carried out one of his periodic Cabinet reshuffles, appointing Kengo Wa Dondo as First State Commissioner (Prime Minister) in place of Sambwa Pida Mbagui. During his tenure of the premiership from 1982 to 1986, Mr Kengo won a reputation among Western diplomats of being 'a model student of the IMF'. His return to high office was interpreted as a move by the President to meet external demands for reform of the country's economy and more vigorous action on the problem of a foreign debt of $7,000 million.

RWANDA AND BURUNDI

Rwanda
CAPITAL: Kigali   AREA: 26,300 sq km   POPULATION: 6,200,000 ('86)
OFFICIAL LANGUAGES: French and Kinyarwanda   POLITICAL SYSTEM: presidential, one-party state
RULING PARTY: National Revolutionary Movement for Development
HEAD OF STATE AND PARTY LEADER: President (Maj.-Gen.) Juvénal Habarimana (since July '73)
INTERNATIONAL ALIGNMENT: NAM, OAU, ACP, Francophonie
CURRENCY: Rwanda franc (end-'88 £1=RF138.84, US$1=RF76.75)
GNP PER CAPITA: US$290 ('86)
MAIN EXPORTS: coffee, tea, tin

Burundi
CAPITAL: Bujumbura   AREA: 28,000 sq km   POPULATION: 4,800,000 ('86)
OFFICIAL LANGUAGE: French and Kirundi   POLITICAL SYSTEM: military regime
HEAD OF STATE: Maj. Pierre Bugoya, Chairman of Military Council for National Salvation
   (since Sept '87)
INTERNATIONAL ALIGNMENT: NAM, OAU, ACP, Francophonie
CURRENCY: Burundi franc (end-'88 £1=FBu269.50, US$1=FBu148.98)
GNP PER CAPITA: US$240 ('86)
MAIN EXPORTS: coffee, tea

IN mid-August northern BURUNDI was the scene of massacres affecting both the minority but dominant Tutsi and the majority Hutu. Ever since the massacres of 1972, in which several thousand Tutsi and at least 100,000 Hutu lost their lives, Burundi had experienced what outside observers described as 'a state of chronic tension' between the two groups. A number of immediate causes provoked the latest bloodbath. Rough action by the army, nearly all of whose members were Tutsi, in attempting to curb the smuggling of coffee to Rwanda, combined with the deceitful practices of rich Tutsi coffee merchants, inflamed Hutu feeling, leading to a mood of hysteria in which a number of Tutsi were attacked and killed. The army then retaliated with great brutality. Official sources admitted that 5,000 people had been killed. Hutu refugees in Rwanda put the number at 50,000. A group of Hutu intellectuals sent a courteously-worded letter to President Pierre Bugoya, urging the Government to set up a commission of inquiry into the killings. The Government rejected the request and most of the signatories of the letter either 'disappeared' or fled into exile.

On 19 October President Bugoya announced the formation of a new Government in which the office of Prime Minister, abolished in 1965, was revived and given to a Hutu, Adrien Sibomana. Another 11 of the 23 Cabinet posts were also given to Hutu. These changes were interpreted as a response to the international outcry over the massacres and the threat made by members of the European Community to cut aid to Burundi. They seemed far less significant, however, when it became apparent that all the most important Ministries, including Defence and Foreign Affairs, remained in Tutsi hands. Moreover, the real decision-making body was seen to be the Military Council for National Salvation, set up after the coup of September 1987: all 31 members of the Council were Tutsi.

The people of RWANDA were reported to have been more shocked by the 1988 Burundi massacres than by the much more extensive bloodletting of 1972. The 1988 massacres occurred in districts adjoining Rwanda and thousands of Hutu refugees poured across the border. Their number was put at 63,000 but fell to 45,000 by the end of the year, a number that still represented a very heavy burden for people living in one of the most densely populated regions of Rwanda.

GUINEA-BISSAU AND CAPE VERDE

Guinea-Bissau
CAPITAL: Bissau   AREA: 36,000 sq km   POPULATION: 905,000 ('86)
OFFICIAL LANGUAGE: Portuguese   POLITICAL SYSTEM: presidential, one-party state
RULING PARTY: African Party for the Independence of Guinea and Cape Verde
HEAD OF STATE AND PARTY LEADER: President (Brig.-Gen.) Joao Bernardo Vieira (since Nov '80)
INTERNATIONAL ALIGNMENT: NAM, OAU, ACP, Francophonie
CURRENCY: Peso (end-'88 £1=PG1,174.23, US$1=PG649.10)   GNP PER CAPITA: US$170 ('86)
MAIN EXPORTS: groundnuts, agricultural products

Cape Verde
CAPITAL: Praia   AREA: 4,000 sq km   POPULATION: 335,000 ('86)
OFFICIAL LANGUAGE: Portuguese   POLITICAL SYSTEM: presidential, one-party state
RULING PARTY: African Party for the Independence of Cape Verde
HEAD OF STATE AND PARTY LEADER: President Aristides Maria Pereira (since July '75)
INTERNATIONAL ALIGNMENT: NAM, OAU, ACP
CURRENCY: Cape Verde escudo (end-'88 £1=CVEsc129.61, US$1=CVEsc71.65)
GNP PER CAPITA: US$460 ('86)
MAIN EXPORTS: fish, agricultural products

ACCORDING to an IMF survey for May 1988 the new economic strategies adopted by the Government of GUINEA-BISSAU in 1986 to deal with a steadily worsening economic crisis were beginning to show significant results. As a result of higher prices being paid for agricultural crops, agricultural exports in 1987 increased by 70 per cent in value and 34 per cent in volume. To counteract the effects of higher food prices on urban groups the Government, with assistance from aid donors, established a temporary relief programme through which food was provided for distribution to the lowest-paid Government employees. Considerable concern was expressed by West European environmentalists when it became known that the Government had signed contracts agreeing to accept toxic waste from a number of European companies. But after a meeting of the OAU in Addis Ababa had passed a resolution condemning the use of Africa as a dumping ground for waste from industrialized countries, the Minister of Natural Resources announced that the contract, which would have earned $600 million over a five-year period, had been cancelled.

CAPE VERDE continued to serve as a model of sustainable development for other Third World countries. The islands' tree-planting programme, described by aid workers as 'unparalleled in Africa for its scope and success', was linked to successful schemes for water preservation through the construction of dams, dykes and wells. The islands' economy was, however, seriously affected by the impact of US sanctions against South Africa. With South African Airways (SAA) being denied the right to land in the United States, many fewer SAA planes made use of the international airport on the island of Sal: earnings from SAA fell from $10 million a year, half the islands' foreign exchange earnings, to $3 million. Relations with Guinea-Bissau, severely strained after the coup of November

1980 (AR 1980, p.247), were reported to have improved after the signature in February of an agreement on bilateral cooperation.

SÃO TOMÉ & PRÍNCIPE

CAPITAL: São Tomé   AREA: 965 sq km   POPULATION: 111,000 ('86)
OFFICIAL LANGUAGE: Portuguese   POLITICAL SYSTEM: presidential, one-party state
RULING PARTY: Movement for the Liberation of São Tomé and Príncipe
HEAD OF STATE AND PARTY LEADER: President Manuel Pinto da Costa (since July '75)
PRINCIPAL MINISTERS: Celestino Rocha da Costa (prime minister), Carlos da Graça, (foreign affairs), Raul Bragança Neto (defence and security), Agapito Mendes Dias (economy and finance), Francisco Fortunado Pires (justice)
INTERNATIONAL ALIGNMENT: NAM, OAU, ACP
CURRENCY: dobra (end-'88 £1=DB134.60, US$1=DB74.41)   GNP PER CAPITA: US$340 ('86)
MAIN EXPORTS: cocoa, copra

ON 8 March the Government of President Manuel Pinto da Costa survived an attempted coup, capturing most and killing some of the 50 members of an invading force which had set sail from bases in Equatorial Guinea. The invaders, led by Alfonso dos Santos, were reported to be members of the National Resistance Front: some of them had received training from South Africans in Walvis Bay.

The extent to which São Tomé's relations with the West had improved in recent years was shown by the volume of foreign aid being received for the period 1987–89 ($108 million), France, Portugal and West Germany being the main donors. Cuba also provided technical assistance. During the year relations with Gabon were notably cordial. After the coup attempt the United States gave São Tomé two patrol boats.

MOZAMBIQUE

CAPITAL: Maputo   AREA: 800,000 sq km   POPULATION: 14,200,000 ('86)
OFFICIAL LANGUAGE: Portuguese   POLITICIAL SYSTEM: presidential, one-party state
RULING PARTY: Front for the Liberation of Mozambique (Frelimo)
HEAD OF STATE AND PARTY LEADER: President Joaquim Alberto Chissano (since Nov '86)
PRINCIPAL MINISTERS: Mario da Graça Machungo (prime minister, planning), Pascoal Mocumbi (foreign affairs), Lt.-Gen. Alberto Joaquim Chipande (defence), Manuel António (interior), Abdul Magid Osman (finance), Ossmane Ali Dauto (justice)
INTERNATIONAL ALIGNMENT: NAM, OAU, ACP, Comecon (observer)
CURRENCY: metical (end-'88 £1=MT1,131.23, US$1=MT625.33)   GNP PER CAPITA: US$210 ('86)
MAIN EXPORTS: seafood, cashew nuts, tea

FEW Governments in Africa were regarded with as much sympathy and good will by the outside world as the Frelimo Government of Mozambique, yet the country remained in a state of chaos, largely because of the activities of the insurgent National Resistance Movement (MNR). 'Mozambique can hardly be described as a state any more', wrote a correspondent in *The Independent* (London) in

February. 'The Government controls hardly anything outside the capital and a handful of towns. Apart from a few units the Frelimo Government's army has disintegrated and it relies heavily on up to 10,000 Zimbabwean troops sent in to protect key points. In the countryside there is mass starvation. The administrative centres are under siege and inundated with refugees. They are fleeing some of the worse atrocities ever committed in Africa.'

These atrocities were authoritatively documented in a report commissioned by the US State Department and based on the research of Robert Gersony, a consultant to the Department's bureau for refugee programmes. Mr Gersony visited 25 refugee camps in five countries, interviewed almost 200 Mozambican refugees and spoke to 50 Government officials, priests and aid workers. From all this evidence he concluded that the MNR's level of violence against the civilian population had been 'extraordinarily high', leading to the murder 'at a conservative estimate' of 100,000 civilians. To these deaths must be added 'extremely high levels of abuse' through 'systematic forced porterage, beatings, rapes, looting, burning of villages, abductions and mutilations'. The MNR's relationship with the civilian population 'revolved almost exclusively around a harsh extraction of labour and food, with virtually no attempt being made to win the people's loyalty or to explain to them the purpose of the insurgency'. Although some complaints against Government soldiers were recorded, their number was 'very low' in comparison with those made against the MNR and there were only isolated incidents of violence by 'free-lance bandits'.

During the year reports increased of division within the ranks of the rebel movement. Some divisions could be ascribed to tribal differences, the dominant position of the Ndau in the MNR leadership being resented by members of other ethnic groups. Another source of division derived from arguments over the continuation of the war, some rebels hoping for a negotiated settlement, others taking the line of 'bitter-enders'. There was also evidence of factional bitterness, leading on occasion to murder, among MNR supporters outside Mozambique in South Africa, Portugal and the United States. The movement was also weakened by defection, some of the defectors providing the Frelimo Government with evidence of the continued support being given by South Africa to the rebels.

Nevertheless, in spite of these indications of MNR weakness, the war continued with no significant diminution in the number of reports of MNR attacks on towns, roads and railways. This overall insecurity led an increasing number of aid agencies to point out to donor Governments that there was little to be gained from the provision of aid unless aid projects could be effectively defended. Some estimates put the value of aid given to Mozambique in 1987-88 at $1,000 million. Of this amount $100 million came from the United States and made Mozambique the single largest recipient of US aid in sub-Saharan Africa. Sweden gave more aid to Mozambique than to any other country in the world and Mozambique came high on the list of African countries receiving aid from Britain. British aid was used to repair the Limpopo railway, one stretch of which was guarded by a company of Mozambican troops trained by the British military mission in Zimbabwe. Portugal too provided training for Mozambican officers, while Spain's Civil Guard organized a counter-insurgency force to protect a Spanish agricultural project. Meanwhile the Soviet Union and other Eastern bloc countries remained the largest providers of military equipment and instructors. Zimbabwe continued to maintain a force, estimated at between 8,000 and 12,000, deployed along the Beira corridor. But the contingent of Tanzanian troops stationed in northern Mozambique was withdrawn in November.

As Western influence steadily grew, it was clear that the Frelimo Government was moving away from the rigid marxist orthodoxy of its early years. Consumer subsidies were reduced and private enterprise was actively encouraged so that more goods began appearing in the shops of Maputo, even if at prices beyond the reach of most workers. There was some evidence of an upturn in the economy, but with close on one-third of the population living in refugee or resettlement camps and with the volume of food aid put at close on one million tonnes, the problems of effective development were as acute as ever. Some observers began warning of the harmful economic consequences of an excessive reliance on food handouts.

In September Pope John Paul II paid a four-day visit to Mozambique. His visit served to emphasize the remarkable change that had taken place in relations between the Frelimo Government and the country's religious communities, both Christian and Muslim. Official hostility to religion, so marked in the early years of independence, was replaced by tolerance and even, according to the Anglican Bishop of Maputo, 'an appreciation of the role of the Church in society'. Many church buildings commandeered in 1975 were handed back, the ban on Jehovah's Witnesses was rescinded and for the first time in a decade Muslims were allowed the foreign exchange needed for a pilgrimage to Mecca. In August the Frelimo Government reversed its policy of discouraging any attempt by church leaders to negotiate with the MNR and provided a committee of churchmen with a list of the addresses of MNR leaders. But the Government remained sceptical of the possibilities of effective negotiation with a movement so lacking in cohesion and with no unified leadership.

The only avenue for effective negotiation seemed to lie with

South Africa. In June a joint agreement was signed in Lisbon between South Africa, Portugal and Mozambique for reactivating the hydroelectric works at Cabora Bassa through repairing the pylons between the dam and the South African border, many of which had been destroyed by the MNR. South Africa agreed to meet half the cost, estimated at £40 million, of these repairs. Following up this agreement, President P.W. Botha visited Mozambique on 12 September for his first meeting with President Chissano, which was held at Songo close to the Cabora Bassa dam. The two Presidents pledged themselves to revive the Nkomati Accord of 1984 (see AR 1984, p. 349), to rebuild and defend the power lines from Cabora Bassa and to step up economic cooperation in other fields. As an earnest of its goodwill, the South African Government sent a naval vessel to Beira at the end of November to unload 'non-lethal' military equipment, worth £2.5 million, intended for the units of the Mozambique army that were to be deployed along the 500 miles of power lines. It remained uncertain whether in fact Pretoria would be able to restrain powerful members of South African Military Intelligence from continuing to give effective aid to the MNR.

ANGOLA

CAPITAL: Luanda   AREA: 1,247,000 sq km   POPULATION: 9,000,000 ('86)
OFFICIAL LANGUAGE: Portuguese   POLITICAL SYSTEM: marxist-leninist one-party state
RULING PARTY: Popular Movement for the Liberation of Angola-Workers' Party (MPLA-PT)
HEAD OF STATE AND PARTY LEADER: President José Eduardo dos Santos (since Sept '79)
PRINCIPAL MINISTERS: Afonso Van-Dúnem Mbinda (external relations), Col.-Gen. Pedro Maria Tonha Pedalé (defence), Augusto Teixeira de Matos (finance), Lt.-Col. Pedro de Castro Van-Dúnem Loy (petroleum and energy), Fernando José França Van-Dúnem (justice)
INTERNATIONAL ALIGNMENT: NAM, OAU, ACP, Comecon (observer)
CURRENCY: kwanza (end-'88 £1=Kw54.59, US$1=Kw30.18)   GNP PER CAPITA: US$470 ('80)
MAIN EXPORTS: oil, coffee, diamonds

'TODAY', said President dos Santos in his New Year address for 1988, 'the general tendency of international policy is gradually to replace military confrontation with the search for negotiated political solutions.' Nevertheless, when the year opened, the chances of a negotiated settlement to the 12 years of conflict since Angola achieved independence in 1975 seemed as slight as ever. The war in the south had reached a new intensity, after Government forces, checked in their offensive against the important Unita base of Mavinga in October 1987, had been driven back by a joint Unita-South African force and obliged to retreat to Cuito Cuanavale. This small town, given strategic importance by its air base, was to become the scene of the toughest fighting of the whole war. As Government forces concentrated on its defence, other areas were left vulnerable to Unita attacks. Among the places captured by Unita in January was Munhango on the Benguela railway, noted as the birthplace of the Unita leader, Jonas Savimbi. Yet even while the fighting, into which both Cuban and South African troops had been drawn, was continuing, the US Assistant Secretary of State for African Affairs, Chester Crocker, visited Luanda to discuss a possible Cuban withdrawal. Much significance was seen in the presence for the first time in such negotiations of a Cuban representative, Jorge Risquet, a member of the Cuban Politburo.

By March the battle for Cuito Cuanavale was being seen by Government supporters as a Stalingrad, by their opponents as a possible Dien Bien Phu. By this time a large South African force, put at 8,000 by Luanda, was being deployed: to keep their own casualties low, the South African relied on heavy artillery and on air strikes. But with Government forces well dug in, artillery bombardments proved ineffective, while the sophisticated radar and anti-aircraft weapons supplied by the Soviet Union together with MiG-23s flown by Cuban pilots deprived the South African air force of its hitherto undisputed mastery of the skies. Further reinforcements, including the crack 50th Division, were sent from Cuba, bringing the total number of Cuban troops in Angola to over 50,000. Later Fidel Castro was to claim that these reinforcements brought about 'a total change in the balance of power'. By April it had become clear to South African generals that Cuito Cuanavale could be taken only by a frontal assault that would involve an unacceptably high number of white South African casualties.

Increasingly resentful of US policy over Angola, which was interpreted as a form of betrayal, Pretoria attempted to deal directly with Moscow, when the South African Defence Minister, General Malan, proposed a joint Soviet-South African agreement on Angola on lines similar to the solution being proposed for Afghanistan by Mr Gorbachev. This proposal was promptly turned down by the Soviet Union. Meanwhile, Dr Crocker was continuing his quest for peace, having secret meetings in March with both the Angolans and the South Africans and finally persuading all the parties—South African, Cuban and Angolan — to come to a meeting under his chairmanship held in London at the beginning of May. It was to be the first in a series of meetings that were to continue at roughly monthly intervals throughout the year.

The next meeting was held at Brazzaville at the end of May. 'We have to create a situation', said one of the participants, 'in which everyone wins.' Informally the South Africans conceded that if agreement could be reached on a timetable for the withdrawal of Cuban troops from Angola, then Pretoria would have no alternative but to concede Namibian independence in accordance with the terms of UN Security Council Resolution 435 of 1978. Meanwhile on the battlefront the siege of Cuito Cuanavale was coming to an end and a powerful Cuban-MPLA force was advancing towards the western stretch of the Namibian border. At the end of June a Cuban attack on the Calueque dam just north of the border killed at least 12 white South Africans—an incident deemed highly significant for the indication it provided of a substantial change in the military balance.

Another indication of change in the Angolan situation came in reports of serious internal rifts within Unita, Jonas Savimbi being criticized by a group of dissidents in Lisbon for his 'dictatorial' manner and for causing the disappearance of influential critics within the movement. There were also hints of war weariness among Unita supporters, but the movement was still strong enough to launch attacks on Government positions in Bie province. Moreover, Mr Savimbi found on his visit to Washington in June that he could still count on firm US backing, with US military equipment reaching Unita from bases in Zaïre.

'Vitriolic exchanges' between Cuban and South African delegates came close to ruining the third round of negotiations, which took place in Cairo at the end of June. It required intervention by the Soviet observer at the talks to bring the discussions back on course by showing that the proposals put forward by the two sides were sufficiently close to make a compromise solution possible. The fourth round of negotiations, in which only 'technical teams' participated, took place on Governor's Island in New York harbour in mid-July and produced what Dr Crocker described as a 'structure', in the form of a two-page document called 'Principles for a peaceful settlement in south-western Africa'; but there was still uncertainty as to whether Pretoria would really be prepared to accept Namibian independence. A fifth round of negotiations held in Geneva in early August was described as 'positive and productive' but immediately after the talks the South African Government publicly proposed that both Namibian independence and the Cuban withdrawal from Angola should be achieved by 1 June 1989 together with the dismantling of all ANC bases in Angola—a proposal which Cuban and Angolan spokesmen described as 'showing bad faith and a lack of seriousness'. Nevertheless, this contretemps did not prevent the two sides from agreeing to a ceasefire involving the withdrawal of all South African troops from Angola by 1 September, a joint military commission, on which Cuban, Angolan, South African and US officers would be represented, being established to monitor the border.

A sixth round of discussions in Brazzaville in late September failed to bring about an agreement on the timetable for a Cuban withdrawal.

There followed further meetings in New York in October and Geneva in November before an agreement was finally reached, the terms being set out in a protocol signed in Brazzaville on 13 December, while the formal signing of a tripartite agreement between Angola, Cuba and South Africa and of a bilateral agreement between Cuba and Angola took place at the UN headquarters in New York on 22 December (see DOCUMENTS). The tripartite agreement set 1 April 1989 as the starting date for the implementation of Resolution 435 in Namibia. The bilateral agreement set out the stages for 'the redeployment to the north and the staged and total withdrawal of Cuban troops from Angola'. All Cuban troops were to be withdrawn north of the 15th parallel by August 1989. By the end of 1989 half the Cuban force was scheduled to have left the country, the remaining troops to be withdrawn in stages until the process was completed in June 1991.

Significantly, Unita had played no part in the negotiations, both the Cuban and the US representatives arguing that negotiations between the MPLA and Unita must be regarded as a purely internal matter. Nevertheless, Dr Crocker repeatedly affirmed his Government's intention of continuing to give aid to Unita. In the latter half of the year Unita guerrillas were reported to be achieving considerable success in northern Angola and there was much talk of Unita transferring its main base from Jamba in the south-east to another location in the north or east. At the same time many Unita supporters were reported to have retreated with the South Africans into northern Namibia, where the South African Defence Force set about strengthening its defences.

In spite of the protracted peace process there could be no guarantee that peace was coming to Angola; but the prospects for that war-wracked land certainly looked less bleak than they had done at the start of the year.

Chapter 2

ZAMBIA—MALAWI—ZIMBABWE—NAMIBIA—BOTSWANA — LESOTHO—SWAZILAND

ZAMBIA

CAPITAL: Lusaka   AREA: 750,000 sq km   POPULATION: 6,700,000 ('86)
OFFICIAL LANGUAGE: English   POLITICAL SYSTEM: presidential, one-party state
RULING PARTY: United National Independence Party
HEAD OF STATE AND PARTY LEADER: President Kenneth Kaunda (since Oct '64)
PRINCIPAL MINISTERS: Kebby Musokotwane (prime minister), Luke Mwananshiku (foreign affairs), Lavu Mulimba (defence), Gibson Chigaga (finance and planning), Gen. Malimba Masheke (home affairs), Frederick Chomba (legal affairs)
INTERNATIONAL ALIGNMENT: NAM, OAU, ACP, Cwth.
CURRENCY: kwacha (end-'88 £1=K17.25, US$1=K9.54)   GNP PER CAPITA: US$300 ('86)
MAIN EXPORTS: copper, zinc, cobalt

IN May 1987 President Kaunda broke off relations with the IMF and announced that in its economic strategy the Zambian Government would go it alone (see AR 1987, p. 273). The consequences of this decision became increasingly apparent in the course of 1988. Both the World Bank and Western Governments held back funds for aid projects to the value of $350 million. Inflation rose to an annual rate of 60 per cent. There was a crippling shortage of foreign exchange and a steady expansion of the black market, which offered goods at prices which fewer and fewer people could afford. In an attempt to eliminate the black market, the National Assembly passed a law in February giving the Government the right to seize businesses thought to be trading illegally. 'We have been forced to do this', the President explained, 'to deal with the selfish minority of businessmen because we must protect the silent majority'. Many of the businesses seized belonged to Asian shopkeepers. Among the Asian community, which numbered no more than 8,000, the feeling grew that they were being made into scapegoats for the country's mounting economic difficulties. Some months later the President confessed that some shops had been taken over 'by error'. But Asian confidence had been dealt a severe blow and Western embassies reported a sharp rise in requests for immigration applications.

As economic difficulties mounted, criticism of President Kaunda became more vocal. Resentment was expressed about his frequent absence from the country on OAU and 'front-line' business and about his unwillingness to delegate power, so that during his absences government ground to a halt. After 24 years as head of state, it was argued, the President had 'outlived his political usefulness'. The most vocal opposition came from the backbenchers of the National Assembly, where a number of Bills presented with presidential approval had been rejected. The familiar method of muzzling critical assemblymen, by appointing them to ministerial posts, proved ineffective when those so appointed began to make a point of using the official information to which they had access to brief their backbench colleagues.

In order to counter this erosion of his influence the President announced a number of constitutional changes at a national congress of the ruling United National Independence Party (UNIP). Parliamentarians were to lose their salaries and left with only their attendance allowances. The party's central committee was to be enlarged from 25 to 68, the new members including Cabinet Ministers, security chiefs, the heads of parastatals and prominent trade unionists. From this body would be selected a committee of chairmen which would fulfil the role of a Politburo. In this way the influence of Parliament would be downgraded. To make assurance doubly sure, a more stringent system of vetting parliamentary candidates for the general election of 26 October was introduced. As many as 130 candidates were later reported to have been rejected, among them several sitting members of the National Assembly.

On 5 October, three weeks before the election, the Government detained a small group of army officers and civilians, following reports of 'alleged subversive activities'. The detainees were named on 4 November: the most prominent among them was General Christon Tembo, former air force commander, recently appointed ambassador to Bonn. The other detainees were middle-ranking army officers and civilians. By the time their names were released, the general election was over. Mr Kaunda was the only candidate for the presidency. He received 95 per cent of the votes cast. In his first press conference after the election the President warned new members of the National Assembly that they must not use their position to attack the policies of the ruling party. The Government continued to deny that it was proposing to approach the IMF, but on 8 November the kwacha was devalued by 20 per cent and interest rates increased from 20 to 25 per cent, moves interpreted as a narrowing of the gap between the Government and Western aid donors.

MALAWI

CAPITAL: Lilongwe   AREA: 118,500 sq km   POPULATION: 7,400,000 ('86)
OFFICIAL LANGUAGE: English   POLITICAL SYSTEM: presidential, one-party state
RULING PARTY: Congress Party
HEAD OF STATE AND PARTY LEADER: President Hastings Kamuzu Banda (since July '66)
PRINCIPAL MINISTERS: Maxwell Pashane (without portfolio), Louis Chimango (finance), Robson W. Chirwa (trade and industry)
INTERNATIONAL ALIGNMENT: NAM, OAU, ACP, Cwth.
CURRENCY: kwacha (end-'88 £1=MK4.59, US$1=MK2.54)   GNP PER CAPITA: US$160 ('86)
MAIN EXPORTS: tobacco, tea, sugar

REFUGEES from Mozambique continued to flood into southern Malawi (see AR 1987, p. 274), the number increasing from 70,000 in May 1987 to 500,000 in May 1988, when at least 300 refugees a day were still crossing the border. In some districts the number of refugees exceeded that of the local population. Malawi continued to provide a small contingent of troops to assist the Government of Mozambique in counter-insurgency operations, but the Mozambican authorities suspected that the insurgent National Resistance Movement (MNR) was still receiving some support from within Malawi.

On 13 September President P.W. Botha of South Africa paid his first visit to Malawi and was received by President Banda at Mzuzu, 180 miles north of Lilongwe. The two leaders were reported to have discussed economic and security matters, including South African aid to Malawi.

Observers began taking a more critical view of Malawi's 'economic miracle', which made it one of the few countries in Africa capable of feeding its population. It was pointed out that more than half the country's peasant population had access to less than one hectare of land: such smallholders were forced to buy food if they could afford so to do. Malawi's infant mortality rate—320 out of every 1,000 children dying before the age of five—was one of the highest in Africa. Acute rural poverty contrasted with the apparent prosperity of the major towns, with their new office buildings and well-stocked supermarkets.

ZIMBABWE

CAPITAL: Harare   AREA: 390,000 sq km   POPULATION: 8,700,000 ('86)
OFFICIAL LANGUAGE: English   POLITICAL SYSTEM: presidential, one-party state
RULING PARTY: Zimbabwe African National Union—Patriotic Front
HEAD OF STATE AND PARTY LEADER: President Robert Mugabe (since Dec. 87, previously Prime Minister)
PRINCIPAL MINISTERS: Simon Vengesai Muzenda (Vice-President), Joshua Nkomo (senior minister, local government), Maurice Nyagumbo (senior minister, political affairs), Bernard Chidzero (senior minister, finance and economic planning), Nathan Shamuyarira (foreign affairs), Enos Nkala (defence), Moven Mahachi (home affairs), Emmerson Munangagwa (justice)
INTERNATIONAL ALIGNMENT: NAM, OAU, ACP, Cwth.
CURRENCY: Zimbabwe dollar (end-'88 £1 = Z$3.48, US$1 = Z$1.93)   GNP PER CAPITA: US$620 ('86)
MAIN EXPORTS: tobacco, gold, cotton

ZIMBABWE began the year with a newly-titled head of state. On 30 December 1987 Robert Mugabe, formerly Prime Minister and first secretary of the ruling Zimbabwe African National Union (Zanu-PF), had been elected unopposed as the country's first executive President. The following day the former Deputy Prime Minister, Simon Muzenda, was appointed Vice-President and on 2 January the composition of the new 29-member Government was announced. Notable among the new appointments was that of Joshua Nkomo, leader of the former Zimbabwe African People's Union (PF-Zapu), to the post of Minister of State in the office of the President. Two other former Zapu members also joined the Cabinet, acknowledging the recent merger between the two parties (see AR 1987, p. 276).

The unity agreement signed on 22 December 1987, and confirmed at an extraordinary congress of Zanu-PF on 9 April, ended 24 years of often bitter rivalry and mutual harassment between Zanu-PF and Zapu. It presaged a one-party state and, according to Mr Mugabe, 'a new discipline' in which contradictions 'are better resolved by discussion and negotiation than by quarrels and fights'. More immediately the dissolution of Zapu signalled a return to peace in Matabeleland, its regional stronghold in the south-west of the country. The end of the five-and-a-half year insurgency campaign, estimated to have cost 1,500 lives, was marked on 19 April by a general amnesty for former dissidents and political fugitives. At the close of the six-week amnesty, 113 guerrillas had surrendered to the police. The solution of the security problem, which had inhibited agricultural production, discouraged tourism and restricted the growth of Zimbabwe's second city, Bulawayo, brought hopes of a real upturn in Matabeleland's economic fortunes.

If the Zanu-PF/Zapu fusion effectively silenced formal political opposition, the year saw a striking growth in extra-parliamentary criticism of the Government, matched by a perceptible decline in official tolerance of it. The principal external enemy remained the South African Government, allegedly the source of covert operations against African National Congress (ANC) targets within Zimbabwe since 1981. On 15 February the Foreign Minister, Nathan Shamuyarira, announced the cracking of a South African-sponsored sabotage network and the arrest of six men following a bomb attack on an ANC house in Bulawayo on 11 January. Three of those arrested received death sentences in November. Military operations against guerrillas of the South African-supported Mozambique National Resistance Movement (MNR) continued throughout the year, involving upwards of 8,000 Zimbabwe troops at an estimated cost of £250,000 a day (see p. 282).

Within the country fresh attacks on government policy came from students at the University of Zimbabwe. A campus boycott on minor university issues at the beginning of April escalated by September into a campaign of peaceful demonstrations against 'creeping corruption' in government. On 29 September police used rubber bullets and tear gas to prevent students from marching into the capital, while on 7 October a Kenyan-born law lecturer at the university, Shadrack Gutto, was deported for incitement, ironically on the day Amnesty International's world tour of musical superstars played its first African concert in Harare.

Government sensitivity to the serious charge of corruption was plainly linked to growing evidence of official financial malpractice, together with the uncomfortable allegation that over eight years of avowedly marxist-leninist government many senior Ministers and party officials had amassed substantial personal fortunes. In April Chief Justice Enoch Dumbutshena described corruption as 'a cancer creeping through Zimbabwean public life'. In November the report of the Comptroller and Auditor-General exposed, as in previous years (see AR 1987, p. 277), excessive and unauthorized departmental expenditure and regular breaches of treasury instructions. The report cited examples of financial indiscipline in most government departments, including unauthorized expenditure by the Ministry of Defence of a total of Z$8 million during the 1986-87 financial year. The Government hence took steps, in the second half of the year, to quell public disquiet. At one level, the President delivered unequivocal assurances that corruption would be rooted out and eliminated. At another, critics were disciplined. On 21 November Edgar Tekere, an MP and former secretary-general of Zanu-PF, was expelled from the party for 'continuously breaching party protocol'. Mr Tekere had made repeated public attacks on the Government, referring to Ministers' alleged Swiss bank accounts and describing democracy in Zimbabwe as 'in the intensive care unit'.

As Zimbabwe entered its ninth year of independence, the familiar problems of budgetary deficits, low investment levels and foreign exchange shortages appeared endemic to the country's economic life. Presenting his Budget to Parliament on 28 July, the Minister of Finance, Economic Planning and Development, Dr Bernard Chidzero, described it as a 'standstill package'. Forecasting a record budget deficit of Z$1,149 million, the fourth in four years (see AR 1987, p. 277), Dr Chidzero observed that the burden of debt servicing both contributed to the inflation rate of 8 per cent and pre-empted resources badly needed for the restructuring of the economy and for the expansion of employment opportunities.

Despite the budget deficit the economy showed an overall growth rate of 6 per cent for the year, in large part the result of a good agricultural season and rising prices for Zimbabwe's exports on world markets. Tobacco represented the country's main foreign exchange earner, with sales of over Z$600 million for the year. Maize production hit the record level of 2.25 million tonnes, two-thirds of the harvest coming from peasant growers and communal farms. Export earnings for mineral production exceeded the 1987 record level of just over Z$1,000 million, and promised further growth in 1989 in response to government plans for export promotion.

Manufacturing output grew by 5 per cent in 1988, foreign investors contributing heavily to major industrial projects. The Z$38 million Mazwikadei dam, built with Italian aid, was opened in April, while the British companies Cluff Oil Holdings and Lonrho signed major contracts for petroleum and mining installations during the year. The United States, after a two-year suspension, resumed aid to Zimbabwe in September with a US$17 million programme; since independence the country had received US$382 million in direct bilateral aid from the United States.

A notable visitor to Zimbabwe in September was Pope John Paul II. Less conspicuous was the British Labour opposition leader, Neil Kinnock who, on a visit to the border with Mozambique in July, went unrecognized and was briefly detained by the security forces.

NAMIBIA

CAPITAL: Windhoek   AREA: 824,000 sq km   POPULATION: 1,200,000 ('86)
STATUS: de facto South African control (regarded as illegal by the UN), due to give way to full independence on the basis of democratic elections to be held in November 1989

IN 1988 Namibia was at last placed on the road to sovereign independence in terms of Resolution 435 of the UN Security Council (1978) (see also pp. 286, 297 and DOCUMENTS). Yet many Namibians were sceptical, noting the ten years which had elapsed since the adoption of Resolution 435 and fearing that yet further delays could be in store.

In February it appeared that Angola and Cuba were prepared to accept a Cuban troop withdrawal from Angola as part of the UN independence plan for Namibia. In April President P.W. Botha and four senior Cabinet colleagues met members of the six-party transitional Government in Windhoek and announced that the powers of South Africa's Administrator-General in the territory, Louis Pienaar, would be expanded to include powers to act against anyone or any section of the media which, in his opinion, was 'promoting terrorism and subversion'. It seemed that the probable targets of such measures included the outspoken *Namibian* newspaper. The new powers threatened to plunge the transitional Government into crisis as several Ministers contemplated resignation, but President Botha refused to withdraw the powers.

The political parties in the transitional Government announced in July that they would go ahead with their own plans for a new constitution in spite of the recent agreement in London between South Africa, Angola and Cuba to implement Resolution 435. The transitional constitution would help Namibians to prepare for independence, it was argued. In August South Africa unveiled a surprise peace plan at Geneva which set 1 November 1988 as the date for the commencement of the terms of Resolution 435. This date was widely felt to be unrealistic, but the talks continued fruitfully and a ceasefire in the Namibian war was announced on

8 August as a first step towards a peace agreement. In the same month the South African Minister of Information, Stoffel van der Merwe, announced that a Swapo Government in Namibia would be acceptable to the South African Government if the Cubans left Angola.

Sam Nujoma, president of Swapo, said in an interview that an independent Namibia would probably not allow bases of the African National Congress (ANC) on its territory. Swapo acknowledged the importance of a multi-party democratic system and there would be no blanket policy of nationalization of private land, industries or buildings. Meanwhile, talks continued under the chairmanship of Dr Chester Crocker, US Assistant Secretary of State, mainly in Brazzaville (Congo) between Angola, Cuba and South Africa, to prepare a detailed timetable of Cuban troop withdrawal from Angola and withdrawal of the South African military from Angola and Namibia.

In September UN Secretary-General Pérez de Cuellar visited Pretoria for discussions with President Botha and with Mr Pienaar. He said he was relying on Pretoria's goodwill to implement Resolution 435 and then left for consultations in Luanda.

After further talks in Brazzaville, agreement was finally reached on a timetable for troop withdrawals and implementation of Resolution 435, 1 April 1989 now being agreed as the starting date. Treaties were signed between South Africa, Cuba and Angola at the UN in December (see DOCUMENTS). After nearly 70 years of South African administration of the territory, formerly known as South-West Africa, the stage was set for the independence of Namibia.

BOTSWANA

CAPITAL: Gaborone AREA: 580,000 sq km POPULATION: 1,130,000 ('86)
OFFICIAL LANGUAGE: English POLITICAL SYSTEM: presidential democracy
HEAD OF STATE AND GOVERNMENT: President Quett Masire (since July '80)
RULING PARTY: Democratic Party
PRINCIPAL MINISTERS: Peter Mmusi (Vice-President, finance and planning), Gaositwe Chiepe (external affairs), Englishman Kgabo (home affairs)
INTERNATIONAL ALIGNMENT: NAM, OAU, ACP, Cwth.
CURRENCY: pula (end-'88 £1=P3.47, US$1=P1.92) GNP PER CAPITA: US$840 ('86)
MAIN EXPORTS: diamonds, copper-nickel, beef

A South African raid into Botswana, which left four people dead in a house in Gaborone, was condemned by UN Secretary-General Pérez de Cuellar on 28 March. He called on Pretoria to refrain from further attacks and to respect the territorial integrity and sovereignty of Botswana. Britain and the United States joined in the condemnation of the raid, which was seen in Pretoria as a successful military operation against the African National

Congress (ANC), whose guerrillas were believed by Pretoria to be using Botswana as an infiltration route into the country. Botswana said the victims were civilians, three of them women. Following the March incident, relations between the two countries deteriorated.

In June two South Africans, apparently commandos attached to the South African security forces, were arrested at a road block following a shooting incident in which three Botswana policemen were injured. Their trial, on charges of attempted murder and violations of the National Security Act, which specified penalties of up to 30 years, began in September. Also in June, the South African police announced that 23 recently-arrested ANC guerrillas had received their weapons and instructions in Botswana.

President Quett Masire was slightly injured in August when his aircraft was accidentally attacked by the Angolan air force when he was en route to a meeting of southern African heads of state in Luanda.

As South Africa suffered its worst-ever succession of urban bombings, the Minister of Foreign Affairs, Pik Botha, warned in September that the Government reserved the right to take whatever steps it deemed to be appropriate to protect South Africans against further acts of terrorism. It was evident, he said, that Botswana was not taking the steps needed to prevent guerrilla infiltration from its territory. He rejected Botswana's denials that the country was a through-route for ANC guerrillas. In November, Mrs Lynda Chalker, a British Foreign Office Minister, visited Botswana and, after touring the site of the March commando raid, called on all sides to find a way to negotiate a suspension of violence.

In December the Minister of Foreign Affairs, Dr G. Chiepe, met her South African counterpart, Mr Botha, as well as the South African Ministers of Defence and Law and Order, for discussion of the security situation. Sources indicated that Dr Chiepe protested to Pretoria against South African raids into Botswana while the South African delegation called on Botswana to take positive action to prevent the ANC from using its territory for infiltration.

On 18 December it was reported that two people were killed when mystery raiders attacked a village in southern Botswana near Goodhope. Botswana said the raid was carried out by a heavily-armed group whose tracks were traced to the South African border.

LESOTHO

CAPITAL: Maseru   AREA: 30,300 sq km   POPULATION: 1,600,000 ('86)
OFFICIAL LANGUAGES: English and Sesotho   POLITICAL SYSTEM: monarchy, under military rule
HEAD OF STATE: King Moshoeshoe II (since Oct '66)
HEAD OF GOVERNMENT: Maj.-Gen. Justin Lekhanya, Chairman of Military Council (since Jan '86)
PRINCIPAL MINISTERS: Col. Thaabe Letsie (foreign affairs), Michael Sefali (planning and economic affairs), Chief Mathealira Seeiso (interior), Bennett Makalo Khaketla (justice)
INTERNATIONAL ALIGNMENT: NAM, OAU, ACP, Cwth.
CURRENCY: maloti (end-'88 £1=M4.30, US$1=M2.38)   GNP PER CAPITA: US$370 ('86)
MAIN EXPORTS: diamonds, wool

IN January Lesotho's military ruler, Major-General Justin Lekhanya, marked two years in power with a military parade but made no reference to earlier promises to set up a National Assembly and return to barracks as soon as peace was restored after the coup which toppled Chief Leabua Jonathan in 1986.

In March strong international interest was widely reported in the R 4,200 million Lesotho Highlands Water Scheme, with British, US, West German, French and South African companies competing to win sections of the contract. The scheme would boost the Lesotho economy by selling water to the rich industrial areas of South Africa and would also supply power to Lesotho and South Africa. In May the first major contract, worth R 97 million, was awarded to LTA of South Africa to build a stretch of access road to the proposed Katse dam.

A member of the African National Congress of South Africa, Mazizi Attwell Maqekeza, was shot dead in his hospital bed in Maseru in March. No arrests were made. In April General Lekhanya declared a state of emergency on account of 'worsening crime in the country', but his order was ruled by Chief Justice Brian Cullinan to be null and void. In September, on the eve of a visit by Pope John Paul II, General Lekhanya again declared a state of emergency. The order was signed by King Moshoeshoe II. The reason for the emergency declaration was not immediately apparent.

The papal visit began on 14 September, after the Pope had travelled to Maseru by car from Johannesburg, his aircraft having been unable to land in Lesotho because of low cloud. The visit was marred by an incident in which guerrillas—reportedly of the Lesotho Liberation Army—hijacked a bus and forced it to drive to the British high commission in Maseru. The South African Defence Force was called in and the impasse was resolved in a shoot-out which took place as the Pope was arriving in Maseru. Six people died, including the four hijackers. The high point of the papal visit was the beatification of the nineteenth-century Jesuit missionary Father Joseph Gerard, who brought Christianity to the kingdom.

In October King Moshoeshoe II visited Pretoria for a meeting with President Botha to discuss matters of mutual concern.

SWAZILAND

CAPITAL: Mbabane   AREA: 17,350 sq km   POPULATION: 689,000 ('86)
OFFICIAL LANGUAGES: English and siSwati   POLITICAL SYSTEM: monarchy
HEAD OF STATE AND GOVERNMENT: King Mswati III (since April '86)
PRINCIPAL MINISTERS: Sotsha Dlamini (prime minister), Sir George Mamba (foreign affairs), Sibusiso Barnabas Dlamini (finance), Senzenjani Enoch Tshabalala (interior), Reginald Dladla (justice)
INTERNATIONAL ALIGNMENT: NAM, OAU, ACP, Cwth.
CURRENCY: emalangeni (end-'88 £1=E4.30, US$1=E2.38)   GNP PER CAPITA: US$690 ('86)
MAIN EXPORTS: sugar, agricultural products

TWO members of the African National Congress (ANC) of South Africa were arrested by Swazi police in a raid on a house in Manzini, it was reported on 30 January. Further arrests of ANC members were made in July, when it was announced that seven others had been deported to Zambia.

In March it was disclosed that Prince Mfanasibili Dlamini, formerly a dominant figure in the royal family, had been convicted, with eight associates, of high treason and sentenced at a closed trial to 15 years in prison. The verdicts were announced by Chief Justice Nicholas Hannah, chairman of the special tribunal set up to try the case. The charges dated from palace feuds during the minority of King Mswati III (who did not assume the throne until 1986) and involved allegations of breaches of Swazi custom.

In April the South African Foreign Minister, Pik Botha, paid a short visit to Swaziland for talks with King Mswati. The Minister of Foreign Affairs of Swaziland, George Mamba, said in August that his country would be prepared to enter into diplomatic relations with South Africa once Pretoria took positive steps to scrap apartheid.

On 6 September, Swaziland celebrated 20 years of independence when about 30,000 people packed the national stadium for a military parade, displays of dancing and gymnastics. Later in the same month there were further arrests of suspected ANC guerrillas who were to be charged with illegally importing weapons into the country.

In October the Prime Minister, Sotsha Dlamini, made his strongest protest yet over violations of the country's territory by South African security forces. He described the killing of a Swazi citizen by South African soldiers in south-western Swaziland as an atrocity and an act of aggression against the sovereignty of an independent state.

In November King Mswati issued a controversial decree giving his Government powers over the ownership and sale of property in Swaziland. The country's Law Society requested an audience with the King to express its concern about the effects of the decree on the economy and potential investment. The King said afterwards that the 'misunderstanding' over the decree had been resolved.

Chapter 3

REPUBLIC OF SOUTH AFRICA

CAPITAL: Pretoria   AREA: 1,220,000 sq km   POPULATION: 32,500,000 ('86, including homelands)
OFFICIAL LANGUAGE: Afrikaans and English
POLITICAL SYSTEM: presidential, under white minority rule (democracy for whites, partial representation for coloured and Asians)
HEAD OF STATE AND GOVERNMENT: President P.W. Botha (since Sept '84, previously Prime Minister)
RULING PARTY: National Party
PRINCIPAL MINISTERS: Roelof F. (Pik) Botha (foreign affairs), Gen. Magnus A. Malan (defence), Chris Heunis (constitutional development), Barend J. du Plessis (finance), J.C.G. Botha (home affairs), Kobie Coetsee (justice)
CURRENCY: rand (end-'88 £1=R6.96, US$1=R3.84)   GNP PER CAPITA: US$2,260 ('84)
MAIN EXPORTS: precious and base metals, minerals

IN 1988 the National Party Government celebrated its 40th anniversary (commemorating the 1948 election victory of Dr D.F. Malan) amid a spate of urban bombings. Press censorship and a state of emergency continued in force and further measures were taken to suppress the extra-parliamentary opposition. It was another year of violent stalemate in the Pretoria Government's long-running conflict with the African National Congress (ANC).

The most notable happening of the year was Pretoria's decision, after many years of stalling, to cooperate in carrying out UN Resolution 435 (1978) which provided for UN-supervised elections and independence for the former German colony of Namibia (South-West Africa), which Pretoria had administered since the 1919 Treaty of Versailles. For a decade Pretoria had fought off the Angola-based insurgency of the South-West African People's Organization (Swapo), which was expected to be the dominant force in the Government of an independent Namibia.

The turning-point came when Pretoria resolved to withdraw its troops from neighbouring Angola, having invaded that territory in operations against Swapo and in support of the Unita rebellion against the MPLA Government in Luanda. Increased South African support for Unita was more than matched by massive reinforcement of the Cuban forces fighting in defence of the Luanda Government. In a precarious military situation outside the town of Cuito Cuanavale (see pp. 283–5), Pretoria resolved to disengage and cooperate with US-led efforts to secure the peace of the region. The long-running negotiations were successfully concluded at a formal treaty-signing ceremony at the UN in December. The agreement (see DOCUMENTS) provided for the phased withdrawal of Cuban troops from Angola and the implementation of Resolution 435, South Africa having insisted on linkage of these key elements in a regional settlement.

Internally, however, there was no significant movement towards negotiation with the ANC, which stepped up its urban bombings in the first half of the year. At the same time, the ANC continued its discussions with white South African liberals and published constitutional guidelines which incorporated a Bill of Rights and seemed intended to reassure apprehensive whites. The intensified bombing campaign seemed in part a response to the assassination of an ANC representative in Paris, Miss Dulcie September, and a car bombing in Maputo in which ANC legal specialist Albie Sachs lost an arm. A number of similar incidents elsewhere in the region were widely attributed to agents of the South African Government.

A disquieting trend which continued in the year was the succession of devastating sabotage actions against left-wing organizations and the anti-apartheid Christian churches, culminating in a fire-bomb attack on Khanya House, headquarters of the Southern African Catholic Bishops' Conference in Pretoria, in which staff members narrowly escaped with their lives. Previously the Johannesburg headquarters of the South African Council of Churches, the Black Sash and other liberal organizations had been destroyed by a massive explosion, apparently originating in a motor vehicle parked in the basement. This followed the destruction by similar means of the building occupied by the trade union federation, COSATU, also in Johannesburg. In no case were any arrests made by the authorities. At the end of the year these incidents remained unexplained and unsolved.

The ANC's sabotage campaign proceeded at an unprecedented rate in the first half of the year, when there were bombing incidents of varying seriousness almost every week. In March a powerful car bomb exploded outside the Krugersdorp magistrate's court, killing three and injuring 22 people. In June four people were killed and 19 injured in explosions which rocked a Roodepoort shopping centre, while in July a car bomb exploded as crowds were leaving the Ellis Park rugby stadium in Johannesburg, killing two people and injuring 34. Limpet mine explosions were reported at regular intervals in the major cities, taking a steady toll in injuries and being particularly directed at a popular chain of hamburger restaurants.

While the ANC continued to claim that its policy was to avoid civilian casualties if possible, it was evident that the organization was split between those who wanted to attack white civilian targets and those who sought to maintain a distinction between hard targets with some strategic rationale and soft targets involving the killing of civilians. In the second half of the year there was a falling-off in the frequency of bombings in the urban areas. Throughout the year hand grenade attacks, often followed by shoot-outs with police, were reported in the black townships.

Until the October municipal elections showed his fears to be exaggerated, President Botha was preoccupied with the political threat posed to his Government by the white ultra-right Conservative Party (CP) of Dr A.P. Treurnicht, a breakaway from his own National Party. For most of the year President Botha's tentative reform programme was in abeyance as his Government seemed intent on mollifying the right while cracking down more heavily than ever on the extra-parliamentary left.

The pattern was set in late February when the state imposed restrictions just short of outright prohibition on the United Democratic Front (UDF), Azapo and 17 other organizations of the extra-parliamentary opposition. Under the emergency regulations the UDF, a multi-racial organization with similar goals to the ANC although opposed to violence, was prohibited from functioning in any way at all. Stringent restrictions were also placed upon COSATU, preventing it from playing any role in politics. Nevertheless, there was a successful three-day workers' stay-away in June, traditionally a month of extra-parliamentary protest.

Of the security/political trials which ended in 1988, the most notable was the marathon trial of the 'Delmas 22' on charges of treason and subversion. It ended with the conviction of 11 of the accused in a judgment which appeared to limit the scope of an extra-parliamentary opposition more stringently than ever.

Inside President Botha's tricameral parliamentary system, the main focus of anti-apartheid resistance to Government policies was Rev Allan Hendrickse's Labour Party, the majority party in the coloured (mixed-race) House of Representatives. Mr Hendrickse obstructed the Government's legislative programme at every turn and threatened that he would continue to do so in 1989 as long as President Botha refused to scrap the Group Areas Act, which provided for racially-separate residential areas.

President Botha was eventually obliged to withdraw a retrogressive amending Bill which would have increased the penalties for flouting the Group Areas Act, but he refused to repeal the original measure. Two other amending Bills, easing the application of the Group Areas Act in some respects, by providing for limited multi-racial areas, were eventually enacted by President Botha, using his reserve powers to refer blocked legislation to the President's Council for resolution.

In the (white) House of Assembly, the small opposition group to the left of the Government tended to be overshadowed by the CP opposition on the Government's right flank. There were sustained efforts throughout 1988 to unite the liberal opposition into a single party, incorporating the Progressive Federal Party, now led by Dr Zach De Beer, the Independent movement led by Dr Dennis Worral and Wynand Malan's National Democratic Party. Negotiations were still in progress as the year ended.

The controversial tricameral constitutional system, rejected by its critics as an apartheid structure, was taken a step further in October when for the first time (racially-separate) local government elections were held simultaneously for all population groups. In the white elections, the right-wing Conservative Party gained control of a number of town and city councils in the Transvaal and proclaimed its intention of reintroducing racial separation in municipal facilities. The first local municipality to do so was Boksburg, which subsequently suffered a ruinous boycott by black consumers which cut the turnover of some shops by as much as 85 per cent and threatened to put them out of business. The CP did not do as well as it had expected at the polls, so that a serious question-mark was raised over its chances of beating the National Party in the next parliamentary election.

The black municipal elections, boycotted by the left, took place against a background of widespread detentions and a call by the Archbishop of Cape Town, the Most Rev Desmond Tutu, that blacks should stay away from the polls. As it turned out, the response at the polls was very disappointing from the Government's point of view, even if the official percentage poll figure of 25 per cent was accurate. The Government's strategy of building constitutional structures from the bottom up had got off to a shaky start. The plan was to erect regional and, ultimately, national tiers of government on a sub-structure of local government; however, it seemed that acceptance in the community would be lacking and the legitimacy of the scheme doubtful.

The Botha Government was emboldened by its performance against the CP in the white municipal elections and took important forward-looking steps as the year was ending, making peace in Angola/Namibia, reprieving the 'Sharpeville Six' as they awaited execution in Pretoria, and announcing that ANC leader Nelson Mandela would not return to prison after his recovery in hospital from a bout of tuberculosis. It transpired that Mr Mandela, a prisoner for 25 years, would be accommodated in a house with swimming pool in the grounds of the Victor Verster prison in the Western Cape province. But Mr Mandela remained a prisoner, however comfortable his quarters, and the Botha Government seemed as unlikely as ever to release the ANC leaders and invite them to negotiate. Yet these concessions to international opinion were thought to have eased the threat of further economic sanctions against the country.

If the right-wing electoral threat was receding, white extremism seemed likely to pose a continuing threat to public safety. In November a young Afrikaner ex-policeman went on the rampage in central Pretoria, shooting 23 blacks at random, six of them fatally, before police were able to stop him. He was said to belong to an organization called the 'White Wolves'.

In December Mother Theresa of Calcutta visited South Africa to establish a branch of her worldwide foundation at Khayelitsha, a sprawling black area outside Cape Town.

VIII SOUTH ASIA AND INDIAN OCEAN

Chapter 1

IRAN—AFGHANISTAN

IRAN

CAPITAL: Tehran   AREA: 1,650,000 sq km   POPULATION: 49,930,000 ('87)
NATIONAL LANGUAGE: Farsi (Persian)
POLITICAL SYSTEM: Islamic republic
SPIRITUAL LEADER: Ayatollah Ruhollah Khomeini
DESIGNATED SUCCESSOR: Ayatollah Hossein Ali Montazeri
HEAD OF STATE: President Seyed Ali Khamene'i (since Oct '81)
SPEAKER OF ASSEMBLY: Hojatolislam Hashemi Ali Akbar Rafsanjani
PRINCIPAL MINISTERS: Mir Hussain Mousavi (Prime Minister), Ali Akbar Vellayati (foreign affairs), Gholamreza Agazadeh (oil), Ali Akbar Mohtashemi (interior), Muhammad Javad Iravani (economic affairs and finance), Hassan Ebrahim Habibi (justice)
INTERNATIONAL ALIGNMENT: NAM, Opec, ICO
CURRENCY: rial (end-'88 £1=R1s125.28, US$1=R1s68.81)   GNP PER CAPITA: US$3,625 ('87)
MAIN EXPORTS: oil and gas

IRAN accepted a ceasefire in the Gulf War effective from 20 August (see also pp. 215–7). In doing so it ended the bitter war with Iraq which had begun in September 1980 and acknowledged its inability to pursue hostilities in the face of severe reverses on the battlefield. The first major setback came on 28 March, when the National Liberation Army managed by the dissident mujahideen-i-khalq was able to drive a 30-km wedge in Iranian lines in Khuzestan. On 15 April the strategic enclave held by the Iranians around the Iraqi outport of Fao was overrun by the Iraqi army without real resistance and it became clear that the Iranians, far from being in a position to launch their long-heralded 'final attack', were so weak that they could not hold sections of their main defensive line. A minor diversionary move by the Iranians in the northern mountains around Halabja on 16-17 March was more important for its unveiling of Iraqi chemical warfare against its own Kurdish civilian population than for its military impact. A further significant loss for the Iranians began on 25 May. Iraqi forces pushed forward throughout the Fish Lake region and retook all the ground east of Basra as far as Shalamcheh so painfully won by the Iranians in the famous Karbala 4 and 5 campaigns in the spring of 1987 (see AR 1987, p. 287). In June Iran lost Halabja in the north and the Majnoon marshes in the south together with Mehran, the latter falling to the mujahideen.

Iranian difficulties on the battlefield stemmed from a chronic depletion of weapons and men. The Karbala offensives of early 1987 saw the loss of a high percentage of trained Iranian officers from the

Revolutionary Guards units. By March 1988 it was estimated that only 13 per cent of the Guards battalions were made up of volunteers, the balance being short-term conscripts. At the same time, the quality of Iran's weaponry had massively deteriorated during the course of the war, given the failure of the regime to find regular and reliable supplies of basic armour and aircraft abroad. Iran appeared not to have the will or the means to retaliate against the use by Iraq of chemical weapons. Reports from the battlefields during 1988 also indicated that Iran's once great advantage over the Iraqis, the total dedication of its troops to its cause, had evaporated, leaving morale at a low ebb. There was an increasing shortage of volunteers to go to the front.

The war in the air also turned markedly against Iran. During the year Iraqi air attacks on oil facilities, tankers and strategic industrial targets were intensified. Kharg Island in particular became untenable as a dependable export terminal and even the loading points further east in the Gulf were vulnerable to attack, Larak being savagely bombed on 15 May. The Iranian air force had been more or less in severe inferiority against Iraqi forces since 1982 and by 1988 was so run down as to be entirely ineffective. Perhaps the most damaging change in the pattern of the air war occurred on 29 February and subsequent days, when a barrage of Iraqi missiles was delivered on Tehran. Iran was caught unawares by the scale and efficiency of the Iraqi missile arsenal and had no means of adequate response. There was a considerable exodus of population from Tehran and the Iranian Government's inadequacies in facing total war were brutally exposed.

Iranian difficulties in handling the war against Iraq were severely compounded by its isolation from, and apparently aggressive intent towards, the international community. The consolidation of the multinational minesweeping force in the Gulf and the increasing activities of the US naval squadron served to reduce Iranian scope for retaliation against Iraq and its Arab allies. Indeed, the confrontation with the USA proved to be a serious and damaging military distraction for Tehran. The US navy destroyed Iranian offshore platforms at Sassan and Sirri oilfields on 18 April in retaliation for an alleged mining by Iran of a US warship, the *Samuel B. Roberts*, on 14 April. The Iranians attempted to make a stand against the US fleet on 18 April, but in so doing lost two frigates and four gunboats, representing a substantial portion of its naval vessels. Although there were continuing small-scale naval actions by the Iranians against neutral shipping after that date, they were unable to reestablish a credible presence in the Gulf against the USA and other foreign naval might.

During a skirmish between Iranian and US naval vessels near

Bandar Abbas on 3 July missiles were launched in error by the USS *Vincennes* against an Iranian civilian airliner. Crew and passengers, in all totalling 290 persons, were killed when the Iran Air airbus crashed into the sea.

A move towards an Iranian reappraisal of the war was foreshadowed on 18 April when Hashemi Rafsanjani stated that 'time is no longer on our side'. Mr Rafsanjani took charge of all the armed forces on 2 June, from that point assuming a leading role in the political management of the Islamic republic. The shooting-down of the airliner in July gave opportunity for the Iranian Government to back out of what was clearly an unwinnable war. On 18 July the Iranian President, Ali Khamene'i, wrote to the UN Secretary-General accepting UN ceasefire Resolution 598 (see AR 1987, p. 548). Acknowledgement of the ceasefire was obtained from both combatants by 8 August and the guns fell silent on 20 August. A UN Iran-Iraq Military Observer Group was moved into the war front to oversee the ceasefire on 19 August.

Peace talks began under UN auspices in Geneva and New York in August. There were immediate difficulties over the status of the Shatt al-Arab, the Iraqis demanding the abrogation of the 1975 'Thalweg' division along the middle of the waterway's deepest point and the reinstitution of the 1937 arrangements under which Iraq held rights to the river west of the low-water mark on the Iranian side of the channel. By the end of the year little progress had been made towards preparing a peace treaty.

Iranian foreign relations were disastrous in the first part of the year. Attempts to re-establish links with the USSR were entirely frustrated by Soviet insistence on peace in the war against Iraq. Later in the year the USSR made efforts to repair its connections with Iran to protect its withdrawal from Afghanistan (see p. 112). The Arab states became increasingly open in their antagonism to the Islamic republic. A Kuwaiti airliner was hijacked to Masshad in north-eastern Iran on 5 April and in the Arab world the Iranian authorities were assumed to have been implicated in the event (see also p. 224). On 26 April Saudi Arabia broke off diplomatic relations with Iran following disputes over Iranian participation in the pilgrimage to Mecca (see p. 219) and attacks on Saudi Arabian shipping in the Gulf. Even links with Syria, Iran's close ally, were damaged during the year as a result of rivalries in Lebanon and Iranian inability to service concessionary oil deliveries to Syria.

In the aftermath of the ceasefire the Iranian Foreign Ministry was at great pains to find allies and rebuild fences with the outside world. New approaches were made to the Arab states in the Gulf. West European countries were singled out for special treatment as potential suppliers during the reconstruction process. Iran had some small success in facilitating the release of French hostages in the Lebanon in May and in consequence there was a restoration of Irano-French relations on 18 August. After extended negotiations new arrangements for diplomatic representation were made with the United Kingdom in the later part of the year.

Domestic politics were dominated by the emergence of Hashemi Rafsanjani and his allies as the principal managers of the Government. The success of Mr Rafsanjani in taking over the most important reins of power came despite an indication in January that Ayatollah Khomeini was veering towards greater support of the Islamic radicals and the results of the spring elections, in which 160 out of 260 seats were won by the more extreme elements in the regime. Mir Hussain Mousavi was retained albeit as a reluctant Prime Minister after the ending of the war. Ayatollah Khomeini became perceptibly less of a commanding figure during 1988, though he remained the ultimate arbiter within the regime.

The failure of the Iranian economy was an important contribution towards ending the war effort. In particular, the oil sector became adversely affected by Iraqi disruption and falling prices for crude oil on the international market. Oil output ran at two million barrels per day during the first half of the year, less than the 2.369 million bpd Opec quota. The falling oil price, which averaged $13.8 per barrel in the first nine-months of 1988, added to Iranian discomfiture, and oil income for the year as a whole was forecast at $8,800 million, down by a fifth on 1987 estimates. Elsewhere in the economy there was disinvestment and neglect allied to unemployment, inflation and shortages of goods brought on by ten years of revolutionary turmoil and war. Foreign exchange reserves were admitted to be negligible in 1988 and informal foreign debt was considerable. The year ended with the Government promising a reconstruction of the productive sectors of the Iranian economy and creation of a new financial framework, both of which were urgently needed but outside the immediate abilities of the Islamic republic to achieve.

AFGHANISTAN

CAPITAL: Kabul   AREA: 650,000 sq km   POPULATION: 15,000,000
OFFICIAL LANGUAGES: Pushtu and Dari (Persian)   POLITICAL SYSTEM: presidential
HEAD OF STATE AND GOVERNMENT: President Mohammed Najibullah (since Nov '87, previously Chairman of Revolutionary Council)
RULING PARTY: People's Democratic Party of Afghanistan (heading National Front)
PRINCIPAL MINISTERS: Mohammed Hasan Sharq (prime minister), Abdul Wakil (foreign affairs), Lt.-Gen. Shanawaz Tanay (defence), Hamidollah Tarzi (finance), Maj.-Gen. Mohammed Aslam Watanjar (internal affairs), Mohammed Bashir Baghlani (justice)
INTERNATIONAL ALIGNMENT: NAM, Comecon (observer), ICO
CURRENCY: afghani (end-'88 £1=Af99.25, US$1=Af54.86)   GNP PER CAPITA: US$168 ('82)
MAIN EXPORTS: agricultural products

EACH year since 1980 a resolution sponsored by Pakistan on Afghanistan had been endorsed by a large majority at the UN General Assembly. Each of these resolutions called for the immediate withdrawal of all foreign (i.e. Soviet) troops from Afghanistan, genuine self-determination for the Afghan people, the return of refugees in safety, and the restoration of Afghanistan's status as an independent and non-aligned country. After nearly six years of talks led by the UN Secretary-General's personal representative, Diego Cordovez, this Pakistan resolution, or something approximating to it, came nearer than ever before to implementation when on 14 April 1988 deadlines for Soviet withdrawal were laid down in accords signed in Geneva by Afghanistan and Pakistan and their guarantors, the Soviet Union and the United States (see DOCUMENTS).

It was agreed that 50 per cent of the foreign troops would leave in the first three months, between 15 May and 15 August, and the remainder by 15 February 1989. Even so, the Geneva accords offered only a partial and ambiguous solution to the question of the immediate political future of Afghanistan. They made no attempt to suggest how an internal settlement could be reached which would be mutually satisfactory and workable to three main, hitherto contending, elements among the Afghan people: (i) the mujahideen (resistance) forces living within Afghanistan and their families and supporters; (ii) the various resistance groups and refugees living outside Afghanistan's frontiers (mainly in Pakistan and Iran); and (iii) those Afghans living in cities or rural areas which since 1979 had been under the administration of the Soviet-imposed communist regime.

President Najibullah visited New Delhi in early May for detailed discussions with Rajiv Gandhi and other Indian leaders, during which he called for full and proper implementation of the Geneva accords. He claimed then, and continued to do so throughout the year, that his Government's policy of 'national reconciliation' offered enough concessions to make it worthwhile for the resistance to become reconciled. However, this view was repudiated by virtually all spokesmen for the resistance.

President Najibullah claimed that in general elections held in April—although without pretence of a secret ballot—over 1.5 million people had voted; but, even if genuine, this was only a small proportion of the adult population. Some non-members of the marxist People's Democratic Party of Afghanistan (PDPA)—the ruling communist party—were elected, but they were mostly from pro-regime, 'front' organizations. The subsequent formation of a two-chamber National Assembly, in which seats were kept open for opposition members, was described by the President as a major step towards national reconciliation. This was not a view which received much acceptance, not least because the Assembly held only two brief meetings during the year and did not deal with matters of great importance.

Estimates of the number of Soviet troops in Afghanistan at the time of the Geneva accords varied, even in Soviet statements, between 100,000 and 120,000. There were conflicting reports from May onwards about the scale and pace of Soviet troop withdrawals. The UN Secretary-General several times expressed satisfaction with the pace of withdrawal—although it was at a standstill between mid-August and early October. The Soviet Foreign Minister, Eduard Shevardnadze, told reporters at UN headquarters on 27 September that the Soviet Union would 'wait and see' with regard to further withdrawals, as he claimed that 'violations' of the Geneva accords had occurred.

During the last week of December the exiled King of Afghanistan, Zahir Shah, was invited by Soviet leaders to take part in negotiations to form a transitional Government designed to steer the country towards free elections. This invitation followed the first direct talks between a high-level Soviet representative (Yuri Vorontsov, ambassador to Kabul and a Deputy Foreign Minister) and the King, who since his deposition from the throne in 1973 had lived in a modest villa on the outskirts of Rome. The USSR, although committed by the Geneva agreements to withdrawing all its troops by 15 February 1989, was obviously at pains to avoid abdicating power to a weakened leadership that could be toppled by Islamic fundamentalists. On the other hand, rivalries within the ranks of the various Peshawar-based resistance groups to the Kabul regime continued to fragment their opposition and to weaken their credibility as a single alternative to the Najibullah Government. Four of the seven Peshawar-based groups expressed strong disapproval of Mr Vorontsov's meetings with ex-King Zahir Shah, and joined mujahideen based in Iran in interpreting these as deliberate attempts to create divisions and to save the Kabul communist regime. They summarily rejected a ceasefire offer by President Najibullah, which was proposed to take effect on 1 January 1989.

Chapter 2

INDIA—PAKISTAN—BANGLADESH—SRI LANKA—NEPAL

INDIA

CAPITAL: New Delhi   AREA: 3,287,000 sq km   POPULATION: 781,400,000 ('86)
OFFICIAL LANGUAGES: Hindi and English   POLITICAL SYSTEM: parliamentary democracy
HEAD OF STATE: President Ramaswamy Venkataraman (since July '87)
RULING PARTY: Congress (I)
HEAD OF GOVERNMENT: Rajiv Gandhi, Prime Minister (since Oct '84)
PRINCIPAL MINISTERS: P.V. Narasimha Rao (external affairs), K.C. Pant (defence), S.B. Chavan (finance), Buta Singh (home affairs), Madhavsingh Solanki (planning), J. Vengala Rao (industry), B. Shankaranand (law and justice)
INTERNATIONAL ALIGNMENT: NAM, Cwth., SAARC
CURRENCY: rupee (end-'88 £1=Rs27.00, US$1=Rs14.92)   GNP PER CAPITA: US$290 ('86)
MAIN EXPORTS: precious stones, textiles, tea

THIS was a year of contrasting political ups and downs for Rajiv Gandhi's Government, with small electoral successes and some bigger setbacks and much activity on a number of foreign-policy issues, with the clear prospect by the end of the year that more changes of consequence were impending.

Again, as in 1987, the ostensibly 'ruling' Congress (I) party, for all its large majority in Parliament (secured in the 1984 general election—see AR 1984, pp. 272-3), demonstrated more than once that it was part of the persisting problem of maintaining a credible all-India polity. Far from countering disruptive forces decisively, the Congress itself was rent by internal forces and often was unable to act effectively. Thus, Mr Gandhi sought again to purge the party of several old-style power brokers but several times found himself, or rather his supporters, losing state elections and sometimes recourting some of the same old Congress hacks he had earlier so unceremoniously dismissed.

In late June Mr Gandhi reshuffled his Ministry for the 24th time in three and a half years. In a major reallocation of portfolios, he inducted three former Chief Ministers—S.B. Chavan (from Maharashtra), who became Finance Minister, Vir Bahadur Singh (from Uttar Pradesh) as Minister of Communications, and Mr Madhavisan Solanki (from Gujarat) as Planning Minister and Deputy Chairman of the Planning Commission. Mr B. Shankaranand, who had recently headed the joint parliamentary committee which had investigated the Bofors affair (see AR 1987, pp. 294-5), got back a portfolio he had held earlier, that of Water Resources, with the additional responsibilities of Law and Justice. The Prime Minister gave up the External Affairs portfolio to P.V. Narasimha Rao, saying that he wished to give up all the major portfolios he held in order to devote more time to political work.

The reshuffle was seen as the Prime Minister's response to poor by-election results in mid-June, when the ruling Congress (I) and the opposition parties won eight seats each in contests for seven Lok Sabha and eleven state Assembly seats. The Jan Morcha leader and former Union Cabinet Minister, V.P. Singh, won in Allahabad as the combined opposition candidate. The results indicated that, while the Congress (I) could no longer bank on the wave of sympathy on which they had ridden to a three-fourths majority in Parliament in the 1984 general elections, opposition hopes that they were now mounting a swelling, combined anti-Congress (I) movement were not compellingly demonstrated. The opposition fared well wherever it put up a united front, as in Gujarat and Uttar Pradesh. However, it had to concede to Congress (I) in its strongholds such as Rajasthan. V.P. Singh's personal victory in Allahabad advertised his role as the only apparently credible, all-nation opposition leader, but his standing, support and reputation suffered some fluctuations during the year. On 6-7 August seven opposition parties formed themselves into a National People's Front (Rashtriya Morcha), with N.T. Rama Rao (Chief Minister of Andhra Pradesh) being elected chairman and V.P. Singh convenor.

One highly controversial matter which preoccupied press and some public attention for several months was the Press Defamation Bill. It was introduced into Parliament on 30 August to the accompaniment of much press and opposition criticism and protest, was then withdrawn, somewhat modified, reintroduced and passed by the Lower House on 15 December. It still left much room for improvement, many said, since it did not seriously deal with crucial issues concerning the abuse of power and of money either by political parties, or by the press, or by the Government.

The annual report of the Ministry of Home Affairs for 1987-88, released in mid-year, claimed that the communal situation in the country remained comparatively peaceful except for riots in Uttar Pradesh, Gujarat and Delhi and their aftermath from the previous summer. The year witnessed a spurt in extremist activities in Assam, and the north-east. Indeed, scattered Hindu-Muslim clashes throughout northern India and the continuing violence of Sikh terrorists kept communal tensions sensitively high.

The activities of terrorist and secessionist elements in the Punjab and the north-east had been continuously engaging the attention of the Government and its security forces. Anti-terrorist activities were intensified and village-level peace committees formed to enlist the cooperation of local people in combating terrorism. In order to combat extremist elements in the north-east, particularly in Manipur, Tripura and Nagaland, the Centre, in consultation with the state governments, took various steps, such as the banning of some extremist organizations as unlawful, increased use of the Armed Forces (Special Powers) Act 1958, the strengthening of border patrols and the heightening of intelligence pooling, and planning joint security measures. The GNLF agitation in the Darjeeling Hills of West Bengal continued during the year.

An accord providing for the setting-up of a Darjeeling Gorkha Hill Council, with the aim of satisfying the aspirations of Nepali-speaking Indians, was signed, however, in Calcutta on 22 August. The signatories were the president of the Gorkha National Liberation Front, Subash Ghising, the central Home Secretary, and the chief secretary of the West Bengal state government. They were witnessed by the central Home Minister, Buka Singh, and the Chief Minister of West Bengal, Jyoti Basu.

Overall, the year produced a gruesome record of 1,567 killings in the Punjab. The battle against terrorism continued unabated in this fertile but deeply troubled north-western Indian state, where extremists seeking a separate Sikh homeland were active for the sixth year in succession. Terrorist activities were concentrated in the three districts of Amritsar, Gurdaspur and Ferozepur. According to figures released by the Punjab government at the end of the year, 1,210 of those killed were innocent Hindus and Sikhs (the victims of terrorists), 74 policemen and 283 'hard-core' terrorists.

At the end of the year, India's critical balance-of-payments situation caused the Government to revise its earlier plan to import an additional 2 million tonnes of wheat, although food stocks were only about half the 10 million tonnes thought necessary to be an adequate buffer stock for the country. The decision to halt wheat imports was taken after a review of foreign exchange reserves revealed that they were only about $3,500 million, approximately equal to three months of imports. This was considered dangerously low. Reserves had fallen mainly because of the growing trade gap and had been aggravated by heavy payments for imported defence equipment, a fall in soft loans from India's traditional creditors, and heavy imports of cooking oil and food grains following the protracted drought of 1987 (see AR 1987, p. 296).

The central Budget for the financial year 1988-89 was presented to the Lok Sabha by the Finance Minister, Narain Dutt Tiwari, on 29 February, in one of the longest budget speeches of recent years. His proposals included an increase in public spending for rural development, some measures intended to benefit weaker groups of society, and the introduction of incentives for selected industries. He sought to encourage the import of essential components and technology for machinery and to promote exports by exempting export profits from income tax. The amount assigned to defence was Rs 130,000 (about 20 per cent of total expenditure); the revised estimate for 1987-88 had been Rs 120,000. Most of this increase was due to the cost of mounting and maintaining the Indian Peace Keeping Force (IPKF) in Sri Lanka.

Among notable official visitors to India during the year, the most significant were the Italian Prime Minister (in January), President Najibullah of Afghanistan (May) and, especially, President Mikhail Gorbachev of the Soviet Union (in November). As a number of commentators did not fail to point out, the timing of Mr Gorbachev's visit, his second to India in successive years, was significant in the light of the thesis he had lately been propounding to New Delhi and others—that 'normalization' of relations between India, China, and the Soviet Union could and would be crucial for Asia and the world, but need not impair the hitherto close relations between India and the Soviet Union.

Four Indo-Soviet agreements and a protocol were signed, covering exploration and the use of outer space, economic and technical cooperation in power projects, a cultural agreement, an agreement to supply India two 1,000-MW nuclear power reactors on a turnkey basis, avoidance of double taxation, and the setting up of a 6,000-MW thermal power plant, for which the Soviets promised to provide their biggest-ever credit to India—Rs 3,400 million (US$234.48 million) for 20 years at 2.5 per cent annual interest.

In April Mr Gandhi inaugurated the Festival of India in Japan; in June he made brief visits in turn to Syria, the Federal Republic of Germany and Hungary. He then went to New York, where he addressed the United Nations on nuclear disarmament. In July he made a four-nations-in-ten-days tour to Jordan, Yugoslavia, Spain and Turkey. In late September he was in Bhutan, where he had talks with the King. In December came his most important foreign visits—to the People's Republic of China and to Pakistan.

After several years of relatively unpublicized, rather unproductive talks between Chinese and Indian officials, Rajiv Gandhi went to China from 19-22 December, the first such visit by an Indian Head of Government since that of his grandfather, Jawaharlal Nehru, in 1954. This was a clear indication on both sides of a willingness to try to improve their relations. Specific bilateral agreements—on civil air services, science and technology, and cultural exchanges—were signed. Mr Gandhi readily and publicly stated that Tibet was a province of China. No agreement was reached over the Sino-Indian border dispute, except to try to unravel and resolve differences quietly and practically, if possible. But a constructive start to improving general relations was apparently under way, despite complaints from Mr Gandhi's critics at home that he was bartering away Indian interests and getting nothing substantial in return.

In a dramatic move towards a measure of Indo-Pakistan detente at the December summit of the South Asian Association for Regional Cooperation (SAARC) in Islamabad (see also p. 315), Mr Gandhi and Miss Benazir Bhutto, the new Prime Minister of Pakistan, met for the first time, got on remarkably well and agreed to meet at least twice in 1989. The two sides signed a treaty (which had been ready in draft form for a few years) providing that they would not attack each other's nuclear plants; they also agreed to exempt each other's airlines from double taxation, and to cooperate on cultural and education matters.

Both leaders frankly faced up to the fact that some outstanding problems remained. Mr Gandhi listed them as India's suspicion that Pakistan was assisting Sikh terrorism in India's state of Punjab, continuing military confrontation between their respective armies on the Siachen glacier (which earlier had led to Indian accusations in January, for instance, that Pakistani troops were firing on Indian emplacements), and India's suspicion that Pakistan was acquiring a nuclear weapons capability. Miss Bhutto said that official representatives of the two countries had been instructed to try to settle these questions in carefully prepared meetings to be held within a few months.

In mid-1988 Rajiv Gandhi announced in both Houses of Parliament that India had joined a select group of only four other countries (the United States, the USSR, France and China) which had produced and successfully tested a fully indigenous surface-to-surface missile. India's military capability was also evident in the successful expedition by a force of paratroopers to the Maldives in early November to crush a coup attempt by dissidents and mercenaries (see p. 327).

PAKISTAN

CAPITAL: Islamabad   AREA: 804,000 sq km   POPULATION: 99,200,000 ('86)
OFFICIAL LANGUAGE: Urdu   POLITICAL SYSTEM: parliamentary democracy
HEAD OF STATE: President Ghulam Ishaq Khan (since Aug '88)
RULING PARTY: People's Party
HEAD OF GOVERNMENT: Benazir Bhutto, Prime Minister (since Dec '88)
PRINCIPAL MINISTERS: Sahabzada Yaqub Khan (foreign affairs), Aitzaz Ahsan (interior), Syed Iftikhar Hussain Gilani (law and justice), Syed Faisal Saleh Hayat (commerce)
INTERNATIONAL ALIGNMENT: NAM, ICO, SAARC
CURRENCY: rupee (end-'88 £1=PRs34.00, US$1=PRs18.79)   GNP PER CAPITA: US$350 ('86)
MAIN EXPORTS: cotton, textiles, rice

THE year was Pakistan's most eventful since 1971, when the country assumed its present shape. President Zia-ul-Haq was killed in an air crash in August and the year ended with Benazir Bhutto of the Pakistan People's Party (PPP) ensconced in power as the country's

Prime Minister following elections in November. The wheel had thus come full circle since her father was deposed in 1977 and later executed during the martial law period in 1979 (see AR 1977, p. 267 and 1979, pp. 275–6). In a very real sense, however, she was able to come to power only with the agreement of the army and her position as Prime Minister was far from secure.

At the beginning of the year the Muslim League Government of Mohammad Khan Junejo was apparently making some headway in building up support through programmes of judicious patronage, although violence in Karachi and elsewhere and difficulties caused by the presence of Afghan refugees were still problems. In an unexpected move at the end of May, however, the Government was dismissed by President Zia-ul-Haq. It was generally assumed that President Zia felt that Mr Junejo was taking too independent a line, in particular on the role of the army and on policy towards Afghanistan, although a public statement spoke only of corruption and the need to press ahead faster with Islamicization programmes. Fresh elections to the National and provincial Assemblies were announced. In June the Government introduced an ordinance to give greater weight to Islamic law in the country's legal system.

The political situation was transformed by the death in a plane crash on 17 August of President Zia (see OBITUARY), along with the two most senior army generals, 19 other senior officers and the US ambassador to Pakistan. It was generally assumed, although not finally established, that the crash was the result of sabotage. One widely-held theory was that it was the work of the Afghan secret service concerned to eliminate the most intransigent of the supporters of the mujahideen, but other plausible hypotheses were also advanced. After President Zia's death the presidency was assumed, in line with the constitution, by the chairman of the Senate, Ghulam Ishaq Khan. It was noticeable that there was no move by the army to take power and it was clear that widespread support existed for the idea that only through elections could a legitimate Government emerge.

Elections for the National Assembly were held on 16 November and following a court decision they took place on a party basis. In the weeks preceding the poll two broad groupings of parties emerged. The first was the Islami Jamhoori Ittehad (IJI) or Islamic Democratic Alliance. At its centre was the Pakistan Muslim League, whose dominant figure was the Chief Minister of the Punjab, Nawaz Sharif, a protegé of President Zia and a representative of a newer generation of politicians. The IJI also contained the Jamaat-i-Islami, the principal fundamentalist party in Pakistan, and the National People's Party, a breakaway group from the PPP. The second grouping consisted of the PPP itself, together with a couple of small groups at the local level. The campaign threw up few sharply-defined issues of policy and revolved instead around style and personality. While the PPP and Miss Bhutto reiterated that the party stood for the legacy of the late Mr Bhutto, the IJI ignored the late General Zia almost completely and emphasized its own commitment to Islamicization while depicting the PPP as a potentially authoritarian Government.

The results of the election (in which the turnout was a low 42 per cent) gave the PPP a clear plurality, with 93 of the 207 seats in the Assembly allocated for the Muslim population. The IJI won 55, with the balance held by smaller parties, notably the Mohajir Qaumi Movement (MQM), which represented the interests of the Urdu-speaking population of Karachi and Hyderabad and which won 13 seats in the two cities, and independents. Shortly after the election Nawaz Sharif, who on 19 November won the Punjab provincial assembly poll, claimed the right to try to form a Government. Political and constitutional confusion then reigned for several weeks. Eventually, on 2 December, Benazir Bhutto was asked by the President to form a Government. She did so, but only after coming to an agreement with the MQM. Thereafter she had no difficulty winning a mandatory vote of confidence in the Assembly, although the IJI dominated the Senate, which was not dissolved in May. The PPP thus appeared to have no chance of obtaining sufficient support in the two houses combined to secure the two-thirds majority necessary for constitutional changes.

Although Miss Bhutto had emphasized throughout her campaign her intention to rule in the people's interests, she had also made it plain that there would be no dramatic policy initiatives either domestically or internationally, being aware that any such radical moves would be likely to bring about renewed pressure from the military. Further evidence that there would be no dramatic break with the previous regime was provided both by the continuation in office of the Foreign Minister, Sahabzada Yaqub Khan, and by the willingness of the PPP to support Ghulam Ishaq Khan as President when elections were held in December. Further restrictions on the PPP's freedom of action came from its failure to win the provincial Assembly elections except in Miss Bhutto's home province of Sind. In particular, the IJI was able to form the ministry in the Punjab, with Nawaz Sharif at its head.

Despite these inhibitions Benazir Bhutto took a number of steps during her first few weeks in office to indicate that there would be a more relaxed approach to government. Many prisoners were released or had death sentences commuted to life imprisonment. Student unions which had previously been banned were again permitted to function and it was announced that the National Press Trust would be dissolved, thus allowing greater diversity in the press. Promises were made to introduce major new programmes in health, literacy and housing. There was, however, a political crisis in Pakistan's smallest province, Baluchistan, where many observers felt that the governor had shown favouritism to the PPP-backed ministry there.

In economic terms, Pakistan had another relatively good year, with growth in GDP in 1987-88 put provisionally at 5.8 per cent thanks largely to a boom in cotton exports. The sixth five-year plan finished on 30 June with growth during the whole period estimated at 6.3 per cent per annum. The underlying structural problems of the economy remained as obdurate as ever, however, with large trade and fiscal deficits and a constant danger of inflation. Attempts to rationalize the tax system in the Budget in June, so as to increase revenue from industry and commerce, met with fierce resistance from those affected, while the agricultural sector remained free from direct taxation. A worsening balance-of-payments situation forced the outgoing Government to go to the IMF for a loan of approximately $830 million. Miss Bhutto made no major changes to the management of the economy, and emphasized that there would be no nationalization of industries.

In foreign affairs, the most important development during 1988 was the April signing of the Geneva accords between Pakistan and Afghanistan for the withdrawal of Soviet troops from Afghanistan (see p. 306 and DOCUMENTS). While the agreement was welcomed in Pakistan, opinions varied as to how far the opportunity should be taken for the mujahideen to strive for a final victory. By the end of the year substantial numbers of Soviet troops had withdrawn, but in the meantime almost all the refugees remained in Pakistan.

The Geneva accords had their impact on relations with India when the latter appeared to the Pakistan Government to be attempting to obtain a voice in arrangements after the Soviet withdrawal. India continued to claim that Pakistan was involved in fomenting terrorist activity among Sikh militants, and in general relations remained at a low ebb for most of the year. After the success of Benazir Bhutto in the elections, however, an opportunity clearly existed for a new beginning and the annual summit meeting of SAARC held in Islamabad provided the occasion for talks between Rajiv Gandhi, who was born in 1944, and Benazir Bhutto, born in 1953. The immediate outcome was the formalization of an agreement made in 1985, but never ratified, to refrain from attacks on each other's nuclear installations. It was agreed to continue talks at a high level on other contentious issues.

BANGLADESH

CAPITAL: Dhaka   AREA: 144,000 sq km   POPULATION: 103,200,000 ('86)
OFFICIAL LANGUAGE: Bengali   POLITICAL SYSTEM: presidential, under military tutelage
HEAD OF STATE AND GOVERNMENT: President (Lt.-Gen. retd.) Hussain Mohammad Ershad (since Dec '83)
RULING PARTY: Jatiya Party
PRINCIPAL MINISTERS: A.K.M. Nurul Islam (Vice-President, justice), Moudud Ahmed (prime minister, industry), M.A. Matin (deputy premier, home affairs), Anisul Islam Mahmud (foreign affairs), Wahidul Huq (finance)
INTERNATIONAL ALIGNMENT: NAM, ICO, Cwth., SAARC
CURRENCY: taka (end-'88 £1=Tk57.00, US$1=Tk31.51)   GNP PER CAPITA: US$160 ('86)
MAIN EXPORTS: jute, fish

THREE months of sometimes violent strikes and public protests against the continuance in office of President Ershad brought Bangladesh virtually to a political stalemate by the middle of February, prior to the holding of parliamentary elections on 3 March. At the end of January the Ershad Government banned all anti-election propaganda in what appeared to be a determined bid to hold elections even without opposition participation, and issued warnings that stern action would be taken against any violators. In the elections the ruling Jatiya Party won an 'overwhelming victory'—an unsurprising result considering that the three major opposition alliances and the fundamentalist Jamaat-e-Islami, which had been campaigning for President Ershad's removal from office, all boycotted the poll (see AR 1987, p. 300).

The election results showed that the Jatiya Party had won 251 of the 300 seats in Parliament. With more than a three-quarters majority, the Government would thus have no trouble in marshalling sufficient votes should it wish to bring in any constitutional amendments. The 76-party Combined Opposition (COG), led by the controversial A.S.M. Abdur Rab, won only 18 seats, the Freedom Party 2, Jatiya Samajtantrik Dal 2 and independents 26. Voting in one constituency was postponed after a candidate was shot dead; it was later won by Jatiya. The poor showing of COG, an alliance cobbled together from dozens of small parties, most of them proclaiming pro-Government views, was surprising since it was thought of as a 'loyal opposition'. The Islamic Khilafat Andolan, the Ganotantra Bastabayam Party (a 23-party alliance) and the Jama Dal were completely unsuccessful. In all, 977 candidates were contestants, a much smaller number than in the three previous general elections.

President Ershad announced on 27 March a new 23-member Cabinet, dropping five Ministers in all, including the Prime Minister, Mizanur Rahman Chowdhury, and elevating the Deputy Premier, Moudud Ahmed, in his place. The Foreign Minister, Humayun Rasheed Chowdhury, kept his post but his deputy was dismissed. A number of new faces were inducted into the 32-member Administration in what seemed like an effort to improve the image and energy of a Government which had been sagging since the mainstream opposition launched a vigorous anti-Ershad campaign in November 1987. In a further Cabinet reshuffle on 10 December, President Ershad appointed the former Irrigation and Education Minister, Anisul Islam Mahmud, as Foreign Minister, replacing H.R. Chowdhury, who had resigned following a scandal over the shipping of personal effects as official documents. The appointment of Mr Mahmud, who enjoyed close ties with India, was balanced by that of the new Irrigation Minister, Mahbubur Rahman, who by repute was pro-Pakistan.

Parliament passed a Bill on 7 June that amended the constitution to make Islam the state religion. The Bill, submitted at the President's behest by the ruling Jatiya Party, was approved by a 254-0 vote in the 300-member Parliament and sent to the President for his signature. About 30 members from the main opposition group walked out in protest against what was known as the 'Eighth Amendment Bill'. President Ershad had promised at a religious meeting in March to make Islam the state religion 'in deference to the wishes of the majority people'—a promise which elicited criticism from many segments of society. About 85 per cent of the country's 103 million people were Muslims; the rest were Hindus, Christians and Buddhists. During the year Bangladesh's Red Cross Society was renamed the Red Crescent Society.

A few weeks after the leader of the so-called 'Biharis' (Pakistan citizens stranded in Bangladesh ever since 1971) had gone on hunger strike in an attempt to put pressure on Islamabad to accept them, the Bangladesh Foreign Ministry announced that 'We are in touch with Pakistan, which has agreed in principle to accept and absorb them'.

The worst monsoon floods ever recorded hit Bangladesh in late August and early September, causing widespread deaths and much damage to the country's infrastructure. At the height of the flooding, in early September, over 75 per cent of the country was submerged and an estimated 25 million people, about one-quarter of the entire population, had been left homeless. Ten million people were marooned on roofs, trees and the few unflooded areas of high ground. Official figures for the period to 13 September recorded 1,139 deaths, but many unofficial estimates suggested that at least 3,000 people had lost their lives.

SRI LANKA

CAPITAL: Colombo   AREA: 64,500 sq km   POPULATION: 16,117,000 ('86)
OFFICIAL LANGUAGES: Sinhala, Tamil and English   POLITICAL SYSTEM: presidential democracy
HEAD OF STATE AND GOVERNMENT: President Junius R. Jayawardene (since Feb '78, previously Prime Minister)
PRESIDENT-ELECT: Ranasinghe Premadasa (elected Dec '88)
RULING PARTY: United National Party
PRINCIPAL MINISTERS: Ranasinghe Premadasa (prime minister), Shahul Hameed (foreign affairs), M.H.M. Naina Marikkar (finance and planning), K.W. Devanayagam (home affairs), Paul Perera (justice)
INTERNATIONAL ALIGNMENT: NAM, Cwth., SAARC
CURRENCY: rupee (end-'88 £1=SLRs59.50, US$1=SLRs32.89)   GNP PER CAPITA: US$400 ('86)
MAIN EXPORTS: tea, rubber

CIVIL disorder, guerrilla warfare and the mass murder of civilians continued in Sri Lanka throughout the year, with the crisis moving from the Tamil north to the Sinhalese south. However, there were attempts to maintain normal political life, with provincial elections in June, a presidential election on 19 December and the promise of general elections by February 1989. The ten-year-rule of President J.R. Jayawardene came to an end on 31 December. The Indian peacekeeping force remained in the country and actively engaged Tamil guerrillas led by the Liberation Tigers of Tamil Eelam (LTTE), who had failed to surrender their arms under the Indo-Sri Lankan agreement of July 1987 (see AR 1987, p. 305 and pp. 549-51).

The presence of the Indians in the Tamil north gradually reduced the hold of Tamil separatist guerrillas, who were themselves very divided. A degree of order was restored in Jaffna, refugees began returning under the supervision of the UN High Commissioner for Refugees, and communal tension was most marked in the eastern province where Tamils, Sinhalese and Muslims lived together. By late August 23,000 refugees had returned from Tamil Nadu. However, the situation was complicated by the internecine relations amongst the Tamil groups and by continued attacks on Sinhalese and Muslim villagers and the murder and abduction of Tamils held to be cooperating with the authorities. Former Senator S. Nadarajah was killed in Jaffna in March, Father Chandra Fernando was killed in Batticaloa in June and on 19 June the much respected K. Kanthasamy, director of the Tamil Information Centre in London, was abducted and presumed killed in Jaffna. In February India announced an increase in its troops to 70,000 and despite talks with LTTE in August, operations were resumed on a major scale when no agreement to surrender arms could be reached. The leader of the Tamil United Liberation Front (TULF), Appapillai Amirthalingam, and his former parliamentary colleagues, felt it safe to return to Colombo (after five years in India) at the end of June. But the TULF had little influence on Tamil affairs, which had passed under the control of the warring separatist factions.

Major Tamil attacks on civilians included the massacre of 70 people in the Trincomalee district in March, prompting a visit to New Delhi by Cabinet Minister Gamini Dissanayake and the commander of the Sri Lanka army, to explore the possibility of greater Sri Lankan involvement in the eastern province campaign. Another major massacre took place near Anuradhapura on 9 October when 45 villagers were hacked to death. Tamil militancy washed over into the Maldives on 3 November when a group attempted to overthrow the Government in a mysterious and short-lived coup (see p. 327).

Despite these outbreaks, the Tamil militants were fairly effectively contained and, on the last day of the year, it was announced that India would start to withdraw its troops in early 1989. The major problem for the Government was now in the south, where the Janatha Vimukthi Peramuna (JVP), under the leadership of Rohan Wijeweera, began a campaign of terror against all those it saw as betraying the Sinhalese to the Indians. On 16 February the JVP killed the popular film star Vijaya Kumaranatunga, who had broken from his mother-in-law Mrs Sirima Bandaranaike in 1984 to form the left-wing Sri Lanka Mahajana Party (see AR 1984, p. 282). He had been expected to lead the left in the presidential elections. While the JVP was said to be divided about this assassination, it continued to harass members of all other political parties. This led the ruling United National Party (UNP) to form the 'Green Tigers' to defend their politicians, each one of whom was allocated 150 of these guards in February. Among acts of JVP terror were a bomb attack on the Matara council meeting on 20 March, the attempted murder of Assistant Minister Gamini Athukorale on 27 June and a bombing of the UNP Colombo offices on 25 October. Suspected JVP supporters were arrested in large numbers and the high incidence of unexplained disappearances caused Amnesty International in London to call for an inquiry into alleged official murders in June.

In an attempt to restrain the JVP, Minister Lalith Athulathmudali signed an 'agreement' with an alleged representative on 10 May. But this was repudiated by Mr Wijeweera. It was also rumoured that Mrs Bandaranaike, in preparation for the presidential elections, was prepared to accept JVP support and they were mentioned as one of the parties endorsing her in November. However, the JVP not only boycotted all elections during the year, but specifically threatened and terrorized anyone taking part in them in the southern area in which JVP influence had always been strongest. Several candidates and organizers were killed and voters discouraged from turning out. Most of the terrorist and guerrilla activity of the JVP was carried out by the Deshapremi Janatha Vyaparaya (DJV or Peoples' Patriotic Movement). The campaign escalated in November, with a three-day general strike which was effective in most Sinhalese areas. By then large parts of the Galle and Matara districts were said to be under JVP control, as they had been in its original uprising in 1971 (see AR 1971, pp. 282-4).

Despite the JVP campaign political life became livelier in the expectation of the first major elections since 1977. On 18 January Finance Minister Ronnie de Mel resigned from the Government and on 12 August he joined Mrs Bandaranaike's Sri Lanka Freedom Party (SLFP), from which he had defected in 1976. In March various parliamentary left parties, including the Communists, the SLMP and the Lanka Samasamaja Party (LSSP), formed a United Socialist Alliance (USA) to contest the new provincial councils. The USA did well in the June elections in the absence of the SLFP, which refused to stand. Although the UNP won all the Sinhalese-dominated councils, the USA was a close second. In the two Tamil provinces, elections held on 19 November returned a coalition of the Eelam National Democratic Liberation Front (ENDLF) and the Eelam People's Revolutionary Liberation Front (EPRLF), with the major separatist guerrilla groups boycotting. In by-elections held for four Sinhalese parliamentary seats on 14 July, the UNP held three but lost Ratnapura to the SLFP. In most elections in Sinhalese areas turnout was down in the face of JVP threats, and this was most marked in the southern province where only 28 per cent voted, with the UNP as the victor.

The presidential election of 19 December was contested by Ranasinghe Premadasa for the UNP, Sirima Bandaranaike for the SLFP and Ossie Abeygunasekera for the USA. There was no Tamil candidate, although the Tamil Congress gave its support to the SLFP and the mainly Tamil Ceylon Workers Congress supported the UNP. On a very low turnout of 53.4 per cent, the UNP gained 50.4 per cent, the SLFP 45 per cent and the USA only 4.6 per cent. The winning candidate had previously been Prime Minister; unlike President Jayawardene, he had entered politics after independence and was not a member of the two family networks which had dominated Sri Lankan politics for 50 years.

NEPAL

CAPITAL: Kathmandu   AREA: 147,000 sq km   POPULATION: 17,000,000 ('86)
OFFICIAL LANGUAGE: Nepali   POLITICAL SYSTEM: monarchy, panchayat (council) democracy
HEAD OF STATE AND GOVERNMENT: King Birendra Bir Bikram Shah Deva (since Jan '72)
PRINCIPAL MINISTERS: Marich Man Singh Shrestha (prime minister, defence), Shailendra Kumar Upadhya (foreign affairs), Prakash Bahadhur Singh (panchayat affairs), Badri Prasad Mandal (law and justice)
INTERNATIONAL ALIGNMENT: NAM, SAARC
CURRENCY: rupee (end-'88 £1=NRs43.36, US$1=NRs23.97)   GNP PER CAPITA: US$150 ('86)
MAIN EXPORTS: agricultural products, basic manufactures

A football stadium disaster, a major earthquake, severe floods, two major Cabinet reshuffles, King Birendra's chairmanship of the SAARC, arms purchases from China, and some slight economic progress—these were the main events of 1988 for Nepal.

About 100 football fans, including children, were reported to have been killed and over 350 injured in a stampede at the national stadium in Kathmandu on 12 March. More than 25,000 spectators were watching a match between Bangladeshi and Nepalese teams when a hailstorm broke over the stadium; the crowd panicked, with the result that children and elderly people were trampled in the frenzied rush for shelter. On 21 May King Birendra dismissed the Sports Council, after an inquiry had held it responsible for the deaths of about 70 people in the stampede.

On 21 August a devastating earthquake rocked the eastern and central parts of Nepal, especially the Himalayan foothills on the India-Nepal border, killing over 800 people. The earthquake was followed later the same month by flooding, which severely afflicted the terai of Nepal as well as much of northern India and Bangladesh (see also p. 317). At the end of talks in Kathmandu between King Birendra and President Ershad of Bangladesh, the two leaders agreed on 1 October to set up a joint study group into ways of controlling the floods which tended to wreak great damage every year.

On 9 March, the Council of Ministers underwent a major change. The overall size of the Ministry was increased to 33 from 17, but four Cabinet Ministers and two Ministers of State were dropped. The reshuffle was justified in terms of a determined fight by the Prime Minister, Marich Man Singh Shrestha, against widely-alleged administrative malpractices. There was a further substantial Cabinet reshuffle on 31 October when the King, acting on the recommendation of the Prime Minister, dropped 11 Ministers. Mr Shrestha was said by informed commentators to be trying to isolate potential rivals and re-establish his grip on the national Parliament well ahead of the next general election, scheduled for May 1991. It was noteworthy that he retained his Foreign Minister, S.K. Upadhya, as 'number two' in the Cabinet, notwithstanding reports that he had wanted to drop this potential rival from his team.

On 17 February King Birendra appointed Bindeswari Shah as ambassador to India, the first Nepalese woman to be appointed ambassador. With Nepal's territory touching that of India on three sides, the New Delhi ambassadorship was usually regarded as Nepal's most sensitive diplomatic post.

At a meeting with a delegation from the Nepalese Parliament in Beijing on 18 March, the Chinese Vice-Premier, Qiao Shi, said that China 'strongly supports' the proposal that Nepal should become a zone of peace, a project reaffirmed by King Birendra and endorsed by his hosts during his visit to China in 1987 (see AR 1987, p. 307). Speaking to the same delegation on 19 March, President Li Xiannian thanked the Nepalese Government for making it possible for 10,000 Tibetans to live in peace in Nepal. The chairman of the Nepalese delegation said that his Government would never permit the Tibetans to live other than in peace in Nepal. According to the Japanese news agency Kyodo, Nepal's Prime Minister confirmed on 8 September that his country had recently purchased anti-aircraft weapons from China.

The Nepalese economy showed some general improvement in the year 1987-88, GDP growing by 7.1 per cent and inflation falling to 11.4 per cent. A substantial balance-of-payments surplus accrued, largely because of a 15 per cent increase in revenue from the private sector and a large seizure of gold from smugglers. These factors helped to mitigate another, otherwise large, deficit on current account. Indeed, despite a 40 per cent growth in the value of Nepal's exports in the financial year ending 15 July, the trade deficit widened by NRs 2 million to NRs 9 million, compared with the previous year. A Ministry of Finance official said that the main reason for the increased deficit was the import of heavy equipment to implement major foreign aid projects, in compliance with IMF advice, and also the purchase of a Boeing 757 aircraft for Royal Nepal Airlines.

Chapter 3

SEYCHELLES—MAURITIUS—MADAGASCAR AND COMOROS—MALDIVES

SEYCHELLES

CAPITAL: Victoria   AREA: 454 sq km   POPULATION: 66,000 ('86)
OFFICIAL LANGUAGE: Creole   POLITICAL SYSTEM: presidential, one-party state
RULING PARTY: People's Progressive Front
HEAD OF STATE AND PARTY LEADER: President France-Albert René (since June '77)
PRINCIPAL MINISTERS: James Michel (education, information, youth), Rita Sinon (internal affairs), Jacques Hodoul (national development)
INTERNATIONAL ALIGNMENT: NAM, OAU, ACP, Cwth., Francophonie
CURRENCY: rupee (end-'88 £1=SR9.50, US$1=SR5.25)   GNP PER CAPITA: US$2,430 ('83)
MAIN EXPORTS: copra, fish

ECONOMIC issues preoccupied the Government of Seychelles in 1988. According to the central bank's annual report there were some tentative signs of economic recovery by the end of 1987. For the first time since 1980 the balance of payments recorded an overall surplus of SR 23.7 million. The current-account deficit of SR 96 million compared with a deficit of SR 207 million in 1986, while there was also a reduction in the central Budget deficit. Yet despite these improvements the financial situation continued to cause concern and commercial banks continued to be required to put 60 per cent of their deposits into treasury bonds. A sharp reduction in agricultural production in 1987 necessitated the import of 2,353 tonnes of food. Inflation rose to 2.5 per cent and although progress was reported in creating employment the central bank claimed that the job supply was still inadequate.

President René announced major tax reforms when he unveiled his 1988 Budget to Parliament on 29 December 1987. Income tax was abolished and taxation on business profits was reduced. It was anticipated that revenue lost through tax reforms would be recovered through higher social security contributions from employers. While the Budget provided for a small pay rise, wages overall were reduced by the amount previously deducted in income tax. A new business tax was imposed on companies and the self-employed, although farmers and fishermen were exempted. Noting the dramatic rise in foreign exchange reserves from $7.8 million to $17 million in 1987, President René undertook not to devalue the Seychelles rupee nor to introduce exchange controls.

On the domestic front the People's Assembly amended the country's constitution in May, enabling the President to designate a member of the ruling People's Progressive Front to replace any deputy absent from Parliament.

Seychelles' external affairs concentrated on reinforcing relations with other Indian Ocean states. At the end of June President René's Government and the Government of Mauritius formalized their bilateral relationship by establishing diplomatic relations. On 30 June the Government of Comoros agreed to establish diplomatic relations and to exchange ambassadors with Seychelles. In a joint statement both Governments expressed their desire to strengthen the existing ties of friendship and to intensify cooperation in all fields.

Other developments emphasized the importance of tourism and the fishing industry to the archipelago's economy. The airport on Praslin, rebuilt after being destroyed by fire, was inaugurated on 2 June at a cost of SR 6.3 million. Its improved facilities, including night-landing equipment, were expected to attract more tourists to the islands. In August Air Seychelles announced its purchase of a Boeing 767 to begin operating on routes to Europe, Japan and Australia from July 1989.

In March the UN Development Programme announced that it would provide $1.7 million to assist seven Indian Ocean countries, including Seychelles, to attain self-sufficiency in monitoring their fisheries, planning and management activities. Other sources of financial assistance to Victoria included a $1.2 million interest-free development loan from China to fund economic and technical projects.

There was encouragement for the Government and the fishing industry with the publication of the 1988 issue of the Seychelles Fishing Authority's *Tuna Fishery Bulletin*. This estimated that foreign trawlers based in Port Victoria, including vessels from France, Spain and the USSR, caught approximately 160,000 tonnes of tuna fish in 1987—an increase of 12 per cent over the previous year.

MAURITIUS

CAPITAL: Port Louis   AREA: 2,040 sq km   POPULATION: 1,000,000 ('86)
OFFICIAL LANGUAGE: English   POLITICAL SYSTEM: parliamentary democracy
HEAD OF STATE: Queen Elizabeth II   GOVERNOR-GENERAL: Sir Veerasamy Ringadoo
RULING PARTIES: coalition of Mauritian Socialist Movement (MSM), Mauritius Labour Party
   (MLP), Assembly of Mauritian Workers (RTM), and Organization of the Rodrigues People
   (OPR)
HEAD OF GOVERNMENT: Sir Aneerood Jugnauth (MSM), Prime Minister (since June '82)
PRINCIPAL MINISTERS: Sir Satcam Boolell (MLP/deputy premier, external affairs, justice), Seetanah
   Lutchmeenaraidoo (finance), Beergoonath Ghurburrun (RTM/planning and economic
   development)
INTERNATIONAL ALIGNMENT: NAM, OAU, ACP, Cwth., Francophonie
CURRENCY: rupee (end-'88 £1=MauRs24.74, US$1=MauRs13.68)
GNP PER CAPITA: US$1,200 ('86)
MAIN EXPORTS: sugar, textiles, manufactured goods

WHILE Mauritius experienced a politically eventful year in 1988, and the drama of an assassination attempt on Prime Minister Sir Aneerood Jugnauth in November, the island's economy continued into its fifth year of unprecedented growth. Rising prosperity seemingly encouraged a centrist shift in political attitudes. In the international sphere the Government remained committed to its policy of non-alignment and in January the Prime Minister reiterated his country's claim to Diego Garcia, and his concern to create a zone of peace in the Indian Ocean. However, despite the Government's opposition to the US military base on Diego Garcia, a pragmatic interpretation of non-alignment allowed the acceptance of Washington's assistance in creating and equipping a coastguard to combat drug-trafficking. Interest in party politics revived in June when Harish Boodhoo, latterly a prominent critic of the Government, officially relaunched the Mauritian Socialist Party (PSM).

A crisis emerged within the governmental coalition when the Deputy Premier, Sir Gaëtan Duval, and his brother Hervé Duval resigned on 12 August. The conflict between the Duval brothers (both Social Democrats) and the Prime Minister came to a head over the allocation of coalition seats in the forthcoming local elections and the sacking of 3,000 Sino-Tex workers in mid-July. The Government reshuffle announced on 15 August named Sir Satcam Boolell (Labour Party) as Deputy Premier. Held on 23

October, the elections were boycotted by Sir Aneerood's Mauritian Socialist Movement and the Labour Party, with the result that the parliamentary opposition alliance of Prem Nababsingh's Mauritian Militant Movement and the Democratic Labour Movement led by Anil Baichoo won all 126 seats. Only 40.5 per cent of registered voters took part in the election.

It was reported in April that the island's economic growth had exceeded official estimates of 7.9 per cent for 1986 and 6.1 per cent for 1987. The revised figures of 9 per cent and 7.6 per cent indicated that the economy had surpassed that of most of the industrialized world and was being favourably compared with the performance of the newly-industrialized countries of South-East Asia. The predicted growth rate for 1988 was 6 per cent. An expected rise in the annual rate of inflation to just over 1 per cent was seen to represent the price of success as the influx of money into the economy outstripped the supply of goods. The rapid expansion also brought with it environmental problems such as pollution. Unemployment all but disappeared and external trade reportedly increased by 28 per cent. Exports, principally textiles, sugar and manufactured goods, rose to Rs 12,034 million while imports were estimated at Rs 13,042 million.

As the booming textile industry (Mauritius became the world's third largest exporter of knitwear) attracted considerable investment from France and Hong Kong, the traditional sugar industry established new export markets in Europe and the Pacific. The rise in the size of tuna catches in the Indian Ocean led to expansion plans in the fishing industry involving the United States and Australia. The Government extended its trading horizons in April when a barter deal agreement was signed with Egypt. Towards the end of the year the Finance Minister predicted a period of consolidation and restructuring in the Export Processing Zone (EPZ)—the linchpin of Mauritius' economic success. The Government's economic plans also anticipated the start of offshore banking and eventually a free port in 1992.

Tourism continued not only to fuel the island's economy but also to consolidate its position as the hub of communications in the Indian Ocean. The expansion of the Air Mauritius fleet, the increase in the number of weekly flights to Europe, the opening of new routes to Singapore and Kuala Lumpur, new air links with Zimbabwe and Tanzania, and the dramatic rise anticipated in the number of passengers using the new international airport in the next decade encouraged optimistic forecasts about the island's potential as a regional centre.

MADAGASCAR AND COMOROS

Madagascar
CAPITAL: Antananarivo   AREA: 587,000 sq km   POPULATION: 10,600,000 ('86)
OFFICIAL LANGUAGES: Malagasy and French   POLITICAL SYSTEM: presidential
HEAD OF STATE AND GOVERNMENT: President (Adml.) Didier Ratsiraka (since June '75)
INTERNATIONAL ALIGNMENT: NAM, OAU, ACP, Francophonie
CURRENCY: Malagasy franc (end '88 £1=FMG2,513.05, US$1=FMG1,389.19)
GNP PER CAPITA: US$230 ('86)   MAIN EXPORTS: coffee, vanilla, cloves

Comoros
CAPITAL: Moroni   AREA: 1,860 sq km   POPULATION: 409,000 ('86)
OFFICIAL LANGUAGES: Arabic and French   POLITICAL SYSTEM: presidential, one-party state
RULING PARTY: Union for Comorian Progress
HEAD OF STATE AND PARTY LEADER: President Ahmed Abdallah Abderrahman (since Oct '78)
INTERNATIONAL ALIGNMENT: NAM, OAU, ACP, Francophonie
CURRENCY: CFA franc (end-'88 £1=CF547.88, US$1=CF302.86)   GNP PER CAPITA: US$320 ('86)
MAIN EXPORTS: vanilla, agricultural products

FOR eight years MADAGASCAR had been one of the 'star pupils' of the IMF and World Bank, restructuring the economy after a decade of socialism. Although President Ratsiraka still proclaimed himself on the left, his policies had all been in the direction of liberalization, deregulation and, notionally, privatization. In January 1988 he was rewarded by praise from a World Bank consultative group, and a commitment to $700 million of new aid. The austerities of structural adjustment had taken their toll, however, and real income per head was still declining, however favourable other statistics might look. New investment was also slow in coming, and government finances were hit by low agricultural commodity prices. The country also received some attention because of an alarming recrudescence of malaria at the beginning of the year in an area from which it had been eliminated for 25 years, causing a probable 25,000 deaths because of the lack of immunity.

Madagascar also achieved fame for being, with Mali, the first country to experience a debt rescheduling (in November) under new more favourable rules on debt approved in principle by the Toronto economic summit in June.

The COMOROS were also in serious economic troubles because of the low price of vanilla and cloves, serious indebtedness, and the doubling of its civil service in four years, one of the obstacles to any assistance from the World Bank or the IMF. There were continued well-confirmed reports of a South African commercial presence in the capital, Moroni, mainly in the tourist sector.

MALDIVES

CAPITAL: Malé   AREA: 300 sq km   POPULATION: 189,000 ('86)
OFFICIAL LANGUAGE: Divehi   POLITICAL SYSTEM: presidential
HEAD OF STATE AND GOVERNMENT: President Maumoun Abdul Gayoom (since July '78)
PRINCIPAL MINISTERS: Fathhulla Jameel (foreign affairs), Umar Zahir (home affairs), Ahmed Zaki (attorney-general)
INTERNATIONAL ALIGNMENT: NAM, Cwth., SAARC
CURRENCY: rufiya (end-'88 £1=R15.89, US$1=R8.79)   GNP PER CAPITA: US$310 ('86)
MAIN EXPORTS: fish, coconuts

PRESIDENT Gayoom was re-elected unopposed for a third successive five-year term on 23 September, receiving 96 per cent of the votes cast. Six weeks later, on 3 November, the presidential palace and other government buildings in the capital were attacked and about 20 people killed during an attempted coup by some 150 armed insurgents who had arrived by boat from Sri Lanka. The coup attempt was quickly put down by a 300-strong force of Indian paratroopers invited in by the Maldives Government. Two Ministers and a parliamentary deputy were among 20 hostages rescued from the raiders on 6 November as they attempted to escape by boat, although at least four other hostages were killed.

The insurgents, most of whom were captured, were found to be led by Maldives dissidents believed to be connected with former President Ibrahim Nasir, whom President Gayoom had replaced in 1978; they also included a number of Tamil separatists recruited in Sri Lanka as mercenaries. Reporting to the Indian Parliament on 4 November, Prime Minister Rajiv Gandhi declared that the Indian military intervention had frustrated an 'attempt to spread terror and undermine peace and stability in our region'.

IX SOUTH-EAST AND EAST ASIA

Chapter 1

BURMA—THAILAND—MALAYSIA—BRUNEI—SINGAPORE—
INDONESIA—PHILIPPINES—VIETNAM—KAMPUCHEA—LAOS

BURMA

CAPITAL: Rangoon   AREA: 676,500 sq km   POPULATION: 38,000,000 ('86)
OFFICIAL LANGUAGE: Burmese   POLITICAL SYSTEM: under military rule
HEAD OF STATE AND GOVERNMENT: Gen. Saw Maung, Chairman of State Law and Order Restoration Council and Prime Minister (since Sept '88)
PRINCIPAL MINISTERS: Rear-Adml. Maung Maung Khin (planning, finance and energy), Maj.-Gen. Phone Myint (home affairs), Maj.-Gen. Sein Aung (industry)
CURRENCY: kyat (end-'88 £1=K11.33, US$1=K6.26)   GNP PER CAPITA: US$200 ('86)
MAIN EXPORTS: rice, teak, minerals

AFTER 25 years of 'the Burmese road to socialism' under General Ne Win's military-run command economy, Burma had by early 1988 been reduced from a prosperous exporter of rice, crude oil and other commodities to 'least developed country' status with the United Nations. Bureaucratic inefficiency and corruption had created shortages of most domestic commodities, including even rice and oil products, and the economy was saved from collapse only by a large and active black market. A normally compliant public had been angered by galloping inflation and demonetization of bank notes, which cancelled private savings without compensation in most cases. In 1987–88 export earnings continued to dwindle and import costs to rise, worsening the trade deficit, sharply increasing foreign debt and almost eliminating foreign exchange reserves, despite foreign aid and a loan from the Asian Development Bank to pay for the costs of imported crude oil, petroleum products and spare parts for the oil production industry. Meanwhile, the regime continued its ruthless, but costly and unending, campaign to beat the ethnic minorities into abandoning well-founded claims to a measure of autonomy.

Riots against demonetization in September 1987 were largely confined to students. In March a teahouse brawl escalated into street riots in Rangoon, when police responded brutally to student protests and public resentment brought crowds into the streets in support of the students. In the summer texts were circulated of letters to Ne Win from a former supporter, Aung Gyi, criticizing economic and political policies and performance. These letters had wide influence. Peaceful demonstrations by students followed, and the Government closed several higher educational institutions, setting off violent street fighting, which spread to major provincial towns. Over the following three months there were increasingly large demonstrations against the regime with reports of some army units declining to fire on crowds and of professional people, civil servants and even armed services personnel, as well as students, monks and ordinary workers, marching in demonstrations. Finally, a violent response by the police and army raised deaths in the year, on foreign estimates, to several thousand.

Ne Win also took political steps to control the situation. It was announced that the Burma Socialist Programme Party (BSPP) would hold a congress on 23 July to discuss economic and political reforms. At the congress Ne Win resigned as leader of the BSPP and San Yu as State President, but other resignations were rejected as was a resolution permitting multi-party politics. Greater private enterprise, joint ventures with foreign firms and reduced controls on domestic trade were approved. General Sein Lwin, who was hated for his use of riot police, was elected BSPP chairman and, by the People's Assembly, State President. Aung Gyi and other critics were arrested and martial law was declared. Sein Lwin's election provoked further demonstrations and a general strike, while exports and the official economy came to a halt, and he resigned on 12 August. Dr Maung Maung, the one civilian leader of the BSPP, was elected party chairman and President on 19 August. He lifted martial law, released leading detainees and conceded early free elections. The security forces exercised greater restraint and members of the armed forces and civil service were banned from membership of the BSPP and other parties.

The military, however, had meanwhile organized looting and food shortages as an excuse for a coup (announced on 18 September) under the leadership of General Saw Maung, the Defence Minister, at the head of an 'Organization for Building Law and Order in the State'. He abolished the People's Assembly and promised to organize democratic multi-party elections after restoring law and order, which he attempted with renewed random firings on crowds and executions of suspects. Militant students fled to rebel territory along the Thai border and few doubted that Ne Win had conducted all these developments and remained firmly in control. Numerous political parties were registered, but scepticism persisted about the real prospects for free elections. The leading parties appeared to be the National Unity Party, a reincarnation of the BSPP, and the National League for Democracy, of which the daughter of the revered independence leader Aung San was secretary-general. The main pressure on the regime, however, came from the state of the economy and a refusal by most foreign Governments, especially the major suppliers of aid, to recognize the new Administration.

THAILAND

CAPITAL: Bangkok   AREA: 513,000 sq km   POPULATION: 52,600,000 ('86)
OFFICIAL LANGUAGE: Thai   POLITICAL SYSTEM: parliamentary, under military influence
HEAD OF STATE: King Bhumibol Adulyadej (Rama IX) (since June '46)
RULING PARTIES: coalition of Chart Thai (CT), Social Action (SAP), Democrat (DP), Rassadorn (RP), United Democracy and Muan Chon parties
HEAD OF GOVERNMENT: Maj.-Gen. Chatichai Choonhavan (CT), Prime Minister (since Aug '88)
PRINCIPAL MINISTERS: Pong Sarasin (SAP/deputy premier), Bhichai Rattakul (DP/deputy premier), Gen. Thienchai Sirisamphan (RP/deputy premier), Air Chief Marshal Siddhi Savetsila (SAP/foreign affairs), Pramual Saphavasu (CT/finance), Maj.-Gen. Pramarn Adireksarn (CT/interior), Police Lt.-Gen. Chamras Mangkalarat (CT/justice)
INTERNATIONAL ALIGNMENT: Asean
CURRENCY: baht (end-'88 £1=B45.50, US$1=B25.15)
GNP PER CAPITA: US$810 ('86)   MAIN EXPORTS: textiles, rice, tapioca, rubber

ON 29 April the Prime Minister, General Prem Tinsulanonda, countersigned a royal decree dissolving Parliament and calling new elections for 24 July. The immediate cause was the resignation of 16 Democrat Party Ministers after half the Democrat MPs had withdrawn support for a Bill to amend copyright legislation. The Bill was passed, but then lost because of the dissolution. (Difficult negotiations with the USA on intellectual property continued throughout the year.) The underlying cause of the dissolution was a parliamentary campaign of criticism not only of individual Ministers, but of the Government as a whole and of Prem in particular; indeed, Prem's position as an unelected Prime Minister was a principal issue in the election. On 22 April the army commander, General Chaovalit Yongchaiyut, announced that he wished to retire on 27 May; Prem, however, did not accept the resignation, so preventing Chaovalit, who was seen as a possible future Prime Minister, from entering politics before the election.

The coalition parties won a comfortable majority of votes and seats, but the balance within the coalition changed, with the Democrats, previously the largest party, whose dissidents had departed to form a rival party, losing over half their seats and the other partners gaining seats. General Prem was proposed as Prime Minister, but declined the invitation. In over eight years as Premier, even though not himself an MP, he had done much to strengthen both the prospects for continued democracy and the economy; however, he had always disliked political infighting and perhaps regarded eight years as a sufficient tour of duty. Instead Major-General Chatichai Choonhavan, leader of the Chart Thai Party, now the largest in the lower house, was appointed Prime Minister on 4 August.

In the political field Chatichai implemented a decision by Prem's Cabinet to amnesty senior personalities charged with involvement in the September 1985 coup attempt (see AR 1985, p. 283) and offered the southern Muslims greater religious and cultural autonomy, while Chaovalit was given a free hand to use the annual reshuffle of armed services posts to promote a wide range of younger officers. In the foreign field the Foreign Minister, Siddhi Savetsila, had already seen signs, especially at a meeting in June with his Vietnamese colleague, of a narrowing of differences with Hanoi. Chatichai advocated a further flexibility in relations with Vietnam and an ultimate aim to turn Indochina 'from a battleground into a trading market' once Vietnamese forces had left Kampuchea, while Chaovalit continued to foster better relations with the Laotian and Burmese military.

Under Prem the economy had enjoyed substantial improvements in economic growth, trade and investment, helped by the depreciation of the US dollar, to which the baht was linked, and by declining debt service ratios. In 1988 exports benefited from the rapid expansion of manufactures, such as textiles, electrical and electronic goods and processed foods and from a recovery of international commodity prices. Imports grew even faster than exports, but with a heavy weighting of investment goods, and, while the visible trade deficit increased, a thriving tourist trade and foreign investment kept the balance of payments in surplus. Real economic growth rose in 1988 to 11 per cent and strained infrastructure, notably port facilities and communications.

Having supported Prem's economic policies, Chatichai appointed a panel of respected academics to advise him on policy options in fields such as rural development, labour relations and promotion of private investment and exports. However, there was some concern that Chart Thai's business, rather than technocrat, orientation might make it less easy to resist corruption and wasteful spending on grandiose projects, to which some earlier Thai Governments had been prone. It was also feared that action or promises to increase civil service, police and military salaries, the statutory minimum wage and social security benefits might overheat the economy. Some efforts were made in the autumn to cool the economy, but the Budget was more expansionary than under Prem.

MALAYSIA

CAPITAL: Kuala Lumpur   AREA: 132,000 sq km   POPULATION: 16,100,000 ('86)
OFFICIAL LANGUAGE: Bahasa Malaysia   POLITICAL SYSTEM: federal parliamentary democracy
SUPREME HEAD OF STATE: Tunku Mahmood Iskandar Ibni al-Marhum, Sultan of Johor (since April '84)
RULING PARTY: National Front coalition
HEAD OF GOVERNMENT: Dr Mahathir Mohamad, Prime Minister (since July '81)
PRINCIPAL MINISTERS: Abdul Ghafar Baba (deputy premier, development), Haji Abu Hassan Omar (foreign affairs), Ahmad Ritthauddeen (defence), Daim Zainuddin (finance)
INTERNATIONAL ALIGNMENT: NAM, Asean, ICO, Cwth.
CURRENCY: ringgit (end-'88 £1=M$4.90, US$1=M$2.71)   GNP PER CAPITA: US$1,830 ('86)
MAIN EXPORTS: oil, palm oil, timber, rubber, tin

ON 4 February the federal High Court ruled that the United Malays

National Organization (UMNO)—the dominant party in the governing National Front coalition—was an unlawful society because 30 of its branches had not been properly registered when its annual assembly and triennial elections were held in April 1987. Eleven dissident UMNO members had requested nullification of those elections, which had returned Prime Minister Dr Mahathir Mohamad as party president by a narrow majority (see AR 1987, p. 315). His political opponents attempted to set up an alternative party called UMNO Malaysia but were prohibited by the registrar of societies. Dr Mahathir then secured permission to register a party called UMNO (New). He announced that all members of the deregistered UMNO would have to apply for admission to the new party and that those who had worked against its interests would be excluded. The 11 UMNO members who brought the law suit appealed to the Supreme Court to reinstate the deregistered party.

In March a constitutional amendment was approved transferring control of the legal process from the judiciary to the federal Parliament. The threat to judicial interpretation posed by its terms reflected the open annoyance of Dr Mahathir at the alleged obstruction of his Government by members of the judiciary. An amendment to the Societies Act 1966 facilitated retention by UMNO (New) of the financial assets of its deregistered predecessor.

On 26 May, shortly after having set a date for the Supreme Court to hear the appeal concerning the legal status of UMNO, Tun Mohamad Salleh Abas, Lord President and head of the judiciary, was suspended from office by the King on the recommendation of the Prime Minister. His suspension was justified with reference to letters which he had written to the King and to state rulers expressing concern at public criticism of the judiciary by the Prime Minister. A tribunal of local and foreign judges to adjudicate on charges against him began closed hearings at the end of June. At the beginning of July, a temporary stay on their proceedings was ordered by five Supreme Court judges sitting in emergency session. Within days all five judges were suspended, charged with gross misbehaviour, and ordered to appear before a judicial tribunal after representations to the King by the acting Lord President, Chief Justice Tan Sri Abdul Hamid Omar, then chairman of the tribunal proceeding against his suspended predecessor. Two of the five judges were dismissed in October.

On 6 August the suspended Lord President was removed formally from office by the King on the grounds of misconduct following a recommendation by the judicial tribunal. Three days later a reconstituted Supreme Court upheld the illegality of UMNO and also set aside the earlier High Court ruling that officials elected at the party assembly in 1984 remained lawful office bearers. At the end of the month, Dr Mahathir suffered a political reverse. Datuk Shahrir Abdul Samad, a former Minister and ally of the Prime Minister's main political rival, Tengku Razali Hamzah, resigned his federal parliamentary seat in Johor and then regained it with an increased majority at a by-election fought on the reputation of Dr Mahathir.

In mid-September, 13 Malay members of the federal Parliament, including Tengku Razali, resigned from the National Front to sit as independents. They were joined in October by former Deputy Prime Minister Datuk Musa Hitam. The same month, Dr Mahathir's political fortunes revived slightly when his candidate narrowly won a by-election for the state assembly in Johor. The predominantly Malay electorate was influenced by the Prime Minister's gesture of reconciliation in inviting his political opponents to join UMNO (New). At the end of October, at the inaugural assembly of UMNO (New), at which he was confirmed as President by nominated delegates, Dr Mahathir invited his principal political rivals, Tengku Razali and Datuk Musa, to join his Cabinet as Ministers without portfolio. Their negative response to this ostensible demonstration of commitment to Malay unity served to ensure his continued political dominance.

In March opposition MP Karpal Singh, who had been arrested under the Internal Security Act in 1987, was freed from detention by the Perak High Court, which granted his application for a writ of *habeas corpus*. He was rearrested the same day. In July the federal Parliament amended the Internal Security Act to prohibit a detainee from seeking recourse to a court to secure release.

In June Singapore's Prime Minister, Lee Kuan Yew, visited Kuala Lumpur, where he signed a memorandum of understanding on the purchase of water and natural gas from Malaysia. During a visit to London in September, Dr Mahathir signed a memorandum of understanding with Prime Minister Margaret Thatcher for arms sales with an estimated value of over £1,500 million, including Tornado fighter-bombers and Rapier anti-aircraft missiles.

BRUNEI

CAPITAL: Bandar Seri Bagawan   AREA: 5,765 sq km   POPULATION: 232,000 ('86)
OFFICIAL LANGUAGES: Malay and English   POLITICAL SYSTEM: monarchy
HEAD OF STATE AND GOVERNMENT: Sultan Sir Hassanal Bolkiah (since Oct '67)
PRINCIPAL MINISTERS: Prince Mohamad Bolkiah (foreign affairs), Prince Jefri Bolkiah (finance), Pehin Dato Haji Isa (internal affairs), Pengiran Bahrin (law)
INTERNATIONAL ALIGNMENT: ICO, Asean, Cwth.
CURRENCY: Brunei dollar (end-'88 £1=B$3.51, US$1=B$1.94)
GNP PER CAPITA: US$15,400 ('86)   MAIN EXPORTS: oil and gas

IN January the registration of the new National Democratic Party was cancelled and its president and secretary-general were detained. During the course of the year, 38 political detainees were released including Abdul Hamid Munap, who had been arrested after the rebellion in 1962, and Awang Abdul Samad Jamaluddin, former secretary-general of the banned Brunei People's Party, who had also been arrested in 1962 but had escaped from prison in 1973 and was rearrested on his return to Brunei in 1987. In a Cabinet reshuffle in December, designed to improve diversification of the economy, Minister of Education Abdul Rahman Taib was appointed to a newly-created portfolio of Industry and Primary Resources.

President Aquino visited Brunei in August and secured the Sultan's support for a US$10,000 million multinational aid plan for the Philippines.

SINGAPORE

CAPITAL: Singapore   AREA: 620 sq km   POPULATION: 2,600,000 ('86)
OFFICIAL LANGUAGES: Malay, Chinese, Tamil and English   POLITICAL SYSTEM: parliamentary
HEAD OF STATE: President Wee Kim Wee (since Aug '85)
RULING PARTY: People's Action Party
HEAD OF GOVERNMENT: Lee Kuan Yew, Prime Minister (since June '59)
PRINCIPAL MINISTERS: Goh Chok Tong (first deputy premier, defence), Ong Teng Cheong
  (second deputy premier), Wong Kang Sen (foreign affairs), Richard Hu (finance), Shanmugam
  Jayakumar (home affairs and law)
INTERNATIONAL ALIGNMENT: NAM, Asean, Cwth.
CURRENCY: Singapore dollar (end-'88 £1 = S$3.51, US$1 = S$1.94)   GNP PER CAPITA: US$7,410 ('86)
MAIN EXPORTS: machinery and equipment, petroleum products

GENERAL elections were held on 3 September for an expanded Parliament of 81 seats, 39 of which were grouped into three-member constituencies in which teams of contesting politicians were obliged to include a minority (i.e. non-Chinese) candidate. The ruling People's Action Party (PAP) was returned to office with 80 seats and 63.8 per cent of the valid votes and 61.8 per cent of the total votes cast. These figures represented a swing against the Government of 1.6 per cent of the valid votes and 1.1 per cent of the total votes cast from the previous elections in December 1984. The sole opposition member, Chiam See Tong of the Singapore Democratic Party, retained his seat. Former Solicitor-General Francis Seow, detained under the Internal Security Act in May and released in July, stood for the Workers' Party in a group constituency with Dr Lee Siew Choh and Mohamad Khalit Baboo. They were narrowly defeated.

After the elections the first Deputy Prime Minister, Goh Chok Tong, announced that he would be ready to take over as Prime Minister from Lee Kuan Yew in two years, an arrangement confirmed publicly by Mr Lee. Mr Goh revealed that Lee Kuan Yew would then remain in the Cabinet with the status of Senior

Minister. Minimal Cabinet changes included the assumption of the Foreign Affairs portfolio by Wong Kang Sen.

In April nine former detainees, who had been arrested and released in 1987, published an open letter denying being party to an alleged marxist conspiracy, complaining of brutal interrogation by members of the Internal Security Department and charging that they had been intimidated into making false confessions on television. Eight of the nine were rearrested (the other signatory being abroad), together with Patrick Seong, a human rights lawyer who had helped prepare the letter. The Government announced that it would set up an inquiry into the charges but reversed its decision when all the rearrested detainees signed statutory declarations retracting their allegations. In May, shortly after applying to the High Court for the release of four of the detainees, Francis Seow was arrested because of his association with a US diplomat, Mason Hendrickson, who was expelled for allegedly interfering in domestic politics. Mr Hendrickson was accused of encouraging disaffected lawyers to stand for election against the PAP. The US State Department repudiated this accusation and retaliated by expelling a first secretary from Singapore's embassy in Washington.

Another former detainee was rearrested in May, while three of those rearrested earlier were released. Francis Seow signed a statutory declaration, after ten days of detention, revealing that he had explored the prospect of being granted political asylum in the United States and Britain (were he to stand for Parliament). The series of arrests prompted open criticism from former President Devan Nair, who charged that they were intended to prevent the appearance of a more effective political opposition. He called on Prime Minister Lee to resign and claimed that in the 1960s, while Singapore was part of Malaysia, Mr Lee had acted similarly to Francis Seow. This statement provoked a libel suit against Mr Devan Nair, who then left Singapore to take up a fellowship at an American university.

In October the judicial committee of the Privy Council ruled that J.B. Jeyaretnam, former secretary-general of the Workers' Party, imprisoned on a fraud charge and expelled from Parliament in 1986, had been wrongly disbarred from practice by Singapore's Law Society and that the court decision which led to it was 'a grievous injustice'. In early December four of the rearrested detainees successfully applied for a writ of *habeas corpus* before the Court of Appeal but were immediately reapprehended. Later, Frances Seow was fined S$19,000 for tax evasion which disqualified him from becoming one of two non-constituency members of Parliament.

In July Malaysia's King paid the first official visit by a reigning monarch of the Federation to Singapore since constitutional separation in August 1965. The visit set a ceremonial seal on the substantial improvement in bilateral relations since the political row caused by the visit to Singapore in November 1986 of the President of Israel (see AR 1986, p. 295).

INDONESIA

CAPITAL: Jakarta AREA: 1,905,000 sq km POPULATION: 166,400,000 ('86)
OFFICIAL LANGUAGE: Bahasa Indonesia POLITICAL SYSTEM: presidential
HEAD OF STATE AND GOVERNMENT: President (Gen. rtd.) T.N.J. Suharto (since March '68)
RULING PARTY: Joint Secretariat of Functional Groups (Golkar)
PRINCIPAL MINISTERS: Lt.-Gen. (rtd.) Sudharmono (Vice-President), Adml. (rtd.) Sudomo (political affairs and security coordination), Radius Prawiro (economy, finance, industry and development supervision), Ali Alatas (foreign affairs), Gen. L.B. (Benny) Murdani (defence), J.B. Sumarlin (finance), Lt.-Gen. (rtd.) Ismail Saleh (justice)
INTERNATIONAL ALIGNMENT: NAM, Asean, ICO, Opec
CURRENCY: rupiah (end–'88 £1=Rp3,106.69, US$1=Rp1,717.35)
GNP PER CAPITA: US$490 ('80) MAIN EXPORTS: oil and gas

THE greater willingness to debate sensitive issues which in 1987 marked elections to the DPR (legislature—see AR 1987, p. 319) was reflected also in the MPR, which consisted of the DPR with additional appointed political, functional and regional members. In January the MPR, having discussed the Government's draft outline of state policy, failed to reach consensus on the coming five-year programme. Amendments were proposed by both the nationalist PDI and the Muslim PPP. The PDI withdrew amendments once it thought that its points had been taken on board by the Government, but the PPP insisted on pressing two amendments to the vote, in order, by displaying independence, to recover popular support. It made a similar demonstration at the voting in March for President and Vice-President. General Suharto was unopposed for President, but the PPP nominated its chairman for the post of Vice-President against the State Secretary and Golkar chairman, Lieut.-General Sudharmono, and only withdrew its nomination when Suharto indicated his preference for Sudharmono, having earlier hoped to leave the decision to the MPR. On this and subsequent occasions it was clear that Sudharmono did not have the confidence of the Armed Forces (Abri); in consequence, he relinquished the chairmanship of Golkar.

Following these elections there were numerous changes in ministerial and Abri posts. Half the Cabinet was replaced and many of the retained Ministers were moved to other portfolios. The economic coordinating Minister, Ali Wardhana, was succeeded by the Finance Minister, Radius Prawiro; General Rudini, who was expected to conduct a campaign against corruption, became Interior Minister; and General Benny Murdani—who had been succeeded in February as Abri commander by the army chief of staff, General

Try Sutrisno—became Defence Minister. Kopkamtib, a military command dealing with internal security, was replaced by a new agency, Bakorstanas, with somewhat reduced powers, some civilian members and a more advisory and less directly executive role. Whereas General Murdani had controlled Kopkamtib, General Sutrisno became head of the new body, although the change reflected some reduction in Abri's exclusive control of security. A Bill passed on 22 February sought, inter alia, to define Abri's military and political functions and to raise the retiring age for senior officers to 60. In December the new security coordinating Minister, Admiral Sudomo, suggested that Indonesia should perhaps cease to execute people convicted many years earlier of subversion.

The new Foreign Minister, Ali Alatas, a career diplomat, intended a more active foreign policy and devoted attention to bringing together the various factions and countries involved in the struggle for Kampuchea, to fostering the revival of contacts with China and to easing the acerbic relationship with Australia. An agreement was reached in September on the division of revenues from future offshore oil production from a disputed area between Timor and Australia. A state visit by the Premier of Papua New Guinea in January passed off well, but frequent Indonesian incursions across the border from West Irian against separatists led to renewed protests. Enforcement of a 200-mile exclusive economic zone, especially the temporary closure of the Lombok and Sunda Straits in September in apparent contravention of the Law of the Sea Convention, provoked protests from leading maritime and trading nations. Some relaxation of military pressure on East Timor was apparent, and, following a proposal by the East Timorese governor in June, it was announced in December that the territory would be declared an open province on 1 January 1989.

The process of liberalizing or deregulating import monopolies, export restrictions, the stock market, foreign investment, tourism, official procurement, the shipping industry and domestic and foreign banks was carried forward actively. Growth in the economy rose to about 5 per cent and a sharp increase was recorded in non-oil exports, notably plywood, rubber, palm oil, shrimps, textiles, clothing and handicrafts, giving a stronger visible trade surplus. There was, however, a prospect that rice imports might be required. The aid consortium pledged a considerable increase in assistance, partly to offset a large increase in debt-servicing requirements related to the strength of the yen.

PHILIPPINES

CAPITAL: Manila AREA: 300,000 sq km POPULATION: 57,300,000 ('86)
OFFICIAL LANGUAGE: Filipino POLITICAL SYSTEM: presidential democracy
HEAD OF STATE AND GOVERNMENT: President Corazon Aquino (since Feb '86)
PRINCIPAL MINISTERS: Salvador Laurel (Vice-President), Raul Manglapus (foreign affairs), Gen. Fidel Ramos (defence), Vincente Jayme (finance), Sedfrey Ordonez (justice)
INTERNATIONAL ALIGNMENT: Asean
CURRENCY: peso (end–'88 £1=P37.50, US$1=P20.73) GNP PER CAPITA: US$560 ('86)
MAIN EXPORTS: electrical goods, textiles, agricultural products, minerals

LOCAL government polling in January completed the initial round of free elections. Around 150,000 candidates campaigned for election to some 16,000 posts of councillor, mayor or provincial governor. There was some vote-buying and sufficient violence for polling to be postponed in 11 of the 73 provinces to enable the Armed Forces of the Philippines (AFP) to concentrate their peacekeeping efforts. Over 80 participants were killed, including 30 or 40 candidates, but this casualty rate was lower than normal. Four-fifths of those eligible voted. In September the first convention of a new party, the LDP, was attended by some 5,000 politicians claiming to support Mrs Aquino and this seemed, with the revival of the Liberal Party under the Senate president, Jovito Salonga, to point to a renewal of a two-party system at national level.

Opinion polls indicated that most Filipinos continued to support Mrs Aquino's policies and conduct of affairs. Her Government, after substantial changes in earlier years, seemed to become an increasingly competent administration and efforts to destabilize it, by Marcos supporters, some right-wing military and the left, grew less threatening, while the influence of senior politicians dismissed from the Cabinet dwindled. A number of extremist right- and left-wing leaders were arrested, although incompetence or disaffection by some AFP personnel allowed a leading right-wing dissident and the supposed commander of the communist New People's Army to escape. The arrests of major communist leaders suggested that the AFP had penetrated the Communist Party apparatus. In January the Defence Secretary, Rafael Ileto, resigned because of slow progress with AFP reform. General Fidel Ramos succeeded him and was himself succeeded as AFP commander by his deputy, Major-General Renato de Villa. There were signs that the AFP was beginning to use more balanced, subtle and effective methods of controlling NPA insurgency.

Criticism of the Government centred around complaints of a revival of corruption and of human rights violations by AFP elements. In July the Presidential Commission on Good Government, set up to recover the proceeds of corruption, was itself attacked for incompetence and corruption and was reorganized, while in

October Mrs Aquino issued instructions ordering officials not to grant concessions or privileges to any of her relatives or pretended relatives. In July she condemned killings of human rights activists and spoke of replacing suspect civilian vigilante groups with better controlled organizations, while the AFP sought to teach troops to respect human rights. There was scepticism about the Agrarian Reform Bill, passed and signed in June, to be implemented in stages over ten years. It made all agricultural land potentially subject to redistribution in lots of up to three hectares, with existing landowners allowed to retain five hectares. Land was to be paid for over 30 years. Where it was not economically sound to redistribute, alternatives were offered such as worker shareholdings. Redistribution was started, but the Government had still to raise the enormous sums required to finance it.

Restructuring agreements on official external debt were signed with various European countries, Japan and the USA, and a further rescheduling was sought with commercial banks. The formation of a more formal aid consortium was also mooted and there were lengthy negotiations on US payments for its Philippine bases. Agreement was reached in October on US$481 million a year for 1990 and 1991, to which the USA was to add contributions under the aid consortium scheme. In discussions on further support the IMF urged cautious budgeting for fear of crowding out private investment and causing overheating. Real economic growth was about 6 per cent, despite heavy damage from typhoons in the autumn. Whereas in 1987 growth had been consumption-led, primed by government spending, in 1988 it was increasingly fuelled by private investment, with a prospect for 1989 of export-led growth helped by improved commodity prices and the rapid increase in manufacturing production. The inflation rate doubled to 8 per cent. A World Bank report drew attention to the danger to the economy posed by population growth of 2.8 per cent a year, an intractable problem in a largely Roman Catholic country.

VIETNAM

CAPITAL: Hanoi   AREA: 330,000 sq km   POPULATION: 63,300,000 ('86)
OFFICIAL LANGUAGE: Vietnamese   POLITICAL SYSTEM: socialist republic under communist rule
HEAD OF STATE: Vo Chi Cong, President of Council of State (since July '87)
RULING PARTY: Communist Party of Vietnam (CPV)
PARTY LEADER: Nguyen Van Linh, CPV General Secretary (since Dec '86)
PRINCIPAL MINISTERS: Do Muoi (prime minister), Gen. Vo Van Kiet (first deputy premier), Nguyen Co Thach (deputy premier, foreign affairs), Gen. Le Duc Anh (defence), Maj.-Gen. Mai Chi Tho (interior), Hoang Quy (finance), Phan Hien (justice)
INTERNATIONAL ALIGNMENT: NAM, Comecon
CURRENCY: dong (end-'88 £1=D5,058.20, US$1=2,796.13)   GNP PER CAPITA: US$100 ('84)
MAIN EXPORTS: coal, agricultural products, seafood

UNDER pressure from economic decline and the USSR, Vietnam signalled a readiness to withdraw from Kampuchea, to reduce its hegemony in Indochina and to seek better relations with its Asean neighbours and the major powers. In February the Foreign Minister said that the army would be withdrawn from Kampuchea during 1990. In May Vietnam promised a first withdrawal of 50,000 troops, out of some 140,000. In June large numbers withdrew accompanied by the Vietnamese command, leaving the remaining troops nominally under Kampuchean command. In July Nguyen Van Linh spoke of total withdrawal by early 1990. It was later indicated that in due course over 300,000 troops, almost a quarter of the army, would be demobilized.

Steps were taken to remove offensive references to China, France, Japan and the USA from the constitution. It was agreed to resettle in the USA all children of American fathers and their close Vietnamese relatives. Hanoi became more helpful to the search for remains of Americans missing in action and in November suggested that the USA open offices throughout Vietnam to deal with this matter, while the US Administration encouraged private humanitarian aid and discussed rehabilitation of disabled Vietnamese. China proved stiffer. There was shelling on the border and in September Beijing insisted that all Vietnamese troops must leave Kampuchea before relations could be normalized. China later seemed to become more gracious, despite conflict over footholds in the Spratly Islands group (see also p. 348). Beijing appeared anxious to assert a right to sovereignty in this wide area of reefs and islets, in which several other countries had claims, before there was a regional settlement. The importance of the group lay in its position along the South China Sea shipping routes and the possibility that oil deposits were present.

The National Assembly was told in December that, despite increases in food grain output to 19 million tonnes, exports and industrial production, living standards, infrastructure and quality of products were still deteriorating; that inflation, unemployment and budget deficits were alarming; and that farmers lacked fertilizer and industry raw materials and spare parts. Assembly members were sharply critical of illogical tax systems and incompetent state banks and pressed for privatization of schools and state industries, while southern peasants demonstrated against local party abuses. Hyper-inflation compelled a devaluation of the dong on 10 November from D 368 to D 2,600 to the US dollar, still well short of the market rate. Inadequate banking systems and infrastructure and suffocating bureaucracy limited the attractions of the new liberal foreign investment law, but investment in offshore oil exploration seemed nevertheless attractive. There were also proposals for export processing zones. Heavy unemployment induced severe birth control regulations in October.

The Prime Minister, Pham Hung, died in March (see OBITUARY) and was succeeded by Do Muoi, while Linh expressed a wish to retire because of illness and age, a condition which, with incompetence and inertia, afflicted many officials at lower levels and hampered implementation of reform.

KAMPUCHEA

CAPITAL: Phnom Penh   AREA: 181,000 sq km   POPULATION: 7,200,000 ('84)
STATUS: People's Republic of Kampuchea regime under Heng Samrin is not recognized by UN majority, which recognizes Democratic Kampuchea coalition government

GROWING detente amongst external powers and increasing Vietnamese readiness to withdraw troops improved prospects for an acceptable settlement. Prince Sihanouk and Hun Sen, the Prime Minister of the Heng Samrin regime, met again in January. They identified areas of agreement, but remained far apart on others. Later many of these were resolved, the main remaining difference being on how best to neutralize the extremist Khmer Rouge (KR) leadership. By July the Vietnamese had withdrawn considerable forces and concern began to shift from doubt about Vietnamese willingness to depart to alarm at the possibility of a KR return to power. On 25 July a conference in Djakarta enabled the four Khmer factions to have informal discussions with each other and with Vietnam and the Asean countries. The only agreements reached were to establish a working group of officials and to hold further meetings, but differences were clarified and it became clear that a key issue was linkage between Vietnamese withdrawal and control of the KR.

Meanwhile, China had begun to indicate that the KR should not be allowed to monopolize power and that international supervision and a peacekeeping force were desirable. On 22 October the KR representative, Khieu Samphan, stated that they would accept an international peacekeeping force. On 3 November the UN General Assembly passed, with an even larger majority than hitherto, a new version of the annual resolution which called for international supervision of withdrawal of foreign forces and, in effect, the exclusion of Pol Pot and other KR extremists. In November and December the Chinese Prime Minister stated that China would withdraw support for the resistance forces, that is mainly the KR, in step with Vietnamese withdrawal and proposed a method of forming a four-party Government which would exclude the extremists. Khieu Samphan, after talks with Prince Sihanouk in France, tried to imply that Pol Pot was not still directing the KR.

The KR itself concentrated on getting troops, labour and supplies into position inside Kampuchea, on attacking and weakening the other resistance forces and on trying to establish their guerrillas more widely in the countryside. Willing peasant support was inhibited by the appalling record of the KR in power and Phnom Penh sought to use the hatred generated by this to build up a determined armed village militia. The KR also tried to seize strategic hill positions along the border as bases for their operations, but, in the one major action—an attempt to recover Phnom Milai—it made little progress against the Heng Samrin defending forces and pulled back when Vietnamese units were brought in.

The economy was supported by a flourishing and officially-encouraged free market and informal trade with Thailand. The riel remained relatively stable by Indochinese standards, with a floating rate related to the free market rate, but weakened on the announcement of Vietnamese troop withdrawals. There was little development of industrial activity and in the spring a UN team reported a shortage of rice due to poor rains in 1987, when only some 180 million acres of rice were sown as against 260 million acres twenty years earlier.

LAOS

CAPITAL: Vientiane   AREA: 237,000 sq km   POPULATION: 3,700,000 ('86)
OFFICIAL LANGUAGE: Lao   POLITICAL SYSTEM: people's republic under communist rule
HEAD OF STATE: Phoumi Vongvichit, Acting President (since June '86)
RULING PARTY: Lao People's Revolutionary Party (LPRP)
HEAD OF GOVERNMENT: Kaysone Phomvihane, Prime Minister and LPRP General Secretary
    (since Dec '75)
PRINCIPAL MINISTERS: Gen. Sipaseuth (deputy premier, foreign affairs), Gen. Khamtay Siphandon
    (deputy premier, defence), Saly Vongkhamsao (deputy premier, economy,
    planning and finance), Asang Laoli (interior), Kou Souvannemethi (justice)
INTERNATIONAL ALIGNMENT: NAM, Comecon (observer)
CURRENCY: new kip (end–'88 £1=KN776.79, US$1=KN429.40)   GNP PER CAPITA: US$80 ('81)
MAIN EXPORTS: minerals, timber, coffee, electricity

A border dispute resulted in January in sharp fighting in a remote area claimed by Thailand as part of their Phitsanulok province. On 17 February the senior military officers of the two countries signed a ceasefire agreement in Bangkok. This was followed by political talks and in March agreement to reactivate border cooperation committees. In January the Thais temporarily closed part of the border and forbade export to Laos of many products, but by October relations had so improved that the Thai Supreme Commander visited Vientiane, followed in November by the Thai Prime Minister. It was agreed to set up a joint border demarcation committee and for Thailand to help Laotian export industries and development of communications, energy and agriculture. In December Thailand further reduced, from 61 to 29, the number of items banned from export to Laos. Relations with the USA also improved, an ambassador was appointed to Beijing, and there were high-level visits to Japan and from Malaysia, while Vietnam cut its troop strength in Laos quietly but substantially.

Dismantling of rural collectivization and control of trade had brought food production closer to basic demand by 1987, although distribution remained inadequate. A drought, however, reduced the 1988 harvest by a fifth. In August 48 people, including a Party provincial secretary, were convicted of processing heroin and the Government persuaded the UN Fund for Drug Abuse to help finance crop substitution. Elimination of restrictions also continued in industry and commerce. Many state enterprises were required to operate profitably and allowed to fix prices and wages themselves; a liberal foreign investment law and new banking policies were approved; the first joint venture, with a Thai garment company, was launched; and it was expected that Lao businessmen would return to resume business. It was proposed to draft a constitution and elections were held for district assemblies in June and provincial assemblies in November.

Chapter 2

CHINA—TAIWAN—HONG KONG—JAPAN—SOUTH KOREA—
NORTH KOREA

PEOPLE'S REPUBLIC OF CHINA

CAPITAL: Beijing   AREA: 9,570,000 sq km   POPULATION: 1,054,000,000 ('86)
OFFICIAL LANGUAGE: Chinese   POLITICAL SYSTEM: people's republic
HEAD OF STATE: President Yang Shangkun (since April '88)
RULING PARTY: Communist Party of China (CPC)
PARTY LEADER: Zhao Xiyang, CPC General Secretary (since Jan '87)
PRINCIPAL MINISTERS: Li Peng (premier), Yao Yilin (vice-premier, state planning commission), Qian Qichen (foreign affairs), Qin Jiwei (defence), Jia Chunwang (state security), Wang Bingqian (finance), Cai Cheng (justice)
INTERNATIONAL ALIGNMENT: independent, oriented to Third World
CURRENCY: yuan (end-'88 £1=Y6.69, US$1=Y3.70)   GNP PER CAPITA: US$310 ('86)
MAIN EXPORTS: oil, manufactured goods, textiles, agricultural products

THE main events of the year could, in various ways, all be linked to the on-going reform process, notably economic reforms, which had been promoted for almost a decade and reconfirmed at the 13th congress of the Communist Party of China (CPC) in late 1987 (see AR 1987, pp. 328–9). The issue attracting the most attention at home and abroad was the state of the Chinese economy, in which inflation was posing major economic, social and, potentially, political problems. As in previous years but, arguably, to a greater degree, corruption and nepotism were evident, attracting national and international attention, as did confrontations at the end of the year between African and Chinese students in several university cities. Foreign relations were subordinated to the main trend of economic reform: links with the Soviet Union improved; in South-East Asia there were positive signs of a breakthrough in the political stalemate affecting the Indochina peninsula, to some extent meeting Chinese pre-conditions, while steps were being taken cautiously to improve links with the offshore 'province' of Taiwan, autonomously governed by the Chinese Nationalist Party since 1949 (see p. 349).

The economic and political reform programme dominated the proceedings of both a plenary meeting of the CPC Central Committee on 15–19 March and the first session of the seventh National People's Congress (NPC), the Chinese Parliament, held from 25 March to 13 April. In a major report to the earlier meeting CPC General Secretary Zhao Xiyang called for greater openness in Party and state affairs and proposed that the NPC and the State Council (Cabinet) should introduce a 'spokesman system' to provide regular briefings to the media and that all government institutions should reduce their staffs, overcome bureaucracy and raise work efficiency. He also called for an acceleration of the development of the country's urban coastal regions, reiterating the thrust of his first major policy statement, made in January, in which he had identified these areas as the key to a strategy of economic growth based on export-oriented industries. His speech and the timing of the plenum were seen by some observers as an attempt to upstage the imminent debut performance of the then acting Premier, Li Peng, at the NPC; others suggested that the CPC General Secretary was primarily concerned to clarify the division of authority between Party and state, itself a key political reform objective.

Elections to the seventh NPC had been held early in the year, the 2,970 deputies being elected indirectly by people's congresses in the provinces, municipalities and autonomous regions and by units of the People's Liberation Army (PLA). For the first time the number of candidates had exceeded the number of seats in some electoral divisions; only 863 deputies were re-elected from the sixth NPC and about a third of those elected were not CPC members. The NPC session itself was notable for the extent of the critical comment expressed by deputies and reported in the Chinese media, a phenomenon described by one Chinese diplomat as a 'national civics lesson' to teach the Chinese people that differences of view could exist and be expressed without necessarily implying life-or-death political struggle.

The experiment in greater democracy continued in the NPC elections to the top state leadership posts. On 8 April Yang Shangkun (a PLA leader, CPC Politburo member and one of the few surviving Long March veterans in the leadership) and Wang Zhen (a prominent conservative) were elected respectively President and Vice-President of the People's Republic (in succession to Li Xiannian and Ulanhu), in both cases with around 200 dissenting votes. On the same day Deng Xiaoping (84), China's 'elder statesman' and still the most influential leader, was unanimously re-elected chairman of the powerful Central Military Commission (CMC), while on 9 April Li Peng secured formal election as Premier of the State Council with minimal opposition. Also on 9 April the NPC approved a major restructuring of the State Council, in which 12 Ministries or Commissions were abolished, nine new ones created and the others massively reorganized. It was officially stated that this restructuring, which the NPC approved only after securing significant modifications to the original proposals, was intended to strengthen government organs in the areas of policy-making, consultation, supervision and dissemination of information.

In a 'Government work report' to the NPC on 25 March, Li Peng described the country's economic development during the previous five years as 'excellent', but admitted that inflation was a serious outstanding problem and had resulted in a fall in living standards in some urban areas. Reform of the pricing system would continue, however, so that moderate levels of inflation were unavoidable, even desirable, although the Government would attempt to maintain relatively stable overall price levels. Looking to the next five years, the Premier presented a broad reform programme in the form of 'ten main tasks' for the State Council and stressed the importance of stepping up agricultural production, developing basic industries and infrastructure and implementing the aforementioned strategy for coastal regions. He also set a production target for grain of 500 million tonnes by the year 2000, approximately 25 per cent higher than the current level.

Economic policy prescriptions featured prominently in the resolutions adopted by the NPC, which included a new state industrial enterprises law (under discussion since the late 1970s) effectively giving professional managers a much freer hand in running factories and making them fully responsible for the 'bottom line' of profit or loss. Also approved were a foreign joint ventures law, enabling overseas partners to chair the boards of such ventures without government interference, and amendments to the 1982 constitution legitimizing the private economic sector and legalizing the right to buy and sell land. Another resolution approved the upgrading of Hainan island, hitherto part of Guangdong province, to provincial and special economic zone status. Also adopted was the 1988 draft Budget presented by Finance Minister Wang Bingqian, forecasting economic growth of 7.5 per cent (some two points down on the level achieved in 1987), state revenue of Y 255,450 million, expenditure of Y 263,450 million and thus a deficit of Y 8,000 million, marginally less than the 1987 outturn.

With the issue of price inflation continuing to dominate internal affairs, Premier Li Peng was quoted in late September as acknowledging that the rate ranged from 15–20 per cent. It was evident, however, that in the case of individual items, and in certain parts of the country, this was a very conservative estimate; unofficial reports indicated a range of 40–50 per cent. The response of the general public to rapid rises in prices—which to some of the senior officials who recalled the demise of the Nationalist Government in the late 1940s in face of hyper-inflation represented an alarming trend—was to withdraw savings from banks and engage in what the press observed as panic-buying and the stockpiling of a wide variety of products. The environment thus became one of fear of a rapid decline in the value of money coupled with strong incentives to speculate, which inevitably fostered widespread social discontent and doubts as to the correctness of the economic reform programme.

The central issue of price reform to achieve market-oriented levels was the main item discussed at high-level CPC conferences in the summer. A meeting of the Politburo in June was reported to have formulated an anti-inflation policy and measures to improve discipline in commercial enterprises, the latter to enhance efficiency as a prerequisite for further price and wage reform. There followed two high-level meetings in July and August at the resort of Beidaihe. The outcome of these deliberations, based on measures drawn up by the Politburo, was endorsed by the State Council on 30 August, when it was decided to aim for the removal of price controls over an extended period of five years or more. However, during 1989, the first year of the programme, the State Council would adopt measures to control further price increases and no radical steps would be taken in price reform. Linked to the main thrust of policy, the State Council also ordered the People's Bank of China to adjust interest rates on deposits to protect their value. At the end of the year, it was reported that depositors enjoyed an interest subsidy to protect the value of their money and to provide a return on investment, of the order of 16 per cent, the cost of which to the banking system would be met by enhanced rates for bank loans. The overall package also included the suspension of the public buildings programme, fulfilment of state procurement quotas for grain, cotton and edible oil, the maintenance of market supplies and measures to curb the excessive issue and circulation of currency.

Another aspect of the general economic situation to attract attention throughout the year was the incidence of corruption and criminal activities within both Party and Government ranks. It was clear that economic reform measures and the associated development of a commodity economy had not been achieved without the creation of many loopholes which certain cadres, officials and merchants were exploiting to gain privilege, preference and pecuniary advantage for themselves and members of their families in tangled webs of relationships. The Party acknowledged the link between corruption and reform, noting that many of the malpractices were a product of the transitional nature of China as it changed from a product economy to a commodity economy. To combat corrupt and criminal practices, the CPC central discipline inspection commission issued new rules governing internal discipline and provisional regulations on disciplinary action. Interim measures against corruption by state administrative office workers were also adopted.

Dissatisfaction among students, which was already evident, was dramatically manifested in an entirely unexpected manner at the end of the year when serious disturbances were reported between Chinese and African students on the campuses of certain universities and colleges in Nanjing, Hangzhou and, to a lesser extent, Beijing. The centre of the unrest was the Chinese students' perception that certain African students were behaving in an intolerable manner in their associations with Chinese women students. The unrest took the form of demonstrations outside the foreign students' dormitories, eliciting a series of violent reactions causing injuries to students and security officials and leading in some instances to the siege of the dormitories. As the local authorities strove to contain the situation, many African students expressed the wish to leave China, while the central authorities did their best to minimize the damage to China's hitherto good image as an exemplar to and benefactor of the Third World. By the end of the year, when the situation had been brought under control, it was evident that while China's image in Africa and internationally had been impaired by what appeared to be racism, these incidents were symptomatic of more pervasive sentiments of dissatisfaction emerging from the difficult economic circumstances encountered by Chinese students.

Shortly after the four days of demonstrations affecting the African students, a large group of Chinese Uygur students studying in Beijing demonstrated against the screening of two films at the Central Institute for Nationalities, claiming they were disrespectful and distorted the history and culture of the Uygur Muslim nationality, some 6 million of whom lived in the Xinjiang autonomous region. The demonstrators paraded with banners seeking greater human rights and an end to what was viewed as national discrimination.

Among other disturbances recorded were those involving Tibetan Lamas who, on 5 March, were reported to have surrounded a police station and the office of the Buddhist Association in Lhasa, injuring policemen and damaging property, while on 17 December Tibetan students were reported to have marched to Tiananman Square to protest following the action of the army in opening fire on a procession in Lhasa. During the year the authorities condemned the Dalai Lama's proposal that Tibet be transformed into a 'self-governing political entity'.

Reflecting the priority accorded to economic advancement and the need to promote international trade, China's foreign relations improved throughout the year. The most noteworthy shift was in Sino-Soviet relations where, following indications of a settlement of the Kampuchea-Vietnam issue involving the withdrawal of Vietnamese troops and a weakening of Vietnamese hegemony (see p. 340), high-level contacts, including a visit to Moscow at the end of the year by Chinese Foreign Minister Qian Qichen, appeared to presage closer political relations and further expansion of economic, trade, technical, educational and cultural exchanges. In the context of Indochina, the Middle East and the future of Taiwan there were signs, reflected in the outcome of visits to China by the US Secretaries of State and Defense, of a coordination of stance, and the Chinese side, despite reservations about protectionist sentiment expressed in the US Trade Bill, made no secret of their preference that George Bush would emerge as the next President.

Against the background of 1988 Sino-Japanese trade exceeding US$20,000 million, the visit by Prime Minister Takeshita appeared to mark a further advance in bilateral relations in which existing issues of dispute such as the Japanese inclination to rewrite recent history, the symbolism of visits by Japanese politicians to the Yasakuni Shrine, the questions of ownership of the Kokaryo dormitory and limitations on manufactured exports to China would be approached sympathetically by Japan. During the visit Mr Takeshita pledged loans of Y 810,000 million to assist in 42 modernization projects for the 1990–95 period.

Modernization of the armed forces continued and it was revealed that the navy was now armed with tactical guided missiles and strategic nuclear missiles. However, it was evident that strict control was being imposed on the military budget, with the emphasis being placed on qualitative rather than quantitative improvements, and on greater professionalization, as indicated by the reintroduction from 1 October of insignia of rank.

Apart from the problems of managing the economic modernization programme, difficulties continued to be encountered in the control of population growth. Implicitly encouraged by the family-based system in the agricultural sector, the current growth rate threatened to take the population to 1,284 million by the end of the century.

TAIWAN

CAPITAL: Taipei   AREA: 36,000   POPULATION: 19,700,000 ('86)
OFFICIAL LANGUAGE: Chinese   POLITICAL SYSTEM: presidential
HEAD OF STATE AND GOVERNMENT: President Lee Teng-hui (since Jan '88)
RULING PARTY: Kuomintang
PRINCIPAL MINISTERS: Yu Kuo-hwa (premier), Shih Chi-yang (vice-premier), Lien Chan (foreign affairs), Cheng Wei-yuan (defence), Shirley Kuo (finance), Hsu Shui-teh (interior), Hsiao Tien-tsan (justice)
CURRENCY: Taiwan dollar (end-'88 £1=T$50.47, US$1=T$27.90)
GNP PER CAPITA: US$3,046 ('84)
MAIN EXPORTS: textiles, plastic goods, electronics

EVENTS in Taiwan were dominated by the death of President Chiang Ching-kuo on 13 January (see OBITUARY), the succession of Vice-President Lee Teng-hui and, in the summer, the holding of the 13th national party congress of the ruling Kuomintang (KMT). Although not unexpected, and therefore the subjects of careful contingency planning over a protracted period, the outcome of each of these events was unpredictable. However, Taiwan emerged from 1988 with its characteristically sound economic programme relatively unimpaired and its fragile pluralism and fledgling democratic political system still intact.

The death of Chiang Ching-kuo was significant because it marked the end of the direct domination of Nationalist Chinese politics by the Chiang family and the ascendancy of a Taiwanese President. The late President had succeeded his father Chiang Kai-shek, who died in 1975, and had by all accounts steered Taiwan through a period of sustained economic growth, initially gradual but lately quickening political reform and, most recently, towards a positive and potentially dynamic *modus operandi* with the People's Republic of China. Accordingly, the Chiang legacy or the Lee inheritance, while their respective orientations were never in doubt, nevertheless posed questions as to the ultimate destination of the politics of Taiwan, now for the first time under a native Taiwanese leader. The fact was that Chiang Ching-kuo's death had prevented a charismatic reforming President and party leader from completing the long overdue reform of Taiwan's political institutions, a task which now fell, by virtue of the constitutional line of succession, to Lee Teng-hui.

Unlike his predecessor, President Lee (65), an American-trained former agricultural economics professor at Taiwan National University, although nurtured by the KMT and a close associate of the late President, enjoyed no particular support in the traditional alternative power centres such as the armed forces and the security system. Implicit in these aspects of the succession was that for the new President to succeed in completing the reform programe following his inauguration on 22 February, he would have to forge an alliance with the people of Taiwan, satisfying the aspirations of both the native population, whose collective memory remained influenced by the killing of an estimated 20,000 Taiwanese during the suppression of resistance against Kuomintang rule in 1947, and of the mainlanders, at a time when closer links with the mainland were an issue of much debate. At the same time, the leadership and authority of the ruling party were being challenged by the recently-formed Democratic Progressive Party.

In these circumstances, it was essential for the new President to carry with him the confidence and support of the KMT, itself now increasingly aware of the uncertainties of political pluralism. These elements in concert made the 13th KMT congress, held from 7-13 July, an unusually significant event. It was also remarkable since delegates to the congress had been elected rather than appointed, breaking with past practice. On the first day of the congress Lee Teng-hui was formally elected chairman of the party central committee. The latter was itself elected on 12 July following, for the first time in KMT history, an open nomination process.

At the congress, the delegates reviewed the major measures adopted since the 12th KMT congress, among which were lifting the emergency decree imposing martial law for the past 38 years; instituting a new national security law and a law to confer freedom to hold assemblies, rallies and parades; revising existing law to confer the right to form associations; facilitating the registration of new newspapers; drafting a programme to provide for improved representation in the National Assembly, Legislative Yuan, Control Yuan and local government institutions; relaxing travel restrictions for those citizens wishing to visit the mainland; and granting amnesties to large numbers of petty criminals. Regarding the future, the major proposals discussed at the congress included, in the category of ideology and thought, the substitution of 'democracy, the equitable distribution of wealth through economic development and the promotion of reunification on those foregoing bases' in place of 'nationalism, democracy and people's livelihood', the previous order of priorities; amendment of party rules so that they incorporated Chiang Ching-kuo's final instruction, namely to promote democratic constitutional government; the reform of party affairs to meet the anticipated challenge from the Democratic Progressive Party, aimed at improving both efficiency and image; and replenishing the membership of the National Assembly, currently still dominated by ageing mainland representatives.

It was evident after the congress that the KMT would, in common with the Communist Party of China, have a collective rather than one-man leadership. Supporting the new President were Lee Huan, the party secretary-general, Prime Minister Yu Kuo-hua, Chief of Staff Hau Pei-tsun and Chiang Wei-go, the late President's brother, a retired general and secretary-general of the National Security Council. The new President and KMT leader adopted a low-profile approach in his first year in office, apparently devoting much attention to securing support on a national basis. However, he did show his mettle in dealing decisively with two potentially serious issues early in his term of office. On 13 May he ordered the National Security Council promptly to return to Beijing a mainland airliner hijacked by two Chinese youths. Shortly after, on 20 May, he was challenged by a farmers' protest calling for medical insurance and an improved rice price support policy, issues reflecting tensions generated by increasing urban-rural, industrial-agricultural worker disparities, which developed into serious sustained rioting. The President responded by indicating his intention to uphold law and order, and subsequently by introducing reforms to mitigate the grievances.

HONG KONG

CAPITAL: Victoria   AREA: 1,068 sq km   POPULATION: 5,500,000 ('86)
OFFICIAL LANGUAGES: Chinese and English   GOVERNOR: Sir David Wilson
STATUS: UK dependency due to revert to Chinese sovereignty in 1997
CURRENCY: Hong Kong dollar (end–'88 £1=HK$14.12, US$1=HK$7.80)
GNP PER CAPITA: US$6,700 ('86)   MAIN EXPORTS: manufactured goods, textiles

INDEPENDENT opinion polls showed a growing majority in favour of direct elections of some Legislative Council members in 1988. A White Paper published on 10 February admitted this wish for direct elections, but claimed a division of opinion on timing and proposed postponement until 1991 and then direct election of only ten out of 56 seats. This decision, while supported by much of the senior business community and a majority of sitting Legislative Councillors, was criticized by other Hong Kong opinion and, in November, by the UN Human Rights Commission. A draft of the Chinese Basic Law for Hong Kong, published on 28 April, was widely seen as rendering nugatory provisions of the 1984 Sino-British Joint Declaration (see AR 1984, pp. 512–24) on human rights, the rule of law, judicial independence and the degree of local economic and political autonomy. Elections on 10 March for 230 District Board seats showed a lower turnout among the 1.6 million registered voters than in 1985. Liberal candidates won 70 per cent of the seats they contested, over twice the success rate of communist-supported candidates; each group contested about 100 seats.

Opinion showed a sharp divergence between corporate business confidence and fading trust in Beijing's intentions amongst individual Hong Kong Chinese. This was due in part at least to ineptly disobliging statements by second-rank Chinese officials and in May a Chinese Vice-Premier visited Hong Kong to praise the territory's capitalist economy and the valuable lessons to be learnt from it. Fear, however, that illiberal mainland bureaucrats would be unable to resist meddling with a society they did not comprehend, contributed to a growing net exodus of local people, skilled workers, technicians, professionals and managers, who were crucial to economic success. Around 50,000 of such people, especially the young middle-aged, departed in 1988, against only some 5,000 returning, and firms found themselves having to employ more expatriates. Both the Governor and Chinese representatives expressed concern at this trend.

Stock and futures markets were reorganized following the closure in 1987. Real GDP growth fell from 13.6 per cent in 1987 to about 7 per cent, with both imports and total exports running in the fourth quarter a third above 12 months earlier. The USA, the largest market despite some loss of share over the decade, withdrew GSP concessions as from January 1989 and the EEC threatened to impose high anti-dumping duties, despite the impossibility of dumping profitably from an unprotected home market. Kwai Chung became the world's busiest container port, traffic having increased by a quarter in 1987. The standard rate of tax dropped again, from 16.5 to 15.5 per cent, and corporation tax from 18 to 17 per cent, while bank rate rose steadily. Residential and commercial property prices strengthened markedly. Full employment continued, improving wages and driving labour-intensive processes into China. The inflation rate rose to almost 8 per cent in the fourth quarter. Average income a head was around the equivalent of £5,500 per annum in September and investment continued to flood in from Japan and elsewhere.

JAPAN

CAPITAL: Tokyo   AREA: 378,000 sq km   POPULATION: 121,500,000 ('86)
OFFICIAL LANGUAGE: Japanese   POLITICAL SYSTEM: parliamentary democracy
HEAD OF STATE: Emperor Michi no Miya Hirohito (since Dec '26)
RULING PARTY: Liberal Democratic Party
HEAD OF GOVERNMENT: Noboru Takeshita, Prime Minister (since Nov. '87)
PRINCIPAL MINISTERS: Sosuke Uno (foreign affairs), Tatsuo Murayama (finance), Hajime Tamura (international trade and industry), Shigenobu Sakano (home affairs), Kichiro Tazawa (defence agency)
INTERNATIONAL ALIGNMENT: OECD
CURRENCY: yen (end-'88 £1=Y226.00, US$1=Y124.93)   GNP PER CAPITA: US$12,840 ('86)
MAIN EXPORTS: machinery and transport equipment, manufactured goods

EARLY in the year communications between the islands in the Japanese archipelago improved in two respects. Firstly, the Seikan Tunnel, the longest undersea tunnel in the world, was opened in March. It joined the northern island of Hokkaido with Honshu and reduced to 11 hours the rail journey-time between Tokyo and Sapporo. Secondly, a land route was opened up between Honshu and Shikoku island in April. The six elegant suspension bridges which made up the new system completed the link-up of the rail network throughout Japan and carried a motor expressway on the upper deck. These developments greatly improved communications between the outlying islands and Japan's main industrial centres, which formerly relied on ferries.

During the year two serious national tragedies occurred. In March a train collision near Shanghai in the People's Republic of China caused the deaths of one teacher and 26 school-children out of a touring party from Kochi prefecture. Later, on 23 July, a head-on collision took place between the submarine *Nadashio* and the fishing-boat *Fuji Maru*, which sank off Yokosuka. The accident killed 22 people and was the worst of its kind involving the Maritime Self-Defence Forces. The Maritime Court held both captains to be responsible, and the head of the Self-Defence Forces offered a public apology.

Throughout the year the Japanese economy was in remarkably good shape. In the early months the official statistics revealed that Japan's trade surplus was 25 per cent lower than the previous year. This seemed to show the success of the Government's programmes for economic restructuring and 'improved market access' for foreign goods, policies which had been pursued since 1985. But later in the year Japan's exports to the American, European and South-East Asian markets soared, after experiencing three difficult trading years, suggesting that its massive trade surpluses would continue, aided by the reduction in the oil price. While imports to Japan did rise, exports also increased. Government officials, who were hoping by their trade adjustment policies to steer a course towards economic expansion based on domestic rather than foreign demand, registered some disappointment at the outcome.

Like his predecessor Yasuhiro Nakasone, Prime Minister Noboru Takeshita spent much of the year travelling. He paid visits twice to the UK and Europe as part of a policy of diversifying foreign policy, it being said that Japan was rather tired of US 'Japan-bashing' and wanted to show itself as a world power, the partner of all. Japan was prominent at the Toronto economic summit in June, as it had been at the earlier Venice and Tokyo summits. Mr Takeshita signed an agreement on science and technology cooperation while in Toronto. Thereafter he visited various cities in the US. Later in the year he visited Oceania, Australia and New Zealand. In March he affirmed the need for closer ties with the newly-elected President Roh of South Korea. It appeared that Japan was helpful in preparations for the Seoul Olympics in September and Mr Takeshita was present at the opening ceremony. A Korean-Japanese commission for the 21st century was set up in order to plan a new era of cordial relationships. While Mr Takeshita thus continued Mr Nakasone's policy of travel and contact, it was hard to say whether he made as much impact abroad. But it was certainly important that Japanese leaders had as much exposure as possible to the often-hostile trends of public opinion abroad.

Following preliminary soundings by Foreign Minister Sosuke Uno in April, Mr Takeshita made his first contact with the Chinese leadership from 25 to 30 August. His trip celebrated the tenth anniversary of the Sino-Japanese treaty of peace and friendship, concluded in 1978. In recent years relations had been impaired by minor disputes over student dormitories and commercial wrangles. In offering gestures of substantial economic and cultural cooperation, the Prime Minister announced a Y10,000 million loan package for the period 1990–95 (double that for 1984–89), covering railway and harbour projects and six chemical fertilizer plants (see also p. 348). There was to be a bilateral conference on technology exchange envisaging more active Japanese private-sector participation in economic development projects in China's special economic coastal zones (see p. 344). The likelihood of increased participation was greater now that Mr Takeshita had resolved a tricky issue which had held up agreement for some two years: Japanese concerns were to enjoy the same treatment as Chinese companies under an agreement for investment protection.

Since the coming to power of Mr Gorbachev, Japan's attitude to the Soviet Union had been one of hope, although during 1988 no substantive changes took place in bilateral relations. When Mr Nakasone met the Soviet leader in Moscow in July to discuss the prickly problem of the Northern Territories, he failed to break any new ground. The Soviet side could not see any advantages from a conference on the subject, but promised to review the matter. In the light of the Soviet leader's subsequent statement to the UN General Assembly at the end of the year (see DOCUMENTS), the Japanese remained hopeful of a breakthrough.

Eduard Shevardnadze, the Soviet Foreign Minister, visited Tokyo from 18 to 21 December to attend the eighth session of the Soviet-Japanese consultation commission. During these talks he hinted that President Gorbachev had it in mind to visit Japan, but nothing more concrete emerged. The communique stated that the two sides had failed to make progress in resolving the Northern

Territories dispute and indeed admitted that there were radical differences in attitude between them. An agreement to set up a joint committee to examine the dispute potentially took it out of the realm of loudspeaker diplomacy, but for the present this single issue remained a serious obstacle to the development of relations between the two countries.

The second half of the year was marred by three major crises: the Government's difficulties in pushing through its tax reforms; the Recruit scandal; and the illness of the Emperor. The tax problem, which successive Liberal-Democratic Governments had been addressing, had been caused by the soaring of land prices in the cities, the steady increase in share values and the unequal burden of taxes which this had created. The Government was anxious to move from direct to indirect taxation, with the introduction of a sales tax which would overcome recurrent shortfalls from tax income. An additional purpose was to secure revenue for the next five-year economic plan and, by reducing income tax, to stimulate domestic consumption and expand imports.

On 26 July the Cabinet agreed to push through a package of six taxation Bills which were known to be controversial. In view of the complexity of the legislation, Mr Takeshita had to extend the Diet sessions. Eventually, at an extraordinary Diet session towards the end of December, the Government secured the passage of its legislation. This owed much to the patient lobbying and persistence of the Prime Minister. Two of the four opposition parties hostile to the Bills were so implicated in scandals that they could not risk a general election and showed themselves willing to vote on the taxation package. The ruling Liberal Democrats were more resolute than they had been when this controversial legislation was first introduced in 1987 and a revolt of younger party members representing urban constituencies was overcome by persuasive backroom negotiation.

Among the consequences of the reform would be the introduction of a consumption tax of 3 per cent on goods and services, a 1 per cent capital gains tax on securities transactions and a reduction of corporate and income tax rates. A provision affecting foreign imports was the modification of taxes on imported alcohol, which would have the effect of halving the price of Scotch whisky, much to the chagrin of Japanese whisky producers.

One of the causes for the unforeseen delays in the Diet was that, since the summer, Japan had been rocked by the Recruit scandal. It appeared that in 1986 a number of prominent politicians had been offered shares in Recruit's Cosmos real estate company prior to its public flotation and anticipated sharp rise in share values. Amid much wild rumour it emerged that some Cabinet members had, either directly or indirectly through their staffs, been implicated in this attempt to purchase political favours at the top and had made windfall profits on a considerable scale. The Diet set up a committee to probe the affair. Opposition politicians boycotted the debates on the Government's tax legislation while they demanded that Ministers should throw light on their part in the scandal. Eventually it appeared that Kiichi Miyazawa, the Finance Minister and a contender for the premiership in 1987, was most directly and conspicuously involved. From the infighting and bargaining between Government and Opposition, it transpired in December that Mr Miyazawa would tender his resignation and the Opposition would allow the parliamentary discussion of the controversial tax Bills to proceed before the end of the parliamentary session. The end-result was the sad humiliation of one of Japan's leading statesmen of the past decade and the passing of the unpopular tax legislation.

In mid-September Emperor Hirohito, who had undergone internal bypass surgery in 1987 (see AR 1987, p. 337), had a serious recurrence of his illness. Reports on the health of the 87-year-old Emperor stated that he was suffering from considerable internal bleeding and was receiving frequent blood transfusions; he continued to be bed-ridden, and his constitutional functions were assumed by his son, Crown Prince Akihito. The Japanese Government went into a state of court mourning and companies and the general public responded by cancelling social events. Thousands of Japanese citizens queued outside the imperial palace in Tokyo, often in inclement weather, and offered get-well messages, though these well-wishers were drawn mainly from the older generation who had lived under the Emperor in pre-war days. Many Japanese were puzzled by the veneration which the Emperor attracted, since his public appearances had been comparatively few since 1975 and he had performed merely the role of a constitutional monarch, a symbol of the Japanese state and of the unity of the Japanese people. Foreign criticism of the Emperor in certain London newspapers, notably *The Sun* and *The Star*, in connection with his role in the war, caused considerable resentment at a time of national mourning in Japan. But the long drawn-out nature of the Emperor's illness gave the Japanese people ample time for reflecting upon his role in the past and led to some reassessment of the place of the monarch in contemporary Japanese society.

In the last days of the year Mr Takeshita carried out a major reshuffle of his Ministers, replacing 15 members of his Cabinet. It was a sign both of a new confidence derived from his success in eventually pushing through the unpopular tax Bills and of a desire to throw off the taint of corruption by bringing in new faces. Even then the Minister of Justice had to resign a few days later because of his involvement in the Recruit scandal. There could therefore be no doubt that the Liberal Democratic Party, the Prime Minister and his Cabinet had been badly wrong-footed by the affair, which had annoyed public opinion more than financial scandals in the past. Their future fortunes would depend on any further revelations in the offing.

SOUTH KOREA

CAPITAL: Seoul   AREA: 99,143 sq km   POPULATION: 41,600,000 ('86)
OFFICIAL LANGUAGE: Korean   POLITICAL SYSTEM: presidential
HEAD OF STATE AND GOVERNMENT: President Roh Tae Woo (since Feb '88)
RULING PARTY: Democratic Justice Party
PRINCIPAL MINISTERS: Kang Yung Hoon (premier), Cho Soon (deputy premier, economic planning board), Choi Ho Joong (foreign affairs), Lee Han Dong (home affairs), Lee Kyu Sung (finance), Lee Sang Hoon (defence), Huh Hyung Koo (justice)
CURRENCY: won (end-'88 £1=SKW1,225.45, US$1=SKW677.42)
GNP PER CAPITA: US$2,296 ('86)
MAIN EXPORTS: transport equipment, electrical goods, textiles and clothing

SOUTH Korea hosted the most successful Olympics of the modern era in September 1988, when 9,627 athletes from 160 nations took part in the XXIV Olympiad at Seoul (see also Pt. XVII, SPORT). The Games were a fitting tribute to the country's remarkable achievements. A war-ravaged agricultural country only 30 years ago, South Korea was today the twelfth largest trading nation and the seventeenth largest economy in the non-communist world. Prosperity had touched most South Korean homes, improving health, education and material progress at a rate rare anywhere else in the world.

On 26 April the electorate had thrown South Korean politics into some confusion when for the first time it denied the ruling Democratic Justice Party an overall majority of the National Assembly's seats. President Roh, elected by direct suffrage the previous December (see AR 1987, pp. 340–41), had been keen to hold legislative elections at an early date to capitalize on the Opposition's disarray. Sure enough, efforts to present a unified front to the Government at the elections foundered and the opposition fought as three separate parties. Despite this advantage the DJP ran into immediate difficulties as news of a major financial scandal surfaced during the campaign. The story concerned the embezzlement of a fortune by Chun Kyung Hwan, brother of the previous President, as head of the Saemaul Udong Movement development agency in 1981–87. The Government was accused of a cover-up. Chung Kyung Hwan was arrested on 30 March and after confessing was charged with expropriating SKW 6,600 million, taking bribes and other offences. Former President Chun Doo Hwan apologized publicly for his brother's scandalous behaviour and for his own failure to prevent it. He resigned his remaining official positions, including that of honorary chairman of the DJP and chairman of the Council of Elder Statesmen.

Inevitably the scandal focused public attention on the DJP's record of corruption. As a gesture of national reconciliation, on 1 April President Roh's Government formally apologized for the way in which the 1980 Kwangju uprising (see AR 1980, p. 312) had been put down—an important concession to the opposition. These moves could not save the Government's embarrassment and within hours of the closure of the polls on 26 April it became clear the Government had been heavily defeated. In the event it took 34 per cent of the vote and remained the largest party within the new National Assembly, but without an overall majority. The voting also confirmed big splits in public opinion along regional lines.

It was largely on calls for the democratization of society that the opposition's strength was felt. The opposition-controlled National Assembly set up committees to investigate the iniquities of the previous regime. By the year's end nine members of the Chun family were either in gaol or being investigated for embezzlement. Former President Chun himself went into voluntary internal exile, in a traditional form of penance. An unprecedented clamour by the opposition led to the resignation on 17 June of Chief Justice Kim Yong Chul, who had been strongly criticized for rulings supporting President Chun and for having ignored human rights abuses.

Violence was largely restricted to student protests. On 16 May anti-Government protests flared after the suicide of a student protesting at the continued imprisonment of allegedly political prisoners. The Government refused opposition demands for a general amnesty, insisting instead on a case-by-case review. The protests grew until on 18 May 40,000 students demonstrated against the Government and called for the withdrawal of US troops and Korean reunification. The lack of support shown to demonstrators by opposition parties tended to emphasize the isolation of violent protestors.

NORTH KOREA

CAPITAL: Pyongyang   AREA: 122,370 sq km   POPULATION: 20,900,000 ('86)
OFFICIAL LANGUAGE: Korean   POLITICAL SYSTEM: people's republic
RULING PARTY: Korean Workers' Party (KWP)
HEAD OF STATE AND PARTY LEADER: Kim Il Sung, President of Republic and KWP General Secretary (since Dec '72 and June '49 respectively)
PRINCIPAL MINISTERS: Yon Hyong Muk (premier), Kim Yong Nam (deputy premier, foreign affairs), Hong Song Nam (deputy premier, chairman of state planning commission), Vice-Marshal Oh Jin Wu (armed forces), Yun Ki Chong (finance)
INTERNATIONAL ALIGNMENT: NAM, Comecon (observer)
CURRENCY: won (end-'88 £1=NKW1.75, US$1=NKW0.97)   GNP PER CAPITA: US$1,123 ('86)
MAIN EXPORTS: magnesite, cement, metal ores

THE world's most closed society and the most orthodox present-day practitioner of stalinism, North Korea had also become an economic failure. Only 30 years earlier it had been richer than the South; now its GNP per capita was less than half of that enjoyed in the South. The state owned everything, by no means only the means of production. A bankrupting 20–25 per cent of GNP was dedicated to defence (compared to 6 per cent in the South). Politically, the country appeared as ossified as ever. Kim Il Sung, the world's longest-ruling dictator and hailed as the Great Leader, continued to preside over the country, as he had since 1946.

A few notable changes occurred in 1988, nevertheless. The Chief of Staff, General O Guk Ryol, was unexpectedly replaced on 12 February by Choe Kwang, a Deputy Prime Minister. An extensive Cabinet reshuffle on 2 June, mainly affecting economic portfolios, was seen as further evidence of the North's continuing economic problems. Proof of the North's stagnation was offered by the fact that 1993 annual production targets set by the current seven-year-plan were the same as the targets fixed in 1980 for achievement by 1989. North Korea made some progress on rescheduling its debts, estimated at about US$3,000 million. Having initially defaulted on debts of US$770 million to Western banks, the North presented the banks with a goodwill payment of US$5 million on 1 June 1988 and agreed to pay off 30 per cent of its agreed debts by 1991.

In an unexpectedly benign concession to religion, some 60 North Korean Catholics were allowed to attend a Mass celebrated in November in Pyongyang by two South Korean priests. The priests were said to have visited the North Korean capital as special envoys of the Vatican.

Despite many positive-sounding statements from both sides, the process of negotiations between North and South remained suspended. Pyongyang failed to become a 'joint host' to the Olympics and its call for a boycott was disregarded by most other communist states, including China and the USSR.

X AUSTRALASIA AND SOUTH PACIFIC

Chapter 1

AUSTRALIA—PAPUA NEW GUINEA

AUSTRALIA

CAPITAL: Canberra AREA: 7,682,000 sq km POPULATION: 16,000,000 ('86)
OFFICIAL LANGUAGE: English POLITICAL SYSTEM: parliamentary democracy
HEAD OF STATE: Queen Elizabeth II GOVERNOR-GENERAL: Sir Ninian Stephen
RULING PARTY: Labor Party
HEAD OF GOVERNMENT: Robert (Bob) Hawke, Prime Minister (since March '83)
PRINCIPAL MINISTERS: Lionel Bowen (deputy premier, attorney-general), Gareth Evans (foreign affairs and trade), Kim Beazley (defence), Paul Keating (treasurer), Peter Walsh (finance), John Button (industry, technology and commerce)
INTERNATIONAL ALIGNMENT: Anzus Pact, OECD, Cwth.
CURRENCY: dollar (end-'88 £1=A$2.12, US$1=A$1.17) GNP PER CAPITA: US$11,920 ('86)
MAIN EXPORTS: minerals, meat and agricultural products, basic manufactures

AUSTRALIANS of non-Aboriginal origin celebrated the bicentenary of European settlement, with support from some two million visitors, mainly from Britain, Japan, New Zealand, Canada and the USA. A generously-funded federal Bicentennial Authority organized or sponsored Australia-wide exhibitions, musical, theatrical, filmic and sporting events, and publications. These included much material about Aboriginal history and culture, but the Aboriginals for the most part ignored the event, and some demonstrated against it. On the bicentenary date, 26 January, the Prince of Wales took the salute at a sail-past of 'tall ships'—square-rigged giants from many countries—in Sydney Harbour, and in September the Duke and Duchess of York similarly saluted a sail-past of warships from 19 nations.

There was a parallel outpouring of visual and literary material by performers and publishers not associated with the Authority, including Australian histories from many special points of view. An international exposition at Brisbane attracted 18 million visitors and all sorts of races and other special events were staged. Some eminent Australians declined to cooperate, out of sympathy with the dispossessed Aboriginals, or because they considered that the centenary of unified nationhood in 2001 would be a more appropriate date for such celebration, or because of dismay at the environmental consequences of the past 200 years. The prevailing tone was self-critical as well as celebratory.

On 2 May Queen Elizabeth II opened the new Houses of the Parliament of the Commonwealth, moulded into the summit of

Capital Hill on the southern aspect of Canberra City. This classic of contemporary design, the joint work of an Australian and an Italo-American architect, provided ample accommodation for the legislative and executive arms of the federal Government.

Australian Labor Party (ALP) Governments continued in power federally and in Victoria, South Australia and Western Australia, a National Party Government in Queensland, and a Liberal Party Government in Tasmania. In New South Wales, however, a general election on 19 March resulted in the defeat of the previous Unsworth ALP Government by a Liberal-National coalition, which came to power under the Liberal leader, Nick Greiner, with a majority of seven seats in the Legislative Assembly. In the Legislative Council, the balance of power was held by two small parties, one generally supporting the Greiner Government and the other generally critical, with some consequent instability. Thus ended 12 years of ALP rule in New South Wales, with serious implications for the position of the federal ALP, since New South Wales had been its electoral sheet-anchor.

In Victoria, at a general election on 1 October, the Cain ALP Government retained power with a Legislative Assembly majority reduced to four seats, and with the Liberal-National majority in the Legislative Council increased to seven.

Despite these adverse voting trends, Bob Hawke, the federal ALP Prime Minister, maintained a commanding position in his party and Parliament, and opinion polls suggested that the electors strongly preferred him to the Liberal federal leader, John Howard. Nevertheless, the ALP's federal position was weakened by forced resignations from office and from Parliament of two senior Ministers for inappropriate—though not particularly wicked—conduct, and by suggestions of rivalry between the Treasurer, Paul Keating, and the Prime Minister.

Another setback for Mr Hawke was the decisive rejection by the voters of four proposals for constitutional change put to referendum on 3 September. The proposals were: (i) to extend the term of members of the House of Representatives from three to four years; (ii) to guarantee fair and democratic parliamentary elections for federal and state institutions; (iii) to give federal 'recognition' to state local government authorities; (iv) to require jury trial in both federal and state courts of serious criminal charges, and to extend to the states the existing federal guarantees of religious freedom and of just terms for government acquisitions of property. The Liberal and National parties vigorously opposed all four proposals, as being either unnecessary or dangerous, and an invasion of state rights; the supporting campaign lacked vigour.

Bill Hayden, Minister for Foreign Affairs and a former leader of the ALP, resigned from his Ministry and from Parliament in August on the announcement by the Prime Minister, with the approval of the Queen, that Mr Hayden would succeed Sir Ninian Stephen as Governor-General when Sir Ninian's term of office ended in early 1989. The appointment was strongly criticized by the opposition parties, and caused considerable public discussion, because of Mr Hayden's political associations and because he had previously advocated a republican system for Australia. However, Mr Howard undertook on behalf of the Liberals that, once the appointment took effect, criticism would cease and the appointee be treated with due courtesy. Combined with the appointment of Brian Burke, till then ALP Premier of Western Australia, to a diplomatic post (ambassador to the Irish Republic and the Holy See) and other less important appointments, these episodes gave the federal opposition parties a 'jobs for the boys' theme with which to attack the ALP.

The long-standing bipartisan policy of a non-racial basis for immigration policy was qualified, although not altogether abandoned, when Mr Howard, with some support from a commission of inquiry into migration problems, suggested that attention might sometimes need to be given to the social consequences of large immigration from particular countries. The risks of importing the racial conflicts of other countries were illustrated in December, when a demonstration by Croat migrants against the Yugoslav consulate in Sydney led to a major diplomatic incident (see also p. 135). Such problems, and relations with Australia's northern neighbours, in particular Indonesia, Fiji and Vanuatu, provided an immediate testing ground for Mr Hayden's successor at Foreign Affairs, Senator Gareth Evans.

Mr Keating again followed the course of making a preliminary budget statement in April, followed by the opening of the formal 1988–89 Budget on 24 August. He was able to show a budget surplus for 1987–88 of A$2,000 million, instead of the merely balanced budget forecast, and he predicted a surplus of $5,500 million for the coming financial year. This was partly the result of unexpectedly buoyant tax revenues, including more effective collection of previously-evaded taxes, some reduction in government spending, and a considerable economic upturn in primary and secondary industry, and in retail trade. Export prices for Australia's principal outputs—wool, coal, grain, gold and meat—increased. Fine wool in particular reached record price levels, and replaced coal as principal export earner, with an almost complete clearance of current output and stocks. There was some growth in manufactured exports, but insufficient to reduce materially the reliance on primary exports which the Hawke Government wished to lessen.

The state and territory budgets directly controlled by their respective Treasurers were also in balance, so that no loan programme was required for the expenditure plans of either those Governments or the federal Government—the first such happening for more than 50 years. The surplus enabled Mr Keating to make a number of small increases in funding of social services, in particular retraining of long-term unemployed, and assistance to children in poverty. He did not, however, make any immediate cuts in personal tax rates, but promised some to take effect in 1989 subject to movements in wage rates; company tax was to be cut from 49 to 39 per cent.

A contentious provision was to qualify the principle of free university education, established by the Whitlam ALP Government in 1975; in future, university students were to be required after graduation and after their income equalled average wage rates to pay back 20 per cent of the costs of their course. Gold production, hitherto untaxed, was made subject to tax. The Treasurer repaid part of the large overseas debt in the following months, reducing it from 26 to 18 per cent of GDP. The postponement of tax reductions was in part designed to prevent a blow-out of public spending, since by August the domestic economy was overheating. It also suited the political programme of the Hawke Government to have vote-winning tax measures in 1989.

The economic optimism of August was qualified by developments in later months. The export prices of wool, gold and grain dropped, and exports generally were handicapped by the sharp appreciation of the (floating) Australian dollar against the US dollar. In terms of a trade-weighted average of currencies, in particular yen, Deutschmark and sterling, the appreciation was less, but most export contracts were negotiated in US dollars. This reduced the return to Australian exporters and encouraged imports, with a resultant growth in the net deficit in the trade balance for private overseas transactions; the unfavourable balance was exacerbated by substantial private overseas borrowings and borrowings by statutory independent public authorities.

The 1986 Accord (see AR 1986, p. 320) continued to keep official wage rates at reasonable levels. However, in February the Arbitration Commission granted a flat 6 per cent wage increase across the board; then in August it announced the abandonment of such annual increases, replacing them with 3 per cent rises granted in detail on condition of satisfactory agreements modifying restrictive work practices. There was an increase in the incidence of strikes, but the level of days lost remained much less than in pre-Accord times. Unemployment declined from 8 per cent in the first quarter to 6.7 per cent in the fourth quarter; inflation remained at about 7 per cent. Interest rates declined in the first half of the year, but then increased again to levels much higher than in major overseas markets, attracting volatile speculative investment from overseas and necessitating a tight Reserve Bank policy.

Most Australian manufacturing, trading and financial institutions announced substantial profits; The second stock market crash predicted by many analysts after the 1987 crash (see AR 1987, p. 346) did not occur. However, the Western Australian merchant bank then saved by joint action (ibid.) was finally forced into liquidation, to the embarrassment of the state Government which had assisted the rescue attempt. In this mix of favourable and unfavourable factors, Mr Keating announced in December that budget projections of 4.5 per cent inflation and a current overseas trade deficit reduced to A$9,500 million were unlikely to be met.

A sombre background to the year's festivities was provided by two royal commissions. One was an inquiry into allegations of police and political corruption in Queensland. This was an outcome of a palace revolution in the Queensland National Party, which had resulted in late 1987 in the departure from the premiership and state parliament of Sir Johannes Bjelke-Petersen, that party's long-time leader, and his replacement by Mike Ahern. The National Party's independent majority in the state legislature was not affected. The other inquiry under federal authority was into the alarmingly high rate of deaths, officially from suicide, of Aboriginals while in police custody pending or during trial; starting with a few cases mainly in New South Wales, it was soon found that there were such cases in all mainland states, extending back for many years; additional commissioners had to be appointed to cope with the work load. Neither commission had reported by year's end, but the proceedings were fully reported in the media, and it had become likely that prosecutions would ensue; in the Queensland case, a special prosecutor had already been appointed.

There was also much dispute about education policy, especially in its tertiary phases. The nation's first private, mainly fee-paying, university was established on Queensland's Gold Coast, and others were planned. Although the general control of university education was a state matter, the federal Government had some express powers and much greater influence through the power of the purse; since 1975 it had taken over from the states the main burden of financing tertiary institutions. The Hawke Government used its authority to pressure tertiary institutions in three directions: amalgamation of neighbouring institutions to secure administrative economies, strategies to increase training in knowledge and skills required to improve the national economy, and research programmes with a greater emphasis on achieving results capable of useful application.

PAPUA NEW GUINEA

CAPITAL: Port Moresby   AREA: 463,000 sq km   POPULATION: 3,600,000 ('86)
OFFICIAL LANGUAGE: Pidgin, Motu and English   POLITICAL SYSTEM: parliamentary democracy
HEAD OF STATE: Queen Elizabeth II   GOVERNOR-GENERAL: Sir Kingsford Dibela
RULING PARTIES: six-party coalition headed by Pangu Pati
HEAD OF GOVERNMENT: Rabbie Namaliu, Prime Minister (since July '88)
PRINCIPAL MINISTERS: Akoka Doi (deputy premier, public service), Michael Somare (foreign affairs), Arnold Marsipal (defence), Paul Pora (finance and planning), Timothy Bonga (home affairs), Bernard Narakobi (justice)
INTERNATIONAL ALIGNMENT: Cwth., ACP
CURRENCY: kina (end-'88 £1=K1.48, US$1=K0.82)   GNP PER CAPITA: US$720 ('86)
MAIN EXPORTS: copper, coffee, palm oil, cocoa

IN Papua New Guinea 1988 was a year of continuing political uncertainty but general economic optimism. July brought a change of Government with the return to power of the Pangu Pati under the leadership of Rabbie Namaliu, with Pangu's founder and the country's first Prime Minister, Michael Somare, becoming Foreign Minister. The new Government was formed after a parliamentary vote of no-confidence in the unravelling coalition of parties, party splinters and independents pulled together by People's Democratic Movement leader Paias Wingti after the 1987 election (see AR 1987, pp. 347–8).

The pressures on the Wingti coalition were typical of those which had become endemic to Papua New Guinea's modified Westminster system of government. Parliament continued to be dominated by individuals representing essentially localized interests. In consequence, political parties were unstable, often transitory and generally incapable of imposing discipline on their members. Backbench support for the Government was usually offered only in return for the promise of office or other preferment, and the distribution of state resources was increasingly determined by considerations of political advantage.

A major support of Mr Wingti's coalition was the Papuan bloc of MPs led by the 'suspended' Foreign Minister, Ted Diro, who at the beginning of 1988 faced serious charges of financial misbehaviour (see AR 1987, p. 348). Mr Diro's demands for political rehabilitation in the post of Deputy Prime Minister became more insistent towards the end of the six months post-election 'grace period' in which votes of no-confidence could not be tabled. Mr Wingti's increasingly desperate attempts to retain power began with a tactical adjournment of Parliament on the eve of a no-confidence debate in April and the simultaneous readmission of Mr Diro to the Cabinet as Minister without portfolio. When this produced not governmental stability but the makings of a constitutional crisis, Mr Wingti dramatically changed tack and attempted unsuccessfully to establish a 'grand coalition' with the Pangu-led opposition which would have freed him of Mr Diro's Papuan bloc entirely. The success of the subsequent vote of no-confidence was guaranteed by the defection of the outraged Papuans to the opposition. The 'Diro problem' was thus inherited by the new Government, although by the end of the year the ex-Minister had yet to press his claims for Cabinet office.

Mr Namaliu, a widely respected figure from the dwindling minority of political leaders untouched by scandal, committed the new Government to wide-ranging economic and social measures designed to create a more attractive climate for foreign investment. The major features of this were tax reform and a commitment to deal with the country's chronic law and order problems—priorities which were reflected in the annual Budget statement in November. The potential wealth from the main focus of this investment—the incipient 'mineral boom' from gold and oil extraction—sustained a generally optimistic economic outlook. The Government's efforts to improve the investment climate were, however, set back by a wave of labour disputes in the second half of the year and by continuing wrangles over land rights.

The change of Government brought something of a shift of emphasis in foreign policy. The strong commitment of the Wingti Administration to pan-Melanesian cooperation (with the Solomon Islands and Vanuatu) was not shared by Mr Somare, who regarded such sub-regionalism as unnecessarily divisive in the broader South Pacific context. The recently more cordial relationship with Jakarta was strained during the year following incursions into PNG by Indonesian troops in pursuit of Irian Jayan separatist guerrillas (see also p. 337). Overall, the relationship with Australia was better in 1988, as Canberra's increasing concern with the strategic situation of the South-West Pacific led to a greater sensitivity in its regional diplomacy.

Chapter 2

NEW ZEALAND

CAPITAL: Wellington AREA: 270,000 sq km POPULATION: 3,300,000 ('86)
OFFICIAL LANGUAGE: English POLITICAL SYSTEM: parliamentary democracy
HEAD OF STATE: Queen Elizabeth II GOVERNOR-GENERAL: Sir Paul Reeves
RULING PARTY: Labour Party
HEAD OF GOVERNMENT: David Lange, Prime Minister (since July '84)
PRINCIPAL MINISTERS: Geoffrey Palmer (deputy premier, justice), Russell Marshall (external relations and trade), Bob Tizard (defence), David Caygill (finance), Michael Bassett (internal affairs)
INTERNATIONAL ALIGNMENT: OECD, Cwth., Anzus Pact (suspended)
CURRENCY: dollar (end-'88 £1=NZ$2.87, US$1=NZ$1.58) GNP PER CAPITA: US$7,460 ('86)
MAIN EXPORTS: meat and meat products, wool, dairy products

CONTINUING recession and the increasingly unsettled politics of Prime Minister David Lange's Cabinet characterized the year. Unemployment exceeded 150,000, being particularly high in rural districts, secondary centres and among the unskilled. Continuing high interest rates curbed growth, investment and job creation, the Government remaining active in its borrowing for rising public spending on health, education and such benefits as unemployment pay and superannuation. Throughout the year rates for 90-day commercial bills rarely fell below 14 per cent.

These costs were underlined by an inflation rate running at 5 per cent annualized to September, and wage settlements averaging only 4 per cent. Buoyant international commodity prices for wool, dairy produce and aluminium, allied to a decline in imports, produced the best terms of trade for a decade. Although the currency remained over-valued for much of the year, pumped up by offshore money attracted by high interest rates, the balance of payments improved markedly to stand at a deficit of NZ$1,160 million to the October year, this halving the corresponding 1987 figure.

In October tax cuts were introduced, of benefit to the better paid, but a dilution from the flat tax proposals outlined by Finance Minister Roger Douglas in his December 1987 announcement. Here, Prime Minister Lange made unilateral alterations to the flat tax proposal in January, when Mr Douglas was abroad, this permitting a more equitable graduated tax scale, but causing a deepening quarrel between these powerful figures. For Mr Lange it was essential that the country should have more time to adjust and accommodate to the rapid scale of economic change and public sector reorganization. This would entail not just a chance to build public support, but a halt to rising unemployment widely attributed to the policies of restructuring. For Mr Douglas and a number of Cabinet colleagues, having got thus far down a monetarist path by squeezing inflation out of the economy, any halt would jeopardize the painful advances already made.

In June the divide between Mr Lange and Mr Douglas widened when the Prime Minister forecast a future internal budget deficit exceeding NZ$3,000 million, while his Finance Minister maintained that it would be but a third of that figure. Then in November the Minister for State-owned Enterprises with responsibility for the sale of state assets, Richard Prebble, ranked fifth in Cabinet, was sacked by Mr Lange. A close ally of Mr Douglas, the outgoing Minister had offended opinion at home and business interests abroad by his abrasive handling of post office closures, an abrupt cancellation of the sale of Petrocorp (a government-owned energy concern) to British Gas, and in his disputed handling of the sale of Air New Zealand—subsequently sold in December to a consortium dominated by Brierley Investments and Qantas.

In a further unilateral act, Mr Lange dismissed a key parliamentary aide to Mr Douglas, a removal symptomatic of the sniping between ministerial offices that had intensified as deregulation permitted Ministers to hire staff on contract outside the career public service. Often outnumbered in Cabinet on economic policy, Mr Lange gained support by appealing for unity at the Labour Party conference in September. This gathering approved a consultative process obliging the Government to engage relevant party committees in matters where a conflict with existing manifesto or conference decisions could arise. Mr Douglas and other Ministers, however, were openly contemptuous of a procedure they regarded as an unwarranted interference in their government responsibilities.

A decisive and swift climax to the conflict occurred in mid-December when Mr Douglas convened a press conference saying that if Mr Lange were to remain as Prime Minister into 1989, then he could no longer serve under him since his leadership was tearing the country apart. He was then promptly dismissed by the Prime Minister and replaced as Finance Minister by David Caygill. The non-Cabinet Minister for Customs and Revenue, Trevor de Cleene, resigned in sympathy with Mr Douglas. Although the latter retained some support for the challenge he put down at a pre-Christmas parliamentary caucus meeting brought forward from February to consider the Labour leadership, Mr Lange easily retained a comfortable majority. Nevertheless, his Government was running far behind the National Party opposition in the public opinion polls.

The momentum of sustained public policy change and reform continued unabated. This included replacement of the outdated hospital board administrative structure with fewer but stronger area health authorities; continuing amalgamation of local government units to perform as bigger regional structures; far-reaching changes in educational administration, consequential upon the 1988 Picot report recommending wider, more diverse, community participation in the management and curriculum of schools; port and harbour rationalization, with abolition of the Waterfront Industry Commission presaged; plans consequential upon the 1988 Hawke report for the reorganization, control and funding of the universities, including abolition of the university grants committee; the corporatization of the Ministry of Works and Development; the creation of a new Ministry of External Relations and Trade, incorporating Foreign Affairs and the trade division of the former Department of Trade and Commerce; and the replacement of a permanent head of the civil service system with senior executives hired on five-year contracts under a new State Services Act.

More contentious was the Government's state asset sale programme designed to help reduce the country's oppressive foreign public debt of over NZ$30,000 million. Under the hammer came energy, transport and forestry enterprises. Proposals to sell the Bank of New Zealand and Postbank generated resentment within the Labour Party and its caucus. A prominent backbencher and former party president, Jim Anderton, was disciplined by a loss of the whip for abstaining in a parliamentary vote on the relevant sale legislation.

Wider controversy occurred after May when the Waitangi tribunal published its interim finding over the fishing claims of the Muriwhenua (Maori) northern tribes. This found that the Crown had been in breach of the original Treaty of Waitangi principles insofar as the claimants' fishing activities had not been protected, but rather undermined by non-Maori fishing activity conducted without consent. The tribunal also found that the Muriwhenua fishing interest extended to the continental shelf and had a commercial dimension that included a right to expand into new technologies. This finding followed a decision of the Waitangi tribunal—widely hailed throughout Maoridom as a great symbolic victory—to return 70 hectares of prime vacant property at Bastion Point, Auckland, to tribal owners.

In a year which saw attacks on incompetence in Maori affairs administration, pakeha resentment at the growing use of Maori in schools and the media, and the race relations office criticized for failing to censure some extremist anti-white statements by Maoris, the Government faced an increasingly delicate race relations problem. On fisheries, it introduced legislation planned to grant Maoris 2.5 per cent of fishing quotas, this amount to be retained if used in the preceding year. The Government also announced financial support to Maori fishing interests in process of establishment.

An extensive, widely-awaited royal commission on social policy produced its report, although the Government's lack of response to it was widely criticized. The report said that New Zealand would have to do better in race relations and improving chances for women; that to achieve a fairer society, economic and social policies would have to provide more employment opportunities; that state organization needed to cater for more effective participation; and that existing social and economic policy needed better joint designation, monitoring and assessment.

In foreign relations, links with France improved with moves to reach a settlement in New Caledonia (see pp. 146, 372), although the return of Dominique Prieur from Hao atoll to France in May revived the *Rainbow Warrior* dispute (see AR 1985, pp. 313–4; 1987,

p. 351). After exhausting diplomatic attempts to reach a settlement to the dispute arising from this breach of agreement, the matter was submitted to third-party legal resolution (see also p. 145).

As regards the European Economic Community, a cut in the tonnage of New Zealand's primary exports was accepted in return for a relaxation of relevant levies. In relations with Australia, the key issue was Canberra's enthusiasm for New Zealand's purchase of four frigates costing NZ$2,100 million over a 20-year period. This proposal saw the Labour caucus divided over cost and suitability considerations. On the 1983 Closer Economic Relations Agreement, Australia and New Zealand signed protocols involving commitments to move to a single 'trans-Tasman' market by July 1990.

An international convention on the regulation of Antarctic minerals resources was adopted in Wellington in June and opened for signature in November. While New Zealand officials played a key role in the formulation of the new convention, environmental interests were unimpressed, condemning the final accord as providing inadequate safeguards.

The year also saw a devastating cyclone hitting the east coast of North Island in March, a visit by King Juan Carlos of Spain, and the establishment of public radio and television as state-owned enterprises.

Chapter 3

SOUTH PACIFIC

New Caledonia
CAPITAL: Nouméa   AREA: 19,000 sq km   POPULATION: 150,000 ('86)
STATUS: French overseas territory
French Polynesia
CAPITAL: Papeete   AREA: 4,200 sq km   POPULATION: 170,000 ('86)
STATUS: French overseas territory
Fiji
CAPITAL: Suva   AREA: 18,375 sq km   POPULATION: 707,000 ('86)
OFFICIAL LANGUAGES: Fijian and Hindi   POLITICAL SYSTEM: presidential/military republic
HEAD OF STATE: President Sir Penaia Ganilau (since Nov '87)
HEAD OF GOVERNMENT: Sir Kamisese Mara, Prime Minister (since Dec '87)
CURRENCY: Fiji dollar (end-'88 £1=F$2.51, US$1=F$1.39)   GNP PER CAPITA: US$1,810 ('86)
MAIN EXPORTS: sugar, agricultural products
Vanuatu
CAPITAL: Port Vila   AREA: 12,000 sq km   POPULATION: 135,000 ('86)
OFFICIAL LANGUAGES: English, French and Bislama   POLITICAL SYSTEM: parliamentary
HEAD OF STATE: President George Ati Sokomanu (since July '80)
HEAD OF GOVERNMENT: Fr Walter Lini, Prime Minister
CURRENCY: vatu (end-'88 £1=VT182.60, US$1=VT100.94)   GNP PER CAPITA: US$880 ('85)
MAIN EXPORTS: copra, agricultural products
Belau
CAPITAL: Koror   AREA: 500 sq km   POPULATION: 15,000
STATUS: US commonwealth
American Samoa
CAPITAL: Pago Pago   AREA: 195 sq km   POPULATION: 35,000 ('85)
STATUS: US dependency
Solomon Islands
CAPITAL: Honiara   AREA: 28,000 sq km   POPULATION: 267,000 ('86)
OFFICIAL LANGUAGE: English   POLITICAL SYSTEM: parliamentary democracy
HEAD OF STATE: Queen Elizabeth II   GOVERNOR-GENERAL: Sir Baddeley Devesi
HEAD OF GOVERNMENT: Ezekiel Alebua, Prime Minister (since Nov. '86)
CURRENCY: dollar (end-'88 £1=SI$3.79, US$1=SI$2.09)   GNP PER CAPITA: US$510 ('86)
MAIN EXPORTS: timber, copra, fish
Nauru
CAPITAL: Domaneab   AREA: 21.4 sq km   POPULATION: 8,500 ('86)
OFFICIAL LANGUAGES: Nauruan and English   POLITICAL SYSTEM: presidential
HEAD OF STATE AND GOVERNMENT: President Hammer deRoburt
CURRENCY: Australian dollar (*see above*)   GNP PER CAPITA: US$20,000 ('86)
MAIN EXPORTS: phosphates
Cook Islands
CAPITAL: Avarua   AREA: 235 sq km   POPULATION: 20,000 ('86)
STATUS: New Zealand associated territory
Western Samoa
CAPITAL: Apia   AREA: 2,830 sq km   POPULATION: 165,000 ('86)
OFFICIAL LANGUAGES: Samoan and English   POLITICAL SYSTEM: monarchy
HEAD OF STATE: Susuga Malietoa Tanumafili II (since Jan '62)
HEAD OF GOVERNMENT: Tofilau Eti Alesana, Prime Minister (since April '88)
CURRENCY: tala (end-'88 £1=WS$3.42, US$1=WS$1.89)   GNP PER CAPITA: US$680 ('86)
MAIN EXPORTS: cocoa, copra, agricultural products

THE dominant development in NEW CALEDONIA was one of tragedy followed by reconciliation. In May Kanak militants killed four French gendarmes and then took further French police and soldiers hostage within caves on the island of Ouvéa. French troops then stormed these caves, killing 19 Kanaks and losing two of their number dead. In the charged atmosphere just prior to the first round of the French presidential elections this violence saw the territory teetering on the brink of civil war. However, after the fall of the Chirac Government (which had adopted a hard line against independence) and its replacement by the Rocard Administration (see p. 142), moves were quickly put in hand to defuse the situation.

In late June, under the Matignon Accord, M. Rocard succeeded in getting the leaders of settler and independence interests, MM. Lafleur and Tjibaou respectively, to agree to a formula under which Paris would exercise direct rule for a year. This would be followed by a period of economic, social, educational and land reform designed to alleviate disparities between settler and indigenes, a final referendum on full independence being scheduled for 1998. An operative statute approved by referendum in October—but with a poor turnout of voters in metropolitan France—divided New Caledonia into three provinces, each with an elected Assembly responsible for land reform, public works and economic development, but with France retaining control of foreign relations and defence. It was also agreed that only those locals qualified to vote in the 1988 referendum, and their descendants subsequently of voting age, could qualify as electors in the ultimate act of political determination scheduled for 1998.

In FRENCH POLYNESIA, the authorities of the nuclear weapons testing programme announced a relocation to Fangataufa atoll. Naval Commander Thireaut conceded that this followed concern that repeated underground blasts would eventually damage the geological foundations of Muroroa atoll. Eight tests were conducted during the year, bringing to 103 the total for all detonations in French Polynesia.

In FIJI, a draft constitution giving ethnic Fijians political supremacy was published. It recommended a unicameral legislature of 71 members, who would consist of 36 Fijians, of whom 28 would be elected by 14 Fijian provinces and eight nominated by the Great Council of Chiefs (but one of whom would have to be commander of the armed forces); 22 Indians; eight returned by 'general' electors (Europeans, Chinese and other minorities); one by the Rotumans; and four nominated by the Prime Minister. All voting for the legislature was to be from separate ethnic electoral rolls; powers to declare conditions of emergency were granted the President; and a general immunity from civil and criminal prosecution was granted the military. This draft was repudiated as totally unacceptable by Dr Timoci Bavadra, the Prime Minister ousted in the May 1987 military coup led by Colonel Rabuka. From the latter came a warning in

December that if the draft constitution was not promulgated, then a third military coup could not be ruled out.

Improved sugar production and prices, an upturn in tourism and a decline in imports led to an improvement in Fiji's balance of payments, although inflation ran at 11 per cent and unemployment increased. Concerned to enhance its legitimacy abroad, the regime actively solicited aid and investment from Japan, France, Malaysia and China, while interim Prime Minister Ratu Sir Kamisese Mara was welcomed by Mrs Thatcher on a visit to Britain. Under some international pressure, particularly an Australian threat to withhold an aid increase, the regime relaxed certain stringent internal security measures which had been employed in the arbitrary arrest and detention of journalists, lawyers, academics and opponents of the Government.

In VANUATU, May riots saw one person killed and widespread property destruction in the capital, Port Vila. The disturbance grew out of a protest at Prime Minister Lini's decision to close down the Vila Urban Land Corporation because of alleged financial misman- agement. Minister of Tourism Barak Sope, an active board member of the organization involved, led the protest, was then sacked from Fr Lini's Cabinet, and suspended as general secretary of the ruling Vanua'aku Party. Utilizing tactics of parliamentary obstruction, Mr Sope and four colleagues were then suspended from Parliament for a period, similar tactics then being adopted by the official opposition. This necessitated December by-elections which confirmed Fr Lini's parliamentary majority.

This outcome was immediately followed by the bombshell decision of President George Sokomanu (Mr Sope's uncle) to dismiss the Lini Government on the spurious grounds that a 37 per cent turnout at the recent by-elections had been insufficient. President Sokomanu attempted to install an interim Government headed by Mr Sope, who was promptly arrested on the orders of Fr Lini (who had retained control of the police and paramilitary forces). The Supreme Court then ruled that the President's decision to dismiss the Lini Government had been completely unconstitutional and steps soon followed to remove the President from office.

In BELAU, President Lazarus Salii was shot dead in August under suspicious circumstances. Most interpretations suspected suicide when it was revealed that, two days prior to his death, President Salii had received information from the US General Accounting Office that he was under investigation over a huge loans scandal involving British interests in a collapsed power project. He was succeeded in an acting capacity by Vice-President Thomas Remengesau, until a presidential election in November was won by Ngiratkel Etpison. The longrunning impasse over implementation of the 'compact of free association' with the US (see AR 1987, pp. 357–8) remained unresolved, amid further legal wrangling and official US inquiries into the manner in which majority approval for the compact had been obtained from Belau voters (see also p. 386).

In AMERICAN SAMOA, Fofo Sunia, the country's delegate to the US House of Representatives, was gaoled for a term of five to 15 months for payroll fraud.

The SOLOMON ISLANDS celebrated a decade of independence in July, Prime Minister Alebua warning that without vast improvement in national management the country could face economic collapse.

In NAURU, a five-month airline strike damaged external receipts as did continuing financial problems for the shipping line Nauru Pacific.

A third political grouping was formed in the COOK ISLANDS with the formation of the Labour Party. It pledged to field a full slate of candidates for the January 1989 general election.

A February election in WESTERN SAMOA initially produced a stalemate when both major political groupings won 23 seats in the Assembly. Following two months of political uncertainty, Tofilau Eti Alesana emerged as Prime Minister with sufficient support from his Human Rights Protection Party to form a Government.

XI INTERNATIONAL ORGANIZATIONS

Chapter 1

THE UNITED NATIONS AND ITS AGENCIES

DESCRIBING 1988 as 'a time of pride for the United Nations', Secretary-General Javier Pérez de Cuellar asserted that there had been a vindication of the concept of multilateralism, 'so the pride we feel is not ours alone: it is shared by all Governments who have contributed to the results that have been achieved'. In his annual report to the General Assembly, Sr Pérez de Cuellar mentioned specifically the Geneva accords on Afghanistan (see DOCUMENTS), the ceasefire in the Iran-Iraq conflict, improved prospects (later a firm agreement) for the independence of Namibia (see DOCUMENTS), new moves on the question of Cyprus, progress on the problem of Western Sahara and better hopes for peace in South-East Asia. He welcomed the working relationship with the Security Council which had 'rarely if ever been closer', but insisted that the 'financial health of the organization must immediately be restored'. The United Nations, he said, could not function without money and the organization was still seriously short of funds.

FINANCE. As of the end of October, member states owed some $450 million in assessed contributions to the regular UN budget, plus about $347 million for peacekeeping operations. Even after recent payments the United States still owed some $337 million, which was made up of $215 million in its assessed contributions for 1988 and $122 million for previous years. In current and accumulated contributions, South Africa owed $34 million, Brazil $18 million, Iran $12 million and the Soviet Union $7 million. Major contributors to the regular budget who were fully paid up on 31 October included Japan, West Germany, France, the United Kingdom, Italy and Canada.

STATUS OF PLO. On 29 February the Assembly resumed its 42nd session to consider the possible closing of the observer mission of the Palestine Liberation Organization (PLO) to the United Nations (see also Pt. XV, Ch. 1). The PLO was granted observer status by the Assembly in 1974 but its failure had been threatened by legislation adopted by the United States Congress calling for the closure of the mission by 21 March. The Assembly adopted two resolutions on the subject. The first—approved by 143 votes to 1 (Israel)—reaffirmed that the PLO observer mission was covered by the provisions of 1947 UN-US Headquarters Agreement and that therefore it should be enabled to establish and maintain premises and its personnel to enter and remain in the United States to carry out their official functions. The second resolution adopted by an identical vote, asked the International Court of Justice (ICJ) for an advisory opinion on the question. The United States did not participate in either vote.

The US representative explained that his Government had made no final decision concerning the application or enforcement of recently-passed US legislation with respect to the observer mission of the PLO. It remained the US intention to find an appropriate resolution of the problem in the light of the Charter, the Headquarters Agreement and the laws of the United States. Nevertheless, on 23 March the Assembly reaffirmed that a dispute existed between the United Nations and the Unites States and that dispute settlement procedures should be set in motion. A resolution was adopted by a vote of 148 to 2 (Israel and USA) requesting the United States to name its arbitrator to the ICJ.

The ICJ subsequently handed down its opinion on the status of the PLO observer mission to the United Nations. It stated that the United States was under an obligation, in accordance with its 1947 Headquarters Agreement with the United Nations, to enter into arbitration for the settlement of a dispute between itself and the United Nations. Later, however, a federal district court in New York ruled against the implementation of the congressional legislation requiring the closure of the PLO office. The decision of the US Administration not to appeal against this ruling was officially welcomed by the United Nations.

The respite was short-lived. In late November the United States refused to grant a visa to Yassir Arafat, head of the PLO, to enable him to take part in the 43rd General Assembly debate on Palestine in New York. Announcing the refusal, the US Secretary of State George Shultz said it was because 'PLO elements have engaged in terrorism against Americans and others', and that the 'PLO chairman knows of, condones and lends support to such acts'. The decision aroused immediate widespread anger and dismay and the Assembly promptly passed a resolution calling upon the United States to reverse its stand. The vote was 151 to 2 (Israel and USA), with the United Kingdom as the sole abstainer.

When the United States refused to rescind the ban, the Assembly took the unprecedented step of switching the debate on Palestine to the UN's European headquarters in Geneva from 13-15 December. The resolution to approve the move was adopted by 154 votes to 2 (Israel, USA), with the United Kingdom again abstaining. For the United States, Herbert Okum said his country would be represented at the Geneva meeting, but was against the resolution because of its 'unacceptable language'. The Assembly's administrative and budgetary committee approved a report from the Secretary-General indicating that the cost of holding the debate in Geneva would be about $440,000. (For the continuation of the debate see below under POLITICAL/PALESTINE.)

43RD GENERAL ASSEMBLY. The Assembly began on 20 September at the UN Headquarters in New York, and elected the Foreign Minister of Argentina, Dante Caputo, as its President. It had previously been determined that the President of this session should be elected from the region of Latin America and the Caribbean, and in a secret ballot Sr Caputo received 91 votes, with 66 countries voting for Dame Nita Barrow of Barbados. Addressing the Assembly after his election, Sr Caputo spoke of positive developments on the international scene in recent months, citing agreements between the United States and the Soviet Union and progress on regional issues, but he noted that the situations in the Middle East and Central America had not shown comparable positive developments.

The Assembly adopted a 149-item agenda which included several new items. One was on the conservation of climate as part of the 'common heritage of mankind' and the danger posed to world health and development by the 'greenhouse effect' (see Pt. XIV, Ch. 1). Another was on the promotion of peace, reconciliation and dialogue in the Korean peninsula.

Colombia, Ethiopia, Canada, Malaysia and Finland were elected as non-permanent members of the Security Council, to replace Argentina, the Federal Republic of Germany, Italy, Japan and Zambia, whose two-year terms expired at the end of the year. Five members had a further year to serve—Algeria, Brazil, Nepal, Senegal and Yugoslavia.

POLITICAL

DISARMAMENT. The General Assembly held its third special session on disarmament from 31 May to 26 June but failed to achieve consensus on a final set of recommendations. The session considered issues ranging from nuclear and conventional disarmament to verification and confidence-building measures. The UN Secretary-General, in adding his regrets, reminded the Assembly that member states had come close to an agreement on most of the provisions contained in a draft prepared by the chairman of the 'committee of the whole'. In the end, however, basic national principles had not been amenable to a compromise text, although he was sure that efforts of member states to formulate a common strategy would continue in various UN organs, including the Assembly. Sr Pérez de Cuellar also expressed his gratification of the unprecedented participation of many national leaders—10 Heads of State, 13 Prime Ministers and 55 Foreign Ministers—as well as the sincere interest shown by non-governmental organizations.

The major breakthrough on disarmament came unexpectedly when President Mikhail Gorbachev addressed the General Assembly in December (see DOCUMENTS)—the first Soviet head of state to do so since Nikita Khrushchev in 1960. In an hour-long review of world affairs, the Soviet leader announced that within the next two years the numerical strength of the Soviet armed forces and the Soviet arsenal of conventional weapons would be substantially reduced, and would take place unilaterally, without any relation to the ongoing talks in Vienna (see Pt. XII, Ch. 2). On the theme of Soviet-US relations, Mr Gorbachev said that while the seriousness of the differences should not be underestimated, the two countries had begun to understand each other and to seek solutions in both their own and the common interest. He spoke of items on their agenda, mainly in the area of disarmament, and emphasized the need for progress towards a 50 per cent reduction in strategic offensive arms while preserving the 1972 Treaty on the Limitation of Anti-Ballistic Missile Systems (ABM); he also called for a convention against chemical weapons and a reduction in conventional armaments in Europe.

Reaction in UN circles to Mr Gorbachev's address ranged from the cynical to the euphoric, but once the media headlines had died down delegates in general felt that a big unilateral step forward had been taken which should lead to a more positive approach to the whole complex question of disarmament.

AFGHANISTAN. After nearly six years of indirect negotiations between Afghanistan and Pakistan, with Diego Córdovez of the UN acting as personal representative of the Secretary-General during successive rounds of proximity talks, agreements were signed in Geneva on 14 April for the settlement of the situation relating to Afghanistan (see DOCUMENTS). At the signing ceremony Sr Pérez de Cuellar said the accords represented a 'major stride in the effort to bring peace to Afghanistan', and showed the capacity of the United Nations 'to attain positive results on the most complex of issues when backed by the political will of its member states'. He added that the challenge facing the people of Afghanistan was great but had to be met by them alone, and that the agreements laid the basis for the exercise by all Afghans of their right to self-determination.

Under the agreements, Afghanistan and Pakistan undertook non-interference in each other's internal affairs and accepted provisions for the voluntary return of refugees. The United States and the Soviet Union agreed to act as guarantors of the accords, which included provision for the withdrawal of foreign troops from Afghanistan to a timetable agreed by the Soviet Union and Afghanistan. The agreements took effect on 15 May and stipulated that half of the troops should be withdrawn within three months from that date, and that the withdrawal of all troops would be completed within nine months.

The accords also called for the establishment of a UN observer mission to monitor their implementation, to which end an operational team arrived in Islamabad on 25 April and Kabul on 1 May. The team, named the UN Good Offices Mission in Afghanistan and Pakistan (UNGOMAP) and led by Maj.-Gen. Rauli Helminen of Finland, consisted of some 50 political and legal advisers and military officers from ten countries. In mid-May Prince Sadruddin Aga Khan was appointed co-ordinator for UN humanitarian and economic assistance relating to Afghanistan. He had previously held a number of senior UN positions, including that of UN High Commissioner for Refugees in 1965-77.

The first conference to receive pledges for the assistance programmes obtained promises of contributions amounting to $795 million, including $600 million from the Soviet Union. The pledges were received from 18 countries in addition to members of the European Community and the Holy See. Prince Sadruddin said that the amount pledged represented nearly 70 per cent of the estimated $1,670 million needed for the first, 18-month, phase of recovery operations. He hoped donor countries would continue to be generous, and that the Afghan people would never again be 'the hostage of useless political confrontations'.

On 3 November the General Assembly called on the parties to the Afghanistan settlement to work for the faithful implementation of the Geneva agreements, which would enable the 'Afghan refugees to return voluntarily to their homeland in safety and honour'. In a resolution adopted without a vote and without debate, the Assembly also emphasized the need for a dialogue on establishing a broad-based Government with the participation of all segments of the Afghan people.

When addressing the General Assembly in December, Mr Gorbachev paid tribute to the UN Secretary-General and his representatives for their work in Afghanistan and said that the agreements reached earlier in the year needed to be supplemented by specific measures. He called for an effective ceasefire everywhere by 1 January 1989, with an end to arms supplies to all the belligerents, and for a UN peacekeeping force to be sent to Kabul and other strategic centres while a broad-based Government was being established. He also proposed an international conference on the neutrality and demilitarization of Afghanistan.

IRAN-IRAQ WAR. On 8 August the UN Secretary-General announced that a date for a ceasefire in the war between Iran and Iraq had been agreed and that as of 0300 hours GMT on 20 August 1988 both sides would observe a ceasefire and discontinue all military action on land, at sea and in the air (see pp. 215–8, 302–4). At a later meeting of the Security Council, Sr Pérez de Cuellar said that he had been assured by the two parties to the conflict that they would observe the ceasefire 'in the context of the full implemenatation of Resolution 598'. Both countries had agreed to the deployment of a team of United Nations observers at the time of the ceasefire. He also appealed 'in the strongest possible terms' to all concerned to exercise restraint and to refrain from any hostile activity in the period before the ceasefire took effect. He was sure that restoration of peace would bring to the peoples of both countries 'victories far greater than those of war'.

Iran had informed the United Nations on 18 July that it accepted Security Council Resolution 598—adopted on 20 July 1987 (see AR 1987, pp. 548-9)—as a formula for ending the war. Resolution 598 demanded an immediate ceasefire in the conflict, an end to all military actions on land, at sea and in the air, and the withdrawal of all forces to the internationally-recognized boundaries without delay. It asked the Secretary-General to send a team of UN observers 'to verify, confirm and supervise the ceasefire and withdrawal'. It also stipulated that in consultation with Iran and Iraq the Secretary-General should 'explore . . . the question of entrusting an impartial body with inquiring into responsibility for the conflict and to report to the Security Council as soon as possible'.

On 9 August the Security Council voted unanimously to establish a team of UN observers to supervise the ceasefire, to be known as the United Nations Iran-Iraq Military Observer Group (UNIIMOG) which would be set up for an initial period of six months. Direct talks between the representatives of Iran and Iraq under the auspices of the Secretary-General began in Geneva on 25 August.

It was announced on 14 September that Sweden's UN ambassador, Jan Eliasson, had been appointed as the Secretary-General's representative on Iran-Iraq. Sr Pérez de Cuellar said that he would be working closely with Mr Eliasson, and hoped that the United Nations could accelerate the peace talks without imposing anything on the parties. Ambassador Eliasson had accompanied the late Prime Minister of Sweden, Olof Palme, on missions to Iran and Iraq on behalf of the United Nations during the period from 1980 to 1986.

Addressing the General Assembly on 3 October, the Foreign

Minister of Iran, Ali Akbar Vellayati, said that what was needed for the success of the talks, which were continuing under UN auspices, was the withdrawal of forces without delay, and also the establishment of the impartial body, provided for in the resolution, for identifying the aggressor. Iran, he said, had unilaterally begun the repatriation of prisoners-of-war even while Iraq, in violation of the ceasefire, had taken further Iranian prisoners.

On the following day, the Foreign Minister of Iraq, Tariq Aziz, told the Assembly that Iran's conduct in the Geneva negotiations between the two countries had been 'characterized by evasiveness'. He said that Iraq called for unobstructed freedom of navigation for all shipping in the international waters of the Gulf and in the Hormuz Straits. Iraq also proposed that the United Nations should clear the Shatt al-Arab, which was Iraq's only outlet to the high seas, and ensure safe navigation without prejudice to the legal status of the waterway.

The peace talks between Iran and Iraq, after being adjourned in September, were briefly resumed in New York earlier in October. A third session at the level of Foreign Ministers opened in Geneva on 31 October, at the conclusion of which Mr Eliasson said on 11 November that they had taken place in a 'constructive, sober and positive atmosphere' but had produced no break-through on major issues.

MIDDLE EAST. While the General Assembly's annual debate on the question of Palestine took place in Geneva from 13-15 December, its consideration of the overall situation in the Middle East had opened in New York on 5 December. In his report to the Assembly, the UN Secretary-General said that any initiative on the Arab-Israeli conflict was bound to encounter difficulty, but he was confident that with the full support of the Security Council, and in particular the permanent members, there could be progress towards a just and lasting peace in the Middle East. He said that the uprising in the occupied territories showed the commitment of the Palestinians to their legitimate rights, and the recent session of the Palestine National Council in Algiers (see DOCUMENTS) had generated a new momentum in the diplomatic process.

On 6 December three resolutions were adopted. The first, repeating the Assembly's call for an international peace conference under UN auspices and with the permanent members of the Security Council taking part, was adopted by 103 votes to 18, with 30 abstentions. In other provisions, the resolution condemned Israel's occupation of Arab territories and reaffirmed that the question of Palestine was the core of the Middle East conflict. It said that the peace conference should have authority to achieve a solution based on

Israeli withdrawal from occupied Palestinian territory, including Jerusalem, and other Arab territories, and on the attainment by the Palestinian people of their inalienable rights in accordance with UN resolutions.

Those not supporting this resolution were mainly Western countries, as was the case with the second resolution—adopted by 83 votes to 21, with 45 abstentions—which stressed the illegality of Israel's occupation of the 'Syrian Arab Golan', declared that Israel was not a peace-loving state, and called on members to cease all dealings with Israel in order to isolate it in all fields. The third resolution asserted that Israel's administration of Jerusalem was 'illegal, null and void', and deplored the transfer to Jerusalem of some countries' diplomatic missions. The voting on this was 143 to 2 (Israel, El Salvador), with seven abstentions.

The mandate of the UN Disengagement Observer Force (UNDOF) in the Golan Heights between Syria and Israel was extended for six months by the Security Council on 30 November. There were some 1,300 personnel serving there in contingents from Austria, Canada, Finland and Poland.

The Security Council had previously also extended the mandate of the UN Interim Force in Lebanon (UNIFIL) until 31 January 1989. While expressing concern over the situation in Lebanon, the Council condemned the abduction of the chief of the military observers of the UN Truce Supervision Organization (UNTSO), Lieut.-Colonel William R. Higgins of the United States, who was assisting UNIFIL in its peacekeeping task.

PALESTINE. In an address lasting nearly one and a half hours to the Assembly's Geneva session on the Palestine question, the PLO chairman, Yassir Arafat, said that the leaders of Israel should come to Geneva to work out a peaceful Middle East settlement within the framework of an international conference convened by the United Nations. He said that the PLO would seek a comprehensive settlement guaranteeing all parties to the conflict, including Palestine, Israel and their neighbours, the right to live in peace and security. Mr Arafat called for temporary supervision of the Israeli-occupied territories to oversee the withdrawal of Israeli forces, and for the formation of a committee of the five permanent members of the Security Council to prepare for the holding of a full international peace conference. He could not accept demands for further PLO 'concessions' to Israel as a condition for direct talks; the PLO, he said, was being asked to accept positions which could not be determined before negotiations.

In reply, Johanan Bein of Israel said that the PLO had not departed from 'extreme and uncompromising positions'. The proclamation of a Palestinian state with no territory and no borders and with

Jerusalem, the capital of Israel, as its capital had no meaning. He said the PLO had cited Security Council Resolutions 242 and 338 only in conjunction with other UN resolutions that sought to impair Israel's legitimacy and existence, and it had not abandoned terrorism.

Vladimir Petrovsky (Soviet Union) said Mr Arafat's peace initiative had opened new opportunities to resolve the Middle East conflict. With the PLO having expressed its desire to coexist with Israel in conditions of peace and security, and having condemned terrorism in all its forms, it was now 'up to the other side to respond'. General Vernon Walters (United States) said Israel had to face up to the need for withdrawal from the occupied territories, and the need to accommodate legitimate Palestinian political rights.

The debate, in which 96 countries and organizations took part, ended with the adoption of resolutions calling for an international peace conference on the Middle East and for Israel's withdrawal from occupied territory, including Jerusalem. The Assembly also decided that the UN system should use the name 'Palestine' rather than 'Palestine Liberation Organization'.

CYPRUS. After talks with the Secretary-General in New York on 22-23 November, the leaders of the Greek Cypriot and Turkish Cypriot communities agreed to further meetings in a continuing effort to solve the Cyprus problem (see pp. 194, 197), and accepted Sr Pérez de Cuellar's invitation to meet him again in March 1989.

On 15 December, the Security Council approved unanimously a recommendation from the Secretary-General to extend the mandate of the UN Peacekeeping Force in Cyprus (UNFICYP) for a further six months.

WESTERN SAHARA. The Secretary-General informed the Security Council on 20 September that the parties to the conflict in Western Sahara—Morocco and the Polisario Front—had agreed to proposals for a peace settlement (see pp. 237-9, 242-3); these had been put forward by the chairman of the Organization of African Unity (OAU) and himself, and the United Nations would be involved. The following month he appointed Hector Gros Espiell (Uruguay) as his special representative for Western Sahara with responsibility for monitoring the ceasefire and supervising a referendum in which the people would be able to exercise their right to self-determination.

NAMIBIA. The importance of early progress towards the independence of Namibia was stressed when the UN Council for Namibia held special meetings on 27 October to mark the start of a 'week of solidarity with the people of Namibia and their liberation movement, the South West Africa People's Organization (Swapo)'. The occasion marked the 22nd anniversary of the decision of the General Assembly to terminate South Africa's mandate over the territory and to make it a direct responsibility of the United Nations.

The UN Secretary-General welcomed the prospect of independence for Namibia following the news that the interested parties in talks in Geneva (Angola, Cuba, South Africa and the United States) had confirmed their agreement with decisions reached. He urged all parties to redouble their efforts so that the UN plan to bring Namibia to independence (Security Council Resolution 435 of 1978) could be implemented. He also said that during his visit to southern Africa the previous month he had made a preliminary review of the practical requirements of the UN Transition Assistance Group (UNTAG), which would be involved in the UN plan.

After the General Assembly had adopted its customary series of resolutions on the Namibia question on 17 November, events moved rapidly to a resolution of outstanding differences between the interested parties. On 22 December agreements were signed at UN headquarters in New York providing for a full implementation of Resolution 435 starting on 1 April 1989 in the context of a phased withdrawal of Cuban troops from Angola (see pp. 285–6 and DOCUMENTS). On the day before this historic occasion, the UN Commissioner for Namibia, Bernt Carlsson of Sweden, was killed in the Lockerbie air disaster in Scotland (see OBITUARY).

NOBEL PEACE PRIZE. The announcement of 29 September that the Nobel Peace Prize for 1988 had been awarded to the UN Peacekeeping Forces was greeted by the Secretary-General as a 'source of pleasure and pride to the organization'. In a statement to the General Assembly, Sr Pérez de Cuellar said that, in making the award, the Nobel Committee had recognized that the quest for peace was a universal undertaking involving all the nations and peoples of the world. The award was a tribute, he said, to the idealism of all who had served the United Nations and in particular to the 'valour and sacrifices of those who had contributed, and continued to contribute, to its peacekeeping operations.' The President of the Assembly, Sr Caputo, said the new international climate provided expanded opportunities for UN peacekeeping operations, and the award was a tribute to the organization and to the Secretary-General.

Nearly 500,000 personnel from 58 countries had served in peacekeeping operations since their inception, of whom 733 had lost their lives. At the time of the award 35 countries were providing peacekeeping forces.

The Secretary-General accepted the Peace Prize at ceremonies in Oslo on 10 December. He was accompanied by the former UN Under Secretary-General, Sir Brian Urquhart, who for many years had supervised UN peacekeeping operations, and by his successor in that responsibility, Under Secretary-General Marrack Goulding. Also present were officers, men and women representing current UN peacekeeping operations.

OTHER UN ACTIVITIES AND AGENCIES

ECONOMIC AND SOCIAL. The Economic and Social Council concluded on 3 August the work of its two regular sessions of 1988. Consideration was given to the major problems of economic and social policy, focusing in particular on the 'highly precarious' international economic situation and waning confidence in current debt-management strategy. During the second session, which opened in Geneva on 6 July, a recurring theme was the need to revitalize the Council in order to make it truly the principal UN organ devoted to economic and social questions.

The Council's traditional debate on international economic and social policy examined the impact of structural imbalances in the world economy on the developing countries. The discussion was based on the World Economic Survey 1988, which provided a review and analysis of the global economic situation, including the effects of indebtedness on the international economic environment (see also Pt. XVIII, Ch. 1).

The Council decided to initiate a comprehensive process for the preparation of an international development strategy for the fourth UN Development Decade (1991-2000). It urged all UN bodies to develop and implement comprehensive policies for the advancement of women and to incorporate them in their medium-term plans, statements of objectives, programmes and other major policy statements. The preferential treatment accorded to the least-developed countries was extended to the occupied Palestinian territories, and Mozambique was also included in the list.

The Council called for a series of studies on environmental issues, with special attention to hazardous wastes, and urged the speedy completion of a global convention on the control of trans-boundary movements of such wastes. It also urged Governments to ensure that transnational corporations should cease to contribute to maintaining the policies of apartheid in South Africa and its illegal occupation of Namibia, and condemned those transnationals which continued systematically to circumvent the laws imposed by the Governments of their home countries. Particular concern was expressed that some transnationals had relocated environmentally-dangerous operations in developing countries.

TRUSTEESHIP. The Trusteeship Council (consisting of the five permanent members of the Security Council) began a four-week session in New York on 10 May, during which it reviewed progress on the attainment of self-government, as well as economic and social developments, in the UN Trust Territory of the Pacific Islands, the last remaining such territory under the International Trusteeship System. It also examined the report of the administering authority, the United States, as well as written petitions and communications from concerned individuals and organizations.

Of the Territory's four administrative entities, the Marshall Islands, the Federated States of Micronesia and the Northern Mariana Islands had reached agreement with the United States on their future status as US dependencies. According to the US administering authority, voters in the fourth, Belau, had finally approved a 'compact of free association' with the United States in two referendums held in 1987 (see AR 1987, pp. 357-8); these had been observed by UN missions, which had reported that they had been conducted fairly. On that basis the Trusteeship Council at its mid-1988 meeting approved the compact by a vote of three (USA, Britain and France) to one (USSR), with China not taking part. However, in the absence of precise precedent it was believed that formal termination of the Pacific trusteeship required endorsement by the Security Council, in which any of the five permanent members could exercise a veto. Moreover, the procedure by which the compact had secured referendum approval in 1987 continued to be subject to legal challenge by local opponents who saw it as conflicting with the anti-nuclear provisions of the Belau constitution (see also pp. 373-4).

HUMAN RIGHTS. The United Nations marked the 40th anniversary of the adoption of the Universal Declaration of Human Rights on 10 December. Commemorated in a solemn ceremony at the General Assembly on 8 December, the anniversary was also marked by a series of discussions and symposia organized by the United Nations and others and by concerts, exhibits, films, TV documentaries and celebrity readings in New York, Geneva, Vienna and other UN offices around the world from 1 to 9 December.

The Universal Declaration was in great part the work of the Commission on Human Rights, with the valuable contribution of such members as Eleanor Roosevelt (USA), Charles Malik (Lebanon), René Cassin (France), Zafrullah Khan (Pakistan) and others. It was adopted by the General Assembly without a dissenting vote in Paris in 1948.

FINANCIAL AND MONETARY. The 43rd annual joint meetings of the board of governors of the International Monetary Fund (IMF) and the World Bank were held in West Berlin on 27-29 September. In its annual report the IMF announced that it expected to be a net lender of money in 1989 for the first time since 1985. In recent years there had been a sustained criticism of the Fund because it had become the recipient of funds from developing countries in repayment of loans. The IMF already had a net flow of funds to Africa, and Japan announced a multi-billion dollar boost to IMF lending to developing countries. Michael Camdessus, the Fund's Managing Director, proposed a five-year programme to tackle Third World debt problems.

The World Bank issued a statement deploring deforestation and promising the highest priority for the protection of the tropical jungles following a meeting with environmental pressure groups.

The UN Conference on Trade and Development on 2 September called for a cut of at least 30 per cent in the debts owed by Third World countries to commercial banks, since existing measures for dealing with the debt crisis were proving inadequate.

WORLD HEALTH ORGANIZATION. Some 1,200 delegates representing the 166 member states of the World Health Organization (WHO) met in Geneva, on 2 May 1988 for the 41st World Health Assembly. On 4 May the Assembly approved the appointment of Dr Hiroshi Nakajima (Japan) as the new WHO Director-General, replacing Dr Halfdan Mahler (Denmark), who had held the post for three successive five-year terms. Dr Nakajima was previously director of WHO's regional office for the Western Pacific in Manila.

On the final day of its proceedings (13 May), the Assembly adopted by consensus a resolution stating that respect for the rights and dignities of those infected with the human immunodeficiency virus (HIV) was vital to the success both of national programmes and of global strategy to combat the spread of the acquired immune deficiency syndrome (AIDS). It was subsequently announced that 1 December 1988 would be the first World Day on AIDS aimed at promoting information and education on the disease. (For WHO statistics on AIDS, see Pt. XIV, Ch. 1.)

FOOD AND AGRICULTURE ORGANIZATION. Early in 1988 it became apparent that the financial crisis in the FAO was deepening. As a result, the United Kingdom and Denmark separately decided to delay their respective financial contributions, while the US representative, Fred Eckert, demanded details of administrative practices inside the agency. Reports indicating a serious budget deficit were finally confirmed at a meeting of the FAO Council in May.

At the meeting a 13-member group of experts was set up and given the responsibility of first setting out the 'role, priorities, goals and strategies of the FAO', and secondly, recommending 'measures to strengthen the organization's capacity to respond to the demands of the future with greater efficiency and effectiveness'.

In September, the FAO Director-General, Edouard Saouma, warned that extensive drought in North America, floods in parts of Africa and Asia and the danger to crops from locusts in Africa posed a threat to world food security. 'While there is no risk of a world food crisis in the immediate future', he said, 'there is every reason for concern for the next year or so'.

Chapter 2

THE COMMONWEALTH

FOLLOWING the turbulence of 1987 over South African sanctions and the lapsing of Fiji's membership, 1988 was in Commonwealth terms internationally and domestically calmer. Only four of the 48 member-countries acquired a new Head of Government—Cyprus, Papua New Guinea, Sri Lanka and Western Samoa. Hopes of an early return to membership of Fiji faded as racial tensions there showed no sign of abating and a new constitution failed to materialize (see p. 372).

Politically, South Africa remained the subject of widest concern to the Commonwealth. The eight-nation Commonwealth Committee of Foreign Ministers, set up by Heads of Government in Vancouver in 1987, met twice—in Lusaka (1-2 February) and Toronto (2-3 August). Britain, which had declined to join the Committee, remained aloof from the rest of the Commonwealth on South Africa, preferring to work mainly bilaterally in terms of economic help and military training for the front-line states, while supporting Commonwealth schemes of education and civilian training for South African blacks inside and outside the country.

The Committee of Foreign Ministers was set up to further Commonwealth programmes in the region as well as to intensify sanctions. In 1988 no new sanctions were put in place, but studies into their effect showed that South Africa had become particularly vulnerable to financial pressures. Appeals were made to persuade countries to tighten existing sanctions. Preliminary findings showed that the squeeze by the banks, particularly those in the US, was hurting the South African economy more than any other sanction. Countries circumventing or breaking sanctions were named: Japan, Taiwan, West Germany, Switzerland, Italy, Spain and Turkey. The Foreign Ministers, chaired by Joe Clark of Canada, considered in Toronto ways of countering South African censorship and propaganda. Canada put down $1 million for this work.

Although the Commonwealth was not directly involved in the negotiations between South Africa, Angola and Cuba that led in December to agreement on the withdrawal of Cuban troops and the independence of Namibia (see pp. 285–6 and DOCUMENTS), it stepped up its training programmes to prepare Namibians to help administer their country. By the end of the year Commonwealth-supported training programmes for Namibian exiles and South Africans had benefited 8,000 people. The offer of Commonwealth membership for an independent Namibia had been lying on the table ever since it was made by Heads of Government at their Jamaica summit in 1975.

Many Commonwealth countries were concerned about growing indications that Britain was quietly downgrading the Commonwealth in its foreign policy considerations. Tensions over South Africa strained the relationship between Britain and the Commonwealth secretariat under Secretary-General Shridath Ramphal, now in the last two years of his third five-year term. The problem went deeper: an influential, if small, right-wing lobby in London argued that the Commonwealth was becoming increasingly irrelevant to British interests and, worse, served to divert the country's attention from more pressing considerations.

Manifestations of this thinking emerged in British Government attitudes to the budgeting of the secretariat and funding for the Commonwealth Institute in London. At the biennial meeting of senior officials in Seychelles (23-25 November) Britain sought zero growth in a secretariat budget that was in danger of being cut in real terms by the imposition of fierce rent increases for buildings occupied during the years-long renovation of Marlborough House. Britain withdrew its paper on the subject in Seychelles when other countries argued that the budget should not suffer because local rents were being raised. In the case of the Institute, almost wholly British-funded, severe cutbacks forced senior staff layoffs and reductions in programmes of an organization primarily aimed at educating the British public about the Commonwealth.

In September a memorandum signed in London set up what was to be known as the Commonwealth of Learning, intended to promote cooperation in distance learning from its base in Vancouver. A board of 15—nine nominees of Governments and six individuals—met in November and elected as president Dr James Maraj (Trinidad), a former Commonwealth assistant secretary-general and vice-chancellor of the University of the South Pacific. Eight Governments pledged a total of £15 million to the project.

The expert group on climatic change and sea level rise held its first meeting in London (19-20 May) under the chairmanship of Dr Martin Holdgate (Britain), director-general of the International Union for Conservation of Nature and Natural Resources. Its members came from nine countries. In 1988 two serious cyclones in Bangladesh underlined the urgency of their work.

Another Commonwealth preoccupation—the vulnerability of small states, subject of a report in 1985—was highlighted by the unsuccessful invasion of Maldives on 7 November by a group of mercenaries from Sri Lanka (see p. 327).

The Commonwealth scheme by which the UN missions of small states were able to maintain a permanent presence in New York by sharing a single office—an idea put forward and first funded by Australia—proved such a success that in 1988 the office was doubled to accommodate more missions. It now housed the representatives of ten countries from the Caribbean, Pacific and African regions.

Two Commonwealth programmes attracted increased funding. Before the Finance Ministers meeting (21-22 September) the board of the Commonwealth Fund for Technical Cooperation agreed in Nicosia that 1988-89 expenditure should rise to £23.2 million and in Apia (Western Samoa) the Commonwealth Youth Affairs Council pledged a 20 per cent rise in funds to £1.18 million for the Commonwealth Youth Programme.

In September Commonwealth magistrates and judges met in Ottawa and parliamentarians held their annual conference in Canberra. In October publishers and editors of the Commonwealth Press Union met in Victoria Falls, Zimbabwe.

An important Commonwealth development in London was the coming together of two of the oldest voluntary organizations—the Royal Commonwealth Society (which dated back to 1868) and the Victoria League for Commonwealth Friendship (founded in 1901). The two formed a joint body to be known as the Commonwealth Trust and planned to turn their headquarters, now renamed Commonwealth House, into an increasingly important centre of activity for Commonwealth non-governmental organizations. Sir Zelman Cowan, former Governor-General of Australia, became the Trust's first president and Sir Peter Marshall, who retired as Commonwealth Deputy Secretary-General (Economic) on 31 December, was elected chairman.

Sir Peter's successor at the secretariat was Peter Unwin, former British ambassador to Denmark. Another major secretariat change was the replacement of Hugh Craft as director of the international affairs division by another Australian, Max Gaylard. Charles Gunawardene (Sri Lanka) retired as director of the information division and was succeeded by his deputy, Mrs Patsy Robertson (Jamaica).

Chapter 3

THE EUROPEAN COMMUNITY

BY the end of 1988 it was clear that the European Community had rediscovered its political momentum. A package of measures agreed at the Brussels summit in February had laid to rest for at least four years the budget problems which had dogged Community affairs since the 1973 enlargement; nearly half the legislation needed to create a single European market had been adopted by Ministers; and the target date of 1992 had come to exert a powerful influence on European business and industry as well as on the general public, at least in some member countries. The world's attitudes towards the Community reflected this new sense of commitment. The US Government and Japanese industry underlined their fears of 'fortress Europe'; the Efta countries nervously considered the implications for them of a genuine common market; while the Soviet Union and the countries of Eastern Europe sought closer economic ties with the Community.

There remained plenty of problems to resolve. Indeed, as progress was made in clearing away obstacles to the single European market, new ones became more apparent. Harmonization of indirect taxes presented special difficulties, as did the removal of frontier formalities between member states. Both aims trespassed on jealously-guarded areas of national competence. The development of monetary policy also promised fireworks ahead as a special committee considered the feasibility and desirability of a European central bank. At a speech in Bruges in September, British Prime Minister Mrs Margaret Thatcher made clear her own reservations about these developments.

DELORS PACKAGE. After two unsuccessful meetings in the previous year, and somewhat gloomy prognostications over the chances for progress, Community leaders finally agreed to a complex package of budgetary measures at the Brussels European Council of 11-13 February. Their decisions were largely based on the proposals put forward one year earlier by the European Commission under its President, Jacques Delors (France). The summit decision completed the triptych which M. Delors had seen as essential to the reinvigoration of the Community: adoption of the Single European Act which modified the Treaty of Rome (see AR 1987, pp. 534-8), commitment to the creation of the European single market by the end of 1992 and agreement on new resources and new priorities for the Community budget.

The Brussels summit agreed a substantial increase in the size of the Community budget. The ceiling for total spending was set at 1.3

per cent of total Community gross national product, compared with current spending of about 1.18 per cent, thus providing an increase over and above that allowed by economic growth. A fourth income source relating to GNP was added to the traditional 'own resources' of import levies, customs duties and up to 1.4 per cent rate of VAT. There was still special provision to reduce the level of the UK contribution in so far as this was distorted by Britain's small share of Community agricultural expenditure. Community leaders also accepted a major shift in priorities away from agricultural spending towards regional and employment-related expenditure in the less prosperous regions. There was a commitment almost to double the structural funds between 1988 and 1992, up from 7,400 MECU[1] to 13,000 MECU a year, providing new investment, especially in the southern parts of the Community and in Ireland, amounting to 52,000 MECU over the five-year period.

This diversion of resources to the less prosperous regions was to be accompanied by the introduction of stricter budget discipline in agriculture to be achieved by a series of specific measures whereby the level of farm price support would diminish as production rose. The summit agreed that the annual rate of increase in spending on the farm price guarantee budget should not exceed 74 per cent of the growth in GNP, implying a gradual reduction of agricultural expenditure as a proportion of the budget as a whole. For cereals, oilseeds and protein products, guarantee thresholds were set. Should production rise above these levels, the intervention prices would be cut the following year. Better budget management would be assured in agriculture with the development of an early warning system to detect rising expenditure trends in good time.

The Brussels summit was a triumph for Chancellor Kohl of West Germany, as president of the Council for the first half of 1988, and also for M. Delors himself, who had been instrumental in developing a formula acceptable to all 12 member countries. The package was welcomed in the European Parliament by unanimous adoption of a special resolution at its March session. By the time of the Hanover summit in June, the task of giving legislative form to the package was largely complete and M. Delors had been nominated to continue in office when his four-year term ended early in 1989.

SINGLE EUROPEAN MARKET. December 1988 marked the midway point between the launching of the idea of the single European market in 1985 and the target date of 1992. By the year's end, the Commission had submitted 90 per cent of the 279 proposals for legislation which would allow the removal of barriers within the Community and the

[1] Million European Currency Units. In January 1988 1 MECU=£695,000; in December 1988 1 MECU=£641,000.

Council of Ministers had adopted about 40 per cent into Community law. At the Hanover summit in June the heads of government were able to declare that progress towards the completion of the internal market 'has now reached the point where it is irreversible, a fact accepted by those engaged in economic and social life'.

A study carried out on the Commission's behalf assessed the impact of 'non-Europe'. Known as the Cecchini Report, this analysis examined the costs to business and industry of the barriers existing within the common market. The authors estimated that the economic gains from the creation of the single European market could amount to 200,000 MECU or more. This would add about 5 per cent to the Community's GDP, create new jobs and bring down consumer prices by an estimated 6 per cent over the years to 1992. Although some observers argued that the study ignored the negative employment impact of increased competition in the market place, there was no denying the widespread influence of the 1992 idea on commerce and industry as well as on politics. At a political level it became one of the major themes of the French presidential election; at a commercial level it was a widely-used justification for takeover bids, mergers and working arrangements between companies. The force of the idea went far beyond the technical measures adopted within the Council. Council decisions remained essential however, and the use of qualified majority voting, which had been brought in by the Single European Act, helped to accelerate the pace. A whole range of decisions of far-reaching economic importance was adopted during the year.

Among important decisions taken for a free internal market in goods were major framework directives for pressure vessels, toys, construction materials and machine safety. Measures were agreed for coordinating procedures for awarding public supply contracts, and for liberalization of the road transport market. The mutual recognition of professional qualifications after three years training was also adopted by Ministers.

In June the Council of Ministers reached agreement on the liberalization of short-term capital movements. Within two years member states would free all capital movements between them with safeguards to counter short-term speculative movements; would introduce the principle of extensive liberalization to and from third countries; and would establish a mechanism to support member states' balance of payments in case of difficulty. Spain, Portugal, Greece and Ireland would have until the end of 1992 to introduce the changes, with a further three years' transition for Greece and Portugal should this prove necessary. The new measures would effectively mean the end of exchange controls on private and commercial capital movement. This measure provided an important basis for a series of decisions in the financial services sector, covering non-life insurance, banking standards and investment services. The question of supervision was usually the most difficult aspect of these measures; the principle of home country control was usually accepted, with certain rules applied by the host country on matters such as advertising.

Significantly, it was in areas where majority voting was not provided that the slowest progress was made. This included fiscal harmonization. The Commission was convinced of the need to narrow the discrepancies between VAT rates in different member states and to standardize excise duties, regarding this as essential if the internal market were to be created without frontier controls and economic distortions. The Commission had proposed two bands for VAT, a normal rate of 14-20 per cent and a reduced rate of 4-9 per cent. The main opposition to these proposals came from Britain and France. The British were avowedly keen to maintain a zero rate for foodstuffs and other essentials and argued that the divergencies between VAT rates would gradually disappear as a natural result of a liberalized market. The French Government was eager to see progress on taxation of savings as part of the freeing of capital movements within the Community and did not put a high priority on VAT harmonization. An informal meeting of Finance Ministers in Greece towards the end of the year failed to break the deadlock.

Outgoing Commission vice-president Lord Cockfield (UK), who had been the architect of the internal market programme and had been responsible for piloting it through the Council, expressed his own disappointment at the slow progress on fiscal reform and also on the reluctance of member countries to facilitate frontier procedures for travellers or ensure the rights of citizens from one member country to take up residence in another.

AGRICULTURE. Although Ministers of Agriculture quickly agreed a political commitment to implement the disciplines demanded by the Brussels summit, adopting the necessary legislation proved much more difficult and it was not until late July that price proposals for 1988-89 were finally agreed, following numerous abortive marathon sessions. The Greek Government, by then holding the presidency of the Council of Ministers, surrendered its demand for substantial further increases in guaranteed prices for Greek farmers. There were similar difficulties at the end of the year, when the Council failed to agree measures for cutting the costs of the beef price support system in the face of British and Irish opposition; the question had to be carried forward into 1989. Beef remained a sector where official intervention stores remained relatively full, while for milk products and cereals the surpluses had virtually disappeared.

One of the conditions demanded by the German Government at the Brussels summit was that the Community should introduce its own set-aside scheme for taking agricultural land out of production. This was accordingly introduced during the year. The Council also discussed, without reaching conclusions, Commission proposals for a system of direct aid to farmers' incomes.

BUDGET. For the first time in many years, the Council of Ministers and the European Parliament, as the two arms of the budget authority, were able to agree the 1989 budget within the deadline laid down in the Treaty so that it could take effect from the beginning of the New Year. Furthermore, the budget provided for a cutback in agricultural spending for the first time in Community history. This reflected both the development of the common agricultural policy and strong world market prices consequent on the American drought. Total spending was set at 44,800 MECU compared with 43,800 MECU in 1988, with agriculture for the first time taking less than 60 per cent of the total.

Agreement on the 1988 budget, in contrast, had been a slower process. The conclusions of the Brussels summit had to be taken into account, presenting particular problems to the Italians because of the means used to calculate the additional GNP-related resource and the reimbursement mechanism for the UK. The budget was not finally adopted until the end of May.

ECONOMIC AND MONETARY UNION. Political opinion within the Community moved increasingly towards the idea of a European central bank. At the Hanover summit in June it was agreed, despite British reticence, to establish a committee under the chairmanship of Commission President Delors to study what positive steps were needed to achieve economic and monetary union. The committee was asked to report to the Heads of Government at their meeting in Madrid in June 1989. The committee was to include the presidents or governors of all the Community's central banks, as well as three coopted members.

Britain stayed outside the exchange-rate mechanism of the European Monetary System during the year, but in the autumn issued the Community's first ECU-denominated treasury bills—an indication, according to Mrs Thatcher, of Britain's practical rather than theoretical approach to economic and monetary integration.

EXTERNAL TRADE RELATIONS. The Community's progress towards a single market had far-reaching implications for its trading partners, who saw a threat that the European economy would increasingly seek to exclude others. On banking and insurance, for example, where financial institutions established in one EC country would be free to offer their services in all other member states, the Commission proposed that reciprocal access should be a condition for third-country banks and other financial institutions to set up in the Community. The Commission argued that this was consistent with work already under way in GATT and in discussions with the Efta countries. It was not a means of isolating the Community but of ensuring better access for European institutions to international markets.

Implications of the single market for Japanese companies were highlighted by the difficulties faced by Nissan in selling cars made in the United Kingdom into France, where the national authorities claimed that the local content of the finished product was not high enough for the cars to be described as being of Common Market origin. The Community continued its pressure on Japan to open up its markets, with bilateral talks on various specific issues such as pharmaceutical products and alcoholic drinks—discussions which produced a generally positive response from the Japanese. The tone of the relationship remained essentially calm.

Trade relations with the United States saw various skirmishes during the year, the European Airbus being the most contentious issue during the early months of 1988 and agricultural tensions growing during the autumn and winter. The conditions for European financial assistance to the Airbus programme were more clearly defined after ministerial discussions in March, and further work of definition was left to officials. The divisions over agriculture were more profound. The December mid-term review of the Uruguay Round of GATT in Montreal was dominated by the US demand for a phasing-out of farm subsidies, especially those paid for exports. The Community refused to accept this and the meeting was suspended until a further session in April 1989. The imposition of a Community ban on meat treated with hormones as from 1 January 1989 also heightened tension. This ban would affect about $100 million of US exports to Europe and the US Administration announced a series of reprisals on European exports. As the year ended, the Community was debating what its counter-reaction should be.

SOVIET UNION AND EASTERN EUROPE. The year saw a major breakthrough in relations between the Community and the state-trading countries of Eastern Europe. Throughout the 1980s the Community had maintained its 'twin-track' approach, insisting on the need to negotiate individual agreements tailored to the conditions of each East European country as well as more general agreements with Comecon itself. This approach came to fruition as diplomatic relations were established between the Community and the USSR, East Germany, Bulgaria, Czechoslovakia, Hungary and Poland.

Negotiations with Hungary resulted in an agreement that all import quotas on Hungarian exports to the Community should be abolished by 1995 in return for a Hungarian guarantee not to discriminate against Community products and a promise to provide better facilities for businessmen from member countries. An agreement on trade in manufactures was also signed with Czechoslovakia (see p. 401) and exploratory talks opened for trade agreements with Poland, Bulgaria, the USSR and East Germany. Continuing talks with Romania made little progress. A joint declaration with Comecon was signed in June on the establishment of formal relations between the two organizations and the creation of a framework for future cooperation.

POLITICAL COOPERATION. The Community remained an interested observer rather than direct participant in the major political changes taking place in the world. It welcomed the Soviet withdrawal from Afghanistan, the end of the war between Iran and Iraq and the increasing momentum towards disarmament. Its most direct concern was over the situation in the Middle East, and especially the deteriorating conditions in the Israeli-occupied territories. Ministers urged the setting-up of an international peace conference under UN auspices. However, attempts by the Greek presidency at the Rhodes summit to persuade the Community to take a more active role in the Middle East peace process were rejected after objections from the northern countries. The statements made by Yassir Arafat in December on the PLO position (see p. 205) were welcomed by the Community. The PLO leader had already taken his diplomatic initiative to the European Parliament, receiving a sympathetic reception at its October session.

Chapter 4

ORGANIZATION FOR ECONOMIC COOPERATION AND DEVELOPMENT—COUNCIL FOR MUTUAL ECONOMIC ASSISTANCE—NON-ALIGNED MOVEMENT

ORGANIZATION FOR ECONOMIC COOPERATION AND DEVELOPMENT

ADDRESSING the Assembly of the Council of Europe on 5 October 1988, OECD Secretary-General Jean-Claude Paye said that the previous 12 months had brought two surprises on the economic front. The first was the suddenness of the stock market shock in October 1987 (see AR 1987, pp. 507-10). The second was the fact that the grave dangers then perceived for OECD countries had failed to materialize. Economic activity had remained extremely robust. The stock market crash had been absorbed without any major upset, thanks, in particular, to the abundant injection of liquidity by central banks. Economic confidence had been boosted by effective cooperation between monetary authorities and by the structural reforms undertaken almost everywhere.

Nevertheless, M. Paye pointed to a number of dangers. Inflation in OECD countries was rising. While the unemployment rate had fallen, the level of unemployment was still dangerously high in many OECD countries. Worrying imbalances in current international payments had been diminished by measures taken by the three strongest members—the USA, West Germany and Japan—but the deficits of other European countries, especially the UK, had grown worse. Not only structural reform but also efforts in micro-economic policy were needed, for instance in respect of education and training, new technology, environmental concerns, agriculture and financial regulation.

These views were echoed in OECD's official statements. Its *Economic Outlook*, issued in December, reported that conditions in the OECD area appeared more buoyant than at any time since the early 1970s. Output had been growing at an annual rate of over 4 per cent, led by private non-residential investment. Inflation, however, had edged up to an average of 4 per cent and to alarmingly high levels in North America and the UK. Financing the US trade deficit set a big problem, and there was a danger of further pressure on interest rates; this would dampen investment, threaten domestic solvency in the US, and worsen the load of debt on developing countries, which was still menacing despite some improvement. Fiscal restraint, structural economic reform, easing of rigidities in the labour market and continued international cooperation were keys to a more secure future.

Protectionism remained a current problem: the trade regimes of many OECD member countries were, on balance, less liberal than they had been ten years earlier. In particular, discriminatory measures targeted at newly-industrialized countries in Asia would raise prices, restrict choice and increase OECD countries' vulnerability to supply bottlenecks. At their May meeting OECD Ministers had expressed both hopes and anxieties about GATT and the future of the Uruguay Round. The climate of negotiation would inevitably be affected by the behaviour of member countries themselves; it was therefore essential to roll back long-standing protectionist measures and to avoid misuse of anti-dumping and countervailing procedures.

OECD's annual *Employment Outlook*, published in September, noted that employment had continued to grow and unemployment was less than had been expected, but no further improvement in

Europe and Japan was foreseen. In many European countries unemployment had remained stable since 1983 despite substantial increases in job vacancies, suggesting that the mismatch between the skills of the unemployed and the needs of industry and commerce had grown worse. The answer lay in greater emphasis on education and training, aimed particularly at disadvantaged groups like the long-term unemployed and older workers, as well as in further structural reform. Unemployment rates varied greatly in different OECD countries, Ireland and Spain recording nearly 20 per cent, followed by Turkey, the Netherlands, Italy, Belgium and France, all with over 10 per cent, with the UK close behind; the OECD average in 1988 was 7.5 per cent, but its European component was over 10 per cent.

OECD's manpower and social affairs committee met at ministerial level in July. Its communique observed that new challenges for systems of social protection were emerging in an environment of high unemployment. At the same time, populations were ageing, family structures were changing, many more women were entering the labour market, and greater affluence led to demands for higher quality provision for education and health, while economic trends were leaving significant regions and population groups behind in poverty and disadvantage. Greater efficiency and flexibility in social services were needed.

The OECD Council issued in April a call for stronger cooperation and the removal of barriers in the field of science and technology. Necessary governmental action included support of basic research, education and training of scientific and technical personnel, international mobility of scientists and engineers, and open access to the results of research, data banks and scientific meetings.

Members of OECD's Development Assistance Committee (DAC), joined by representatives of the World Bank, the IMF and the UN Development Programme at their annual high-level meeting in December, agreed to review in 1989 the major development issues ahead and to seek consensus on how aid programmes should be structured for the 1990s. They expressed concern at the recent faltering of total aid volume, thanks mainly to cuts in US aid. Total net disbursements by DAC countries had declined in real terms by 2 per cent between 1986 and 1987, despite a big increase in Japan's overseas aid, opening the prospect of its becoming the world's largest single aid source. The DAC identified a whole series of problems likely to affect the development environment in the coming decade, including carry-over of heavy debt burdens, technological advance which left commodity-dependent, low-income countries at a disadvantage, environmental degradation and the need for international help in basic education, industrial training and primary health. Members of the committee expressed strong support for a common set of principles which had been devised for the appraisal, selection, design and monitoring of all development projects, and undertook to review their own programmes in the light of them.

COUNCIL FOR MUTUAL ECONOMIC ASSISTANCE

A 'joint declaration on the establishment of official relations', valid in the 17 languages of the two organizations, was signed on 25 June in Luxembourg by the chairman of the Executive Committee of the Council for Mutual Economic Assistance (CMEA or Comecon) Rudolf Rogliček and the president of the European Community's Council of Ministers, Hans-Dietrich Genscher. For the two other signatories—Vyacheslav Sychev, Secretary of Comecon, and Willy de Clercq, European Commissioner for External Relations—it was the personal culmination of negotiations initiated by the Comecon summit of 1984 (see AR 1984, p. 360).

Taken at its face value, the declaration appeared less committing to the two sides than the draft which had almost reached finality in the 1970s: also started at Comecon's request in 1973 (see AR 1973, pp. 377-8), those discussions had foundered in 1980 as a political consequence of the Soviet invasion of Afghanistan (see AR 1980, pp. 363-4). The agreement then emergent would have named specific areas of EC-Comecon cooperation and would have been signed by the seven European members of Comecon together with the Comecon Secretary. The 1988 declaration had virtually only one substantive, but very broad, undertaking—of 'cooperation in areas which fall within their respective spheres of competence and where there is a common interest'. The differences between the negotiations of the late 1970s and the late 1980s testified, however, to the latter's more extensive applicability to East-West economic relations in Europe.

In the first place, the environment for those relations had by 1988 been greatly improved in political terms, symbolized by the year's superpower summit. The economic context, secondly, had been transformed by Mikhail Gorbachev's *perestroika*. Commenting on the declaration, I. Frantseva observed in *Izvestia* (6 September) that 'implementing economic reforms in the CMEA countries will make the existing relations even more complete'. 'Economic relations,' she went on, 'cannot be confined to trade...the launching of joint ventures is a major area of potential development.' The very breadth of the joint declaration allowed exploration of all the new features of market mechanisms in planned economies, notably those measures which dissolved the monopoly of national

Ministries of Foreign Trade and opened domestic territory to the installation of Western equity capital. Thirdly, whereas only seven Comecon signatories had been envisaged in 1979, eight of the 10 full members had meanwhile established diplomatic relations with the Commission (Romania and Mongolia being the exceptions) and all seven European members had instituted negotiations for bilateral treaties.

In November 1988 the European Community concluded an agreement on trade and commercial and economic cooperation with Hungary (see p. 397) and one on trade in industrial products with Czechoslovakia (some import restrictions to be lifted in return for undertakings by Czechoslovakia on business access and information). Progress was still not made on a trade and economic cooperation agreement with Romania (see AR 1987, p. 393), partly because of Western distaste for Ceauşescu's domestic policy (see p. 127), but informal discussions continued with Bulgaria and Poland (pending establishment of a formal negotiating mandate) and were initiated with the GDR and the USSR. At the July meeting of the Foreign Affairs Council the Community stressed that such agreements must be concluded on the basis of reciprocity and mutual benefit. This view was endorsed at the EC summit in Rhodes in December.

Finally, the 1988 negotiations settled the long-standing dispute over the inclusion of West Berlin within the Community's common external tariff and other instruments. The Federal Republic's chairmanship of the European Council in those final months to June was decisive and included a personal visit by Herr Genscher to Moscow in May. The solution was a parallel statement (*zayavlenie*) by all Comecon Members that 'nothing in the declaration (*deklaratsiya*) affected the Quadripartite Agreement on Berlin of 3 September 1971'.

The new openness of European Comecon members to the West was illustrated not only by further concessions to foreign companies (limitation to minority share-holding being relaxed in 1988 in Poland and the USSR) but also by plans to open duty-free zones in Cracow and Szczecin-Swinojuście in Poland and at Soviet Baltic, Black Sea and Pacific ports. It contrasted with their persistent inhibitions to exchanges among themselves.

The worst bilateral examples were between the three most-industralized members, Czechoslovakia, the GDR and Poland. In November Czechoslovakia imposed severe limits on the export of consumer goods by individual travellers. Poles were predominantly affected and a Czechoslovak reporter (in *Rudé právo*, 19 November) observed of the confiscated products at the border railway station: 'Sacks of oranges, sweets, ground coconut, cocoa powder, coffee, peanuts, toothpastes, shampoos, cases of bananas, Christmas confectionery, tinned meat, semolina: all of that collected within a day.' A Polish diplomatic protest proved unavailing. Similar divergence of prices and availabilities clogged the implementation of 'direct links' at the commercial level, as promoted by the 1987 Comecon summit (see AR 1987, p. 393). A Czechoslovak enterprise director wrote that cooperation with East Germany was precluded because for his product the import price of components was twice the price of the finished product; he added: 'This nonsense will last until 1990 because the contract is valid until 1990 and the GDR insists on its fulfilment' (*Rudé právo*, 8 November).

A Hungarian authority on intra-Comecon relations, Kálmán Pécsi, interviewed in *Magyar Nemzet* (12 November), 'considered the question whether Hungary should leave Comecon and whether this would improve our situation' and pertinently asked 'when the Western world is trying to get into the Soviet market, why should it be an ambition of ours to leave it?' While concluding that Hungary should not quit Comecon, he called for some bilateral schemes to be abrogated (the Nagymaros dam with Czechoslovakia, the exploitation of Soviet oil and gas at Tengiz and Yamburg and car-industry cooperation with the USSR) and for 'small-scale integration' to be fostered transnationally between enterprises, perhaps by an 'East European Council for Corporate Cooperation.' He continued: 'The principle of mutual economic assistance is out-of-date and should be replaced by mutual efficiency.'

Only towards the end of the year did such strictures gain some prospective action within the Comecon organization, seemingly due to the personal efforts of József Marjai, just retired as Deputy Premier and participating for the last time as Hungarian permanent representative. The 129th session of the Executive Committee (Moscow, 10-11 October) resolved with two dissentients (GDR and Romania) to form 'a common market within CMEA member states'; the GDR accepted steps towards this provided that it could choose which measures to apply to its own practice. Even so, Mr Marjai afterwards admitted that the 'front lines' in the CMEA remained unchanged in the major issues and only small 'cosmetic' changes had taken place in minor issues. One major issue where different policies proved irreconcilable was the application of uniform price relativities in joint investment projects. The USSR and the three developing member countries, Cuba, Mongolia and Vietnam, maintained that accounts be on the basis of national prices and standards (i.e. qualities and the like). With that, Mr Marjai declared, Hungary lost all interest in joint ventures with those states and pointed to the consequence that investment in Ust-Ilimsk cellulose or Yamburg gas would cost far more per unit of product than Hungary could earn in normal trade with the USSR.

If the official communiques were a sufficient guide, the October meeting, the last Executive of the year, was the only one to get to grips with the key problems of inter-member pricing. The other top-level meetings carried on the rationalization of the organization called for by the 1987 summit (see AR 1987, pp. 392-3). The first Executive of the year in Moscow in February approved a reorganization of commissions and Secretariat (for 'systematic analyses and forecasts of the state of inter-member cooperation') as well as reviewing a series of sectoral configurations (electronics, transport and legal aspects of 'direct links'). The second Executive in May drafted a 'collective concept for the international socialist division of labour for 1991-2005' including special programmes for machine-building, radio engineering, electronics and chemicals, and approved shorter-term collaborative measures in the medical equipment and pharmaceutical industries and in restructuring information systems.

The only other Executive meeting took place as usual in conjunction with the 44th full session, held in Prague in July under the chairmanship of Lubomír Štrougal (soon to lose the Czechoslovak premiership—see p. 121). The session reverted to the standard practice (omitted in 1987) of welcoming observers from developing countries 'of socialist orientation', the full list for 1988 being Afghanistan, Angola, Ethiopia, Laos, Mozambique, Nicaragua, South Yemen and Yugoslavia. There was particular concern for Comecon's own less-developed full members—the special relationships discussed at the 1987 session being elaborated more fully with Cuba, Mongolia and Vietnam—while protocols were published on the statute of three mixed commissions comprising Comecon on the one hand and Angola, Ethiopia and South Yemen respectively on the other.

On a more commemorative note, the May Executive approved plans for celebrating the 40th anniversary of Comecon, founded in January 1949, but the epigraph was Kálmán Pécsi's in the interview cited above: 'According to the original concept of the socialist countries, they were going to form an integration in the region based on a customs union and a political confederation. In 1948 the Soviet Union pointed out that it did not agree with it and stressed that the flag of national independence should be raised high. Comecon was then formed on this ideological and political basis in 1949. Comecon meant national isolation, centralized management and basically its concept is still the same as it was 40 years ago.'

No major developments attended the two banks whose membership coincided with that of Comecon—the International Bank for Economic Cooperation and the International Investment Bank—although they could not have regarded with equanimity the increase in their members' debts through banks and non-trade credit. OECD and BIS estimates released in July showed these to have risen (on a gross basis) from $95,863 million at the end of 1986 to $110,646 million, at the end of 1987.

NON-ALIGNED MOVEMENT

JUST as the re-emergence of detente between the United States and the USSR and progress with the major regional conflicts led to a general sense of optimism in East and West, the Non-Aligned Movement (NAM) welcomed the 'positive developments on many fronts'. The INF treaty, the ceasefire in the Gulf, the Geneva accords on Afghanistan and the moves towards a settlement in Kampuchea were all taken as vindicating long-standing NAM policy positions. In the case of the regional conflicts, they also removed problems which throughout the 1980s had embarrassed and divided the movement. The result was that the major triennial conference of Foreign Ministers—held in Nicosia, Cyprus, from 5-10 September with 93 of the 102 members represented—was one of the most harmonious ever held and initiated a forward-looking review of the Movement's policy and its institutions.

There had also been significant progress in several minor regional disputes since the eighth NAM summit in Harare in 1986. Libyan troops withdrew from Chad, leaving the Aozou strip dispute to be resolved by peaceful means (see p. 233). Negotiations were resumed between Belize and Guatemala (see p. 97). Intercommunal talks between the two main groups in Cyprus were resumed under UN auspices (see p. 194). Finally, there was satisfaction with the new French policy towards New Caledonia (see p. 372), which opened up the possibility of a peaceful transition to independence for the territory. Thus in Nicosia the NAM Foreign Ministers were able to concentrate on the four substantive issues—disarmament, southern Africa, the Middle East and development—on which they were virtually unanimous. Even the one issue on which a hard choice had to be made, the venue for the next summit in 1989, was handled smoothly when the two rival contenders, Nicaragua and Indonesia, withdrew in favour of Yugoslavia.

While the INF treaty was warmly welcomed, it was seen only as a starting-point towards the elimination of 50 per cent of strategic weapons in the near future and a nuclear-weapon-free world subsequently. Earlier in the year there had been an extraordinary ministerial meeting of the Coordinating Bureau in Havana (26-30 May), convened to prepare Non-Aligned positions for the UN General Assembly's third special session on disarmament (which opened on 31 May—see p. 377). The highest priority was given to a comprehensive nuclear test ban and support expressed for the steps taken by Indonesia, Mexico, Peru, Sri Lanka and Yugoslavia to initiate a review conference under the provisions of the 1963 Partial Test Ban Treaty to make it comprehensive.

At the Nicosia conference the Governments of Angola and Cuba obtained endorsement of their negotiations with South Africa and the US to seek a comprehensive settlement in south-western Africa (see DOCUMENTS). But the text suggested that Swapo was not fully confident of its position, as the section on Namibia repeated earlier attacks on 'the discredited policy of linkage' between independence for Namibia and the withdrawal of Cuban troops, without mentioning the negotiations at all. The Africa Fund, established at Harare to offer solidarity to the countries of southern Africa, made progress during the year, receiving pledges totalling US$250 million. The nine-member Fund committee held meetings in Brazzaville in January and in Lima in August. They were able to initiate cooperation with the Commonwealth, IFAD and the UN Special Committee Against Apartheid. Two projects with Commonwealth support, to assist the electrical industry in Botswana and the railways in Zambia, got under way. Plans also started for the Africa Fund to create a strategic relief reserve for the front-line states.

The conference of Foreign Ministers came in the period when the PLO was in intensive ferment, although its new policy positions had not yet been adopted. The section on the Middle East in the political declaration was toned down as compared with the 1986 Harare text, notably by the omission of negative references to Zionism; however, some remnants of the text from as far back as the 1979 Havana summit, condemning the Camp David agreements, were still retained. The uprising in the West Bank and Gaza was acknowledged in a new special section, which described the Palestinians' *intifada* as 'an irreversible historical event and tangible evidence of their determination to have a state of their own'. The conference called for the Security Council to place the territories under temporary UN supervision.

Throughout the year the NAM Committee of Nine on Palestine, the Coordinating Bureau in New York and representatives of Zimbabwe (currently holding the NAM chairmanship) were all highly active on the question of Palestine. The main issue for the first half of the year was to support the PLO against the call of the US Congress for the closure of its office in New York. The Bureau was responsible jointly with the Arab League for reconvening the UN General Assembly three times to maintain pressure on the US Administration, which eventually decided not to appeal against a US federal court ruling on 29 June that the US had an international obligation not to hinder UN meetings.

A similar dispute arose in December when US Secretary of State Shultz declined to issue a visa for PLO chairman Yassir Arafat to address the General Assembly. This time the delegates resolved the matter by transferring the Assembly to Geneva, where Mr Arafat was duly heard. In November President Mugabe, acting as the NAM chairman, welcomed the Palestine National Council's declaration of Palestinian independence (see p. 204 and DOCUMENTS) and urged 'all members of the Movement seriously to consider recognizing the newly-proclaimed state'.

The political optimism was matched by deep pessimism over economic questions, although there was some progress in advancing NAM policy positions. The ministerial meeting on the global system of trade preferences, held in Belgrade in April, was able to finalize an agreement, which was signed by 48 Non-Aligned and other developing countries. The standing ministerial committee for economic cooperation, set up at the eighth summit, held its first substantive meeting in Harare in July and produced an analysis of the history of North-South dialogue together with powerful arguments for its revitalization. The 'South-South' Commission also started work with meetings in Mexico City on the Uruguay Round and in Kuala Lumpur on debt. On the other hand, neither the NAM Action Programme nor the Group of 77's Caracas Programme appeared to make any progress in 1988.

Chapter 5

COUNCIL OF EUROPE—WESTERN EUROPEAN UNION—EUROPEAN FREE TRADE ASSOCIATION—NORDIC COUNCIL

COUNCIL OF EUROPE

As the Council of Europe prepared to celebrate its 40th anniversary in 1989, the approaching challenges of 1992 resulted in some introspection about the Council of Europe's future. There was a feeling that the Council of Europe was being bypassed by the constant evolution of the European Community. The traditional distinction between 'integration' Europe (the Community) and 'co-operation' Europe (the Council of Europe) was felt to be no longer realistic. Furthermore, attempts to give the Council of Europe the role of a bridge between the Community and non-Community countries had not overcome the latter's preference for negotiating bilateral agreements with the Community or using other multilateral frameworks such as Efta.

The Council of Europe's activities fell within three main

areas of its distinctive competence: human rights, problems of society and European cultural identity. In the field of human rights the European Court of Human Rights delivered an important judgment (*Brogan and others*) in November that, although the detention of a person under the United Kingdom's Prevention of Terrorism (Temporary Provisions) Act 1984 was inspired by the legitimate aim of protecting the community from terrorism, detention for four days and six hours in police custody without appearance before a judge or other judicial officer impaired the very essence of the right to prompt judicial control protected by Article 5(3) of the European Convention on Human Rights. The UK Government entered a temporary derogation under Article 13 so that the Act remained effective and enforced, while entering into discussions with the British judiciary on whether a practicable way could be found to implement the Court's decision without losing a valuable weapon against terrorism.

On the problems of society, the Council of Europe's Parliamentary Assembly commended a revised code of social security and approved reports on the fight against drugs, AIDS in prisons, territorial asylum, improving community relations and family policy. Concern for the family was the central message in the address given to the Parliamentary Assembly by Pope John Paul II in October.

In the cultural field, one of the most important subjects was the preparation of a convention on trans-frontier television broadcasting due for signature in 1989. The technological changes in broadcasting underlined the importance of agreeing Europe-wide standards in an area which had hitherto been regulated by widely-differing national codes. European Cinema and Television Year 1988, jointly sponsored by the Council of Europe, was an appropriate background to the agreement finally reached in Stockholm in November which included a limitation on the number of commercial breaks in programmes shown across national boundaries. A French-inspired move to set quotas for European-made programmes was not adopted. In October the Parliamentary Assembly approved a draft charter for regional and minority languages prepared by the standing conference of local and regional authorities of Europe.

Two important campaigns reflecting the wider concerns of the Council of Europe were concluded in 1988. The Campaign for Countryside drew attention to the problems of the rural world, with a large number of events throughout member countries ranging from international conferences to local competitions and exhibitions at agricultural shows. The first prize in the 'Citizen's Europe' journalism competition, awarded in 1988 for work on the theme 'a better life in the countryside', was won by two British journalists, Debbie Bartlett and Jane Flatt of the *Eastern Daily Press*.

The European Campaign on North-South Interdependence and Solidarity was inaugurated at the Parliamentary Assembly in January by King Juan Carlos of Spain, the campaign's honorary president. The Assembly also saw a recorded video message from President Abdou Diouf of Senegal. A number of round table discussions on different themes took place in the early part of the year, including a conference in London on debt (February), leading up to the Madrid conference of parliamentarians and non-governmental organizations (June). The latter conference closed on 3 June with the adoption of the Madrid Appeal, which called for measures to revitalize international trade and economic growth and reduce the burden of debt to the benefit of the world's poorest countries. The Appeal requested an increase in development aid designed to foster self-reliance and help create a world where every citizen could be free from hunger, oppression and discrimination. The benefits to the North of such measures to strengthen and protect the economies of the South were underlined in the document which also referred extensively to the need to take full account of the role played by women in the productive resources of the Third World, and to the importance of giving recognition and encouragement to participation in development activities by young people.

On a more domestic scale, San Marino became the 22nd member state of the Council of Europe in October. Finland was expected to accede in 1989, thereby completing the maximum possible number of members among the sovereign plural democracies in Europe. The reports debated in the Parliamentary Assembly on wider international issues tended to concentrate on human rights questions, for example, the situation of Jews in the Soviet Union or Palestinian refugees in the occupied territories. Particular concern was expressed over the situation in Romania (see p. 127) during several of the debates during the Parliamentary Assembly session in October.

The year opened with a serious threat to unity as the Assembly condemned the French policy—introduced by the conservative Government of Jacques Chirac after a spate of outrages in the autumn of 1986—of requiring visas from nationals of countries outside the Community (except Switzerland and Liechtenstein). The January part-session of the Assembly was cut short in protest, and throughout the year many Assembly committee meetings were held outside France as a further sign of displeasure with the attitude of the French authorities. Nevertheless the Assembly avoided any action which would have looked like interference in the French presidential and parliamentary election campaigns. The visa measures were rescinded by the new French Government in December, leaving Turkey as the only Council of Europe member state whose nationals still required a visa to enter France.

WESTERN EUROPEAN UNION

ON 14 December Spain and Portugal acceded to WEU, having accepted the rights and duties prescribed by the (modified) Brussels Treaty whereby it was founded. It was 'an historic day for Europe', said Sir Geoffrey Howe, the British Foreign Secretary, at an accession ceremony in London (the United Kingdom having succeeded the Netherlands in the chair of the Union in mid-year). 'As a club of nine'—the original seven being Belgium, France, West Germany, Italy, Luxembourg, the Netherlands and the UK—'we will be well placed to face the challenges of the 1990s in the security field'. Some hopeful observers thought that WEU, developing in parallel with the European Community, would come to serve as the latter's defensive and political arm.

The reactivation of WEU as the voice of Western Europe in all matters of defence, which had been proclaimed in 1984 (see AR 1984, p. 351; 1985, p. 341; 1986, pp. 353-4), proceeded mostly at governmental level in 1988, and much of the action was necessarily hidden from its 'parliament' and the public. An encouraging exception was the organization by WEU's Council of combined activity by European warships to protect navigation in the Gulf. While applauding this success, the parliamentary Assembly felt neglected. At its June session it passed a resolution lamenting its 'impossible position. . .because of the Council's reluctance to inform the Assembly of its activities', and 'noting that international public opinion is still hardly aware that WEU is being reactivated.' By the time of its December session the Assembly had been somewhat mollified, although it again demanded to know how the Council intended to implement the promised political impetus, and to be given much other information by the ministerial organ. A single permanent seat for all the institutions of the Union was badly needed, but member countries continued to disagree on its location.

There had been some plain speaking on defensive burden-sharing at the June session. David Mellor, a British Minister of State, claimed that the UK was spending well above the WEU average on defence and sharply criticized Italy, Luxembourg, Belgium and Denmark for inadequate contributions to common security. The Italian official spokesman protested that Italy had fulfilled its Nato undertaking to raise its defence budget by 3 per cent in real terms, and was embarking on a ten-year programme of strengthening its conventional forces.

Besides its constant concern for European cooperation in such matters as weapons procurement and standardization, WEU spent much thought and debate during 1988 on the consequences for Europe of the INF treaty and the evolving new relationship between the USSR and the USA and other Western powers. There were signs of unease lest the nuclear shield be weakened, the unacceptable concept of a limited war in Europe take root, US land forces on the continent of Europe be cut, and the balance of conventional arms remain tilted in favour of the Warsaw Pact. Differences of view on all this appeared within the Union, both between the several countries and between parliamentary groups, broadly right and left.

EUROPEAN FREE TRADE ASSOCIATION

THROUGH 1988 Efta was preoccupied with its relations with the European Community, as the single European (that is, Community) market loomed ever nearer. The abolition in 1983 of tariff barriers and quantitative restrictions on industrial products traded bilaterally between the two groups (see AR 1983, p. 352) had been followed by their joint Luxembourg Declaration of April 1984 (see AR 1984, p. 353) setting the common goal of a comprehensive European Economic Space (EES). Meanwhile, however, the scene had changed. The Community had been expanded by the adherence of Spain and Portugal. Not only had it set its 1992 deadline; it had been working hard at all the legal and administrative problems involved in the single market objective, leaving Efta behind and somewhat disadvantaged by its lack—unlike the EC—of any mandate or apparatus for imposing multilateral solutions. Thoughts of individual Efta members' cutting the knot by joining the Community were whispered in some quarters, but this course seemed unlikely, if only because it would probably take just as long as the run-up to 1992.

The first EC-Efta ministerial meeting since Luxembourg 1984 was held in Brussels on 2 February. Although it reaffirmed the joint commitment to a dynamic EES, it poured a cool shower on easy Efta hopes; for it became clear that because of the different structures and powers of the two institutions progress in cooperation had to be made piecemeal, bilaterally or multilaterally, while the Community would brook no check upon its own unifying processes to accommodate Efta's needs. The Ministers agreed that certain new steps were now timely, notably the pursuit of an efficient pan-European standardization code for the regulation of trade, common simplification of rules of origin, and 'greater transparency' in regard to state aid to industry, public procurement policies and price adjustments on processed agricultural products.

Later in February a meeting of EC and Efta parliamentarians added to the agenda an urgent call for cooperation on protection of the environment; and in June a joint meeting of the EC's economic and social committee and its Efta counterpart urged that priority be given to fighting pollution of the atmosphere, water and soil, problems of toxic waste, environmental accidents and exhaust emissions. Standards for these matters and means of enforcing them should be harmonized throughout Europe.

The collaborative process was taken a stage further at a meeting between Efta Ministers and EC Commissioner Willy de Clercq, held in Tampere, Finland, on 15 June. The meeting welcomed an Efta convention, signed on that day, granting mutual recognition of technical tests by member countries, as a step towards negotiating a similar regime for the whole European Economic Space. Other areas in which collaborative progress was noted included education and training, international transport, indirect taxation, product liability, copyright and financial services.

In one important sphere the EES concept took legislative form in 1988. On 17 September, at Lugano, representatives of the 12 EC and six Efta member states signed a convention extending to Efta countries the EC Brussels Convention of 1968 on jurisdiction and judgment enforcement in civil and commercial disputes, enhancing the ability of a litigant to secure damages or other redress, awarded by a domestic court, from a defendant in any other signatory country, and enabling an aggrieved consumer to sue, in a court in his own country, a foreign producer of a defective or harmful product. The Lugano convention was regarded as a model for EC-Efta regimes concerning other aspects of civil and commercial intercourse in Europe.

Efta leaders again took the opportunity of their ministerial council meeting on 28-29 November in Geneva to review EC-Efta relations with M. de Clercq. On a wide range of issues they found a healthy state of progress, but it was plain that a great deal remained to be done.

Within Efta itself, the Geneva ministerial council received a progress report from a working group, set up in June, on liberalization of trade in fish, a problem vital for Efta members but complicated by their practice of state aid to the fishing industry. They also welcomed a revised system of Efta rules on public procurement, designed to match the Community's system and to enable public procurement markets to be opened up on a reciprocal EC-Efta basis.

Efta maintained its historic special interest in two non-members, Portugal and Yugoslavia. The Efta-Yugoslavia joint committee, meeting in September, noted a satisfactory fall in Yugoslavia's trade deficit with Efta, and welcomed Yugoslav reforms aimed at a more open and market-oriented economy (see p. 132). The Efta Industrial Development Fund for Portugal approved new loans totalling US$12 million, raising the total of loans granted to Portugal since 1977 to US$212 million and contributing to an investment of nearly three times that sum.

On 16 April Per Kleppe of Norway, Secretary-General of Efta since 1981, was succeeded by Georg Reisch, until then Austria's permanent ambassador to the international organs in Geneva.

NORDIC COUNCIL

THE 36th session of the Nordic Council (consisting of parliamentarians from the five Nordic countries) was held in Oslo on 7-11 March. The Council adopted 42 recommendations for action by the Council of Ministers, ten of them based on recommendations from the Council of Ministers itself. They included the adoption of cooperation programmes in the fields of traffic safety, culture, biotechnology, foodstuffs and development aid; the establishment of a Nordic industrial centre in Oslo and a Nordic Development Fund; and the establishment on a permanent basis of the Nordic Investment Bank's regional loan system and the Nordic Project Export Fund.

The Council adopted 12 recommendations on the environment. Two, aimed at tightening restrictions on smoking, recommended that the Governments should examine even stricter rules on where smoking was allowed, on advertising and on health warnings, and work for such restrictions at the international level. The Council recommended the systematic inclusion of environmental considerations in the Nordic plan for economic development and full employment. In the field of air pollution it recommended that the Governments investigate the economic consequences of imposing a drastic reduction on emissions of sulphur dioxide and nitrogen oxide by 1995, and work for a 30 to 50 per cent reduction of sulphur dioxide emissions by all European countries by 1993 and a European convention to reduce nitrogen oxide emissions by half by the mid-1990s.

Other environmental recommendations from the parliamentarians to their Governments included a draft programme for environmentally-friendly waste disposal and recycling, a plan to combat ocean pollution, intensified research into the seal population and its marine environment, an investigation into the use of economic methods such as the taxation system to attain environmental objectives, and the presentation by the Council of Ministers of an annual report on Nordic environmental policy.

Recommendations from the communication committee adopted by the Nordic Council included the introduction of regulations to ensure the safe use of mobile car telephones, an investigation into ways of developing tourism in the North Nordic animal parks, the preparation of a report on the traffic problems of the region's large cities and alternative strategies for solving them, and the introduction of measures to speed up postal services within the region. In the social and health sector the Council recommended the preparation of a new cooperation programme by the Council of Ministers, and an intensification of cooperation to combat alcoholism and drug abuse. From the economic committee came recommendations that the Nordic countries intensify their cooperation in the use of natural gas with the aim of increasing its role in the region's energy supply as a contribution to the aim of reducing dependence on nuclear energy.

In the field of cultural cooperation the Council recommended the institution of a Nordic technology prize, a deepening of cooperation on adult education, and continued support for the strengthening of links between the youth organizations and schools of the five countries. Legal committee recommendations adopted included the harmonization of quality regulations for foodstuffs and the establishment of a working party to examine methods of improving cooperation in criminal investigations.

A prominent theme in the Council's general debate was the Nordic countries' relations with the European Community and in particular their response to the development of the EC's single European market. The Danish Prime Minister, Poul Schlüter, argued that a dynamic response in the direction of adapting to the EC internal market regulations could prove a positive development in Nordic cooperation itself. Ingvar Carlsson, Sweden's Prime Minister, stressed the need both to influence EC decisions on the internal market and to adjust in so far as politically possible to these developments, a position similar to that taken by the Prime Ministers of Norway and Finland. Iceland's then Prime Minister, Thorsteinn Pálsson, stated that his country could never consider EC membership as this would require opening its labour market and surrendering sovereignty over its fishing waters. Carl Bildt, leader of Sweden's Moderate Party and chief spokesman for the Conservative Group, proposed the establishment of a Nordic Council working party to consider the region's relations with the EC.

Another prominent theme was Council members' criticism of the Council of Ministers for failing to produce a detailed programme to combat ocean pollution in time for adoption at the 36th session. This led to demands for an extraordinary session in November at which such a programme could be adopted. The Council of Ministers—in this case the representatives of Finland, Norway and Sweden—were also criticized for failing to take a political decision on the future of the Nordic television satellite Tele-X, due to be launched in 1989. This was because of disagreements over the number of channels and whether, after the planned three-year experimental period, the broadcasts would become permanent. On 3 May the three countries decided that, in the absence of agreement on a permanent exchange of Nordic television programmes via Tele-X, there was no justification for beginning the three-year experimental period. The Tele-X project was therefore abandoned without a decision on a use for the satellite.

On 16 November the Nordic Council met in extraordinary session and approved an ocean pollution plan. This called on the Nordic countries to cut by a half by 1995 the discharge of phosphates, nitrogen and heavy metals into the ocean areas affected by pollution.

Chapter 6

AFRICAN CONFERENCES AND ORGANIZATIONS—SOUTH ASIAN ASSOCIATION FOR REGIONAL COOPERATION—
SOUTH-EAST ASIAN ORGANIZATIONS—SOUTH PACIFIC REGIONAL COOPERATION—ORGANIZATION OF AMERICAN STATES—CARIBBEAN ORGANIZATIONS

AFRICAN CONFERENCES AND ORGANIZATIONS

THE deteriorating economic condition of the continent continued to dominate African conferences and organizations in 1988, although the international conference on African indebtedness (called for at an emergency summit of the Organization of African Unity (OAU) at the end of 1987) did not materialize, because the major creditor countries continued to oppose it. There were signs, however, that the international community increasingly recognized that more needed to be done for 'low-income, debt-distressed' countries in sub-Saharan Africa, as the leaders of the Group of Seven put it in Toronto in June. This was reconfirmed at the World Bank meeting in West Berlin in September, and in November two countries, Mali and Madagascar, were the first to benefit from more favourable terms for debt rescheduling.

In this climate it was not surprising that the OAU marked its 25th anniversary at the end of May in an atmosphere of 'nothing to celebrate', although over 30 heads of state, a record attendance, turned up to show their continuing support for the OAU idea. In a keynote address, the outgoing chairman, President Kenneth Kaunda of Zambia, stressed the present 'deplorable state' of African economies. While praising the nobility of the ideal of pan-Africanism, Dr Kaunda thought that the vision of the founders appeared to have gone into limbo, and urged his fellow Africans to rededicate themslves to the OAU Charter, as well as mobilizing the support necessary for the hard task of maintaining African independence.

This sentiment was also contained in an anniversary declaration which said that 'unity, solidarity, liberation and development' would be the guiding philosophy of the OAU for the next two decades. Although this was mainly a political document concerned with such issues as southern Africa, the Western Sahara and the Middle East, the leaders also reaffirmed their commitment to the establishment of an African economic community 'as enshrined in the Lagos Plan of Action' of 1980, and expressed serious concern at the debt problem. They also called on the international community to honour its commitment to the UN Programme of Action 1986-90, stressing: 'We believe that world economic growth and stability cannot be achieved without a lasting solution to Africa's crisis'.

There was also a separate resolution on debt, mandating the new OAU chairman, President Moussa Traoré of Mali, to continue efforts to sensitize the international community, and repeating the call for a conference on the subject. Other resolutions were passed on the subject of AIDS, refugees, Afro-Arab cooperation, and human rights, urging those countries which had not yet ratified the African Charter on Human and Peoples' Rights, adopted at the Nairobi summit in 1981, to do so.

Major decisions and negotiations about Africa continued to take place outside the umbrella of the OAU, however. Only three weeks before the anniversary, crucial peace talks began involving South Africa, Angola and Cuba on possible independence for Namibia. Meeting in a variety of venues from Brazzaville to Geneva, with assistance from the United States and the UN, they were able to sign a pact on Namibian independence in December (see DOCUMENTS), which was to be implemented in 1989 and beyond. Although the Congo Government played a useful intermediary role, the OAU's input was marginal.

The OAU had been slightly more involved in the peace process in Chad, even if a reconciliation meeting between Presidents Habré and Qadafi which had been scheduled to take place in Addis Ababa during the summit did not happen because of the absence of Col. Qadafi (see p. 273). However, by October Chad and Libya had resumed diplomatic relations, and the ceasefire along the border was more or less intact.

There was a higher OAU input in the peace moves on the Western Sahara, if only because the Saharan Arab Democratic Republic (SADR) had been recognized by a majority of OAU states since 1984, and had not only a seat at the OAU but a vice-chairmanship, even if most of the territory claimed as SADR was in the possession of Morocco, which also claimed it. At the end of August, the United Nations announced a ceasefire and the beginning of peace negotiations, although the conditions for holding a UN-managed referendum were still not clearly established (see p. 238). Before the end of the year, Morocco made a major concession in agreeing to hold meetings with the Polisario Front, the SADR's political movement.

Morocco, which left the OAU in protest against the SADR's admittance in 1984, was also pursuing a policy of wooing African countries. In December King Hassan was able to play host in Casablanca to the Franco-African summit, an annual 'family gathering of France and its friends in Africa'. Thirty-seven countries were represented, 22 by heads of state, including several who had recognized the SADR, and the meeting, which seldom produced much substance, was generally reckoned a diplomatic success for King Hassan, who had now also agreed to host, in 1990, the Pan-African Festival (FESPAC), which Senegal had been obliged to abandon in November because of financial and administrative problems.

Apart from sundry dependent bodies of the OAU which held meetings (such as the Liberation Committee, and Ministers of Information and Culture), the impetus was maintained, however haltingly, behind the wide range of regional groupings. These included the economic communities of West and Central Africa (ECOWAS and CEEAC) and the Preferential Trade Area (PTA) in East and Southern Africa, as well as more ad hoc bodies, including those concerned with commodities such as cocoa, rice and groundnuts, science (anti-locust research) and the development of river basins, notably the Senegal, the Niger, and the Nile, to name but a few. The ten-nation airline Air Afrique was experiencing such a serious economic crisis that its members decided to sack its Congolese chairman and bring in a French expert, Yves Roland-Billecart, to knock the airline, which in the 1960s had made a handsome profit, back into shape. The condition of Air Afrique was seen as symbolic of the continent's general economic deterioration.

This was the major preoccupation of the two major African economic institutions, the African Development Bank (AfDB) and the UN Economic Commission for Africa (ECA). The former, refreshed with its 1987 capital enlargement and admission of outside shareholders, was playing, under its Senegalese president Babacar Ndiaye, a more crucial role in development funding, and was turning its attention increasingly to helping solve the major drama of African indebtedness by promoting debt-equity swaps. The

ECA, which had small access to funds of its own, continued in its 30th anniversary year to play a major advocate's role in putting forward the continent's problems on the international stage. For example, it helped to organize a meeting on 'adjustment with a human face' in Khartoum in March, seeing its current role particularly as helping to bridge the gap between short-term adjustment and longer-term development needs.

SOUTH ASIAN ASSOCIATION FOR REGIONAL COOPERATION

WHAT looked like being, for several months, a year of frustration and postponements for SAARC ended up, at the very end of the year, with a much publicized and rather successful summit conference in Islamabad. The frustrations and postponements derived principally from the fact that the venue and the timing of the summit had to be changed not once but twice. First, it was decided not to go ahead with the original plan for the summit to be held in Colombo, because of the continuing tension there, especially between Sinhalese and Tamils. Then, following President Zia's death in August, the timing of SAARC's Islamabad summit was postponed until December so as not to clash with Pakistan's general election in November (see pp. 313–4).

Otherwise, most of the new routines of SAARC (see AR 1987, pp. 398-9) continued unobtrusively. A South Asian food security reserve was set up in August and the SAARC Agricultural Information Centre (SAIC) at Dhaka. The Foreign Ministers' meeting in July attracted little press comment or publicity, and the participants contented themselves mostly with restating familiar positions.

At the December summit most public interest and publicity centred on the various meetings between Rajiv Gandhi and Benazir Bhutto, whose partial restoration of cordial Indo-Pakistan relations overshadowed everything else (see p. 315). Nevertheless at the end of three days of hectic talks, many bilateral sessions and banquets, the seven SAARC leaders issued two agreed documents (on 31 December) which indicated that they had produced some results of substance or of promise.

The final communique (of some 29 paragraphs) was called the Islamabad Declaration, and was accompanied by a joint press release, of some 22 paragraphs. These two documents did a number of different things: they offered a record of SAARC projects in progress, some commentary on international trends relevant to the interests of the participating countries and their region, and some proposals for their future action in common. The summit also agreed to study the 'greenhouse effect', and the raising of world sea levels currently under way which threatened to inundate large areas of Bangladesh's mostly low-lying land and perhaps totally to submerge the Maldives within 20 years.

The creation of a SAARC travel document to do away with visa requirements, initially for members of Parliament and Supreme Court judges travelling between various member states, was justified not only for itself but also as a start to a process of reducing bureaucratic controls and impediments to travel throughout the SAARC region.

Trade patterns in 1988 within SAARC also clearly indicated both India's primacy and the association's relative unimportance, so far, in regional trade terms. Trade within SAARC amounted to less than 3 per cent of the total trade of the seven member-countries, and in the five years ending in 1988 India's imports from SAARC countries amounted to less than 1 per cent of its total imports.

SOUTH-EAST ASIAN ORGANIZATIONS

ASEAN again devoted much attention to the Kampuchean issue, on which there was considerable movement owing to the progress of Sino-Soviet detente, consequent Vietnamese readiness to moderate its Indochinese ambitions and to withdraw troops from Kampuchea (see pp. 340-2) and more flexible attitudes to Vietnam by China and Thailand. There was even a Vietnamese suggestion that Vietnam's 'special relationship' with Laos and Cambodia and the related economic coordination commissions should be abandoned and all three countries join Asean. Indonesia, on behalf of Asean, organized a series of informal meetings in Java of the four Kampuchean factions, Vietnam, Laos and the Asean states. China indicated that it would phase out support for the Kampuchean resistance in step with Vietnamese troop withdrawals, that it did not want either the Khmer Rouge or the Heng Samrin regime to have a monopoly of power and that it approved of a peacekeeping force and an international commission to oversee installation of a four-party coalition Government led by Prince Sihanouk. The annual Asean UN resolution, which was overwhelmingly approved, was modified along similar lines and included both the long-standing demand for a Vietnamese withdrawal and measures to prevent Pol Pot returning to power.

The 21st Asean conference called for a UN conference to discuss measures to deal with the increase in refugees from Vietnam. These were increasingly ethnic Vietnamese and many of the boat people arriving in Hong Kong from North Vietnam seemed to be fleeing from bad economic conditions rather than political oppression. Vietnam agreed to expand the 'orderly departure programme' and to negotiate voluntary repatriation, subject to assurances on treatment of those returning; it also took steps to limit the renewed exodus. Asean's industrial development policies made little progress, being hampered as always by economic nationalism and by the economies being competitive rather than complementary. This appeared likely to be the fate of an attempt in October to revive the motor-car co-production scheme by committing Governments to some further mutual tariff cuts on car components. A meeting of Asean and industrialized countries in July, however, produced confirmation of Asean agreement to join in helping the Philippines restore its economy, the first offer of aid to a member country by the Association and one of interest to the Indochinese countries and Burma.

Escap showed concern for the massive destruction of tropical forest by uncontrolled logging, fuel-gathering and conversion of land to agriculture and for the related problem of population pressure; here some success was recorded, the birth rate in the Escap region having been brought down from 2.8 per cent a year in 1969 to about 1.7 per cent. The region again achieved much higher economic growth than elsewhere, real growth in Escap developing countries averaging 8 per cent in 1988, although this average concealed little or no growth in 11 land-locked, small island, or command economy countries. Escap developing country exports grew by over 30 per cent in US dollar terms, helped by improved international prices for commodities, a new and rapid growth in intra-regional trade and a shift of investment in labour-intensive industry from the region's developed countries to the developing.

SOUTH PACIFIC REGIONAL COOPERATION

IN March representatives from Papua New Guinea, the Solomons and Vanuatu, signed an understanding as to 'agreed principles of cooperation'. Locally termed the Spearhead Group, these Melanesian countries accorded priority to continuing political contact, harmonization of trade, investment and tourism policies, yet not in ways that would supplant the primacy of the South Pacific Forum (SPF).

The SPF held its annual meeting in September in Tonga. The most significant advances were organizational, with the former Bureau for Economic Cooperation now officially designated the Forum Secretariat. It was allocated more resources to service the organization, and directed to facilitate greater regional trade, investment, tourism, job-training and economic planning. The need to deal with Japanese fishing interests in the South Pacific on a collective basis was emphasized, as were proposals to combat terrorism, halt French nuclear testing and implement proposals for upgrading regional telecommunications facilities.

Representing the interim regime of his country (see p. 372), Ratu Sir Kamisese Mara, Prime Minister of Fiji, found that the Fijian political situation was conspicuously absent from the formal Forum agenda. Towards New Caledonia (see pp. 371–2), the meeting supported what it called a 'new spirit of constructive dialogue'.

The South Pacific Commission met in Rarotonga, the Cook Islands, in October. Deliberations were completely overshadowed by the resignation of the organization's head, Palaunui Tuisosopo, following allegations that he had granted himself excessive salary, expense and travel claims.

ORGANIZATION OF AMERICAN STATES

THE year began inauspiciously with some US$36 million still outstanding in membership quotas, of which five-sixths represented the contribution of the United States. Inevitably, in the early part of the year, US attempts to force the resignation of the Panamanian leader, General Noriega, led to the OAS being drawn into the tragi-comedy (see pp. 88–9). At a special meeting of consultation on 27 February, delegates invited to consider the crisis in Panama voiced support for President Delvalle but failed to vote either for the United States or for General Noriega. Following the 26 June decision of the US Senate which led to the recall of the Panamanian ambassador and a diplomatic protest at US interference in Panama's internal affairs, an extraordinary session of the OAS convened at Panama's request resolved by 17 votes to one (the United States) that US activities in Panama constituted 'unwarranted interference' in Panama's internal affairs.

Fortunately, the other work of the OAS and its related agencies went on despite its political paralysis. On 20 January Honduras, the first Latin American Government to be arraigned before the Inter-American Court of Human Rights, was held guilty of maintaining army death squads responsible for the 'disappearance' of named civilians (see also p. 87). At a meeting in Honduras on 15 October the OAS, the Inter-American Development Bank (IDB), the Inter-American Institute for Agricultural Cooperation (IIAC) and the Central American Bank for Economic Integration (CABEI), in conjunction with the European Community, agreed to fund US$878 million of the cost of the Trifinio Plan. The plan, the brainchild of Vice-President Jorge Carpio Nicolle of Guatemala, consisted of 220 projects to be implemented over a 10-year period and sought to bring economic stability to the Central American region by creating a three-nation conservation park on the shared frontiers of Guatemala, El Salvador and Honduras, which would include a 'multiple-use' zone to promote economic and social development.

CARIBBEAN ORGANIZATIONS

THE annual summit of the 13-member Caribbean Community (Caricom), held in St John's (Antigua) from 4–8 July, was dominated by three issues: the political situation in Haiti (see p. 85); US anti-drug strategies in the region; and the persistence of trade restrictions between member states, notwithstanding the 1987 summit's setting of end-September 1988 as the deadline for their elimination (see AR 1987, p. 400). The summit also decided to grant Caricom observer status to the Netherlands Antilles.

The heads of government remained sharply divided over whether the observer status of Haiti should be suspended until democracy was restored in that country. The outgoing Caricom chairman, Prime Minister John Compton of St Lucia, called for disapproval to be shown to the Namphy military regime which had seized power (for the second time) in June but stopped short of urging Haiti's suspension. Other members, notably Antigua & Barbuda, favoured a conciliatory approach, whereas Prime Minister Erskine Sandiford of Barbados called for Haiti's suspension from certain Caricom ministerial committees. Such divisions had already been apparent at an emergency Caricom summit held in Barbados on 6 January shortly before the first Namphy regime finally allowed elections to be held. An active role in promoting dialogue rather than confrontation with Haiti was taken by a new regional grouping called the 'Concerned Caribbean Leaders', launched by the Jamaican Prime Minister, Edward Seaga, late in 1987 and including the Bahamas, St Lucia, Dominica and St Vincent & the Grenadines.

The St John's Caricom summit registered its opposition to what was seen as the US Government's claim to 'extraterritorial jurisdiction' in its fight against drug-trafficking in the region, against a background of persistent US allegations that leading Caribbean politicians were involved in the trade. In the words of Antiguan Deputy Premier Lester Bird, the heads of government 'condemn trafficking in drugs but they are determined that the matter of the US Justice Department wishing to have its writ run in sovereign countries outside of its territory is of deep concern'. Of the Caribbean leaders against whom drug-running allegations had been made in the US,

Prime Minister Sir Lynden Pindling of the Bahamas asserted at the summit that the US Monroe Doctrine of 1823 (rejecting interference in the Americas by outside powers) had now been replaced by an ideologically-motivated interventionist policy.

The summit failed to agree on the dismantling of all trade barriers between members states by the envisaged target date of 1 October. Accepting instead the arguments of smaller states that the removal of tariff and quantitative restrictions would cause unacceptable damage to some sectors, the heads of government decided instead that protection could be maintained on certain products until 1991. The list of 23 such items, which was not published, was to be reviewed periodically. The summit also agreed to abandon previous plans for a Caribbean export bank and instead to establish an export credit facility (ECF) through the Caribbean Development Bank, as proposed at the 1986 Caricom summit (see AR 1986, p. 369).

XII DEFENCE AND ARMS CONTROL

Chapter 1

THE ARMS TRADE

THE year 1988 was one of paradoxes and ironies. Positive short-term developments encouraged a degree of optimism about international security and stability that had not been evident throughout the 1980s. At the same time, it was possible to discern longer-term developments which were more disquieting and potentially destabilizing.

On the one hand, there were several developments which encouraged the belief that 'peace was breaking out' in the world. Not only did the superpowers continue to pursue policies of detente—albeit a detente without a name—but also there was the beginning of an end to at least some of the regional conflicts which had been in progress throughout most of the 1980s and in some cases even longer. The Soviet decision to withdraw from Afghanistan was followed by the ending of the Iran-Iraq war as well as by agreement on the future of Namibia, a move which went some way towards reducing tension in southern Africa. On the other hand, there were some disturbing trends in the pattern of arms supplies to, and in some instances from, Third World states. Furthermore, although the winding-down of regional conflicts was an encouraging development, it was not self-evident that this marked more than a temporary respite in regions long characterized by turmoil and instability.

Peace by exhaustion was not the same as a settlement which eliminated the underlying sources of tension and animosity. The endemic insecurity bedevilling much of the Third World, therefore, looked unlikely to diminish. The problems of secession, of regional arms racing, of poverty and civil war had not disappeared. In short, while 1988 was certainly not a year without hope, developments during the year did not warrant euphoria. Indeed, several trends were evident which, if left unchecked would add an additional overlay of instability to conflicts in the Third World.

Perhaps the first of these was the continuing trend towards indigenous arms production and supply by Third World nations themselves. This was partly the result of the cost of the sophisticated weapons systems developed by advanced industrialized nations, many of them with capabilities well beyond the needs of most Third World states. It was not surprising, therefore, that recipient states had begun to look for alternative supplies of systems which were cheap but suitable for the kinds of conflict in which they were most likely to be involved. Partly in response to this demand, nations such as Brazil and Argentina had become significant arms suppliers to the Third World and had also had some success in selling systems to the more advanced industrialized states.

In recent years Brazil had found its largest markets in Iraq and Saudi Arabia. In 1988 Saudi Arabia agreed to purchase the Osorio main battle tank from Brazil's armoured vehicle producer Engesa—a sale achieved despite strong competition from the United States, Britain and France. This deal followed an earlier reported one in which the Saudis agreed to purchase the Brazilian Asros II rocket launcher from Avibras. Moreover, Embraer of Brazil had a 30 per cent stake in a joint venture with Italy to build the AMX subsonic tactical fighter and also produced military trainer aircraft whose purchasers included the Royal Air Force.

The lack of political conditions attached to Brazilian arms sales, and the fact that Brazil did not prohibit onward transfer to third parties, gave it important advantages; at the same time, such factors rendered its actions highly controversial in some instances. This was particularly the case in early 1988 when a senior Libyan delegation visited Brazil to purchase a range of equipment including tanks and medium-range ballistic missiles. The reported decision to supply Libya with Sonda missiles with a range of around 600 miles was characterized as 'regrettable' by the US Government, which claimed that they were the same kind of weapons as those used by Libya against Chad. They were also of such a range that they would concern at least some of the states on Nato's southern flank as well as Israel and Egypt. As far as Brazil was concerned, however, the deal was both timely and opportune and would provide a much needed inflow of funds to finance the further development of the missile.

Brazil was not the only Third World supplier of arms involved in controversial sales. It was reported in June that Argentina was supplying Mirage-3 fighter-bombers to South Africa in defiance of the UN arms embargo. But perhaps the most controversial arms supplier of all during the year was China: following its earlier sale of Silkworm missiles to Iran, the People's Republic agreed in 1988 to supply Saudi Arabia with its East Wind-3 (CSS-2) intermediate-range ballistic missiles, with a range over 2,500 km. Once again, the US expressed strong disapproval of the Chinese action, a Reagan Administration official suggesting that China was 'a rogue elephant in the arms market, ready to sell anything for money'. The sale, which some reports suggested had been agreed two years earlier rather than in response to the Iran-Iraq 'war of the cities', was doubly ironic if there was any accuracy in reports in April that Israel had been supplying high technology to China, including missile warheads, armour-piercing devices and radar technology from the cancelled Lavi fighter project. Although the specifics of the reports were denied by the Israeli Defence Minister, it was fairly clear that considerable cooperation had taken place between the two countries in the 1980s.

There were several footnotes to the Saudi-Chinese deal which were of considerable importance. The first was that President Reagan, in response to a report in *The Washington Post*, warned Israel not to take any military action against the Saudi missiles. A White House spokesman also emphasized that the Saudis and the Chinese had given categorical assurances that nuclear warheads for the missiles would be neither sought nor supplied. The second footnote came in September when the Chinese assured the visiting US Secretary of Defense, Frank Carlucci, that China would act responsibly in relation to arms sales. The third was that during 1988 Syria concluded a deal for the acquisition of the M-9 missile (with a range of 600 km) currently being developed by China.

Concern over the acquisition of ballistic missiles by Third World states was intensified but not created by the Chinese and Brazilian sales during 1988. Syria and Egypt for example, had possessed Soviet Scud missiles for some time. The Gulf 'war of the cities', however, revealed that Third World states were capable of modifying these missiles to increase their range, thereby highlighting another development that could become more pronounced in the future. Both Israel and Taiwan had major programmes for ballistic missile development, and in September Israel launched its first satellite into orbit.

Not all the important developments were in the Middle East, of course. On 25 February India announced that it had successfully tested a ballistic missile, the Prithvi, with a range of 250 km. It was clear too that India had the capacity to extend the range of the system and that, when deployed, it would enable New Delhi to strike at almost any target in Pakistan. These missiles, like those supplied to the Saudis by China, would be capable of launching nuclear as well as conventional warheads. Although the acquisition of such missiles was often justified in terms of enhancing deterrence, they added potential instabilities in regions that were already highly dangerous.

The year's developments in the spread of both ballistic missiles technology and completed weapon systems highlighted a problem which had been growing for some years and of which the United States, in particular, had long been aware. In 1983 the Reagan Administration had initiated negotiations with its major economic partners—Britain, France, Canada, Italy, Japan and West Germany—to establish a convention or regime designed to restrict missile technology exports, resulting in the establishment in April 1987 of the 'missile technology control regime'. The events of 1988, however, suggested that this regime—which did not have the status of a fully-fledged international treaty—was seriously flawed in that it failed to deal adequately with either the supply or demand sides of the ballistic missile proliferation problem. It was, moreover, too restrictive in its membership, did nothing to minimize the incentives for Third World states to acquire missiles and contained no agreement on implementation, compliance and verification.

Nevertheless, the regime did provide a basis on which it might be possible to build. If the Soviet Union and China could be persuaded to accept the restrictions agreed upon by the Western powers, then their efficacy would be considerably enhanced. Promising signs that this might be possible included the initiation of US-Soviet bilateral discussions on the subject and China's agreement, in response to US urgings, not to provide ballistic missiles to Libya. The proliferation of ballistic missiles to the Third World, however, was something that could be slowed down rather than halted. In retrospect, the most significant development of 1988 could prove to be not the ending of the Gulf war, but the Iranian and Iraqi missile attacks on each other's cities in the months preceding the cessation of hostilities. The model thus provided for Third World warfare could increasingly be emulated.

None of this could obscure the fact that the arms trade continued to be dominated by the major powers, namely the USSR, the United States, France, Britain and West Germany, with China emerging as a significant new force. The US and USSR still retained their positions as the world's foremost arms suppliers, and although the role competition of newcomers was growing the main competition came from established sellers like France and Britain. The US in particular found itself at a disadvantage in one of the most lucrative regions for the arms suppliers, the Middle East. Although Washington had, since the mid-1970s, attempted to play the role of even-handed mediator in the Arab-Israeli dispute, its efforts to supply arms to friendly and moderate Arab Governments had frequently run into difficulties with a Congress sympathetic to Israel and highly sensitive to pressure from the Jewish lobby in the US, with the result that states like Jordan and Saudi Arabia looked elsewhere for suppliers. It was not entirely surprising, therefore, when it was announced in July that Britain had won a £10,000 million order from Saudi Arabia to supply 50 Tornadoes, 50 Hawk aircraft, 90 helicopters, and six minesweepers. The scale of the package was surprising, however, not least because there had been rumours of problems attendant upon an earlier agreement signed in 1985. Whatever the case, the order meant that Britain replaced the US as Saudi Arabia's largest supplier, and ensured that around 18,000 jobs in British Aerospace were safeguarded. It was also indicative of the success of the systematic efforts made in recent years by Britain to expand its arms sales.

If 1988 was primarily the year of the missile, underlying much of the concern was the future possibility that missile technology available to Third World states such as Libya could be combined with nuclear weapons. There was a more immediate reminder of the nuclear proliferation problem when, in August, the South African Foreign Minister acknowledged that South Africa had the capability to make nuclear weapons. Although the statement revealed nothing that was not widely known already, it was in effect the first time that the Government had acknowledged the possibility of a 'bomb in the basement', thereby ending a long period in which South Africa had been very cautious about either confirming or denying the existence of its nuclear programme. Although considerable uncertainty remained about the extent to which South Africa had already stockpiled nuclear weapons, it was clear that the horizontal proliferation of nuclear weapons would demand increasing attention in the years ahead.

Chapter 2

THE CENTRAL BALANCE

THE superpowers were expected to move rapidly in 1988 towards a strategic arms reduction (START) agreement as a follow-up to the INF Treaty, signed in December 1987, which provided for the removal from Europe of all land-based nuclear missiles with a range between 500 and 5,500 km (see AR 1987, pp. 414-5, 558-66). In the event, progress was much slower than expected. On 27 May the INF Treaty was overwhelmingly approved in the US Senate, where only five members voted against it; but Senate action had been neither as prompt nor as unqualified as had been hoped. The debate revealed considerable anxiety over the direction of US arms control policy, with particular concern over verification.

The Senate vote consenting to ratification of the INF Treaty occurred while President Reagan was in Moscow for another summit with Mr Gorbachev. Although this was regarded as successful, and produced some modest progress on mobile missile verification and air-launched Cruise missile counting rules, the momentum that had seemed to some to be developing in the strategic arms control negotiations was not maintained. To some extent this was inevitable. The presidential election created uncertainties over the approach of the next Administration and resulted in what was virtually a political hiatus in the US Government. There were also substantive problems involved in START which significantly hindered progress during 1988. In November, at the end of the 11th US-Soviet negotiating session, President Reagan stated that there was a solid foundation for the next Administration but that 'major areas of disagreement' remained.

The first of these issues, which had been evident for several years, concerned the linkage between START and strategic defence. A compromise formula agreed at the Washington summit of December 1987 left considerable room for the US to claim a permissive interpretation of the activities permitted under the ABM Treaty of 1972 and the Soviet Union to adopt a more restrictive stance about precisely what was allowed. A second source of contention related to sea-launched Cruise missiles (SLCMs). In effect, the US wanted freedom to deploy about 750 nuclear SLCMs, as part of a diversified deterrent capability, and justified this with the claim that, in view of the difficulties of differentiating them from conventionally-armed SLCMs, effective verification of nuclear SLCMs was impossible. The USSR, which was still attempting to catch up with the US in terms of SLCM technology, preferred either a total ban or a limit of 400, which they claimed could be adequately verified.

It also became increasingly evident during 1988 that START would not bring about the significant reduction in forces sometimes claimed for it. Because of the counting rules, the reductions would be more in the region of 25-30 per cent than the 50 per cent figure generally used in public discussion. Furthermore, the negotiations would not prevent the further modernization of Soviet and US strategic armories. Indeed, during 1988 there were several important developments in terms of both Soviet and US force modernization. The number of Soviet mobile missiles increased markedly during the year, while the US unveiled its new and very expensive B-2 'Stealth' bomber, intended to be undetectable to Soviet radar. One task of the B-2 (assuming it survived the defence budget cuts likely to be a feature of the Bush Administration) was to target Soviet command centres and mobile missiles. Not surprisingly, therefore, the B-2 proved enormously controversial. Its unveiling in November was preceded by critical statements from both the Union of Concerned Scientists and the Federation of American Scientists recommending against production.

In terms of strategic armaments, 1988 was a period of ambivalence, when the trends towards arms control and budget cutting on the one side sat rather uneasily with continued military modernization on the other. It was also the year when the dreams of President Reagan about building an astrodome strategic defence over the US were, more obviously than ever before, relegated to the status of long-term wishful thinking. Although there had been considerable scepticism over the President's SDI vision ever since its unveiling in March 1983, the Pentagon had been very optimistic about the programme. In late 1988 it bowed to budget and technical realities by acknowledging that its plans for early deployment were being scaled down and delayed. It was announced that the number of space-based interceptors would be reduced by half from those initially planned, while the number of ground-based defensive missiles would be increased by up to 70 per cent. The projected cost of the deployment was reduced from $115,000 million to $69,000 million and it was acknowledged that the initial operational capability for the system had slipped to the late 1990s if not beyond. The election victory of George Bush cast further doubt on the scheme; his comments during the election revealed that he was far less enthusiastic about SDI than President Reagan. Moreover, the director of the programme, General Abrahamson, resigned during the year, thereby providing another indication of its faltering momentum.

At the level of strategic arms control, therefore, 1988 could be understood as the year in which reality crept back into the discussions. The idea of a nuclear-free world, as generated by SDI, Reykjavik and the INF Treaty, was shown to be little more than rhetoric. Nevertheless, it also became clear that the US strategic modernization programme would be seriously hampered by budgetary stringency and that the incoming Administration would face difficult and painful choices. How the dilemmas and difficulties were resolved would not only impinge upon the strategic balance, but also upon the situation in Europe.

Chapter 3

NATO AND THE WARSAW PACT

IN Europe 1988 was characterized by gradual moves towards new talks on conventional stability. Within Nato there were continued attempts to come to terms with the consequences of the INF Agreement, while the Warsaw Pact nations were adjusting to the Gorbachev reforms and assessing what they might mean for Eastern Europe in the longer term. It was a year when, apart from Mr Gorbachev's announcement at the UN that Soviet conventional force levels were to be substantially reduced (see DOCUMENTS), there was little that was dramatic. Yet there were certain changes and developments which could be a foretaste of things to come in the 1990s.

For Nato, 1988 was not a bad year. There were several successes for the Alliance, not the least being the way in which it dealt with the question of the US F-16s based in Spain. Although the US wanted to retain the base at Torrejón, it was politically important for the Spanish Government to be seen to reduce the US presence. Consequently, the US agreed to remove its F-16s from this base while agreement was reached on the retention of three military facilities elsewhere in Spain. The F-16 wing was successfully relocated in Italy, with the costs being met by Nato.

If this issue was managed quite effectively by the Alliance, other issues appeared rather more intractable. These included the re-emergence of the debate over burden-sharing between the US and its allies. Although this issue was never far below the surface, and did not in fact play as large a role in the US presidential election campaign as some Europeans had feared, it became clear that the Alliance would have to deal seriously with the matter over the coming years. Part of the difficulty was that there were two separate strands in the US demand for burden-sharing. The one, represented by Senator Sam Nunn, was a demand that the allies did more in order to reduce Nato's reliance on nuclear weapons. The second, represented by Representative Patricia Schroeder, equated burden-sharing with burden-shedding or burden-relief. In effect, it demanded that the Allies should do more so that the US could do less.

The Alliance acknowledged that the issue had to be dealt with and at the March summit between the 16 heads of government the Allies reaffirmed their willingness to share fairly the risks, burdens, and responsibilities of the common defence effort. By the end of the year, Nato had produced a major analysis of the problem which not only placed the emphasis on the sharing of 'risks, roles and responsibilities' but also highlighted specific ways in which this might be achieved. The assessment included a country-by-country study and pinpointed ways in which national contributions might be enhanced—something that had not been done before.

An additional element in the European response to US pressure over burden-sharing was to emphasize the progress towards West European defence cooperation. The notion of a European pillar in the Atlantic Alliance had long been on the agenda. The difficulties had concerned how best to achieve it in view of continued differences of perspective amongst the European allies, especially France, Britain and West Germany. In 1988 there were some moves towards closer relations between the three major European powers and some setbacks. Perhaps the most important development was the creation by France and Germany of a joint defence and security council—intended to give 'visibility and permanence' to their new cooperation—and the establishment of a joint brigade. Although closer Franco-German cooperation reflected French concerns over a possible West German drift towards neutrality as well as German desires to bring France closer to Nato's integrated military structure, it was also seen as the nucleus of a West European defence identity.

Critics claimed that the cooperation was symbolic rather than substantive and that little was being done to enhance real military effectiveness. At one level Franco-German cooperation was far less extensive than that between Britain and West Germany, although most of the latter took place in Nato rather than outside. In response to the lack of visibility of Anglo-German defence cooperation, the Ministers of Defence of the two countries agreed to take measures to give the relationship greater prominence.

It was in the third bilateral relationship, however, that there was greatest disappointment. In the aftermath of Reykjavik, the incentives for closer Anglo-French nuclear cooperation had seemed greater than ever before, and in 1987 Britain and France initiated discussions about developing a stand-off missile for their aircraft—weapons which would go some way to substituting for the removal of the Cruise and Pershing II missiles from Western Europe. By the end of 1988, however, it was clear that Britain intended to acquire an American system rather than the French missile, the ASMP, which would also be available. The British Government claimed that the French missile had not met requirements in terms of range. Others contended that the problem stemmed from a British reluctance to depart from the entrenched pattern of Anglo-American collaboration in favour of European partners.

The other problem faced by the Alliance was what to do about short-range nuclear forces. The INF Agreement aroused considerable anxiety in several West European states. These concerns, however, did not take the same form. Mrs Thatcher was most worried that INF would lead to 'cascading denuclearization' in Western Europe, thereby undermining deterrence and stability. In Bonn, by contrast, the concern over a weakening of deterrence was outweighed by the belief that with the second 'zero', i.e. the removal of short-range intermediate nuclear forces (SRINF), Nato was left with an absurd posture and West Germany was left hosting nuclear weapons which could only be used on German territory. As a result, the Bonn Government felt that it had been 'singularized' i.e. placed in a position where it faced risks that were far greater than those confronting any of its Allies.

This led to a somewhat bitter debate in the Alliance over short-range nuclear force (SNF) modernization, with Britain and the US lined up against West Germany, backed to some extent by France. Although Chancellor Kohl rejected the third 'zero' desired by Moscow, it was difficult for him to make a commitment to deploy a follow-on to the ageing Lance missile which would require replacement by the mid-1990s. Although several compromise formulae were available (one possibility being the elimination of

Nato's nuclear artillery in return for German support for the Lance follow-on), the issue became bound up with the German proposal, still far from complete by the end of the year, for a 'comprehensive concept' for the Alliance. The difficulties were exacerbated by splits within the coalition Government itself, Foreign Minister Genscher being more favourable to the third 'zero' than was Chancellor Kohl. In effect, the issue was placed on the agenda in 1988, but by the end of the year was still far from resolution. In short, the disputes over Nato's military posture post-INF proved divisive within Europe as well as across the Atlantic, and took some of the momentum out of the movement towards the creation of a West European pillar within Nato.

If there were setbacks for West European defence cooperation in 1988, some progress was also made. The Western European Union (WEU) followed up its widely-applauded activity in coordinating European naval activities in the Gulf by enlarging its membership through the accession of Spain and Portugal (see p. 409). Steps were taken by Britain and France to open up their defence markets, while the Independent European Programme Group continued in its task of facilitating collaboration in procurement. Perhaps most important of all there was growing excitement about the creation of a single European market by the end of 1992 and a feeling that this might give a considerable boost to the cooperative process in defence.

Some progress had been made throughout 1987 in discussing conventional arms control and there were signs that Mr Gorbachev was far more sensitive than his predecessors to Western concerns over Soviet force structure and doctrine. This flexibility was evident when he and other Soviet spokesmen acknowledged that there could be asymmetrical reductions in Nato and Warsaw Pact forces, each side focusing on areas where it had the advantage. Although Nato was anxious to see reductions in Soviet tanks, there were many who saw the corresponding demand for a major reduction in Nato's strike aircraft as a continuation of the traditional Soviet aim of weakening Nato's nuclear capacity. Nevertheless, during 1988 Soviet proposals became more detailed and specific.

In June and July a multi-stage proposal for force reductions and restructuring was enunciated by the USSR. The proposal was presented initially at the Moscow summit between Mr Reagan and Mr Gorbachev and subsequently elaborated by Soviet Foreign Minister Eduard Shevardnadze. The proposal envisaged a three-stage process, the first stage to consist of data exchange and on-site inspections to identify 'imbalances and asymmetries' as well as the elimination of these asymmetries. The second stage would involve a reduction of half-a-million men on both sides and would be followed by a third phase in which the remaining forces would be restructured to ensure that they were capable of only defensive operations.

The Atlantic Alliance found it difficult to agree on a response that had the same kind of long-term vision as the Soviet proposal. The development of the Western position was also hampered by differences between France and the US over procedural issues. Gradually, however, Nato and the Warsaw Pact moved towards agreement on the mandate for the 'conventional stability talks' (CST), although at the end of the year there were still a few issues which had yet to be resolved.

In the event, the prospects for the CST were given a considerable boost by Mr Gorbachev's 7 December speech at the United Nations (see DOCUMENTS). The Soviet leader declared the Cold War to be over, offered a vision of a 'common European home' from the Urals to the Atlantic and announced his decision to make large and unilateral force reductions in Eastern Europe and to restructure Soviet forces towards a more defensive posture. Among the specific elements of the Gorbachev plan were a 500,000 unilateral cut in Soviet forces with accompanying reductions in armaments, and the removal of 10,000 tanks, 8,500 artillery pieces, and 800 combat aircraft from Eastern Europe and the western Soviet Union. This was to include the withdrawal of six tank divisions from Eastern Europe, which would reduce Soviet forces deployed there by 50,000 men and 5,000 tanks. It seemed likely that four divisions would be removed from East Germany and one each from Hungary and Czechoslovakia. Other measures included the withdrawal of assault troops and bridge-crossing units which were necessary for a rapid *Blitzkrieg*, and the reorganization of the remaining units to produce a much more clearly defensive force posture.

There were several ambiguities in the Gorbachev statement. It was not clear, for example, how much bridging equipment would actually be removed. If it was simply the equipment in the departing divisions, those that remained would still have a considerable capability for offensive operations. Despite this uncertainty, however, the initiative suggested that there was indeed a possibility of taking serious steps to dismantle the military confrontation in Europe.

On 8 December Nato released some details of its own proposals for the negotiations on conventional stability. As well as welcoming the Gorbachev announcement, Nato Ministers announced that they would propose overall limits on levels of arms in Europe. These would include a limit of 40,000 on the number of tanks. In addition, no one country would be entitled to more than a fixed proportion (e.g. 30 per cent) of total holdings, and there would be both limits and sub-limits on stationed forces. These limits would be reinforced by measures designed to achieve greater military transparency, and constraints on the deployment and readiness of forces. In addition, the

Alliance made clear that it regarded the conventional stability talks as part of a wider process, in which the negotiations on confidence- and security-building measures among all 35 signatories of the Helsinki Final Act were crucial.

Despite important differences of perspective between Nato and the Warsaw Pact on the specifics of arms reductions, there was some convergence on the underlying principles of defensive force structures. Consequently, Mr Gorbachev's recognition that certain aspects of Soviet force posture and strategy appeared threatening to the West was particularly welcome. Although this had been acknowledged in earlier statements by the Soviet President, it now appeared that he was willing to take unilateral action to provide reassurance that the USSR had only defensive intentions.

At the same time, there was a strong element of caution in the Western response. This had several sources. It stemmed partly from a recognition that, in one sense at least, the Soviet leader was engaging in a very skilful public relations campaign and was obtaining considerable credit for his statement even though there was a potential gap between decision and implementation. Concerns over implementation were exacerbated by the possibility that Mr Gorbachev did not have the full support of the Soviet military for his proposal, a possibility that was underlined by the resignation of Marshal Akhromeyev, the chief of the Soviet General Staff, ostensibly on grounds of health. A second source of caution in the official reaction stemmed from the fact that the unilateral reductions were unlikely to shift fundamentally the military balance in Europe. For the sceptics, Mr Gorbachev's reductions simply highlighted the extent of the superiority of Soviet and Warsaw Pact forces over those of Nato. If some were doubtful about the overall effect of the initiative, others saw it as having an ulterior motive of dividing Western Europe from the US and rendering Nato's decisions about nuclear modernization even more problematical. Nevertheless, the UN speech ensured that a year in which progress on arms control had been slow, steady and unspectacular ended on an optimistic note.

XIII RELIGION

RUSSIAN MILLENNIUM. A thousand years after the arrival of Orthodox Christianity at Kiev in the Ukraine celebrations were held in major cities of the USSR, with far greater freedom than anticipated owing to the policy of *glasnost*. On 19 April Patriarch Pimen and members of the Holy Synod met Mikhail Gorbachev in the Kremlin, the first such encounter for over 40 years, and he hailed believers as 'Soviet people, working people, patriots'. *Izvestia* carried a series of articles about the Church and *Pravda* noted its positive attitude towards reforms. The principal Church events in Moscow, from 5-12 June, began with liturgy in the Patriarchal Cathedral of the Epiphany attended by over 400 representatives from other churches and countries, including the Archbishop of Canterbury. The foundation stone of a church to commemorate the Millennium was laid in the outskirts of Moscow, claimed by the Chairman of the Council for Religious Affairs, Konstantin Kharchev, as a symbol of *perestroika* in Church-State relations. A Millennium concert at the Bolshoi Theatre was attended by President Gromyko and Mrs Gorbachev.

At Kiev a 'jubilee ceremony' in a theatre was presided over by Metropolitan Filaret; Soviet officials were present, and guests addressing the gathering included the Roman Catholic Cardinal Willebrands (Netherlands) and American evangelist Billy Graham. Part of a historic Monastery of the Caves in Kiev was returned by the State to the Orthodox Church and 650 other churches were opened in the USSR during the year. Unofficial meetings were also organized, some by dissidents, others by Roman Catholics and Baptists, 5,000 of the latter holding an open-air gathering at the statue of St Vladimir in Kiev, 75 being baptized publicly in the River Dnieper.

In the church of St Sergi at Zagorsk nine new saints of previous centuries were canonized, but calls by independent church activists for commemoration of modern martyrs were not acknowledged. Especially important was a council (*sobor*) at Zagorsk from 6 to 9 June presided over by the Primate with Chairman Kharchev beside him throughout. The chief item was the Church's new statute (*ustav*), replacing one adopted and revised under governmental pressure in 1945 and 1961 and providing a new guide for Church order. The statute had 15 sections dealing with organization, theological education, finance and property. A 1961 amendment passed at the height of Khrushchev's anti-religious campaign was overturned and priests reinstated as head of parish assemblies. Patriarch Pimen was ageing and in poor health and provisions were made for retirement and a successor, who must be a Soviet citizen and have theological education. Parishes and monasteries could buy property and disburse income for charitable purposes. Mr Kharchev estimated that 30 per cent of children in the USSR were baptized, approximately 21 million in 1971-1987, but Metropolitan Vladimir of Rostov considered the figure to be 30 million.

In Lithuania the Roman Catholic cathedral in the capital Vilnius, which had been used as a picture gallery, was restored to the Church in October and Mass celebrated for the first time in 38 years. In Latvia the Protestant cathedral in Riga was returned to the Church. But in the German Democratic Republic demands for social and political reform by the Evangelical Church were met with official denial that changes were needed. Wittenberg Pastor Friedrich Schorlemmer published 20 theses at a synod in Halle stating 'we consider it necessary that the Communists renounce the monopoly of truth which they exercise by force'. The Evangelical Church had sought to be 'a Church in socialism' but alternative Church movements, 'the Church from the bottom', demanded radical protest and one of its founders, Mrs Vera Wollenberger, was imprisoned in January but later released.

The Church in Hungary was allowed to transport 50,000 Catholics to a Mass celebrated by Pope John Paul II at Trausdorf in Austria, but Czechoslovaks were refused such permission. No new bishops had been appointed in Czechoslovakia since 1973 and there were ten vacant sees, because of the refusal of the Vatican to accept a governmental demand that bishops should belong to the state-backed Pacem in Terris clergy organization. The 88-year-old Primate, Cardinal Frantisek Tomasek, wrote to the Prime Minister supporting a nationwide petition for more religious freedom and in April talks between the Vatican and Prague ended with agreement on three new bishops, none belonging to Pacem in Terris but two of them being auxiliaries and the third not a residential bishop. In Romania the planned 'systemization' of agricultural land, entailing destruction of thousands of villages and their churches (see p. 126), brought protests from Hungarian leaders whose fellows were affected, with letters from Cardinal László Paskai and the Hungarian Ecumenical Council.

LAMBETH AND BEYOND. The ten-yearly Lambeth Conference of bishops of the Church of England met for three weeks in July at the University of Kent in Canterbury with 524 bishops for the 70 million Anglican communion worldwide (see AR 1978, p. 359). Among many subjects discussed the ordination of women priests was prominent, the General Synod in England having reaffirmed earlier that legislation should be prepared to allow female ordination. The Archbishop of Canterbury, Dr Robert Runcie, thought the move 'not opportune', but the Archbishop of York, Dr John Habgood, said the measure would 'allow the Church at large to discuss this legislation' which could not be put into effect before 1993 at earliest. Women priests functioned in the US, Canada, New Zealand, Kenya and Uganda but were banned from officiating in England. In October Rev Suzanne Fageol of Chicago was refused entry to St Benet's Chapel in east London and celebrated the Eucharist outside with 100 supporters from St Hilda's community.

The Lambeth Conference was even more disturbed over the possibility of women becoming bishops. Bishop John Spong of New Jersey spoke in their favour and was attacked by Bishop Graham Leonard of London. The Archbishop of Canterbury moved to avert schism by appointing a commission, but American Anglicans would not be held back. In September Rev Barbara Harris, aged 59, a black divorcee, was elected suffragan bishop of Massachusetts.

Less publicized, but historic, was the unanimous commendation by the Lambeth Conference of a document urging dialogue with Jews and Muslims in understanding and sharing. It admitted past anti-Jewish prejudice which provided the soil for 'the evil weed of Nazism', rejected conversionism and recognized the validity of the Jewish relationship with God. But some evangelicals feared that recognition of Judaism undermined Christian faith.

A new Education Reform Act came into force in Britain in September after much debate with religious bodies. It decreed that the 'basic curriculum' in all maintained schools must include religious education for all pupils up to the age of 18, although not as one of ten examinable subjects. Daily collective school worship, required since the 1944 Act but often ignored, was mandatory and to be 'wholly or mainly of a broadly Christian character' yet 'without being distinctive of any particular Christian denomination'. A conscience clause allowed exemption for non-Christians and in the small number of schools, estimated at fewer than 500, where the majority was other than Christian, variant forms of worship could be used.

There were many pronouncements on religion and politics. The Bishop of Durham, Dr David Jenkins, declared government policy towards the poor was 'verging on the wicked', and he was called 'an Antichrist' by a Conservative MP. On 21 May the Prime Minister, Mrs Thatcher, addressed the General Assembly of the Church of Scotland, saying that the distinctive marks of Christianity 'stem not from the social but from the spiritual side of our lives'. In a presidential address to the Methodist Conference in June Rev Richard Jones declared: 'Almost all current political systems are streaked with cruelty. Our British brand of capitalism is no exception. What may be called the harsh underbelly of capitalism treats the poor with a mixture of contempt and patronizing charity.' The Chief Rabbi of the

Orthodox Hebrew congregations, newly ennobled as Lord Immanuel Jakobovits, held that 'government policies have a big element of caring', but 'many people in this country are work-shy'.

PAPAL CONCERNS. Pope John Paul II undertook his 37th international 'pilgrimage' in May with another visit to Latin America, concerned with the inroads of television evangelists and marxism disguised as 'liberation theology'. In an encyclical in February he blamed both 'liberal capitalism and marxist collectivism' for blocking the development of the Third World. A visit to southern Africa in September was marred by the hijacking of a pilgrim bus of nuns and children in Lesotho. This caused the papal aeroplane to be diverted to Johannesburg, originally absent from the Pope's schedule, and South African commandos were brought in to storm the hijacked bus (see p. 295). Although nearly half the people of Lesotho were Catholics, only some 10,000 attended the principal Mass.

In an apostolic letter, *Mulieris Dignitatem* (Dignity of Women), in September the Pope reiterated opposition to women in the priesthood, which was a masculine characteristic in which woman 'could deform and lose all that makes her essential richness'. An editorial in the *Catholic Herald* remarked that 'the Pope is a skilled theologian and has the keenest pastoral awareness, but he is not a woman'. He 'hammers out the hackneyed arguments about the 12 being male, about Christ being male', and was preoccupied with distinctions between male and female. In Italy the birth-rate was among the lowest in Europe, indicating the use of contraceptives against papal directives.

A film, *The Last Temptation of Christ*, which included a sequence of Jesus fantasizing about a sexual liaison with Mary Magdalene, was widely condemned as blasphemous and anti-Christian. The Holy Shroud of Turin, revered for centuries, was finally declared by experts from carbon-dating not to be that of Christ but originating in the fourteenth century (see also p. 488).

Negotiations by the Vatican with the rebel Archbishop Marcel Lefèbvre (see AR 1987, p. 420) finally broke down when on 30 June the Archbishop, against Vatican orders, consecrated the first four bishops of his traditionalist movement. A congregation of thousands from several countries assisted and the Archbishop accused Rome of the sins of 'liberalism, socialism, modernism and Zionism', but his schism entailed automatic excommunication.

For over a year there was controversy between Catholics in Cologne and the Vatican over the appointment of a new archbishop. The cathedral chapter proposed three candidates, all of whom were rejected by the Pope, and in December he made his own conservative choice in Cardinal Joachim Meisner, an action regarded by many Catholics as undemocratic and authoritarian.

Only 34 per cent of the Roman Catholic population in the UK attended Mass regularly, some 2 million compared with 4.5 million at Protestant churches.

TRAVAIL. American evangelist Jimmy Swaggart (see AR 1987, p. 420), who had accused rivals of immorality, went before his 7,000-strong congregation in Louisiana in February, weeping and confessing his own adultery. This humiliation led the elders of his Assemblies of God to give him a second chance after suspension for three months.

In December the Lord Chancellor of Britain, Lord Mackay of Clashfern, was suspended as an elder of the Scottish Free Presbyterian Church because he had attended Roman Catholic Masses for two of his deceased friends.

In South Africa Archbishop Desmond Tutu and other Church leaders were briefly detained by police after a protest march in Cape Town in February, and in September police seized the text of the Archbishop's sermon calling for a boycott of local government elections in defiance of an official prohibition of abstention. In March the Roman Catholic newspaper *New Nation* was banned for three months and accused of 'communism'. In August the headquarters of the South African Council of Churches in Johannesburg was bombed (see p. 298), and in October arsonists set fire to Roman Catholic offices. In December Fr Smangaliso Mkhatshwa was awarded R 25,000 and legal costs by the Ministers for Law and Order in settlement of a damages claim for torture (see AR 1986, p. 391).

In Tibet hundreds of monks and laymen detained after demonstrations in autumn 1987 were released in January, but there were further riots in Lhasa in March, September and December, several demonstrators being killed by police. The Dalai Lama, visiting London and Geneva, spoke of 'over-caution' and proposed a five-point peace plan for Tibet, but other exiled leaders called for armed struggle against Chinese occupation (see AR 1987, p. 422).

WIDER FUNDAMENTALISM. Elections in Israel reflected a trend towards religious extremism, the tolerant Meimad Party receiving no seats but right-wing Shas and Agudat Israel holding the balance of power after rabbis pronounced curses on opponents on television. Ultra-religious parties sought to ban abortions, to close cinemas and beaches on the Sabbath, and to undermine reform Judaism. The Law of Return, guaranteeing a homeland in Israel to overseas Jews, should be changed to allow only those who conformed to rules established by special rabbinical authorities. Widespread protests, especially from the US where most Jews identified with Reform or Conservative movements, influenced the formation of a further coalition between the major Likud and Labour parties without the participation of the ultra-religious formations (see pp. 200–1).

Increasing numbers of Jews were allowed to emigrate from the USSR, although most opted not to go to Israel. An international conference in Oxford, 'Remembering for the Future', considered the causes and lessons of the Holocaust, and in November there was widespread commemoration of the 50th anniversary of *Kristallnacht* when many Jews in Germany had been killed and persecuted and synagogues destroyed. The director of the International Red Cross accepted that this organization had failed to save many Jews from the Nazis.

In March President Ershad declared that Islam was the state religion of Bangladesh and its laws would conform to the Sharia code of conduct, but political opponents called this a diversion and religious leaders said they alone could effect the change. Similar moves in Sudan intensified the conflict between the Arab and Muslim north and the black African non-Muslim south. Hardliners in Egypt called for a breach of the peace treaty with Israel and declaration of Holy War.

Salman Rushdie's novel *The Satanic Verses* aroused protests among Muslims, supported by Chief Rabbi Lord Jakobovits. Mr Rushdie, a lapsed Muslim, took his title from a disputed verse of the Koran and claimed to write of an imaginary prophet, but a ban was demanded by a Society for the Promotion of Religious Tolerance. The winner of the 1988 Nobel Prize for literature, Naguib Mahfouz of Egypt, also suffered demands for bans on his novels from religious groups. (For further details, see Pt. XVI, Ch. 3.)

Sikh extremists seized control of the Golden Temple of Amritsar in May and were expelled only after 30 were killed by Indian army commandos. In July high priest Sohan Singh and a temple official were killed by Sikh separatists in Ludhiana (see AR 1987, p. 422).

BOOKS OF THE YEAR. John Romer's *Testament*, a book and television series on archaeology and faith, was praised by Jewish and Christian critics. Happy cooperation appeared in *Better Together* by Anglican David Sheppard and Roman Catholic Derek Worlock, bishops in Liverpool. John Bowden, director of the Student Christian Movement Press, in *Jesus: The Unanswered Questions*, thought that images of Christ were culturally conditioned, and Lucas Grollenberg in *Unexpected Messiah* criticized interpretations of prophecy. Norman Lewis in *The Missionaries* blamed them for cultural and economic changes, and Peter de Rosa in *Vicars of Christ* exposed the dark side of the papacy. *The World's Religions*, edited by Stewart Sutherland and others, provided a massive guide to historical and living faiths, while *The Myth of Christian Uniqueness* edited by John Hick and Paul Knitter tackled problems of religious encounter and proposed a pluralistic compromise. Jacob Neusner in *Christian Faith and the Bible of Judaism* reflected the dialogue of religions, which was taken further in *The Gospels and Rabbinic Judaism* by Rabbi Michael Hilton and Fr Gordian Marshall. In *T.S. Eliot and Prejudice* Christopher Ricks indicated the poet's anti-semitism, and in *The Six Days of Destruction* Elie Wiesel and Albert Friedlander suggested meditations towards hope after the Holocaust. *The Politics of Islamic Revivalism* edited by Shireen Hunter shed light on diversity, while Leonora Petts in *Women of Marrakech* and Veronica Doubleday in *Three Women of Herat* revealed female conditions under Islam. *The British Discovery of Buddhism* by Philip C. Almond painted a historical picture, while Richard F. Gombrich in *Theravada Buddhism* provided social and religious history from India to Sri Lanka.

XIV THE SCIENCES

Chapter 1

MEDICAL AND SCIENTIFIC RESEARCH

MEDICAL RESEARCH. No cure was found for AIDS (acquired immune deficiency syndrome), the progressive and eventually fatal weakening of the human immune system caused by infection with the human immune virus (HIV). Vaccines intended to protect against infection were being tested in humans, but the unusual nature of infection with HIV, which replicated inside and inactivated the class of white blood cells (T-cells) which normally identified and destroyed foreign organisms entering the body, made the devising of an effective vaccine a very formidable challenge for immunologists. Neither an effective vaccine nor a cure was expected for several years, and existing treatments, of which the most effective was with Zidovudine, AZT, did no more than slow down the progressive loss of immunity.

Meanwhile the spread of the disease continued. By 1 November over 120,000 cases of AIDS had been reported to the World Health Organization from over 140 nations, although WHO estimated that the true total of cases was around 300,000. The symptoms of AIDS were known frequently to be obscured by other syndromes such as malnutrition, especially in parts of Africa. Statistics concerning the incidence of AIDS were, like other medical statistics, hard to gather in nations with limited resources of medical manpower. Some African countries were suspected of under-reporting the incidence of AIDS for fear of losing valuable tourist and other trade.

The numbers infected with HIV greatly exceeded those as yet showing symptoms. WHO's best estimate was that between five and ten million people worldwide were infected with HIV. The period between infection and the first appearance of symptoms, usually of lung infections or rare forms of cancer which normally would have been beaten off by the intact immune system, varied from a few months to eight or more years, with the average incubation period being around 28 months. WHO anticipated a minimum of one million cases of AIDS by the early 1990s, two million by 1994 and three million by 1996.

The AIDS epidemic appeared most serious in large areas of central and eastern Africa, North America and the Caribbean. It was becoming serious in parts of Latin America and Western

Europe. The pattern of infection varied. In what WHO designated Pattern I, apparent in North America, Western Europe, Australia, New Zealand and urban areas in Latin America, transmission was principally through homosexual intercourse or the injection of drugs of abuse, although changing homosexual behaviour was reducing the rate of spread. Relatively few women had been infected but more rapid spread into the heterosexual community via bisexuals and drug abusers who injected was anticipated. In Pattern II areas, namely sub-Saharan Africa, the Caribbean and rural Latin America, sexual transmission was predominantly heterosexual, for reasons which were not fully understood but which possibly included a higher incidence of sores in the genital area (allowing infection through the blood) and more common practice of heterosexual anal intercourse. In Pattern III areas (mainly Eastern Europe and Asia), HIV appeared to have been introduced later, in the early to mid-1980s, so that infections had not yet penetrated into the general population, although prostitutes and people who injected drugs were increasingly at risk.

In the absence of a cure or protective vaccine, and with several hundred million people in the world at clear risk of infection through their sexual or drug-abusing behaviour, WHO saw the role of the media as all-important. Only through ceaseless, frank publicity could people be persuaded to avoid promiscuous behaviour. Anal intercourse with any but a wholly faithful partner to whom one was wholly faithful; any form of sexual intercourse with a new partner without a condom; drug injecting with shared needles: these were the principal activities leading to a high risk of infection with HIV.

The most significant scientific development of the year in combating AIDS was probably the successful transplantation, by a number of US research groups, of the complete human immune system into mice which had had their own immune systems effectively removed, so as to allow human immune cells to be implanted without being rejected by the mice. This made it possible to test the effects of medical drugs designed to try to interfere with the replication of HIV in T-cells (thymus derived lymphocytes) without risking unacceptable side effects on human subjects.

In September 1987 in Mexico City brain tissue taken from a 13-week foetus had been transplanted into the brain of a 50-year-old man severely affected by Parkinson's syndrome, a progressive and incurable disease characterized by uncontrollable shaking and paralysis. The hope was that the living brain cells would supply the neurotransmitter (the brain chemical L-dopa), which is deficient in Parkinson's disease. During 1988 at least 12 similar operations were carried out in the United Kingdom, by a team led by Professor Edward Hitchcock at the Midlands Centre for Neurosurgery near Birmingham. Others were carried out in Sweden and the USA. British scientists had led the way in the animal research needed to prepare the way for this treatment. At the end of the year some of the patients were said unofficially to have shown some improvement, but no formal results had been published and it was too early to know whether any improvement would be maintained.

The technique raised ethical issues. One dispute was, of course, between those who opposed abortion on principle and those who supported legally-controlled abortion and believed that, since foetuses were made available through abortion, it was logical to make use of any available foetal material to help people regain health. But some who favoured controlled abortion were uneasy about the removal of living brain material from foetuses, even though the brain from which it came was at such an early stage of development that it could not have been conscious. The British Medical Association published guidelines to try to ensure that no woman would undergo an abortion simply to provide material for treating Parkinson's disease. But it was clear that if the treatment proved successful, perhaps also for other common brain conditions such as Alzheimer's syndrome, then the demand for foetal brain tissue might become so strong that women in the poorest countries of the world especially might become pregnant in order to sell foetal tissue for use in brain implants.

Psychiatrists at the Middlesex Hospital in London published research findings indicating a strong link between schizophrenia and inherited genetic factors. Another study, published in the same issue of *Nature*, found no such link. Earlier studies of identical twins had provided evidence for a genetic link. The general picture emerging, as with manic-depressive disease, was one of inherited predisposition to mental illness, probably caused by several different genetic factors, which could be triggered into active illness by a number of different environmental factors. Hopes accordingly centred around the possibility of using genetic probes to identify those at greatest risk of illness, and then protecting them against the environmental factors which might trigger it.

Another controversial research result came from Swansea University in Wales, where Gwilym Roberts, a schoolteacher who had become convinced of a decline in his pupils' intelligence over the past eight years, decided to test his hypothesis that the decline might be due to the growing consumption of convenience foods such as chips and ice-cream. A properly-controlled study of 60 pupils, organized by Mr Roberts and a university psychologist and first revealed in a widely-publicized television programme, revealed a substantial and statistically significant improvement in the non-verbal intelligence of the children who had been given vitamin tablets daily for nine months. A similar experiment carried out on children in a juvenile detention centre in the US at about the same time gave similar results. Together these studies implied that the most fundamental parameters of intelligence could be improved by vitamin supplementation of an impoverished diet. Other psychologists strongly disputed the theory, however, and its findings remained controversial.

A survey of 22,000 men in the US over five years showed that one aspirin tablet taken every day halved their average risk of a coronary heart attack. The findings suggested that men from families with a history of heart disease would be well-advised to take an aspirin every other day, in addition to other precautions such as not smoking, drinking little alcohol, eating only small amounts of animal fat and taking moderate exercise.

An important advance in cancer treatment was begun by the use of so-called 'chimaeric' or 'humanized' antibodies to treat leukaemia. These were antibodies made, in the bodies of rats, to react selectively with cancer cells. The use of such antibodies in cancer therapy had been severely limited by the fact that, being made in the bodies of rats or mice, they were recognized as foreign by the body of the cancer patient into whom they were injected and rapidly eliminated by the rejection process. A team led by Dr Greg Winter of the Cambridge Laboratory for Molecular Biology used genetic engineering techniques (now referred to as protein engineering when used for such purposes) to reshape the anti-cancer antibodies and to surround the reactive sites made in rats with human antibody material, so the antibodies were effectively disguised as human material and were no longer rejected. Very good results were obtained in treating two leukaemia patients who had failed to respond to other treatments, using humanized anti-cancer antibodies. Plans were made to use the same technique to treat several other conditions including other forms of cancer and toxic shock, and to prevent the rejection of grafted organs.

New techniques developed and tested in the UK made it possible to identify abnormalities caused by genetic defects so early that no abortions would be needed to prevent the birth of babies affected by them. Dr Marilyn Monk of the Medical Research Council's Mammalian Development Research Unit in London showed that it was possible to fertilize an egg cell outside the body, to remove one cell from the resultant embryo at the very early eight-cell stage, while the embryo was still just a microscopic clump of undifferentiated cells, and to test that single cell to see if the embryo was affected by a genetic defect. If the embryo was affected it could be destroyed, but if it was unaffected it could be reimplanted to continue its development to a normal birth. In this way, women at risk of giving birth to babies with serious inherited defects could be protected against such births, while avoiding the trauma of repeated abortion.

Dr Monk and her colleagues stressed, however, that more research on early human embryos was needed before the technique could be made reliable enough for routine use. If future legislation placed a ban on embryo research, then a succession of abortions would remain the only way to avoid the birth of children doomed to an early death because of genetic abnormalities. The Government's failure to introduce legislation to provide accepted guidelines for embryo research in 1988 was strongly criticized.

SPACE AND AVIATION. The first US space shuttle to fly since the disastrous explosion of *Challenger* in January 1986 (see AR 1986, pp. 48-50, 399, 402) lifted off on 29 September. *Discovery* was equipped with rebuilt solid fuel boosters, a joint failure in one of which had caused the 1986 disaster. It had a successful mission, during which the crew of five deployed a communications satellite designed to enable future shuttle missions to keep in touch with ground control over longer periods. A second US shuttle, *Atlantis*, was launched on 2 December, officially as a secret military mission. However, aviation magazines were able to piece together enough data to establish that its purpose was to launch a low-altitude reconnaissance satellite able to image military manoeuvres on land and sea in all weathers using very powerful radar.

After delays lasting several months the first Soviet space shuttle, named *Buran* (meaning Snowstorm), made its maiden flight, unmanned, for just two orbits under radio control from the ground. Several other Soviet shuttles were said by a Soviet spokesman to be under construction. Like US shuttles, which it closely resembled, *Buran* was launced vertically by rocket but landed like an aeroplane. Unlike US shuttles, *Buran* had no onboard rocket engines. All power for the launch was provided by the giant *Energia* liquid-fuel launch vehicle, the most powerful in the world. Also unlike US shuttles, *Buran* had jet engines for manoeuvring on the way down to land, giving it much more flexibility in its landing path and in the choice of a landing ground than US equivalents. Soviet spokesmen said *Buran* was intended to ferry future crew to and from space stations, and to help assemble space stations in orbit. It and other Soviet shuttles were not intended to take over virtually all space launching tasks, as the US shuttle had originally been planned to do. The majority of Soviet satellite launches were to continue to be made using conventional rocket boosters.

On 21 December two Soviet cosmonauts, Vladimir Titov and Musa Manarov, returned to Earth after spending 366 days in orbit in the space station *Mir*. With them was a French astronaut, Jean-Loup Chrétien, who was the 14th foreign national to have flown a Soviet-sponsored space mission.

On 20 December the US National Aeronautics and Space Administration (NASA) unveiled plans for a manned mission to Mars. These plans, which were to be put to the US Congress for approval, included several options, the most ambitious of which could put Americans on Mars by the year 2004. No cooperative effort with the USSR was envisaged.

One of two Soviet *Phobos* probes launched towards Mars during the year eventually ceased to function, because ground control had issued an incorrect radio command to it, causing the probe's power-collecting solar panels to swing away from the Sun. The other *Phobos* probe was suffering severe mechanical problems at the end of the year, when it seemed probable that the entire mission was heading for total failure.

The experimental US B-2 bomber, which used so-called 'Stealth' technology to make it invisible to radar as well as other techniques to avoid heat-seeking missiles, was shown briefly to reporters on 2 November (see also p. 428). Shaped like a smoothly-curved boomerang with no sharp protuberances, the B-2 was said to use carbon-fibre materials and special paint which absorbed rather than reflected radio waves, so as to prevent radar beams being reflected from its fuselage. Because the amount of detectable heat produced by the aircraft's four engines had been reduced at the cost of engine efficiency and speed, the B-2 could travel only at subsonic speeds.

ASTRONOMY AND PARTICLE PHYSICS. A new array of radio telescopes was opened in September in Calgoora, 350 km north-west of Sydney, Australia. The Australia Telescope, the most powerful in the southern hemisphere, comprising eight receiving dishes at three locations, was to be used to examine the southern hemisphere in the same detail as the northern. It was hoped that it would help to solve such puzzles as whether or not our own galaxy, the Milky Way, had a black hole swallowing stars at its heart.

The discovery, announced during the year, of a large planet orbiting a nearby star was the first absolute proof of the existence of planets other than those of the Solar System in the Universe. Although this particular planet was much too hot to support life, its discovery greatly strengthened the case for the existence of extra-terrestrial life and intelligence.

On 10 November the US Energy Secretary, John Herrington, announced the winner of a year-long contest between 25 states to become the home of the world's largest-ever scientific instrument, the Superconducting Supercollider (SSC). Subject to congressional approval of funding the SSC would be built in Texas, at Waxahachie just south of Dallas, and would be 20 times more powerful than the most powerful machines already in operation. It would incorporate a subterranean tunnel 82 km in circumference, in which subatomic particles were to be accelerated to near the speed of light, moving in opposite directions before colliding into each other head-on. Questions which it might answer included: whether all sub-atomic particles are made of different combinations of just two basic particles, quarks and leptons; and whether the apparently different forces which hold matter together are really different manifestations of one basic force.

MOLECULAR GENETICS. The year's single most important discovery in the field of molecular biology and genetic engineering was probably that by Professor John Ellis of Warwick University and others of substances nicknamed 'molecular chaperones', because their task was to ensure that reactions proceeded in the proper manner and at the proper pace. Without their chaperones, it was becoming clear, vital enzymes such as those responsible for photosynthesis could not perform their tasks properly. From the point of view of biotechnology, this meant that enzymes being harnessed for use in industry, or transferred into new organisms so as to 'clone' new drugs, would have to be accompanied by their chaperones. This discovery made a huge area of biotechnology potentially twice as difficult and expensive to develop.

On 13 October, in Turin, the famous shroud, a relic kept in the cathedral and believed by some earlier authorities to have been the burial cloth of Christ, was officially declared a medieval fake dating from between 1260 and 1390 AD. Samples had been tested in three laboratories in Zürich, Arizona and Oxford, using a dating technique in which a few threads of material were treated to separate the isotope carbon 14 from the more common carbon 12. Carbon 14 was continually replenished in living material but decayed (changed to carbon 12) at a steady rate. When the flax from which the shroud had been made was gathered and became lifeless, the proportion of carbon 14 relative to carbon 12 in it would have begun steadily to decrease. In this way the age of the shroud was reliably assessed to within approximately one hundred years.

NOBEL PRIZES. The Nobel Prize for Medicine went to two Americans, Gertrude Evans and George Hitchins, and a Scotsman, Sir James Black. The American work had led to drugs to combat herpes, leukaemia and malaria and to prevent the rejection of transplanted organs. Sir James Black's work had led to the development of drugs to treat heart disease and to prevent the recurrence of stomach ulcers. Three West Germans, Dr Johann Deisenhofer, Professor Robert Huber and Dr Hartmut Michel, shared the Chemistry Prize for work which had led to a better understanding of photosynthesis, the complex series of chemical reactions on which all life on Earth ultimately depended. The Physics Prize went to three Americans, Drs Leon Lederman, Melvin Schwartz and Jack Steinberger, for their discovery of the subatomic particle, the mu-neutrino. This discovery showed that subatomic particles formed a symmetrical family group, and also showed how other subatomic particles might be dissected to reveal how they were composed of still smaller particles.

Chapter 2

TECHNOLOGY

ARTIFICIAL INTELLIGENCE. The year marked an important stage in the controversial attempt by researchers working for the Japanese Government to develop a new generation of 'intelligent' computers, the so-called fifth generation. An international conference in Tokyo in November launched the final stage of the ten-year project, which began in 1982. Its goal was to develop a computer capable of human-like abilities of reasoning and the ability to process knowledge rather than numbers. Experts in artificial intelligence were impressed by some of the fifth generation project's achievements. Among them was a machine called the Multi-PSI, which consisted of 64 different processing circuits connected in parallel, to tackle problems simultaneously rather than sequentially as with conventional computers. This was hailed as the first step towards a computer consisting of 1,000 parallel processors which, the Japanese team said, would be capable of genuine artificial intelligence. Another computer on display demonstrated one attribute of artificial intelligence—the ability to answer questions on a piece of text by inferring facts not explicitly stated within it.

Despite the successes of the fifth generation project, experts around the world were questioning whether the Japanese were approaching artificial intelligence in the right way. The Japanese team conceded that it still faced many problems, particularly in designing programmes which would run on the new parallel computers, and that it might not reach its goal by the target year of 1992. By 1988 most computer scientists believed that artificial intelligence was possible, but arguments continued to rage about how to define the concept.

COMPUTER DEVELOPMENTS. In the realm of more conventional computers, the year saw a comeback by Steve Jobs, the Californian entrepreneur who helped create the microcomputer business in 1977 with his company Apple Computers. Mr Jobs, who had been ousted from Apple in 1986 by a new management, unveiled a new personal computer which he called NeXT, aimed at the education market. In many ways, the computer reflected the state of the art of personal computing in the late 1980s, based around a 32-bit microprocesor, the Motorola 68030, with eight megabytes of random-access memory. One breakthrough, however, was the NeXT computer's disc storage device. Unlike previous microcomputers which had relied on magnetic storage, either in removable floppy discs capable of storing at most one megabyte of information, or fixed 'Winchester' discs with capacities of between 20 megabytes and 40 megabytes, NeXT employed optical technology.

The computing world had long pondered such a changeover, because optical discs could hold vastly more data than magnetic ones. But the difficulty of recording new information on optical discs held back their everyday use. NeXT's secret was a hybrid magneto-optical disc, developed by the Japanese company Canon, which had 256 megabytes of capacity, enough to store more than 300 complete books. To 'write' information on the disc, a magnetic field was applied and a laser heated up a tiny spot, changing the alignment of crystals; the same laser 'read' or retrieved information, but without the magnetic field. The technology, which several other companies were developing, promised to free computers from the limits of magnetic storage. However, its further development needed to overcome the computer industry's old bugbear, the lack of technical standards to make one manufacturer's disc run in another make of computer.

SOFTWARE STANDARDS. Efforts continued around the world to create international software standards, which would allow programmes to work on computers regardless of make. In May, International Business Machines (IBM) of the US, by far the world's largest maker of computers, joined six other manufacturers in an organization called the Open Software Foundation. The companies agreed to introduce standard operating systems—software which converted useful programmes into instructions that the computer could understand—based on the Unix programme. However, the company which originally invented Unix, American Telephone and Telegraph (AT&T), promptly organized a rival group based on another version of the software.

Independent arbitrators settled one of the computer industry's longest-running legal battles, over Fujitsu's duplication of IBM's software. Under an agreement announced in November, the Japanese company agreed to make payments totalling $833 million to use the software. Litigation continued to fly elsewhere in the computer industry, with Apple bringing suits against companies for allegedly copying features of its pioneering Macintosh microcomputer.

HACKING AND VIRUSES. A rash of incidents involving 'hacking' (unauthorized tapping into computers) raised fears about the security of the world's computer systems. In April, investigators revealed that a mysterious West German programmer had managed to gain entry to more than 30 computers in military bases in the US, Japan, West Germany and Canada. In May, a computer 'virus'—a section of programme designed to duplicate itself and spread to other computers through telephone lines—was detected in thousands of computers in Israel. The virus, nicknamed 'Black Friday', was constructed to shut down any computer it infected on Friday 13 May. Finally, in November, a virus created by an American computer student caused chaos at hundreds of government and university computers throughout the United States. Computers belonging to the US Air Force and the Lawrence Livermore National Laboratory, which designed nuclear weapons, were among those infected.

Meanwhile, in Britain the House of Lords finally cleared two enthusiasts who had used home computers to gain access to British Telecom's electronic mail system. The Lords were upholding an earlier decision by the Appeal Court that such hacking was 'trickery, but not illegal'.

OPTOELECTRONICS. Optoelectronic technology, in which pulses of light rather than electricity carry information, made some significant inroads into people's everyday lives. In December 1988, the first transatlantic optical fibre telephone cable went into service, linking Britain and France with the United States. The cable, called TAT-8, could handle 40,000 simultaneous telephone conversations, transmitted as pulses of laser light through 5,000 kilometres of hair-thin optical fibres. The newest conventional copper cable, laid five years before, could carry 8,500 conversations. Work also began on an optical fibre cable under the Pacific Ocean between Japan and the United States.

COMPACT DISCS. Even closer to most people's everyday lives, 1988 was the year when the compact disc, which stored recorded music as a digital code to be read by a laser, began to eclipse the mechanical long-playing record. Compact discs, developed by Philips of the Netherlands in partnership with Japan's Sony, first went on sale in 1982. After a slow start, mainly because of record companies' reluctance to release music in the new format, compact discs rapidly caught on. By 1988, several specialist record companies had stopped releasing material on mechanical long-players. In November 1988, the first major company to follow suit, CBS/Sony, said it would stop producing mechanical records in spring 1989.

Meanwhile, the electronics company Tandy of the United States announced in May that it had developed a compact disc capable of recording as well as playing back music. The company could not say when the system would become a reality. Apart from technical obstacles, it faced potential opposition by record companies, worried about copyright infringements. By 1988 the record industry had effectively killed another high-quality recording technology, digital audio tape, which Japanese electronics companies had unveiled two years previously.

TELEVISION AND VIDEO. The consumer electronics industry was wrestling with an even bigger technical and political transition—the next generation of television. The Olympic Games in Seoul provided Japan's electronics companies, which dominated the world's consumer electronics industry, with a chance to demonstrate their system, called high-definition television. During the Olympics, a satellite relayed television pictures made up of 1,125 picture lines, twice as many as normal, to special screens set up in department stores and public areas. Japanese consumers reacted enthusiastically to the pictures, which were far sharper than those of conventional broadcasts. But, elsewhere in the world, Governments and broadcasters viewed the system with suspicion, fearing that the new technology would give a huge advantage to Japanese companies. The announcement in May that the last British-owned television manufacturer, Fidelity, would close, underlined such anxiety.

In response, government organizations in Europe and the United States tried to organize their own electronics industries to develop domestic technologies for high-definition television, a market expected to be worth $100,000 million by 1991. In October, the European Community and Japan agreed to work together to develop guidelines for high-definition television. The US, however, seemed set to develop its own system, financed by the Department of Defense, with the aim of supporting America's electronics industry.

Undeterred, Japan's electronics companies ploughed ahead in new directions. In June, the innovative Sony unveiled a pocket-sized combined video-tape recorder and television set. The device, called the Video Walkman, played 8-mm video cassette tapes on a flat colour screen. The company hoped the technology would spawn a new industry producing 'video magazines' and other programmes on 8-mm tapes, but by the end of the year it was too early to say whether the idea would catch on.

SILICON CHIPS. The silicon integrated circuit, the technology at the heart of these electronic innovations, continued to shrink. During the summer, Japanese manufacturers released first samples of dynamic random-access memory chips, also known as DRAMS, capable of holding 4 million bits (four megabits) of information. The new chips packed 9 million components into a circuit 5-mm wide and 15-mm long. They were among the first built with true sub-micron technology, containing structures less than 1 micron (one micrometre) in size.

Electronics companies were already working on the next step, DRAMS with capacities of 16 megabits, with structures half a micron in size. The Japanese giant NEC said it was setting up a pilot production line for such chips. Its rival, Hitachi, decided to join forces with Texas Instruments of the United States to develop the technology. Meanwhile, engineers working for Fujitsu, Japan's largest computer company, announced that they had created the basic structure for a 64-megabit DRAM. Such chips would be capable of storing 256 newspaper pages in a piece of silicon the size of a fingernail.

SATELLITES AND SPACE. For Britons, direct broadcasting of television programmes by satellite came a step closer in December when a European Ariane rocket launched the *Astra* direct broadcasting television satellite. It was a flawless year for Arianespace, the French-dominated consortium which operated Ariane. The Ariane 4 rocket, which was capable of boosting a payload of 4.2 tonnes into space, seemed set to become the workhorse of commercial space until the end of the century. Its main challengers in the business of commercial satellite launches were China's Long March 2 rocket and the Soviet Union's tried and tested Proton, both of which were heavily promoted by their respective Governments. (For US and Soviet space shuttle flights see pp. 60-1, 446-7; for broadcasting satellites see pp. 494-5.)

In July, the British Government announced that it would end funding for the Hotol spaceplane, a concept proposed by British Aerospace and Rolls-Royce for an unmanned craft which could fly from runways into earth orbit at a fraction of the cost of conventional rockets. However, Britain reluctantly agreed to join the 13-nation European Space Agency's long-term plan, 'Horizon 2000', which involved creating an independent European presence in space over 20 years.

Chapter 3

ENVIRONMENT

MID-WESTERN North America experienced one of its worst-ever droughts in 1988; hurricane 'Gilbert', one of the most powerful tropical storms of the century, tore across Jamaica and into Mexico; much of Bangladesh was flooded. And 1988 joined 1980, 1981, 1983 and 1987 as among the warmest years on record. These may all have been random natural events. But they were the sort which computer models of the planet's climate had forecast would be associated with a gradual, pollution-driven warming of the globe—the so-called 'greenhouse effect'. Dr James Hansen of the US National Aeronautics and Space Administration (NASA) told the US Congress that the Earth was warmer during the first five months of 1988 than at any time since measurements began 40 years ago. According to Dr Hansen, it was 99 per cent certain that the warming was caused by a build-up of carbon dioxide and other 'greenhouse gases' in the atmosphere.

In Toronto, more than 300 researchers and policy-makers from 48 nations met in June and announced: 'Humanity is conducting an enormous, unintended, globally pervasive experiment whose ultimate consequence could be second only to a global nuclear war.' The conference agreed that the mean surface temperature of the earth would rise by 1.5-4.5°C by the middle of next century (but twice this in the higher latitudes) and sea levels by 30 cm to 1.5 m. These effects were thought to be induced by increased levels of carbon dioxide from power plants, by the burning of forests and by other 'greenhouse' gases such as methane, nitrous oxide and chlorofluorocarbons (CFCs).

A study by an international scientific committee released in Washington in March found that the stratospheric ozone layer, which protected living things from ultra-violet radiation, was thinning by 6 per cent in the Northern latitudes each winter; this annual loss was much more than had been predicted. The panel concluded that the thinning, which replicated the thinning of ozone over the Antarctic, was due to the release of CFCs used in aerosols, refrigerators, air conditioners and in various industrial processes.

Such findings and events possibly helped to convince several national leaders to pronounce themselves environmentally concerned. British Prime Minister Margaret Thatcher warned the Royal Society that humankind, in its environmental mismanagement, 'may have unwittingly begun a massive experiment with the system of this planet itself'. She added: 'We need to identify particular areas of research which will help to establish cause and effect.' Her speech raised expectations that a 'Green Bill' bringing together various environmental concerns would emerge in 1989.

US Vice-President George Bush campaigned successfully for the presidency partly as an environmentalist. Soviet Foreign Minister Eduard Shevardnadze proposed to the UN General Assembly that nations should abolish some military programmes and use the funds released for 'an international regime of environmental security'. Brazilian President José Sarney promised in October that his nation, which contained one-third of the world's rainforests, would protect these forests. He said that his Government would restrict subsidies to farmers in the Amazon region, ban the export of all logs and subject every forest project to environmental controls. The Prime Ministers of Canada and Norway—Brian Mulroney and Gro Harlem Brundtland respectively—called in June for a 'law of the atmosphere' to protect the planet from atmospheric pollution.

Evidence emerged during the year that northern industrial nations were systematically dumping toxic and/or hazardous wastes in developing southern nations. Nigeria charged Italy with dumping waste at its port of Koko (see also p. 259), and Guinea arrested a Norwegian diplomat for representing a US firm which deposited fly ash on an island near the capital. The freighter *Karin B*, carrying over 2,000 tonnes of toxic waste from the Koko site, was given permission to tie up at Livorno, Italy, in October after six European countries had refused to let it dock. An OAU meeting in Addis Ababa in May denounced the 'increasing tendency' of African nations to accept such refuse, along with nuclear wastes. The UN Environment Programme (UNEP) began work on a treaty to control such deposits.

In a development which caused considerable ire among environmental groups trying to protect Antarctica as a 'world park', 33 nations concluded six years of negotiations on a treaty to open all of the continent to regulated development of its oil and mineral resources. The treaty, initialled on 2 June in Wellington, New Zealand, was to take effect after ratification by 16 of the 20 voting members of the Antarctic Treaty.

Several events in 1988 could not be explained by scientists, but had an effect upon the public's environmental fears. An epidemic which was thought to have taken the lives of thousands of bottle-nosed dolphins off the US east coast—over 800 bodies were washed ashore—ended in March. A virus similar to that which caused rhinderpest killed thousands of common seals in the Baltic, the North Sea and the Irish Sea. Algal blooms off the coasts of Norway, Sweden and Denmark killed all marine life they encountered and wreaked havoc among salmon farms, doing at least £2 million worth of damage.

Numerous theories linked these events to various forms of

pollution (acid rain and fertilizer run-off for the algae and seal deaths), but scientists could find no such causes. At one point the dolphins were thought to be suffering a form of AIDS, as their natural immunity systems seemed to have been degraded. Hospital waste, including vials of AIDS antibodies, were washed up during the year on north-eastern US beaches. The AIDS theory was later discounted, but one possibility that remained was that the dolphin deaths were due to stress caused by hotter than usual water. Such disasters, and increased concern over global warming amd ozone depletion, were all likely factors in a Gallup poll finding, published by the *Daily Telegraph* in November, that damage to the environment was seen as among the three greatest threats to humankind, alongside war between the superpowers and nuclear destruction.

In a development related to the general issue of global warming, scientists found that much of the clearing of the Amazonian rainforests was being accomplished by burning, which released carbon-dioxide into the atmosphere very rapidly. Brazilian scientists reported that 77,000 square miles of forest were burned in 1987, and that preliminary data for 1988 indicated an even larger area of such destruction.

The World Bank, often criticized for its own projects in Amazonia, completed the creation of its new Environment Department. Kenneth Piddington, former New Zealand environment commissioner, was appointed director of the department, whose staff of 40 represented a seven-fold increase over the old system. The Bank created an environmental division for each of its four geographic regions.

A report by the UN Environment Programme and the World Health Organization, based on 15 years of monitoring in more than 60 nations, found that most of the world's 1,800 million urban dwellers were breathing air of unacceptable quality. According to the report, cities such as Milan, Seoul, Rio de Janeiro and Paris all suffered air pollution averaging above the WHO guidelines, the problem being concentrated in Third World urban areas.

In October, the signatory nations of the 1972 London Dumping Convention agreed in Washington to minimize or reduce the incineration of toxic wastes at sea by 1991 and to end all such burning by 1994 if acceptable alternatives could be developed. The agreement also banned the export of liquid toxic wastes for incineration or other disposal harmful to the environment. At about the same time the US Congress agreed to ban the ocean dumping of sewage sludge after 1991.

In Europe, a protocol covering nitrous oxide emissions—a major cause of acid precipitation—was added to the UN Economic Commission for Europe's Geneva Convention on Long-Range Air Pollution. The European Community formally agreed emission standards for small cars that were laxer than US standards but tighter than members such as the UK, France, and Italy had wanted.

An earlier ruling by the European Court of Justice that the Danish Government could require beer and soft drinks to be sold only in returnable bottles was criticized as an unfair trade barrier by countries importing beverages to Denmark. Nevertheless, the ruling was potentially profoundly significant for the 1992 goal of a single European market, since it appeared to put environmental considerations above free trade requirements. Following agreement at the European summit meeting in February, several EEC nations initiated in mid-year programmes to 'set aside' proportions of productive agricultural land, a practice pioneered in the United States. While in theory this could have beneficial environmental effects, such as the creation of more wildlife habitats, observers were concerned that it could have negative effects, such as encouraging farmers to use more fertilizers and chemicals on land still in production.

The British Government introduced Bills to 'privatize' both water and energy. The former legislation would create a relatively powerful National River Authority; but strengthened environmental regulations would require more investment in pollution controls, so that water was expected to become more expensive. The move to privatize energy demonstrated that entrepreneurs wanted nothing to do with nuclear power, with the result that the Government was forced to require that after privatization power companies should continue to buy 20 per cent of their power from nuclear plants.

In an environmental drama which caught the attention of the world towards the end of the year, Soviet ice-breakers helped to free two grey whales trapped in a tiny, ice-locked patch of open water off northern Alaska. But US environmental groups charged that this concern covered up the fact that the US Government was refusing to use strict economic sanctions against Japan, Norway and Iceland to force them to stop whaling. The Soviet Union announced in 1988 that it had ceased whaling.

Finally, the Swedish Government, reacting to a campaign by 81-year-old children's story writer Astrid Lindgren, established perhaps the world's most stringent programme to protect the rights and improve the welfare of farm animals.

XV THE LAW

Chapter 1

INTERNATIONAL LAW—EUROPEAN COMMUNITY LAW

INTERNATIONAL LAW

As in 1987, the International Court of Justice did not give judgment on the merits of any contentious case, although it had five such cases before it. Proceedings in the case brought by Nicaragua against Honduras, *Border and Transborder Actions*, had been retarded at the request of both parties (See AR 1987, p. 440), but they were resumed when Nicaragua requested the Court to indicate provisional measures, including the assignment of observers to monitor border incidents. Although Nicaragua later withdrew this request, the hearings on jurisdiction and admissibility continued. The Court unanimously decided that it had jurisdiction in this dispute over the activities of armed bands allegedly operating from Honduras against Nicaragua.

The Court based its jurisdiction on the 1948 Pact of Bogatá (i.e. the America Treaty on Pacific Settlement). It rejected Honduras's argument that the unilateral declarations it had made in 1986 in an attempt to limit the Court's jurisdiction under the Optional Clause could operate to restrict jurisdiction based on the Pact of Bogotá. Honduras also objected to the admissibility of Nicaragua's application, first on the ground that the application was politically inspired. The Court observed that it could not concern itself with the political motivation which may have led a state at a particular time to choose judicial settlement. As to Honduras's argument that the result of Nicaragua's action was 'an artificial and arbitrary dividing up of the general conflict existing in Central America', the Court repeated the view it had taken earlier in the *Iranian Hostages* case (see AR 1980, pp. 398–9) that the Court would not decline to take cognizance of one aspect of a dispute merely because that dispute had other aspects, however important. The Court also rejected Honduras's arguments that the application was too vague, and that the dispute should be settled by direct negotiation or by the Contadora process.

The Court delivered an Advisory Opinion on the *Applicability of the Obligation to Arbitrate under Section 21 of the United Nations Headquarters Agreement* in response to problems arising out of the relations between the United States as host state of the United Nations and the PLO (see also pp. 375–7). The US Congress had passed the 1987 Anti-Terrorism Act 'to make unlawful the establishment and maintenance within the United States of an office of the PLO'; under this Act the Attorney-General brought an action in the United States courts to close the office of the PLO observer mission to the UN.

The UN Secretary-General protested that the Anti-Terrorism Act violated the Headquarters Agreement. This agreement, he maintained, imposed a treaty obligation on the United States to allow personnel of the PLO mission, invited by the General Assembly in 1974 to participate in its work as an observer, to enter and remain in the United States to carry out their official functions. The Secretary-General called on the United States to submit the dispute to arbitration as required by the Headquarters Agreement. The US Secretary of State agreed that the closing of the mission would violate the Headquarters Agreement, but argued that no dispute existed between the United States and the United Nations because the Anti-Terrorism Act had not yet been implemented. He said that they should await the outcome of the US litigation before resorting to arbitration.

On 29 February the General Assembly voted to ask the International Court of Justice for an Advisory Opinion on the question whether the United States was under an obligation to enter into arbitration in accordance with the Headquarters Agreement for the settlement of the dispute between itself and the United Nations.

The Court accelerated the normal procedure because of the urgency of answering the question before the United States implemented the Anti-Terrorism Act. It found unanimously that there was a dispute between the United Nations and the United States concerning the interpretation and application of the Headquarters Agreement; this was a matter for objective determination and did not depend on mere assertions of the parties. The possibilities of negotiation between the United States and the United Nations had been exhausted and there was no legal duty to wait for the decisions of the US court. Indeed, the purpose of the Headquarters Agreement was to settle disputes between the United Nations and the host state without prior recourse to municipal courts; therefore the United States was under an obligation to enter into arbitration. In the event, however, the US court subsequently ruled against implementation of the 1987 Act in respect of the PLO office, and the US Government decided not to lodge an appeal.

A new case was brought to the Court by Denmark against Norway; this was the latest in a long line of maritime boundary cases but was only the second application (the first was the *Gulf of Maine* case, see AR 1984, p. 409) to request the delimitation of a single maritime boundary for both fishing zones and continental shelves. Denmark asked the Court to decide in accordance with international law where a single line of limitation should be drawn in the waters between Greenland and the Norwegian island of Jan Mayen.

Judge Nagendra Singh (India) died on 11 December (see OBITUARY). Judge José Maria Ruda (Argentina) was elected President of the Court and Judge Kéba Mbaye (Senegal) was re-elected Vice-President.

The *Taba* arbitration between Egypt and Israel which had begun in December 1986 ended with the five-member international arbitration panel finding in favour of Egypt. They held that the Taba strip, a border area south of Eilat on the Sinai coast which Israel had retained after its withdrawal from the Sinai in 1982, should be returned to Egypt (see also p. 206).

In the year in which the United Nations celebrated the 40th anniversary of the adoption of the Universal Declaration of Human Rights there were several important developments in the international and regional protection of human rights. The *Convention against Apartheid in Sports* entered into force on 3 April. This requires states parties not to permit sports contact with a country practising apartheid and to take appropriate action to ensure their sports bodies, teams, and individual sportsmen do not have such contact. The *First Protocol to the European Social Charter* opened for signature on 5 May. This extends the rights set out in the Charter: contracting states undertake to accept as a policy aim the realization of certain social and economic rights such as equal opportunities in employment, workers' rights to consultation and to participation in decisions on conditions in the workplace, and the right of the elderly to social protection. Contracting states also undertake to be bound by at least one of these rights immediately.

The Inter-American Court of Human Rights gave its first decision on the merits of a contentious case. It unanimously held that the disappearances of Velásquez Rodríguez and others in Honduras in 1981-82 entailed that state's responsibility for violation of the rights to life, humane treatment and personal liberty. Also for the first time, the Court exercised its powers to order Honduras to pay fair compensation to the victims' next of kin.

The African Commission, established under the *African Charter on Human and People's Rights* (which entered into force 21 October 1986), adopted rules of procedure to clarify its functions in securing the implementation of the African Charter. The Committee against Torture, a panel of ten independent experts established under the *Convention against Torture* (see AR 1987, p. 442), held its first session to monitor the behaviour of states parties to the Convention.

The European Court of Human Rights ruled on 29 November

that the United Kingdom had violated Article 5(3) of the *European Convention on Human Rights* by its application of the Prevention of Terrorism (Temporary Provisions) Act 1984. The ruling related to four persons detained by the police in Northern Ireland in 1984 under the Prevention of Terrorism Act, allowing the police to hold suspects without charge for up to seven days. They were held for periods of between four days six hours and six days 16 hours. None was charged or brought before a judicial authority before being released. By 12 votes to 7 the Court held that the United Kingdom had violated Article 5(3), which provides that everyone arrested and detained shall be brought promptly before a judge or other officer authorized by law to exercise judicial power. At the end of the year the United Kingdom was still considering its response to this ruling.

Certain new treaties were opened for signature. The *Convention on the Regulation of Antarctic Mineral Resources*, initialled on 2 June (see p. 455), provides a framework for prospecting and exploration for minerals in the Antarctic and creates institutions to control these activities.

In response to the *Achille Lauro* hijacking (see AR 1985, pp. 137–8), the International Maritime Organization drew up (in March) the *Convention for the Suppression of Unlawful Acts against the Safety of Maritime Navigation* and an associated *Protocol on Fixed Platforms Located on the Continental Shelf*. Both agreements are designed to strengthen co-operation against terrorism and both are based on the 'prosecute or extradite' principles found in the Montreal Convention on aircraft hijacking. Another treaty against terrorism opened for signature was the *Protocol for the Suppression of Unlawful Acts of Violence at Airports Serving Civil Aviation*, drawn up under the auspices of the International Civil Aviation Organization.

EUROPEAN COMMUNITY LAW

THIS was a year of consolidation and deepening as the image of 1992 and the single European market began to bite. The pace of legislative enactment perceptibly increased, helped by the new parliamentary procedures of the Single European Act (see AR 1987, pp. 535–48), including a widened majority voting, and the political pressures on the member states not to hinder the completion of the internal market. These pressures also brought into the open the political dimension of the Community, which was given particularly dramatic form in an intense clash between the policy attitudes of the British Prime Minister, Mrs Thatcher, as defined in a key speech at Bruges, and the President of the European Commission, Jacques Delors (see p. 391). There was also a parallel increase in the high constitutional law cases before the European Court and in political tensions between the Community and the outside world, notably with Efta, the USA and Japan.

The previous year's surge in interest among the Efta countries in joining the Community calmed down but did not go away. The Community's negative attitude, however, increased; and it seemed that it would even welcome a strengthening of Efta itself if that would remove the pressures for enlargement. This was linked to signs of a rapidly developing 'Community chauvinism', an unwillingness of some to share the perceived advantages of the Community with outsiders, whether they be fellow-Europeans or on other continents.

There were also fears that the benefits of the truly common market would be seized by foreign enterprises which would take advantage of the resulting economies of scale quicker than the industries within the Community, particularly in the field of services, where the continental member states had never been very willing to relinquish national controls. The suggestion was therefore aired that non-EEC service enterprises such as banks, even if having an EEC subsidiary, should not enjoy freedom of services unless their home state granted reciprocal rights to Community enterprises. This idea was resisted by the United States and was added to that country's existing irritation over new Community legislation prohibiting the administration of certain growth hormones to beef cattle. The US retaliated against Community exports, but both sides, although firm, showed a distaste for the trade war which might ensue.

The United States also became a favourite target for Community anti-dumping proceedings, although the most extreme interpretation of the anti-dumping regulations was adopted by the European Court in the *Tokyo Electric Company* and associated appeals (electronic typewriters). To strengthen the Commission's powers further, the basic regulation was amended and consolidated during the year (Reg. 2523/88). Japanese companies in Europe were also hit by the imposition of quasi-dumping duties on several 'screwdriver assembly' operations, as the 1987 regulation came into full use. This reached such an extent that Japan asked GATT to refer the issue to a GATT panel, a move which the Community strongly resisted. Dumping between EEC member states themselves, for which there was normally no special remedy, was the subject of a prohibition under Reg. 812/86, applicable during the transitional period following Iberian accession, on a Belgian company dumping chemical products onto the Spanish market.

The Hormones Regulation was annulled by the European

Court at the beginning of the year because it had been adopted by a majority vote of the Council (which was indeed permissible under Art. 43 EEC on which it was properly based, but was not allowed if the Council's 'written procedure' was used). It was then immediately re-enacted properly, whereupon an Art. 177 reference was made by the English High Court to the European Court to test whether the second regulation was valid. The *Battery Hens* case revealed more disturbing practices. A directive regulating the conditions of battery hens was attacked by the UK, which not only voted against it but also contended that, as it was aimed at animal welfare, it should have been based on Art. 100 (requiring unanimity). The Court held that the directive was correctly based on Art. 43 (which allowed majority voting) as it was concerned with agricultural production; however, the Council secretariat had, without authority, tampered with the preamble by deleting a significant clause and adding Art. 42 as a further base. The text as published and notified to the member states was therefore unauthorized and the whole directive was annulled. Both these cases illustrated a relatively new phenomenon linked to 1992: the search for a replacement for the lost veto power of the states as more and more legislation was passed by majority vote. What seemed therefore to be a purely legalistic dispute in reality expressed a fundamental struggle for political power.

The European Court itself went through a controversial and changeable year. The publication of reports of its decisions reached a record delay of 30 months. The delays in delivery of judgment too stretched out to some 18 months on average for references, and sometimes two years, while actions against member states were taking up to 2½ years. There were disturbing rumours of bureaucratic attitudes and even cliques in the Court and at least one member complained of the immense burden of paper work without assistance of counsel. The Court's proffered solution, a new lower Court of First Instance, was agreed by the Council but only after the vested interests of the Commission and of France had succeeded in removing anti-dumping cases from its jurisdiction.

Even the renewal of the Court was controversial since the 13th Judge (who rotated among the Big Five) would through normal alphabetical order have passed from France to Italy. But Spain claimed it had been promised the extra judgeship during its accession negotiations and eventually won the day. The Court underwent a major reshuffle on 6 October, in addition to the change of the 13th Judge. The President, Lord Mackenzie Stuart (UK), retired from the Court and promptly received a peerage (previously he was using merely the courtesy title granted to all Scottish judges); he was succeeded by sitting Judge Ole Due (Denmark). For the first time an advocate-general (indeed two) was appointed Judge: both Sir Gordon

Slynn (UK) and Signor Federico Mancini (Italy) returned to the Court to sit on the full bench; and also for the first time, an ex-legal secretary, Professor Francis Jacobs, was appointed advocate-general.

The major change in the composition of the Court stimulated a strong sense of urgency to clear some of the long-standing files, and during the weeks leading up to 6 October an unusually large number of judgments was delivered, many of them showing signs of hasty decision-making. Among these was *Wood Pulp*, an appeal from a Commission decision of December 1984 fining companies in the USA, Canada, Sweden and Finland for operating a price cartel, even though many of them had no presence at all within the EEC. The Court supported the Commission by holding that a company was present within the Community (and therefore subject to its laws) if its agreement was implemented there. As the cartel had agreed on prices to be applied in the EEC, its members were deemed to be present there whether they were or not.

Several distinct judicial trends could be seen in the year. VAT continued its high profile both for judgments and for new cases. Particularly noteworthy was the pair of cases brought by the Commission against the UK and Ireland respectively, querying the validity of their use of zero-rating. The English courts were persuaded that the restrictive UK Sunday trading laws might impede free movement of goods under Art. 30 EEC and some dozen Art. 177 references were made to the European Court. This was quickly followed by a similar spate of references in prosecutions relating to sex shops; but the Court of Appeal in *Noncyp* denied that Art. 30 could apply to restrict the Customs prohibition of obscene publications. Danish laws prohibiting the use of non-returnable beer cans were, however, accepted by the European Court as a legitimate restriction on trade in the interests of the environment (see p. 457). It also agreed, in the *Daily Mail Trust* case, that companies could not use the freedom of establishment rules to relocate themselves in other member states in order to avoid payment of taxes. The Commission, among many anti-trust decisions, caused consternation by holding that resale price maintenance for books in Britain (under the Net Book Agreement) breached Art. 85 EEC and that so did the publication monopoly of television programme information held by the listing magazines in Ireland and Northern Ireland. This was paralleled on the legislative side by a Commission Green Paper on copyright and by a draft directive on copyright in computer programmes.

The most important piece of legislation was undoubtedly the Lugano Convention on jurisdiction and enforcement of judgments, extending the existing EEC Brussels Convention 1968 to the Efta countries (see also p. 411). The Diplomas Directive was finally agreed, to ease the exercise of freedom of establishment by members of the regulated professions where there had been no harmonization of professional qualifications. The group exemption regulations for franchising and know-how agreements and for air transport were also enacted, while the draft Mergers Regulation was revived and promoted with great energy. The draft Statute for a European Company, which had been dormant for many years, was also revived and a new draft directive on one-man companies was introduced.

Chapter 2

LAW IN THE UNITED KINGDOM

LEGAL administration and the structure of the legal profession were the subject of considerable scrutiny. The Lord Chancellor's *Civil Justice Review*[1] made sweeping proposals designed to accelerate legal proceedings and to reduce their cost, principally by means of a fundamental shift of balance between the High Court and the county courts, involving an expansion of the jurisdiction of the county court, an increase of the jurisdiction of county court registrars, and the further extension of the already highly successful small claims procedure. The Marre Committee on the legal profession made significant recommendations, including the reform of legal education, an extension to Crown courts of the right of audience of solicitors, the recruitment of judges from the solicitors' branch of the legal profession, and the removal of the rule preventing access to a barrister except through a solicitor[2]. Both the Bar and the Law Society initiated amendments to their rules in response to the Marre report[3]. New principles behind the working of the system of legal aid were introduced by the *Legal Aid Act*, designed to ensure that it operated as cost-effectively as possible.

The litigation concerning the Government's attempts to restrain the publication of the book *Spycatcher* finally ended with the House of Lords refusing to grant a permanent injunction, holding that the information contained in the book was so freely available that it could no longer be regarded as confidential[4] (see DOCUMENTS). The newspaper which had wrongfully published extracts from the book at a time when the information was truly confidential, however, was required to account for the profits which it had made from this publication, and it was stressed that contracts concerning the publication of improperly divulged information should not be enforceable in the courts. In part precipitated by the *Spycatcher* litigation, in part by an earlier private member's

Bill, the Government introduced a White Paper on the reform of the law relating to official secrets, and towards the end of the year presented a Bill to Parliament for the amendment of the much-criticized Section 2 of the *Official Secrets Act* of 1911 (see also p. 36).

The *Local Government Act* restricted the power of local authorities to undertake certain types of work directly, specifying that this should be permissible only if a competitive tender by the private sector had revealed that the cost of the work could be minimized only by the local authority's performing it through its own employees. After much controversy, both within Parliament and outside, section 28 of the Act was finally passed; this prohibited the intentional promotion of homosexuality by a local authority, its publication of material with such an intention, and the promotion of the teaching in any maintained school of the acceptability of homosexuality as a pretended family relationship. Further weakening of the powers of local authorities was contained in Part III of the *Housing Act*, which facilitated the transfer of residential rented accommodation from public authorities to private landlords; and by the *Education Reform Act*, which introduced a national curriculum into secondary education and gave schools the choice whether to opt out of being controlled by local education authorities.

Among its many minor reforms the *Criminal Justice Act* abolished the requirement that a child's unsworn evidence must be corroborated, and made provision for the admissibility as evidence in cases involving sexual or violent assaults of a written or recorded statement from a child, removing the need to call the child as a witness unless cross-examination was necessary. Also abolished was the peremptory right of the defendant in a criminal trial to challenge jurors, this being balanced by the introduction of limitations on the prosecution's right to require jurors to stand down. The power of the Court of Appeal to award a retrial after allowing an appeal against conviction on the grounds of a misdirection at the trial was significantly extended.

The *Landlord and Tenant Act*, adopting a report of the Law Commission, gave a tenant a right to damages against a landlord who improperly refused consent to the transfer of the leased property; and the *Landlord and Tenant Act 1987* was brought into force, further increasing the rights of long-term tenants against their landlords. In *AG Securities* v. *Vaughan* and *Antoniades* v. *Villiers*[5] the House of Lords refused to countenance sham transactions designed to circumvent the protection afforded to tenants under the Rent Acts; but both the House of Lords and the Court of Appeal stressed that not all agreements drawn up with a view to the avoidance of the Rent Acts should be treated as shams[6]. Outside the courts, the position of landlords of privately rented accommodation was improved enormously by Part I of the *Housing Act*, which largely abolished the regime of controlled rents which had formerly prevailed.

An overdue, if minor, reform of the land registration system was achieved by the enactment of the *Land Registration Act*, introduced as a private member's Bill, which opened the register to public inspection for the first time. A more substantial overhaul and rationalization of the system was presaged by the inclusion of a draft Bill in the Law Commission's *Fourth Report of Land Registration*; meanwhile, a number of long-standing difficulties concerning the operation of the doctrine of notice as applied to the rights of persons in actual occupation of registered land were considered by the Court of Appeal[7], and a strongly conservative approach was taken to the effect of contractual licences on third-party purchasers of real property[8].

The law relating to the privilege attaching to certain classes of documents was clarified by a series of cases. In *Balabal* v. *Air-India*[9] the Court of Appeal allowed the application of legal professional privilege to any document passing between solicitor and client which had been made confidentially for the broad purpose of giving or receiving legal advice. In *Francis and Francis* (a firm) v. *Central Criminal Court*[10] it was held by the House of Lords that the exclusion of legal professional privilege from documents held with the intention of furthering a criminal purpose applied even when the criminal intention was not of the holder but of a third party. In *Rush and Tompkins Ltd* v. *Greater London Council*[11] the same court extended the privilege attaching to documents written 'without prejudice' in the course of negotiations to any litigation on the same subject matter after the initial negotiations had been completed.

A confusion in the law of criminal evidence was removed by the decision of the House of Lords that a voluntary statement made by a person accused of a crime was admissible fully as evidence of the facts contained in it even though it was only in part an admission and in part consisted of exculpatory matter[12]. In the Court of Appeal it was held that legal professional privilege could be claimed in a statement made by an accused person to his solicitor which might tend to exonerate his co-accused only if the maker of the statement had an interest in the assertion of the privilege sufficient to outweigh the prejudicial effect that the exclusion of the evidence might have on the co-accused[13].

In the law of torts, the House of Lords and the Court of Appeal continued their retrenchment of a restrictive approach to liability, resiling from the expansive attitude of the late 1970s and early 1980s. In several cases, and in a variety of contexts, it was reiterated that pure economic loss should not normally be recoverable[14]; the House of Lords refused to impose on the police a duty towards the general public to use reasonable care in the apprehension of a suspect[15]; and limits were placed on the right of plaintiffs who had suffered loss by relying on statements made to third parties to recover damages from the representor[16]. The House of Lords refused to allow an injured party to recover compensation against a negligent doctor in the absence of clear proof that the injury had in fact resulted from the negligent conduct, even though there was clear evidence that the conduct of the defendants had materially increased the risk to the plaintiff of the injury which actually occurred[17]; and a robust approach was adopted to the problem of the assessment of damages when a plaintiff who had been contributorily negligent sought compensation from two independent tortfeasors[18]. In large personal injury claims, the attraction of reaching a settlement in terms of structured periodical payments rather than a single lump sum was enhanced by a tax concession granted by the Inland Revenue[19].

In two important cases the House of Lords developed the 'equal pay for work of equal value' procedures as an effective tool for women seeking equality with men. In *Hayward* v. *Cammell Laird Shipbuilders Ltd*[20] it held that an employer could not defend a claim for equal wages by pointing to collateral benefits enjoyed by women alone; and in *Pickstone* v. *Freemans plc*[21] it emphasized that it was not sufficient for an employer simply to show that a woman claimant was being paid at the same rate as some man if the generality of men in comparable occupations were paid at a higher rate. The House was unwilling to extend this wide interpretation, however, to a claim by a woman whose annual wage was less than that of a man in a comparable occupation if the reason for this was that her working year was shorter, so long as their hourly rates of pay were broadly equivalent[22]. Notwithstanding the provisions of the European Community's *Equal Treatment Directive* of 1976, the House of Lords would not interpret the *Sex Discrimination Act* in such a way as to render illegal an employer's imposition of discriminatory retirement ages on men and women[23]. The Court of Appeal held that aggravated or exemplary damages could be awarded in a claim under the *Race Relations Act 1976*[24]; the effects of this were soon visible in actions brought before industrial tribunals[25]. The rights of trade unions to discipline individual members who had failed to act in accordance with decisions reached by a majority of members were severely circumscribed by the *Employment Act*.

The law relating to intellectual property was updated and consolidated in the *Copyright, Designs and Patents Act*, although significant problems continued to be raised by the improper interference with computers and computer programs. In *R* v.

Gold the House of Lords upheld the refusal of the Court of Appeal to interpret the offence of forgery as extending to the gaining of unauthorized access to a computer databank[26] (see p. 451); the Law Commission issued a consultation paper on computer misuse generally.

Several important statutes on family law came into force: the *Family Law Act 1986* (dealing *inter alia* with the problem of child abduction by estranged parents and the recognition of foreign decrees of nullity of marriage); the *Adoption Act 1976* (regulating the adoption of children); and much of the *Family Law Reform Act 1987* (finally abolishing the legal disadvantages suffered by illegitimate children). The Law Commission completed its major review of *Child Law, Guardianship and Custody*; this was followed by the introduction into Parliament of a consolidating *Children Bill*. The paramountcy of the interests of the child was again stressed by the House of Lords in the context of both adoption[27] and wardship[28]. Similar criteria were applied to authorize the abortion and sterilization of a mentally handicapped woman[29]. In a novel application, the Court of Appeal held that there was no jurisdiction to make an order of wardship over an unborn child[30].

Among other Acts emanating from an active parliamentary session were two major consolidatory statutes, the massive *Income and Corporation Taxes Act* and the *Road Traffic Act*. The *Malicious Communications Act*, implementing a Law Commission report on poison pen letters, introduced a criminal offence of unjustifiably telling a lie in a letter with the object of causing distress or anxiety to the recipient. The *Access to Medical Reports Act* laid down that patients should have an automatic right of access to medical reports provided in connection with applications for employment or insurance. The *Licensing Act* extended the permitted opening hours of licensed premises, and a provision of the *Local Government Act* abolished the dog licence.

---

[1] *The Times* 8 June 1988.
[2] *The Times* 14 July 1988.
[3] [1988] *New Law Journal*, p. 923.
[4] *Attorney-General* v *Guardian Newspapers Ltd (No 2)* [1988] 3 All E.R. 545.
[5] [1988] 3 All E.R. 1058.
[6] *Otter* v. *Norman* [1988] 2 All E.R. 897; *Hilton* v. *Plustitle and Rose* [1988] *New Law Journal*, p. 340.
[7] *Lloyds Bank* v. *Rosset* [1988] 3 All E.R. 915.
[8] *Ashburn Anstalt* v. *Arnold* [1988] 2 All E.R. 147.
[9] [1988] 2 All E.R. 246.
[10] [1988] 3 All E.R. 775.
[11] [1988] 1 All E.R. 737.
[12] *R* v. *Sharp* [1988] 1 All E.R. 65.
[13] *R* v. *Ataou* [1988] 2 All E.R. 321.

[14] *Simaan General Contracting Co* v. *Pilkington Glass Ltd [1988] 1 All E.R. 791; Greater Nottingham Co-op Society Ltd* v. *Cementation Piling and Foundations Ltd* [1988] 2 All E.R. 971; *D & F Estates Ltd* v. *Church Commissioners for England* [1988] 2 All E.R. 992.
[15] *Hill* v. *Chief Constable of West Yorkshire* [1988] 2 All E.R. 238.
[16] *Harris* v. *Wyre Forest DC* [1988] 1 All E.R. 691; *Caparo Industries plc* v. *Dickman, The Times* 5 August 1988.
[17] *Wilsher* v. *Essex Area Health Authority* [1988] 1 All E.R. 871.
[18] *Fitzgerald* v. *Lane* [1988] 2 All E.R. 961.
[19] [1988] *New Law Journal*, p. 660.
[20] [1988] 2 All E.R. 257.
[21] [1988] 2 All E.R. 803.
[22] *Leverton* v. *Clwyd County Council* [1988] *New Law Journal*, p. 365.
[23] *Duke* v. *GEC Reliance* [1988] I.R.L.R. 118.
[24] *Alexander* v. *Home Office* [1988] 2 All E.R. 118.
[25] [1988] *New Law Journal*, p. 188.
[26] [1988] 2 All E.R. 186.
[27] *Re C (a minor)* [1988] 1 All E.R. 705.
[28] *Re K D (a minor)* [1988] 1 All E.R. 577.
[29] *T* v. *T* [1988] 1 All E.R. 613.
[30] *Re F (in utero)* [1988] 2 All E.R. 193.

Chapter 3

LAW IN THE UNITED STATES OF AMERICA

LARGE damage awards to consumers and employees for tortious violations of their rights served as a major indicator for directions in the law: a federal jury awarded $7,975,000 to the estate of an IBM executive and his wife who were killed in an airplane crash in 1985, the largest award for such deaths.[1] (A study of settlements in airplane crash cases for the 1970–1984 period found the average settlement to be $362,943 and for 1984–1987 to be approximately $500,000.) Searle & Co. was ordered to pay one plaintiff $8,150,000 in connection with use of the Copper-7 intrauterine device.[2] A jury in New Jersey awarded $400,000 to the husband of a women who, as a result of cigarette smoking, died of lung cancer; this was the first wrongful death verdict against a cigarette producer.[3] A California court awarded $7 million in a libel action by a rancher against the University of California and three scholars for 'scholar malpractice'.[4] A federal court in Georgia ordered Miles Laboratories Inc. to pay more than $1 million to a plaintiff who contracted AIDS from blood supplied by Miles, which bought it from an unemployed man;[5] and a California court held Irwin Memorial Blood Bank liable for damages where, after refusing to allow family members to donate blood for the heart surgery of their five-year-old son, he contracted AIDS from the blood supplied by the defendant.[6] The California Supreme Court held that the Unification Church could be sued by its former members for intentional infliction of emotional distress and fraud, because of its practice of concealing its identity in order to bring outsiders into its structured environment.[7]

However, in other decisions the California Supreme Court established highly important limits on consumers' and employees' rights: The Court, in *Naradi-Shalal* v. *Fireman's Fund*,[8] reversed its prior decision, in 1979, which allowed a victim to claim against the tortfeasor's insurer where the insurer declined to bargain with that victim in good faith.[9] In employment law, the Court reversed prior decisions of the lower courts in California which held, in the late 1970s and early 1980s, that an employee could proceed against his former employer for bad faith dismissal;[10] by 1988 some 40 states had followed these decisions. (A study of awards in 120 wrongful dismissal cases between 1980 and 1986 found median awards of approximately $170,000.) The day before the Court's decision an appellate court upheld an award to Racquel Welch for $2 million in compensatory damages and $8 million in punitive damages for her dismissal by Metro-Goldwyn-Mayer from the film *Cannery Row*.[11]

In *Matter of Baby M*[12] the New Jersey Supreme Court held illegal a contract entered into before a woman became pregnant wherein that woman, for compensation, agreed to carry a foetus and to surrender its custody after birth. The US Supreme Court affirmed a decision of the Indiana Supreme Court, which held that a husband had no constitutional right to veto his wife's decision to have an abortion.[13] The US Supreme Court also dismissed an appeal by an unwed father who claimed a constitutional right to veto a mother's decision to offer her child for adoption; the Court ruled that a state could accord priority to the right of the child over those of the unwed father.[14]

The right of a person terminally ill to decline the assistance of life-support facilities received conflicting treatment in the courts. The Missouri Supreme Court denied a request by a family to disconnect such facilities, rejecting their claim on behalf of the patient that there was a right to die.[15] A lower court in California, on the other hand, held that a family could disconnect the feeding tubes which had kept alive for five years a 44-year-old comatose man.[16] The US Supreme Court declined to hear an appeal in such a right-to-die case, leaving the matter to be resolved by state courts.[17]

In the sphere of equal protection, handicapped persons and blacks achieved significant gains in respect of greater access to housing. The Fair Housing Amendments Act 1988,[18] enacted by Congress, established standards for new multi-family residential units, so that they would be accessible to persons using wheelchairs, whereas previously such standards were applicable to housing constructed with some assistance from federal governmental funds. The US Supreme Court held unconstitutionally discriminatory the practice of Huntington, New York, of continually siting low-income housing development in areas occupied by non-whites and scheduled for urban renewal.[19]

No major precedents were set in criminal law, although by the end of the year the number of persons sentenced to death and awaiting execution exceeded 2,000. The US Supreme Court, in a divided decision, held unconstitutional the death sentence for an offender who was 15 years old when he committed the murder; Justice O'Connor, whose vote favoured the holding, declined to state categorically that the death sentence for persons under the age of 16 at the time of their crime was constitutionally impermissible.[20] A federal district court in Virginia departed from an established precedent when it sentenced a corporation to prison for three years, the effect of which would have been a seizure of the physical assets of the offender and a closure of its operations; the Court suspended the sentence and placed the offender on probation for three years, leaving for a future date the legality of incarceral sentences for corporate offenders.[21]

[1] *Estridge v. Delta A. Lines* (S.D–N.Y6t. 85 Civ. 7975, April 4, 1988).
[2] *Kociembu v. G.D. Searle & Co.* (3–85–1599).
[3] *Cipollone v. Ligget Group Inc.* (D–N.J., 83–2864) (June 27, 1988).
[4] *Neary v. Regents of University of California* (525839) (October 3, 1988).
[5] *Jones v. Miles Laboratories Inc.* (N.D. GA., 86–CU.–83).
[6] *Osborn v. Irwin Memorial Blood Bank* (S.F. Sup. Ct., December 5, 1988).
[7] *Molko v. Holy Spirit Association* (1988) 46 Cal.3d 1092.
[8] (1988) 45 Cal. 3d 1122.
[9] *Royal Glove Insurance v. Superior Court*, (1979) 23 Cal.3d 880.
[10] *Foley v. Interactive Data Corp.* (1988) 254 Cal. Rptr. 211; Commercial Life Insurance Company v. Superior Court (1988) 47 Cal. 3d 473.
[11] *Welch v. Metro-Goldwyn-Mayer* (1988) 207 Cal.App.3d 164.
[12] (1988) 525 A2d 1128.
[13] *Conn v. Conn* (1988) 109 S.Ct. 391.
[14] *McNamara v. San Diego* (1988) 109 S.Ct. 546.
[15] *Cruzan v. Harmon* (1988) 760 S.W.2d 409.
[16] In re conservatorship of the person of William Drabik III (1988) 200 Cal.App.3d 185; Conservatorship of Morrison (1988) 206 Cal.App.3d 304.
[17] *Brown v. Southern Maryland Hospital Center* (1988) 109 S.Ct. 107.
[18] 102 Stat. 1619.
[19] *Town of Huntington, N.Y. v. Huntington Branch, NAACP* (1988) 109 S.Ct. 276.
[20] *Thompson v. Oklahoma* (1988) 479 U.S. 1084.
[21] *United States v. Allegheny Bottling Co.* (E.D. Va., 87–123–N).

XVI THE ARTS

Chapter 1

OPERA—MUSIC—DANCE/BALLET—THEATRE
—CINEMA—TELEVISION AND RADIO

OPERA

NO major trend was apparent during the year, apart from a general tendency towards more adventurous repertories. The lack of any centennial anniversaries encouraged managements to look in various directions. Leoš Janáček, who died 60 years ago, received many productions: *Katya Kabanova* at the Paris Opéra, Glyndebourne, and Geneva; *The Cunning Little Vixen* in Zürich; *The Makropoulos Case* in Munich; *From the House of the Dead* in Paris, were among the more interesting.

Franz Schreker, the Austrian composer born 90 years ago, also attracted attention: *Der ferne Klang* and *Die Gezeichneten* were given in Brussels; *Das Spielwerk und die Prinzessin* at Wiesbaden; and *Der Schatzgräber* in St Gallen, Switzerland. Sergey Prokofiev was another popular choice, with *The Fiery Angel* staged in Geneva and at the Adelaide Festival, while *Love for Three Oranges* opened Opera North's tenth season, which also introduced Georges Bizet's *Les pêcheurs de perles* to Leeds.

In London, the most significant events included the retirement of Sir John Tooley as managing director of the Royal Opera and his replacement by Jeremy Isaacs, whose tenure was inaugurated with *Das Rheingold*, intended as the start of a new cycle of Richard Wagner's *Ring*, directed by Yuri Lyubimov and conducted by Bernard Haitink. However, owing to differences of opinion between director and conductor, Lyubimov resigned from the production; Götz Friedrich's Berlin staging would be substituted in 1989.

Other notable events at Covent Garden were new productions of Michael Tippett's *Knot Garden*, directed by Nicholas Hytner, and of Giuseppe Verdi's *Rigoletto*, staged by Nuria Espert. English National Opera offered Benjamin Britten's *Billy Budd*, Nikolay Rimsky-Korsakov's *Christmas Eve* and the first British performance of Philip Glass's *Making of the Representative for Planet 8*, which had its world premiere at Houston on 8 July. Another Glass opera, *The Fall of the House of Usher*, was premiered in Louisville, Kentucky, on 31 May.

Welsh National Opera scored a triumph with Peter Stein's production of *Falstaff*; the same opera, directed by Peter Hall as part of the Verdi series at Glyndebourne, was less successful. Scottish Opera presented Tippett's *Midsummer Marriage*, while the same composer's *King Priam* received its first French production at Nancy. Meanwhile, Britten's *Peter Grimes* was staged in Florence by Jean-Pierre Ponnelle, three months before the French director-designer's untimely death (see OBITUARY).

A new opera house, designed by Alvar Aalto, opened in Essen (25 September) with *Die Meistersinger*. Other interesting Wagner productions included *Tristan und Isolde*, staged by Ruth Berghaus at Hamburg; *Der fliegende Holländer*, directed by Michael Hampe, in Milan; Peter Sellar's controversial staging of *Tannhäuser* in Chicago; the completion of Otto Schenk's production of *Der Ring des Nibelungen* at the Metropolitan, New York. Complete cycles of *The Ring* were given at Turin and Orange, while Harry Kupfer unveiled his new staging at Bayreuth.

Munich Festival opened with *Der Liebe der Danae*, directed by Giancarlo del Monaco and continued with performances of Richard Strauss's 14 other operas. Santa Fe offered two lesser-known Strauss works, *Feuersnot* and *Friedenstag*, as well as the first American production of Krzysztof Penderecki's *Schwarze Maske*. Both Aix-en-Provence and Salzburg Festivals opened with Wolfgang Amadeus Mozart's *Clemenza di Tito*. Pesaro gave the chance to hear Gioacchino Rossini's *Otello*, while Edinburgh included the British premiere of John Adams' *Nixon in China*. Buxton successfully exhumed Gaetano Donizetti's *Torquato Tasso*, while Wexford unearthed Giuseppe Gazzaniga's version of *Don Giovanni*, together with Ferruccio Busoni's *Turandot*. The Gazzaniga also surfaced at Montpelier.

Other rarities staged during the year included Rossini's *Viaggio a Reims* in Vienna; Niccolò Jommelli's *Fetonte* in Milan; Donizetti's *Parisina* at Basel; and Eugen d'Albert's *Golem* at Ulm. Arrigo Boito's *Mefistofele*, which opened the 1988–89 season at both Geneva and Zürich, was also given in Marseilles. Franz Schubert's *Fierrabras*, directed by Berghaus in Vienna, was repeated in London; Berghaus also staged Alban Berg's *Lulu* in Brussels; *Lulu* was successfully performed in Madrid, while Berg's *Wozzeck*, directed by David Alden, opened the Los Angeles season.

The Metropolitan chose Verdi's *Trovatore* for opening night; La Scala, Milan, reopened with Rossini's *Guillaume Tell*; Rome Opera with Donizetti's *Poliuto*; Bologna with Giacomo Puccini's *Madama Butterfly*; Florence with Verdi's *Simon Boccanegra*; Venice with Vincenzo Bellini's *Sonnambula* and Turin with Amilcare Ponchielli's *Gioconda*. Strasbourg, rather more enterprising, began with a magnificent production of Bernd-Alois Zimmermann's *Soldaten*, staged by Kupfer.

World premieres in 1988 included Karl-Heinz Stockhausen's *Montag aus Licht* (Milan, 7 May); Sylvano Bussotti's *Ispirazione* (Florence, 26 May); Maurice O'Hana's *Céléstine* (Paris, 13 June); Mark-Anthony Turnage's *Greek* (Munich, 17 June); Robin Orr's *On the Razzle* (Glasgow, 27 June); Brian Howard's *Whit Sunday* (Sydney, 2 September); Gerhard Konzelmann's *Gauklermärchen* (Cologne, 4 September); Jay Reise's *Rasputin* (New York, 17 September); Peter Maxwell-Davies's *Resurrection* (Darmstadt, 18 September); Marc Neikrug's *Los Alamos* (Berlin, 1 October); René Koering's *Marche de Radetsky* (Strasbourg, 11 October) and Dominick Argento's *Aspern Papers* (Dallas, 19 November), adapted from Henry James.

Olivier Messiaen's 80th birthday (10 December) was celebrated by the British premiere of his opera, *St François d'Assise*, in London. Thea Musgrave's *An Occurrence at Owl Creek Bridge* and Michael Finnissey's *Undivine Comedy* received their first British performances at, respectively, Bracknell and the Almeida Festival, London.

Deaths were announced of Thomas Walsh, Irish writer and founder of Wexford Festival; Kurt Herbert Adler, American administrator; Gerald Abrahams, British musicologist; Nicola Benois, Italian designer; Mauro Pagano, Italian designer; Ita Maximovna, Russian designer; Sir Frederick Ashton, British choreographer and director (see OBITUARY); Rudolf Hartmann, German director; Dennis Arundell, British author and director; and Arwel Hughes, Welsh composer.

Singers who died included Bruno Prevedi, Italian tenor; Afro Poli, Italian baritone; Gianna Pederzini, Italian mezzo-soprano; Raffaele Arie, Bulgarian bass; John Reardon, American baritone; James McCracken, American tenor (see OBITUARY); Anneliese Burmeister, German mezzo-soprano; Heinz Rehfus, German baritone; Richard Holm, German tenor; Petre Munteanu, Romanian tenor; Gladys Parr, British mezzo-soprano; and two famous Austrian sopranos, Hilde Gueden and Irmgard Seefried (see OBITUARY), who both excelled in the Mozart and Strauss repertory for over three decades.

MUSIC

THE momentum of musical activity was fully sustained throughout 1988. Indeed, in the great world centres like London and New York, such was the level of activity that it would be possible to write separate accounts about, for example, early, classical, contemporary, popular or 'ethnic' music.

If London was the clearing-house for European music, the obligatory port-of-call for touring soloists, groups, orchestras, opera and dance companies, then New York was the musical supermarket of America. Every weekday ten or twelve events took place—recitals, concerts, operas—and at weekends there were even more. Although of necessity familiar classics provided the staple fare, some noteworthy performances of early and Renaissance music were also to be heard, from such groups as the *Pomerium Musices* of Alexander Blackley, or the choir of St Thomas's, Fifth Avenue. New York was the opera centre of America—where the Metropolitan offered its customers a widely varied diet: the best music and the most expensive names that money could buy. There was a revival of *Turandot*, in Zeffirelli's production; *L'Elisir d'amore*, with Pavarotti; *Lulu* under James Levine. The Met, together with other of the world's opera houses, proved that traditional grand opera thrives best under the star system.

Nor was the living composer disregarded in America. The Residencies Scheme, under which an American composer was assigned to an orchestra for a two-year period, during which time he would be responsible for steering his own works (and those of other American composers) through rehearsal and performance, was firmly established by 1988. Its worth was proved, and it was unique to America and the envy of European composers. There were also other outlets; in New York the American Symphony Orchestra continued its valiant support for the American composer, however unknown or obscure. Joan Tower, for instance, was a name unfamiliar outside a limited circle.

Apart from New York, Boston, for example, took pride in its elegant colonial past, deriving direct benefit from it, and its links with the eighteenth century. The Handel and Haydn Society was an active force in the city's music; the 200th anniversary of the death of C.P.E. Bach was aptly celebrated. In April the city played host to a major festival of Soviet music, of which the highlights were an opera by Shchedrin, *Dead Souls*, and *Offertorium* by Sofiya Goubaydulina. The latter composer had a further success in 1988 when her *Stimmen . . . Verstummen* was conducted in London by her fellow countryman Gennady Rozhdestvensky. Soviet music proved distinctly exportable. Schnittke was everywhere; and the Estonian composer Arvo Pärt (see AR 1986, p. 428) found himself almost becoming a cult-figure in the West, when his *St Johannes Passion*, with its discreet mixture of folk melody, religious ritual and repetitive minimalism captured one of the chief trends of the late 1980s.

If the Russians exported their music extensively in 1988, American music was equally represented in Europe. The Bath Festival featured George Crumb and Elliott Carter (who was 80 in

1988), as well as Robert Shaw and the Atlanta Symphony Chorus. Not to be outdone, the Edinburgh Festival put on *Nixon in China*, by the minimalist John Adams, after it had been performed in Houston and elsewhere earlier in the year. Unfortunately, all the American flair for energy and showbiz display could not disguise the threadbare nature of the musical material. Much greater success attended another American, Leonard Bernstein, whose 70th birthday was marked by a revival of his musical *Candide*. Berlin, designated European City of Culture for 1988, selected an opera, *Los Alamos*, from a little-known American Marc Neikrug. His idiom proved accessible, being drawn from various traditional sources, including Mahler, coupled with the now almost obligatory folk-song source, in his case simple ethnic Indian music.

The Australian bicentenary provided many opportunities for Australian music, and outlets for Australian composers, many of whom were little known, if at all, outside their own country. The best-known Australian composer, Peter Sculthorpe, found himself much in demand. His official work, *Child of Australia*, was interrupted during its premiere in the forecourt of Sydney Opera House when it clashed with a better-attended spectacular fireworks display in Sydney Harbour, introduced by an 88-gun salvo. In the course of the year, Australians welcomed many eminent musicians, chiefly the 80-year-old Messiaen, and Boulez with his Ensemble Intercontemporain.

Elsewhere, many of the year's premieres were operatic. Stockhausen's *Montag* was produced in Milan, the latest in the pretentious week-long operatic cycle *Licht*. Two successful performances marked other European festivals. Sylvano Bussotti's *L'ispirazione* was produced in Florence, as a cornerstone of the Maggio Musicale; a multi-media confection of music, ballet, design and costume. In Munich the new Biennale, under the direction of Hans Werner Henze, presented an unusual operatic project from the America of the 1920s—George Antheil's *Transatlantic*. Short operas by Hartman, together with all 15 of the Strauss operas, made this Bavarian festival a memorable occasion.

The London scene was more memorable for its back-stage manoeuvres than for its tangible achievements. By the autumn of 1988, the new administration of the South Bank had shaken off the previous stranglehold of the London orchestras, with the immediately visible result that concerts began to be given in planned series rather than as isolated events. *Beethoven Plus* and *Schoenberg—The Reluctant Revolutionary* were two examples of this trend, each extending over several months. In fact the second series showed greater flair and imagination than the first, even though it did illustrate the extent to which the planners were still mesmerized by pre-1914 Vienna. The first series was little more than an excuse to present the same mixture as before, with little evidence of imaginative thought.

At the BBC, John Drummond, Director of Radio 3, demonstrated all too clearly the absence of accepted aesthetic standards in contemporary music. He was 'a Birtwistle man'; Mozart was 'wallpaper music'; those who criticized Radio 3 were 'unhelpful'. On the evidence of output alone, BBC policy was little altered. Living British composers were allotted less than 2 per cent of total musical output; BBC public concerts continued to be 'ghetto concerts', moving in an exclusive orbit, esoteric, and appealing to a minority. The year began with a Birtwistle Festival at the Barbican, at which the lack of artistic substance became more and more obvious as the days passed. Birtwistle's novelty was indisputable and no one could seriously doubt his invention of new textures; but these qualities were no guarantee of the finished art-work. To pretend otherwise (as many did) could greatly harm the standing of the contemporary composer with the ordinary listener. The performances of Act II of *The Mask of Orpheus*, and of *Endless Parade*, were revelatory in this respect.

Claudio Abbado left the London Symphony Orchestra, Michael Tilson Thomas arrived; but it would have been mistaken to expect radical changes in this or any other London orchestra. The London scene was fixed. Perhaps the securest place in the repertory was that of Mahler, with Shostakovitch a strong challenger. Among conductors, Simon Rattle at Birmingham maintained his position as the most committed, if image-laden, of his profession. Someone even wrote a biography of him in 1988, though he was still in his early thirties. Changes also took place in Amsterdam, where the centenary of the Concertgebouw was marked by five performances of Mahler's *Resurrection Symphony* and Bernard Haitink stood down after 27 years as principal conductor, having been replaced by Riccardo Chailly.

The publication of a new edition of Mendelssohn's organ works generated the year's unsolved mystery. A manuscript in Cracow, which purported to be Mendelssohn's autograph, was copied by an American musicologist William A. Little and raised a question about the source of the existing edition, which had been available for many years; for there were very significant differences between the two. Interestingly, no reviewer understood the importance of this matter.

On the other side of the cultural divide, pop music had, on the whole, a somewhat fallow year. However, the singer-songwriter Michael Jackson enjoyed considerable success with his world tour, which included dates at Wembley, one of which was attended by the Prince and Princess of Wales. A major concert was also held at Wembley to celebrate the 70th birthday of the gaoled ANC leader, Nelson Mandela, raising the sum of £2 million. A concert by the French electronic musician-composer Jean-Michel Jarre, called *Destination Docklands*, was a spectacle combining lasers and fireworks, given in London's Docklands. It was a financial disaster, however, because bad weather reduced the audience well below the anticipated numbers.

Among those who died in 1988 were the oboeist Léon Goossens, the violinists Manoug Parikian and Henryk Szeryng, the cellist Andre Navarra, the pianists Solomon and Denis Matthews, the conductors Yevgeny Mravinsky, Paul Steinitz and Antal Dorati, the composer Kenneth Leighton, and the scholar Frank Ll. Harrison. (For Goossens, Szeryng, Solomon, Mravinsky and Dorati, see OBITUARY.)

BOOKS OF THE YEAR. Outstanding books published in the year were few and far between. Just two can be recommended: *1791: Mozart's Last Year*, by H. C. Robbins Landon, and *The Early Music Revival: a History*, by Harry Haskell.

DANCE/BALLET

THE year 1988 saw the barriers down and great, historic collaborations between Soviet dancers and the West. Mikhail Baryshnikov danced in a Boston gala honouring Maya Plisetskaya and the Bolshoi Ballet; Andris Liepa and Nina Ananiashvili of the Bolshoi danced with New York City Ballet; Altynai Asylmuratova and Faroukh Ruzimatov of the Leningrad Kirov Ballet danced with American Ballet Theatre; Natalia Makarova danced with her old company, the Kirov, in London and as a result was invited to return to Leningrad early in 1989 where she received a tumultuous welcome.

Furthermore, when the Royal Opera House, Covent Garden, hosted a gala in aid of the Armenian disaster, stars of the Kirov and Bolshoi companies came to London to take part. Ananiashvili's partner had to cancel at the last moment, so she appeared with a Royal Ballet dancer, young Errol Pickford, thus cementing friendships between dancers and nations.

The Royal Ballet in London, under the direction of Anthony Dowell, began the year well with a meticulous revival of Frederick Ashton's Hans Werner Henze ballet, *Ondine*. Ashton, who was to die only a few months later, consented to the revival and was very well pleased by the result and by the cast headed by Maria Almeida, Jonathan Cope, Deanne Bergsma and Stephen Jefferies. Some beautiful performances of the title role (created for Fonteyn) were also given by the American ballerina Cynthia Harvey who, at the end of the summer season, elected to return to her home company, American Ballet Theatre.

Thereafter the Royal Ballet settled for a limited and mostly traditional repertory. The prolific David Bintley continued to make new works, full of ideas, using his dancers well but signifying little. Antoinette Sibley and Dowell were reunited as a great partnership in *Manon* and *A Month in the Country*. Fiona Chadwick and Almeida made strong claims to their ballerina status; Jonathan Cope emerged as a true *danseur noble*; Bruce Sansom danced a most elegant Oberon in *The Dream*. Jennifer Penney announced her retirement and returned to her native Canada. Nureyev brought one of his young stars from the Paris Opéra, Sylvie Guillem, to dance with him in *Giselle* as a guest at Covent Garden; she was to return later in the year to dance, with even greater effect, in more modern works. There was indeed a most welcome invasion of French dancers to the Royal Ballet companies. Isabelle Guérin, Elisabeth Maurin and Laurent Hilaire appeared at Covent Garden. With Sadler's Wells Royal Ballet another Paris *étoile*, Monique Loudières, danced in *Giselle* with the Romanian star Georghe Iancu.

Sadler's Wells Royal Ballet undertook a big tour of the Far East which cut down on time and opportunity for the creation of new works but at the beginning of the 1988–89 season staged excellent revivals of two Balanchine masterworks, *Theme and Variations* and *Concerto Barocco*. By the end of the year it was resolved that the company would make its home theatre, from August 1990, at the Hippodrome Theatre, in Birmingham, which had been in effect its second home for nearly a decade. With very generous funding from Birmingham, and the superb facilities of the Hippodrome, director Peter Wright foresaw an exciting future for his company.

Of the other important British companies, Rambert Dance Company continued to stage new works by director Richard Alston, the Royal Ballet's Ashley Page, Siobhan Davies and others and to maintain its record of fine design. London Contemporary Dance Theatre continued important residencies and education work and performed well in a repertory that had grown somewhat desiccated. Robert Cohan, who had guided its fortunes from the beginning, retired and Dan Wagoner, the American who had danced with the Graham, Cunningham and Paul Taylor companies, was named as his successor.

London Festival Ballet continued to tour full length classics of proven box-office attraction and staged a *Swan Lake* by Natalia Makarova which took an idiosyncratic look at the work but was, as always with *Swan Lake*, popular. A memorable night was the single performance with the company by Lynn Seymour, in the role of Tatiana in Cranko's *Onegin*.

To the autumn Dance Umbrella season was added a new showcase for contemporary and post-modern dance at The Place Theatre, called Spring Loaded and offering some 44 attractions of, inevitably, uneven quality. The Umbrella's big success in 1988 was DV8 Physical Theatre in *Dead Dreams For Monochrome Men*—a terrifying, yet utterly compassionate, work based on the Denis Nielson murders which dealt with homosexual loneliness, violence and despair.

The year 1988 in London was memorable as the time of the summer ballet marathon. No fewer than five classical ballet companies were to be seen in the capital: London Festival Ballet; the Kirov Ballet from Leningrad; the Australian Ballet; Dance Theatre of Harlem; and the Moscow Classical Ballet. All were competing for audiences; all were drawing them, even to the giant auditorium at the Design Centre in Islington, converted by the Entertainment Corporation to house both the Kirov and Moscow Classical companies.

The visit of the Kirov, returning to Britain for the first time in 18 years and bringing a new generation of dancers to reaffirm the purity and beauty of the Kirov training, dominated the year for ballet lovers. Dancing first in Dublin in the 4,000-seat Simmond Court Pavilion (in *Swan Lake*, which alas did not come to London), they gave us first sight of the incandescent partnership of Asylmuratova and Faroukh Ruzimatov, their wonderful young principals and soloists, and incomparable corps de ballet. Subsequently, at the London Coliseum, the Design Centre and Covent Garden they showed that in classical choreography their school, which celebrated its 250th birthday during 1988, remained unrivalled in the world. They danced a magical *Giselle*, delicious extracts from ballets like *Paquita, La Esmeralda* and *La Vivandière*, and at Covent Garden the full-length *Corsaire*, with its gallimaufry of exotic setting, hotchpotch of a score, and wealth of bravura dance.

The Australian Ballet proved to be young and vital in dancing, weak in repertory. Harlem brought a good revival of Eugene Loring's *Billy the Kid*; Moscow Classical brought a poor version of *Swan Lake*, decked out in designs by a British designer, and some terrible modern choreography. On the name of Moscow alone, they were a sell-out, and they did have good young male dancers such as Malakhov, Terentyev, Galimullin and Isayev.

After all these visitors had departed, a Spanish troupe called Cumbre Flamenca (Supreme Flamenco) consisting of five dancers, four singers and four guitarists made a tremendous impact during a short season at Sadler's Wells.

In Paris, the school continued to feed Nureyev's company with beautifully trained dancers—as the School of American Ballet continued to feed New York City Ballet. There was criticism of Peter

Martins' direction of NYCB—and his American Music Festival in the spring employed far too many inferior choreographers. However, it did import the entire Paul Taylor Dance Company with his *Danbury Mix*. Taylor, with the older Cunningham and the younger Mark Morris, continued to create magnificent work. Cunningham's *Five Stone Wind* and Morris's *Drink To Me Only With Thine Eyes* for American Ballet Theatre, and Morris's *L'Allegro, Il Penseroso ed il Moderato* for his new company in Brussels, were the outstanding choreographic achievements of the year.

Two remarkable women were in the limelight during 1988. Dame Ninette de Valois CH, DBE, celebrated her 90th birthday on 6 June and the British dance world honoured the founder of The Royal Ballet to her huge enjoyment. In America, Martha Graham at the age of 94 revived her *Deep Song* and embarked on a new work.

The dance world suffered its most grievous loss in the death of Sir Frederick Ashton OM, CH, CBE, England's greatest choreographer who helped mould the English style of classical ballet (see OBITUARY). Other losses were Dora Stratou, pioneer researcher into Greek folk dance; Douglas Kennedy of the English Folk Dance and Song Society; Maria-Theresa Duncan, the last of Isadora Duncan's adopted daughters; Robert Joffrey, founder and director of the Joffrey Ballet in New York (see OBITUARY); Arnie Zane, former partner of Bill T. Jones also in New York; the great Danish mime Gerda Karstens, and the Danish teacher and expert on Bournonville's ballets, Hans Brenaa; the dancer and teacher Hélène Wolska in London; the English dancer and photographer Hugh Laing in New York; the internationally famous teacher Anna Northcote in London; the dancers Graham Bart and Robert Mead; and Sir Donald Albery, theatrical impresario who rescued the then Sadler's Wells (now Royal) Ballet during the war years and subsequently saved Festival Ballet from financial troubles.

BOOKS OF THE YEAR. *Siva in Dance. Myth and Iconography,* by Anne-Marie Gaston; *Days on Earth. The Dance of Doris Humphrey,* by Marcia B. Siegel; *Theoretical and Practical Treatise on Dancing,* by Gennaro Magri (translated by Mary Skeaping with Irmgard Berry); *The World of Greek Dance,* by Alkis Raftis; *Dance Technique and Injury Prevention,* by Justin Howse and Shirley Hancock.

THEATRE

THIS was a year in which the scene appeared to be dominated by productions of Shakespeare, good, bad and, for the most part, indifferent, emanating not only from such expected sources as the National and the Royal Shakespeare theatres but also from touring companies, commercial managements, and even from the fringe. The Royal Shakespeare Company (RSC) in Stratford began the year badly with that enchanting comedy *Much Ado About Nothing*, which the director, Di Trevis, contrived to turn into a deadeningly humourless three hours of tedium, with the leading roles of Beatrice and Benedick seriously undercast. This was followed by a *Macbeth* in which the absence of leading players of real stature was again greatly damaging to the rather low-key production.

The standard of these and other RSC productions was so low, and the quality of the verse-speaking so poor, that a newspaper campaign to 'Save Shakespeare from Stratford', although launched not altogether seriously, attracted huge support from playgoers disenchanted with bad acting, irrelevant directorial 'concepts' and the automatic updating of the plays to a modern period in order to make them more relevant. (In 1988, the Edwardian era seemed to be the flavour of the year.)

Fortunately, the RSC redeemed itself at Stratford in the autumn with *The Plantagenets*, which consisted of the *Henry VI* trilogy plus *Richard III*, cut and rearranged to make three plays. A particular strength of Adrian Noble's staging was that it refrained from playing the fashionable game of relocating characters and events to make Shakespeare more 'relevant'. The playwright's concern for a social order based on submission to a just, or even an unjust, authority was allowed to make its uncomfortable points without impeding the narrative flow of the plays. A new young Shakespearian actor of great promise was revealed in Ralph Fiennes (Henry VI), and the only major disappointment was the comic-strip Richard III of Anton Lesser.

Shakespeare fared well at the National Theatre when, for his farewell as artistic director, Sir Peter Hall chose to produce, on consecutive evenings, the Bard's last three plays: *Cymbeline, The Winter's Tale* and *The Tempest*. In Hall's production, *Cymbeline* seemed a different play from the one which was being performed simultaneously under the same title by the RSC in the Barbican. More than the other two late plays, it is at the mercy of its director, for its disparate elements are not easily assembled into a coherent whole. At the Cottesloe auditorium in the National Theatre, the play blossomed, thanks to a director who was properly equipped to offer authoritative intellectual and aesthetic guidance to his cast.

Peter Hall's staging of *The Winter's Tale*, a play in which Shakespeare returned to the theme of lives destroyed by jealousy, which he had first explored years earlier in *Othello*, maintained a fine balance between sound and sense, often by the simple expedient of having the actors pause ever so slightly to acknowledge the line endings. *The Tempest* was, in many ways, the best of the three productions. The nature of the play allows for more spectacular effects than do the other two plays, and Hall responded with an especially imaginative opening scene of the storm at sea, all the more effective for not being delivered at breakneck speed, and a masque of beauty and charm, much of which was provided by Harrison Birtwistle's music (see also p. 478).

Shakespeare returned to the West End when Kenneth Branagh's Renaissance Theatre Company staged a season of three plays at the Phoenix Theatre, an interesting feature of the enterprise being that all three plays were directed by experienced Shakespearian players, each of whom was making his or her directorial debut. Kenneth Branagh, who had established himself as a leading actor while still in his twenties, appeared in every production. In Judi Dench's intelligent and perceptive staging of *Much Ado About Nothing,* he and Samantha Bond conducted the merry war of Beatrice and Benedick with the freshness and underlying good humour of youth. There was no trace of that cynical rancour which can infest middle-aged portrayals of these famous roles.

Geraldine McEwan directed *As You Like It* to great acclaim, and Derek Jacobi brought a lively but at times misguided actor's intelligence to his production of *Hamlet,* in which Branagh offered a not unsympathetic portrayal of the title role, although one which will surely, when he returns to it in years to come, find more poetry and introspection in the character. This Hamlet gave one the impression that he would have been capable of killing his uncle within five minutes of having been commanded to do so by his father's ghost.

The Renaissance Company, which had spent much of the year touring the regions, received no Arts Council subsidy, though it certainly merited support from the public purse. The company's season at the Phoenix Theatre in London was followed immediately, in the last weeks of the year, by another season of Shakespeare at the same theatre, in which Derek Jacobi starred in *Richard II* and *Richard III.* The latter play would not open until early in 1989, but Jacobi's Richard II was an arresting and unusual interpretation, eschewing the elegiac self-pity which actors traditionally find in the role, and opting instead for hysteria. Jacobi was supported by a strong company, and by Clifford Williams's intelligent staging of the play.

Of the many other Shakespeare productions mounted during the year, two in particular deserve to be mentioned. In *The Tempest* at the Old Vic, Jonathan Miller's amusing and highly personal gloss on the play, stressing those aspects which he saw as relating to the experience of colonialism, was thoroughly enjoyable, although Max von Sydow's Prospero was strangely tentative. The indefatigable company which braves the elements to bring Shakespeare to Regent's Park each summer presented an extremely lucid and good-humoured account of *A Midsummer Night's Dream*, the archetypal open-air play.

The National Theatre during the year displayed more taste and discernment in its choice of new plays than the RSC. Its two most distinguished offerings were new pieces by David Hare and Nicholas Wright. Wright's *Mrs Klein* is about a weekend in the life of Melanie Klein, the famous Viennese specialist in the psychoanalysis of children, during which it both comically and tragically transpires that she has not had a pronounced success with her own children; it was literate, intelligent, amusing and, finally, very moving. David Hare's *The Secret Rapture*, ostensibly a play concerned with family tensions, contained an interesting sub-text about the acquisitive society of the 1980s. Hare's dialogue was both elegant and witty, and his willingness to present his characters for what they are, or seem to be, without passing judgment on them, was most welcome. The more overtly political works favoured by the RSC were of less value.

One company dedicated to the revival of first-rate plays of the past disappeared from the scene, while another, with a similar aim, took its place. The Royalty Theatre Company, which had begun operations the previous year with luxuriously cast productions of Graham Greene and Oscar Wilde, faded away in the spring after an immaculate production of Terence Rattigan's double-bill, *The Browning Version* and *Harlequinade*, in which superb performances were given by Dorothy Tutin and Paul Eddington in the contrasting roles of the vain pair of actors in the second play and the unpopular housemaster and his snobbish wife in the first.

As though to replace the Royalty Company, the Old Vic Theatre under the artistic directorship of the ubiquitous Jonathan Miller mounted a highly eclectic season of revivals. It began with Racine's *Andromache*, a brave experiment spoiled by a last-minute change of translator, continued somewhat moodily with minor German, Russian and English classics, and ended successfully with Shakespeare's *Tempest* and Leonard Bernstein's *Candide*.

That once lively home of new drama, the Royal Court Theatre, for the most part produced trivia, both in its main auditorium and in its studio Theatre Upstairs. It also displayed an unfortunate fondness for the works of a not very impressive contemporary German playwright, Manfred Karge, two of whose peculiarly depressing pieces of pseudo-Brecht (*Man to Man* and *The Conquest of the South Pole*) were staged during the year. The Royal Court redeemed itself, however, with a revival of Farquhar's *The Recruiting Officer*, produced wittily in tandem with a new play, *Our Country's Good* by Timberlake Wertenbaker, which was about an attempt by the convicts of Australia's first settlement to put on a peformance of *The Recruiting Officer*.

With the exception of the enterprising King's Head Theatre Club, London's fringe theatres did not have a particularly good year. The erratic Bush Theatre seemed especially determined to give its stage over to work unlikely to appeal to more than a handful of people, and even the usually reliable Hampstead Theatre produced only one worthy play, *Aristocrats*, Brian Friel's examination of the decline of the Catholic upper class in Ireland. However, the Riverside Studios presented *No Sugar,* an impressive crypto-autobiographical play by Jack Davis, an Australian Aborigine, and Ted Hughes's powerful version of Seneca's *Oedipus* was staged at the Almeida.

One new fringe theatre opened during the year. This was the Lilian Baylis Theatre, carved out of a back-stage area at the Sadler's Wells Theatre. Its first two offerings were a minor American comedy, *House of Blue Leaves* by John Guare, and a poorly-cast revival of Giraudoux's *Madwoman of Chaillot*. One had the distinct impression that there were now many more fringe theatres in and around London than there were good new plays for them to stage.

In the West End, one of the best of the revivals was R. C. Sherriff's moving corrective to the romantic conception of war, *Journey's End*, at the Comedy Theatre, meticulously directed by Justin Greene, and beautifully acted by Nicky Henson and Andrew Castell. The cast of Chekhov's *Uncle Vanya* at the Vaudeville Theatre was rather like the curate's egg, but Michael Blakemore's direction was almost faultless.

Having left the National Theatre, and the contemporary brutalism of its three auditoria, Peter Hall formed his own company to present revivals of classical and modern plays at the elegant, early nineteenth-century Haymarket Theatre. His season was launched with Tennessee Williams's flawed but fascinating *Orpheus Descending*, Hall's production successfully combining fidelity to the letter and spirit of the play with great imaginative flair. The leading roles were admirably portrayed by Vanessa Redgrave, now firmly established as one of the finest actresses of her generation, and Jean-Marc Barr, a newcomer to the English stage.

With the exception of Alan Ayckbourn's bleakly hilarious *Henceforward*, the year's new plays tended to be slight. Three of them, however, were immensely entertaining, and contained splendid roles for some of the theatre's senior knights and dames. It was good to see Sir John Gielgud back on stage after an absence of some years, in Hugh Whitemore's *The Best of Friends*, in which Rosemary Harris and Ray McAnally were also excellent, and to find Dame Wendy Hiller in such sprightly form in an engaging American play, *Driving Miss Daisy*, by Alfred Uhry. Another American play, *A Walk in the Woods* by Lee Blessing, brought Sir Alec Guinness back to the West End in a performance of great subtlety and humour. His American co-star, Edward Herrmann, stood up to him well, and Ronald Eyre demonstrated, not for the first time, that he was one of Britain's most reliable directors.

The only good new musical was an American import, *Sugar Babies*, a raucously amusing tribute to the great days of vaudeville, which starred those survivors from American film musicals of the forties, Mickey Rooney and Ann Miller. There were several revivals of such popular shows of past years as Noël Coward's *Bitter Sweet*, which went in and out of Sadler's Wells Theatre rather quickly, and the Rodgers and Hammerstein *South Pacific* which stayed at the Prince of Wales Theatre for the entire year, and then went on tour. Two other revivals, *Brigadoon* and *Can-Can*, were botched in production, but proved successful at the box office, so starved was the British public for first-rate musical shows.

NEW YORK THEATRE. As usual, Broadway theatre was dominated by the musical, which is not to say that major new works of musical theatre were presented, merely that a large number of musical shows were produced, few of them successfully. The long-running British imports, *Cats, Me and My Girl, Les Misérables* and *Starlight Express*, were joined by Andrew Lloyd Webber's *The Phantom of the Opera*, whose success was not threatened in the slightest by the almost uniformly unfavourable notices which greeted it.

One of the most engaging, literate and entertaining of the year's new plays was staged off-Broadway (though at a theatre which is literally *on* Broadway). This was A. R. Gurney's *The Cocktail Hour*, which dealt with the attempt of a white Anglo-Saxon Protestant family to come to terms with the fact that the son of the family had written a play about them. Broadway's most commercially successful new play was the meretricious and dramatically unconvincing *M. Butterfly* by David Henry Hwang, based on the real-life romance between a transvestite Chinese opera performer and a French diplomat who, after they had lived together for some years, apparently still believed his lover to be a real woman.

Speed-the-Plow, David Mamet's satire on Hollywood, was generally considered to be his best play to date, as scathing as *Glengarry Glen Ross*, and as funny as *American Buffalo*. Mamet is the poet among American playwrights of today, with an ear finely attuned to the sounds of urban life. Neil Simon's new comedy, *Rumors*, disappointed those who had come to expect from Simon something more than the kind of farce with which he began his career. For the rueful comedy of his most recent three autobiographical plays, the playwright substituted a series of wisecracks and mechanically contrived situations. The play, however, was well acted by Ron Leibman and Jessica Walter, and slickly directed by Gene Saks.

Michael Weller's *Spoils of War*, an engaging new play about the efforts of a prep-school boy to reunite his divorced parents, had a disappointingly brief run despite a bravura performance by Kate Nelligan as the boy's mother. Two distinctly less good plays fared better. Richard Greenberg's *Eastern Standard*, a comedy of New York life, was preparing to transfer from the Manhattan Theatre Club to Broadway at the end of the year, and the performances of Denzel Washington and Ruby Dee enlivened Ron Milner's flatly written domestic comedy, *Checkmates*.

Revivals included *Ain't Misbehavin'*, a celebration of the music and the comic spirit of Fats Waller, which was first seen on Broadway some ten years ago. Most of the original company had been reassembled, and the show proved as exhilarating as it had the first time around. A production by Steven Berkoff of *Coriolanus* did great violence to Shakespeare, and Mike Nichols's staging of *Waiting for Godot* with personalities instead of actors in the leading roles did equal violence to Samuel Beckett. Much more attractive was *Cafe Crown*, a 1942 comedy about Yiddish actors, writers and intellectuals of New York's Lower East Side, revived at the Public Theatre with Eli Wallach as a former star and Bob Dishy as a bossy waiter.

CINEMA

WHEN most people think of films, they still think of Hollywood, despite the fact that Hollywood ceased to exist as a film factory some years ago, unless one counts the hundreds of television dramas that are turned out annually in places like Universal Studios. Hollywood, however, still cobbles together the finances for films, which are then made all over the world with American money and American stars, and on subjects that will hopefully appeal to the American public first and the world afterwards.

So it was not such a surprise that in 1988 the American Motion Picture Academy gave several major Oscars to the British-produced, Italian-directed and fully international *The Last Emperor*, a giant epic about the last Emperor of China that had to have Chinese cooperation too before it could be made there. Bernardo Bertolucci's film became an international success but never performed really well on the US market, which is by some way the biggest anywhere. However, that market was in 1988 sated with films everyone wanted to see, like

Fatal Attraction, Wall Street, Broadcast News, Beverly Hills Cop II, Crocodile Dundee II, Big, Three Men and A Baby and *Who Framed Roger Rabbit?* It was a year with plenty of failures, notably Richard Attenborough's *Cry Freedom* in the USA (if not elsewhere), but enough successes to counteract the delays and uncertainties caused by a 22-week writers' strike, which only ended in August after much compromise.

It was a year when Hollywood went in for a whole series of films that did not necessarily require viewing by a teenage or under-25 audience only, although that age group still dominated the ratings. It was, in fact, realized that a much wider audience would eventually see most of the top movies either on video or television (both considerable sources of financial gain, even when a film did not do well in the cinema). If any particular themes emerged, apart from the usual ones which form the basis of the lucrative horror or thriller markets, it was those contained in the baby films (babies were the subject of a whole string of movies apart from the mildy amusing *Three Men and A Baby*, the top example) and in films about body transference. As usual, American films topped the box-office league tables in eight out of ten countries where this sort of thing is measured. Thus a good year for the American box-office meant a good year for most other countries too.

It was, without doubt, a very reasonable year for the British cinema which, through the London-based producer Jeremy Thomas, had a significant part-share in *The Last Emperor*, and also won two top prizes at the still very prestigious Cannes Festival. There cinematographer Chris Menges's debut as director, *A World Apart* (like *Cry Freedom*, about apartheid in South Africa), was honoured, and the International Critics' Prize for the best film out of competition went to Terence Davies's *Distant Voices, Still Lives*. These were the two outstanding wholly British films of the year, also winning several other festival citations. The Davies film, about his own family in Liverpool during and after World War II, was also nominated five times—more than any other—in the first-ever European Film Awards, held in West Berlin in November.

In general, British films, particularly those financed on comparatively small budgets by Channel Four and the British Screen Consortium, continued to be admired, and sold, throughout the world. At the end of the year, however, it was generally agreed that the strain put upon their directors by budgetary constraints would soon have to be alleviated. And bigger budgets meant reliance on more foreign money, particularly from America, which in turn would mean some sort of compromise.

This compromise was very successfully achieved by one film in particular—Charles Crichton's *A Fish Called Wanda*. Written by John Cleese and shot in Britain with the veteran director of *The Lavendar Hill Mob*, the comedy starred Cleese and Michael Palin but also Kevin Kline and Jamie Lee Curtis, two popular American stars. The result of this careful tailoring for both the British and US market was a sensational financial success, which was not achieved by Neil Jordan's *High Spirits*, another comedy that used British actors like Peter O'Toole with American stars Darryl Hannah and Steve Guttenberg.

Late in the year, there were four favourable omens for the future of films in the UK. The first was an announcement by David Puttnam, now back home after his troubled sojourn as head of Columbia in Hollywood, that he had secured some £50 million from various sources to make films either in Britain or using British talent. The next was the even more impressive amount, almost twice as large, that Jeremy Thomas had gathered, mostly from Japanese sources, to finance six films also using British talent and British post-production facilities. The third was the announcement from the British Screen Consortium that the Government had extended the repayment of its debt for a further two years, so that it could continue in full operation. And the fourth was the BBC's decision to go into feature films in the same way as Channel Four, having at last come to a satisfactory arrangement with the unions after several years of negotiation.

As for British cinemas, it appeared that audiences were still increasing, albeit from the disastrously low base of the early 1980s. If this was largely due to the success of a few very popular Hollywood films, particularly *Fatal Attraction, Crocodile Dundee II* and *Who Framed Roger Rabbit?*, there was no doubt that the new multiplex cinemas, with six to ten screens apiece, were another spur to distribution and exhibition.

In Europe, the most important event of the year may turn out to have been the institution of the European Film Awards as an annual event. The idea was conceived and paid for in 1988 by the West Berlin Senate, who hoped that other countries would take turns to stage the awards, for which every country in Europe could enter two films. In 1988, the television spectacular at which the awards were announced, and which was staged in West Berlin at the Theater des Westons, was watched by around 300 million viewers all over Europe. The winning film was from Poland—Krzyztof Kieslowski's controversial *A Short Film About Killing*—and the best director was adjudged to be Wim Wenders, the West German maker of *Wings of Desire*. A highlight of the show, attended by an impressive array of European film personalities, was the presentation of career awards to Ingmar Bergman, the great Swedish director, and to Marcello Mastroianni, the evergreen Italian leading man. Europe, however, did not otherwise have a very impressive year, either with new films that made an international impact or with audiences, which on the whole remained either static or declined a little.

Nevertheless, the three major European festivals each displayed and gave prizes to top-class European films, which proved some compensation. Aleksandr Askoldov's *The Commissar*, a Soviet film made in 1967 but banned for 20 years, was much admired at the Berlin Festival; Bille August's *Pelle The Conqueror*, from Denmark, won the Cannes Golden Palm; and Venice's Golden Lion went to Ermanno Olmi's *Legend of the Holy Drinker*. Europe also had a notable success when Gabriel Axel's *Babette's Feast*, again from Denmark, won the Hollywood Oscar for Best Foreign Film and went on to do splendid business around the world.

Elsewhere, the emerging Chinese cinema went back into its shell a little after *Red Sorghum* had won the Berlin Festival's Golden Bear. A bad dip in Chinese cinema-going habits, probably because of the spread of television, was one reason; another was the Government's uncertainty about the audacious but not necessarily popular work of China's new young directors.

Japan and India had good years, both at home and abroad, with Mira Nair's *Salaam Bombay*, from India, winning the Camera d'Or at Cannes for Best First Feature and selling all over the world, and Juzo Itami, from Japan, having national and international success with no fewer than three films—*Tampopo, The Funeral* and *A Taxing Woman*. India's declining if still massive audiences made few producers happy, while on Indian television Govind Nihilani's *Tamas*, a brave and successful attempt to explain Partition through the lives of ordinary people, survived court action to become massively popular and a real landmark on the Government-controlled network.

South America and Cuba, both renowned for their film-making in the past, did not achieve any real breakthroughs during the year, although as many people as ever seemed to be going to the cinema. Africa came up with a rare international success in *Yeelen*, Souleymane Cisse's epic from Mali. This might well encourage others in the always difficult effort to finance films on that continent. Ousmane Sembene's *Camp De Thiaroye*, from Senegal, also won a prize at Venice. It was the first film for nearly a decade by a director often referred to as the father of the African cinema.

Deaths during the year included: Sir John Clements (British actor), Nat Cohen (British producer), Allan Cuthbertson (British actor), I. A. L. Diamond (American scenarist and producer), Trevor Howard (British actor), Raj Kapoor (Indian producer, director and actor), Alf Kjellin (Swedish actor and director), Jesse Lasky Jr (American scenarist), Robert Livingstone (American actor), Colleen

Moore (American actress), Eva Novak (American actress), Emeric Pressburger (British producer), Ella Raines (American actress), Irene Rich (American actress), Renato Salvatore (Italian actor), Kenneth Williams (British comedian), John Houseman (American producer and actor), Lois Wilson (American actress), Andrew Cruickshank (British actor) and Hal Ashby (American director). (For Clements, Houseman, Howard and Pressburger, see OBITUARY.)

BOOKS OF THE YEAR. *Silent Magic*, by Ivan Butler; *That Was Hollywood: The 1930s*, by Allan Eyles; *City of Nets*, by Otto Friedrich; *The Classical Hollywood Cinema*, by David Bordwell and others; *The British Film Institute Book of the Western*, edited by Ed Buscombe; *Ozu And The Poetics of Cinema*, by David Bordwell; *Bertolucci By Bertolucci*, edited by Don Ranvaud and Enzo Ungaro; *The Magic Lantern*, by Ingmar Bergman; *The Last of England*, by Derek Jarman; *Eisenstein Writings*, Vol. 1, edited by Richard Taylor; *The French Through Their Films*, by Robin Buss; *The 1988 International Film Guide*, edited by Peter Cowie; *Third World Film Making And The West*, by Roy Armes; *The Film Factory*, by Richard Taylor and Ian Christie; *Mass Observation at The Movies*, by Jeffrey Richards and Dorothy Sheridan; *Hollywood*, by Joel Finler.

TELEVISION AND RADIO

ONE of the most dramatic periods of change since the introduction of commercial television in Britain in 1955 was heralded by a radical government White Paper, designed to increase choice and competition, and the launch of a new age of satellite television. A powerful mixture of technology and the free market principles of Mrs Thatcher, the Prime Minister, were combining to pose a series of unprecedented challenges to existing broadcasters, the BBC and the ITV companies.

Change became inevitable in December when the 16-channel television satellite, *Astra*, was successfully launched from French Guiana. At least nine of the channels would be in the English language and no less than six of them would be controlled by Rupert Murdoch, chief executive of News International, the newspaper group which owned five of Britain's national newspapers.

In the longer term, the changes resulting from the Government's White Paper, *Broadcasting in the '90s: Competition, Choice, and Quality*, published in November, could be even more dramatic. The White Paper proposed a significant degree of deregulation—a growing international trend in broadcasting—including awarding future ITV franchises to the highest bidder after an initial quality test, and removing many of the barriers which had prevented commercial broadcasting companies from being taken over on the stock exchange. The Government said its aim was to open the door so that individuals could choose from a much wider range of broadcasting and to place 'the viewer and listener at the centre of broadcasting policy'.

According to the White Paper 'the Government believes that with the right enabling framework, a more open and competitive broadcasting market can be attained without detriment to programme standards and quality'. Apart from encouraging change, which the Government said was not only inevitable but desirable, an important theme running through the White Paper was an emphasis on creating more internal competition within the broadcasting market by breaking up its monolithic structures. Under the White Paper proposals, which were expected to form the heart of a new Broadcasting Bill to be introduced in the House of Commons in the autumn of 1989, commercial television would face the greatest changes. ITV would lose its special status as a national network and instead 10-year national, regional and local television licences would be awarded to the highest bidder.

A new Independent Television Commission (ITC) was also proposed, to regulate all forms of commercial television with 'a lighter touch', replacing both the Independent Broadcasting Authority and the Cable Authority. As a result of the changes, Channel 4 could become the only truly national commercial channel, although a new Channel 5, capable of reaching up to 70 per cent of the country, was to be launched in 1993 with the possibility of an even more limited sixth channel in the mid-1990s. Under the new proposals, the new ITV companies, with their regional roles re-emphasized and their channel re-named Channel 3, would not have to form a national network and many of their public service obligations would be removed.

Channels 3, 4 and 5, which could be funded by any mixture of advertising, subscription and sponsorship, would have to show high-quality news and current affairs and provide 'a diverse programme service calculated to appeal to a variety of tastes and interests'. The new local television stations would be able to use cable or local microwave 'over-the-air' transmitters or any mixture of the two. However, the network owners would not be able to sell the programme services—that was to be the task of a new breed of local retailers. The Government also wanted to see the existing national television transmission system, run by the IBA and the BBC, replaced by 'a regionally based, privatized transmission system designed to promote competition'.

The only area where the Government showed any sign of doubt was over the future of Channel 4, which was to retain its programming remit to be innovative but in future it would have to sell its advertising in competition with the other commercial stations. The Government had not, however, decided what its future constitution should be and put forward three options—that it should be a straight private-sector body or a non-profit making subsidiary, or that there should be a link between Channel 4 and Channel 5.

The BBC appeared to emerge from the reform proposals virtually unscathed, except for the planned removal of one of its national early morning television channels and its allocation as a commercial service. The Government, however, issued a longer-term threat which could in the end undermine the BBC as a universal broadcaster to the nation. The BBC was to 'have in mind' the eventual replacement of the licence fee by subscription and, to provide a financial incentive after April 1991, the Government intended to agree licence fee increases of less than the retail price index (the present method of calculating licence fee increases) 'in a way which takes account of the BBC's capacity to generate income from subscription'. Moreover, it was made clear that the entire role of the BBC would be fully reviewed when its Royal Charter came up for renewal in 1996.

The White Paper also confirmed previous proposals for several hundred local and community radio stations, the creation of three new national commercial channels, to be awarded to the highest bidder, and the setting-up of a new Radio Authority. The IBA was also given permission to advertise 20 new 'incremental' radio stations—new stations to be set up under existing legislation in areas which already had an independent local radio station.

Home Secretary Douglas Hurd said of the White Paper: 'It is a difficult balance but I think we have got it about right.' Lord Thomson, retiring chairman of the IBA, saw it rather differently: 'There is astonishingly no mention of the need to continue religious programming. There is no obvious peg in the text of the Government's document on which to hang documentaries, drama or science and children's programmes.' Lord Thomson added in a valedictory address: 'Most striking of all, it will not be any part of the positive duty of the ITC to promote a national spine of network programmes.' Also critical was the Cable Authority, which attacked the Government's proposals as 'nonsense' and said that it would award as many franchises under existing legislation as the market demanded.

Apart from the long-awaited declaration of the Government's policy, the story of the year concerned the relentless media ambitions of Mr Murdoch, who first announced in June that he was taking four channels on *Astra,* and then increased the number to six, all under the banner of Sky Television. Four channels—Sky News (a 24-hours-a-day news channel), Sky Movies, Eurosport (a joint venture with public service broadcasters such as the BBC) and the existing Sky entertainment channel—were all scheduled for launch from the direct-to-the-home satellite in February 1989. The Disney Channel and Sky Arts were due for launch later in the year.

Mr Murdoch said that before the end of 1989 both Sky Movies and the Disney Channel would be scrambled and offered as a subscription package at £12 a month. He also promised to spend more than £100 million a year on programmes, although the number of homes which Sky guaranteed to advertisers that it would reach in the first year had to be reduced from 2.5 million to 1.15 million. Alan Sugar, chairman of Amstrad Consumer Electronics, undertook that in the first 12 months his company would manufacture 1 million units of basic receiving equipment for the *Astra* channels, at a retail cost of £199 (not including installation). As at year's end, however, sales of the new equipment were far behind original expectations.

Apart from Sky, W. H. Smith, the retail group, took two channels on *Astra* for its Screen Sport and Lifestyle channels, while the pop music station MTV (Europe), controlled by publisher Robert Maxwell, was also scheduled to move to *Astra*. The other two channels so far allocated were for Scansat, a Scandanavian company planning to broadcast to Scandinavia from London. Several of the channels, such as MTV and Eurosport, were to be aimed at audiences all over Western Europe.

As *Astra* went into orbit, Sky's main rival in the UK, the British Satellite Broadcasting (BSB) consortium, pushed ahead with preparations for its launch in September 1989 of a three-channel, high-power, direct-broadcasting-by-satellite (DBS) service. The main battle between the satellite rivals was fought over rights to feature films for their respective pay television channels. BSB bought up the libraries and future output of more Hollywood studios than Sky, but had to commit more than $700 million to guarantee that Mr Murdoch did not get them. To stay in this battle, BSB had to get a further £131 million in backing from its investors (in addition to the £222.5 million already raised) in advance of going to the City, probably through a public flotation, to ask for yet more. BSB also announced the arrival of the 'squarial', a flat aerial system, to enable reception of the three BSB channels and the additional two DBS channels which the IBA intended to advertise.

The Government's enthusiasm for freedom of choice for viewers did not always extend to freedom for broadcasters to decide what programmes should be shown. Lord Rees-Mogg was appointed head of a new Broadcasting Standards Council to monitor the portrayal of sex and violence in all the electronic media, although there were signs that his planned code of practice would not differ greatly from the standards already operated by the BBC and the IBA.

The greatest point of tension between broadcasters and the

Government concerned the reporting of terrorism. Broadcasters in Northern Ireland were threatened with prosecution under the Prevention of Terrorism Act to make them hand over untransmitted footage of an IRA atrocity. After the murder of eight soldiers in a bomb attack, the Government banned Britain's broadcasters from interviewing members of the IRA or their supporters face-to-face, although their words could be carried in reported speech. The ban included members of Sinn Féin, the political wing of the IRA, even though the party was legal and had local councillors and a Westminster MP.

The biggest row was over a Thames Television documentary *Death on the Rock*, which looked into the circumstances of the shooting by the SAS of three IRA terrorists in Gibraltar and was broadcast in March (see p. 188) before the inquest was held. The IBA turned down a formal request from the Foreign Office not to show the documentary, which carried eye-witness accounts by individuals who said that the terrorists had been given no chance to surrender and that at least one had been shot while on the ground. Mrs Thatcher was described as being 'beyond fury' at the decision to transmit the programme and the political pressure was such that Thames Television set up an independent inquiry into the making of the programme, under the chairmanship of Lord Windlesham, a former Conservative Minister. (Eventually held in September, the inquest returned verdicts of lawful killing.)

Elsewhere, the process of deregulating broadcasting and the spread of new channels continued apace. The first satellite television channels with commercials began broadcasting in Denmark and there was a new cultural channel in the Netherlands. In May the Spanish Parliament finally passed legislation enabling the creation of three new private television channels. The French finally launched their direct broadcasting satellite *TDF-1* in October, although there was little agreement on the uses to which it should be put. The election of the Socialist Government of Michel Rocard led to promises to replace the new independent broadcasting authority, the CNCL, and to bring in a new regulatory structure for broadcasting—the tenth since the war and the third change since 1982. In West Germany the rise of private television was symbolically marked when the publishers Bertelsmann, with a stake in RTL-Plus, the German satellite channel, beat public service broadcasters ARD and ZDF to exclusive television rights to the German football league.

In the US the gradual advance of cable television and the independent television stations at the expense of the networks continued. In November, for instance, the three networks had a total audience share of 67 per cent in prime time, compared with 71 per cent in 1987 and 76 per cent in 1986. Things were much less gloomy for broadcasters in the Soviet Union, where it was the year in which *glasnost* came to television. As a result, there was a new openness in the portrayal of the top institutions and a new honesty in dealing with national disasters such as the earthquake in Armenia (see p. 113).

Chapter 2

ART—ARCHITECTURE—FASHION

ART

THE year was one in which blockbuster shows and auctions made news and the art market escalated even higher, with records made only to be broken. Sotheby's announcements were typical of figures which seemed to be heading into the stratosphere; its 1988 auction season reported an overall increase of 27.5 per cent over 1987 and established a new record annual sales total for any auction house. The art market was on a permanent high of hype, media attention and dollar signs: in sterling, Sotheby's total was £1,015,768,000.

Perhaps the most startling pointer to future trends was the sale of Jasper Johns's *False Start* for $17,050,000, a world record both for contemporary art and work by a living artist. Following in the contemporary stakes at Sotheby's, Robert Rauschenberg's *Rebus* fetched $6,300,000 and Andy Warhol's *Marilyn* $3,960,000. The extraordinary variety of objects and materials consigned for sale in the year included such things as Kafka's manuscript of *The Trial* (£1,100,000) and Orson Welles' typescript of the *War of the Worlds* (£74,500), a console table made for Marie Antoinette (£1,650,000), and a Guarneri violin (£572,000)—all records in their fields.

Christie's too had an extraordinary season: the autumn period alone (August to December) was reckoned at £398 million, a 61 per cent increase on the corresponding period in 1987. Moreover, the most expensive painting—and indeed most expensive item at auction during the year, also setting a record for a twentieth-century painting—was Picasso's *Acrobate et Jeune Arlequin*, sold by Christie's for £20,900,000 to a Japanese department store.

Geraldine Norman, the respected art market commentator for *The Independent*, suggested that the most remarkable trend was the new passion for twentieth-century, and in particular contemporary, work. For example, two other works by Johns went for enormous prices at auction: his *Diver*, sold at Christie's in May for $4,180,000, held the record for work by a living artist, until it was surpassed, also at Christie's, by his *White Flag* at $7,040,000.

Van Gogh, Monet and Picasso were the world leaders in

painting prices at auction in 1987–88: but Johns was not too far behind in this improbable race, which of course benefited owners and auction houses rather than artists. And coming up strong were other painters like Rothko, Warhol, Pollock and Rauschenberg, not to mention Francis Bacon and de Kooning. By the end of 1988, the top ten prices ever paid at auction included eight late-nineteenth- and twentieth-century paintings; Johns's *False Start* was seventh, sold for much more than any Rembrandt, Velasquez or Goya; only Mantegna, in tenth place, represented the Old Masters.

Mega-millionaires dominated the overheated salerooms, led by Americans, with some Europeans and Japanese also to the fore. The most disturbing factor, in our museum age, was that the buyers were all private or corporate. Investment dominated aesthetics. No public museum or gallery could compete, so that it was likely to be a substantial period before some of these paintings came into the public domain. Even the director of the oil-rich Getty Museum in Malibu, California, publicly declared in November that the auction prices were 'just plain mad'.

Personal collections, on two levels, were also brand leaders. First, there was stardom in the pop and art worlds. The posthumous sale of the eclectic Andy Warhol collections, ranging from art deco to cookie jars to American Indian art to American federal furniture, realized over $25 million, all to benefit the Andy Warhol Foundation, which in turn would benefit the arts. Also well-publicized was the summer sale by Sotheby's (for £2 million) of art and artifacts collected by the pop singer Elton John. It was preceded by a controversial exhibition of the items at the Victoria and Albert and many commented on the use of the national museum of applied and decorative arts as, in fact, an extension of an auction saleroom. (The V & A was also at the centre of controversy over its Saatchi and Saatchi advertisements using the slogan 'An ace caff with quite a nice museum attached'.)

London remained the centre of the Old Masters trade, and a new commercial gallery dedicated to Old Masters, the Walpole, opened in the West End gallery belt in the summer. The showing of the Thyssen collection of Old Masters at the Royal Academy fuelled a media campaign to have the collection, especially Holbein's *Henry VIII*, permanently in Britain. Existing national museums, drastically underfunded, were outraged at the apparent ability of the Government to find £150 million to house and maintain the Thyssen collection. In the event, the paintings were to go on loan to Madrid (the present Baroness Thyssen's native country) for a decade, occupying buildings earmarked for the expansion of the Prado (thereby enraging the Prado).

The Western public was, however, not entirely neglected (although the quality exhibitions often seemed to bypass Britain).

The *Degas* and *Gauguin* exhibitions were stunning and revelatory. The *Degas* started at the Grand Palais (Paris), went on as the prestigious inaugural show for the new buildings of the National Gallery of Canada in Ottawa and then to the Metropolitan in New York, in each case with a surprisingly different selection, due to the difficulties of securing the same loans for three different venues. The *Gauguin* started at the National Gallery in Washington, then went on to Chicago's Art Institute—which also inaugurated superb new buildings for its twentieth-century collections—and would go finally, in 1989, to the Grand Palais. In both cases the shows were as inclusive as possible, to a degree which seemed nothing short of miraculous.

Other exhibitions contributed mightily to scholarship and to enlightening pleasure around the world, from Basle, with its dazzling show of drawings by Holbein, to the Kimbell Museum in Fort Worth (Texas), which put on *Poussin: The Early Years in Rome*. Of special note were *Goya and the Age of Enlightenment* (Prado, Madrid), *Art at the Court of Rudolf II* (Kunsthistorisches Museum, Vienna), *Early Cézanne* (Royal Academy, London; Musée d'Orsay, Paris) and *Courbet Rediscovered* (Brooklyn Museum, New York). Other wonderful shows included *Late Picasso* (Pompidou, Paris; MOMA, New York; Tate); *Van Gogh in Paris* (Musée d'Orsay, Paris); *Giacometti* (Hirshhorn, Washington; San Francisco); Picasso's *Bathers* (Paris); and *The Age of Dürer and Holbein, German Drawings 1400–1550*, an exemplary museum show at the British Museum in London. What John Russell of the *New York Times* called an *annus mirabilis* closed with an exceptional showing of Sienese paintings at the Metropolitan Museum in New York.

One of the most poignant, devastating and soul-searching shows of the decade was *Statione der Moderne*, in West Berlin's Martin Gropius Bau, which did nothing less than examine the growth of modernism in Germany from the early years of the century, through the Nazi period, up to the great Documentas of the 1950s when modern art returned. Incidentally, the 70th anniversary of the Armistice was celebrated with a sad and revelatory show called *The Fallen* at Oxford's Museum of Modern Art, which looked at nine of the artists, including Marc and Macke, who did not survive World War I.

The British sculptor Tony Cragg had a fine exhibition at his home base, the Lisson, which coincidentally opened the week after he won the 1988 Turner Prize (worth £10,000) for the most outstanding contribution to British art in 1988, and by general consent at the 1988 Venice Biennale. Richard Deacon, the 1987 Turner Prize winner, had an excellent show of recent sculpture at the Whitechapel.

That very fine abstract painter, Jennifer Durrant, won the £25,000 Athena Prize, and the Athena competition showing at the Barbican demonstrated how much very good painting, much of it abstract, was going on in Britain. Gillian Ayres, who ended the year with a superb show of euphoric abstract south-of-France landscapes at Kasmin, won the Critics' Prize at the Royal Academy Summer Show; she was also one of the eight Athena finalists. A major show at the Mappin Art Gallery in Sheffield, *The Presence of Painting*, surveyed the past 30 years of British abstract painting, in all its skilled diversity. Leon Kossoff had a rare exhibition of fine painting, based on London landscapes, interiors and portraits, at Anthony d'Offay. David Hockney's retrospective was the fourth most popular show ever held at the Tate, beaten only by Constable, the Pre-Raphaelites and Dali.

Historic twentieth-century Britain art was not neglected, with a showing of David Bomberg at the Tate, a selection of which went onto the Paul Mellon Center for British Art at Yale, USA, in the autumn. Lucian Freud's retrospective was a huge success at the Hirshhorn, Washington, and at the Hayward Gallery, London, but had a mixed reception at the Pompidou, Paris. In West Berlin, his small portrait of Francis Bacon was stolen during the showing at the New National Gallery. The art of Francis Bacon went to Moscow, to almost universal acclaim, the first time an 'advanced' painter had been properly shown in the USSR for 60 years. (Masses of contemporary Russian art, much of it mediocre, poured out to Western commercial galleries, and Sotheby's held the first auction of modern and contemporary Russian art by a Western auction house in Moscow.)

For all the riches of British art, there was many an ironic paradox. So strapped for cash was the Church of England that at year's end the dean and chapter of Hereford Cathedral took the controversial decision to sell their thirteenth-century *Mappa Mundi* (World Map) to raise funds to restore, endow and protect the cathedral itself. The national galleries and museums were desperately short of funds for staff, their buildings, conservation, and acquisition. In May, the Tate Gallery Liverpool (TGL) opened in converted buildings at Albert Dock, with masterly surveys for the following six months of British sculpture this century; but even though TGL was a great popular success there were worries about adequate revenue funding.

There were some significant changes at the top of the museum and gallery world. Nicholas Serota, who had re-energized the Whitechapel Art Gallery, took over from Sir Alan Bowness at the Tate; his plans included a radical reinstallation of the collection. Catherine Lampert, of the South Bank Centre, took over at the Whitechapel. On the publications front, a new quarterly journal called *Modern Painting*—its title cheekily echoing one of Ruskin's masterworks—was launched in March, founded and edited by the controversial critic Peter Fuller.

While public museums and institutions struggled practically everywhere, private and corporate art collecting and buying continued to boom. Major British companies such as ICI, Unilever and BOC expanded their significant collections, as did American companies, the leaders in the field since the 1950s. The outstanding trend in the United States, however, was the private museum. In November the Broad Foundation (Eli Broad is a Los Angeles construction, property and insurance millionaire) opened its major contemporary American collection in its own building in Santa Monica, which would be a loan facility for museums and open for viewing to art professionals. The de Menil Museum in Houston (housing the superb and wide-ranging collections of Dominique de Menil and her late husband) and the Terra Museum in Chicago (American art) also opened in 1988.

BOOKS OF THE YEAR. *Degas*, by Robert Gordon and Andrew Forge; *Degas: The Nudes*, by Richard Thomson; *Impressionism*, by Robert Herbert; *Michelangelo and his Drawings*, by Michael Hirst; *Goya: In Pursuit of Patronage*, by Sarah Symmons; *Sporting Art in Eighteenth-Century England*, by Stephen Deuchar.

ARCHITECTURE

THIS was another year dominated by the Prince of Wales, who finally made clear the content of his architectural manifesto and raised public interest in architecture to an unprecedented level in Britain. He began his architectural year by opening the vast and as yet incomplete Broadgate office development at Liverpool Street, London. Seeking royal approval for this American-inspired complex, the developers were mortified when the Prince simply made no comment beyond the tersest pleasantries. The architectural press rightly interpreted this reticence as a sign of disapproval for such colossal office schemes.

Later in the year Prince Charles lent his wholehearted support to the neo-classical scheme shown to the public as a counter-proposal to the long-talked-of redevelopment of Paternoster Square flanking St Paul's Cathedral. This populist proposal, designed by the classicist John Simpson, was a serious challenge to the official scheme designed by Arup Associates. The degree of popular support for Simpson's proposals led to Arup Associates withdrawing quietly, only to re-emerge towards the end of the year with fresh proposals that bore all the hallmarks of a conversion to neo-classicism by a practice that had long championed intelligent modern architecture.

Prince Charles followed this off-stage victory with his long-awaited television documentary *Visions of Britain,* commissioned by Christopher Martin of the BBC. In the 75-minute film, the Prince launched a scathing attack on modern architecture and supported community-based architectural projects as well as vernacular and classical design. He also called for 'ten commandments' by which the laws of architecture would be known.

Throughout the year neo-classical architecture was in the ascendant. The redevelopment of the riverside site at Richmond-upon-Thames opened to great acclaim. Designed by Quinlan Terry, a Suffolk-based architect responsible for classical buildings throughout his increasingly successful career, the new buildings facing the Thames at Richmond Bridge were designed in a highly mannered mix of classical devices. The fact that what might have passed for eighteenth-century facades in the popular imagination hid conventional offices with suspended ceilings and uniform fluorescent lighting seemed to worry no one.

As if to ram home the case against modern architecture, a damning report written by the community architects Hunt Thompson Associates examined the Maiden Lane estate in the London Borough of Camden, completed in the early 1980s by the dogmatic modernists Benson & Forsyth, and found it more than somewhat lacking. Designed in a style reminiscent of Le Corbusier at his toughest, the estate had been heralded by the *Architectural Review* only a few years before as a triumph of housing design. Hunt Thompson's report concluded with the grim finding that this last of the post-war concrete local authority housing estates had caused the 'self-destruction of the Maiden Lane community'.

The Royal Institute of British Architects, however, chose to ignore populist feeling and awarded the Royal Gold Medal to the severe American modernist Richard Meier. There was much upset over the decision, as many members of the profession and critics thought the award should have gone to an architect such as Aldo Van Eyck, who had fought for and created a high standard of community architecture over the past three decades. However, enthusiasm for community architecture was dampened by the news that Newcastle City Council had issued a writ against Ralph Erskine for defects in the much-publicized and approved-of Byker housing scheme. Erskine was awarded the Royal Gold Medal in 1987 (see AR 1987, pp. 484–5).

If 1988 was the year of the Prince, it was also the year of the Americans. American architects won numerous lucrative commissions in London during the year. The most notable event was the unveiling of Cesar Pelli's design for the 800-ft office tower intended to dominate the Canadian-financed Canary Wharf development in the Isle of Dogs. The Royal Fine Art Commission approved Pelli's choice of stainless steel finishes to the exterior of this all-American giant. On the other hand, Skidmore Owings & Merrill, the American practice given the responsibility of master-planning both Canary Wharf and the Broadgate office development, were ousted by the British practice Foster Associates in the competition to control the master-plan of the King's Cross development, said to be the largest slice of urban real estate in Europe. By the end of the year Foster Associates had made limited progress on an extremely demanding and controversial brief. However, during the course of the year this high-tech practice, best known for its design of the critically-acclaimed Hong Kong and Shanghai Bank, won several prestigious commissions, including the design of the new ITN headquarters in Gray's Inn Road (London), the new Montjuish Communications Tower in Barcelona, as well as three buildings in Japan and a new museum in Jerusalem. Clearly the British brand of modern architecture was popular abroad if not at home.

Although popular debate on architecture raged fiercely, the Government took a typically detached and even contrary stance. Lord St John of Fawsley initiated the first-ever House of Lords debate on architecture, attended by fewer than 20 peers. Meanwhile Environment Secretary Nicholas Ridley pushed ahead with disturbing plans to litter south-east England with privately-developed suburbia. Nevertheless, the Government was to be congratulated on finally approving changes in legislation governing the listing of historic buildings, meaning that buildings over 30 years old were now eligible for listing. The first 18 buildings chosen from the years 1946–58 were a mixed bag and, as expected, excluded post-war housing schemes. The new listing could not save the brutal yet fascinating architecture of the controversial Hungarian emigré architect Erno Goldfinger, whose Alexander Fleming House at the Elephant and Castle was threatened with destruction, while his Odeon cinema nearby was pulled down. A sudden spot-listing of *The Economist* buildings in St James's Street, designed by Alison and Peter Smithson, prevented the American practice Skidmore Owings & Merrill from remodelling this rare high-quality group of early 1960s office buildings.

The year effectively marked the end of public architecture in Britain. Under the rulings of Nicholas Ridley's extraordinary Local Government Act, local authority architects were unable to tender for local government commissions under their own steam, preventing them from going it alone as public architects' departments closed. In the meantime it was announced that the Property Services Agency (the Government's official architects' department) was to be hived off to private enterprise by 1993. The imprisonment of three PSA officials on sentences of corruption did little to inspire potential buyers, nor did the news that a House of Commons committee had charged the PSA with 'insanity' after it was discovered that expenditure on new work at Broadmoor Hospital was 90 per cent above the original PSA estimate.

As public architecture ground to a halt, British cities were blighted with a massive increase in the number of shopping malls, theme parks and leisure centres. Few intelligent architects were called upon to design these ubiquitous British building types, although there were honourable exceptions. Hi-tech architect Richard Rogers won a contract for the design of a large shopping complex in Docklands, while another, Nicholas Grimshaw, completed the new Sainsbury supermarket in Camden Town as well as the Sainsbury-owned Homebase DIY warehouse in Brentford, Middlesex.

The intellectual current of the year was 'deconstructionism'. Based on the fashionable French philosophy of the 1970s, deconstructionism in architectural terms proved to be a confused rag-bag of ideas. Deconstructionists favoured an architecture in which buildings were composed of fragments of twentieth-century modern architectural icons propped together in unlikely and hugely fashionable angles, contortions and bricolage. The movement, which was looking exhausted even before the year was out, was pushed forward by the maverick octogenarian Manhattan architect Philip Johnson. In London, Johnson was busy redesigning London Bridge City Two, a complex of offices on the Thames designed to resemble Barry and Pugin's Palace of Westminster.

The year's greatest tragedy, however, was President Ceauşescu's continuing assault on traditional Romanian architecture, involving in recent years the destruction of 30 churches and over 4,000 houses in Bucharest alone. According to the Union of International Architects, hundreds of villages were under threat and many thousands of rural settlements were to be bulldozered (see also p. 126).

The year saw the deaths of Sir Ove Arup, the great architectural engineer, at the age of 92 (see OBITUARY), and of the brilliant critic Peter Reyner Banham, aged 66.

FASHION

AS promised, this was the year that started with short skirts and ended with an 'any length goes' story. The uncertainty brought back the wide-legged trouser and the all-in-one garment as soft options for anyone deciding to skirt the hemline issue. Overall it was the year that saw play-safe power dressing, with its short sharp suits and hard-edged tailoring, slip into softer jersey draped and wrapped skirts and tops.

This was also the year of colour, as black was finally pushed to one side by the introduction of pretty pales for summer and rich tapestry shades such as old gold, cognac, aubergine, greens and purples for the autumn. Looking rich and flamboyant, they were just right for the dandy mood, particularly for waistcoats, that was so prevalent in the winter. In the world of couture, Yves Saint Laurent fought back as his arch-rival Christian Lacroix moved down the Seventies' hippy trail. The year also saw the return of 'ethnic' fashion, which got its seal of approval when the designer of the year award went to Turkish-born Rifat Ozbek. Hard on its heels came fashion collections full of eastern promise with sumptuous silks and satins and richly embroidered gold and silver exploding just in time for Christmas.

The fashion mail-order business continued to expand, helped in part by the attraction of top Hollywood stars modelling their own clothes and leading fashion designers presenting capsule collections at high-street prices. In January, Next launched its own directory designed to change the face of home shopping. However, in December came the year's biggest retailing shock, when George Davies, chairman and chief executive of Next, was sacked by the company he had transformed from an ailing menswear chain to an £11,000 million retail empire. A crippling postal strike and interest-rate rises dampened consumer demand. Retailing was hit at every level, resulting in a substantial increase in mark-down sales.

Designer thefts were also on the increase, with burglaries being reported from some of the country's top fashion boutiques. Clothes were copied in the Far East and sold in the high street.

As a final unabashed statement of luxury, the year closed with cashmere capes, shawls and 'throws' luxuriously tossed over new interpretations of the classic tweed suit. The scarf in all its variations was the accessory of the year.

The classic English lifestyle continued to be the keynote in men's fashion with a Thirties' and Forties' styling of tweeds, cords, and cricketing flannels.

Chapter 3

LITERATURE

AFTER the frantic activity in the British publishing scene during 1987, 1988 proved quieter. There were no major changes in ownership, although the pattern of integration of publishing interests on both sides of the Atlantic continued with the purchase by Robert Maxwell of

Macmillan New York (not connected to the British firm of the same name), while the French conglomerate, Les Presses de la Cité, also established a substantial presence in the United States. At the end of the year the sale of one of the largest independent publishing companies, William Collins, to Rupert Murdoch's News International, already the owner of 41.7 per cent of the shares, was imminent.

One of the main talking points of the book trade was the ending of the Net Book Agreement (NBA), the legal accord between publishers and booksellers, signed in 1902, that books (other than those supplied to schools) should only be sold at the price indicated on the jacket. The trend in recent years for chains of booksellers to spread out to all the main centres of population at the expense of the small, individually-owned shop, accelerated during 1988, with the result that there was an increasing desire for the NBA to be discontinued. Most publishers and booksellers (even including the largest of the chains, W. H. Smith) preferred to continue the NBA system, but at the end of the year Terry Maher, the head of the Pentos group, declared his intention to breach the agreement in the near future. Although the Publishers' Association prepared to take legal action to preserve the agreement, there was growing support for the contention that the NBA was out of date and ripe for change. The fears in 1987 that the next year would bring the imposition of VAT on books in Britain in order to bring that country into line with other EEC members proved to be groundless.

Once again the awarding, and in one case the non-awarding, of the major literary prizes aroused a certain amount of controversy, although not so much as in some years. The Nobel committee once again showed its preference for a writer whose books were banned in his own country, in this case, the Egyptian novelist Naguib Mahfouz. Mahfouz, whose best-known novel, *The Children of Gebelawi*, remained banned in Egypt, was the first writer in Arabic to be made a Nobel laureate. Another major prize was withheld, namely the $50,000 Ritz Paris Hemingway award. It had been expected to go to the black American writer Toni Morrison, author of the 1987 novel *Beloved*, but in the event the donors changed their minds. Miss Morrison was, however, awarded the 1988 Pulitzer prize for fiction.

In Britain, there was general agreement that the Booker prize judges had chosen well in naming Peter Carey's *Oscar and Lucinda* as the winner. It was the second time that this Australian writer had been on the short-list. The judges declared that their choice had been easy (the deliberations lasted for less than an hour instead of the normal three or four). In a controlled yet seemingly freewheeling way the novel moved from Britain to Australia in the middle of the nineteenth century, describing the lives of two gamblers from radically different backgrounds and examining the ways in which their compulsive gaming affected them. The brilliance of Mr Carey's performance depended on the intricacy in which the relatively simple story was presented—every character was analysed, each background carefully detailed.

The ease with which the Booker judges reached their decision did not mean that it was a poor year for fiction. Indeed, the short-list contained books that might in another year have won. Two previous winners were included: Penelope Fitzgerald with *The Beginning of Spring* and Salman Rushdie with *The Satanic Verses*. Most critics thought that Miss Fitzgerald's latest work was superior to *Offshore* (her 1979 Booker winner). A tragi-comedy set in Moscow in 1913, the new novel vividly described the lot of an Englishman deserted by his wife trying to cope with life in a city ripe for revolution.

Rushdie's novel was less well received critically. Many were overwhelmed by the sheer mass of words and kaleidoscope of events in this study of the war between good and evil, into the narrative of which fables and folk tales were incorporated. Devout Muslims took great exception to the theme of the novel and endeavoured to prevent booksellers from stocking it. The campaign against the book included a protest march through London, the first to protest against the publication of a book, it was thought, for many years.

The runner-up for the Booker was David Lodge's *Nice Work,* a witty description of life as seen by a rather stuffy academic woman and the practical managing director of an engineering factory. Comparatively few English novels have described the industrial scene. For this fact, and the fact it was done so well, the novel was widely welcomed. Bruce Chatwin's *Utz* was another of his mélanges of fact and fiction, this time describing the life of a Czech who gave his whole life to the collection of fine porcelain. This obsession had caused him to lose touch with humanity; only the collection's loss could bring him back into the world. The most lightweight of the novels shortlisted for the Booker prize was Marina Warner's *The Lost Father*. This cleverly-constructed book-within-a-book combined the romantic story of the central character's grandfather who had fought a duel many years before and her own humdrum existence in southern Italy. But was the grandfather's existence so romantic and the present-day one so dull?

The prize scene in France remained to cynics much the same, the awards being shared out among the principal publishers. The Prix Goncourt winner, *L'Exposition Coloniale* by Erik Orsenna, baffled many. Indeed, one critic wondered whether it was a serious novel or a gigantic joke. In loose picaresque form, the story concerned a man, born at the end of the nineteenth century, who had given his life to the culture, manufacture and use of rubber. The scene changed constantly and the inventiveness and hilarity were occasionally clever but more often wearisome. The winner of the Prix Fémina was 23-year-old Alexandre Jardin, whose *Le Zèbre* was something of a fairy story in which a husband tried to revive his cold marriage by inventing a mistress and then preparing for his own death. Only then was his wife's passion reawakened.

Tom Wolfe's *Bonfire of the Vanities*, published late in 1987 (see AR 1987, p. 489), remained the most talked-about book of 1988. The satire of life in New York appealed to a world audience. Rivalling Wolfe's success was that of the Colombian winner of the 1982 Nobel Prize, Gabriel García Márquez, whose *Love in the Time of Cholera* was rightfully highly praised. With all the passion and panache associated with South American writing of the magical realistic school, Márquez presented a romantic story of enduring love. Florentino, the libertine, had long loved Femina, the wife of a gifted doctor. It was not until old age that they came together. The meaning of the title became clear as the reader discovered that symptoms of love are similar to those of cholera. Latin America also played its part in the long-awaited Graham Greene novel, *The Captain and the General*, not one of his master-works but a satisfying, wide-ranging story.

Three British novelists who made their names in the 1950s returned to that stamping-ground: Muriel Spark wrote a particularly lively account of the world of the small publisher and the fledgling author in *A Far Cry from Kensington,* while John Wain, rather less successfully, began a novel sequence, to be set in and around Oxford, with a first volume, *Where the Rivers Meet,* which described undergraduate days very similar to his own. Kingsley Amis revived the central character from *A Girl Like Me* to be the catalyst for one of his customary grumbles about the world in which he was growing old, *Difficulties with Girls.*

There was some disappointment with John Updike's *S* and Alison Lurie's *The Truth about Lorin Jones,* neither anywhere near to their author's best form. The best volume of short stories was undoubtedly *Elephant and Other Stories.* Sadly, the collection's author, Raymond Carver, died of cancer a week before the book's publication. It showed all Carver's grittiness in describing urban life. A young fellow countryman of Carver's Ethan Canin, made an impressive debut as a short story writer with *Emperor of the Air.* Young British writers who made an impression with their first books were Candia McWilliam (joint winner of the Betty Trask Award) with *A Case of Knives,* David Profumo with *Sea Music* and Alan Hollinghurst with *The Swimming Pool Library.* There was also the surprising debut as a novelist of the 79-year-old poet,

Sir Stephen Spender, who felt that at last he could produce a revised version of the unpublished homosexual novel, *The Temple*, which he had written more than 50 years earlier. In the event, it produced more wonder that anyone should have bothered to publish it than praise or dispraise.

The volume of poetry that sold far more than any other was Anthony Thwaite's edition of *Philip Larkin: Collected Poems*. There was controversy, too, because Thwaite, one of Larkin's literary executors, had included unpublished work and fragments discovered among the poet's papers. Larkin's will was ambiguous but it was widely thought that he had requested that all unpublished writings should be destroyed. No work of real significance had been discovered. The other controversial publication in this field was *New Verses by William Shakespeare,* which Peter Levi, Professor of Poetry at Oxford, claimed to have discovered and had edited for publication. These uninspired works, evidently written to celebrate a wedding, were immediately seized upon by Shakespearean scholars who asserted that they were not new (the manuscript was widely known) and that they were certainly not by Shakespeare. A brief storm in a teacup was over. Professor Levi had come across these verses while he was researching his critical work, *The Life and Times of William Shakespeare*. Although the reception of this book, published shortly after the 'doubtful' poems, was slightly muted, it was clearly a work of some scholarship.

Heathcote William's *A Whale Nation,* a long reverie (a mixture of evocative poetry and some poetic prose) about the fate of the sea mammals, was an experiment that came off remarkably well. More conventionally, there were good collections by established poets, among them Kit Wright (*Poems 1974–87*), George Barker (*Seventeen*) and Michael Hamburger (*Selected Poems*). New voices that were welcomed included Mark Imlack, who was much praised for his *Birthlights,* and Peter Scupham (*The Air Show*).

In the centenary year of T. S. Eliot's birth, it was only to be expected that there would be a number of studies of the poet, as well as the publication of the first volume of *The Collected Letters of T. S. Eliot*. The last, edited by his second wife Valerie and covering as it did the period up to 1922, proved to be disappointingly unrevealing. However, *T. S. Eliot and Prejudice* by Christopher Ricks stirred up a great deal of argument in that it pointed out the possibility of interpreting some passages in Eliot's work as being antisemitic. The measure of the passion that was aroused could be judged by the fact that the committee of the London Library, to which the poet was devoted and to whom he had been generous in the gift of manuscripts, spent considerable time in discussion as to whether to use Eliot's name in the appeal for funds to modernize the library's premises. Professor Ricks had written a scholarly work covering many areas where Eliot showed prejudice but it was the emotive subject of antisemitism that was seized upon.

The former Leader of the Opposition in the House of Commons, Michael Foot, provided, in *The Politics of Paradise*, a lively and cogent account of Byron as a political animal. The poet Seamus Heaney's collection of critical writing, *The Government of the Tongue*, showed that he was an inspired assessor of other writers' work. Ralph Kenner's at times hysterical denunciation of post-war writing in Britain, *A Sinking Island*, caused a number of ruffled feathers, although it was admitted that, however overstated, there was more than a little truth in what he had written.

It was an exceptionally strong year for literary biography, with the first volume of Michael Holroyd's much-awaited life of the playwright, *Bernard Shaw: the Search for Love*, for which the largest advance for a work of non-fiction (£625,000) in British publishing history had been paid. Although a work of great scholarship and well written, it was thought unlikely that such a book would in fact earn the vast sum paid for it. Some took great exception to the fact that the notes and references were to be supplied in a separate volume. In his *Tolstoy*, A. N. Wilson managed to confine an examination of a writer who lived almost as long as Shaw, and had a more complicated career, to a single volume; although it had little to offer in the way of new facts, this was a sensitive and acute portrait.

Ian Hamilton's *In Search of J. D. Salinger* was written against the wishes of the reclusive novelist, who indeed went to court to try to prevent the publication of the book but ultimately failed to do so. The main success of the account of a not very eventful life lay in the author's revelations of his troubles in researching the book. Had he lived to read it, it is unlikely that Truman Capote would have objected to the biography of him (*Capote*) by his friend and admirer Gerald Clarke, although it is possible that such a vain writer might have thought it insufficiently fulsome. Alan Bishop's *Gentleman Rider: the Biography of Joyce Cary* served to remind readers of a novelist neglected in the years following his death in 1957. Another author somewhat out of fashion was dealt with rather unimaginatively by Vincent Brome in *J. B. Priestley*. There was rather a mixed reception for Bevis Hillier's *Young Betjeman*, which many considered was an over-sentimental and, certainly, over-long account of the first half of the life of the poet John Betjeman. Much greater praise was forthcoming for the biography of another poet, *Stevie Smith*. Frances Spalding's portrait was clear-eyed and revealing.

The year saw the end of one great enterprise and the beginning of another. A quarter of a century after Randolph Churchill set out to write the life of his father, the eighth and final volume of this monumental work was completed by Martin Gilbert, who had originally been Randolph Churchill's chief assistant in the enterprise. This last part, dealing with Churchill's post-1945 political and private life, was entitled *Never Despair*. It was followed by the first volume (of two) of the official life of another Prime Minister, Alistair Horne's *Macmillan*. Notable for its forthrightness and objectivity, it received a wide welcome, not least because Harold Macmillan (who died in 1986) had decreed that no official life should be published during his lifetime. Less interest was aroused in the second volume of another biography of Winston Churchill, *The Caged Lion*, by William Manchester. It was thought to be too adulatory and to lack the massive authority of Martin Gilbert's work.

There was the usual crop of political memoirs. The one most talked about was Norman Tebbit's *Upwardly Mobile*, which proved to be sharp and opinionated, the testament of a Thatcher man. In contrast, the memoirs of Lord Carrington, another former member of Mrs Thatcher's Cabinet, *Reflection on Things Past*, proved to be as starchy and discreet as the title suggested. The practice of Labour Cabinet Ministers to publish the diaries that they had kept whilst in office continued with a further instalment of Tony Benn's political testament, *Office Without Power*. The best-timed of all political books in 1988 was Benazir Bhutto's *A Daughter of the East*, published in the week that she became the first woman Prime Minister of Pakistan (see p. 314). The fact that it was not a particularly revealing book did not take away from the interest that it caused. Another book that was carefully timed, in this case intentionally, was Anthony Holden's *Charles*, a biography scheduled to coincide with the Prince of Wales's 40th birthday. It was sufficiently intimate in detail to incur royal displeasure, but insufficiently revelatory to satisfy the avidity of the tabloid press for Buckingham Palace gossip. Another biography to arouse 'establishment' wrath was Arianna Stassinopoulos Huffington's *Picasso: Creator and Destroyer*, thought by many, particularly art critics, to be deficient in its assessment of the artist's work and over-sensational in its treatment of his private life.

Notable among the autobiographies of those involved in the entertainment world was William Gaskill's amusing but, on occasions, bitter account of the birth pangs of the New English Theatre Company at the Royal Court Theatre in London, *A Sense of Direction, Life at the Royal Court*. Alasdair Milne, dismissed as director-general of the BBC in 1987, wrote a rather tame memoir, less full of rancour or a desire to 'spill the beans' than had been hoped. It was entitled *DG: the Memoirs of a British Broadcaster*. The literary critic, Peter Conrad, produced in *Down Home* an amused if slightly despairing account of his return to his native Tasmania after several decades of teaching at Oxford. There were very divided opinions of Ralph Glasser's *Gorbals Boy at Oxford,* a sequel to his much admired childhood memoir, *Gorbals Boy.* Many found it touching and realistic while the Chancellor of the university, Lord Jenkins, who noted that he must have been an undergraduate at the same time as Mr Glasser, found the book wholly unconvincing.

Perhaps the most unlikely best-seller of the year was a truly remarkable book, *A Brief History of Time.* Stephen Hawking, one of the leading theoretical physicists of his time, had written an account of the development of the Universe from its supposed origins onward in a way that not only satisfied his fellow scientists but was appreciated by non-specialist readers who were prepared to take the trouble to understand the professor's arguments. The book remained in the best-seller list longer than all but the most popular novels.

The work of conventional history that aroused the greatest interest was R. F. Forster's *Modern Ireland, 1670–1972.* That someone should have managed to produce a major study of the changes in Ireland which was regarded equally highly by Catholics and Protestants was truly remarkable. Michael Prestwich's biography of *Edward I* was an addition to the scholarship surrounding this monarch, while John Kenyon's *The Civil Wars of England* was a major work of assimilation of a vast number of facts. So far as social history was concerned, the outstanding work was *In Sickness and in Health: the British Experience, 1650–1820* by Roy and Dorothy Porter, which described in graphic detail just exactly how it was to be ill in Stuart and Hanoverian times. Michael Fishman's *East End, 1888* was more limited in scope but equally rich in detail of working-class life.

Among those literary figures who died was Alan Paton, the South African novelist, who failed by a few weeks to see published the second volume of his remarkable autobiography, *Journey Continued.* Raymond Williams, novelist, critic and left-wing polemicist also died during the year, as did the poet and architectural writer, Sir Sacheverell Sitwell, the last survivor of the celebrated children of Sir George Sitwell, who in the 1920s constituted a poetical faction on their own. Another critic who died was Marghanita Laski, at one time the chairman of the literary committee of the Arts Council (and later the Council's deputy chairman). Two notable thriller writers, both with actual experience on clandestine operations, also died. They were Geoffrey Household and Lord Clanmorris, who wrote as John Bingham. Science fiction lost one of its most accomplished practitioners, Robert Heinlein, and the cowboy novel its most popular contemporary writer, Louis L'Amour. (For Paton, Williams, Sitwell, Laski and Household, see OBITUARY.)

Among the interesting new books published during the year were:

FICTION: *Difficulties with Girls* by Kingsley Amis (Hutchinson); *Latecomers* by Anita Brookner (Cape); *Emperor of the Air* by Ethan Canin (Picador); *Oscar and Lucinda* by Peter Carey (Faber); *Elephant and Other Stories* by Raymond Carver (Collins Harvill); *Utz* by Bruce Chatwin (Cape); *Deceits of Time* by Isabel Colegate (Hamish Hamilton); *Fatal Light* by Richard Currie (Faber); *The Lyre of Orpheus* by Robertson Davies (Viking); *Libra* by Don DeLillo (Viking); *Scandal* by Shusako Endo (Owen); *Rock Springs* by Richard Ford (Collins Harvill); *The Captain and the Enemy* by Graham Greene (Reinhardt); *The Swimming Pool Library* by Alan Hollinghurst (Chatto); *Le Zèbre* by Alexandre Jardin (Gallimard); *Loving and Giving* by Molly Keane (Deutsch); *Leaving Home* by Garrison Keiler (Faber); *Quinn's Book* by William Kennedy (Cape); *The Fifth Child* by Doris Lessing (Cape); *Nice Work* by David Lodge (Secker); *The Truth about Lorin Jones* by Alison Lurie (Michael Joseph); *Love in the Time of Cholera* by Gabriel García Márquez (Cape); *A Case of Knives* by Candia McWilliam (Bloomsbury); *Mother London* by Michael Moorcock (Secker); *Summer's Lease* by John Mortimer (Viking); *The High Road* by Edna O'Brien (Weidenfeld); *L'Exposition Coloniale* by Erik Orsena (Editions de Seuil); *Black Box* by Amos Oz (Chatto); *Sea Music* by David Profumo (Secker); *A Season in the West* by Piers Paul Read (Alison/Secker); *The Satanic Verses* by Salman Rushdie (Viking); *A Far Cry from Kensington* by Muriel Spark (Constable); *The Temple* by Stephen Spender (Faber); *A Wedding of Cousins* by Emma Tennant (Viking); *The Skeleton in the Cupboard* by Alice Thomas Ellis (Duckworth); *Rebuilding Coventry* by Sue Townsend (Methuen); *S* by John Updike (Deutsch); *The House of Stairs* by Barbara Vine (Viking); *Bluebeard* by Kurt Vonnegut (Cape); *The Lost Father* by Marina Warner (Chatto); *Where the Rivers Meet* by John Wain (Hutchinson); *Second Fiddle* by Mary Wesley (Macmillan); *Incline Our Hearts* by A. N. Wilson (Hamish Hamilton); *Happiness* by Theodore Zeldin (Collins Harvill).

POETRY: *Interluna* by Margaret Atwood (Cape); *Seventeen* by George Barker (Greville); *Moonlight* by Douglas Dunn (Faber); *The Grey among the Green* by John Fuller (Chatto); *Selected Poems* by Michael Hamburger (Carcanet); *Birthlights* by Mark Imlack (Chatto); *New Verses by William Shakespeare* introduced by Peter Levi (Macmillan); *Pencil Letters* by Irina Ratushinskaya (Bloodaxe); *Collected Poems and Selected Prose of A. E. Housman* edited by Christopher Ricks (Allen Lane); *The Air Show* by Peter Scupham (Oxford); *Philip Larkin: Collected Poems* edited by Anthony Thwaite (Faber/Marvell); *Whale Nation* by Heathcote Williams (Cape); *Poems 1974–87* by Kit Wright (Hutchinson).

LITERARY CRITICISM: *MacDiarmid* by Alan Bold (Murray); *Unsent Letters* by Malcolm Bradbury (Deutsch); *The Modern Social Conflict: an Essay on the Politics of Liberty* by Ralf Dahrendorf (Weidenfeld); *Fields of Vision* by D. J. Enright (Oxford); *The Politics of Paradise: a Vindication of Byron* by Michael Foot (Collins); *The Government of the Tongue* by Seamus Heaney (Faber); *The Poetry of Marianne Moore* by Margaret Holley (Cambridge); *Intellectuals* by Paul Johnson (Weidenfeld); *A Sinking Island* by Hugh Kenner (Barrie & Jenkins); *The Life and Times of William Shakespeare* by Peter Levi (Macmillan); *The Pursuit of Happiness* by Peter Quennell (Constable); *T. S. Eliot and Prejudice* by Christopher Ricks (Faber); *A Ring of Conspirators: Henry James and his Literary Circle* by Miranda Seymour (Hodder); *The Trial of Socrates* by I. F. Stone (Cape).

BIOGRAPHY: *Gentleman Rider: a Biography of Joyce Cary* by Alan Bishop (Michael Joseph); *Rich: the Life of Richard Burton* by Melvyn Bragg (Hodder); *J. B. Priestley* by

Vincent Brome (Hamish Hamilton); *Dickens: a Biography* by Fred Caplan (Hodder); *Capote: a Biography* by Gerald Clarke (Hamish Hamilton); *Elizabeth Barrett Browning* by Margaret Forster (Chatto); *Freud: a Life in Our Time* by Peter Gay (Dent); *Many Masks: the Life of Frank Lloyd Wright* by Brendan Gill (Heinemann); *In Search of J. D. Salinger* by Ian Hamilton (Heinemann); *Young Betjeman* by Bevis Hillier (Murray); *Charles* by Anthony Holden (Weidenfeld); *Bernard Shaw. Vol. I: The Search for Love* by Michael Holroyd (Chatto); *Macmillan, 1894–1956. Volume I of the Official Biography* by Alistair Horne (Macmillan); *Nora* by Brenda Maddox (Hamish Hamilton); *Wittgenstein: a Life. Young Ludwig, 1889–1921* by Brian McGuinness (Duckworth); *The Life of a Provincial Lady: a Study of E. M. Delafield* by Violet Powell (Heinemann); *Jack: C. S. Lewis and His Times* by George Sayer (Macmillan); *Stevie Smith: a Critical Biography* by Frances Spalding (Faber); *Picasso: Creator and Destroyer* by Arianna Stassinopoulos Huffington (Weidenfeld); *Sylvia Plath; a Biography* by Linda Wagner-Martin (Chatto); *The Secret Lives of Trebitsch Lincoln* by Bernard Wasserstein (Yale); *Tolstoy* by A. N. Wilson (Hamish Hamilton).

AUTOBIOGRAPHY AND LETTERS: *Office Without Power: Diaries, 1968–72* by Tony Benn (Hutchinson); *The Magic Lantern: an Autobiography* by Ingmar Bergmann (Hamish Hamilton); *A Daughter of the East* by Benazir Bhutto (Hamish Hamilton); *Selected Letters of Eugene O'Neill* edited by Travis Bogard and Jackson R. Bryer (Yale); *The Tongue Set Free* by Elias Canetti (Deutsch); *Reflection on Things Past: a Memoir* by Lord Carrington (Collins); *Something to Hold Onto: Autobiographical Sketches* by Richard Cobb (Murray); *Down Home: Revisiting Tasmania* by Peter Conrad (Chatto); *The Letters of T. S. Eliot. Vol. I: 1898–1922* edited by Valerie Eliot (Faber); *A Sense of Direction: Life at the Royal Court* by William Gaskill (Faber); *Gorbals Boy at Oxford* by Ralph Glasser (Chatto); *A Local Habitation* by Richard Hoggart (Chatto); *A Life* by Elia Kazan (Deutsch); *The Drowned and the Saved* by Primo Levi (Michael Joseph); *The Letters of Edith Wharton* edited by R. W. B. and Nancy Lewis (Simon & Schuster); *DG: the Memoirs of a British Broadcaster* by Alasdair Milne (Hodder); *Journey Continued* by Alan Paton (Oxford); *The Faber Book of Letters: Letters Written in English, 1578–1979* edited by Felix Pryor (Faber); *Coastwise Lights* by Alan Ross (Collins Harvill); *Fear No Evil* by Nathan Scharansky (Weidenfeld); *Upwardly Mobile* by Norman Tebbit (Weidenfeld); *Riding the Iron Rooster* by Paul Theroux (Hamish Hamilton); *Monkeys, Men and Missiles* by Solly Zuckerman (Collins).

HISTORY: *Edmund Burke: His Life and Opinions* by Stanley J. Ayling (Murray); *Douglas Haig, 1861–1928* by Gerard de Groot (Unwin Hyman); *East End, 1888* by Michael J. Fishman (Duckworth); *Modern Ireland, 1600–1972* by R. F. Forster (Allen Lane); *Never Despair: Winston Churchill, 1945–65* by Martin Gilbert (Heinemann); *The Essential Gesture* by Nadine Gordimer (Cape); *A Brief History of Time* by Stephen W. Hawking (Bantam); *Munich: the Eleventh Hour* by Robert Kee (Hamish Hamilton); *The Civil Wars of England* by John Kenyon (Weidenfeld); *The Missionaries* by Norman Lewis (Secker); *The Caged Lion: Winston Spencer Churchill, 1932–40* by William Manchester (Michael Joseph); *In Sickness and in Health: the British Experience, 1650–1820* by Roy and Dorothy Porter (4th Estate); *Edward I* by Michael Prestwich (Methuen); *The French Revolution* by George Rude (Weidenfeld).

XVII SPORT

THE OLYMPICS. This was the year of the sweet and sour XXIV Olympiad. For once boycotts and politics hardly intruded, yet despite brilliant staging in Calgary and Seoul the Games' image was tarnished by scandals.

These were Games of contrasts. The myth of amateurism was exposed as millionaire tennis players competed alongside athletes with million-dollar sponsorships at stake. Yet real amateurs still had a place, as Britain's hockey team demonstrated. For many, winning was more important than taking part; as Australian swimming coach Laurie Lawrence voiced it: 'Stuff the silver. We came for gold.' Yet for most it was still a joy to be part of the occasion. The aim was sporting excellence, yet a most popular competitor was the incompetent British ski-jumper Eddie Edwards. The unhealthy reactions to Ben Johnson's crowning and crucifying showed distorted values in sport. Yet this too was offset, as 'Eddie the Eagle' captured hearts by proving that if something was worth doing, it was worth doing badly.

The one depressing aspect of the colourful Calgary winter Olympics was the chinook wind howling off the Rockies, although the only real depression it caused was for ABC TV, as postponements snarled up schedules. Expectations of a return on investment of £309 million were further dampened when the Soviets' invincible 'red machine' ensured an early exit for the US ice-hockey team. So TV fell back on building into a superstar the anti-athlete Eddie, who landed a full 40 feet short of the real star, Matti Nykaenen, in the competition, yet outjumped him in publicity. Nykaenen won the 70 and 90 metre towers and also inspired a Finnish team win to take three golds, like speed skater Yvonne van Gennip.

The Swiss dominated the prestigious men's downhill. Pirmin Zurbriggen sped down the 3,147-metre course in under two minutes, outpacing close rival Peter Müller. In the ladies' downhill West Germany's Marina Kriehl proved fastest, while in the combined it was Austrian Hubert Strolz who strolled to victory when Zurbriggen fell. The confident Italian, Alberto Tomba, made good his boast to win two slalom golds.

Other outstanding performers were the East German luge competitors and their charming figure-skater, Katerina Witt. She recognized the attractions of her own figure by commenting: 'Men prefer looking at a well-built woman to someone the shape of a rubber ball.' Another to catch the eye was the tiny Russian Ekaterina Gordeeva who partnered Sergei Grinkov to the pairs title. The USSR and East Germany headed the medal table, as they did later in the summer Olympics.

In Seoul 160 countries competed, undeterred by North Korean posturing, a Cuban boycott, or threats of student violence. Yet the friendly atmosphere was soon sullied by sporting scandal. The minor one, in contrast to all else in Korea, shamed the host nation. A defeated Korean boxer staged a 63-minute protest and officials violently assaulted the referee. Minimal action by the boxing authority was followed by outrageous decisions, as when middleweight Park Si Hun was awarded the gold after being battered round the ring by American Roy Jones. No wonder IOC President Juan Antonio Samaranch expressed doubts about boxing's place in future Olympics.

All that was of little significance compared with the drug furore which then engulfed the Seoul Olympics. Concern started with the weight-lifters, when positive tests halted the too successful Bulgarians. In a peripheral sport this caused muted reaction and often jocular comment, as when a trio of Canadians were among others banned and their team was said to be 'four cleans and three jerks'. Then came the most publicized event as rivals Ben Johnson of Canada and Carl Lewis of the US battled for the title of fastest man on earth in the 100-metre sprint.

Johnson became Canada's hero, as he set a new world record well ahead of Lewis and third-placed Linford Christie (UK), the first European to break ten seconds. Public adulation was rapidly followed by vilification, as his use of anabolic steroids was proved. 'From hero to zero in 9.79 seconds' was one of the milder comments. Bill Shankly once joked of a Liverpool football match that it wasn't a matter of life or death, it was much more important than that. People who treated sport as if that were sensible comment and those who turned the Olympics into a vast commercial enterprise were more to blame than Johnson. As Samaranch commented, Johnson was guilty, but those who surrounded him were guiltier.

The glad confident opening in Seoul was irretrievably clouded despite many fine performances. Korea had success in archery, judo, boxing and the new Olympic event of table tennis. The Kenyans dominated the middle and long-distance track events with John Ngugi outstanding in the 5,000 metres. The Russians inflicted a rare basketball defeat on the Americans, who retaliated by beating them in the volleyball final. Amid its disgrace, weightlifting produced a shining star in the Turkish competitor Naim Süleymanoglu (who had defected from Bulgaria in 1986—see AR 1986, pp. 120, 177). America's Matt Biondi won five golds, a silver and a bronze in swimming, but the IOC nominated Kristin Otto of East Germany as the outstanding competitor of the Games for her six swimming golds. America's Greg Louganis was many people's choice as the most courageous competitor for his skill in winning both springboard and highboard titles (as in Los Angeles) despite needing seven stitches in his head after hitting a board. Mark Todd (New Zealand) and his horse Charisma won great respect for repeating their 1984 win in the testing three-day event.

Lewis was given gold in the 100 metres and also won the long-jump, but was beaten into second place in the 200 metres. The most colourful figure of the Games and undisputed queen of the track was Florence Griffith-Joyner of the USA. 'Flo Jo' broke the world record in the semi-final of the 200 metres and broke it again in the final. She was just as impressive in winning the 100 metres, although she had to settle for silver in the relay. Sister-in-law Jackie Kersee-Joyner added to the family success with golds in the heptathlon and long-jump.

As usual some world beaters were themselves beaten. The ageless Ed Moses had to give best at last, taking the bronze in the 400 metres hurdles won by his fellow-American Andre Phillips. Moroccan Said Aouita's boasts of a string of golds in long-distance running transmuted into just one bronze. Despite the unprecedented intervention of Samaranch on his behalf, Britain's Sebastian Coe was not even selected for a second defence of his 1,500 metre title, while Steve Cram had a double failure, if coming fourth in the 1,500 metres Olympic final rates as failure. Certainly Daley Thompson's fourth place in the decathlon qualified for the red badge of courage for an ageing and injured British athlete in the world's toughest event. Mary Slaney (USA) and Ingrid Kristiansen (Norway) were other great athletes whose day had passed.

The USSR made a clean sweep of the men's gymnastics and dominated the women's except that Romania's Daniela Silivas exchanged perfect tens and golds with Elena Chouchounova. Britain's most heartwarming gold was the triumph of the hockey team. They qualified for the semi-finals by beating eight-times Olympic champions India and then beat world champions Australia. In the final Sean Kerly's eighth goal of the tournament helped towards a 3-1 win over West Germany. Another impressive British gold was Malcolm Cooper's in the rifle-shooting, a repeat of his Los Angeles success. The hardest-won was swimmer Adrian Moorhouse's 100 metres breast-stroke win by one-hundredth of a second. Most against the odds was the performance of Mike McIntyre and Bryn Vaile in sailing to gold in the Star class after needing a win in their last race *and* a failure to finish by their closest rivals (who suffered a broken mast). Most courageous was the gold won by Steven Redgrave and Andy Holmes in the coxless pairs as part of an exhausting series of races which also brought them bronze in the coxed pairs. Britain finished a creditable 12th in the medal table which was dominated as usual by the USSR, East Germany and the USA, with the Americans in an unaccustomed third position. However, in athletics America had 13 golds to Russia's ten and East Germany's six.

When the captains of sport departed, Seoul played host to the Paralympic Games, the large and enthusiastic crowds proving a great encouragement to these courageous athletes in rising above their disabilities. Britain sent 242 competitors, won 179 medals and set 16 world records, finishing third in the medals table, behind the USA and West Germany.

ASSOCIATION FOOTBALL. The main event of the year was the finals of the European Championship in West Germany. England went there with a fine qualifying record, but the forwards in particular failed to live up to the expectations of manager Bobby Robson. Their first match was against the little-fancied Irish Republic, managed by England's Jack Charlton. A headed goal from Ray Houghton, coupled with many missed chances by Gary Lineker and other English forwards, gave victory to the Irish. While England stumbled to defeats against the Netherlands (for whom Marco Van Basten scored a brilliant hat-trick) and the Soviet Union, the Irish team almost qualified for the semi-final. Ronnie Whelan's instinctive volley gave them a win over the powerful Russian team and they were within eight minutes of putting out the Dutch team when a freak goal at last defeated their resolute defence.

Van Basten and Ruud Gullit were the outstanding Dutch players who finally ensured that the Netherlands at last won its first international football championship. Against West Germany in the semi-final it was Van Basten's last-minute goal which sent them through to take on the fast and fit Russian side in the final. There Van Basten made the opening for Gullit to head the first goal, before himself deciding the issue with a remarkable volley which beat a Russian goalkeeper rated as the best of the championship. That Dutch football had recovered some of its glory of the 1970s was further confirmed when club champions PSV-Eindhoven won the 1988 European Champions Cup.

With English clubs still barred from Europe because of football hooliganism interest at home centred mainly on the League, which was dominated throughout the 1987-88 season by Liverpool. With John Aldridge scoring freely, and Peter Beardsley and John Barnes torturing defences with their skill, their football was as attractive as it was successful. At the back the admirable Hansen marshalled a blanket defence which smothered the hopes of so many opponents and gave Liverpool their ninth championship in the last 13 years. The double also seemed at their mercy when they took an unfancied

Wimbledon in the FA Cup final at Wembley. It was only 11 years since Wimbledon had been a non-League side and the critics derided their direct and physically forceful style of play. However, Wimbledon matched Liverpool for skill and determination, with Laurie Sanchez's goal proving decisive when Aldridge had his penalty saved by Dave Beasant, Wimbledon's captain and calming influence.

Ray Harford's good management helped Luton to win the Littlewoods Cup, but perhaps the most remarkable performance of the season was by Steve Bull in scoring 52 goals to take Wolverhampton Wanderers to the fourth division championship and the Sherpa Van Trophy. In Scotland Glasgow Celtic celebrated their centenary with an impressive double. They regained the premier league championship from Glasgow Rangers then beat Dundee United in the Scottish Cup Final, with Frank McAvennie scoring twice.

At the start of the 1988-89 season the English League was no longer a Merseyside preserve. Despite the return of Ian Rush from Italy, the goals dried up for Liverpool, while the absence of Hansen unsettled their defence. Everton too, like Manchester United, had an unimpressive start. So it was left to the lesser-known teams like Norwich and Millwall to make the running, with Arsenal the most formidable of the big name clubs. Bobby Robson's nightmare continued as England could only draw 0-0 in their home World Cup qualifier with Sweden and were then held to another draw in an away friendly with Saudi Arabia.

The Football League meanwhile continued to take avoiding action over any serious steps to combat the hooliganism which was keeping English clubs out of Europe. Indeed, their only policy seemed to unite in opposition to the Government's declared plan to impose a membership scheme such as had already worked well in the case of Luton Town.

RUGBY FOOTBALL. In rugby union this was the year in which Wales touched the heights and sank to the depths. In the five nations championship they won the triple crown, sent on their way by an impressive win over England at Twickenham. Adrian Hadley's two tries there emphasized the team's attacking flair and against Scotland at Cardiff it was Jonathan Davies who starred with two dropped goals and a clever try. But this close-fought contest was won by the heroics of the Welsh pack, who finally set up Ray Evans for a brilliant and decisive try. Against the Irish in Dublin one of Paul Thorburn's huge kicks won the match in injury time, to give Wales the triple crown. From there it was all down-hill as France shared the championship by winning a single-point victory over the Welsh in Cardiff, as a downpour turned the pitch into a quagmire. Crushing defeats by the All-Blacks on a

Welsh tour to New Zealand then showed a humiliating difference in the standard of rugby out there. Finally, at the year's end, Wales suffered the unthinkable of a home defeat by Romania.

England too suffered humiliation in their sterile performances in the championship and in their heavy defeats when touring Australia. In the winter, however, a new spirit of hope was kindled under the leadership of Will Carling. He inspired a win over the touring Australians, with Underwood's two tries outstanding in a match full of fine attacking moves. The quality of that win was further underlined by the Australians' easy 32-12 win over Scotland at Murrayfield. In club rugby a world record 56,000 crowd saw Llanelli take the Schweppes Trophy in Wales, while in England Leicester won the first Courage League title.

In rugby league too England had a rare victory over Australia. After losing the first two Tests of their tour they won the next and more important World Cup match. That was brief triumph, as the all-conquering New Zealanders then snuffed out England's World Cup hopes. The player of the year in English club rugby league was Martin Offia, whose 44 tries helped Widnes to the League and Premiership double. The cup, however, was won yet again by Wigan, whose decisive defeat of Halifax was a record fifth win at Wembley.

GOLF. Once more Europe's golfers were in fine form with Seve Ballesteros (Spain), Sandy Lyle (Scotland) and Nick Faldo (England) outstanding. To emphasize further that the USA no longer dominated the scene the Great Britain and Ireland ladies' team won the Curtis Cup at Royal St George's, while Sweden's Liselotte Neumann won the US Ladies' Open and England's amateurs won the prized Eisenhower trophy.

Sandy Lyle became the first British winner of the US Masters at Augusta when he defeated Mark Calcavecchia (USA) by one stroke. The shot which won him the title was played with a seven iron, sending his ball 150 yards to within ten feet of the 18th hole. Warren Wind, the doyen of American golf writers, had this to say: 'There is little question that Lyle's shot on the 18th stands as the greatest bunker shot in the history of the game.' Lyle's boyish charm could not conceal the determined professionalism of his play. This brought him seventh place in the US PGA tour money list, with $726,934, coupled with fifth place in the Volvo order of merit for the European tour, with earnings of £186,017. His other notable successes were in the Dunhill British Masters and in the Suntory World Matchplay. The latter was the sweetest success of all for Lyle, following his defeats in the four previous finals.

The finalist Lyle beat in the Suntory was no stranger either to the disappointments of coming second. Nick Faldo was the season's most consistent golfer yet always seemed to miss out on the main prizes. In the US Open he tied with the American Curtis Strange, but lost the play-off. It was just his luck to be beaten by Strange, who had a reputation for being America's main money winner without ever winning anything. For Faldo there were consolations, however, in winning the French Open and the Volvo Masters. And although he was inevitably second in the Volvo European order of merit, that was worth £347,971, with another $179,120 coming from the US tour.

Top of the European money winners was Seve Ballesteros, back to his best form and clearly enjoying the game to the full once more. Of his takings of £451,559, the £80,000 for winning the British Open at Royal Lytham & St Anne's was the most memorable. Playing with all his old flair he finished with an irresistible round of 65 to shake off the challenge of Nick Price and Nick Faldo. With another $165,202 from his US ventures, Ballesteros still rated as one of Europe's big three and that in turn made him one of the best in the world.

Ian Woosnam never quite recaptured the form which made him the Ritz golfer of the year in 1987, but he did recover well after a dismal start. His mood and his plans changed dramatically after winning the Volvo PGA championship in May. As his confidence returned he added the Irish Open and the European Open to finish fourth in the order of merit. Woosnam disappointed himself by his poor results on the US tour, and many of his fans by refusing to help Wales retain the World Cup, which went to the USA this time.

In Europe there was a wealth of young players coming to the fore to win occasional championships, but it was José-Maria Olazabal of Spain, third in the order of merit, who looked most likely to join the big names in the near future. In contrast to his consistency, one of the established stars, the West German Bernhard Langer, had a relentless struggle to maintain form as the dreaded putting 'twitch' returned to ruin his game. In America too there were many new names figuring as tournament winners. Too many, some said, as no-one seemed capable of establishing the mastery of a Jack Nicklaus of old. Curtis Strange came nearest, again heading the money list with over $1 million, well in front of Chip Beck and Joey Sindelar. For Australia Greg Norman was outstanding as always and his country's Dunhill Nations Cup team were favourites to win. But it was the unfancied Irish who took this prestigious title at St Andrews.

The standard of ladies' golf reached new peaks. In Europe the leaders were Lorenzi de Taya followed by Alison Nicholas, Corinne Dibnah and Dale Reid, with Laura Davies back to eighth place. In America Sherrl Turner won $350,851 with Patty Sheehan,

Rosie Jones, Nancy Lopez, Colleen Walker and Ayako Okamoto also grossing over $300,000.

TENNIS. The old order changed in tennis as Ivan Lendl (Czechoslovakia) and Martina Navratilova (once Czech, now American) no longer dominated. Lendl had his victories still, but it was Swedish players who took most of the major honours. The number one player was Mats Wilander, who won the French, Australian and US tournaments, while Stefan Edberg took the most coveted trophy at Wimbledon. In ladies' tennis the phenomenal Steffi Graf of West Germany was irresistible, the first person ever to win the 'grand slam' and Olympic titles (tennis having been readmitted to the Olympics after an interval of 64 years).

Wimbledon provided many highlights in a season of high-class tennis. Defending men's champion Pat Cash (Australia) went out in the quarter-final to Boris Becker (West Germany), who seemed set to win again on the Wimbledon grass so suited to his power game. In the semi-final he confirmed that impression by overwhelming Lendl after losing the first set. In the other semi-final Yugoslavia's Miloslav Mecir, the subtlest of touch players, so outwitted Stefan Edberg in the early play that he cruised to a two-set lead. Edberg fought back with skill and spirit to battle his way through to the final. There Becker was the firm favourite, particularly after taking the first set; but again Edberg rallied and his cool courage gave him the title, to the joy of his English coach, Tony Pickard.

In the ladies' event the oustanding match was the semi-final between Martina Navratilova and Chris Evert of the USA. This was the 78th time these two champions had met and Navratilova finally won the close-fought three-set match full of fine shots and delicate placings, but sadly decided by a disputed line call. Meanwhile, Steffi Graf had overwhelmed all opponents, but appeared unusually hesitant as Navratilova took the first set of the final. Graf's response was dramatic, with Navratilova winning only three more games as the power of her young opponent proved too great to handle. At 19 Graf was the youngest Wimbledon winner since Maureen Connolly (Little Mo) in 1952. She was the complete player on all surfaces and to emphasize her supremacy she swept to victory in the Seoul Olympics, crushing Argentina's Gabriela Sabbatini in the final. At Seoul Mecir also had reward for much fine play when he beat Tim Mayotte (USA) to take the men's title.

At the end of the season West Germany provided its most remarkable result by winning the Davis Cup 4-1 in Sweden. It was the first time the Germans had ever won the event. Becker was dominant throughout, and received unexpectedly firm support from his partners in overcoming the talented Swedes.

CRICKET. The West Indies swept all before them on the field. But this was a year in which international cricket was beset by rows as a game which was once a by-word for fair play was brought into disrepute by bad sportsmanship and political wrangles.

The frustrations of touring teams with the notoriously biased umpiring and pitch preparation in Pakistan flared again as Australia suffered. Less than a year after English anger boiled over in Mike Gatting's notorious confrontation with umpire Shakoor Rana, the Australians were equally enraged by Mahboob Shah. So enraged in fact that after their innings defeat in the first Test this team too was only prevented from returning home by a direct order from their Board. As captain Allan Border put it: 'You don't have a chance here. It's a conspiracy from the word go.' While ordering their team to continue playing, the Australian Board gave full backing to their complaints. Manager Colin Egar issued an agreed statement reading: 'We fully support Allan Border in comments on playing conditions in Pakistan. Other visiting countries have drawn attention to pitches and umpiring decisions which are clearly unsatisfactory and contrary to the spirit of the game. The situation is unacceptable and damaging to international cricket, yet nothing seems to be done.'

Controversy flared again as India refused entry to some England players and the tour was cancelled. The Indian Government saw the appointment of Graham Gooch as captain as particularly insensitive because of his South African connections. The English view was that the South African issue was due for discussion at the next International Cricket Conference and that meanwhile there was agreement to accept any selected team. They therefore claimed compensation, unsuccessfully. A replacement tour to New Zealand, with Pakistan involved, also fell through when Pakistan withdrew for similar reasons.

England's cricket performance was almost as depressing. Only in one-day internationals did they maintain high standards, winning all three Texaco trophy matches against the West Indies. That proved no guide to Test form. After drawing the first, the West Indian tourists easily won the next four. No matter how England permed 28 players and four captains, the West Indies remained a class above. The reluctant Gooch took over for the final Test and then led England to victory over Sri Lanka, so ending their 18-match sequence without a win. By the end of the year the West Indies had scored an equally decisive success over Australia, comfortably winning the first three Tests.

New Zealand's Richard Hadlee established an all-time bowling record with his 374th Test wicket in a series which India won despite his fine bowling. In domestic cricket there was one outstanding performer. The Zimbabwean, Graeme Hick, became only the second batsman since the war to score a thousand runs in May. This included a remarkable 405 not out against Somerset and 172 against West Indies in his last May innings. Worcestershire were the team of the year, winning the county championship by a single point from Kent and also taking the Refuge Assurance League title. Worcestershire also reached the final of the NatWest Trophy, only to lose to Gatting's Middlesex. In the Benson & Hedges Cup Hampshire won, thus taking their first-ever one-day title.

MOTOR RACING. This was the last Grand Prix season for turbo-charged cars and it was dominated throughout by the McLaren MP4/4 with its specially designed Honda RA-168E engine. The McLaren-Honda won the constructors' championship by a remarkable 199 points to Ferrari's 65 and Beneton-Ford's 46. Only once did one of its cars fail to take first place, as Alain Prost's engine failed and Ayrton Senna crashed, allowing Gerhard Berger's Ferrari an appropriate victory in the Italian Grand Prix. For the rest it was usually McLaren first and second. This monotonous sequence was broken only by Berger's Ferrari in Brazil and Monaco, Nigel Mansell's Williams-Judd at Silverstone and in Spain, Michele Alboreto's Ferrari in Italy and Ivan Capelli's March-Judd in Portugal.

This meant that the drivers' championship was between Prost and Senna, with the rest nowhere. But the rivalry of those team mates was intense and the contest so close that it was only decided in Senna's favour in the 15th and penultimate Grand Prix in Japan. The styles of the two also made for a fascinating contrast, with the consistent and reliable Prost careful of taking risks, Senna determined to win at all costs. As John Watson commented on Senna: 'If anybody ever sold their soul to win a championship, Senna did. His commitment was just frightening.' That commitment and readiness to take risks meant that Senna had some unscheduled disasters amid the brilliant drives and was much favoured by a points system which only took account of the eleven best races. On this basis Senna won by the narrow margin of 90 points to 87. But in all the 16 events Prost had 105 points to Senna's 90.

Prost accepted the outcome without bitterness, but with no belief in the fairness of the system: 'I am not world champion because that is the rule and we have to accept it. But it would be best to count all results. No one except myself can understand why I have 105 points to Senna's 90, but I am not world champion.' For Prost, however, there were major compensations. His seven wins (to Senna's eight) took him comfortably past Graham Hill's record of 28 Grand Prix wins overall and made him the most successful championship driver of all time. Moreover, Prost had been involved with turbo development since his early experience with Renault and had helped develop every winning turbo except the first, the BMW in 1983.

As he commented: 'I wanted to finish with a win especially as it was the last race of the turbo engine. I won 15 races with this kind of engine and I really wanted to be the one winning the last one.' Asked about the difference between the early Renault and the current Honda turbo, Prost said: 'The most impressive thing technically is that we can have 700 bhp with 150 litres of fuel. When I was at Renault we had 250 litres for 550 bhp. That explains everything.'

THE TURF. The leading jump jockey, Peter Scudamore, set a new record as the first to reach 100 winners before Christmas. That put him well on the road to beating the previous best season's total of 149. Before the Grand National at Aintree the Princess Royal unveiled a statue of Red Rum, with the horse himself nodding approval. In the race that followed there was indeed a performance worthy of any by Red Rum. Rhyme 'n' Reason ploughed a long furrow after landing over Beechers. Horse and jockey, Brendan Powell, recovered bravely and retained enough strength to win on the run-in. Horse of the year over the jumps was Desert Orchid, winner of more than a score of races, including the Welsh National at the end of December.

David Elseworth won the first trainer of the year award, although this was shadowed by a heavy fine from the Jockey Club when one of his horses gave a positive test for steroids after a race. The problem for Elsworth had been that the use of these steroids was accepted for dealing with injury and the rules on this type of doping clearly needed clarification. Martin Pipe became the first trainer to saddle 100 winners before the year's end. The royal trainer, David Nicholson, had his first win at the Cheltenham Festival for 18 years when Richard Dunwoody rode home Charter Party in the Gold Cup. The Champion Hurdle was won by Peter Scudamore on Celtic Shot.

On the flat the Derby winner Kahyasi also won the Irish Derby. This was a most courageous performance after the horse sustained serious injury four furlongs from home. With Dimuendo winning the Oaks Henry Cecil became champion trainer and Sheikh Mohammed leading owner. Pat Eddery regained the title of leading jockey, although falling short of his target of 200 winners. Steve Cauthen suffered a severe fall at Goodwood in August, concussion and a broken bone bringing an unhappy end to another promising season for him. The horse of the year was M'toto, who failed to find his best form in the French Prix de l'Arc de Triomphe but had a remarkable win when he surged from last to first in the King George and Queen Elizabeth Stakes.

BOXING. Heavyweight boxers having always been the kings of the ring, it was no surprise that one of the most ferocious heavyweight fighters of all time, Mike Tyson of the United States, should hog the limelight all year. For a time it was for the best of boxing reasons, as he shattered Larry Holmes in January, battered Tony Tubbs to defeat in March, and so frightened his next opponent with his awesome reputation that Michael Spinks was like a prey hypnotized by a cobra and helpless against the lethal strike. After these American opponents, Britain's Frank Bruno was to be his next target. But that fight was endlessly postponed as Tyson continued his fighting outside the ring in brawls with other boxers, or court actions with his wife. By the year's end Bruno had been promised a fight in February 1989, but was commenting philosophically that he would be ready any time in the next ten years.

Lloyd Honeyghan was one British boxer to regain a world title, in the middle-weight division. He had surrendered it under controversial circumstances to Jorge Vacca (Mexico), but this time his whirlwind assault knocked out Vacca in the third round. Britain's Duke McKenzie won the IBF flyweight title when the towel was thrown in.

The most controversial fight was that between South African Brian Mitchell and Jim Macdonald in London for the WBC super-featherweight title. The fight went ahead only after a High Court action and with anti-apartheid demonstrators still trying unsuccessfully to disrupt it. Brian Mitchell confirmed the high quality of his boxing with a unanimous points decision over a brave opponent. The most memorable performance was Ray Leonard's eighth-round knock-out of Danny Lalonde in Las Vegas. That made him the first fighter to win world titles at five weights.

AMERICAN ASPECTS. After around 1,000 preliminary games, the NBA Basketball Finals were contested between the Los Angeles (LA) Lakers and Detroit Pistons. For the second successive year it was the Lakers who won, but only after the closest of contests. The Detroit team had won the Eastern division by beating the Boston Celtics 4-2. In the seven-match final Detroit led 3-2 and 103-102 only for Lakers to win that sixth game despite Detroit's Isaiah Thomas scoring 43 points. In the decisive match an injury to Thomas handicapped Detroit, who went down narrowly by 108-105. The Lakers' win was set up by Kareem Abdul-Jabbar and James Worthy, the latter's 35 points resulting in his being named 'most valuable player'.

Los Angeles had further success in another traditional American game, as the LA Dodgers won the World Series baseball comfortably, beating favourites Oakland by 4-1. In ice-hockey too Los Angeles secured a glittering prize when the Kings bought Wayne Gretzky from Canada's Edmonton Oilers. Gretzky was rated the game's greatest current player, and his multi-million transfer by owner Peter Pocklington aroused almost as much emotion in Canada as the later disgrace of sprinter Ben Johnson in the Olympics.

In American football's Super Bowl XXII the Washington Redskins came from behind to beat favourites Denver Broncos by a record 42-10. In the battle of the quarter-backs, Denver's star, John Elway, began brilliantly with a spectacular touch-down pass and by becoming the first Super Bowl quarter-back to receive a pass. But he was then let down by lack of cover against the ferocious assaults of Dexter Manley and Charles Mann. By contrast 'Rifleman' Doug Williams, the first coloured Super Bowl quarter-back, won the 'most valuable player' award for his consistently excellent performance. Other factors in the Redskins' win included a formidable defensive unit and the effective running of rookie Timmy Smith.

In yachting the America's Cup remained American as New Zealand hoisted themselves on their own yardarm by insisting on their sole right to challenge. The result was a farcical mismatch since their yacht, *Majestic*, was far too slow for the catamaran *Stars and Stripes* which Dennis Connor sailed to runaway victory. So San Diego still had the presumptive right to host the biggest and most lucrative America's Cup in 1991, subject to the legal wrangles always surrounding this millionaires' sport.

The United States entered a team for the first time in the World Fly Fishing Championships in Tasmania, finishing 12th out of the 16 competing countries. For the second year the event was won decisively by England, whose team finished first, second, fourth, 12th and 13th out of 80. The individual world champion was John Pawson of England with 692 points.

WORLD CHAMPIONS. The range of British world champions indicates again the wide variety of competitive sport. For the second year England made a clean sweep of the fishing world championships when their coarse fishing team won at Damme in Belgian equal on points with Italy, but winning on heavier weight. Hugh Duff of Scotland won the Indoor Bowls, at 22 the youngest ever to win a Bowls World Championship. By contrast the Outdoor Bowls Championship went to that most consistent of competitors, England's David Bryant. A Briton also won another world title with Janet Acland winning the ladies championship in New Zealand.

England's team won the world snooker title and that remarkable player, Steve Davis, won his 5th world title and was named Sportsman of the Year in the BBC's Review. Norman Dagley became world billiards champion and Alison Fisher the women's winner, while Bob Anderson won the darts.

In cycling Sally Hodges was the ladies' points world winner and in powerboat racing Roger Fletcher won the Class 2 and Neil Holmes the 4-litre off-shore. James Male took the world rackets title, Tim Stevens the under 65 kg karate and Abdy Shaher the under 60 kg, while Great Britain won the team karate title.

In yachting Nigel Buckley and Peter Newlands won the 470 class, Nigel Buckley and Tim Hancock the Flying 15s. In water ski racing Steven Moore added to England's list of champions.

XVIII ECONOMIC AND SOCIAL AFFAIRS

Chapter 1

THE INTERNATIONAL DEBT CRISIS

WHILE the industrialized countries were basking in economic growth of 4 per cent in 1988 the financial problems of the Third World were lying in the background like an unexploded bomb from a forgotten war. Normally when the industrialized nations expanded their economies by 1 per cent they generated growth of around 1.5 per cent in the developing world, thanks to an explosion in demand for commodities and raw materials. This time, with the notable exception of the countries of the Pacific Basin, poorer countries grew by conspicuously less than their industrialized counterparts. Although there were other factors involved (like less reliance on high stocks by the West, the trend towards services rather than manufactures and the reduced demand for materials like copper for hi-tech goods), the main reason was the increasing financial squeeze on the Third World.

In 1988 the international debt crisis went into its sixth year. There was less public concern about a 'great default', partly because it had not happened yet (despite dire predictions) and partly because the Western banks had been taking remedial action. The top 100 banks had set aside $65,000 million in provisions against bad debts and had reduced their exposure to such debts from 125 per cent of their equity in 1982 to 57 per cent by 1987.

Against this, however, the underlying position of the Third World was getting worse each year because, thanks to high interest rates, developing countries were regularly paying more to Western banks in interest than they were receiving in new loans themselves. This reversed the traditional situation in which the Third World was able to rely heavily on a cashflow from richer countries to aid development. In each of the five years to 1988 there was a net transfer of money from the Third World to developed countries. As more than one commentator remarked during the year, this was a bit like curing haemophilia by extracting blood.

The reverse transfer started with $10,000 million passing to the West in 1984 and built up steadily to a record $43,000 million in 1988 as poor countries found that no matter how hard they tried they could not escape from the revenge of compound interest. By the end of 1988, according to the World Bank, the total stock of

Third World debt had risen by 3 per cent to $1,300,000 million after an 11 per cent rise the previous year. This meant that their accumulated debts equalled almost 50 per cent of the combined gross national product of developing countries. Jean Baneth, a World Bank economist, commented: 'The central message is that the debt crisis is still with us and indeed its end is not in sight.' The trouble was that indebted countries could only generate the dollars required for paying interest on their debts (not many could repay capital as well) by running enormous surpluses of exports over imports. This, in turn, meant sharply curtailing domestic spending and growth in order to keep imports out. The global figures, however, concealed different performances by three different kinds of debtors.

First, the poorest countries in the world—mainly in sub-Saharan Africa—were still receiving some net flows of money in 1988. This was largely because they were too poor in the first place to negotiate loans from the commercial banks and so came to rely on loans and grants from Governments which were less hardfaced than the banks in continuing their assistance. About 80 per cent of Africa's $70,000 million debts was owed to Governments. At the Tokyo economic summit in May 1986 (see AR 1986, pp. 482-3), the leading seven industrialized nations had agreed to negotiate a package of measures to alleviate the burden on sub-Saharan Africa by writing off some of its debt and reducing interest rates on much of the rest. During 1988 the economies of sub-Saharan Africa expanded by 3.1 per cent. But as their population increased by even more this implied continuance of the negative growth per capita that had dogged the continent for years.

The second group—the 17 so-called 'highly-indebted middle-income countries'—presented the biggest financial problem. These consisted mainly of the big Latin American debtors like Brazil, Argentina and Mexico, but also included Nigeria and the Philippines. These dispatched over $31,000 million to their creditors in 1988, leaving them to suffer another drop in income per head (of about 0.4 per cent). Most of these debts were owed to commercial banks and Governments refused to bail them out. The World Bank pursued policies along the lines laid down by the Baker Plan of 1985 (named after US Treasury Secretary James Baker—see AR 1985, p. 46), under which debtor countries were to adopt policies of 'structural adjustment' whereby they adjusted their economic policies in exchange for assistance from international lending bodies like the World Bank and the International Monetary Fund. These countries were also encouraged to find other 'market-related' solutions to their problems, like buying back their own (discounted) debts on the open market and exchanging their debts for equity stakes in industry.

The third group of mainly Asian countries including South

Korea and Taiwan—known as the 'tiger economies'—were able to repay their debts early because of their booming economies. They were estimated to have repaid $10,000 million in 1988.

By the end of the year there was a growing consensus that something more would have to be done to alleviate the growing debt burden of developing economies to enable them to break away from a spiral of decline. There was growing acceptance of the need for 'debt reduction' whereby affected countries would be forgiven some of their debts in return for achieving certain economic norms. This would be negotiated on a bilateral basis to avoid the indignity of 'externally-imposed' solutions. Although some banks still remained vulnerable to default, particularly those with exposure in Latin America, most had stacked enough away in the form of reserves during the previous five years to face some write-offs with relative calm. But no one was pretending that the next few years would be easy, particularly as the growing financial problems of individual countries could easily lead to domestic political upheavals with unknown consequences.

Chapter 2

THE INTERNATIONAL ECONOMY

THE 24 nations of the OECD saw their economies expand by about 4 per cent in 1988, compared with 3.6 per cent the previous year and an average of 2.2 per cent between 1983 and 1986. Growth was higher (by a percentage point) than both the IMF and the OECD had forecast in the middle of the year—and much higher than the doom-laden predictions following the world stock market crash of October 1987 (see AR 1987, pp. 507-10). In the circumstances the performance of the world's economies was greeted as something of a minor miracle. The unusually strong performance in 1988 was helped by two factors. First, with the benefit of hindsight, it was apparent that the world's leading economies—helped by a delayed reaction to falling oil prices—were growing faster than realized at the time of the crash. Second, the leading nations linked with each other to take counter-cyclical action (mainly in the form of lowering interest rates) in a successful attempt to prevent the share crash from becoming a re-run of the depression of the 1930s. At the end of 1988 that strategy seemed to have worked.

Among the larger economies Japan led the field with growth of 5.6 per cent followed by the United Kingdom and Canada with around 4 per cent. Both West Germany and Italy ended the year strongly (with growth rates of 3.4 and 3.9 per cent respectively) while France reached an unexpectedly high 3.5 per cent. But the most spectacular growth came, once again, from the Far East, with China, South Korea, Thailand and Singapore all expanding by between 10 and 12 per cent. Countries in the Pacific Basin were benefiting from the effects of the strong yen which was forcing Japanese industries to locate more factories in low-cost countries in the Far East. This was of particular benefit to the newly industrializing economies of East Asia (Hong Kong, Singapore, South Korea and Taiwan) anxious to invest in medium to high technology products and in the process lessen their dependence on the uncertainties of the US export market. This trend had a knock-on effect on the commodity-producing countries of South-East Asia (Thailand, Malaysia, Indonesia and the Philippines), whose relatively high levels of unemployment made them ideal low-cost bases for labour intensive industries like footwear, sports goods, toys and some electrical products.

But the star performer in the Pacific continued to be Japan with economic growth of 5.75 per cent combined with inflation of only 1.2 per cent. 1988 saw a pronounced swing towards domestic demand and imports taking over more of the thrust of growth—but this did not prevent the country from running up another embarrassingly huge current-account surplus of $80,000 million. Japan's financial strength continued unabated and by the end of 1988, according to calculations made by Goldman Sachs, the value of all shares on the Tokyo stock exchange was worth $2,964,600 million, equivalent to 45.2 per cent of the market capitalization of all recorded shares in the world. This compared with a 29.8 per cent market share for Wall Street in 1988. Extrapolations were being made that soon Tokyo would be bigger than the sum of the rest of the world's bourses.

For the sixth successive year OECD countries recorded growth without a revival of inflation. Average inflation (as measured by the GDP deflator) fell from 3.4 per cent to 3.2 per cent during the year. However, inflation in the Pacific Basin crept up from 1.9 per cent in 1987 to 3.5 per cent.

INTERNATIONAL COOPERATION. The members of the Group of Seven leading industrial nations (US, Japan, UK, France, West Germany, Italy and Canada) continued to harmonize their efforts to stabilize currencies, particularly the US dollar, and to coordinate changes in interest rates. This reached a peak in the months after the worldwide crash of share prices in October 1987 when a coordinated reduction of interest rates injected liquidity into the system and helped to prevent the financial crisis from escalating into an economic recession. Cooperation continued, albeit in a lower key, during 1988 in keeping with the February 1987 Louvre Accord to promote currency stability (see AR 1987, pp. 510-11). The unexpectedly high growth during 1988 was due in part to the way (relatively) stable foreign exchange markets helped to boost private sector confidence. However, the scope for extending international cooperation into other areas of economic policy was constrained by the continuance of huge budget and current-account imbalances—particularly the US budget and trade deficits and the huge Japanese trade surplus.

ANNUAL ECONOMIC SUMMIT. The difficulty of doing anything about the aforementioned constraints in advance of the new presidency in the US cast a cloud over the annual economic summit in Toronto in July. Although some important things were agreed (like debt relief for the poorest Third World countries and a new way of measuring commodity prices in an attempt to create an early-warning system of world inflation) the communique papered over the lack of agreement on Latin American debts and the US demand to phase out all agricultural subsidies.

TRADE AND EMPLOYMENT. World trade expanded by 9 per cent in 1988 as against 5.7 per cent the previous year (revised upwards from earlier estimates of 4 per cent). The main thrust of growth in the OECD area was exports and imports of manufactures, both of which grew by 10.75 per cent during 1988. The year also saw the OECD's current-account deficit with the rest of the world worsen from $49,000 million to $61,000 million, while that of Opec—thanks to weaker oil prices—deteriorated from $8,000 million to $21,000 million. If the US deficit of $132,000 million were excluded, however, the rest of the OECD was in surplus by $72,000 million.

Towards the end of the year strong protectionist currents came to the surface when the United States imposed $100 million of 'revenge duties' against EEC countries following the latter's imposition of a ban on imports of US meat which had been treated with hormones to stimulate growth (see pp. 66–7, 396). Earlier in the year the US Congress had adopted strong powers to impose trade barriers against other nations and the Administration had insisted on a non-negotiable policy at GATT of eliminating all agricultural subsidies by the year 2000.

THE NOBEL PRIZE. The $340,000 Nobel Prize for economics went to Maurice Allais, one of the early post-war architects of France's unique tradition of combining market forces with *dirigisme*. Professor Allais, aged 77, published *In Search of an Economic Discipline* in 1943, followed by *Economy and Interest* in 1947. In 1987 he was credited with having been one of the few economists in France to have warned about a possible stock market crash.

Chapter 3

THE ECONOMY OF THE UNITED STATES

THE US economy expanded by almost 4 per cent in 1988, compared with 3.4 per cent the previous year. This marked six years of uninterrupted growth without a serious revival of inflation. By the end of the year the recovery had lasted 40 months longer than the average for the previous 30 economic upswings which historians had traced back to the middle of the last century. Only two upswings had lasted longer and they were both associated with wars (World War II and the conflict in Vietnam).

Modest progress was made during the year in reducing both the trade and budget deficits, but their size was still a major worry to the financial markets at the end of the year. Unemployment declined for the fifth year running to 5.5 per cent, about the level which many US economists regarded as 'full employment' beneath which inflationary pressures could start to rise again.

OUTPUT AND EMPLOYMENT. Expansion was led by a 19 per cent rise in exports compared with 13 per cent in 1987 and 3.0 per cent the previous year. This was considerably higher than the growth of imports (8.75 per cent) and led to a $22,000 million drop in the current-account deficit to $132,000 million in the year to December. Among other expansionary factors were non-residential investment (up 9.5 per cent), private consumption (up 2.75 per cent) and industrial production (up 5.5 per cent).

Fast economic growth brought in its wake big increases in employment in both manufacturing and service industries. Overall employment grew by 2.25 per cent to 112.4 million, the sharpest growth among the Group of Seven leading nations apart from Canada. Employment expanded at the monthly rate of 340,000 in the first half of the year before slowing down to 220,000 a month in the third quarter.

INFLATION AND MONETARY/FISCAL POLICY. Inflation as measured by the consumer prices index actually fell slightly during the year from 4.5 per cent in 1987 to 4.25 per cent in 1988. The more broadly-based gross national product deflator (measuring price rises throughout the economy) dropped from 3.3 to 3.25 per cent. But the continuing strength of the economy and signs of a revival of wage claims reawakened fears about inflation, prompting the Federal Reserve to tighten monetary policy. For most of the year the Fed (in contrast to its tactics in 1987) acted in advance of market pressures. It exerted upward pressure on short-term interest rates from the spring thereby signalling an end to the more permissive period of monetary policy which followed the October 1987 shares crash. The discount rate was raised in August against the background of rapid growth in employment, which raised fears about overheating. Towards the end of the year the monetary aggregates, M_2 and M_3, had slowed down to around the middle of their official target ranges of 4 to 8 per cent.

In the last quarter of the year the markets started to anticipate further turns of the monetary screw as the dollar came under pressure. By this time attention was being heavily focused on what the incoming Administration led by President George Bush would do about the budget deficit in the light of his pre-election pledges not to raise taxes.

The budget deficit narrowed to around $155,000 million in 1988. This compared with a 'balanced budget' target (as laid down by the Gramm-Rudman legislation) of $144,000 million. The budget position was better than it looked in that the surplus in the social security fund (technically not part of the budget, but counting towards the Gramm-Rudman targets) rose from $20,000 million to $39,000 million. This was mainly the result of an increase in the social security tax designed to meet the future burden of an ageing population. The OECD and other forecasters were predicting that this surplus could almost double by 1991 and reach nearly $200,000 million by the year 2005. Theoretically self-contained to provide future pensions, the fund was in practice part of the general pool of revenues and expenditures and its outcome was included in the general government fiscal balance.

PROBLEM OF THE THRIFTS. There were increasing worries about the effect on the budget of bailing out the nation's 'thrift' or savings institutions. Some $8,000 million of government funds were provided at the end of 1988 to prevent a rush of bankruptcies among these funds, which had lent money on fixed interest rates. In its final Budget the outgoing Reagan Administration acknowledged the scale of the problem by providing $64,000 million over five years to the insolvent Federal Savings and Loan Corporation, which insured thrift deposits. This was three times more than estimates made only a few months previously. Some economists were predicting that the crisis in America's home loan industry could eventually cost the US Exchequer $110,000 million.

EXTERNAL TRADE. The current-account deficit fell from $154,000 million in 1987 to $132,000 million in 1988. Exports rose by 27 per cent in the year to November, helped by the continuing 'J' curve effect of earlier devaluations, and imports went up by 8.75 per cent over the same period. Exports tended to stagnate in the second half of the year (although at a very high level) while imports rose steadily. Much of the rise in imports was due to imports of capital goods for investment, which jumped 20 per cent in the year to November compared with the previous year. However, the comparatively weak rise in non-car imports, of only 7 per cent, was due in large measure to the running-down of artificially high stocks. One important redeeming feature about the current-account deficit was that it was financed entirely by the private sector—in contrast to 1987 when members of the Group of Seven central banks had to finance virtually all of it.

By the end of the year the dollar had recovered some of its strength, thereby casting doubt on the longevity of the export boom. Professor Martin Feldstein, one of President Bush's economic advisers, repeated his view at the end of the year that the dollar would have to fall a further 20 per cent if the external deficit were to be eliminated. Other economists were pondering ruefully over the fact that no US economic recovery since World War II had ended voluntarily. Rather, they had in the main ended when the Federal Reserve Board had raised interest rates sharply to combat inflation. Despite six years of continuous growth no one in the US was pretending at the end of 1988 that the Administration had found the economic equivalent of the perpetual motion machine.

Chapter 4

THE ECONOMY OF THE UNITED KINGDOM

THE economy expanded by an estimated 4.0 per cent in 1988, compared with 4.3 per cent in 1987. This was better than the 3.0 per cent forecast at the time of the Budget in March and marked the seventh successive year of economic growth. The UK economy had expanded by just over 3.1 per cent a year since the nadir of the recession in 1981 and by just over 2 per cent since Mrs Thatcher came to power in 1979.

Among the main influences on the economy were an increase of 5.1 per cent in the volume of retail sales, a rise of 9.6 per cent in investment (including a 9.8 per cent increase in manufacturing investment) and a 7 per cent increase in manufacturing output. The strength of consumer spending (much of it financed by a £40,000 million increase in personal borrowing) was such that imports were sucked in strongly, leading to a record of £14,500 million deficit on the current account of the balance of payments. This was the third successive deficit, despite the start of North Sea oil production at the beginning of the 1980s.

OUTPUT AND EMPLOYMENT. Unemployment was reduced by 649,000 during the year to just over 2 million. The number of people in employment (full and part-time) rose by 399,000 to 25.3 million. Virtually all of the new employment was in the service industries and consisted largely of part-time jobs for women. Manufacturing industry continued to shed (mainly male) jobs, although at a much slower rate than most previous years.

The economy's estimated 4 per cent expansion in 1988 was open to wide margins of error because of the absence of adequate data at the time the figures were assembled. In theory all three ways of assessing gross domestic product—by adding up incomes, output and expenditure — should come to the same total. But by the end of 1988 the income total was showing annual growth of 2.8 per cent and the output measure 4.3 per cent, while the expenditure measure suggested that the economy had contracted by 1 per cent. At the start of the New Year economists were regarding 1988 as the year when the forecasters failed to predict the boom in demand and the statisticians to record it once it had happened. This criticism was also levelled at the Chancellor of the Exchequer, who lowered interest rates at the end of 1987 (after the stock market crash) not realizing the gathering strength of the underlying consumer boom despite a strong rise in most of the measures of the money supply.

COSTS AND PRICES. Strong economic growth brought in its wake a renewed burst of inflation which could have been worse had not much of the excess demand for goods been siphoned off into imports. By the end of the year the annual rise in prices (as measured by the retail prices index) reached 6.8 per cent compared with only 3.7 per cent a year earlier. This was easily the highest inflation among the Group of Seven leading industrial nations. Average earnings rose by 8.75 per cent during the year (slightly higher than 1987), although they peaked at 9.25 per cent during the year. Manufacturers were able to absorb most of the increase in their pay bills by another sharp rise in productivity. Output per head in manufacturing rose by 6.9 per cent in the year to December and wage costs per unit of output (the inflation measure most important to manufacturers) increased by only 2.2 per cent.

However, wage pressures were also building up as bargainers sought to offset the effects of rising inflation. Economists were worried that a combination of rising wage pressure and slower economic growth could lead to a further worsening of price inflation unless the Government's high interest policy persuaded companies to resist high wage demands.

EXTERNAL TRADE. Britain recorded a deficit on the current account of the balance of payments of (£14,500 million) in 1988, compared with £2,700 million the previous year. This was the worst current-account deficit ever recorded, but unlike the experience of the 1960s and 1970s had very few destabilizing effects on the value of the pound, which gathered strength against most currencies during the course of the year. The Government's view was that the deficit was not as serious as those of previous decades because it was the consequence of individuals making spending decisions (rather than Governments as in previous periods). The City did not appear unduly worried about the size of the deficit, but there were concerns about the way it was being financed—increasingly by short-term 'hot money' from abroad needing increasingly high interest rates to stay.

The basic problem, once again, was that import volume (up 16 per cent over the year) was racing ahead of exports (up 4 per cent). Many of the goods purchased during the consumer boom were not made in the UK any more (such as colour televisions, videos, computers, cameras etc.) and where they were they tended to be relatively expensive because of the strength of the pound. By the end of the year Britain's deficit on trade in manufactured goods had risen to over £10,000 million compared with £7,500 million in 1987.

GOVERNMENT POLICY. Monetary policy had been deliberately relaxed in the months after the October 1987 shares crash as part of an internationally-coordinated attempt to prevent the share crash from inducing a recession. In fact—as was to become apparent later—it merely stirred up an economy which was already expanding fast because of an explosion of consumer credit, much of which was tied to the value of homes (which rose over 30 per cent during the year). The underlying buoyancy of the economy was further stoked up by fiscal policy in the shape of £4,000 million worth of tax cuts in the March Budget. By May, when the unexpectedly large surge in consumer demand was producing large trade deficits and fresh pressure on the pound, the Chancellor of the Exchequer, Nigel Lawson, started to engineer rises in base rates. There were nine in all, from the year's low-point of 7.5 per cent in April to 13 per cent in November. By the end of the year there were signs that consumer spending was beginning to fall away.

Mr Lawson frequently asserted that he regarded interest rates as his main instrument of policy, to control both domestic demand and the value of the pound on the foreign exchanges. However, there was a change of emphasis during the year, as the Chancellor put more stress on the efficacy of M_o (mainly cash in circulation) as a monetary indicator and on a higher exchange rate as the main means of curbing inflationary pressures. The value of sterling against the key West German Deutschmark rose from under three to the pound in 1987 to 3.21 in December. M_o rose strongly above its 1-5 per cent target range to 7.7 per cent by the end of the year. The Chancellor declared in October that it was his intention to get M_o heading firmly back towards its target range.

The biggest surprise of 1988—for the second year running—was the unexpected strength of the Government's own finances. In his March Budget the Chancellor had predicted a budget surplus of £3,000 million. In the event it turned out to be a surplus of around £13,000 million. Since the scope for returning this to the people in the form of tax cuts (without exacerbating the balance of payments in the process) was limited, the Government introduced a new policy target of using the surplus funds to reduce the national debt. The national debt in 1988 was standing at £178,000 million or 40.1 per cent of GDP. Mrs Thatcher was being advised that on present trends the entire debt could be paid off in under 20 years.

Chapter 5

ECONOMIC AND SOCIAL DATA

The statistical data on the following pages record developments from 1983 to the latest year, usually 1988, for which reasonably stable figures were available at the time of going to press. Year headings 1983 to 1988 are printed only at the head of each page and are not repeated over individual tables unless the sequence is broken by extending series of figures over a longer period than elsewhere on the page.

Pages to which the point is relevant include a comparative price index, allowing the current-price figures to be adjusted in accordance with changing values of money.

Unless figures are stated as indicating the position at the *end* of year, they should be taken as annual *totals* or *averages*, according to context.

Tables, 2, 3, 4 and 5. Statistics which are normally reported or collected separately in the three UK home jurisdictions (England and Wales, Scotland, and Northern Ireland) have been consolidated into UK series only to show general trends. As the component returns were made at varying times of year and in accordance with differing definitions and regulatory requirements, the series thus consolidated may therefore be subject to error, may not be strictly comparable from year to year, and may be less reliable than the remainder of the data.

Symbols: — = Nil or not applicable   .. = not available at time of compilation.

Sources

A. THE UNITED KINGDOM
GOVERNMENT SOURCES
Annual Abstract of Statistics: Tables 1, 2, 3, 4, 5.
Monthly Digest of Statistics: Tables 1, 11, 17, 18, 23, 24, 25.
Financial Statistics: Tables 9, 11, 12, 13, 14, 15, 16, 26.
Economic Trends: Tables 6, 7, 8, 9, 11, 26.
Social Trends: Tables 2, 3, 4, 5, 10.
Department of Employment Gazette: Tables 19, 20, 21, 22.
Housing and Construction Statistics: Table 5.
ADDITIONAL SOURCES
National Institute of Economic and Social Research, *National Institute Economic Review*: Tables 6, 7, 8.
United Nations: *Monthly Bulletin of Statistics*: Table 1.
The Financial Times: Tables 13, 15.

B. THE UNITED STATES
GOVERNMENT AND OTHER PUBLIC SOURCES
Department of Commerce, *Survey of Current Business*: Tables 27, 28, 29, 30, 31, 32, 37, 38, 40.
Council of Economic Advisers, Joint Economic Committee, *Economic Indicators*: Tables 30, 36.
Federal Reserve Bulletin: Tables 33, 34, 35.
ADDITIONAL SOURCES
A. M. Best Co.: Table 35.
Insurance Information Institute, New York: Table 35.
Monthly Labor Review: Tables 38, 39.
Bureau of Economic Statistics, *Basic Economic Statistics*: Table 39.

C. INTERNATIONAL COMPARISONS
United Nations, *Annual Abstract of Statistics*: Tables 41, 42.
UN *Monthly Bulletin of Statistics*: Tables 41, 42, 44.
IMF, *International Financial Statistics*: Tables 41, 43, 45, 46, 47, 48, 49.
OECD, *Main Economic Indicators*: Table 42.
International Institute for Strategic Studies, *The Military Balance*: Table 50.
OECD, *Labour Force Statistics*: Table 51.

ECONOMIC AND SOCIAL DATA
A. THE UNITED KINGDOM

SOCIAL

1. Population

	1983	1984	1985	1986	1987	1988
Population, mid-year est. ('000)	56,377	56,488	56,618	56,763	56,930	..
Crude birth rate (per 1,000 pop.)	12·8	12·9	13·3	13·3	13·6	..
Crude death rate (per 1,000 pop.)	11·7	11·4	11·8	11·6	11·3	..
Net migration ('000)	+17	+37	+59	+37	+2	..

2. Health

	1983	1984	1985	1986	1987	1988
Hospitals:						
staffed beds, end-year ('000)	446·4	430·9	421·2	409·9	392	..
waiting list, end-year ('000)	854	828	803	831	806	..
Certifications of death ('000)(1) by:						
ischaemic heart disease	174·9	175·6	181·9	176·8	173·6	..
malignant neoplasm, lungs and bronchus	39·8	40·0	40·1	39·4	39·4	..
road fatality	5·8	5·7	5·5	5·5	5·4	..
accidents at work (number)	645	626	659	537	525	..

(1) Great Britain.

3. Education

	1983	1984	1985	1986	1987	1988
Schools ('000)	37·1	36·4	36·1	35·6	35·4	..
Pupils enrolled ('000) in schools	10,094	9,877	9,702	9,545	9,407	..
maintained primary(1)	4,758	4,655	4,624	4,521	4,550	..
maintained and aided secondary	4,494	4,385	4,244	4,080	3,902	..
assisted and independent	606	603	605	607	619	..
Further education: institutions (number)	5,328	5,268	4,975	3,627	3,252	..
full-time students ('000)	603	595	594	608	624	..
Universities	46	46	46	46	46	..
University students ('000)	304	301	305	310	316	..
First degrees awarded (number)	74,918	73,841	72,209	70,912	..	..
Open University graduates ('000)	6·7	7·3	8·1	8·0	..	..

(1) Including nursery schools.

4. Law and Order

	1983	1984	1985	1986	1987	1988
Police ('000)						
Full-time strength(1)	132·7	132·2	132·4	133·2	135·7	..
Ulster, full-time strength	8·0	8·1	8·3	8·2	8·2	..
Serious offences known to police ('000)(2)	3,704	4,040	4,085	4,324	4,437	..
Persons convicted, all offences ('000)(2)	2,356	2,004	2,144	..	..	..
Burglary or robbery(3)	79	79	76	63	..	..
Handling stolen goods/receiving, theft	228	226	219	187	..	..
Violence against person	52	48	48	44	..	..
Traffic offences	1,185	1,138	1,111	1,120	..	..
All summary offences	1,667	1,547	1,503	1,542	..	..
Prisons: average population ('000)	51·0	50·3	53·6	54·3	..	..

(1) Police full-time strength: Great Britain only. (2) Because of differences in juridical and penal systems in the three UK jurisdictions, totals of offences are not strictly comparable from year to year: they should be read only as indicating broad trends. (3) Specific offences: England, Wales and N. Ireland.

Overall price index (1985=100)	90·0	95·1	100·0	102·6	107·6	114·4

	1983	1984	1985	1986	1987	1988
5. Housing						
Dwellings completed ('000)						
by and for public sector(1)	55	54	43	35	34	..
by private sector	149	158	154	167	178	..
Homeless households ('000)(2)	81	80	91	101	107	..
Housing land, private sector,						
weighted ave. price (£/hectare)	134,933	150,942	190,450	243,749	327,538	..
Dwelling prices, average (£)(3)	28,593	30,812	33,188	38,121	44,220	54,280

(1) Including government departments (police houses, military married quarters, etc.) and approved housing associations and trusts. (2) Accepted by local authorities as in priority need. (3) Of properties newly mortgaged by building societies.

PRICES, INCOME AND E..PENDITURE

6. National Income and Expenditure
(£ million, 1985 prices)

	1983	1984	1985	1986	1987	1988
GDP(1), expenditure basis	288,965	292,723	304,208	314,330	327,805	336,278
income basis(2)	260,925	278,452	305,262	321,999	352,431	391,543
output basis (1985=100)	94·0	96·6	100·0	103·0	107·8	112·4
average estimate (1985=100)	94·7	96·3	100·0	103·1	107·6	111.6
Components of gross domestic product:						
Consumers' expenditure	204,318	207,927	215,267	227,757	240,100	255,624
General government						
consumption	73,282	73,974	73,995	75,398	76,198	76,601
Gross fixed investment	53,476	58,075	60,283	61,293	66,373	74,219
Total final expenditure	423,474	438,000	453,124	471,744	495,942	519,584
Stockbuilding	1,306	−1,072	569	689	916	1,945
Adjustment to factor cost	46,390	48,514	49,521	51,893	54,767	56,412

(1) At factor cost. (2) Current prices, £ 000 million.

7. Fixed Investment
(£ million, 1985 prices, seasonally adjusted)

	1983	1984	1985	1986	1987	1988
Total, all fixed investment	53,476	58,075	60,283	60,798	64,243	..
Dwellings	12,247	12,571	11,928	12,798	13,445	..
Private sector	39,085	43,845	48,043	48,451	53,080	..
manufacturing	6,422	7,810	8,735	8,478	9,090	..
other	32,663	36,035	39,308	39,973	43,990	..
Government and public corporations	14,391	14,230	12,240	12,347	11,163	..

8. Personal Income and Expenditure
(£ million, seasonally adjusted, current prices unless otherwise stated)

	1983	1984	1985	1986	1987	1988
Wages, salaries and forces' pay	145,469	155,117	168,568	182,621	198,161	..
Current grants	39,843	43,029	46,757	50,729	52,499	..
Other personal income(1)	46,954	52,120	56,227	60,197	64,671	69,907
Personal disposable income	206,132	220,950	238,112	256,072	274,318	..
Real personal disposable income(2)	228,126	232,622	238,112	245,317	253,077	..
Consumers' expenditure	184,619	197,494	215,267	237,644	260,690	..
Personal savings ratio(3)	10·4	10·6	9·6	7·2	5·0	..

(1) From rent, self-employment (before depreciation and stock appreciation provisions), dividend and interest receipts and charitable receipts from companies. (2) At 1985 prices. (3) Personal savings as % of personal disposable income.

Overall price index (1985=100)	90·0	95·1	100·0	102·6	107·6	114·4

UNITED KINGDOM STATISTICS

9. Government Finance(1)
(£ million)

	1983	1984	1985	1986	1987	1988
Revenue(2)	121,841	128,538	139,548	151,305	158,801	174,133
taxes on income	41,843	43,536	48,513	52,442	52,464	58,439
corporation tax	5,564	6,012	8,341	10,708	13,495	15,734
taxes on expenditure	47,029	49,770	53,340	57,687	63,881	69,534
value added tax	13,815	15,218	18,534	19,329	21,377	24,067
taxes on capital(3)	1,401	1,562	1,757	2,356	3,034	3,747
Expenditure(4)	129,527	140,685	151,978	159,776	168,829	177,263
net lending(5)	3,003	−472	−1,706	−2,119	−3,918	−5,171
Deficit(−) or surplus	−7,686	−12,147	−12,430	−8,471	−9,343	−2,775

(1) Financial years ended 5 April of year indicated. (2) Total current receipts, taxes on capital and other capital receipts. (3) Capital gains, capital transfer tax, estate duty. (4) Total government expenditure, gross domestic capital formation and grants. (5) To private sector, public corporations, and overseas.

10. Public Expenditure
(£ billion, constant prices)

	1983	1984	1985	1986	1987	1988
Health and personal social services	20·9	21·4	21·3	22.·3	23·3	23·6
Social security	41·4	42·9	44·1	45·8	45·9	45·9
Education	18·7	18·6	18·1	19·2	20·1	20·1
Housing	5·0	4·8	4·2	3·8	3·5	3·8
Defence	17·6	18·8	18·5	18·1	18·1	17·6
Law and order	6·2	6·7	6·5	6·9	7·5	7·7

11. Prices and Costs (index 1985=100)

	1983	1984	1985	1986	1987	1988
Total UK costs per unit of output(1)	90·0	95·1	100·0	102·6	107·7	114·1
Labour costs per unit of output	92·6	96·0	100·0	104·7	108·7	..
Mfg. wages/salaries per unit of output	91·6	94·2	100·0	104·5	105·3	..
Import unit values	87·8	95·5	100·0	96·0	98·5	99·0
Wholesale prices, manufactures	89·8	95·0	100·0	104·3	108·3	113·2
Consumer prices	89·8	94·3	100·0	103·4	107·7	113·0
Tax and prices	91·6	95·0	100·0	101·9	104·5	107·5

(1) Used as 'Overall price index' on all pages of UK statistics.

FINANCIAL

12. Monetary Sector(1)
(£ million, amounts outstanding at end of period)

	1983	1984	1985	1986	1987	1988
Notes and coins in circulation	11,866	11,542	12,069	12,824	13,593	14,823
M_0(2) (average)	12,859	13,468	14,096	14,663	15,354	16,399
M_3(3)	100,502	110,130	124,918	150,626	184,762	222,716
M_4(4)	175,548	198,902	225,205	261,399	304,278	357,440
Deposits						
domestic	110,347	125,779	140,403	173,922	210,908	251,848
overseas	350,707	453,616	415,995	493,413	474,211	511,137
Domestic lending						
private sector	122,583	150,574	167,676	206,555	250,782	318,763
public sector	20,000	21,537	19,638	18,401	17,677	15,714
Overseas lending	338,325	432,933	403,275	479,735	460,772	483,726

(1) Institutions recognized as banks or licensed deposit-takers, plus Bank of England banking dept. and other institutions adhering to monetary control arrangements. (2) M_0=Notes and coins in circulation plus banks' till money plus bankers' balance with Bank of England. (3) M_3=Notes and coins in circulation plus private sector sight and time deposits. (4) M_4=M_3 plus private sector holdings of building society shares and deposits, less building societies' bank deposits.

Overall price index (1985=100)	90·0	95·1	100·0	102·6	107·6	114·4

	1983	1984	1985	1986	1987	1988
13. Interest Rates and Security Yields(1)						
(% per annum, end of year)						
Treasury bill yield	8·88	9·15	11·17	10·69	8·37	12·91
London clearing banks base rate	9·00	9·63	11·50	11·00	8·50	13·00
2½% consols, gross flat yield(2)	10·24	10·15	10·11	9·47	9·31	9·12
10-year government securities(2)	11·27	11·27	11·06	10·05	9·57	9·67
Ordinary shares, dividend yield(2)	4·58	4·62	4·47	4·01	3·50	4·32
Interbank 3-month deposits	9·38	9·97	11·91	11·25	8·87	12·94
Clearing bank 7-day deposits	5·50	6·25	7·86	6·92	3·58	5·97

(1) Gross redemption yields, unless stated otherwise. For building societies see Table 16. (2) Average during year.

14. Companies
(£ million unless stated)

	1983	1984	1985	1986	1987	1988
Total income	35,660	66,428	75,617	71,417	88,483	..
Gross trading profit in UK	44,372	52,354	59,738	56,146	69,071	..
Total overseas income	6,505	8,654	8,987	7,871	11,455	..
Dividends on ord. shares	4,582	5,139	6,379	8,963	12,375	..
Net profit	26,033	31,948	34,015	33,839	45,335	..
Companies taken over (number)	447	568	474	696	1,125	1,224
Total take-over consideration	2,343	5,475	7,090	14,934	15,364	22,122
Liquidations (number)(1)	13,406	13,721	14,895	14,405	11,439	9,427
Receiverships (number)(1)	7,032	8,229	6,772	7,155	6,994	7,717

(1) England and Wales.

15. The Stock Market
(£ million, unless otherwise stated)

	1983	1984	1985	1986	1987	1988
Turnover (£000 mn.)	287·6	364·7	390·5	646·3	1,757·5	1,602·8
ordinary shares (£000 mn.)	56·1	73·1	105·6	181·2	496·1	405·2
New issues, less redemptions (value)	3,328	2,338	5,175	9,305	15,444	7,544
Government securities	8,183	8,953	9,232	7,169	5,425	−266
Local authority issues(1)	−66	−258	−566	−202	−177	−34
UK companies	2,812	1,721	5,110	8,971	15,433	7,175
FT ordinary share index (1935=100)(2)	693·0	855·03	1,004·64	1,287·11	1,600·01	1,448·73
FT-Actuaries index (750 shares)(3)	434·7	516·68	631·95	782·10	1,025·07	931·67
Industrial, 500 shares	471·23	560·52	692·02	858·57	1,133·51	1,019·76
Financial, 100 shares	323·1	386·72	475·31	590·05	725·37	679·99

(1) Includes public corporation issues. (2) Average during year. (3) 1962=100.

16. Building Societies

	1983	1984	1985	1986	1987	1988
Interest rates (%): end year:						
Paid on shares, ave. actual	7·26	7·74	8·71	8·14	6·51	8·38
Basic rate	7·25	7·75	7·00	5·99	4·02	5·59
Mortgages, ave. charged	11·05	11·84	13·01	12·32	10·34	12·75
Basic rate	11·25	12·50	12·75	12·30	10·30	12·77
Shares and deposits, net (£ min.)	6,839	8,572	7,462	6,592	7,561	13,214
Mortgage advances, net (£ min.)	10,928	14,572	14,711	19,541	15,390	24,737

| Overall price index (1985=100) | 90·0 | 95·1 | 100·0 | 102·6 | 107·6 | 114·4 |

UNITED KINGDOM STATISTICS

	1983	1984	1985	1986	1987	1988
17. Industrial Production (Index, average 1985=100, seasonally adjusted)						
All industries	94·7	94·9	100·0	102·2	105·8	109·8
Energy and water	96·8	88·8	100·0	105·0	103·9	99·7
Manufacturing industries	93·7	97·6	100·0	100·9	106·6	114·2
Food, drink and tobacco	100·0	100·8	100·0	100·9	103·4	105·7
Chemicals	91·4	96·8	100·0	101·8	109·0	114·2
Metal manufacture	93·9	93·6	100·0	99·9	108·6	121·4
Engineering and allied	92·3	96·8	100·0	99·3	104·0	112·2
Textiles	92·5	95·9	100·0	100·8	103·3	102·3
Intermediate goods	95·2	93·2	100·0	103·7	107·0	108·1
Consumer goods	95·7	98·3	100·0	101·6	106·7	112·5
Paper, printing, publishing	93·1	97·8	100·0	104·2	114·3	126·4
Construction	95·3	98·6	100·0	103·3	111·4	..
Crude steel (million tonnes)	14·9	15·2	15·7	14·8	17·4	18·9
Man-made fibres (million tonnes)	0·39	0·38	0·33	0·29	0·27	..
Cars ('000)	1,045	909	1,048	1,019	1,143	1,227
Motor vehicles, cars imported ('000)(1)	1,020	1,006	1,064	1,054	1,041	1,250
Commercial vehicles ('000)	244	225	266	229	247	318
Merchant ships(2) completed ('000 gr.t)	540	411	225	106	247	..

(1) Including imported chassis. (2) 100 gross tons and over.

18. Energy

	1983	1984	1985	1986	1987	1988
Coal, production (mn. tonnes)	119·2	51·2	94·1	108·1	104·4	103·8
Power station consumption (mn. tonnes)	81·6	53·4	73·9	82·6	86·3	..
Electricity generated ('000 mn. kwh.)	260·5	265·7	279·8	282·4	282·4	..
by nuclear plant ('000 mn. kwh.)	45·8	49·4	56·2	54·1	50·4	..
Natural gas sent out (mn. therms)	17,202	17,789	18,390	18,648	19,050	..
Crude oil output ('000 tonnes)(1)	115,200	126,000	127,200	127,200	123,600	114,375
Oil refinery output (mn. tonnes)(2)	64·5	81·4	69·8	69·2	67·5	..

(1) Including natural gas liquids. (2) All fuels and other petroleum products.

LABOUR

19. Employment
(millions of persons, in June each year)

	1983	1984	1985	1986	1987	1988
Working population(1)	26·67	27·11	27·59	27·86	28·21	28·09
Employed labour force(2)	23·57	24·08	24·41	24·59	24·68	25·09
Employees: production industries	6·06	5·91	5·84	5·66	5·54	5·46
Manufacturing	5·42	5·30	5·26	5·13	5·04	4·99
Transport and communications	1·32	1·31	1·30	1·33	1·33	1·35
Distributive trades	3·21	3·32	3·41	3·49	3·29	3·32
Education and health	2·91	2·94	2·97	3·01	2·91	2·95
Insurance, banking, financial	1·82	1·89	1·97	2·06	2·30	2·44
Public service	1·87	1·87	1·88	1·93	1·98	2·02
Total employees	21·06	21·24	21·47	21·54	21·82	22·10
of whom, females	9·11	9·34	9·52	9·66	9·93	10·16

(1) Including registered unemployed and members of the armed services. (2) Including employers and self-employed.

Overall price index (1985=100)	90·0	95·1	100·0	102·6	107·6	114·4

	1983	1984	1985	1986	1987	1988
20. Demand for Labour						
Average weekly hours worked, manufacturing industry, men over 21(1)	42·6	42·8	43·0	42·7	43·5	..
Manufacturing employees:						
Total overtime hours worked ('000)(2)	10,300	11,600	11,940	11,720	12,680	..
Short time, total hours lost ('000)(2)	985	619	416	485	364	..
Unemployed, excl. school-leavers, adult students (monthly ave. '000)(3)	2,970	3,051	3,163	3,185	2,880	2,294·5
Percentage of working population	10·8	11·1	11·3	11·5	10·3	8·1
Unfilled vacancies, end-year ('000)	146·2	153·5	162·1	188·8	235·0	238·3
Job schemes average ('000)(4)	630	650	725	820	925	..

(1) October. (2) Great Britain. (3) Seasonally adjusted. (4) Numbers supported on employment or training schemes.

21. Industrial Disputes

Stoppages (number)(1)(2)	1,352	1,206	887	1,053	1,016	725
Workers involved ('000)(3)	573	1,436	643	538	887	725
Work days lost ('000), all inds., services	3,754	27,135	6,402	1,920	3,546	3,752

(1) Excluding protest action of a political nature, and stoppages involving fewer than 10 workers and/or lasting less than one day except where the working days lost exceeded 100. (2) Stoppages beginning in year stated. (3) Directly and indirectly, where stoppages occurred; lay-offs elsewhere in consequence are excluded.

22. Wages and Earnings

Average earnings index (1985=100)						
Whole economy	87·0	92·2	100·0	107·9	116·3	126·5
Manufacturing	84·4	91·7	100·0	107·7	116·3	126·2
Average weekly earnings(1)(2)						
Men						
Manual	143·6	152·7	163·6	174·4	185·5	200·6
Non-manual	194·9	209·0	225·0	244·9	265·9	294·1
All occupations	167·5	178·8	192·4	207·5	224·0	245·8
Women						
Manual	87·9	93·5	101·3	107·5	115·3	123·6
Non-manual	115·1	124·3	133·8	145·7	157·2	175·5
All occupations	108·8	117·2	126·4	137·2	148·1	164·2
Average hours(3)	40·1	40·3	40·4	40·4	40·4	40·6

(1) In all industries and services, full time. (2) April. (3) All industries and services, all occupations, men and women over 18 years.

23. Productivity
(Index of output per head 1985=100)

All production industries(1)	92·2	94·2	100·0	105·1	111·1	..
Manufacturing	92·0	97·3	100·0	103·1	110·4	..
Minerals	102·1	102·8	100·0	101·6	105·5	..
Metal manufacture	83·6	90·3	100·0	108·1	123·7	..
Engineering	88·8	95·7	100·0	102·8	110·8	..
Textiles	94·1	96·9	100·0	101·3	105·8	..
Chemicals	91·3	97·4	100·0	102·4	110·1	..

(1) Excluding extraction of mineral oil and natural gas.

Overall price index (1985=100)	90·0	95·1	100·0	102·6	107·6	114·4

UNITED KINGDOM STATISTICS

TRADE

24. Trade by Areas and Main Trading Partners

(£ million; exports fob; imports cif)	1983	1984	1985	1986	1987	1988
All countries: *exports*	60,386	70,511	78,416	73,009	80,405	81,703
All countries: *imports*	66,123	78,705	84,697	86,006	95,066	106,865
E.E.C.: *exports*	28,034	33,127	38,226	35,003	39,611	41,082
E.E.C.: *imports*	31,690	37,408	41,474	44,506	49,699	55,972
Other Western Europe: *exports*	5,981	7,132	7,420	6,962	7,747	7,459
Other Western Europe: *imports*	8,872	11,184	12,025	11,864	13,125	13,991
North America: *exports*	9,342	11,406	13,310	12,128	13,214	12,668
North America: *imports*	9,055	11,055	11,703	10,054	10,859	12,916
Other developed countries: *exports*	3,133	3,684	3,792	3,614	4,106	4,503
Other developed countries: *imports*	5,220	5,589	6,379	6,861	7,393	8,534
Oil exporting countries: *exports*	6,110	5,807	5,957	5,494	5,315	5,058
Oil exporting countries: *imports*	2,830	2,862	2,782	1,877	1,746	2,129
Other developing countries: *exports*	6,671	7,550	7,924	7,644	8,549	8,630
Other developing countries: *imports*	6,761	8,568	8,451	8,637	9,685	10,492
Centrally planned economies: *exports*	1,116	1,630	1,587	1,727	1,571	1,623
Centrally planned economies: *imports*	1,542	2,042	1,894	1,865	2,099	2,039
Balance of trade in manufactures	−4,854	−6,314	−5,812	−8,246	−9,946	−17,660

25. Terms of Trade
(Index 1985=100)

Volume of exports(1)	87·2	94·6	100·0	103·4	109·1	109·9
manufactures	86·4	94·3	100·0	103·0	111·3	117·9
Volume of imports(1)	87·2	96·5	100·0	106·5	114·1	129·8
Unit value of exports(1)	88·1	94·9	100·0	91·9	95·6	97·3
manufactures	87·0	94·0	100·0	104·0	108·0	114·0
Unit value of imports(1)	88·0	95·5	100·0	95·8	98·1	98·6
Terms of trade(2)	100·1	99·4	100·0	95·9	97·4	98·6

(1) Seasonally adjusted: Overseas Trade Statistics basis. (2) Export unit value index as percentage of import value index, expressed as an index on the same base.

26. Balance of Payments
(£ million: current transactions seasonally adjusted; remaining data unadjusted)

Exports (f.o.b.)	60,776	70,367	77,988	72,678	79,421	80,157
Imports (f.o.b.)	61,611	74,751	80,178	81,141	89,594	100,714
Visible balance	−835	−4,384	−2,190	−8,463	−10,174	−20,557
Invisible balance	+4,171	+5,857	+5,465	+8,509	+7,475	+6,065
Current balance	+3,336	+1,473	+3,275	+46	−2,699	−14,492
Direct investment overseas(1)	−5,379	−6,118	−8,653	−11,290	−18,775	−14,937
Portfolio investment overseas(1)	−6,810	−9,500	−18,060	−25,644	+1,526	−10,872
Bank lending abroad(1)	−18,332	−14,067	−22,041	−53,809	−50,381	−19,266
Direct investment in UK(2)	+3,386	−181	+4,213	+4,846	+8,108	+7,114
Portfolio investment in UK(2)	+1,888	+1,419	+7,121	+8,066	+9,665	+4,134
UK overseas bank borrowing(2)	+21,137	+24,797	+29,461	+63,780	+52,906	+33,712
Net change in assets/liabilities	−5,085	−7,239	−7,748	−13,851	−9,451	−562
Balancing item	+1,749	+5,766	+4,473	+13,700	+12,356	+15,227
Official reserves, end of year	12,271	13,533	10,753	14,776	23,490	28,589

(1) − = increase, + = decrease. (2) − = decrease, + = increase.

Overall price index (1985=100)	90·0	95·1	100·0	102·6	107·6	114·4

B. THE UNITED STATES

27. Population	1983	1984	1985	1986	1987	1988
Population, mid-year est. (mn)	234·50	236·63	239·28	241·60	243·77	..
Crude birth rate (per 1,000 pop.)	15·5	15·7	15·7	15·5	..	..
Crude death rate (per 1,000 pop.)	8·6	8·7	8·7	8·7	..	..

28. Gross National Product
('000 million current dollars)

Gross national product	3,305	3,775	4,010	4,235	4526·7	4863·1
Personal consumption	2,156	2,423	2,629	2,800	3012·1	3227·2
Gross private domestic investment	472	674	642	671	713	766·1
Net exports, goods and services	−8·3	−59·2	−79·2	−105·5	−123·0	−94·3
Government purchases	686	737	819	870	925	964

29. Government Finance
('000 million dollars, seasonally adjusted)

Federal government receipts	660	726	789	828	916	970
from personal taxes(1)	294	310	346	361	406	413
Federal government expenditure	836	896	986	1,034	1,074	1,117
Defence purchases	214	234	259	278	295	298
Grants to state/local govts.	86	94	100	107	103	111
Federal surplus or (−) deficit	−176·0	−169·6	−196·9	−205·6	−157·8	−137·3
State and local govt. receipts	487·6	540·5	581·8	623·0	655·7	697·3
from indirect business tax(1)	231·0	258·2	278·5	297·6	312·3	332·4

(1) Includes related non-tax receipts on national income account.

30. Balance of Payments
(millions of dollars)

Merchandise trade balance	−61,055	−114,109	−124,289	−144,339	−160,280	−126,525
Balance on current account(1)	−41,562	−107,361	−117,668	−141,355	−153,996	−135,331
Change in US private assets abroad(2)	43,576	13,685	24,711	96,303	86,297	..
Change in foreign private assets in US(2)	79,023	99,481	131,012	185,746	166,522	..

(1) Includes balance on services and remittances and US government grants other than military.
(2) Includes reinvested earnings of incorporated affiliates.

31. Merchandise Trade by Main Areas
(millions of dollars)

All countries: *exports* (f.o.b.)	200,538	219,900	215,935	224,361	252,866	322,245
All countries: *imports* (f.o.b.)	258,048	332,422	338,083	368,700	424,082	440,940
Western Europe: *exports*	55,414	56,867	56,015	60,664	69,718	87,995
Western Europe: *imports*	53,476	72,054	77,454	89,074	99,934	100,515
Canada: *exports*	38,244	53,037	55,390	56,984	59,814	70,862
Canada: *imports*	52,129	67,630	70,394	70,315	71,510	80,921
Latin America						
exports	22,619	29,766	30,788	30,877	31,574	..
imports	35,683	48,364	46,109	41,426	44,371	..
Japan: *exports*	21,894	23,241	22,145	26,361	28,249	37,732
imports	41,183	60,210	65,653	80,764	88,074	89,802

| *Dollar purchasing power (1967=100)* | 34·0 | 33·0 | 31·0 | 31·0 | 30·0 | 29·0 |

32. Merchandise Trade by Main Commodity Groups
(millions of dollars)

	1983	1984	1985	1986	1987	1988
Exports:						
Machinery and transport equipt.	82,524	89,973	94,278	95,289	108,596	135,135
Motor vehicles and parts	14,463	17,548	19,364	18,365	24,632	29,430
Electrical machinery	11,936	13,855	12,489	13,630	16,637	..
Food and live animals	24,168	24,463	19,268	17,303	19,179	26,415
Chemicals and pharmaceuticals	19,752	22,336	21,759	22,766	26,381	32,300
Imports:						
Machinery and transport equipt.	86,208	119,192	137,264	166,240	182,807	201,938
Motor vehicles and parts	35,034	45,412	55,740	57,990	87,479	89,991
Food and live animals	15,408	17,973	18,649	22,395	22,224	21,771
Petroleum and products	52,325	55,906	49,607	39,838	46,724	41,813
Iron and steel	6,799	11,853	11,223	8,900	9,178	..

33. Interest Rates
(per cent per annum, annual averages, unless otherwise stated)

Federal Funds rate(1)	9·09	10·22	8·10	6·80	6·66	7·57
Treasury bill rate	8·61	9·52	7·49	5·98	5·82	6·69
Government bond yields: 3–5 years	10·63	11·83	9·64	7·19	7·68	8·26
Long-term (10 years of more)	10·84	11·99	10·75	8·14	8·39	8·85
Banks' prime lending rate(2)	10·79	12·04	9·93	8·33	8·22	9·32

(1) Effective rate. (2) Predominant rate charged by commercial banks on short-term loans to large business borrowers with the highest credit rating.

34. Banking, money and credit
('000 million dollars, outstanding at end of year, seasonally adjusted)

Money supply M1(1)	522·1	551·9	620·1	725·4	752·3	790·2
Money supply M2(2)	2,185	2,364	2,563	2,808	2,910	3,072
Money supply M3(3)	2,693	2,978	3,196	3,491	3,677	3,918
Currency	146·3	156·1	167·7	180·4	196·4	211·8
Deposits of commercial banks	1,524·8	1,605·9	1,772·5	2,018	2,009	2,121
Advances of commercial banks	1,149·3	1,450·8	1,617·2	1,807	1,899	2,021
Instalment credit	367·9	442·5	517·8	571·8	613·0	667·3
Motor vehicle contracts	143·8	173·7	209·6	246·1	267·2	290·4
Mortgage debt	1,825	2,051	2,290	2,597	2,943	3,154

(1) Currency plus demand deposits, travellers cheques, other checkable deposits. (2) M1 plus overnight repurchase agreements, eurodollars, money market mutual fund shares, savings and small time deposits. (3) M2 plus large time deposits and term repurchase agreements.

35. Insurance
($ million, unless otherwise stated)

Property-liability, net premiums written	108,400	118,200	144,186	176,552	193,246	..
Automobile(1)	47,816	51,285	61,334	73,386	81,199	..
Underwriting gain/loss(2)	−13,322	−21,477	−24,794	−15,913	−9,624	..
Net investment income(3)	15,973	17,760	19,508	21,924	23,960	..
Combined net income(3)	2,651	−3,817	−5,286	+6,012	+14,335	..
Annual rate of return (%)(4)	8·3	1·8	3·8	13·1	12·8	..
Life insurance, total assets, end-year	652,904	722,979	825,901	937,551	1,044,459	..

(1) Physical damage and liability, private and commercial. (2) After stockholder and policy-holder dividends and premium rebates. (3) Property, casualty. (4) Per cent of net worth.

Dollar purchasing power (1967=100)	34·0	33·0	31·0	31·0	30·0	29·0

ECONOMIC AND SOCIAL DATA

36. Companies(1) ('000 million dollars)	1983	1984	1985	1986	1987	1988
Net profit after taxes	86·3	107·6	87·7	83·1	115·6	..
Cash dividends paid	41·5	45·1	45·5	46·0	49·5	..

(1) Manufacturing corporations, all industries.

37. The Stock Market
(millions of dollars, unless otherwise stated)

Turnover (sales), all exchanges	057,118	959,110	1,199,420	1,705,124	2,284,166	..
New York Stock Exchange	815,113	822,617	1,023,179	1,448,235	1,983,311	..
Securities issued, gross proceeds	206,315	238,952	356,372	395,217	389,437	..
Corporate common stock	44,842	22,151	36,242	58,852	65,835	..
Stock prices (end-year):						
Combined index (500 stocks)(1)	164·93	167·24	211·28	242·17	247·08	277·7
Industrials (30 stocks)(2)	1,258·64	1,211·57	1,537·73	1,895·95	1,938·83	2,168·6

(1) Standard and Poor Composite 1941–43=10. (2) Dow-Jones Industrial (Oct. 1928=100).

38. Employment
('000 persons)

Civilian labour force(1)	111,550	113,544	115,460	117,841	119,850	121,666
in non-agricultural industry	97,440	101,679	103,967	106,433	109,229	111,796
in manufacturing industry	18,677	19,412	19,314	18,995	19,112	..
in agriculture	3,381	3,321	3,179	3,165	3,210	3,175
unemployed	10,690	8,539	8,312	8,243	7,410	6,695
Industrial stoppages(2) (number)	81	62	54	69	46	..
Workers involved ('000)	909	376	324	533	174	..

(1) Aged 16 years and over. (2) Beginning in the year. Involving 1,000 workers or more.

39. Earnings and Prices

Average weekly earnings per worker						
(current dollars): mining	479·0	503·6	519·9	525·81	530·85	..
contract construction	441·9	456·9	464·1	466·75	479·68	..
manufacturing	354·6	373·6	386·0	396·01	406·31	..
Average weekly hours per worker						
in manufacturing	40·1	40·7	40·5	40·7	41·0	..
Farm prices received (1977=100)	134	142	128	123	127	138
Wholesale prices (1982=100)	101·6	103·7	104·6	103·2	105·4	108·0
Fuels and power	95.9	94·7	91·4	70·2	70·2	66·8
Consumer prices (1982–4=100)	99·6	103·9	107·6	109·7	113·7	118·4
Food	99·5	103·3	105·7	109·1	113·6	118·3
Dollar purchasing power (1967=100)(1)	34·0	33·0	31·0	31·0	30·0	29·0

(1) Based on changes in retail price indexes.

40. Production

Farm production (1977=100)	96	112	118	111	110	97
Industrial production (1977=100)	109·2	121·4	123·8	125·1	129·8	137·2
Manufacturing	110·2	123·4	126·4	129·1	134·7	142·8
Output of main products and manufacturers						
Coal (million tons)	784·9	895·9	886·1	886·0	915·2	..
Oil, indigenous (000 barrels/day)	8,656	8,757	8,934	8,727	8,347	8,159
Oil refinery throughput (000 barrels/day)	11,672	12,055	13,690	14,522	14,626	13,708
Natural gas ('000 mn. cu. ft.)	16,083	17,393	16,395	16,791	17,155	..
Electricity generated ('000 mn. kwh)	2,287	2,416	2,470	2,487	2,572	..
Steel, crude (million tonnes)	82·6	92·5	88·3	81·6	89·1	..
Aluminium ('000 tonnes)	3,353	4,099	3,499	3,036	3,343	..
Cotton yarn ('000 running bales)	7,500	12,545	12,988	9,438	14,359	..
Man-made fibres (millions lbs.)	9,299	9,433	8,121	8,447	8,921	..
Plastics/resins (millions lbs.)	30,863	35,178	36,583	38,415	32,295	..
Motor cars, factory sales ('000)	6,739	7,621	8,002	7,516	7,085	..

C. INTERNATIONAL COMPARISONS

41 Population and GDP, Selected countries

countries	Area '000 sq. km.	Population (millions) mid-year estimate 1985	1986	Gross Domestic Product (1) US $ mins(2) 1986	1987
Argentina	2,777	30·56	31·03	78,798	..
Australia(3)	7,695	15·76	15·97	168,168	193,602
Belgium	31	9·90	9·91	114,431	142,122
Canada	9,976	25·36	25·61	363,606	414,548
China	9,561	1,045·3	1,065·3	225,614	300,341
Denmark	34	5·11	5·12	81,844	101,320
France	552	55·17	55·39	726,946	878,267
Germany, West (incl. W. Berlin)	248	61·02	61·05	892,010	1,117,781
India (incl. India-admin. Kashmir)	3,268	750·9	766·14	219,063	225,883
Irish Republic	69	3·55	3·54	24,468	29,427
Israel (excl. occupied areas)	21	4·23	4·30	27,587	34,702
Italy	301	57·13	57·22	599,921	758,113
Japan	370	120·75	121·49	1,962,687	2,384,458
Kuwait(4)	18	1·71	1·79	17,075	19,542
Netherlands	34	14·48	14·56	175,335	213,171
New Zealand(4)	104	3·25	3·25	27,703	31,613
Norway	324	4·15	4·17	69,782	82,660
Portugal	92	10·23	10·21	23,640	31,365
Saudi Arabia	2,150	11·54	12·07	77,415	71,466
South Africa (incl. Namibia)	1,221	32·39	32·30	61,578	80,813
Spain	505	38·50	38·67	229,097	289,229
Sweden	450	8·35	8·37	131,404	159,055
Switzerland	41	6·47	6·50	135,416	171,070
Turkey	781	49·27	50·30	58,070	..
USSR	22,402	277·5	281·7	607·7	..
UK	244	56·62	56·76	547,748	669,573
USA	9,363	239·28	241·6	4,194,500	4,484,300

(1) Expenditure basis. (2) Converted from national currencies at average exchange rates. (3) Years beginning 1 July. (4) Years beginning 1 April.

42. World Production
(Index 1980=100)

	1983	1984	1985	1986	1987	1988
Food(1)	106·4	110·0	114·0	116·0	..	..
Industrial production(2)	99·5	105·5	109·0	112·7	118·2	..
Crude petroleum, nat. gas	78·9	81·2	79·0	82·6	83·6	..
Manufacturing	101·9	108·7	112·8	116·7	123·0	..
Chemicals	104·7	111·4	114·8	119·4	125·7	..
Paper, printing, publishing	104·5	111·8	115·8	120·1	126·9	..
Textiles	99·2	100·8	102·5	105·5	108·3	..
OECD	99·5	106·9	108·9	110·1	113·5	..
EEC(3)	96·9	99·9	103·5	105·1	107·4	..
Developing market economies(4)	106·6	115·4	121·4	136·5	158·7	..
Caribbean, C. & S. America	91·3	96·0	102·0	109·8	117·4	..
Asia(5)	125·4	138·9	154·0	182·2	234·6	..
France	98·0	99·4	99·0	101·0	104·0	..
Germany, West	96·3	100·0	105·0	107·0	107·0	..
Italy	92·3	95·4	96·9	99·0	103·0	..
UK	101·9	103·2	108·1	110·0	113·0	..
Japan	105·0	116·5	118·0	118·0	122·0	..
Sweden	103·0	109·0	109·0	110·0	114·0	..
USSR	111·3	115·7	120·2	126·1	130·3	..

(1) Excluding China. (2) Excluding China, N. Korea, Vietnam, Albania. (3) Community of Ten. (4) Manufacturing. (5) Excluding Japan and Israel.

43. World Trade(1)
(millions of US dollars. Exports f.o.b., imports c.i.f.)

	1983	1984	1985	1986	1987	1988
World(1): exports	1,663,600	1,768,200	1,804,000	2,003,200	2,364,800	..
imports	1,737,700	1,842,900	1,881,100	2,059,100	2,424,800	..
Industrial Countries: exports	1,139,400	1,214,600	1,255,900	1,462,500	1,712,300	..
imports	1,200,300	1,309,200	1,360,200	1,357,200	1,794,300	..
USA: exports	200,538	217,890	213,144	217,307	250,405	..
imports	269,878	341,179	361,627	387,081	424,081	..
Germany, West: exports	169,440	171,729	183,913	243,327	294,168	..
imports	152,940	153,007	158,490	191,084	228,346	..
Japan: exports	146,963	169,753	177,139	210,757	228,631	..
imports	126,518	136,148	130,505	127,553	150,496	..
France: exports	94,943	97,566	101,674	124,948	148,534	..
imports	105,416	103,726	107,768	129,402	158,475	..
UK: exports	91,430	93,772	101,248	106,989	131,239	..
imports	100,183	104,863	108,957	126,330	154,454	..
Other Europe: exports	382,601	401,001	422,211	506,658	599,656	..
imports	411,210	417,846	452,020	529,520	645,564	..
Australia, NZ, S. Afr: exports	44,595	46,939	44,983	46,956	55,238	..
imports	42,498	48,356	43,350	45,156	51,923	..
Less Developed Areas: exports	501,470	520,130	525,247	510,286	624,644	..
imports	515,820	514,670	521,191	521,891	607,561	..
Oil exporters: exports	175,660	170,510	148,450	117,300	132,020	..
imports	141,680	128,590	105,220	93,400	97,770	..
Saudi Arabia: exports	47,816	46,857	27,481	20,085	26,975	..
imports	39,197	33,696	23,622	19,112	24,345	..
Other W. Hemisphere: exports	60,562	65,992	63,354	57,324	60,491	..
imports	59,547	55,888	52,636	52,148	59,742	..
Other Middle East(2): exports	15,130	13,417	15,731	14,972	..	..
imports	35,440	37,886	28,219	32,004	44,588	..
Other Asia: exports	137,030	158,038	158,710	174,856	261,002	..
imports	163,818	180,038	187,251	191,547	260,308	..
Other Africa: exports	22,882	24,391	..	..	..	..
imports	29,359	29,226	27,393	29,971	31,002	..

(1) Excluding trade of centrally planned countries (see Table 47). (2) Including Egypt. (3) Unweighted average of IMF series for US$ import and export prices in developed countries.

World trade prices (1980=100)(3)	88·8	86·6	85·9	93·4	103·6	..

44. World Trade of Centrally Planned Countries
(millions of US dollars)

European(1): exports	175,182	177,664	174,834	193,765	204,657	..
imports	158,571	159,786	165,899	184,546	194,307	..
USSR: exports	91,330	91,649	87,201	97,336	..	..
imports	80,267	80,624	82,578	88,906	..	..
China: exports	22,157	24,871	27,343	30,942	39,542	..
imports	21,320	26,185	42,491	42,904	43,392	..
Total: exports	199,161	205,021	204,894	227,722	245,027	..
imports	183,618	190,278	212,101	223,588	243,191	..

(1) Except Yugoslavia and Albania.

45. Prices of Selected Commodities
(Index 1980=100)

	1983	1984	1985	1986	1987	1988
Aluminium (Canada)	81·0	70·5	58·6	64·8	88·2	143·5
Beef, Irish (London)	81·3	69·0	63·8	79·0	88·9	..
Copper, wirebars (London)	72·7	63·0	64·9	62·7	81·5	119·0
Cotton, Egyptian (L'pool)	91·2	106·7	106·8	103·3	106·2	142·3
Gold (London)	69·5	59·3	52·2	60·5	73·1	72·0
Newsprint New York	109·5	108·7	116·0	119·3	116·8	126·9
Rice, Thai (Bangkok)	63·8	58·2	50·1	48·5	53·1	69·6
Rubber, Malay (Singapore)	74·2	66·7	53·3	56·6	69·1	83·2
Soya beans, US (R'dam)	95·1	95·2	75·8	71·4	72·8	102·4
Sugar, f.o.b. (Caribbean)	29·5	18·1	14·1	21·1	23·6	35·6
Tin, spot (London)	77·3	72·8	68·7	38·7	41·5	43·5
Wheat (Canada No. 2 CW)	93·9	88·2	78·6	66·5	65·4	84·1
Wool, greasy (Sydney)	89·2	93·2	85·5	78·7	113·6	..

46. Consumer Prices, Selected Countries
(Index 1980=100)

Argentina	2,403	17,462	134,842	256,335	592,400	..
Australia	134·2	139·6	149·0	162·3	176·0	..
France	138·9	149·3	158·0	161·9	167·9	171·7
Germany, West	115·6	118·4	121·0	120·7	121·1	122·4
India	136·5	148·1	155·9	169·5	184·4	..
Japan	109·6	112·0	114·4	115·3	115·3	116·1
South Africa	148·3	165·5	192·6	228·4	265·1	..
Sweden	132·5	143·2	153·8	160·2	166·9	176·7
UK	127·1	133·4	141·5	146·0	152·1	159·9
US	120·8	126·1	130·5	133·1	138·0	143·5
World trade prices (1980=100)	88·8	86·6	85·9	93·4	103·6	..

47. Industrial Ordinary Share Prices
(Index 1980=100) end of year

	1983	1984	1985	1986	1987	1988
Amsterdam	154	197	255	328	329	..
Australia, all exchanges	100	117	144	193	278	..
Canada, all exchanges	110	110	130	144	168	..
Germany, West, all exchanges	132	150	200	270	249	..
Hong Kong (31 July 1968=100)(1)	867	1,200	1,752	2,568	2,292	2,687
Johannesburg	109	107	115	147	215	..
New York	134	135	155	194	246	..
Paris	115	156	182	281	324	..
Tokyo	136	172	210	277	413	..
UK	165	196	242	300	397	..

(1) Hang Seng index for Hong Kong Stock Exchange only: last trading day of year.

48. Central Bank Discount Rates
(per cent per annum, end of year)

	1983	1984	1985	1986	1987	1988
Canada	9·96	10·16	9·49	8·47	8·75	8·75
France	9·50	9·50	9·50	9·50	9·50	9·50
Germany, West	4·00	4·50	4·00	3·50	2·50	3·50
Italy	17·00	16·50	15·00	12·00	12·50	12·50
Japan	5·00	5·00	5·00	3·00	2·50	2·50
Sweden	8·50	9·50	10·50	7·50	7·50	8·50
Switzerland	4·00	4·00	4·00	4·00	2·50	3·50
UK	9·00	9·63	11·50	11·00	8·50	13·00
USA (Federal Reserve Bank of N.Y.)	8·50	8·00	7·50	5·50	6·50	6·50

49. Exchange Rates
(Middle rates at end of year)

Currency units per US dollar / per £

	1984	1985	1986	1987	1988	1988
Australia (Australian dollar)	1·2115	1·4655	1·5049	1·3897	1·1694	2·1155
Belgium-Luxembourg (franc)	63·25	50·05	40·41	38·00	37·26	67·40
Canada (Canadian dollar)	1·397	1·398	1·381	1·300	1·1907	2·1540
China (yuan)(1)	2·7902	3·2015	3·722	3·722	3·697	6·689
France (franc)	9·6450	7·50	6·425	5·342	6·057	10·958
Germany W. (Deutschmark)	3·144	2·445	1·940	1·574	1·773	3·207
Italy (lire)	1,935	1,670	1,351	1,165	1,306	2,362
Japan (yen)	251·6	200·2	159·9	121·3	124·9	226·0
Netherlands (guilder)	3·557	2·758	2·191	1·772	2·002	3·623
Portugal (escudo)	169·75	157·75	146·1	129·0	146·2	264·5
South Africa (rand)	1·9880	2·5810	2·184	1·988	2·379	4·304
Spain (peseta)	173·30	153·1	131·9	107·75	113·18	204·75
Sweden (krona)	8·980	7·580	6·780	5·785	6·125	11·080
Switzerland (franc)	2·5865	2·0600	1·6230	1·2755	1·5022	2·7175
USSR (rouble)(1)	0·8585	0·7642	0·6783	0·591	0·603	1·0911
UK (£)(2)	1·1590	1·4455	1·4768	1·8785	1·8090	..

(1) Official fixed or basic parity rate. (2) US dollars per £.

50. Defence Expenditure

Expenditure or budget (US $ mn.)

	1984	1985	1986	1987	$ per capita 1987	% of GNP 1987
France	20,113	20,728	28,459	34,530	620	4·7
Germany, East	7,710	7,981	8,948	11,626	700	..
Germany, West (inc. W. Berlin)	20,430	19,922	28,248	34,244	560	3·1
Greece	2,204	2,329	2,418	2,972	285	6·4
Iran	20,162	14,091	5,904	8,956	179	..
Israel	5,798	4,225	5,560	5,136	1,154	14·8
Japan	12,018	14,189	20,930	25,422	207	1·07
Saudi Arabia	22,687	17,693	17,930	16,235	2,360	22·7
South Africa	2,434	2,147	2,340	3,294	95	4·1
Sweden	2,676	3,239	3,832	4,429	528	2·8
Turkey	2,190	2,295	2,770	2,890	55	..
USSR(1)	17·05	19·06	19·06	20·5	1,126	..
UK	21,995	25,356	27,344	31,774	567	4·7
USA	265,160	266,642	281,102	288,433	1,185	6·4

(1) Official budget, Roubles '000 mn.

51. Employment and Unemployment

Civilian Employment ('000)	1983	1984	1985	1986	1987	1988
USA	100,169	105,005	107,150	109,597	112,440	..
Japan	57,294	57,660	58,070	58,530	59,110	..
W. Germany	24,592	24,828	25,000	25,267	25,456	..
France	21,168	20,978	20,916	20,949	20,988	..
UK	23,470	23,739	24,065	24,434	24,987	..
EEC(1), Employment by Sectors (%)						
Agriculture	8·9	8·7	8·4	8·0	7·9	..
Industry	34·5	33·5	33·0	32·9	32·9	..
Services	56·6	57·8	58·6	59·1	59·2	..
Unemployment (%)						
OECD	8·7	8·0	7·9	7·7	7·4	..
EEC	10·5	10·8	10·9	10·9	10·7	..
USA	9·4	7·4	7·1	6·9	6·1	..
Japan	2·6	2·7	2·6	2·8	2·8	..
UK	12·5	11·7	11·2	11·2	10·3	..

(1) Community of Twelve.

XIX DOCUMENTS AND REFERENCE

HOUSE OF LORDS' 'SPYCATCHER' JUDGMENT AND THE LAW OF CONFIDENTIALITY

Below is the speech of Lord Keith of Kinkel, delivered on 13 October 1988, leading the judgment of the House of Lords as court of final appeal in the Spycatcher *case, in so far as Lord Keith dealt with the general law on disclosure of confidences, rather than the particular issues concerning certain British newspapers. In the latter respect, their Lordships ruled that the British Government could no longer prevent British newspapers from publishing any information derived from the book* Spycatcher *(the memoirs of Mr Peter Wright, a former member of MI5), on the grounds that the publication of the book abroad and the ready availability of copies of it in the United Kingdom had destroyed the confidential nature of the book's contents, so that no further harm could now be done to the national interest that had not already been done. The judgment of the five Law Lords was unanimous save that Lord Griffiths would have granted an injunction forbidding further serialization by* The Sunday Times, *on the grounds that the newspaper was so closely associated with Mr Wright's breach of duty that in equity it should be placed under the same restraint as he.*

Attorney-General v The Observer Ltd and Others
Attorney-General v Times Newspapers Ltd and Another

Before Lord Keith of Kinkel, Lord Brightman, Lord Griffiths, Lord Goff of Chieveley and Lord Jauncey of Tullichettle.

The House of Lords dismissed appeals by the Attorney-General from the decision of the Court of Appeal [on 10 February 1988], who had upheld the decision of Mr Justice Scott [on 21 December 1987] in refusing the Attorney-General's claim for permanent injunctions prohibiting the *Observer* and *The Guardian* from commenting or reporting on the contents of *Spycatcher* and prohibiting further serialization of the book in *The Sunday Times*. The House of Lords also dismissed a cross-appeal by *The Sunday Times*.

LORD KEITH said: From 1955 to 1976 Peter Wright was employed in a senior capacity by the counter-espionage branch of the British Security Service known as MI5. In that capacity he acquired knowledge of a great many matters of prime importance to the security of the country.

Following his retirement from the service he went to live in Australia and later formed the intention of writing and publishing a book of memoirs describing his experience in the service.

He wrote the book in association with a man named Paul Greengrass, and it was accepted for publication by Heinemann Publishers Pty Ltd, the Australian subsidiary of a well known English publishing company.

The Attorney-General in right of the Crown, learning of the intended publication of the book, instituted in 1985 proceedings in New South Wales (NSW) against Mr Wright and Heinemann Publishers claiming an injunction to restrain the publication in Australia or alternatively an account of profits . . . .

The Attorney-General's action failed before Powell J and again before the Court of Appeal of NSW. Special leave to appeal was granted by the High Court of Australia, but . . . the book was published in Australia on 13 October 1987, under the title of *Spycatcher*.

On 2 June 1988 the High Court dismissed the Attorney-General's appeal upon the sole ground that an Australian court should not accept jurisdiction to enforce an obligation of confidence owed to a foreign government so as to protect that government's intelligence secrets and confidential political information.

In the meantime *Spycatcher* had on 14 July 1987 been published in the United States of America . . . . Her Majesty's Government had been advised that, in view of the terms of the First Amendment to the United States Constitution, any attempt to restrain publication there would be certain to fail. Publication also took place in Canada, the Republic of Ireland, and a number of other countries.

Her Majesty's Government decided that it was impracticable and undesirable to take any steps to prevent the importation into the United Kingdom of copies of the book, and a very substantial number of copies have in fact been imported. So the contents of the book have been disseminated world wide and anyone in this country who is interested can obtain a copy without undue difficulty. . . .

The Crown's case upon all the issues which arise invokes the law about confidentiality. So it is convenient to start by considering the nature and scope of that law.

The law has long recognised that an obligation of confidence can arise out of particular relationships. Examples are the relationships of doctor and patient, priest and penitent, solicitor and client, banker and customer.

The obligation may be imposed by an express or implied term in a contract but it may also exist independently of any contract on the basis of an independent equitable principle of confidence: *Saltman Engineering Co Ltd v Campbell Engineering Co Ltd* ((1948) 65 RPC 203).

It is worthy of some examination whether or not detriment to the confider of confidential information is an essential ingredient of his cause of action in seeking to restrain by injunction a breach of confidence. Presumably that may be so as regards an action for damages in respect of a past breach of confidence.

If the confider has suffered no detriment thereby he can hardly be in a position to recover compensatory damages. However, the true view may be that he would be entitled to nominal damages.

Most of the cases have arisen in circumstances where there has been a threatened or actual breach of confidence by an employee or ex-employee of the plaintiff, or where information about the plaintiffs business affairs has been given in confidence to someone who has proceeded to exploit it for his own benefit: an example of the latter type of case is *Seager v Copydex Ltd* ([1967] 1 WLR 923).

In such cases the detriment to the confider is clear. In other cases there may be no financial detriment to the confider, since the breach of confidence involves no more than an invasion of personal privacy.

Thus in *Duchess of Argyll v Duke of Argyll* ([1967] Ch 302) an injunction was granted against the revelation of marital confidences. The right to personal privacy is clearly one which the law should in this field seek to protect.

If a profit has been made through the revelation in breach of confidence of details of a person's private life it is appropriate that the profit should be accounted for to that person.

Further as a general rule it is in the public interest that confidences should be respected, and the encouragement of such respect may in itself constitute a sufficient ground for recognising and enforcing the obligation of confidence even where the confider can point to no specific detriment to himself.

Information about a person's private and personal affairs may be of a nature which shows him up in a favourable light and would by no means expose him to criticism.

The anonymous donor of a very large sum to a very worthy cause has his own reasons for wishing to remain anonymous, which are unlikely to be discreditable. He should surely be in a position to restrain disclosure in breach of confidence of his identity in connection with the donation.

So I would think it a sufficient detriment to the confider that information given in confidence is to be disclosed to persons whom he would prefer not to know of it, even though the disclosure would not be harmful to him in any positive way.

The position of the Crown as representing the continuing government of the country may, however, be regarded as being special. In some instances disclosure of confidential information entrusted to a servant of the Crown may result in a financial loss to the public.

In other instances such disclosure may tend to harm the public interest by impeding the efficient attainment of proper governmental ends, and the revelation of defence or intelligence secrets certainly falls into that category.

The Crown, however, as representing the nation as a whole, has no private life or personal feelings capable of being hurt by the disclosure of confidential information. In so far as the Crown acts to prevent such disclosure or to seek redress for it on confidentiality grounds, it must necessarily, in my opinion, be in a position to show that the disclosure is likely to damage or has damaged the public interest.

How far the Crown has to go in order to show this must depend on the circumstances of each case. In a question with a Crown servant himself, or others acting as his agents, the general public interest in the preservation of confidentiality, and in encouraging other Crown servants to preserve it, may suffice.

But where the publication is proposed to be made by third parties unconnected with the particular confidant, the position may be different.

The Crown's argument in the present case would go the length that in all circumstances where the original disclosure has been made by a Crown servant in breach of his obligation of confidence any person to whose knowledge the information comes and who is aware of the breach comes under an equitable duty binding his conscience not to communicate the information to anyone else irrespective of the circumstances under which he acquired the knowledge.

In my opinion that general proposition is untenable and impracticable, in addition to being unsupported by any authority. The general rule is that anyone is entitled to communicate anything he pleases to anyone else, by speech or in writing or in any other way.

That rule is limited by the law of defamation and other restrictions similar to these mentioned in Article 10 of the Convention for the Protection of Human Rights and Fundamental Freedoms (1953)(Cmnd 8969).

All those restrictions are imposed in the light of considerations of public interest such as to countervail the public interest in freedom of expression.

A communication about some aspect of government activity which does no harm to the interests of the nation cannot, even where the original disclosure has been made in breach of confidence, be restrained on the ground of a nebulous equitable duty of conscience serving no useful practical purpose.

There are two important cases in which the special position of a government in relation to the preservation of confidence has been considered.

The first of them is *Attorney-General v Jonathan Cape Ltd* ([1976] QB 752). That was an action for injunctions to restrain publication of the political diaries of the late Richard Crossman, which contained details of Cabinet discussions held some 10 years previously, and also of advice given to Ministers by civil servants.

Lord Widgery said (at p.771) that while the expression of individual opinions by Cabinet Ministers in the course of Cabinet discussions were matters of confidence, the publication of which could be restrained by the court when clearly necessary in the public interest, there must be a limit in time after which the confidential character of the information would lapse.

Having read the whole of volume one of the diaries he did not consider that publication of anything in them, 10 years after the event, would inhibit full discussion in the Cabinet at the present time or thereafter, or damage the doctrine of joint Cabinet responsibility.

He also dismissed the argument that publication of advice given by senior civil servants would be likely to inhibit the frankness of advice given by such civil servants in the future. So in the result Lord Widgery's decision turned on his view that it had not been shown that publication of the diaries would do any harm to the public interest.

The second case is *Commonwealth of Australia v John Fairfax & Sons Ltd* ((1980) 147 CLR 39). That was a decision of Mason J in the High Court of Australia, dealing with an application by the Commonwealth for an interlocutory injunction to restrain publication of a book containing the texts of government documents concerned with its relations with other countries, in particular the government of Indonesia in connection with the "East Timor Crisis".

The documents appeared to have been leaked by a civil servant. Restraint of publication was claimed on the grounds of breach of confidence and also on that of infringement of copyright. Mason J granted an injunction on the latter ground but not on the former.

He said: ". . . the court will determine the government's claim to confidentiality by reference to the public interest. Unless disclosure is likely to injure the public interest, it will not be protected.

"The court will not prevent the publication of information which merely throws light on the past workings of government, even if it be not public property, so long as it does not prejudice the community in other respects.

"Then disclosure will itself serve the public interest in keeping the community informed and in promoting discussion of public affairs. If, however, it appears that disclosure will be inimical to the public interest because national security, relations with foreign countries or the ordinary business of government will be prejudiced, disclosure will be restrained.

"There will be cases in which the conflicting considerations will be finely balanced, where it is difficult to decide whether the public's interest in knowing and in expressing its opinion, outweighs the need to protect confidentiality."

I find myself in broad agreement with this statement by Mason J . . . .

In relation to Mr Wright, there can be no doubt whatever that had he sought to bring about the first publication of his book in this country, the Crown would have been entitled to an injunction restraining him. The work of a member of MI5 and the information which he acquires in the course of that work must necessarily be secret and confidential and be kept secret and confidential by him.

There is no room for discrimination between secrets of greater or lesser importance, nor any room for close examination of the precise manner in which revelation of any particular matter may prejudice the national interest. Any attempt to do so would lead to further damage.

All this has been accepted from beginning to end by each of the judges in this country who has had occasion to consider the case and also by counsel for the respondents.

It is common ground that neither the defence of prior publication nor the so called "iniquity" defence would have availed Mr Wright had he sought to publish his book in England.

The sporadic and low key prior publication of certain specific allegations of wrongdoing could not conceivably weigh in favour of allowing publication of this whole book of detailed memoirs describing the operations of the security service over a lengthy period and naming and describing many members of it not previously known to be such.

The damage to the public interest involved in a publication of that character . . . vastly outweighs all other considerations.

The question whether Mr Wright or those acting for him would be at liberty to publish *Spycatcher* in England under existing circumstances does not arise for immediate consideration. These circumstances include the worldwide dissemination of the contents of the book which has been brought about by Mr Wright's wrongdoing.

In my opinion general publication in this country would not bring about any significant damage to the public interest beyond what has already been done. All such secrets as the book may contain have been revealed to any intelligence services whose interests are opposed to those of the United Kingdom.

Any damage to the confidence imposed in the British Intelligence Services by those of friendly countries brought about by Mr Wright's actions would not be materially increased by publication here.

It is, however, urged on behalf of the Crown that such publication might prompt Mr Wright into making further disclosures, would expose existing and past members of the British Intelligence Services to harassment by the media and might result in their disclosing other secret material with a view, perhaps, to refuting Mr Wright's account and would damage the morale of such members by the spectacle of Mr Wright having got away with his treachery.

While giving due weight to the evidence of Sir Robert Armstrong [Secretary of the Cabinet] on these matters, I have not been persuaded that the effect of publication in England would be to bring about greater damage in the respects founded upon than has already been caused by the widespread publication elsewhere in the world.

In the result, the case for an injunction now against publication by or on behalf of Mr Wright would in my opinion rest upon the principle that he should not be permitted to take advantage of his own wrongdoing.

The newspapers which are the respondents in this appeal were not responsible for the worldwide dissemination of the contents of *Spycatcher* which has taken place.

It is a general rule of law that a third party who comes into possession of confidential information which he knows to be such, may come under a duty not to pass it on to anyone else. Thus in *Duchess of Argyll v Duke of Argyll* the newspaper to which the Duke had communicated the information about the Duchess was restrained by injunction from publishing it. However, in that case there was no doubt but that the publication would cause detriment to the Duchess in the sense I have considered above . . . .

For the reasons which I have indicated in dealing with the position of Mr Wright, I am of the opinion that the reports and comments proposed by *The Guardian* and the *Observer* would not be harmful to the public interest, nor would the continued serialisation by *The Sunday Times*. I would therefore refuse an injunction against any of the newspapers.

I would stress that I do not base this upon any balancing of public interest nor upon any considerations of freedom of the press, nor upon any possible defences of prior publication or just cause or excuse, but simply upon the view that all possible damage to the interest of the Crown has already been done by the publication of *Spycatcher* abroad and the ready availability of copies in this country.

It is possible, I think, to envisage cases where, even in the light of widespread publication abroad of certain information, a person whom that information concerned might be entitled to restrain publication by a third party in this country . . . .

But it cannot reasonably be held in the present case that publication in England now of the contents of *Spycatcher* would do any more harm to the public interest than has already been done.

In relation to future serialisations by *The Sunday Times*, the Master of the Rolls . . . considered that there was a strong public interest in preventing Mr Wright and his publishers from profiting from their wrongdoing. There can be no doubt that the prospect of Mr Wright receiving further sums of money from *The Sunday Times* as a reward for his treachery is a revolting one.

But a natural desire to deprive Mr Wright of profit does not appear to me to constitute a legally valid ground for enjoining the newspaper from a publication which would not in itself damage the interests of the Crown.

Indeed, it appears that Mr Wright would have no legally enforceable claim against *The Sunday Times* for payment, upon the principle of *ex turpi causa non oritur actio* . . . .

The next issue for examination is conveniently the one as to whether *The Sunday Times* was in breach of an obligation of confidentiality when it published the first serialised extract from *Spycatcher* on 12 July 1987. I have no hesitation in holding that it was.

Those responsible for the publication well knew that the material was confidential in character and had not as a whole been previously published anywhere. Justification for the publication is sought to be found in the circumstance that publication in the United States of America was known to be imminent.

That will not hold water for a moment. It was Mr Wright and those acting for him who were about to bring about the American publication in breach of confidence.

The fact that a primary confidant, having communicated the confidential information to a third party in breach of obligation, is about to reveal it similarly to someone else, does not entitle that third party to do the same. The third party to whom the information has been wrongfully revealed himself comes under a duty of confidence to the original confider.

The fact that his information is about to commit further breaches of his obligation cannot conceivably relieve the third party of his own.

If it were otherwise an agreement between two confidants each to publish the confidential information would relieve each of them of his obligation, which would be absurd and deprive the law about confidentiality of all content.

The purpose of *The Sunday Times* was of course to steal a march on the American publication so as to be the first to reveal, for its own profit, the confidential material . . . . There can be no question but that the Crown, had it learned of the intended publication in *The Sunday Times*, would have been entitled to an injunction to restrain it. Mr Neil [*editor of the ST*] employed peculiarly sneaky methods to avoid this.

Neither the defence of prior publication nor that of just cause or excuse would in my opinion have been available to *The Sunday Times* . . . . As to just cause or excuse it is not sufficient to set up the defence merely to show that allegations of wrongdoing have been made. There must be at least a *prima facie* case that the allegations have substance . . . .

In cases where the information disclosed is of a commercial character an account of profits may provide some compensation to the claimant for loss which he has suffered through the disclosure, but damages are the main remedy for such loss.

The remedy is, in my opinion, more satisfactorily to be attributed to the principle that no one should be permitted to gain from his own wrongdoing. Its availability may also, in general, serve a useful purpose in lessening the temptation for recipients of confidential information to misuse it for financial gain.

In the present case *The Sunday Times* did misuse confidential information and it would be naive to suppose that the prospect of financial gain was not one of the reasons why it did so. I can perceive no good ground why the remedy should not be made available to the Crown in the circumstances of this case, and I would therefore hold the Crown entitled to an account of profits in respect of the publication on 12 July 1987.

Lord Keith went on to reject the Attorney-General's claims for permanent injunctions upon the Observer, The Guardian and The Sunday Times, and agreed with the Court of Appeal in rejecting those claims by the Crown.

The final issue is whether the Crown is entitled to a general injunction against all three newspapers restraining them from publishing any information concerned with the *Spycatcher* allegations obtained by any member or former member of the Security Service which they know or have reasonable grounds for believing to have come from any such member or former member, including Mr Wright, and also from attributing any such information in any publication to any member or former member of the Security Service.

The object of an injunction on these lines is to set up a second line of defence, so to speak, for the confidentiality of the operations of the Security Services.

The first and most important line of defence is obviously to take steps to secure that members and ex-members of the service do not speak about their experiences to the Press or anyone else to whom they are not authorised to speak.

Obviously the Director-General of the Security Service is in a position to impose a degree of discipline upon the existing members of the service so as to prevent unauthorised disclosures, and it is reasonable to suppose that in any event the vast majority of these members are conscientious and would never consider making such disclosures.

In so far as unconscientious ex-members are concerned, in particular Mr Wright, the position under existing circumstances is more difficult, although measures may now be introduced which are apt to discourage breaches of confidence by such people.

There are a number of problems involved in the general width of the injunction sought. Injunctions are normally aimed at the prevention of some specific wrong, not at the prevention of wrongdoing in general.

It would hardly be appropriate to subject a person to an injunction on the grounds that he is the sort of person who is likely to commit some kind of wrong, or that he has an interest in doing so. Then the injunction sought would not leave room for the possibility that a defence might be available in a particular case.

If Mr Wright were to publish a second book in America or Australia or both and it were to become readily available in this country, as has happened in regard to his first book, newspapers which published its contents would have as good a defence as the respondents in the present case.

It would not be satisfactory to have the availability of any defence tested in contempt proceedings. In my opinion an injunction on the lines sought should not be granted.

A few concluding reflections may be appropriate. In the first place I regard this case as having established that members and former members of the Security Service do have a lifelong obligation of confidence owed to the Crown.

Those who breach it, such as Mr Wright, are guilty of treachery just as heinous as that of some of the spies he excoriates in his book. The case has also served a useful purpose in bringing to light the problems which arise when the obligation of confidence is breached by publication abroad.

The judgement of the High Court of Australia reveals that even the most sensitive defence secrets of this country may not expect protection in the courts even of friendly foreign countries, although a less extreme view was taken by Sir Robert Cooke in the New Zealand Court of Appeal (*Attorney-General v Wellington Newspapers Ltd* 28 April 1988).

The secrets revealed by Mr Wright refer to matters of some antiquity, but there is no reason to expect that secrets concerned with matters of great current importance would receive any different treatment.

Consideration should be given to the possibility of some international agreement aimed at reducing the risks to collective security involved in the present state of affairs.

The First Amendment clearly poses problems in relation to publication in the United States of America, but even there is the prospect of defence and intelligence secrets receiving some protection in the civil courts, as is shown by the decision of the Supreme Court in *Snepp v United States* ([1980] 444 US 507).

Some degree of comity and reciprocity in this respect would seem desirable in order to promote the common interests of allied nations.

My Lords, upon the whole matter and for the reasons I have expressed, I would dismiss both appeals and also the cross-appeal by *The Sunday Times*.

NATO SUMMIT DECLARATION

Declaration adopted by the Heads of State and Government of the members of the North Atlantic Treaty Organization (Nato), meeting in Brussels, 2-3 March 1988.

A TIME FOR REAFFIRMATION

1. We, the representatives of the 16 members of the North Atlantic Alliance, have come together to re-emphasize our unity, to assess the current state of East-West relations, to review the opportunities and challenges which lie ahead, and in so doing: to reaffirm the common ideals and purposes which are the foundation of our partnership; to rededicate ourselves to the principles and provisions of the Washington Treaty of 1949; [and] to reassert the vital importance of the Alliance for our security, and the validity of our strategy for peace.

THE PURPOSES AND PRINCIPLES OF OUR ALLIANCE

2. Our Alliance is a voluntary association of free and democratic equals, united by common interests

and values. It is unprecedented in its scope and success. Our security is indivisible. Our Alliance is dedicated to preserving peace in freedom and to collective self-defence, as recognized by the United Nations Charter. None of our weapons will ever be used except in response to attack.

3. Our concept of a balanced security policy as set out in the Harmel Report has successfully stood the test of time. It remains valid in its two complementary and mutually reinforcing approaches: political solidarity and adequate military strength, and, on that basis, the search for constructive dialogue and cooperation, including arms control. The ultimate political purpose of our Alliance is to achieve a just and lasting peaceful order in Europe.

4. The security in freedom and the prosperity of the European and North American Allies are inextricably linked. The long-standing commitment of the North American democracies to the preservation of peace and security in Europe is vital. The presence in Europe of the conventional and nuclear forces of the United States provides the essential linkage with the United States strategic deterrent, and, together with the forces of Canada, is a tangible expression of that commitment. This presence must and will be maintained.

Likewise, a free, independent and increasingly united Europe is vital to North America's security. The credibility of Allied defence cannot be maintained without a major European contribution. We therefore welcome recent efforts to reinforce the European pillar of the Alliance, intended to strengthen the transatlantic partnership and Alliance security as a whole.

The Atlantic Alliance cannot be strong if Europe is weak.

5. Our aim will continue to be to prevent any kind of war or intimidation. By maintaining credible deterrence the Alliance has secured peace in Europe for nearly 40 years. Conventional defences alone cannot ensure this; therefore, for the foreseeable future there is no alternative to the Alliance strategy for the prevention of war. This is a strategy of deterrence based upon an appropriate mix of adequate and effective nuclear and conventional forces which will continue to be kept up to date where necessary.

6. While seeking security and stability at lower levels of armaments, we are determined to sustain the requisite efforts to ensure the continued viability, credibility and effectiveness of our conventional and nuclear forces, including the nuclear forces in Europe, which together provide the guarantee of our common security. Taking into account the structure of the Alliance, each of us undertakes to play his part in this joint endeavour in a spirit of solidarity, reaffirming our willingness to share fairly the risks, burdens and responsibilities as well as the benefits of our common efforts.

7. We seek a just and stable condition of peace in which the sovereignty and territorial integrity of all states are respected and the rights of all individuals, including their right of political choice, are protected.

We want gradually to overcome the unnatural division of the European continent, which affects most directly the German people. We will continue to uphold the freedom and viability of Berlin and to support efforts to improve the situation there.

The search for improved and more stable relations with the Soviet Union and the other countries of Eastern Europe is among our principal concerns. We call upon these countries to work with us for a further relaxation of tensions, greater security at lower levels of arms, more extensive human contacts and increased access to information. We will continue the effort to expand cooperation with the East wherever and whenever this is of mutual benefit.

EAST-WEST RELATIONS: THE WAY AHEAD

8. We have noted encouraging signs of change in the policies of the Soviet Union and some of its allies. This creates the prospect for greater openness in their relations with their own peoples and with other nations. We welcome such progress as has been already achieved in certain areas. But we look beyond pronouncements for tangible and lasting policy changes addressing directly the issues dividing East and West.

9. However, we have to date witnessed no relaxation of the military effort pursued for years by the Soviet Union. The Soviet Union persists in deploying far greater military forces than are required for its defence. This massive force, which the Soviet Union has not refrained from using outside its borders, as is still the case in Afghanistan, constitutes a fundamental source of tension between East and West. The steady growth of Soviet military capabilities, as it affects every region of the Alliance, requires our constant attention.

10. We will continue to be steadfast in the pursuit of our security policies, maintaining the effective defences and credible deterrence that form the necessary basis for constructive dialogue with the East including on arms control and disarmament matters.

To meet our security needs in the years to come will require ever greater efficiencies in the application of our scarce resources. We are therefore determined to expand our practical cooperation in the field of armaments procurement and elsewhere. In this context we recognise the challenges to our industrially less advanced Allies and the need to address them through mutual assistance and cooperation.

11. Arms control is an integral part of our security policy. We seek negotiations not for their own sake but to reach agreements which can significantly reduce the risk of conflict and make a genuine contribution to stability and peace. We shall work together vigorously and on the basis of the closest consultation to this end.

12. Our representatives to the North Atlantic Council continue actively the further development of a comprehensive concept of arms control and disarmament as directed in the Statement of our Ministers at Reykjavik in June 1987.

13. The recently concluded INF agreement between the USA and the Soviet Union is a milestone in our efforts to achieve a more secure peace and lower levels of arms. It is the impressive result of the political courage, the realism and the unity of the members of the Alliance. The treaty's provisions on stringent verification and asymmetrical reductions provide useful precedents for future agreements. We look forward to its early entry into force.

14. Consistent with their security requirements, the 15 Allies concerned will make use of all possibilities for effectively verifiable arms control agreements which lead to a stable and secure balance of forces at a lower level. For them, the comprehensive concept of arms control and disarmament includes:

a 50 per cent reduction in the strategic offensive nuclear weapons of the USA and the Soviet Union to be achieved during current Geneva negotiations;

the global elimination of chemical weapons;

the establishment of a stable and secure level of conventional forces, by the elimination of disparities, in the whole of Europe;

in conjunction with the establishment of a conventional balance and the global elimination of chemical weapons, tangible and verifiable reductions of American and Soviet land-based nuclear missile systems of shorter range, leading to equal ceilings.

15. Recognizing the urgency and central importance of addressing the conventional force imbalances in Europe, we have adopted a separate statement on conventional arms control.

16. The resolution of East-West differences will require progress in many fields. Genuine peace in Europe cannot be established solely by arms control. It must be firmly based on full respect for fundamental human rights. As we continue our efforts to reduce armaments, we shall press for implementation on the part of the Governments of the Soviet Union and of other Eastern countries of all of the principles and provisions of the Helsinki Final Act and of the Madrid Concluding Document. We support the continuation and strengthening of the CSCE process. It represents an important means of promoting stable and constructive relations on a long term basis between countries of East and West, and, moreover, enhances closer and more fruitful contacts between peoples and individuals throughout Europe. We call upon all participating states to make every effort for an early conclusion to the CSCE follow-up meeting in Vienna with a substantial and balanced final document.

17. We agree that the speedy and complete withdrawal of Soviet troops from Afghanistan and the effective restoration of that country's sovereignty would be of major significance. It is against these criteria that we shall assess General Secretary Gorbachev's recent statements.

18. We hope that at their forthcoming summit in Moscow President Reagan and General Secretary Gorbachev will be able to build upon the progress achieved at their Washington meeting last December. We strongly support the efforts of the United States. These fully accord with our consistent policy to seek, through high-level dialogue, early and substantial progress with the Soviet Union on a full range of issues, including greater respect for human rights, arms control, a lessening of regional tensions, and improved opportunities for bilateral contacts and cooperation.

19. Reflecting upon almost four decades of common endeavour and sacrifice and upon the results achieved, we are confident that the principles and purposes of our Alliance remain valid today and for the future. We are united in our efforts to ensure a world of more secure peace and greater freedom. We will meet the opportunities and challenges ahead with imagination and hope, as well as with firmness and vigilance. We owe no less to our peoples.

(Greece recalls its position on nuclear matters.)

GENEVA AGREEMENTS ON AFGHANISTAN

Edited texts of the five agreements signed in Geneva on 15 May 1988.

I AFGHANISTAN-PAKISTAN AGREEMENT ON MUTUAL RELATIONS

The Republic of Afghanistan and the Islamic Republic of Pakistan, hereinafter referred to as the high contracting parties, . . . have agreed as follows:

Article I. Relations between the high contracting parties shall be conducted in strict compliance with the principle of non-interference and non-intervention by states in the affairs of other states.

Article II. For the purpose of implementing the principle of non-interference and non-intervention each high contracting party undertakes to comply with the following obligations:

(1) To respect the sovereignty, political independence, territorial integrity, national unity, security and non-alignment of the other high contracting party, as well as the national identity and cultural heritage of its people;

(2) To respect the sovereign and inalienable right of the other high contracting party freely to determine its own political, economic, cultural and social systems, to develop its international relations and to exercise permanent sovereignty over its natural resources, in accordance with the will of its people, and without outside intervention, interference, subversion, coercion or threat in any form whatsoever;

(3) To refrain from the threat or use of force in any form whatsoever so as not to violate the boundaries of each other, to disrupt the political, social or economic order of the other high contracting party, to overthrow or change the political system of the other high contracting party or its government, or to cause tension between the high contracting parties;

(4) To ensure that its territory is not used in any manner which would violate the sovereignty, political independence, territorial integrity and national unity or disrupt the political, economic and social stability of the other high contracting party;

(5) To refrain from armed intervention, subversion, military occupation or any other form of intervention and interference, overt or covert, directed at the other high contracting party, or any act of military, political or economic interference in the internal affairs of the other high contracting party, including acts of reprisal involving the use of force;

(6) To refrain from any action or attempt in whatever form or under whatever pretext to destabilize or to undermine the stability of the other high contracting party or any of its institutions;

(7) To refrain from the promotion, encouragement or support, direct or indirect, of rebellious or secessionist activities against the other high contracting party, under any pretext whatsoever, or from any other action which seeks to disrupt the unity or to undermine or subvert the political order of the other high contracting party;

(8) To prevent within its territory the training, equipping, financing and recruitment of mercenaries from whatever origin for the purpose of hostile activities against the other high contracting party, or the sending of such mercenaries into the territory of the other high contracting party and accordingly to deny facilities, including financing for the training, equipping and transit of such mercenaries;

(9) To refrain from making any agreements or arrangements with other states designed to intervene or interfere in the internal and external affairs of the other high contracting party;

(10) To abstain from any defamatory campaign, vilification or hostile propaganda for the purpose of intervening or interfering in the affairs of the other high contracting party;

(11) To prevent any assistance to or use of or tolerance of terrorist groups, saboteurs or subversive agents against the other high contracting party;

(12) To prevent within its territory the presence, harbouring, in camps and bases or otherwise, organizing, training, financing, equipping and arming of individuals and political, ethnic and any other groups for the purpose of creating subversion, disorder or unrest in the territory of the other high contracting party and accordingly also to prevent the use of mass media and the transportation of arms, ammunition and equipment by such individuals and groups;

(13) Not to resort to or to allow any other action that could be considered as interference or intervention.

Article III. The present Agreement shall enter into force on 15 May 1988.

Article IV. Any steps that may be required in order to enable the high contracting parties to comply with the provisions of Article II of this Agreement shall be completed by the date on which this Agreement enters into force.

Article V. This Agreement is drawn up in the English, Pashtu and Urdu languages, all texts being equally authentic. In case of any divergence of interpretation, the English text shall prevail. Done in five original copies at Geneva this 14th day of April 1988.

For the Government of the
Republic of Afghanistan
Abdul Wakil

For the Government of the
Islamic Republic of Pakistan
Zain Noorani

II AFGHANISTAN-PAKISTAN AGREEMENT ON REFUGEES

The Republic of Afghanistan and the Islamic Republic of Pakistan, hereinafter referred to as the high contracting parties, . . . have agreed as follows:

Article I. All Afghan refugees temporarily present in the territory of the Islamic Republic of Pakistan shall be given the opportunity to return voluntarily to their homeland in accordance with the agreements and conditions set out in the present Agreement.

Article II. The Government of the Republic of Afghanistan shall take all necessary measures to ensure the following conditions for the voluntary return of Afghan refugees to their homeland:

(a) All refugees shall be allowed to return in freedom to their homeland;

(b) All returnees shall enjoy the free choice of domicile and freedom of movement within the Republic of Afghanistan;

(c) All returnees shall enjoy the right to work, to adequate living conditions and to share in the welfare of the state;

(d) All returnees shall enjoy the right to participate on an equal basis in the civic affairs of the Republic of Afghanistan. They shall be ensured equal benefits from the solution of the land question on the basis of the Land and Water Reform;

(e) All returnees shall enjoy the same rights and privileges, including freedom of religion, and have the same obligations and responsibilities as any other citizens of the Republic of Afghanistan without discrimination.

The Government of the Republic of Afghanistan undertakes to implement these measures and to provide, within its possibilities, all necessary assistance in the process of repatriation.

Article III. The Government of the Islamic Republic of Pakistan shall facilitate the voluntary, orderly and peaceful repatriation of all Afghan refugees staying within its territory and undertakes to provide, within its possibilities, all necessary assistance in the process of repatriation.

Article IV. For the purpose of organizing, coordinating and supervising the operations which should effect the voluntary, orderly and peaceful repatriation of Afghan refugees, these shall be set up mixed commissions in accordance with the established international practice. For the performance of their functions the members of the commissions and their staff shall be accorded the necessary facilities, and have access to the relevant areas within the territories of the high contracting parties.

Article V. With a view to the orderly movement of the returnees, the commissions shall determine frontier crossing points and establish necessary transit centres. They shall also establish all other modalities for the phased return of refugees, including registration and communication to the country of return of the names of refugees who express the wish to return.

Article VI. At the request of the Governments concerned, the United Nations High Commissioner for Refugees will cooperate and provide assistance in the process of voluntary repatriation of refugees in accordance with the present agreement. Special agreements may be concluded for this purpose between UNHCR and the high contracting parties.

Article VII. The present Agreement shall enter into force on 15 May 1988. At that time the mixed commissions provided in Article IV shall be established and the operations for the voluntary return of refugees under this Agreement shall commence. The arrangements set out in Articles IV and V above shall remain in effect for a period of 18 months. After that period the high contracting parties shall review the results of the repatriation and, if necessary, consider any further arrangements that may be called for.

Article VIII. This Agreement is drawn up in the English, Pashtu, and Urdu languages, all texts being equally authentic. In case of any divergence of interpretation, the English text shall prevail. Done in five original copies at Geneva this 14th day of April 1988.

For the Government of the
Republic of Afghanistan
Abdul Wakil

For the Government of the
Islamic Republic of Pakistan
Zain Noorani

III US-SOVIET DECLARATION ON INTERNATIONAL GUARANTEES

The Government of the Union of Soviet Socialist Republics and of the United States of America,
expressing support that the Republic of Afghanistan and the Islamic Republic of Pakistan have concluded a negotiated political settlement designed to normalize relations and promote good-neighbourliness between the two countries as well as to strengthen international peace and security in the region;

wishing in turn to contribute to the achievement of the objectives that the Republic of Afghanistan and the Islamic Republic of Pakistan have set themselves, and with a view to ensuring respect for their sovereignty, independence, territorial integrity and non-alignment;

undertake to invariably refrain from any form of interference and intervention in the internal affairs of the Republic of Afghanistan and the Islamic Republic of Pakistan and to respect the commitments contained in the bilateral agreement between the Republic of Afghanistan and the Islamic Republic of Pakistan on the principles of mutual relations, in particular on non-interference and non-intervention;

urge all states to act likewise.

The present Declaration shall enter into force on 15 May, 1988. Done at Geneva, this 14th day of April 1988, in five original copies, each in the Russian and English languages, both texts being equally authentic.

For the Government of the
Union of Soviet Socialist Republics
Eduard Shevardnadze

For the Government of the
United States of America
George Shultz

IV AGREEMENT ON AFGHANISTAN INTERRELATIONSHIPS

1. The diplomatic process initiated by the Secretary-General of the United Nations with the support of all governments concerned and aimed at achieving, through negotiations, a political settlement of the situation relating to Afghanistan has been successfully brought to an end . . .

5. . . . In accordance with the timeframe agreed upon between the Union of Soviet Socialist Republics and the Republic of Afghanistan there will be a phased withdrawal of the foreign troops which will start on the date of entry into force mentioned above [15 May 1988]. One half of the troops will be withdrawn by 15 August 1988 and the withdrawal of all troops will be completed within nine months.

6. The interrelationships in Paragraph 5 above have been agreed upon in order to achieve effectively the purpose of the political settlement, namely, that as from 15 May 1988, there will be no interference and intervention in any form in the affairs of the parties; the international guarantees will be in operation; the voluntary return of the refugees to their homeland will start and be completed within the timeframe specified in the Agreement on the Voluntary Return of the Refugees; and the phased withdrawal of the foreign troops will start and be completed within the timeframe envisaged in Paragraph 5. It is therefore essential that all the obligations deriving from the instruments concluded as component parts of the settlement be strictly fulfilled and that all the steps required to ensure full compliance with all the provisions of the instruments be completed in good faith.

7. To consider alleged violations and to work out prompt and mutually satisfactory solutions to questions that may arise in the implementation of the instruments comprising the settlement, representatives of the Republic of Afghanistan and the Islamic Republic of Pakistan shall meet whenever required.

A representative of the Secretary-General of the United Nations shall lend his good offices to the parties and in that context he will assist in the organization of the meetings and participate in them. He may submit to the parties for their consideration and approval suggestions and recommendations for prompt, faithful and complete observance of the provisions of the instruments.

In order to enable him to fulfil his tasks, the representative shall be assisted by such personnel under his authority as required. On his own initiative, or at the request of any of the parties, the personnel shall investigate any possible violations of any of the provisions of the instruments and prepare a report thereon. For that purpose, the representative and his personnel shall receive all the necessary cooperation from the Parties, including all freedom of movement within their respective territories required for effective investigation. Any report submitted by the representative to the two governments shall be considered in a meeting of the parties no later than 48 hours after it has been submitted.

The modalities and logistical arrangements for the work of the representative and the personnel under his authority as agreed upon with the parties are set out in the Memorandum of Understanding which is annexed to and is part of this Agreement.

8. The present instrument will be registered with the Secretary-General of the United Nations. It has been examined by the representatives of the parties to the bilateral agreements and of the states-guarantors, who have signified their consent with its provisions. The representatives of the parties, being duly authorized thereto by their respective Governments, have affixed their signatures hereunder. The Secretary-General of the United Nations was present.

Done at Geneva, this 14th day of April 1988, in five original copies, each in the Russian, Pashtu, Urdu and English languages, all being equally authentic. In case of any dispute regarding the interpretation the English text shall prevail.

For the Government of the
Republic of Afghanistan
Abdul Wakil

For the Government of the
Islamic Republic of Pakistan
Zain Noorani

In witness thereof, the representatives of the states-guarantors affixed their signatures hereunder:

For the Government of the
Union of Soviet Socialist Republics
Eduard Shevardnadze

For the Government of the
United States of America
George Shultz

V MEMORANDUM OF UNDERSTANDING

I. Basic Requirements. (a) The parties will provide full support and cooperation to the representative of the Secretary-General and to all the personnel assigned to assist him;

(b) The representative of the Secretary-General and his personnel will be accorded every facility as well as prompt and effective assistance, including freedom of movement and communications, accommodation, transportation and other facilities that may be necessary for the performance of their tasks. Afghanistan and Pakistan undertake to grant to the representative and his staff all the relevant privileges and immunities provided for by the Convention on the Privileges and Immunities of the United Nations;

(c) Afghanistan and Pakistan will be responsible for the safety of the representative of the Secretary-General and his personnel while operating in their respective countries;

(d) In performing their functions, the representative of the Secretary-General and his staff will act with complete impartiality. The representative of the Secretary-General and his personnel must not interfere in the internal affairs of Afghanistan and Pakistan and, in this context, cannot be used to secure advantages for any of the parties concerned.

II. Mandate. The mandate for the implementation-assistance arrangements envisaged in Paragraph 7 [of the Interrelationship Agreement] derives from the instruments comprising the settlement. All the staff assigned to the representative of the Secretary-General will accordingly be carefully briefed on the relevant provisions of the instruments and on the procedures that will be used to ascertain violations thereof.

III. Modus Operandi and Personnel Organization. The Secretary-General will appoint a senior military officer as deputy to the representative, who will be stationed in the area, as head of two small headquarters units, one in Kabul and the other in Islamabad, each comprising five military officers, drawn from existing United Nations operations, and a small civilian auxiliary staff.

The deputy representative of the Secretary-General will act on behalf of the representative and be in contact with the parties through the liaison officer each party will designate for this purpose.

The two headquarters units will be organized into two inspection teams to ascertain on the ground any violation of the instruments comprising the settlement. Whenever considered necessary by the representative of the Secretary-General or his deputy, up to 40 additional military officers (some 10 additional inspection teams) will be redeployed from existing operations within the shortest possible time (normally around 48 hours).

The nationalities of all the officers will be determined in consultation with the parties.

Whenever necessary the representative of the Secretary-General, who will periodically visit the area for consultations with the parties and to review the work of his personnel, will also assign to the area members of his own office and other civilian personnel from the United Nations secretariat as may be needed. His deputy will alternate between the two headquarters units and will remain at all times in close communication with them.

IV. Procedure. *(a) Inspections conducted at the request of the parties:* (i) A complaint regarding a violation of the instruments of the settlement lodged by any of the parties should be submitted in writing, in the English language, to the respective headquarters units and should indicate all relevant information and details.

(ii) Upon receipt of a complaint the deputy representative of the Secretary-General will immediately inform the other party of the complaint and undertake an investigation by making on-site inspections, gathering testimony and using any other procedure which he may deem necessary for the investigation of the alleged violation. Such inspection will be conducted using headquarters staff as referred to above, unless the deputy representative of the Secretary-General considers that additional teams are needed. In that case, the parties will, under the principle of freedom of movement, allow immediate access of the additional personnel to their respective territories.

(iii) Reports on investigations will be prepared in English and submitted by the deputy representative of the Secretary-General to the two governments on a confidential basis. (A third copy of the report will be simultaneously transmitted, on a confidential basis, to United Nations headquarters in New York, exclusively for the information of the Secretary-General and his representative.) In accordance with Paragraph 7 a report on an investigation should be considered in a meeting of the parties not later than 48 hours after it has been submitted. The deputy representative of the Secretary-General will, in the absence of the representative, lend his good offices to the parties and in that context he will assist in the organization of the meetings and participate in them. In the context of those meetings the deputy representative of the Secretary-General may submit to the parties for their consideration and approval suggestions and recommendations for the prompt, faithful and complete observance of the provisions of the instruments. (Such suggestions and recommendations will be, as a matter of course, consulted with, and cleared by, the representative of the Secretary-General.)

(b) Inspections conducted on the initiative of the deputy representative of the Secretary-General: In addition to inspections requested by the parties, the deputy representative of the Secretary-General may carry out on his own initiative and in consultation with the Representative inspections he deems appropriate for the purpose of the implementation of Paragraph 7. If it is considered that the conclusions reached in an inspection justify a report to the Parties, the same procedure used in submitting reports in connection with inspections carried out at the request of the Parties will be followed.

(c) Level of Participation in Meetings: As indicated above, the deputy representative of the Secretary-General will participate at meetings of the parties convened for the purpose of considering reports on violations. Should the parties decide to meet for the purpose outlined in Paragraph 7 at a high political level, the representative of the Secretary-General will personally attend such meetings.

V. Duration. The deputy representative of the Secretary-General and the other personnel will be established in the area not later than 20 days before the entry into force of the instruments. The arrangements will cease to exist two months after the completion of all timeframes envisaged for the implementation of the instruments.

VI. Financing. The cost of all facilities and services to be provided by the parties will be borne by the respective governments. The salaries and travel expenses of the personnel to and from the area, as well as the costs of the local personnel assigned to the headquarters units, will be defrayed by the United Nations.

DECLARATIONS OF PALESTINE NATIONAL COUNCIL

Excerpts from the two principal declarations adopted in Algiers on 15 November 1988 by the Palestine National Council, the Palestinian parliament in exile. (English translation supplied by the Palestine Liberation Organization office in London.)

DECLARATION OF INDEPENDENCE

It was in Palestine, cradle of humanity's three monotheistic faiths, that the Palestinian Arab people was born, and it was there that it grew and developed its unbroken, uninterrupted organic relationship with its land and its history moulding its human and national being. With epic steadfastness, the Palestinian people forged their national identity, rising in their tenacious defence of it to miraculous heights. The magic of this ancient land and its location at the crossroads of powers and civilizations aroused ambitions and cravings, inviting invasions that led to the denial of political independence to its people. But the people's perpetual adherence to the land gave the land its identity and breathed the spirit of the homeland into the people . . . .

When the contemporary world drafted its new order of values, the balance of local and international forces denied the Palestinian a share of the general weal, once more demonstrating that justice alone does not turn the wheel of history. The painful inequity poured salt on the Palestinian wound. The people that had been denied independence and whose homeland had become the victim of a new breed of occupation became the target of attempts to propagate the lie that "Palestine is a land without a people". This historical fraud notwithstanding, the international community, in Article 22 of the Covenant of the League of Nations of 1919, and in the Lausanne Treaty of 1923, had recognized that the Palestinian Arab people, like the other Arab peoples that had broken away from the Ottoman Empire, was a free and independent people.

Despite the historical injustice done to the Palestinian Arab people by their dispersion and deprivation of the right of self-determination after the United Nations General Assembly Resolution 181 of 1947, which partitioned Palestine into two states, Arab and Jewish, that resolution still provides the legal basis for the right of the Palestinian Arab people to national sovereignty and independence. The occupation of the Palestinian land and of Arab territory by the Israeli forces, and the uprooting and expulsion of the majority of the Palestinians from their homes by organized terrorism, and the subjection of the Palestinians who remained to occupation, persecution and the destruction of all semblances of national life constitute a flagrant violation of all legal principles, and of the Charter of the United Nations, and of those United Nations resolutions that recognize the national rights of the Palestinian people, including their rights to repatriation, self-determination, and independence and sovereignty on their national soil.

In the heart of our homeland, along its frontiers, and in their exiles near and far, the Palestinian Arab people never lost their deep faith in their right to return and their right to independence. The occupation, the massacres, the dispersion failed to loosen the Palestinian's grip on his national consciousness. He pressed his epic struggle and, through that struggle, continued to crystallize his national identity. And the national Palestinian will formed its own political framework: the Palestine Liberation Organization [PLO], the sole legitimate representative of the Palestinian people, recognized as such by the international community as represented by the United Nations and its institutions and by the other international and regional organizations. Armed with a belief in its people's inalienable rights, and with Arab national unanimity, and with international legitimacy, the PLO led the battles of its great people, a people fused into a solid national unity by the massacres and sieges to which it was subjected in its homeland and outside it. The epic of the Palestinian resistance entered the Arab and international records as one of the most distinguished national liberation movements of this era.

The titanic popular *intifada* waxing in the occupied land and the legendary steadfastness displayed in the camps of the homeland and the diaspora have raised human awareness of the Palestinian reality and the national rights of the Palestinians to the level of mature comprehension, bringing the curtain down on the phase of rampant deception and sedentary consciences, and besieging the official Israeli mentality that had grown addicted to reliance on myth and terrorism in its denial of the existence of the Palestinians. The rise of the *intifada* and the cumulative fruit of the revolution in all its aspects have brought the Palestinian saga to another historic juncture where the Palestinian Arab people must once more claim their rights and affirm their determination to exercise them on their Palestinian soil.

By virtue of the Palestinian Arab people's natural, historic and legal right to their homeland, Palestine, and of the sacrifices of their successive generations in defence of the liberty and independence of their homeland, . . . the Palestine National Council proclaims, in the name of God and the Palestinian Arab people, the establishment of the State of Palestine on our Palestinian land, with the Holy City of Jerusalem as its capital.

The State of Palestine is the state of Palestinians wherever they may be. In it they shall develop their national and cultural identity and enjoy full equality in rights. Their religious and political beliefs and their human dignity shall be safeguarded under a democratic parliamentary system of government built on the freedom of opinion; and on the freedom to form parties; and on the protection of the rights of the minority by the majority and respect of the decisions of the majority by the minority; and on social justice and equal rights, free of ethnic, religious, racial or sexual discrimination; and on a constitution that guarantees the rule of law and the independence of the judiciary; and on the basis of total allegiance to the centuries-old spiritual and civilizational Palestinian heritage of religious tolerance and coexistence.

The State of Palestine is an Arab state, an integral part of the Arab nation and of that nation's heritage, its civilization and its aspiration to attain its goals of liberation, development, democracy and unity. Affirming its commitment to the Charter of the League of Arab states and its insistence on the reinforcement of joint Arab action, the State of Palestine calls on the people of its nation to assist in the completion of its birth by mobilizing their resources and augmenting their efforts to end the Israeli occupation.

The State of Palestine declares its commitment to the principles and objectives of the United Nations, and to the Universal Declaration of Human Rights, and to the principles and policy of non-alignment. The State of Palestine, declaring itself a peace-loving state committed to the principles of peaceful coexistence, shall strive with all states and people to attain a permanent peace built on justice and respect of rights, in which humanity's constructive talents can prosper, and creative competition can flourish, and fear of tomorrow can be abolished, for tomorrow brings nothing but security for the just and those who regain their sense of justice.

As it struggles to establish peace in the land of love and peace, the State of Palestine exhorts the United Nations to take upon itself a special responsibility for the Palestinian Arab people and their homeland; and exhorts the peace-loving, freedom-cherishing peoples and states of the world to help it attain its objectives and put an end to the tragedy its people are suffering by providing them with security and endeavoring to end the Israeli occupation of the Palestinian territories. The State of Palestine declares its belief in the settlement of international and regional disputes by peaceful means in accordance with the Charter and resolutions of the United Nations; and its rejection of threats of force or violence or terrorism and the use of these against its territorial integrity and political independence or the territorial integrity of any other state, without prejudice to its natural right to defend its territory and independence . . . .

To the innocent souls of our martyrs, to the masses of our Palestinian Arab people and our Arab nation, and to all the world's free and honorable people we make this pledge: that we shall continue our struggle to roll back the occupation and entrench our sovereignty and independence. We call upon our great people to rally around their Palestinian flag, to take pride in it and defend it, so that it will remain forever the symbol of our liberty and dignity in a homeland that will forever remain the free homeland of a free people . . . .

POLITICAL STATEMENT

. . . The international community is now more prepared than ever before to strive for a political settlement of the Middle East crisis and its root cause, the Palestinian issue. The Israeli occupation authorities, and the American administration that stands behind them, cannot continue to ignore the international will, which is now unanimous on the necessity of holding an international peace conference on the Middle East and enabling the Palestinian people to gain their national rights, foremost among which is their right to self-determination and national independence on their own soil.

In the light of this, and toward the reinforcement of the steadfastness and blessed *intifada* of our people, and in accordance with the will of our masses in and outside our homeland, and in fidelity to those of our people who have been martyred, wounded or taken captive, the Palestine National Council resolves:

First: on the escalation and continuity of the *intifada*

A. To provide all the means and capabilities needed to escalate our people's *intifada* in various ways and on various levels to guarantee its continuation and intensification.

B. To support the popular institutions and organizations in the occupied Palestinian territories.

C. To bolster and develop the Popular Committees and other specialized popular and trade union bodies, including the attack groups and the popular army, with a view to expanding their role and increasing their effectiveness.

D. To consolidate the national unity that emerged and developed during the *intifada*.

E. To intensify efforts on the international level for the release of the detainees, the repatriation of the deportees, and the termination of the organized, official acts of repression and terrorism against our children, our women, our men, and our institutions.

F. To call on the United Nations to place the occupied Palestinian land under international supervision for the protection of our people and the termination of the Israeli occupation.

G. To call on the Palestinian people outside our homeland to intensify and increase their support, and to expand the family-assistance program.

H. To call on the Arab nation, its people, forces, institutions and governments, to increase their political, material and informational support of the *intifada*.

I. To call on all free and honorable people worldwide to stand by our people, our revolution, our *intifada* against the Israeli occupation, the repression, and the organized, fascist official terrorism to which the occupation forces and the armed fanatic settlers are subjecting our people, our universities, our national economy, and our Islamic and Christian holy places.

Second: in the political field

Proceeding from the above, the Palestine National Council, being responsible to the Palestinian people, their national rights and their desire for peace as expressed in the Declaration of Independence issued on 15 November 1988; and in response to the humanitarian quest for international entente, nuclear disarmament and the settlement of regional conflicts by peaceful means, affirms the determination of the Palestine Liberation Organization to arrive at a political settlement of the Arab-Israeli conflict and its core, the Palestinian issue, in the framework of the UN Charter, the principles and rules of international legitimacy, the edicts of international law, the resolutions of the United Nations, the latest of which are Security Council Resolutions 605, 607 and 608, and the resolutions of the Arab summits, in a manner that assures the Palestinian Arab people's right to repatriation, self-determination and the establishment of their independent state on their national soil, and that institutes arrangements for the security and peace of all states in the region.

Toward the achievement of this, the Palestine National Council affirms:

1. The necessity of convening an effective international conference on the issue of the Middle East and its core, the Palestinian issue, under the auspices of the United Nations and with the participation of the permanent members of the Security Council and all parties to the conflict in the region, including, on an equal footing, the Palestine Liberation Organization, the sole legitimate representative of the Palestinian people; on the understanding that the international conference will be held on the basis of Security Council Resolutions 242 and 338 and the safeguarding of the legitimate national rights of the Palestinian people, foremost among which is the right to self-determination, in accordance with the principles and provisions of the UN Charter as they pertain to the right of peoples to self-determination and the inadmissibility of the acquisition of others' territory by force or military conquest, and in accordance with the UN resolutions relating to the Palestinian issue.

2. The withdrawal of Israel from all Palestinian and Arab territories it occupied in 1967, including Arab Jerusalem.

3. The annulment of all expropriation and annexation measures and the removal of the settlements established by Israel in the Palestinian and Arab territories since 1967.

4. Endeavoring to place the occupied Palestinian territories, including Arab Jerusalem, under the supervision of the United Nations for a limited period, to protect our people, to create an atmosphere conducive to the success of the proceedings of the international conference toward the attainment of a comprehensive political settlement and the achievement of peace and security for all on the basis of mutual consent, and to enable the Palestinian state to exercise its effective authority in these territories.

5. The settlement of the issue of the Palestinian refugees in accordance with the pertinent United Nations resolutions.

6. Guaranteeing the freedom of worship and the right to engage in religious rites for all faiths in the holy places in Palestine.

7. The UN Security Council shall draw up and guarantee arrangements for the security of all states concerned and for peace between them, including the Palestinian state.

The Palestine National Council confirms its past resolutions that the relationship between the fraternal Jordanian and Palestinian peoples is a privileged one and that the future relationship between the states of Jordan and Palestine will be built on confederal foundations, on the basis of the two fraternal peoples' free and voluntary choice, in consolidation of the historic ties that bind them and the vital interests they hold in common . . .

MIKHAIL GORBACHEV'S UN ADDRESS

Edited text of the address delivered to the United Nations' General Assembly on 7 December 1988 by President Mikhail Gorbachev, General Secretary of the Communist Party of the Soviet Union. (English text supplied by Novosti Press Agency.)

I THE FUTURE OF MANKIND

What will mankind be like when it enters the 21st century? People are already fascinated by this not too distant future. We are looking ahead to it with hopes for the best and yet with a feeling of concern. The world in which we live today is radically different from what it was at the beginning or even in the middle of this century. And it continues to change as do all its components. The advent of nuclear weapons was just another tragic reminder of the fundamental nature of that change. A material symbol and expression of absolute military power, nuclear weapons at the same time revealed the absolute limits of that power. The problem of mankind's survival and self-preservation came to the fore.

We are witnessing most profound social change. Whether in the East or the South, the West or the North, hundreds of millions of people, new nations and states, new public movements and ideologies have moved to the forefront of history. Broad-based and frequently turbulent popular movements have given expression, in a multi-dimensional and contradictory way, to a longing for independence, democracy and social justice. The idea of democratizing the entire world order has become a powerful socio-political force.

At the same time, the scientific and technological revolution has turned many economic, food, energy, environmental, information and population problems, which only recently we treated as national or regional ones, into global problems. Thanks to the advances in mass media and means of transportation, the world seems to have become more visible and tangible. International communication has become easier than ever before. Today, the preservation of any kind of 'closed' societies is hardly possible. This calls for a radical review of approaches to the totality of the problems of international cooperation as a major element of universal security.

The world economy is becoming a single organism, and no state, whatever its social system or economic status, can normally develop outside it. This places on the agenda the need to devise a fundamentally new machinery for the functioning of the world economy, a new structure of the international division of labour. At the same time, the growth of the world economy reveals the contradictions and limits inherent in traditional-type industrialization. Its further extension and intensification spell environmental catastrophe. But there are still many countries without sufficiently developed industries, and some have not yet moved beyond the pre-industrial stage. One of the major problems is whether the process of their economic growth will follow the old technological patterns or they can join in the search for environmentally clean production.

And there is another problem: instead of diminishing, the gap between the developed and most of the developing countries is increasingly growing into a serious global threat. Hence the need to begin a search for a fundamentally new type of industrial progress — one that would meet the interests of all peoples and states. In a word, the new realities are changing the entire world situation. The differences and contradictions inherited from the past are diminishing or being displaced. But new ones are emerging. Some of the past differences and disputes are losing their importance. But conflicts of a different kind are taking their place. Life is making us abandon established stereotypes and outdated views, it is making us discard illusions . . .

Today, further world progress is only possible through a search for universal human consensus as we move forward to a new world order. We have come to a point when the disorderly play of elemental forces leads into an impasse. The international community must learn how it can shape and guide developments in such a way as to preserve our civilization, to make it safe for all and more conducive to normal life. We are speaking of cooperation which could be more accurately termed co-creation or co-development.

The formula of development "at the expense of others" is on the way out. In the light of existing realities, no genuine progress is possible at the expense of the rights and freedoms of individuals and nations, or at the expense of nature. If we are to solve global problems, countries and socio-political trends have to arrive at a new scope and quality of their interaction, whatever their ideological or other differences. Of course, radical changes and revolutionary transformations will continue to occur within individual countries and social structures. This is how it was and how it will be. But here too, our time marks a change. Internal transformations no longer can advance their national goals if they develop just along 'parallel courses' with others, without making use of the achievements of the outside world and of the potential inherent in equitable cooperation.

In these circumstances, any interference in those internal developments, designed to redirect them to someone's liking, would have all the more destructive consequences for establishing a peaceful order. In the past, differences often acted as barriers. Now they have a chance of becoming a factor for mutual enrichment and mutual attraction. Behind differences in social systems, in the way of life and in preferences for certain values stand differing interests. There is no escaping that fact. But equally, there is no escaping the need to find a balance of interests within an international framework, which has become a condition for survival and progress.

Pondering all this, one comes to the conclusion that if we are to take into account the lessons of the past and the realities of the present, if we are to reckon with the objective logic of world development, we must look for ways to improve the international situation and build a new world — and we must do it together. And, if so, we ought to agree on the basic, truly universal prerequisites and principles of such action. It is obvious, for instance, that the use or threat of force no longer can or must be an instrument of foreign policy. This applies above all to nuclear arms, but that is not the only thing that matters. All of us, and primarily the stronger of us, must exercise self-restraint and totally rule out any outward-oriented use of force . . . After all, it is now quite clear that building up military power makes no country omnipotent. What is more, one-sided reliance on military power ultimately weakens other components of national security.

It is also quite clear to us that the principle of freedom of choice is mandatory. Its non-recognition is fraught with extremely grave consequences for world peace. Denying that right to the peoples under whatever pretext or rhetorical guise means jeopardising even the fragile balance that has been attained. Freedom of choice is a universal principle that should allow for no exceptions. It was not simply out of good intentions that we came to the conclusion that this principle is absolute. We were driven to it by an unbiased analysis of the objective trends of today.

More and more characteristic of them is the increasingly multi-optional nature of social development in different countries. This applies both to the capitalist and to the socialist system. The diversity of the socio-political structures that have grown over the past decades out of national liberation movements also attests to this. This objective fact calls for respect for the views and positions of others, tolerance, a willingness to perceive something different as not necessarily bad or hostile, and an ability to learn to live side-by-side with others, while remaining different and not always agreeing with each other. As the world asserts its diversity, attempts to look down on others and to teach them one's own brand of democracy, become totally improper, to say nothing of the fact that democratic values intended for export often very quickly lose their worth. What we are talking about, therefore, is unity in diversity. If we assert this politically, if we reaffirm our adherence to freedom of choice, then there is no room for the view that some live on Earth by virtue of divine will while others are here quite by chance. The time has come to discard such thinking and to shape our policies accordingly. That would open up prospects for strengthening the unity of the world.

The new phase also requires de-ideologizing relations among states. We are not abandoning our convictions, our philosophy or traditions, nor do we urge anyone to abandon theirs. But neither do we have any intention to be hemmed in by our values. That would result in intellectual impoverishment, for it would mean rejecting a powerful source of development — the exchange of everything original that each nation has independently created. In the course of such exchange, let everyone show the advantages of their social system, way of life or values — and not just by words or propaganda, but be real deeds. That would be a fair rivalry of ideologies. But it should not be extended to relations among states. Otherwise, we would simply be unable to solve any of the world's problems, such as: developing wide-ranging mutually beneficial and equitable cooperation among nations; making efficient use of the achievements of the scientific and technological revolution; restructuring the world economy and protecting the environment; overcoming backwardness, eliminating hunger, disease, illiteracy and other global scourges . . .

We regard prospects for the near and more distant future quite optimistically. Just look at the changes in our relations with the United States. Little by little, mutual understanding has started to develop and elements of trust have emerged, without which it is very hard to make headway in politics. In Europe, these elements are even more numerous. The Helsinki Process is a great process. I believe that it remains fully valid. Its philosophical, political, practical and other dimensions must all be preserved and enhanced, while taking into account new circumstances. Current realities make it imperative that the dialogue that ensures normal and constructive evolution of international affairs involve, on a continuous and active basis, all countries and regions of the world, including such major powers as India, China, Japan, and Brazil and other countries — big, medium and small.

I am in favour of a more dynamic and substantive political dialogue, of strengthening the political prerequisites needed to improve the international climate. That would make it easier to find practical solutions to many problems. Tough as it may be, this is the road that we must travel . . .

II ROLE OF THE UNITED NATIONS AND SOVIET PERESTROIKA

In this specific historical situation we face the question of a new role for the United Nations. We feel that states must to some extent review their attitude to the United Nations, this unique instrument without which world politics would be inconceivable today. The recent reinvigoration of its peace-making role has again demonstrated the United Nations' ability to assist its members in coping with the daunting challenges of our time and working to humanize their relations.

Regrettably, shortly after it was established, the organization went through the onslaught of the Cold War. For many years, it was the scene of propaganda battles and continuous political confrontation. Let historians argue who is more and who is less to blame for it. What political leaders today need to do is to draw lessons from that chapter in the history of the United Nations which turned out to be at odds with the very meaning and objectives of the organization.

One of the most bitter and important lessons lies in the long list of missed opportunities. As a result, at a certain point the authority of the United Nations diminished and many of its attempts to act failed. It is highly significant that the reinvigoration of the role of the United Nations is linked to an improvement in the international climate. In a way, the United Nations blends together the interests of different states. It is the only organization capable of merging into a single current their bilateral, regional and global efforts.

New prospects are opening up for it in all areas that fall naturally under its responsibility — in the politico-military, economic, scientific, technological, environmental, and humanitarian areas. Take, for example, the problem of development, which is a truly universal human problem. The conditions in which tens of millions of people live in a number of Third World regions are becoming a real threat to all mankind. No closed entities or even regional communities of states, important as they are, are capable of untangling the main knots that tie up the principal avenues of world economic relations — North-South, East-West, South-South, South-East, and East-East. What is needed here is joining the efforts and taking into account the interests of all groups of countries, something that only this organization, the United Nations, can accomplish.

External debt is one of the gravest problems. Let us not forget that in the age of colonialism the developing world, at the cost of countless losses and sacrifices, financed the prosperity of a large portion of the world community. The time has come to make up for the losses that accompanied its historic and tragic contribution to global material progress. We are convinced that here, too, internationalizing our approach shows a way out.

Looking at things realistically, one has to admit that the accumulated debt cannot be repaid or recovered on the original terms. The Soviet Union is prepared to institute a lengthy moratorium of up to 100 years on debt servicing by the least developed countries, and in quite a few cases to write off the debt altogether. As regards other developing countries, we invite you to consider the following: limiting their official debt servicing payments depending on the economic performance of each of them or granting them a long period of deferral in the repayment of a major portion of their debt; supporting the appeal of the United Nations Conference on Trade and Development for reducing debts owed to commercial banks; guaranteeing government support for market arrangements to assist in Third World debt settlement, including the formation of a specialized international agency that would repurchase debts at a discount . . .

International economic security is inconceivable unless related not only to disarmament but also to the elimination of the threat to the world's environment. In a number of regions, the state of the environment is simply frightening. A conference on the environment within the framework of the United Nations is scheduled for 1992. We welcome this decision and are working to have this forum produce results that would be commensurate with the scope of the problem. But time is running out. Much is being done in various countries. Here again I would just like to underscore most emphatically the prospects opening up in the process of disarmament — for environmental revival. Let us also think about setting up within the framework of the United Nations a centre for emergency environmental assistance. Its function would be promptly to send international groups of experts to areas with badly deteriorating environment.

The Soviet Union is also ready to cooperate in establishing an international space laboratory or manned orbital station designed exclusively for monitoring the state of the environment. In the general area of space exploration, the outlines of a future space industry are becoming increasingly clear. The position of the Soviet Union is well known: activities in outer space must rule out the appearance of weapons there. Here again, there has to be a legal base. The groundwork for it — the provisions of the 1967 treaty and other agreements — is already in place.

However, there is already a strongly felt need to develop an all-embracing regime for peaceful work in outer space. The verification of compliance with that regime would be entrusted to a world space organization. We have put forward our proposal to establish it on more than one occasion. We are prepared to incorporate within its system our Krasnoyarsk radar station. A decision has already been taken to place that radar under the authority of the USSR Academy of Sciences . . .

The whole world welcomes the efforts of the United Nations Organization and its Secretary-General, Mr Pérez de Cuéllar, and his representatives in untying knots of regional problems . . . I will single out only Afghanistan. The Geneva accords, whose fundamental and practical significance has been praised throughout the world, provided a possibility for completing the process of settlement even before the end of this year. That did not happen.

This unfortunate fact reminds us again of the political, legal, and moral significance of the Roman maxim: *Pacta sunt servanda*! I do not want to use this rostrum for recriminations against anyone. But it is our view that, within the competence of the United Nations, the General Assembly resolution adopted last November could be supplemented by some specific measures.

In the words of that resolution, for the urgent achievement of a comprehensive solution by the Afghans themselves of the question of a broad-based government the following should be undertaken:

A complete ceasefire, effective everywhere as of 1 January 1989, and the cessation of all offensive operations or shellings, with the opposing Afghan groups retaining, for the duration of negotiations, all territories under their control.

Linked to that, stopping as of the same date any supplies of arms to all belligerents.

For the period of establishing a broad-based government, as provided in the General Assembly resolution, sending to Kabul and other strategic centres of the country United Nations peace-keeping forces.

We also request the Secretary-General to facilitate early implementation of the idea of holding an international conference on the neutrality and demilitarization of Afghanistan.

We shall continue most actively to assist in healing the wounds of the war and are prepared to cooperate in this endeavour both with the United Nations and on a bilateral basis. We support the proposal to create under the auspices of the United Nations a voluntary international peace corps to assist in the revival of Afghanistan.

In the context of the problem of settling regional conflicts, I have to express my opinion on the serious incident that has recently affected the work of this session. The chairman of an organization which has observer status at the United Nations was not allowed by US authorities to come to New York to address the General Assembly. I am referring to Yassir Arafat. What is more, this happened at a time when the Palestine Liberation Organization has made a constructive step which facilitates the search for a solution to the Middle East problem with the involvement of the United Nations Security Council. This happened at a time when a positive trend has become apparent toward a political settlement of other regional conflicts, in many cases with the assistance of the USSR and the United States. We voice our deep regret over the incident and our solidarity with the Palestine Liberation Organization . . .

I would like to join the voice of my country in the expressions of high appreciation of the significance of the Universal Declaration of Human Rights adopted 40 years ago on 19 December 1948. Today, this document retains its significance. It, too, reflects the universal nature of the goals and objectives of the United Nations. The most fitting way for a state to observe this anniversary of the declaration is to improve its domestic conditions for respecting and protecting the rights of its own citizens. Before I inform you on what specifically we have undertaken recently in this respect I would like to say the following.

Our country is going through a period of truly revolutionary uplifting. The process of *perestroika* is gaining momentum. We began with the formulation of the theoretical concept of *perestroika*. We had to evaluate the nature and the magnitude of problems, to understand the lessons of the past and express that in the form of political conclusions and programmes. This was done. Theoretical work, a reassessment of what is happening, the finalization, enrichment and readjustment of political positions have not been completed. They are continuing. But is was essential to begin with an overall concept, which, as now confirmed by the experience of these past years, has generally proved to be correct and which has no alternative.

For our society to participate in efforts to implement the plans of *perestroika* it had to be democratized in practice. Under the sign of democratization, *perestroika* has now spread to politics, the economy, intellectual life, and ideology. We have initiated a radical economic reform. We have gained experience. At the start of next year the entire national economy will be redirected to new forms and methods of operation. This also means profoundly reorganizing relations of production and releasing the tremendous potential inherent in socialist property.

While choosing to pursue such bold revolutionary transformations, we knew there would be blunders and resistance to the new, engendering new problems, and we anticipated delays in some areas. But what makes it certain that the overall process of *perestroika* will proceed steadily ahead and gather momentum is the profound democratic reform of the entire system of government and administration. As the USSR Supreme Soviet has recently introduced constitutional amendments and adopted a new electoral law, we have completed the first stage of the political reform.

Without pausing, we entered the second stage, whereby the paramount task will be to practise coordination between central authorities and republics, to settle ethnic relations in line with the principles of Leninist internationalism, as bequeathed to us by the great revolution, and at the same to reform the administration of local government councils. We have much to do, while at the same time coping with an array of formidable issues. But we are looking with confidence into the future. We have the theory, and the political framework, and the driving force of *perestroika* — the party, which also has been reforming itself in line with new tasks and profound transformations in society. And, most important of all, *perestroika* is supported by all nations and all generations of citizens of our great country.

We have immersed ourselves in constructing a socialist state based on the rule of law. A whole series of new laws have been elaborated or are nearing completion. Many will enter into force in 1989, and, we believe, comply fully with the highest standards in ensuring human rights. Soviet democracy will be placed on a solid normative base. I am referring, in particular, to laws on the freedom of conscience, *glasnost*, public associations and organizations, and many others.

In places of confinement there are no persons convicted for their political or religious belief. Additional guarantees are to be included in the new draft laws that rule out any form of persecution on those grounds. Naturally, this does not apply to those who committed actual criminal offences or state crimes such as espionage, sabotage, terrorism, etc., whatever their political or ideological beliefs. Draft amendments to the penal code have been prepared and are awaiting their turn. Among the articles being revised are those related to capital punishment.

The problem of exit from and entry to our country, including the question of leaving it for family reunification, is being dealt with in a humane spirit. As you know, one of the reasons for refusal to leave is a person's knowledge of secrets. Strictly warranted time limitations on the secrecy rule will now be applied. Every person seeking employment at certain agencies or enterprises will be informed of this rule. In case of disputes there is a right of appeal under the law. This removes from the agenda the problem of the so-called 'refuseniks' . . .

III DISARMAMENT PROPOSALS

Now let me turn to the main issue — disarmament, without which none of the problems of the coming century can be solved. International development and communication have been distorted by the arms race and militarization of thinking. As you know, on 15 January 1986 the Soviet Union put forward a programme of building a nuclear-weapon-free world. Translated into actual negotiating positions, it has already produced material results.

Tomorrow marks the first anniversary of the signing of the INF treaty. I am therefore particularly pleased to note that the implementation of the treaty — the elimination of missiles — is proceeding normally, in an atmosphere of trust and businesslike work. A large breach has thus been made in a seemingly unbreakable wall of suspicion and animosity. We are witnessing the emergence of a new historic reality — a turning-away from the principle of superarmament to the principle of reasonable defence sufficiency. We are present at the birth of a new model of ensuring security — not through the build-up of arms, as was almost always the case in the past, but on the contrary, through their reduction on the basis of compromise. The Soviet leadership has decided to demonstrate once again its readiness to reinforce this healthy process, not only by words but also by deeds.

Today, I can report to you that the Soviet Union has taken a decision to reduce its armed forces. Within the next two years their numerical strength will be reduced by 500,000 men. The numbers of conventional armaments will also be substantially reduced. This will be done unilaterally, without relation to the talks on the mandate of the Vienna meeting. By agreement with our Warsaw Treaty allies, we have decided to withdraw by 1991 six tank divisions from the German Democratic Republic, Czechoslovakia and Hungary, and to disband them. Assault landing troops and several other formations and units, including assault crossing units with their weapons and combat equipment, will also be withdrawn from the groups of Soviet forces stationed in those countries. Soviet forces stationed in those countries will be reduced by 50,000 men and their armaments, by 5,000 tanks.

All Soviet divisions remaining, for the time being, in the territory of our allies are being reorganized. Their structure will be different from what it is now; after a major cutback of their tanks it will become clearly defensive. At the same time, we shall reduce the numerical strength of the armed forces and the numbers of armaments stationed in the European part of the USSR. In total, Soviet armed forces in this part of our country and in the territories of our European allies will be reduced by 10,000 tanks, 8,500 artillery systems and 800 combat aircraft. Over these two years we intend to reduce significantly our armed forces in the Asian part of our country, too. By agreement with the government of the Mongolian People's Republic, a major portion of Soviet troops temporarily stationed there will return home. In taking this fundamental decision, the Soviet leadership expresses the will of the people, who have undertaken a profound renewal of their entire socialist society. We shall maintain our country's defence capability at a level of reasonable and reliable sufficiency so that no one might be tempted to encroach on the security of the USSR and our allies.

By this action, and by all our activities in favour of demilitarizing international relations, we wish to draw the attention of the international community to yet another pressing problem — the problem of transition from the economy of armaments to an economy of disarmament. Is conversion of military production a realistic idea? I have already had occasion to speak about this. We think that, indeed, it is realistic. For its part, the Soviet Union is prepared: in the framework of our economic reform we are ready to draw up and make public our internal plan of conversion; in the course of 1989 to draw up, as an experiment, conversion plans for two or three defence plants; to make public our experience in providing employment for specialists from military industry and in using its equipment, buildings and structures in civilian production.

It is desirable that all states, in the first place major military powers, should submit to the United Nations their national conversion plans. It would also be useful to set up a group of scientists to undertake a thorough analysis of the problem of conversion as a whole and as applied to individual countries and regions and report to the Secretary-General of the United Nations, and, subsequently, to have this matter considered at a session of the General Assembly.

IV RELATIONS WITH UNITED STATES

And finally, since I am here on American soil, and also for other obvious reasons, I have to turn to the subject of our relations with this great country. I had a chance to appreciate the full measure of its hospitality during my memorable visit to Washington exactly a year ago. The relations between the Soviet Union and the United States of America have a history of five and a half decades. As the world changed, so did the nature, role and place of those relations in world politics. For too long a time they developed along the lines of confrontation and sometimes animosity — either overt or covert. But in the last few years the entire world could breathe a sigh of relief thanks to the changes for the better in the substance and the atmosphere of the relationship between Moscow and Washington.

No one intends to underestimate the seriousness of our differences and the toughness of outstanding problems. We have, however, already graduated from the primary school of learning to understand each other and seek solutions in both our own and common interests. The USSR and the United States have built immense nuclear missile arsenals. But they have also managed to realize their responsibility and become the first to conclude an agreement on the reduction and physical elimination of some of those weapons, which threatened our two countries and all the other countries. Our two countries have the greatest and most sophisticated military secrets. But they also have begun and continue to develop a system of mutually verifying the destruction of armaments, their limitation and the ban on their production. Our two countries are accumulating experience for future bilateral and multilateral agreements. We cherish this experience, and we appreciate and value the contribution made by President Ronald Reagan and the members of his administration, especially Mr George Shultz.

All this is capital we have invested in a joint venture of historic significance. It must not be wasted or left idle. The new US administration, to be led by President-elect George Bush, will find in us a partner prepared, without procrastination or backsliding, to continue the dialogue in the spirit of realism, openness and goodwill, and determined to achieve practical results on the agenda which now embraces key issues of Soviet-American relations and international politics. I mean, above all, the consistent advance to a treaty on a 50 per cent reduction in strategic offensive arms with simultaneous observance of the ABM treaty, work to draft a convention to eliminate chemical weapons (we believe that 1989 may become a crucial year in this respect), negotiations on the reduction of conventional arms and armed forces in Europe. I also mean economic, ecological and humanitarian problems in the broadest context . . .

I am concluding my first address to the United Nations with the same feeling that I had when I began it — a feeling of responsibility to my own people and to the world community. We are meeting at the end of a year which has meant so much for the United Nations and on the eve of a year from which we all expect so much. I would like to believe that our hopes will be matched by our joint effort to put an end to an era of wars, confrontation and regional conflicts, to aggressions against nature, to the terror of hunger and poverty as well as to political terrorism. This is our common goal and we can only reach it together. Thank you.

NAMIBIAN INDEPENDENCE AGREEMENTS

Excerpts from the two agreements, one between Cuba and Angola on the withdrawal of Cuban troops from Angola and the other between Angola, Cuba and South Africa on the implementation of UN Security Council Resolution 435 providing for the independence of Namibia, signed at the United Nations in New York on 22 December 1988.

CUBAN-ANGOLAN AGREEMENT ON CUBAN TROOP WITHDRAWAL

The Government of the Republic of Cuba and the Government of the People's Republic of Angola, hereinafter referred to as 'the parties',
Considering
That on 1 April [1989] the implementation of UN Security Council Resolution 435 (1978) on the independence of Namibia will commence,. . .
That, on the same date as the present agreement, a tripartite agreement between the Government of the Republic of Cuba, the Government of the People's Republic of Angola and the Government of the Republic of South Africa, containing the essential elements for the achievement of peace in the south-western region of Africa, is to be signed [see below],. . .
Now therefore hold it to be established
That the conditions have been created which permit the commencement of the return to its homeland of the Cuban military contingent now present in Angolan territory, which has successfully fulfilled its internationalist mission,
And accordingly agree as follows:
Art. 1 The redeployment to the 15th and 13th parallels and the phased and total withdrawal to Cuba of the 50,000-man contingent of Cuban troops dispatched to the People's Republic of Angola shall commence, in accordance with the pace and time-limits established in the annexed timetable, which shall form an integral part of this agreement. The total withdrawal shall be concluded on 1 July 1991.
Art. 2 The Governments of the People's Republic of Angola and the Republic of Cuba reserve the right to modify or alter their obligations arising out of Article 1 of this agreement in the event that flagrant violations of the tripartite agreement are verified.
Art. 3 Both parties, through the Secretary-General of the United Nations, request the Security Council to carry out verification of the redeployment and the phased and total withdrawal of the Cuban troops from the territory of the People's Republic of Angola, and to that end the corresponding protocol shall be agreed upon.
Art. 4 This agreement shall enter into force upon the signature of the tripartite agreement between the Governments of the Republic of Cuba, the People's Republic of Angola and the Republic of South Africa.
DONE on 22 December 1988 at United Nations Headquarters, in duplicate in the Spanish and Portuguese languages, both texts being equally authentic.

For the Republic of Cuba
Isidoro Malmierca Peoli

For the People's Republic of Angola
Afonso Van-Dúnem (Mbinda)

APPENDIX

In compliance with Article 1 of the agreement between the Governments of the Republic of Cuba and the People's Republic of Angola on the conclusion of the internationalist mission of the Cuban military contingent now present in Angolan territory, both parties establish the following timetable for withdrawal:

By 1 April 1989 (day of the commencement of the implementation of Resolution 435 (1978)	3,000 troops
Total duration of the timetable starting from 1 April 1989	27 months
Redeployment northwards:	
To the 15th parallel	1 August 1989
To the 13th parallel	31 October 1989

Total troops to be withdrawn:
By 1 November 1989 — 25,000 (50%)
By 1 April 1990 — 33,000 (66%)
By 1 October 1990 — 38,000 (76%)
By 1 July 1991 — 50,000 (100%)

ANGOLAN-CUBAN-SOUTH AFRICAN AGREEMENT ON NAMIBIA

The Governments of the People's Republic of Angola, the Republic of Cuba, and the Republic of South Africa, hereinafter designated as 'the parties', . . .

Considering the acceptance by the parties of the implementation of UN Security Council Resolution 435 (1978), adopted on 29 September 1978, hereinafter designated as 'UNSCR 435/78',

Considering the conclusion of the bilateral agreement between the People's Republic of Angola and the Republic of Cuba providing for the redeployment toward the north and the staged and total withdrawal of Cuban troops from the territory of the People's Republic of Angola [see above],. . .

Agree to the provisions set forth below.

(1) The parties shall immediately request the Secretary-General of the United Nations to seek authority from the Security Council to commence implementation of UNSCR 435/78 on 1 April 1989.

(2) All military forces of the Republic of South Africa shall depart Namibia in accordance with UNSCR 435/78.

(3) Consistent with the provisions of UNSCR 435/78, the Republic of South Africa and the People's Republic of Angola shall cooperate with the Secretary-General to ensure the independence of Namibia through free and fair elections and shall abstain from any action that could prevent the execution of UNSCR 435/78. The parties shall respect the territorial integrity and inviolability of borders of Namibia and shall ensure that their territories are not used by any state, organization, or person in connection with acts of war, aggression, or violence against the territorial integrity or inviolability of borders of Namibia or any other action which could prevent the execution of UNSCR 435/78.

(4) The People's Republic of Angola and the Republic of Cuba shall implement the bilateral agreement, signed on the date of signature of this agreement, providing for the redeployment toward the north and the staged and total withdrawal of Cuban troops from the territory of the People's Republic of Angola, and the arrangements made with the Security Council of the United Nations for the on-site verification of that withdrawal.

(5) Consistent with their obligations under the Charter of the United Nations, the parties shall refrain from the threat or use of force, and shall ensure that their respective territories are not used by any state, organization, or person in connection with any acts of war, aggression, or violence, against the territorial integrity, inviolability of borders, or independence of any state of south-western Africa.

(6) The parties shall respect the principle of non-interference in the internal affairs of the states of south-western Africa.

(7) The parties shall comply in good faith with all obligations undertaken in this agreement and shall resolve through negotiation and in a spirit of cooperation any disputes with respect to the interpretation or implementation thereof.

(8) This agreement shall enter into force upon signature.

Signed at New York in triplicate in the Portuguese, Spanish and English languages, each language being equally authentic, this 22nd day of December 1988.

For the People's Republic of Angola
Afonso Van-Dúnem (Mbinda)

For the Republic of Cuba
Isidoro Malmierca Peoli

For the Republic of South Africa
R. F. Botha

THE UNITED KINGDOM CONSERVATIVE CABINET

(as at 10 January 1988)

Prime Minister, First Lord of the Treasury and Minister for the Civil Service	Rt. Hon. Margaret Thatcher, FRS, MP
Secretary of State for Foreign and Commonwealth Affairs and Minister of Overseas Development	Rt. Hon. Sir Geoffrey Howe, QC, MP
Chancellor of the Exchequer	Rt. Hon. Nigel Lawson, MP
Lord Chancellor	Rt. Hon. The Lord Mackay of Clashfern
Secretary of State for the Home Department	Rt. Hon. Douglas Hurd, CBE, MP
Secretary of State for Wales	Rt. Hon. Peter Walker, MBE, MP
Secretary of State for Defence	Rt. Hon. George Younger, TD, MP
Secretary of State for Employment	Rt. Hon. Norman Fowler, MP
Secretary of State for Northern Ireland	Rt. Hon. Tom King, MP
Secretary of State for the Environment	Rt. Hon. Nicholas Ridley, MP
Secretary of State for Trade and Industry	Rt. Hon. The Lord Young of Graffham
Secretary of State for Education and Science	Rt. Hon. Kenneth Baker, MP
Chancellor of the Duchy of Lancaster and Minister for Trade and Industry	Rt. Hon. Kenneth Clarke, QC, MP
Minister of Agriculture, Fisheries and Food	Rt. Hon. John MacGregor, OBE, MP
Secretary of State for Scotland	Rt. Hon. Malcolm Rifkind, QC, MP
Secretary of State for Transport	Rt. Hon. Paul Channon, MP
Secretary of State for Social Services	Rt. Hon. John Moore, MP
Lord President of the Council and Leader of the House of Commons	Rt. Hon. John Wakeham, MP
Lord Privy Seal and Leader of the House of Lords	Rt. Hon. The Lord Belstead
Secretary of State for Energy	Rt. Hon. Cecil Parkinson, MP
Chief Secretary to the Treasury	Rt. Hon. John Major, MP

(as at 31 December 1988)

Prime Minister, First Lord of the Treasury and Minister for the Civil Service	Rt. Hon. Margaret Thatcher, FRS, MP
Secretary of State for Foreign and Commonwealth Affairs and Minister of Overseas Development	Rt. Hon. Sir Geoffrey Howe, QC, MP
Chancellor of the Exchequer	Rt. Hon. Nigel Lawson, MP
Lord Chancellor	Rt. Hon. The Lord Mackay of Clashfern
Secretary of State for the Home Department	Rt. Hon. Douglas Hurd, CBE, MP
Secretary of State for Wales	Rt. Hon. Peter Walker, MBE, MP
Secretary of State for Defence	Rt. Hon. George Younger, TD, MP
Secretary of State for Employment	Rt. Hon. Norman Fowler, MP
Secretary of State for Northern Ireland	Rt. Hon. Tom King, MP
Secretary of State for the Environment	Rt. Hon. Nicholas Ridley, MP
Secretary of State for Trade and Industry	Rt. Hon. The Lord Young of Graffham
Secretary of State for Education and Science	Rt. Hon. Kenneth Baker, MP
Secretary of State for Health	Rt. Hon. Kenneth Clarke, QC, MP
Minister of Agriculture, Fisheries and Food	Rt. Hon. John MacGregor, OBE, MP
Secretary of State for Scotland	Rt. Hon. Malcolm Rifkind, QC, MP
Secretary of State for Transport	Rt. Hon. Paul Channon, MP
Secretary of State for Social Security	Rt. Hon. John Moore, MP
Lord President of the Council and Leader of the House of Commons	Rt. Hon. John Wakeham, MP
Lord Privy Seal and Leader of the House of Lords	Rt. Hon. The Lord Belstead
Secretary of State for Energy	Rt. Hon. Cecil Parkinson, MP
Chief Secretary to the Treasury	Rt. Hon. John Major, MP
Chancellor of the Duchy of Lancaster and Minister of Trade and Industry	Rt. Hon. Antony Newton, OBE, MP

THE UNITED STATES REPUBLICAN CABINET

(as at 31 December 1988)

Secretary of Agriculture	Richard E. Lyng
Secretary of Commerce	C. William Verity Jr
Secretary of Defense	Frank C. Carlucci
Secretary of Education	Lauro Cavazos
Secretary of Energy	John S. Herrington
Secretary of Health & Human Services	Otis R. Bowen
Secretary of Housing & Urban Development	Samuel R. Pierce Jr
Secretary of the Interior	Donald Paul Hodel
The Attorney-General	Richard L. Thornburgh
Secretary of Labor	Ann Dore McLaughlin
Secretary of State	George P. Shultz
Secretary of Transportation	James H. Burnley IV
Secretary of the Treasury	Nicholas Brady

CABINET RANK MEMBERS

Vice-President	George Bush
Director of the Central Intelligence Agency	William H. Webster
Director of the Office of Management & Budget	Joseph R. Wright Jr
US Ambassador to the United Nations	Vernon A. Walters
US Trade Representative	Clayton Yeutter
Chief of Staff & Assistant to the President	Kenneth Duberstein
Chairman of Council of Economic Advisers	Beryl W. Sprinkel
President's Assistant for National Security Affairs	Colin Powell

OBITUARY

Abubakar III, Sultan of Sokoto (b. 1903), was a powerful influence in Northern Nigeria throughout his 50 years on the throne. He maintained a simple way of life and a traditional role in government, always conciliatory and open to his subjects. Died 1 November

Addams, Charles (b. 1912), US cartoonist, created in his drawings for the *New Yorker*, over 30 years, the sinister Addams family and their decaying home, which became famous all over the world. Died 29 September

Alvarez, Professor Luis Walter (b. 1911), US scientist, won the Nobel prize for physics in 1968 for his work on nuclear particles. He was professor of physics at the University of California 1945–78. His wide range of interests and activity included aeronautical radar, the atom bomb, palaeontology and electronic monitoring of golf swing. Died 1 September

Andrewes, Sir Christopher, FRS (b. 1896), British physician, was director of the World Influenza Centre 1947–61, and leader of research into the virology of the common cold. Died 31 December

Annigoni, Pietro (b. 1910), Italian artist, sprang from relative obscurity to instant fame in 1955 with his portrait of Queen Elizabeth II in Garter robes. Thereafter he painted other royal and eminent figures, including the Duke of Edinburgh, President Kennedy and Dame Margot Fonteyn; in later life he concentrated on frescoes in the classical tradition for Italian churches. Died 28 October

Arias Madrid, Dr Arnulfo (b. 1901), was three times President of Panama (1940–41, 1949–51 and 1968), but each time was ousted by a military coup, in the last case after only 11 days in office. The intervals he spent in gaol or in exile. His ejection in 1941 had been engineered by the USA because of his pro-Axis policies. Died 10 August

Armstrong, Henry (b. 1913), US boxer, in 1938 simultaneously featherweight, lightweight and welterweight champion of the world. Died 22 October

Arup, Sir Ove (b. 1895), was an engineer who left a strong personal mark upon the architecture of his time throughout the world. Born in England, he was Danish by descent and took his degree in engineering in Copenhagen in 1922. His post as designer to a Danish engineering firm brought him to London, where he became director of several engineering firms, including one of his own. After World War II he set up as a consulting engineer and founded Ove Arup and Partners, whose activity and fame became worldwide. The Sydney Opera House was among the notable buildings for which he was engineering consultant. In 1966 he was awarded the Royal Gold Medal of the RIBA. Died 5 February

Ashton, Sir Frederick, OM, CH (b. in Peru 1904), British choreographer, had determined in childhood to be a ballet dancer, and eventually, against family opposition, studied under Massine and Marie Rambert. His genius for choreography soon found scope, and in 1931 he had vast success with *Façade*, which married the talents of himself, William Walton, Edith Sitwell, Lydia Lopokova and Alicia Markova. For the Vic–Wells Ballet, with which he stayed through its elevation to the Royal Ballet for the rest of his life, he made *Regatta* (1932), *Les Rendezvous* (1933), *Wedding Bouquet* (1937) and *Les Patineurs* (1937), among other works. The list of his later ballets include some of the finest of the century: *Symphonic Variations, Cinderella, Ondine, La Fille Mal Gardée, The Two Pigeons, Daphnis and Chloe, Romeo and Juliet.* He was artistic director of the Royal Ballet 1948–63, and its director 1963–70, but long after his formal retirement he continued to invent new ballets and even to dance. He also produced operas and choreographed films and plays. Many critics ranked him above Balanchine as the world's greatest choreographer of the twentieth century. Died 18 August

Balfour of Inchrye, Lord (Harold Balfour), British airman and politician, Under-Secretary of State for Air 1938–44. Died 21 September

Ballard, Lucien (b. 1904), outstanding US film cameraman. Died 1 October

Baroda, former Maharajah of, (Lieut.-Col. Fatesinghrao Gaekwad, b. 1930), lost his throne in 1971 when Mrs Gandhi's Government abolished the titles and privileges of the Indian princes. Immensely rich, he worked as politician, industrialist and conservator of wild life, and, himself a first-class cricketer, was president of India's cricket board of control 1963–66. Died 1 September

Bellisario, Marisa (b. 1934?), Italian businesswoman, managing director of Italel. Died 4 August

Bhattacharya, Bhabani (b. 1906), Bengali novelist, winner in 1966 of India's highest literary award. Died 9 October

Bikaner, former Maharaja of (Karni Singhji Bahadur, b. 1924), Indian politician (MP 1952–77) and sportsman. Died 4 September

Blaisdell, Thomas C. (b. 1895), US economist, was chief of the US Mission for Economic Affairs in London in 1945, and then as Assistant Secretary of Commerce helped to frame the Marshall Plan. Died December

Brake, Brian (b. 1927), New Zealand photographer, first sprang to world fame in 1960 with his marvellous collection of colour pictures of the Indian monsoon. He specialized in Asian and Australasian subjects. Died 4 August

Brewster, Kingman (b. 1919), US academic, was educated at Yale and Harvard universities and ended life as head of an Oxford college. Meanwhile he had been assistant professor, from 1953 professor, of law at Harvard 1950–60, Provost of Yale 1960–63, and its President 1963–77. There followed four years as US ambassador in London, and in 1985 his election as Master of University College, Oxford. Died 8 November

Brockway, Lord (Archibald Fenner Brockway) (b. 1888), was the outstanding British militant pacifist of his generation. In World War I he was repeatedly sent to prison for his challenges to conscription. A member of the far-left Independent Labour Party from 1912, Brockway was a Labour MP 1929–31 and 1950–64, when he was given a life peerage. Among the movements with which he had been closely linked were No More War, United Socialist States of Europe, the Congress of Peoples Against Imperialism, the Campaign for Nuclear Disarmament and the World Disarmament Campaign. His statue stands in Red Lion Square, London. Died 28 April

Carlsson, Bernt (b. 1938), Swedish Social Democrat and diplomat, UN Commissioner for Namibia from July 1987, formerly general secretary of the Socialist International 1976–83 and Swedish roving ambassador and junior minister 1983–87. Died in the Lockerbie air disaster 21 December

Chiang Ching-kuo (b. 1910), was President of Taiwan from 1978 until his death. The son of Chiang Kai-shek, he became the Generalissimo's political heir and virtual deputy as dictator after the retreat of the Kuomintang to Taiwan in 1949. Sent to Moscow in 1925 to learn military science and engineering, he had remained in Russia until 1937, when he returned to China a dedicated anti-communist but an equally ruthless authoritarian. In high office he was one of the leaders of Taiwan's advance to administrative and military modernity and economic success. In 1969 he was made Deputy Premier and in 1972 Premier (President of the Executive Yuan), and three years after his father's death was elected President. He lifted martial law in 1987, some 38 years after it was first imposed. Died 13 January

Clements, Sir John (b. 1910), British classical actor and theatrical director/manager. Died 6 April

Coutts, Sir Walter (b. 1912), governor 1961–62 and governor-general 1962–63 of Uganda. Died 4 November

Daniel, Yuli (b. 1925), Russian satirist and poet, was tried, along with Andrei Sinyavsky, on charges of literary slander of the Soviet Union, and in 1966 was sentenced, despite international protests, to five years in prison or labour camps. Died 30 December

Dart, Professor Raymond (b. in Australia 1893), was professor of anatomy (1923–58) at Witwatersrand University, South Africa, when in 1924 he identified fossil bones unearthed in Bechuanaland as those of an anthropoid baboon forming a link between apes and men, and implying that southern Africa was the cradle of mankind. From 1966 he was professor of anthropology at the Institute of Achievement of Human Potential in Philadelphia. Died 22 November

Dorati, Antal (b. 1906), Hungarian-born conductor, took US citizenship in 1947, having forestalled Nazi oppression by emigrating first to Paris (1933) and then to New York (1941). He had been taught by both Bartók and Kodály, and Hungarian music was one of his specialities, along with Haydn. He had been principal conductor of the Münster Opera 1929–32, musical director of the Ballets Russes de Monte Carlo 1933–39, Ballet Theater of New York 1939–43, the Dallas (1945–49) and Minneapolis (1949–60) Symphony Orchestras; and principal conductor of the BBC Symphony Orchestra 1963–66, the Stockholm Philharmonic Orchestra 1966–74, and the Royal Philharmonic Orchestra 1975–78. Died 13 November

Downie, Professor Allan, FRS (b. 1901), British virologist, was as much responsible as anyone for the eradication of smallpox which the WHO proclaimed in 1978. In 1943 he became professor of bacteriology at Liverpool University, where he devoted 30 years to the study of smallpox, in cooperation with the WHO. Died 26 January

Drees, Dr Willem, hon. GCMG (b. 1887), was Prime Minister of the Netherlands 1948–58. It was a difficult time for his country, which was still striving to recover from the German occupation in World War II and to halt the loss of its colonial empire in S.E. Asia. Drees, a moderate socialist, achieved economic stability, inaugurated a social security system, and realistically resigned the sovereignty of the Dutch East Indies to the Republic of Indonesia. During World War II he led the coordination of underground political movements. Died 20 May

Eldridge, Florence (b. McKechnie 1902), US actress, married Frederic March in 1928, and they moved into fame together, playing the leading parts in such plays as *Long Day's Journey into Night*, *The Skin of Our Teeth* and *Another Part of the Forest*, and in films like *Les Misérables* and *Mary of Scotland*. But she was a stage star in her own right, and as Mary Tyrone in O'Neill's *Long Day's Journey* (1956) the New York critics named her best actress of the year. Died 1 August

Evans, Dr William (b. 1896), Welsh cardiologist of world-wide fame. Died 20 September

Eyskens, Gaston (b. 1905), was three times Christian Democratic Prime Minister of Belgium, in 1949–50, 1958–61 and 1968–73. A professor of economics at the University of Louvain, he was elected to the Chamber of Representatives in 1919; in 1965 he became a Senator. After action in the Resistance during World War II he became Minister of Finance in 1945, an office to which he returned in 1947–49 and 1965–66. During his second term as Prime Minister his Government ceded independence to the Belgian Congo. Retiring from politics in 1973, he became president of the Kredietbank. Died 3 January

Faure, Edgar (b. 1908), was twice Prime Minister of France, in 1952 and 1955–56. A brilliant scholar, in 1928 he became the youngest-ever member of the Paris Bar. After the fall of France he joined de Gaulle in Algeria. Elected as Radical Party deputy in 1946, he held a number of offices in the Fourth Republic, including the Finance Ministry, as well as the Premiership. De Gaulle made him Minister of Agriculture 1966–68 and then Minister of Education, with the task of reforming the university system after the student revolts of 1968. He was Minister of Social Affairs 1972–73 and President of the National Assembly 1973–78. In 1979 he rejoined the Radicals and was a member of the European Parliament 1979–81. He had been elected to the Académie Française in 1978. Died 30 March

Ferranti, Basil de, MEP (b. 1930), joined the Ferranti electronics firm in 1950 and eventually became its chairman. After a brief interval as Conservative MP and junior Minister he became managing director of a leading manufacturer of computers, for which he perceived a visionary future. Elected to the European Parliament in 1979, he again sought to play a prophetic role as fervent advocate of the single European market. Died 24 September

Ferrari, Enzo (b. 1898), Italian motor engineer and racing driver, became a test driver after service in the artillery in World War I, but he was soon able to add, for Alfa Romeo, his engineering and managerial skills to those of the racing track, and he gave up race driving himself in 1932. His work on aero engines and machine tools in World War II helped him to set up as racing car constructor. In 1951 a Formula One Ferrari won the British Grand Prix at Silverstone, and by 1988 Ferraris had won 93 Grands Prix as well as eight constructors' world championships. Although he sold his company to Fiat in 1965, he retained a close interest in all Ferrari models and stayed in personal control of the racing team. Died 14 August

Feynman, Professor Richard (b. 1918), US scientist, shared with two others the 1965 Nobel prize for physics for their work in quantum electrodynamics, then a comparatively new scientific tool which he sharpened and simplified. After teaching at Cornell University, he became professor of theoretical physics at the California Institute of Technology, where his fame grew as an excellent communicator as much in the public media as in the classroom. He was a member of the team which produced the atom bomb and of the presidential commission of inquiry into the *Challenger* disaster. Died 15 February

OBITUARY

Fornasetti, Piero (b. 1913), Italian designer, was closely associated with the architect Gio Ponti for a quarter of a century from World War II onwards; his fecund, often surrealist, ideas were translated into many products, from silk scarves to china plates, which sold all over the world. Died 15 October

Frenay, Henri (b. 1906), French resistance hero, was an army captain at the start of World War II. Although working with General de Gaulle after 1942, and receiving ministerial office from him after the liberation, they were rivals, and remained so after Frenay's retirement from politics in 1946, opposing as he did the General's 'haughty nationalism' and hostility to socialism. Died 6 August

Fuchs, Dr Klaus (b. 1911), betrayed the secrets of the atom bomb to the Russians after serving (1943–46) on the British Atomic Energy Commission team at Los Alamos; and continued to do so as a member of the Commission's research staff. Though suspect, he was repeatedly whitewashed by Sir Roger Hollis, the head of MI5. In 1949 Fuchs confessed under interrogation, and after trial was sentenced to 14 years in prison. A German from Frankfurt, he had been a member of the Communist Party since 1930; fleeing from the Nazi regime in 1934, he came to Britain, took his doctorate at Edinburgh, was interned and despatched to Canada in World War II, but was allowed to return and became a naturalized British citizen. Released from prison in 1958, he went back to East Germany, where he continued to serve the Soviet bloc as a nuclear research physicist, a prominent Party member and, as he had always been, a rigorous marxist ideologue. Died 28 January

Furstenberg, H.E. Cardinal Maximilien de (b. 1904), though born in the Netherlands was Belgian by family descent and education, and became Rector of the Belgian College in Rome in 1948. Entering the Vatican diplomatic service in the following year as titular archbishop, he served in Japan, Australasia and Portugal, before becoming Head of the Sacred Congregation for Eastern Churches 1968–73. He received the cardinal's hat in 1967. Died September

Ghaffar Khan, Khan Abdul (b. 1890?), popularly dubbed 'the Frontier Gandhi', was a thorn in the flesh of the British Government of India before 1947, and after partition in that of the Government of Pakistan; in all, under the two regimes, he spent over 16 years in prison. With his brother, Dr Khan Sahib, who became Congress chief minister of the N.W. Frontier Province, he led a new party, the Khodai Khidmatgaran, nicknamed the Red Shirts, which was proscribed in 1931. Its philosophy was non-violent, its aim the creation of a separate Pathan state, Pakhtunistan. Not until 1977 did he renounce his separatist agitation. Died 20 January

Goossens, Léon, CBE (b. 1897), British musician, was the foremost oboist of his time. At the age of 17 he became first oboist in Sir Henry Wood's Queen's Hall Orchestra. In World War I he fought as an infantryman and was badly wounded. In 1923 he became a professor at the Royal College of Music and a year later at the Royal Academy of Music. His American debut came in 1928, in New York. He played in the Royal Philharmonic and Covent Garden Orchestras and joined Beecham's London Philharmonic as principal oboist in 1932. Among the composers who wrote music for him were Hindemith, Vaughan Williams, Elgar, Britten, Malcolm Arnold, Bliss, Bax and his brother Eugene Goossens. His technique was impeccable and his style and tone beautiful beyond compare; he was also a fine teacher. Died 12 February

Gorshkov, Admiral Sergei (b. 1910), as commander-in-chief of the Russian navy 1956–85 was credited with turning the Soviet Union into a great naval power. Under Stalin the navy had been little regarded, and Khrushchev believed that nuclear armament should have priority; but Gorshkov, who had held rising command in the Black Sea during World War II, argued that a strong navy was not only effective in upholding national interests all over the globe but also a necessary attribute of any great power. His thesis, expressed publicly in *The Sea Power of the State*, prevailed. In 1965 he was made a Hero of the Soviet Union. Died 13 May

Graham, Sheilah (b. 1904), US author and gossip columnist, mistress and biographer of Scott Fitzgerald. Died 17 November

Grandi, Dino, Count (b. 1895), was a trusted adherent of Mussolini for much of his middle life but eventually helped to accomplish the dictator's downfall. Embracing fascism as a young man, he played an important part in the 1922 March on Rome. Elected to the Chamber of Deputies in 1921, he held office in the subsequent fascist Governments, becoming Foreign Minister in 1929. From 1932 to 1939 he was Italy's ambassador in London, the period of the Abyssinian invasion and the Spanish civil war. Recalled shortly before World War II, he became Minister of Justice and professor of law at Rome University. In July 1943 he introduced in the Fascist Grand Council a motion criticizing Mussolini's conduct of the war and indicating that he should be relieved of his supreme powers: carried by 19 votes to 7, it precipitated the dictator's resignation and flight. Grandi himself fled to Portugal; until 1973, when he returned at last to Italy, he pursued a business career. Died 21 May

Grice, Professor Paul (b. 1913), was greatly admired by philosophers in both his native Britain and the USA. He was a Fellow of St John's College, Oxford, 1939–67 (with a wartime interval in the Royal Navy) and professor of philosophy at the University of California at Berkeley 1967–80. An intellectual perfectionist, he wrote little for publication, but he was an immensely stimulating critic and debater. Died 28 August

Hamengkubuwono IX, Sultan (b. 1912), ninth Sultan of Jogjakarta, Java, occupied one of the few ancient thrones in Indonesia that survived national independence after World War II, perhaps because he had strongly backed the revolutionaries against renewed Dutch colonial rule. He was Vice-President of Indonesia 1973–78. Died 2 October

Hamilton, Sir Denis, DSO (b. 1918), British newspaper man, had a brilliant military career in World War II, ending in command of a regiment at the age of 26. Returning to journalism, his pre-war occupation, he eventually became editorial director of the Kemsley newspaper chain, which in 1959 was sold to Mr Roy Thomson (later Lord Thomson of Fleet). In 1961 he was appointed editor of *The Sunday Times*, and when Thomson bought *The Times* in 1967 Hamilton became chief executive of Times Newspapers. From 1979 he was chairman of Reuters and his negotiation of its public flotation was a final achievement. Died 7 April

Hamilton, Hamish (b. 1900), British publisher, founder of the firm Hamish Hamilton in 1931. Died 24 May

Hancock, Sir Keith, KBE, FBA (b. 1898), Australian historian, was best-known internationally for his volumes in the *Survey of British Commonwealth Affairs* (1937–42), for his editorship of the official history of civil Britain through World War II, to which his own contribution was *British War Economy* (1949), and for his two-volume biography of General Smuts (1962 and 1968). He had been a Fellow of All Souls College, Oxford (1923–30), professor of history at the Universities of Adelaide (1926–34) and Birmingham (1934–41), supervisor of civil histories in the War Cabinet

Office (1941–46), Chichele Professor of Economic History at Oxford (1944–49) and first director of the Institute of Commonwealth Studies in the University of London (1949–56), before returning to his native land as director of the research school of social sciences in the Australian National University (1956–61). When the Australian Academy of Humanities was founded in 1969, he was appropriately honoured with its presidency. Died 13 August

Holmes, Professor John Wendell (b. 1911), Canadian diplomat, was the long-serving director of the Canadian Institute of International Affairs. In that role, and in his previous career in the External Affairs department of the Ottawa Government, he was influential in the development of Canada's foreign policy for half a century. Died 13 August

Household, Geoffrey (b. 1900), British novelist (esp. *Rogue Male* 1939). Died 4 October

Houseman, John (b. in Austria–Hungary 1902), US cinema and theatre producer, director, script-writer and actor, worked with Orson Welles on several famous productions, including the film *Citizen Kane* (1940) and the radio play *The War of the Worlds* (1938) which caused panic among listeners who took it as a report of an actual invasion from Mars. Among Houseman's Hollywood productions were *Julius Caesar* (1953), *Lust for Life* (1956) and *Voyage to America* (1964). As an actor he won an Academy Award for best supporting role in *The Paper Chase* (1974). Entering the theatrical world from a family grain business in 1930, he became head of Negro Theater Project 1934–37 and co-founder of the Mercury Theater in 1937. Among other appointments he was artistic director of the American Shakespeare Festival 1956–59. Died 31 October

Howard, Trevor (b. 1916), British actor, played the London and Stratford stage until after World War II, in which he served in the 1st Airborne Division. He then turned to films and became a star with his part in Noel Coward's *Brief Encounter* (1945). Among later films in which he appeared were *The Third Man* (1949), *An Outcast of the Islands* (1951), *The Heart of the Matter* (1953, perhaps his finest performance), *Sons and Lovers* (1960), *Mutiny on the Bounty* (1962), *Ryan's Daughter* (1970) and *Conduct Unbecoming* (1976). He also acted for television (Emmy award 1963) and returned occasionally to the London stage. Died 7 January

Hulton, Sir Edward (b. 1906), British publisher, who launched *Picture Post* in 1938. Died 8 October

Hunt, General Sir Peter, KCB, DSO (b. 1916), chief of the general staff 1973–76. Died 2 October

Hutchinson, Sir Joseph, CMG, FRS (b. 1902), British plant geneticist, was for many years a member of the advisory board of *The Annual Register*, nominated by the British Association for the Advancement of Science. Much of his career was spent overseas, in Trinidad, India, Uganda, Sudan and East Africa, before he became professor of agriculture at Cambridge in 1957. Died 16 January

Huxley, Sir Leonard (b. 1902), Australian scientist, was Vice-Chancellor of the Australian National University 1960–67 after occupying the Elder chair of physics at Adelaide University 1949–60. Died 4 September

Ikeda, Youson (b. 1896), Japanese artist, concentrated on landscape painting in the traditional Japanese manner, after a period of western-style painting in the 1920s. He received Japan's highest artistic honours, including in 1987, the cultural prize Bunka Kunsho. Died 26 September

Issigonis, Sir Alec, FRS (b. in Turkey 1906), British engineer, was most famed for his design of the Mini motor car, a revolutionary novelty in 1959 and still in production in 1988; but his inventive skill and brilliant engineering produced other highly successful cars. He was a director of the British Motor Corporation 1963–71. Died 2 October

Jacobson, Lord (Sydney), MC (b. 1908), British newspaperman, political editor *Daily Mirror* 1952–62, editor *Daily Herald* 1962–64 and *Sun* 1964–65, editorial director IPC Newspapers 1968–74, deputy chairman 1973–75. Died 13 August

Jewkes, Professor John, CBE (b. 1902), British economist, was a powerful exponent of free market economics. Among his published books were *Ordeal by Planning* (1948), *Sources of Invention* (1958) and *The Genesis of the National Health Service* (1961). He was professor of economic organization at Oxford 1948–69. Died 18 August

Jha, Lakshmi (b. 1913), was one of India's ablest civil servants, well known and admired in the wider world, especially as Indian representative on GATT (chairman 1957–58), Governor of the Reserve Bank of India 1967–70, ambassador to Washington 1970–73 and deputy chairman of the Brandt Commission 1977–81. Among other high posts that he held were those of Finance Secretary 1960–64 and Governor of Kashmir 1973–80. He was secretary to the Prime Minister 1964–67 and remained the trusted economic adviser of both Mrs Indira Gandhi and her son Rajiv. Died 16 January

Joffrey, Robert (b. A.J.A.B. Khan 1930), US dancer and choreographer, founded in 1956, with Gerald Arpino, the Joffrey Ballet company, which from small beginnings became an admired part of the American ballet scene. Died 25 March

Kiesinger, Dr Kurt Georg (b. 1904), was Chancellor of the Federal Republic of Germany 1966–69. A lawyer by profession, he joined the Nazi Party in 1933 and remained a member throughout the Hitler period. He entered federal politics in 1949, but in 1957 became premier of Baden-Württemberg. In 1966 he was the compromise figure chosen to head the 'grand coalition' of Christian Democrats (CDU/CSU) and Social Democrats. After the victory of Willy Brandt in 1969, he continued for two years as chairman of the CDU but then retired to the Bundestag backbenches, where he sat until 1980. Died 9 March

Laski, Marghanita (b. 1915), British novelist, playwright, critic and broadcaster. Died 6 February

Lee of Asheridge, Baroness (Jennie Lee), PC (b. 1904), British Labour politician, Minister for the Arts 1964–70, widow of Aneurin Bevan. Died 16 November

Leiris, Mme Louise (b. 1902), French art gallery owner, was, along with her brother-in-law Daniel-Henry Kahnweiler, the great patron and marketer of the work of Pablo Picasso, among other contemporary artists. In 1984 she, Kahnweiler and her husband, a distinguished ethnologist, gave an unrivalled collection, bearing their two names, of some 200 works of art to the Museum of Modern Art in the Centre Beaubourg. Died 24 September

Loewe, Frederick (Fritz), (b. 1901), US composer, was indelibly linked in the public mind with the librettist Alan Jay Lerner (d. 1986). The Loewe–Lerner partnership began in 1942 with *Life of the Party* and burst into immense success with *Brigadoon* (1947) followed by *Paint Your Wagon* (1951), *My Fair Lady* (1956), *Gigi* (1958) and *Camelot* (1960). In earlier life Loewe, born of a stage family, had been a concert pianist, without much success, and had earned his living by playing the piano in beer halls and the organ in cinemas. Died 14 February

Losev, Sergei (b. 1927), director-general of the Soviet press agency Tass. Died 31 August

MacBride, Seán (b. 1904), Irish politician and internationalist, won the Nobel prize for peace in 1974 for his work as a founder member of Amnesty International and its chairman 1970–73, secretary-general of the International Commission of Jurists 1963–70 and United Nations Commissioner for Namibia 1973–76. He had inherited an intense Irish nationalism from his father, who was executed after the 1916 rebellion, and his mother, the famous Maud Gonne. He rejected the Anglo–Irish treaty of 1921, fought in the ensuing civil war and opposed de Valera's return to constitutionalism in 1926. However, he forsook the IRA in the late 1930s and led a new republican party in the Daíl, becoming Minister for External Affairs 1948–51 in a coalition Government which severed all Eire's links with the Commonwealth and declared the Republic of Ireland. He lost his seat in 1957 and left national politics to champion wider causes. Died 15 January

McCracken, James (b. 1927), American tenor, famed for his Otello. Died 29 April

McMahon, Rt. Hon. Sir William, CH (b. 1908), was Prime Minister of Australia 1971–72. A lawyer by profession, in 1949 he won for the Liberal Party a seat in the Commonwealth Parliament which he held until his retirement in 1982. Though highly successful as a Minister (Treasurer 1966–69 and Minister for Foreign Affairs 1969–71), as Prime Minister he won little applause, and after electoral defeat of the Liberal–Country coalition he was quickly replaced as party leader. Died 31 March

Magnus-Allcroft, Sir Philip, Bt (Philip Magnus) (b. 1906), biographer of Edward VII, Gladstone, Kitchener and others. Died 21 December

Malenkov, Georgiy (b. 1902), was Prime Minister of the USSR 1953–55, having succeeded Stalin as Chairman of the Council of Ministers; but he very soon lost power to Khrushchev, the First Secretary of the Party, while remaining Deputy Prime Minister under Bulganin. Malenkov, a Party member from the age of 18, was closely associated with Stalin and with his ruthless purges from the late 1920s onwards. Having served in Stalin's 'War Cabinet' during World War II, he became a member of the Politburo and Deputy Prime Minister in 1946 and from 1948 was 'number two' to Stalin in the Soviet hierarchy. This personal history was the background to his struggle with Khrushchev in 1957. The latter's victory put an end to Malenkov's political career; expelled from the Politburo and the Central Committee, he spent the rest of his life in obscurity. Died 1 February

Marchand, Senator the Rt. Hon. Jean (b. 1918), Canadian trade unionist and politician, was an ardent advocate of bilingualism and opponent of Quebec separatism. Elected a federal MP in 1965, he was a Minister in Liberal Cabinets from that date until his resignation in 1976, and became a Senator in 1977. Died 28 August

Marshall, Rt. Hon. Sir John, GBE, CH (b. 1908), was Prime Minister of New Zealand for nine months in 1972 before his National Party suffered electoral defeat. He had previously been a Cabinet Minister (for Health, Justice, Overseas Trade, Customs, Industry and Labour) for a total of 18 years, and deputy leader of the Opposition for three years. As Minister of Overseas Trade he negotiated New Zealand's relatively favourable agreement with the EEC when the UK joined the Community in 1973. Died 30 August

Massigli, René (b. 1888), was ambassador of France in London 1944–54 and head of the French Foreign Office 1954–56. His diplomatic career had begun in the secretariats of the Versailles peace conference, the Council of Ambassadors, the Washington Conference of 1921 and the Geneva Conference of 1922. In 1928 he was appointed head of the League of Nations section at the Quai d'Orsay, and in 1937 director of its political section. When World War II broke out he was French ambassador in Turkey; later the Vichy Government dismissed him on Nazi orders. In hiding after the Germans occupied all France, he was rescued by the RAF and joined de Gaulle, who made him commissioner for foreign affairs in the provisional government in Algiers, and then ambassador. From 1958 to 1969 he was French president of the Channel Tunnel Study Group. Among his many honours were those of honorary Companion of Honour, GCVO and KBE. Died 3 February

Melen, Ferit (b. 1906), was Prime Minister of Turkey 1972–73, installed by a military coup and ousted by Mr Bülent Ecevit after a general election. A founder member of a small right-wing party, he had been Minister of Finance 1962–65 and of National Defence 1971–72, and was again Defence Minister 1975–77. Died 3 September

Mendez, Dr Aparicio (b. 1904), was President of Uruguay 1976–81, a civilian figurehead and tame instrument for a military regime which imposed severe restraints on democracy and human rights. Died 27 June

Miki, Takeo (b. 1907), was Prime Minister of Japan 1974–76. His tenure was marked by his campaign against corruption in high places, especially in connection with the Lockheed Aircraft scandal. He had been elected MP in 1937 and held his seat for 51 years. Rich and well-connected, he had courageously resisted the rise of Japanese militarism. Under the post-war constitution, as a leader of the centre-left wing of the conservative Liberal–Democratic Party, he held important ministerial offices, including those of Foreign Minister 1966–68 and deputy Prime Minister 1972–74. Died 8 November

Mitchell, John (b. 1913), American lawyer, US Attorney-General 1969–72, a close associate of President Nixon, was convicted of conspiracy, perjury and obstruction of justice in the cover-up of White House involvement in the Watergate scandal, and served 19 months in prison. He became Mr Nixon's presidential campaign manager in 1969 and again in 1972, shortly before the Watergate break-in. Died 9 November

Mooney, Rt. Rev. Sylvester, OSB (b. 1886), English monk, was Abbot of Douai for forty years, 1929–69. He had been a pupil at Douai when the Benedictine community was expelled from France to England in 1903. Successive Popes honoured his silver jubilee as Abbot and his 100th birthday. Died 5 September

Mravinsky, Yevgeny (b. 1906), was the leading Soviet orchestral conductor for half a century, as chief conductor of the Leningrad Philharmonic from 1938 until his death. He often conducted in Britain and elsewhere abroad, and his renderings of Tchaikovsky and Shostakovich particularly won the applause of the musical world. Died 21 January

Muhammad bin Abdul Aziz, Prince (b. 1908?), was a son of King Ibn Saud, founder of Saudi Arabia. Opposed to Ibn Saud's successor, he strongly supported King Faisal who next took the Saudi throne. Prince Muhammad's

Islamic fundamentalism led him to order the execution of a princess, his granddaughter, for adultery, an episode captured in a film which caused an international furore. Died 25 November

Mulder, Dr Connie (b. 1925), was one of South Africa's most powerful politicians until, in 1978, he was inculpated in the misuse of government funds for the undercover promotion of apartheid. Having first held ministerial office in 1968, from 1972 to 1978 he was Minister of the Interior and of Information and was widely expected to succeed Dr Vorster as Prime Minister, but the 'Muldergate' scandal brought his resignation and eventually the loss of his parliamentary seat. In 1987 he returned as an extreme right-wing MP. Died 12 January

Noguchi, Isamu (b. 1904), US artist of Japanese ancestry, was famed as much for making gardens (notably at the Chase Manhattan Plaza, New York, and Unesco, Paris) and for his designs for domestic objects and the theatre as for his sculpture. Died 30 December

Norstad, General Lauris (b. 1907), US air force officer, was Nato's Supreme Allied Commander Europe (Saceur) 1956–62. After distinguished service in World War II, he took command of Nato air forces in Central Europe in 1951, then of all Nato air forces as deputy to General Eisenhower. As Saceur he promoted a forward strategic policy, first with conventional forces and, if they failed, with tactical nuclear weapons. In retirement Norstad became chairman and chief executive of the Owens–Corning Fibreglass Corporation. Died 12 September

Ofori-Atta, William (b. 1910), Ghanaian politician, Foreign Minister 1970–72. Died 14 July

Onassis, Christina (b. 1950), heiress to half the immense fortune of her father, the Greek shipowner Aristotle Onassis, who died 1975. Died 19 November

O'Neill, Sir Con, GCMG (b. 1912), British career diplomatist, resigned from the Foreign Service in 1939 in protest against 'appeasement' policy, was re-established after World War II and headed the official team which negotiated UK membership of European Communities 1969–72. Died 11 January

Paton, Alan (b. 1903), South African author and politician, earned instant worldwide fame as an opponent of apartheid with his novel *Cry, the Beloved Country*, published in 1948. It became the material first of a musical play and later of a film. A schoolmaster by profession, he had spent 13 years as principal of a reformatory for delinquent boys near Johannesburg. In 1958 he founded the Liberal Party of South Africa, but was obliged to close it down ten years later. His later books included a second novel, *Too Late the Phalarope* (1953), a life of Jan Hofmeyr (1964) and a two-volume autobiography. He was inspired throughout his life by a profound Christian faith. Died 12 April

Peart, Lord (Fred), PC (b. 1914), British Labour politician, Minister of Agriculture 1964–68 and 1974–76. Died 26 August

Perrin, Sir Michael (b. in Canada 1906), British scientist, was one of the experts who worked on the invention of the atomic bomb during World War II; afterwards he served alongside Sir John Cockcroft, Sir Christopher Hinton and Sir William Penney on the development of atomic energy. In 1950 he received from Klaus Fuchs (*q.v.*) the startling confession of Fuchs's comprehensive disclosure of Anglo-American atomic secrets to the USSR. From 1953 to 1970 Perrin was chairman of the Wellcome Foundation. Died 18 August

Peterson, Alec (A.D.C.) (b. 1908), British educationist, was an outstanding pioneer of international education. He led the creation of an international baccalaureat (university entrance qualification) and was the first director-general of its Geneva bureau 1967–77. He was also involved in the founding and conduct of Atlantic College in Wales and the United World Colleges. By profession a school teacher, he was director of education at Oxford University 1958–73. Died 17 October

Pham Hung (b. 1913), died in office as Prime Minister of Vietnam. A communist activist from boyhood, he was sentenced to death by the French colonial regime in 1931; reprieved to serve hard labour for life, he was released in the 1945 uprising, and though a southerner he joined the communists of North Vietnam. After Dien Bien Phu and the Geneva Pact of 1954, he joined the Politburo of North Vietnam and as a deputy Prime Minister played a major part in the subsequent guerrilla war against the South and its US allies. Upon the US withdrawal he became Vietnam's Minister of the Interior, wielding enormous police power, and in June 1987 assumed the prime ministership. Died 10 March

Philby, H.A.R., known as Kim after Kipling's boy hero (b. 1912), British intelligence agent and journalist, betrayed his country and his colleagues on an unexcelled scale. In the 1930s, already a dedicated communist and managed by the KGB, he established his cover as a conservative journalist, gained admittance to the MI6 counter-intelligence service and rose in rank until in 1949 he became its link with the CIA in Washington. Suspected, correctly, of being the 'third man' who enabled the spies Guy Burgess and Donald Maclean to escape to Russia in 1951, he was dismissed but never charged, and from 1956 he continued to assist his Soviet masters while working as a press correspondent in Beirut. In 1956, under pressure to confess, he disappeared, to emerge six months later in Moscow, where he worked, now a Soviet hero, as adviser to the KGB. Died 11 May

Ponnelle, Jean-Pierre (b. 1932), French operatic producer, insisted, after reaching international fame as director of operas, on filling also the role of designer. As such, he was widely criticized for extravagant and distracting stage inventions. However, from 1968 onwards he was greatly in demand by the principal opera houses, and he worked fruitfully with such conductors as Abbado, Karajan, Boehm and Barenboim. Died 11 August

Pressburger, Emeric (b. in Hungary 1902), formed a partnership with the British film director Michael Powell which produced 16 films, among them *49th Parallel, One of Our Aircraft is Missing, A Canterbury Tale, The Red Shoes, The Tales of Hoffmann* and *Ill Met by Moonlight.* In 1942, they had formed their own production company, the Archers, which was dissolved some 20 years later. Pressburger's early life had been spent in Central Europe—he was a scriptwriter for the Ufa studio in Berlin—but, fleeing from the Nazi regime, he settled in England from 1935. Died 5 February

Rabi, Dr Isidor (b. in Austria 1898), won the Nobel prize for physics in 1944 for his work on the properties of atomic nuclei. His knowledge had been invaluable in the making of the first atomic bomb, but his work also had less destructive applications in the fields of radar, laser technology, diagnostic medicine and satellite guidance, among others. He initiated President Eisenhower's atoms-for-peace programme, and helped to create the European Centre for Nuclear Research (CERN). Died 11 January

Ramsey of Canterbury, Rt. Rev. Lord, PC (b. 1904), as Dr Michael Ramsey was Archbishop of Canterbury 1961–74. A theologian rather than an administrator, thinker rather than an activist or diplomat, he brought to the Anglican Church spiritual leadership, but he failed in one of his ambitions, Anglican–Methodist reunion. His visit to the Pope in 1966, the first by an English primate since the Reformation, was another signal of his quest for unity among the Christian churches. He recognized that Christian theology had to tread new paths in the modern scientific world. Pastorally, he became a champion of the rights of coloured peoples and of the poor everywhere. He was professor of divinity at Durham 1940–50, Regius professor of divinity at Cambridge 1950–52, Bishop of Durham 1952–56 and Archbishop of York 1956–61. Died 23 April

Ross of Marnock, Lord, PC (William Ross), (b. 1911), British Labour politician, Secretary of State for Scotland 1964–70, 1974–76. Died 10 June

Rothschild, Baron Philippe de (b. 1902), French wine-grower, sportsman, theatrical director and man of letters, inherited Château Mouton Rothschild, of which he had been manager for 25 years, in 1947, and raised it to a peak of fame among lovers of claret. A member of the French branch of the Jewish Rothschild family, in the 1920s he was in the top rank of racing drivers and ocean yachtsmen. In World War II, after the fall of France, he joined General de Gaulle in London; his first wife died in a Nazi concentration camp. Among his literary output were translations of Elizabethan poems and plays and a volume of his own poems, *Le Pressoir Perdu*. In the theatre he directed the Théâtre Pigalle 1928–31, and founded the repertory Cartel des Quatre. He held the Croix de Guerre and the Commandership of the Légion d'Honneur. Died 20 January

Salem, General Mamdouh Mohamed (b. 1918), was Prime Minister of Egypt 1975–78. He had been police commander in Alexandria 1946–68, Governor of Assiut 1968–70, Minister of the Interior and Deputy Prime Minister 1971–75. After losing the prime ministership he became personal assistant to successive Presidents Sadat and Mubarak. Died 25 February

Saragat, Giuseppe (b. 1898), was President of Italy 1964–71. After serving in World War I he joined the Socialist Party and spent the Mussolini years in exile in Vienna and Paris. Returning after the liberation, he was appointed ambassador to France 1945–47. The Italian socialists were then split between those led by Saragat, who favoured cooperation with the Christian Democrats, and those led by Pietro Nenni who leant towards the Communists. In 1947 Saragat formed his own Social Democratic Party, which entered successive coalition Governments. He was Minister of Merchant Marine 1947–49, Deputy Prime Minister 1947–49 and 1954–57, and Foreign Minister 1963–64. Elected to the presidency in 1964 after 21 ballots, he sought to keep the political centre of gravity in the centre-left, and to promote the European Community. Died 11 June

Sardinias, Eligio (b. 1911), Cuban boxer known as 'Kid' Chocolate, world featherweight and junior lightweight champion in the early 1930s. Died 8 August

Scorza, Carlo (b. 1897), Italian politician, close ally of Mussolini, was the last secretary of the Fascist Party in 1943. Died 23 December

Scott, Sheila (b. 1927), British aviator, flew round the globe in a light aircraft in 1966, and thereafter set many records for light-aircraft flights, including London–Cape Town (1967), London–New York and back (1969), London–Nairobi and Johannesburg–London (1969) and equator to equator over the North Pole (1971). Died 20 October

Seefried, Irmgard (b. in Germany 1919), Austrian soprano, interpreter esp. of Mozart and Strauss. Died 24 November

Sieghart, Paul (b. 1927), Austrian-born British lawyer, a persistent champion of human rights and successful promoter of such legislation as the Data Protection Act, was chairman of the executive of the International Commission of Jurists (British section) and a member of the (Catholic) Bishops' Commission for International Justice and Peace. Died 12 December

Silkin of Dulwich, Lord (Samuel Silkin), PC, QC (b. 1918), British Labour politician and lawyer, Attorney-General 1974–79. Died 17 August

Simon, Dr Ernst (b. in Germany 1899), Israeli academic, became a Zionist in 1918 and ten years later emigrated to Palestine, but throughout his life he worked for Arab–Jewish understanding. He became professor of philosophy and the history of education at the Hebrew University and in 1967 was awarded the Israel Prize, his country's highest honour. Died 18 August

Singh, Dr Nagendra (b. 1914), Indian civil servant and lawyer, was a judge of the International Court of Justice from 1973, and its vice-president 1976–79. Qualified as a barrister in England, he had entered the ICS in 1938, and held high administrative posts in the 1960s. Simultaneously he became recognized as an authority on international law; in 1967 he was appointed to the Permanent Court of Arbitration at The Hague, and in 1969 became vice-chairman (chairman 1971) of the UN commission on international trade law. He also held academic posts and published a number of books on aspects of international law. Died 14 December

Sitwell, Sir Sacheverell, Bt, CH (b. 1897), British author, brother of Osbert and Edith Sitwell, was the youngest of that haughty trio who shook the artistic world in the 1920s and '30s with their promotion of new aesthetic ideas and neglected causes in art, music and literature. His most lasting contributions were his championship of baroque art and a seminal study of *Mozart* (1932). In all he published more than 50 books, some of poetry, some on art, architecture and music, many on exotic travels enlivened by sensitivity to the beautiful or extraordinary. He succeeded Sir Osbert as sixth baronet in 1969. Died 1 October

Solh, Taki Eddine el (b. 1909), was Prime Minister of Lebanon 1973–74 and a prominent member of the Muslim community. His moderation, backed by personal contacts in the Lebanon's rival religious communities, was swept aside by civil war. When he was again asked to form a Government of national unity in 1980, he failed. Died 27 November

Solomon (b. S. Cutner 1902), was one of the most admired concert pianists of his time, especially in the USA. He had made his debut at the age of nine but, sickening of a life fettered to the piano, retired from the platform for two years until 1921, never thereafter looking back. He was famed above all for his interpretation of Mozart, Beethoven, Schumann and Brahms. Died 2 February

Steptoe, Patrick, CBE, FRS (b. 1913), British surgeon, was the global pioneer of human *in vitro* fertilization. After ten years of research and experiment in collaboration with the biologist Dr Robert Edwards, Steptoe delivered the world's first 'test-tube baby', Louise Brown, at the Oldham hospital where he had worked since 1949. He was the first chairman of the British Fertility Society (1973) and in 1980 founded the Centre for the Study of Human Reproduction, where he continued his work for the relief of infertile couples after his retirement from hospital service. Died 12 March

Stevens, Dr Siaka (b. 1905), was Prime Minister of Sierra Leone 1967–71 (interrupted by a brief period in exile) and its President 1971–85. At first a policeman, railway worker and mineworker, as a leading trade unionist he had spent a year at Ruskin College, Oxford. From 1951, politics were his career. He was mayor of Freetown 1964–65, being then leader of the All People's Congress, which won a national majority in 1967. Under him Sierra Leone became an avowedly socialist, one-party, non-aligned state. The multiparty system he held to be a colonial imposition unsuited to a developing nation with tribal divisions. In 1985 he peacefully transferred power to a military but popularly-chosen successor. Died 29 May

Stonehouse, John (b. 1925), British Labour politician, who held ministerial office 1964–70, was imprisoned for fraud and theft 1976 after faking his own death. Died 14 April

Strauss, Franz Josef (b. 1915), was one of the most powerful figures in West German politics for some 40 years. He became secretary-general of the Bavarian conservative party, the Christian Social Union (CSU), in 1949 and its chairman and leader in 1962, meanwhile making it the indispensable ally of the Christian Democrat Union (CDU) in the federal arena. He was taken into Chancellor Adenauer's Cabinet in 1953 (Defence Minister 1956–62) and became Finance Minister in the Bonn 'Grand Coalition' Government 1966–69. A political scandal in 1962 involving Strauss and the magazine *Der Spiegel* stalled his ambition to become Chancellor, but in 1980 he stood, with CDU support, for the highest office, to be defeated by Helmut Schmidt of the Social Democrats. In federal opposition under the Brandt and Schmidt regimes, and thereafter from Munich as Bavaria's Minister–President, he pursued a flamboyant political campaign and a robust life-style. Died 3 October

Strickland, the Hon. Mabel (b. 1899), was the embattled foe of Malta's Prime Minister Dom Mintoff and his Labour Party. Of ancient aristocratic British and Maltese descent, she devoted herself from early life to the causes of the island, from a strongly pro-British and anti-socialist viewpoint. She was principal director of *The Times of Malta* and its editor 1935–50, remaining in post throughout World War II. Died 29 November

Symington, Senator Stuart (b. 1901), US businessman and politician, was drawn into government by President Truman as Assistant Secretary, later Secretary, for Air, then chairman of the National Security Resources Board. He was US Senator for Missouri from 1952 until 1977, and unsuccessfully contested the Democratic nomination for President in 1960. Died 14 December

Szeryng, Henryk (b. in Poland 1918), violinist, became a Mexican citizen in 1946. An international concert performer in the 1930s, during World War II he was a personal aide to General Sikorski. Mexico then became his home, mainly as a teacher and encourager of Mexican musicians and composers, but in 1954 he resumed his concert career, gaining great applause in the USA and in Europe, not least for his renderings of Bach's sonatas and partitas. Died 3 March

Thamrong Navasawat, Luang (b.

1901), was Prime Minister of Siam (Thailand) 1946–47, until overthrown by a military coup. He was one of the leaders of the People's Party who in 1932 negotiated with King Prajadhipok the peaceful change from absolute to constitutional monarchy. Died 3 December

Theotokis, Spyros (b. 1908), Corfiot politician, Greek Foreign Minister 1955–56. Died 7 September

Tinbergen, Professor Nikolaas, FRS (b. in the Netherlands 1907), naturalized British zoologist, shared with Konrad Lorenz and Karl von Freisch the Nobel Prize for Medicine in 1973 for their work on animal behaviour. He and Lorenz, working together since 1937, had revolutionized this branch of zoological science. After imprisonment during the German occupation of Holland, Tinbergen left his professorial chair at Leiden to become lecturer (1949), reader (1960) and professor (1966) of animal behaviour at Oxford. Beyond his ethological research, teaching and writing, he was a fine photographer, and one of his documentary films won the Italia prize in 1960. Died 21 December

Trench, Sir David, GCMG, MC (b. 1915), Governor of Hong Kong 1964–71. Died 4 December

Truong Chinh (b. Dang Xuan Khu 1907), was Secretary-General of the Communist Party of Vietnam, of which he had been a founder member, from 1941 to 1956 and again briefly in 1986. In the first of those periods he was dominated by Ho Chi Minh, and for most of the interval between them by his rival Le Duan, but he imprinted his own radical, Chinese-inspired stamp upon Vietnamese communist strategy, expressed in his 1947 manifesto *The Resistance Will Win.* He was deputy prime minister 1959–60, chairman of the National Assembly 1960–81, and President of the State Council (head of state) 1981–86. Under French rule he had been imprisoned for five years. Died 1 October

Ulanhu (b. Yun-tse 1906), former Vice-President of the People's Republic of China, chairman of its commission for minority affairs and constant champion of his native Mongolia. Died 8 December

Volk, H.E. Cardinal Hermann (b. 1903), was Bishop of Mainz 1962–73. An active ecumenist, he became a cardinal in 1973. Died 1 July

Wankel, Felix (b. 1902), German engineer, inventor of the Wankel rotary engine. Died 9 October

Watt, Sir Alan (b. 1901), Australian diplomat, entered his country's infant diplomatic service in 1937 and rose to be its ambassador in Moscow (1948–50), Tokyo (1956–60) and Bonn (1960–62), and head of the External Affairs department 1950–54. Died September

Williams, Raymond (b. 1921), influential British left-wing writer (esp. *Culture and Society* 1958), critic and thinker; professor of drama at Cambridge University 1974–83. Died 26 January

Wootton of Abinger, Baroness, CH (Barbara Frances Wootton, b. Adam 1897), British social scientist. While spending most of her professional life from 1926 as an academic (reader, then professor, of social studies at London's Bedford College 1944–52, Nuffield research fellow 1952–57), she exerted massive influence on ideas and action mainly through public service and resultant publications. Thus her work as a civil service arbitrator produced *The Social Foundation of Wage Policy* (1955), and half a century as a lay magistrate produced *Social Science and Social Pathology* (1959) and *Crime and the Criminal Law* (1963). She was a member of four royal commissions, the University Grants

Committee, the BBC's governors, the Countryside Commission and many other public bodies. Her sociology was essentially empirical, her politics those of democratic socialism. She became one of the first woman life peers in 1958. Died 11 July

Zia-ul-Haq, General Mohammad (b. 1924), was supreme military ruler of Pakistan from July 1977 until his violent death. The country's self-appointed chief martial law administrator, he made himself President in 1978. He was chief of the army staff when the 1977 general election, won by Zulfiqar Ali Bhutto's Pakistan People's Party, was followed by charges of electoral malpractice and widespread disorder. Zia's seizure of power, accompanied by a promise of an early return to democracy which was several times repeated but never honoured, was popular, but his image was tainted, at home and abroad, by his refusal to reprieve from the gallows his opponent Bhutto, who had been convicted by the civil courts of complicity in a political murder. Relations with the West, chilled by fears that Pakistan was making a nuclear bomb, cooled to frost, but thawed after the Soviet invasion of Afghanistan. Zia secured massive US aid and handled Pakistan's relations with India with skill. At home, Zia's efforts to convert Pakistan's constitution to Islamic principles made little progress and split the country. Died in an air crash 17 August

Zweig, Dr Ferdynand (b. 1896), Polish economist, had a seminal effect on the study of the life of workers and the poor, especially in Britain. A Jewish teacher, he fled the Nazi regime and eventually settled in England. Among his books were *Labour, Life and Poverty* (1948), *The British Worker* (1958), *The Worker in an Affluent Society* (1961), *The New Acquisitive Society* (1976) and two books about Israel, where he was a visiting professor. Died 9 June

CHRONICLE OF PRINCIPAL EVENTS IN 1988

JANUARY

1 New Year messages by President Reagan and Mr Gorbachev were broadcast in USSR and USA respectively.
2 Canada-US free trade agreement signed in separate ceremonies in California and Ottawa.
3 In UK, Mrs Thatcher achieved record as longest-serving PM this century.
7 Erich Honecker began first-ever state visit to France by an East German leader.
8 In USA, New York stock market registered its third-largest one-day fall in history, Dow Jones average closing 140.58 points down on the day; US Brady Commission on October 1987 crash (see AR 1987, pp. 507–10) blamed computerization for exaggerated market swings.
10 In UK, Lord Whitelaw resigned from the Government on health grounds and was succeeded as Lord President of the Council by John Wakeham and as Leader of the House of Lords by Lord Belstead.
12 In UK, Government published White Paper *DTI: The Department for Enterprise* (Cmnd. 278), proposing important changes on mergers and monopolies and an end to regional development grants.
13 Noboru Takeshita began his first visit as Japanese Prime Minister to USA and Canada.
   In Taiwan, President Chiang Ching-kuo died aged 77 (see OBITUARY); he was succeeded by Vice-President Lee Teng-hui.
14 In S. Korea, a former N. Korean secret agent in custody in Seoul admitted responsibility for destruction of S. Korean airliner which crashed in November 1987 with loss of 115 lives (see AR 1987, p. 591).
15 Two-day summit of Central American nations opened in Costa Rica; final communique pledged immediate implementation of Arias peace plan (see AR 1987, pp. 552–5).
17 In Haiti, presidential elections were held amid widespread allegations of voting irregularities; 24 Jan. army-backed candidate Leslie Manigat declared winner; he was inaugurated on 7 Feb., ending nearly two years of military rule (see 20 June).
18 In Argentina, forces loyal to President Alfonsín crushed a military rebellion, the second such insurrection in nine months (see 4 Dec.).
22 W. German Chancellor Kohl joined President Mitterrand in Paris for celebrations marking 25th anniversary of Elysée treaty on Franco-German cooperation.
   In Vienna, third follow-up session opened of 35-nation Conference on Security and Cooperation in Europe; at Geneva US-Soviet disarmament talks US submitted draft space defence treaty.
25 Ramsewak Shankar inaugurated as President of Suriname, ending eight years of military rule.
   Colombian Attorney-General kidnapped and murdered, apparently by drug-traffickers; 27 Jan. President Barco signed emergency decree aimed at countering rising violence by left-wing rebels and drug barons.
   In USA, President Reagan delivered his final State of the Union address, restating the conservative values and policies pursued under his presidency.
26 Health Ministers and experts from 148 countries began three-day London conference on AIDS; in the London Declaration on AIDS, Governments were urged to take urgent action on 'a serious threat to humanity'.
   In Australia, the Prince and Princess of Wales were guests of honour at celebrations

in Sydney, attended by two million people, marking the bicentenary of the arrival of the first European settlers.
West German Chancellor Kohl began two-day visit to Czechoslovakia, the first such for 14 years.
28 Egyptian President Mubarak in Washington for talks on Middle East peace.
In UK, six Irishmen, convicted of Birmingham pub bombing in 1974, lost their appeal, the longest criminal appeal in English legal history.
In Bulgaria, a special two-day Communist Party conference opened, its purpose being to discuss 'qualitative change' and political reforms.
Franco-British summit began annual two-day session in London, focusing on nuclear and defence cooperation and EC budget issue.
29 Angolan-Cuban talks in Luanda, with US participation, concluded with agreement in principle on a Cuban military withdrawal from Angola to pave way for Namibian independence (see 22 Dec.).
In USA, President Reagan signed order withdrawing general preferences from imports from Hong Kong, South Korea, Singapore and Taiwan on grounds of their unfair competitive advantage.
31 Following a weekend summit conference in Davos, Greek PM Papandreou and Turkish PM Özal announced measures and further contacts aimed at improving bilateral relations.

FEBRUARY

1 In Finnish presidential election, President Koivisto failed to achieve 50 per cent of vote for outright win but was re-elected for second term by electoral college on 15 Feb.
Former US Defense Secretary Caspar Weinberger awarded honorary knighthood for services to British interests.
3 In UK, some 2,000 nurses and other health workers at 40 London hospitals held one-day strike over pay amid continuing concern about state of NHS.
4 In UK, Education Secretary Kenneth Baker announced abolition of Inner London Education Authority in 1990.
US Congress rejected President Reagan's request for further military aid for Contra rebels in Nicaragua (see March 31).
In USSR, Supreme Court approved posthumous judicial rehabilitation of Nikolai Bukharin and nine other pre-war Soviet leaders executed or imprisoned in 1938 'show trial' (see 13 June).
8 Mr Gorbachev announced that Soviet troops would begin withdrawal from Afghanistan on 15 May, subject to signature of peace agreement between Pakistan and Afghanistan (see 6, 14 April, 15 May and DOCUMENTS).
In Austria, report of historical commission found that President Waldheim must have been aware of wartime atrocities in the Balkans and had lied about his part, but exonerated him from involvement in war crimes.
9 In UK, House of Commons voted in favour of six-month experiment for televising its proceedings.
UK-US agreement signed in London providing for confiscation of assets of convicted drug-traffickers.
10 Hong Kong Government published White Paper proposing reform of Legislative Council: elections would not be held until 1991; 14 Feb. demonstrators protested at this delay in implementation of democratic system.
S.African troops restored President Mangope in black homeland of Bophuthatswana: he had earlier been overthrown by mutinous army officers.
More than 100 died in violence during local elections in Bangladesh.
11 A two-day 'emergency' summit conference of EC heads of government opened in

Brussels: agreement was reached on reforms to the budget and restrictions on common agricultural policy spending.
14 President Stroessner of Paraguay was re-elected for an eighth term.
In Cyprus, three Palestinian activists died in car-bomb explosion; 15 Feb. ferry chartered by PLO to take expelled Palestinians back to Israel was sabotaged in Limassol harbour.
16 In UK, Government announced that Prevention of Terrorism Act, introduced as a temporary measure in 1974, was to become permanent.
17 In UK, Northern Ireland Secretary Tom King announced inquiry into whether disciplinary action should be taken against RUC members implicated in alleged 'shoot-to-kill' policy in 1982.
In Lebanon, Lt.-Col. William Higgins, chief of UN Truce Supervising Organization, was kidnapped by Muslim extremists, whose claim that he was CIA agent was denied by US.
18 In USA, President Reagan presented $1,094,000 million budget; defence spending pegged but increased spending proposed for education, science and war on AIDS; it called for a reduction in deficit to $129,500 million in fiscal year from October 1988.
19 Laos and Thailand signed ceasefire after Bangkok talks on border dispute; 21 Feb. both sides withdrew troops from battle zone.
Pope John Paul II's seventh encyclical, *Sollicitudo Rei Socialis*, addressed the question of international solidarity and development needs.
21 In the second round of the presidential election in Cyprus, Georgios Vassiliou defeated Glafkos Clerides, President Kyprianou having been defeated in first round on 14 Feb.; Mr Vassiliou took office on 28 Feb.
22 US Navy Secretary James Webb resigned in protest after Navy budget cuts; 23 Feb. President Reagan nominated William Ball as his successor.
23 In Brazil, more than 275 reported dead, 25,000 homeless, following torrential rain in state of Rio de Janeiro.
European Court of Justice ruled that UK was obliged to impose VAT on spectacles, contact lenses and hearing aids.
24 S. African Government announced sweeping new curbs on anti-apartheid movements (see 29 Feb., 6 June).
Foreign Ministers of six Balkan states (Albania, Bulgaria, Greece, Romania, Turkey and Yugoslavia) began three-day conference in Belgrade mainly to discuss greater economic cooperation.
25 US Secretary of State Shultz arrived in Israel at start of Middle East peace mission which later took him to Syria, Egypt, Jordan and London, without success.
In S. Korea, new Administration of President Roh Tae Woo (elected in Dec. 1987) sworn in; Lee Hyun Jae became PM (see 5 Dec.).
In UK, Energy Secretary announced plans for privatization of electricity industry.
26 President Delvalle of Panama was dismissed by Legislative Assembly after attempting to dismiss military leader Gen. Manuel Noriega, who remained effective ruler despite earlier indictment in US for involvement in drugs traffic (see 16 March).
In USSR, Mr Gorbachev made unprecedented television appeal for calm after a week of nationalist demonstrations in Armenia (see 1 March, 11, 23 June, 12 July).
28 In elections in Senegal, President Diouf returned to office for a second term, his Socialist Party retained majority in National Assembly; 29 Feb. opposition leader Abdoulaye Wade and five colleagues temporarily gaoled after insisting that results were fraudulent.
29 In S. Africa, Archbishop Desmond Tutu and 100 clergy arrested in Cape Town while attempting to present petition to Parliament protesting over recent curbs on anti-apartheid organizations (see 24 Feb.); all were later released (see 6 June).

MARCH

1 In USSR, troops were called in to enforce curfew in city of Sumgait in Azerbaijan where at least 31 were later reported to have died in ethnic violence (see 26 Feb.).
2 A two-day summit conference of Nato leaders opened in Brussels: the final communique endorsed Mrs Thatcher's call for modernized nuclear weapons.
  In UK, results of ballot on proposed merger between Liberals and Social Democrats were published; Liberal members voted 7–1 in favour, Social Democrats by 2–1 but 50 per cent of party members failed to vote; the new merged Social and Liberal Democratic Party was launched on 3 March (see 28 July).
3 Bangladesh general elections resulted in a big victory for ruling Jatiya Party led by Gen. Ershad; main opposition parties boycotted polls, which were marred by violence.
  In Turcs & Caicos Islands, opposition People's Democratic Movement won general election marking end of 18 months of direct rule from London.
5 In Tibet, at least eight reported dead in anti-Chinese protests in Lhasa.
6 In Gibraltar, three suspected IRA terrorists shot dead by SAS forces following undercover operation; on 7 March British Foreign Secretary Sir Geoffrey Howe stated that a bomb plot, aimed at British forces on the Rock, had been uncovered (see 16 March, 30 Sept.).
7 Three Palestinians hijackers of bus in the Negev were killed by Israeli troops, three passengers also dying.
  British forces began three-week 'Operation Fire Focus' to test rapid deployment defence capability for Falkland Islands.
8 In São Tomé and Principe, two people killed in unsuccessful coup attempt, allegedly by exiled dissident faction.
  In USSR, five of 11 hijackers of Aeroflot airliner killed when Soviet security forces stormed plan at Leningrad.
10 The Prince of Wales was unharmed in an avalanche which killed one of his companions while skiing in Switzerland.
  President Suharto re-elected unopposed as President of Indonesia.
  Pham Hung, PM of Vietnam since June 1987, died in office (see 22 June and OBITUARY).
11 Giovanni Goria resigned as leader of Italy's 47th postwar Government; a new Government led by Ciriaco De Mita was sworn in on 13 April.
14 Mr Gorbachev began a five-day visit to Belgrade, the first by a Soviet leader to Yugoslavia since death of Marshal Tito in 1980 (see 16 March).
  Three days of clashes began between China and Vietnam over disputed Spratly Islands, both sides admitting casualties.
15 In UK, Budget day: standard income tax reduced to 25 per cent; a single rate of 40 per cent replaced all higher rates (previously up to 60 per cent); separate taxation of married women proposed for 1990; excise duties raised in line with inflation; public sector surplus forecast at £3,000 million in 1988–89.
16 In Panama, coup attempt against Noriega regime failed; 22 March, US rejected Gen. Noreiga's offer of previous day to stand down before 1989 elections if opposition joined in national dialogue (see 26 Feb.).
  In Belgrade, Mr Gorbachev proposed reciprocal US-Soviet freeze on naval forces in the Mediterranean from 1 July; US responded by reaffirming commitments to Nato allies.
  In N. Ireland, three died and more than 50 were injured in grenade and pistol attack by a lone gunman at funeral of three IRA men killed in Gibraltar (see 6, 19 March).
17 US Defense Secretary Frank Carlucci announced in Geneva creation of new US-Soviet military contact body to prevent escalation of military incidents.

19 In N. Ireland, two British soldiers in civilian clothes murdered during savage attack by mob during an IRA funeral in Belfast for one of the victims of the funeral attack on 16 March.
20 In El Salvador, elections to National Assembly won by right-wing Nationalist Republican Alliance.
21 General elections held in Kenya on one-party basis; 24 March, President Moi announced Cabinet changes including appointment of Dr Josephat Karanja as Vice-President.
23 In Nicaragua, a 60-day ceasefire agreement was signed by Government officials and Contra commanders: the two-stage peace process would begin on 1 April (see 23 May, 9 June).
24 General election in Gibraltar won by Socialist Labour Party led by Joe Bossano who was sworn in as Chief Minister on 25 March.
25 Seven alleged ANC guerrillas killed by South African forces, three on Botswana border and four in raid on Gaborone (Botswana); 29 March, ANC representative in Paris, Dulcie September, shot dead by unknown gunman.
27 In Israel, Mordechai Vanunu sentenced to 18 years' imprisonment for disclosing details of Israeli nuclear programme to UK newspaper.
29 In UK, Industry Secretary announced sale of Rover car group to British Aerospace.
31 US Senate approved $47,900,000 package including $17,700,000 in humanitarian aid for Nicaraguan Contras and the same amount for medical treatment of children injured in the war.

APRIL

1 Turkish PM Özal began three-day visit to Baghdad, but mediation attempts in Gulf War overshadowed by alleged Iraqi use of chemical weapons against Kurds.
2 Indian forces moved to seal Pakistan border to stop infiltration of Sikh extremists, after more than 120 reported dead in week of violence in Punjab; some 645 had died since January.
 In UK, Oxford won Boat Race by 5½ lengths.
3 Ethiopia and Somalia concluded provisional peace agreement, thus ending 11 years of border and other conflict.
 In Lebanon, a week of fierce fighting began in the south between the Syrian-backed Amal and pro-Iranian Hizbullah Shia Muslim militias.
4 Tibet's exiled Dalai Lama began a 9-day spiritual visit to Britain.
5 Shia Muslim extremists hijacked a Kuwaiti Airways jumbo jet, forcing it to fly to Iran and later to Cyprus where two passengers were shot dead; the hijack ended in Algiers on 20 April when remaining passengers were freed but terrorists were given safe passage out of Algeria.
6 Mrs Thatcher began a two-day official visit to Turkey, the first by a British PM.
 Mr Gorbachev held two days of talks in Tashkent with Afghan leader Najibullah; a joint communique reaffirmed pledge to withdraw Soviet troops from Afghanistan subject to signing of peace agreement (see 8 Feb., 14 April, 15 May).
 In clash near West Bank village of Beita, Israeli girl was accidentally shot dead by Israeli guard (it later transpired) and two Palestinians also killed; six Beita villagers were among 16 Palestinians deported by Israeli authorities later in month.
 At Brasilia summit, Presidents of Argentina, Brazil and Uruguay signed Act of Alvorada providing for enhanced economic integration.
7 In Brussels, two-day World Food Conference opened to discuss ways of reducing global imbalance of food supplies.
8 Yang Shangkun (81), a former general, elected President of China by National People's Congress (see 12 April).

CHRONICLE OF EVENTS 603

    In Honduras, state of emergency declared in two areas amid anti-US riots protesting against arrest and extradition to US of alleged drug baron.
    In Western Samoa, Tofilau Eti Alesana chosen as Prime Minister by new Assembly.
9 PLO leader Yassir Arafat visited Moscow and was told by Mr Gorbachev that recognition of Israel and its security interests were necessary elements of a peace settlement.
    In UK, Grand National won by Rhyme 'n' Reason at 10–1.
10 In Pakistan, 100 dead, 700 injured in a massive explosion at an army ammunition dump near Islamabad; Afghan agents were believed to be responsible.
12 In China, National People's Congress elected a new State Council: the 41 Ministers included ten new names; Qin Qwei named Minister of Defence and Qian Qichen Minister of Foreign Affairs (see 8 April).
    King Olav of Norway began four day state visit to Britain.
14 Agreements signed in Geneva to resolve international aspects of Afghanistan conflict included one by US Secretary of State Shultz and Soviet Foreign Minister Shevardnadze for the withdrawal of Soviet troops from Afghanistan (see 8 Feb., 6 April, 15 May and DOCUMENTS).
    In Naples (Italy), five people killed in bomb attack on US Navy club, apparently by left-wing extremists; 16 April, the shooting to death of government adviser Roberto Ruffilli was claimed by Red Brigades.
16 PLO military commander Abu Jihad assassinated in Tunis; half a million Palestinians attended funeral near Damascus on 20 April.
18 US planes and warships destroyed two Iranian oil platforms, crippled two frigates and sank a patrol boat in Gulf in retaliation for damage to a US frigate on 14 April; in land war, Iraqi forces recaptured Fao peninsula from Iranians in major offensive in southern sector (see 14 May).
20 HM Queen Elizabeth II and Prince Philip began bicentenary tour of Australia.
21 Israeli PM Shamir and President Reagan signed memorandum providing for five-year continuation of US-Israel 'unique dialogue' and for annual meetings on Israel's defence and economic needs.
22 In New Caledonia, three gendarmes killed and over 20 captured by Kanak separatists; France flew in military reinforcements in effort to restore order (see 5 May).
23 In Lebanon, a Tripoli car bomb, thought to have been planted by right-wing Christians, killed 69 people and injured over 100.
24 In first round of the French presidential elections François Mitterrand (Socialist) established comfortable lead over Jacques Chirac (Gaullist) and Raymond Barre (centrist); unexpectedly placed fourth was extreme right-wing leader Jean-Marie Le Pen, while the Communist candidate won only 6.8 per cent (see 8 May).
25 PLO leader Yassir Arafat began two-day visit to Damascus, his first to Syria for five years.
    In Israel, John Demjanjuk, known as Ivan the Terrible, sentenced to death after conviction of war crimes at gas chambers of Treblinka.
26 In National Assembly elections in S. Korea, ruling Democratic Justice Party lost its working majority.
    Ministers from Opec and seven non-Opec oil-producing countries began three-day meeting, but failed to agree on oil price support measures

MAY

1 In UK, a 13-week dispute at P&O escalated to an all-out strike by members of the National Union of Seamen halting most British ferries; 12 May, NUS called off all illegal secondary picketing at UK ports following High Court's sequestration of its assets.

Three off-duty British soldiers died in two separate IRA attacks in Netherlands.
In Sri Lanka, at least 26 bus passengers killed by land-mine explosion near Trincomalee, Tamil extremists being blamed.
2 Convention on the Regulation of Antarctic Mineral Resource Activities initialled in Wellington (New Zealand) and opened for signature.
Israeli forces began three-day operation against Palestinian and Shia positions in southern Lebanon, three Israelis and some 40 Hizbullah members being killed.
In Poland, seven Solidarity leaders detained by police when thousands of shipyard workers went on strike in Gdansk (see 28, 31 Aug.).
3 Japanese PM Noboru Takeshita on official visit to UK.
4 Three Frenchmen, kidnapped by Islamic Jihad three years ago, released amid allegations that French Government had done a pre-election deal with Iran and hostage-takers.
5 In New Caledonia, French security forces stormed cave where Kanak separatists were holding 22 gendarmes and a French magistrate, 19 Kanaks and three French soldiers being killed (see 22 April).
6 Pope John Paul II began 13-day tour of Uruguay, Bolivia, Peru and Paraguay.
Franco-New Zealand relations badly strained by repatriation to France of agent Dominique Prieur, who had been convicted in New Zealand of 1985 *Rainbow Warrior* sinking and later held in French custody in Pacific.
8 President Mitterrand (Socialist) defeated Jacques Chirac (Gaullist) in second round of French presidential elections, achieving over 54 per cent of poll (see 10 May).
Sr Rodrigo Borja achieved a decisive victory over Sr Abdala Buceara in presidential election in Ecuador.
9 President Chaim Herzog sworn in for second term as President of Israel.
In Belgium, Dr W. Martens sworn in as head of new centre-left coalition: the country had been without a Government since the election of Dec. 1987.
S. African-born athlete Zola Budd announced her withdrawal from international competitive sport: she claimed sickness had been brought on by pressure from anti-apartheid movement.
10 General elections in Denmark resulted in a swing to the right; Poul Schluter resigned as PM but announced formation of new coalition Government on 3 June.
Jacques Chirac resigned as PM of France and was succeeded by Michel Rocard of the Socialist Party (see 12 June).
In Mauritius, a two-day meeting of EEC and ACP Ministers began negotiations on renewal of Lomé Convention (due in 1990).
11 In Guatemala, attempted coup by army officers foiled without bloodshed.
12 A Chinese airliner on internal flight hijacked to Taiwan, where the two hijackers were accepted as refugees.
13 In Iran, completion of elections to Majlis (following first round on 8 April) confirmed growing strength of 'radical' faction in parliament.
14 Iraqi planes attacked Iranian oil terminal in Strait of Hormuz, killing about 20 seamen and hitting five tankers.
15 Soviet forces began to withdraw from Afghanistan after 8½-years presence; the withdrawal was due to be completed by 15 Feb. 1989 (see 14 April).
In Sudan, five Britons and two Sudanese killed in Muslim extremist attacks in Khartoum. Government of national unity formed.
17 In UK, Government published White Paper on Defence (Cmnd. 344) emphasizing need to keep conventional weapons up to date and seek value for money.
Morocco and Algeria resumed diplomatic relations which had been broken since 1976 following the outbreak of the Polisario conflict in W. Sahara.
19 In India, 46 Sikh rebels who had been occupying Golden Temple at Amritsar surrendered to Indian forces: three committed suicide.
20 In Hungary, a Communist Party special conference (the first for 30 years) opened in Budapest; 22 May, Janos Kadar was succeeded as Party General Secretary by

Karoly Grosz; extensive changes to Politburo were announced at end of conference (see 23 June, 23 Nov.).
23 In UK, Government gained majority of 134 in House of Lords for Poll Tax Bill in second-largest turnout of peers this century.
In Nicaragua, President Ortega announced unilateral 30-day extension of ceasefire, but further talks with Contras ended on 27 May without definitive ceasefire agreement (see 23 March, 9 June).
25 Col. Qadafi announced Libyan recognition of Hissène Habré Government in Chad and the end of 'all outstanding differences' between two countries.
US Administration announced collapse of negotiations with Gen. Noriega of Panama intended to secure his removal from effective power (see 26 Feb., 16 March).
In Gulf war, Iran lost further ground in southern sector around Basra and withdrew across Shatt al-Arab waterway (see 18 April, 14 May).
26 Vietnam announced withdrawal of 50,000 of its troops from Kampuchea by late 1988, the remainder being placed under Kampuchean control.
OAU's 25th anniversary summit opened in Addis Ababa; during the three-day meeting President Moussa Traoré of Mali was elected OAU chairman in succession to President Kaunda of Zambia.
27 US Senate voted overwhelmingly to ratify intermediate-range nuclear forces (INF) treaty (see AR 1987, p.558).
29 President Reagan and Mr Gorbachev held a three-day summit conference in Moscow during which a range of agreements on arms control, space and cultural exchanges were signed and the instruments of ratification of INF treaty were exchanged.
In Pakistan, President Zia dissolved National Assembly and dismissed Cabinet of Mohammad Khan Junejo, promising free elections in three months (see 15 June, 17 Aug.)

JUNE

1 In W. Germany, 51 miners died in a colliery disaster near Kassel.
In UK, the Derby was won by the Aga Khan's Kahyasi at 11–1.
2 President Reagan in London for talks with Mrs Thatcher; he addressed a meeting at London's Guildhall on 3 June.
In Australia, Canberra High Court unanimously approved sale in Australia of Peter Wright's *Spycatcher*, dismissing UK Government's final appeal after 18 months of legal proceedings (see 13 Oct.).
3 In USSR, Nobel prizewinner Andrei Sakharov gave unprecedented news conference at Foreign Ministry: he attacked Soviet human rights policies and called for release of dissidents (see 20 Oct.).
4 In USSR, train carrying industrial explosives blew up east of Moscow, killing 84 people and injuring over 700.
5 Archbishop of Canterbury and leading world churchmen in Moscow for celebrations of 1,000 years of Christianity in Russia.
6 In South Africa estimated one million black workers began three-day strike in protest against new labour laws and greater restrictions on anti-apartheid organizations (see 24, 29 Feb.).
7 Arab League summit conference opened in Algiers, ending 9 June.
In UK, MPs voted 341–218 against reintroduction of death penalty.
Bangladesh Parliament approved constitutional amendment to make Islam state religion.
9 In Nicaragua, ceasefire talks between Government and Contras finally broke down (see 23 March, 23 May).

10 Leaders of five Maghreb states (Algeria, Libya, Mauritania, Morocco and Tunisia) concluded Algiers summit with agreement on plans for greater unity.
11 In USSR, it was reported that weeks of strikes and protests by Armenians in disputed enclave of Nagorno-Karabakh had left region paralysed (see 26 Feb., 23 June).
12 In second round of French parliamentary elections, Socialist Party failed to win majority but obtained dominant position in new Assembly; Michel Rocard was reappointed PM on 23 June.
13 Turkish PM Özal in Athens for talks with Greek PM Papandreou on Cyprus and other bilateral issues.

A court in the Irish Republic released a suspected IRA terrorist in spite of an extradition request by Britain; a new extradition treaty between the Republic and Britain had recently been finalized.

In UK, Government announced investigation of role of Department of Trade and Industry in affair of collapsed investment company Barlow Clowes where millions of pounds of investors' money had disappeared.

USSR Supreme Court annulled verdict of treason passed in 1936 on Grigory Zinoviev and Lev Kamenev (see 4 Feb.).
14 83rd Opec ministerial meeting in Vienna concluded with agreement to extend existing production quotas to end-1988; Dr Subtroto (Indonesia) appointed to post of Opec secretary-general, vacant since 1983 (see 28 Nov.).

In W. Germany, riot police attempted to restore order in Düsseldorf where serious violence occurred among British, Dutch and German supporters attending European football championships.
15 In N. Ireland, six soldiers taking part in a 'fun run' died when their van was blown up by an IRA bomb.

In Pakistan, President Zia announced the imposition of Islamic law (Sharia) (see 17 Aug.).
16 Iran and France resumed diplomatic relations.

In India, ruling Congress (I) suffered several by-election defeats; main opposition leader V.P. Singh elected to central Parliament.
18 Turkish PM Turgut Özal survived an assassination attempt in Ankara.
19 An economic summit meeting of the seven major industrialized nations opened in Toronto, ending 21 June, with consensus on the rescheduling of poorest countries' debts.

In Gulf war, Iranian setbacks in central sector around Mehran were blamed by Iran on Iraqi use of chemical weapons.
20 President Leslie Manigat of Haiti deposed in military coup; Gen. Namphy announced formation of military Government and declared himself President (see 17 Sept.).
21 Canada declared 17 Soviet diplomats personae non gratae for alleged industrial espionage; 22 June, USSR took reciprocal action against five Canadian diplomats in Moscow.
22 Do Muoi (71) elected PM of Vietnam by Nationalist Assembly in succession to Pham Hung (see 10 March).
23 About 100 died in landslide in north-western Turkey.

In USSR, *Pravda* reported that Soviet troops had moved into parts of Armenia and Azerbaijan and disputed region of Nagorno-Karabakh where ethnic violence had entered fifth month (see 11 June, 12 July).

Pope John Paul II began five-day visit to Austria intended as 'European mission' to preach also to Catholics in neighbouring Hungary and Yugoslavia; further controversy attended his meetings with embattled President Waldheim (see 8 Feb.).
25 European Community and Comecon Ministers signed declaration of mutual recognition.

CHRONICLE OF EVENTS

In the presidential election in Iceland, President Finbogadóttir was unanimously re-elected for third term.

Laos held first national elections since Communists took power 13 years ago.

French PM Rocard announced that French settlers and indigenous Kanaks had reached agreement on future of New Caledonia: an independence referendum would be held (see 6 Nov.).

27 In France, 59 died in runaway train accident at Gare de Lyon, Paris.

A two-day summit conference of EC Heads of Government opened in Hannover, W. Germany, and declared 1992 goal of single European market 'irreversible'.

In Hungary, large demonstrations took place against Romania's planned destruction of 8,000 Transylvanian villages containing many ethnic Hungarians.

28 In USSR, a national conference of the Communist Party opened in Moscow; in keynote speech Gorbachev outlined plans for changes in administrative structure of state; 30 June, delegates called for resignation of President Gromyko and other officials associated with Brezhnev era; 1 July, conference ended with approval of six resolutions for implementation of *perestroika*.

A car bomb in Athens killed the US defence attaché, an anti-Nato group claiming responsibility.

29 Hungarian Parliament elected Bruno Ferenc Straub (a non-member of the ruling HSWP) as head of state in succession to Károly Németh.

In UK, a White Paper, *Reform of Section 2 of the Official Secrets Act 1911* (Cmnd. 408) was published.

30 Dissident Archbishop Marcel Lefèbvre and four bishops whom he had just consecrated were excommunicated by the Pope for the sin of schism.

JULY

1 Gen. Manfred Wörner succeeded Lord Carrington as Secretary-General of Nato.

3 US warship *Vincennes* shot down Iranian civilian airliner in the Gulf with loss of 290 lives; on 5 July President Reagan told Congress that it was a justified act of self-defence in spite of Iranian allegations of mass murder.

In Turkey, PM Özal opened a second bridge across the Bosphorus, linking Europe to Asia.

4 9th Caricom summit began five-day meeting Antigua; observer status granted to Netherlands Antilles.

5 HM Queen Elizabeth II and Prince Philip in Netherlands for two-day visit to mark 300th anniversary of accession of Prince William of Orange to British throne.

In UK, General Synod of Church of England voted in favour of legislation for ordination of women as priests.

US Attorney-General Edwin Meese resigned following investigation into his personal finances.

In UK, National Health Service celebrated its 40th birthday.

In N. Yemen, elections held to new legislative Council; 17 July, President Saleh re-elected for third term.

6 In UK, 167 died in explosion at North Sea oil platform *Piper Alpha* (see 22 Sept.).

In UK, the report of the inquiry led by Lord Justice Butler-Sloss into handling of alleged child sexual abuse cases in Cleveland in 1987 (see AR 1987, p.33, 449–50) was published: it criticized all agencies and individuals involved and made recommendations for reform of child care law.

In Mexico, presidential election was won by Carlos Salinas de Gortari (of ruling Institutional Revolutionary Party) amid allegations of ballot-rigging (see 1 Dec.).

10 150 died in rail crash in Kerala, S. India.

11 Soviet leader Mikhail Gorbachev began six-day visit to Poland.

In Greece, 11 tourists died in grenade and gun attack on tourist pleasure boat by Arab terrorists.

Nicaragua expelled US ambassador and seven colleagues, accusing them of inciting violent anti-government incidents; 12 July, Nicaraguan ambassador and seven colleagues expelled by US.

In Italy, 13 people sentenced, some to life imprisonment, in connection with 1980 Bologna station bombing.

12 In USSR, Communist Party leadership in disputed Nagorno-Karabakh region voted to secede from Azerbaijan and join Armenia in violation of Soviet constitution (see 26 Feb., 1 March, 11, 23 June).

President Evren of Turkey began three-day state visit to UK.

13 In Liberia, President Doe announced failure of attempted armed incursion led by a former deputy head of state.

16 Warsaw Pact summit concluded with a call for three-stage reduction of conventional forces in Europe.

In UK, 525 Anglican bishops gathered in Canterbury for opening of 12th Lambeth Conference; a compromise resolution on the consecration of women bishops, a resolution to widen the scope of consultation leading to the appointment of the Archbishop of Canterbury and a resolution condemning Irish terrorism were approved by the conference which ended on 6 Aug.

18 The 70th birthday of imprisoned ANC leader Nelson Mandela was marked by worldwide protests and demands for his release from gaol in S. Africa.

Iranian spiritual leader Ayatollah Khomeini announced unconditional acceptance of UN Resolution 598 (see AR 1987, p.548) calling for ceasefire in Gulf War (see 8 Aug.).

In USA, 40th Democratic Party National Convention opened in Atlanta, ending 21 July; Michael Dukakis adopted as presidential candidate (see 8 Nov.).

19 Beacons were lit all over Britain to mark 400th anniversary of first sighting of Spanish Armada.

23 Gen. Ne Win, ruler of Burma for 26 years, resigned amid mounting political and economic chaos; he was succeeded by U Sein Lwin on 27 July (see 12 Aug.).

In Irish Republic, three holidaymakers died in IRA bomb explosion: bomb was believed intended for an Ulster High Court judge.

24 In elections in Thailand, three largest parties gained more than 50 per cent of parliamentary seats (see 11 Aug.).

25 In UK, PM Thatcher announced Cabinet reshuffle and the splitting of the Department of Health and Social Security into two separate departments.

28 In UK, Paddy Ashdown defeated Alan Beith to become first leader of Social and Liberal Democrats (see 2 March).

An Israeli consular delegation began first official Israeli visit to USSR since latter broke diplomatic relations in 1967.

31 King Husain of Jordan announced plans to cut legal and administrative ties with West Bank, in accordance with PLO aspirations.

AUGUST

1 Mrs Thatcher began a five-day bicentenary visit to Australia, the first official visit by a British PM for 21 years.

The first Soviet intermediate-range nuclear weapons to be eliminated under the INF Treaty were destroyed at the Sary-Ozek range in Soviet Kazakhstan (see 29 May).

In first IRA bomb attack in mainland Britain for four years, one soldier was killed and nine injured in an explosion at a barracks in Mill Hill (near London).

3 W. German pilot Matthias Rüst, who had landed his plane in Red Square,

CHRONICLE OF EVENTS

Moscow, in May 1987, released from gaol in USSR on humanitarian grounds (see AR 1987, p.584).
7 In Sudan, over one million people reported homeless and many dead after widespread flooding in Khartoum and surrounding provinces.
President Masire of Botswana suffered slight injuries when his aircraft was accidentally forced down by an Angolan jet fighter.
8 Following acceptance by Iran and Iraq of a UN peace plan, UN Security Council ordered end to hostilities in Gulf; direct peace talks began in Geneva on 25 Aug.
S. African Foreign Minister Pik Botha announced that agreement had been reached with Angola and Cuba for a ceasefire in conflict in Angola; the agreement was signed by Angolan and S. African Governments on 22 Aug. (see 22 Dec.).
10 Rodrigo Borja inaugurated as President of Ecuador in succession to Sr Leon Febres Cordero.
In Burundi, bloody tribal conflict flared up between the majority Hutu and the dominant Tutsi, resulting in many thousands of deaths over the following weeks.
11 Chatichai Choonhavan appointed PM of Thailand (see 24 July).
12 In Burma, Brig.-Gen. U Sein Lwin resigned as President of State Council and Chairman of Socialist Programme Party following a week of anti-Government demonstrations in which 1,000 were believed to have died; he was succeeded by Dr Maung Maung on 19 Aug. (see 18 Sept.).
14 Radio Moscow reported that the withdrawal of half of Soviet forces from Afghanistan had been accomplished, one day ahead of the schedule (see 14 April).
17 In Pakistan, President Zia ul-Haq and US ambassador among some 35 who died when plane exploded in mid-air; a state of emergency was declared and and Ghulam Ishaq Khan named acting President; sabotage was suspected.
In USA, Republican convention meeting in New Orleans adopted Vice-President Bush as presidential candidate (see 8 Nov.).
18 In Lebanon, the National Assembly failed to obtain a quorum to elect a new President.
20 In N. Ireland, eight soldiers died when an IRA bomb blew up their coach near Omagh.
President Lazarus Salii of the US Pacific dependency of Belau was found shot dead in his house; Vice-President Thomas Remengesau became acting President.
21 In Moscow and Prague, police broke up big demonstrations by protesters marking 20th anniversary of Soviet invasion of Czechoslovakia.
In India at least 900 died in earthquake on border with Nepal.
A major earthquake devastated northern Bihar (India) and adjoining areas of Bihar, over 700 people being killed.
24 In Cyprus, the leaders of the Greek and Turkish communities held first meeting for three years, under UN auspices.
25 Japanese PM Takeshita began six-day visit to China, during which he announced soft loan and grant package of US$7,600 million over 1990–95.
A catastrophic fire devastated the historic commercial centre of Lisbon, Portugal.
26 Soviet authorities announced plans for leasing of agricultural land by private individuals.
28 In W. Germany, 70 people died when three jets collided at an air show.
In Poland, General Jaruzelski called for new attempts at national reconciliation as a two-week wave of strikes at steel mills, coal mines and shipyards continued (see 31 Aug.).
Romanian and Hungarian leaders met in Arad (Romania) but failed to resolve differences over Romania's treatment of its Hungarian minority (see 27 June).
30 Representatives of Morocco and the Polisario Front accepted UN plan designed to settle their conflict over Western Sahara.
In N. Ireland, three IRA suspects shot dead by SAS in ambush near Omagh; 31 Aug. W. German police arrested two armed IRA suspects on border.

W. German freighter *Karin B*, carrying 2,000 tonnes of toxic waste, banned from entering Britain; it docked at Livorno on 19 Sept. after 2½ month voyage during which 5 countries refused admission.

31 In Poland, Solidarity leader Lech Walesa held talks with Interior Minister (his first talks with Polish authorities since banning of Solidarity in 1981) following which he urged workers to end strikes (see 28 Aug.).

In Bangladesh some 25 million were left homeless and many hundreds died in flooding which affected widespread areas of country including capital Dhaka.

In UK, postal workers staged a one-day strike but unofficial action brought postal services to a standstill until an agreement was reached on 15 Sept.

SEPTEMBER

1 In Libya, Col. Qadafi made first of series of speeches repudiating many radical domestic and international policies pursued hitherto.

In Chile, a decree allowed return of those exiled before and after 1973 military coup.

3 A general election in Singapore resulted in a further landslide victory for the ruling People's Action Party of Lee Kuan Yew.

4 In Yugoslavia, some 70,000 Serbs and Montenegrins demonstrated in Smederevo calling for martial law in Kosovo province, and demanding protection from Albanian separatists; demonstrations continued in other cities throughout month (see 6 Oct.).

5 In USSR, trial opened in Moscow of Gen. Yury Churbanov, son-in-law of late President Brezhnev; he was gaoled for 12 years for corruption and six others received 8–10 year sentences on 30 Dec.

7 Non-Aligned Foreign Ministers began four-day meeting in Nicosia.

9 India announced that it would refuse entry to England cricket players who had had sporting contacts with S. Africa, forcing England to abandon its planned winter tour.

10 Pope John Paul II began 9-day visit to southern Africa (see 14 Sept.).

11 Some 50 million people worldwide took part in 'The Race Against Time' to raise money to fight diseases that kill 15 million children a year.

12 President Botha of S. Africa held talks in Mozambique with President Chissano: it was Botha's first visit to a black African country.

Some 30 people died when hurricane Gilbert (the strongest ever recorded in Western hemisphere) devastated Jamaica and the Cayman Islands (see 17 Sept.).

13 Two Cuban diplomats expelled from UK after shooting incident in London.

President Reagan ordered the immediate release of $44 million in outstanding US dues to UN and recommended a further payment of $144 million for fiscal year 1988–89.

14 In Maseru, Lesotho, S. African police stormed a hijacked bus carrying pilgrims waiting to see the Pope; three hijackers and a hostage died in shoot-out; incident forced Pope to make unscheduled stopover in S.Africa where he was greeted by Foreign Minister Pik Botha.

16 Mr Gorbachev proposed evacuation of Soviet naval base at Cam Ranh Bay (Vietnam) in return for US withdrawal from bases in Philippines, as part of peace plan involving a freeze on nuclear and naval forces in the Pacific.

17 XXIV Olympiad opened in Seoul, S. Korea, ending 2 Oct. (see 26 Sept.).

In Mexico some 170 people died as hurricane Gilbert struck Monterrey; some 300 reported to have died and one million made homeless in path of hurricane (see 12 Sept.).

18 In Haiti, Gen. Henri Namphy deposed in military coup; Brig.-Gen. Prosper Avril declared himself President (see 20 June).

In Swedish general election, Social Democrats lost three seats but retained majority over non-socialist parties; Greens obtained 20 seats, entering Parliament for first time.

In Burma, Government of President Maung Maung overthrown in military coup led by Army Chief of Staff Gen. Saw Maung; 19 Sept. some 400 died when troops fired on protesters in Rangoon.

19 In Poland, Government of PM Zbigniew Messner resigned because of its failure to deal with country's economic problems (see 26 Sept.).

Israel launched its first satellite, *Horizon*.

In Japan, Emperor Hirohito (87) fell critically ill; 23 Sept., Crown Prince Akihito assumed his father's official duties.

20 43rd session of UN General Assembly opened in New York.

Mrs Thatcher, addressing College of Europe in Bruges, warned against 'folly' of moves towards political and economic union of Europe.

21 Mrs Thatcher in Spain for talks with PM González—first official visit to Spain by a British PM (see 17 Oct.).

In USSR, state of emergency declared in Nagorno-Karabakh in view of worsening ethnic clashes, strikes and demonstrations.

22 In Lebanon, President Gemayel, whose term of office expired at midnight, appointed transitional military Government, under Gen. Michel Aoun, but existing Cabinet headed by Salim al-Hoss refused to recognize it.

In UK, one man missing but 66 rescued when N. Sea oil rig *Ocean Odyssey* exploded.

Brazil concluded agreement with creditor banks, rescheduling debts of US$62,100 million.

Three Czechoslovak diplomats expelled from UK for espionage activities; 28 Sept. two British diplomats expelled from Prague.

23 Nigeria concluded agreement in London, rescheduling US$5,200 million in debts to commercial banks.

25 In USA, a divorcee, Rev. Barbara Harris, elected suffragan Bishop of Anglican diocese of Massachussetts: she would be first woman bishop in Anglican Communion.

26 At Olympic Games, Ben Johnson of Canada, who had won 100 metres in world record time, stripped of gold medal after failing drugs test.

In Poland Mieczyslaw Rakowski appointed PM; he named a 23-man Cabinet on 13 Oct.

At UN General Assembly, President Reagan proposed international conference to reverse erosion of 1925 Geneva protocol banning chemical and gas weapons.

27 The deaths of three Palestinians in Gaza brought the death toll since the *intifada* began in December 1987 to 287.

28 In Iceland, Steingrimur Hermannsson (Agrarian Progress Party) named PM at head of tripartite coalition Government.

29 In USA, space shuttle *Discovery* with five crew launched on four-day mission: it was first shuttle launch since *Challenger* disaster in Jan. 1986.

Nobel Peace Prize awarded to UN Peacekeeping Forces.

29 The annual joint meetings of the IMF and World Bank concluded three-day session in West Berlin.

An international arbitration tribunal ruled that the disputed Taba Strip on the Gulf of Aqaba should be returned to Egypt by Israel.

30 In Gibraltar, an inquest jury returned verdict of lawful killing of three IRA terrorists by SAS on 6 March (see 6 March).

In USSR, an extraordinary plenum of Central Committee of Communist Party was held in Moscow; a purge of senior members of political hierarchy was announced including retirement of President Gromyko and demotion of Gorbachev's No. 2 Yegor Ligachev (see 1 Oct.).

OCTOBER

1 President Botha of S. Africa held summit talks in Zaïre with President Mobutu; Presidents of Angola, Gabon and Congo were holding simultaneous talks in Gabon (see 12 Sept., 15 Oct.).

Mikhail Gorbachev elected President of USSR by Supreme Soviet.

3 Eleven died in freak flooding in Nîmes, southern France.

Chad and Libya formally ended their war and established diplomatic relations (see 25 May).

4 Kuwait Investment Office ordered by UK Government to reduce its holding in BP from 22 to not more than 9.9 per cent.

President Ceauşescu of Romania began three-day official visit to USSR; President Gorbachev not among welcoming party at Moscow airport.

5 In a referendum in Chile, voters rejected a proposal that President Pinochet should remain in power for a further eight years; under the terms of constitution he would remain in office until March 1990.

Amnesty International's annual report said that at least 80 of 135 countries surveyed held prisoners of conscience in 1987 and that torture or ill-treatment was reported in 90.

6 In Algeria, a curfew was imposed in Algiers as President Chadli introduced emergency measures following three days of rioting against rising prices and unemployment; 12 Oct., stage of siege lifted; President announced a referendum in Nov. and unspecified plans for political reform; 200 were reported to have died in unrest (see 3 Nov.).

In Yugoslavia, Communist leadership of Vojvodina region resigned following massive demonstrations by Serbian protesters who accused them of siding with Albanian separatists (see 18 Nov.).

7 S. Korea relaxed ban on trade with North and proposed talks on creating single economic unit.

10 Tamil extremists murdered 47 Sinhalese civilians in North-Central province.

11 Following a session of the Czechoslovak Communist Party Central Committee, major Party leadership and Government changes were announced; Ladislav Adamec replaced Lubomír Štrougal as PM.

Indictments issued in US on Luxembourg-based parent banking company and two subsidiaries for laundering drugs money.

12 In Italy, life sentences passed on 26 Red Brigades members in connection with 1978 murder of Aldo Moro; 127 others convicted of belonging to armed organization.

13 In UK, Law Lords rejected Government's claim for a permanent ban on publication of *Spycatcher* in Britain but condemned its author Peter Wright for a breach of confidentiality (see DOCUMENTS).

The results of carbon-dating tests revealed that the Turin shroud was not the burial cloth of Christ, placing it firmly in the medieval period.

14 Italian PM De Mita began three-day visit to USSR.

16 President Evren of Turkey began four-day visit to West Germany, where he pressed Turkish case for EC membership.

17 US-Philippines agreement reached on continued US use of military bases until 1991 in return for economic and military aid.

In Brussels, trial began of 26 English football supporters charged with causing 39 deaths during May 1985 Heysel stadium riot.

HM Queen Elizabeth II began a five-day state visit to Spain, the first by a reigning British monarch.

An extraordinary meeting of the Central Committee of the League of Communists of Yugoslavia opened in Belgrade; 19 Oct. four members of the Presidium resigned but demands of Serbian leader Slobodan Milosevic for resignation of entire Presidium failed.

Thirty-one died when Uganda Airlines Boeing 707 crashed at Rome airport.
19 In UK, Home Secretary announced a ban on television and radio interviews with representatives of Sinn Fein and 10 other Republican and loyalist paramilitary organizations.
In India, 165 died in two separate air crashes.
20 In USSR, Nobel prizewinner Andrei Sakharov elected to presidium of Academy of Sciences and authorized to travel abroad (see 3 June, 7 Nov.).
21 In Greece, a cruise ship carrying nearly 400 British schoolchildren sank off Piraeus after a collision with an Italian freighter; four died.
24 Chancellor Kohl of W. Germany in Moscow for four days of talks; on 26 Oct. he announced that he had been told that USSR would release all political prisoners.
At least 470 died when a ferry sank in a typhoon off the Philippines.
26 In S. Africa, simultaneous elections to white, black, Coloured and Indian local councils were held for first time; in white elections, Nationalists retained control in spite of challenge from far-right Conservative Party.
Zambian President Kaunda re-elected unopposed for sixth term.
28 Unofficial demonstration in Prague marking 70th anniversary of Czechoslovakia's independence broken up by police.
31 In Argentina, former President Galtieri and two former members of junta gaoled for 12 years for mismanagement of Falklands war in 1982.
Polish Government announced closure of Gdansk shipyard, stronghold of Solidarity movement (see 2 Nov.).

NOVEMBER

1 In Israeli elections there was no clear winner, Likud Party obtaining two seats fewer than previously; 14 Nov. President Herzog invited outgoing PM Yitzhak Shamir to form Government.
China and USSR announced agreement on most of disputed eastern sector of their common border.
2 Mrs Thatcher began a three-day visit to Poland during which she held talks with PM Rakowski and met Lech Walesa at Gdansk shipyard.
In Belau, Ngiratkel Etpison elected President on pro-US platform (see 20 Aug.).
3 Indian troops put down an attempted coup against the Government of President Gayoom in the Maldives.
In Algeria, a referendum approved reduction in power of presidency; 5 Nov., Col. Kasdi Merbah appointed new PM.
6 In France, referendum approval given in low turnout to Government's political and economic development plan for New Caledonia (see 25 June).
Greece's worst post-war political scandal intensified with flight of Bank of Crete chairman George Koskotas, who had been accused of massive embezzlement and other offences; later in month Public Order and Justice Ministers resigned.
In China, more than 700 believed dead in earthquake in Yunnan province.
7 Soviet Nobel prizewinner Andrei Sakharov, visiting USA (his first trip abroad for 30 years), called on the West to back policy of *perestroika* (see 3 June, 20 Oct.).
In UK, a White Paper on Broadcasting (Cmnd. 517), envisaged an enlarged framework for television broadcasting and proposed a fifth terrestrial channel for 1993.
Prince and Princess of Wales began five-day official visit to France.
8 In US presidential election, George Bush (Republican) defeated Michael Dukakis (Democrat) taking 54 per cent of popular vote; in congressional elections Democratic Party increased its majority in Senate and House of Representatives.

GATT concluded 44th annual meeting with assertion that 'Uruguay round' multilateral trade negotiations could only succeed if Third World's need for special treatment were acknowledged by industrialized states.

In Ethiopia, in a major policy switch President Mengistu announced support for private economic investment.

10 UK-Iran memorandum signed in Vienna providing for resumption of normal diplomatic relations.

In UK, Scottish National Party won by-election at Glasgow Govan, overturning Labour majority of 19,500.

In UK, a report on fire at King's Cross Underground station in Nov. 1987 accused London Transport of 'dangerous, blinkered self-sufficiency'; Transport Secretary announced £266 million programme for improved safety.

11 In West Germany, president of Bundestag, Dr Philipp Jenninger, resigned amid controversy over speech the previous day marking 50th anniversary of *Kristallnacht* anti-Jewish pogrom.

14 Spain and Portugal became members of WEU, bringing its membership to nine.

15 PLO leader Yassir Arafat read proclamation of Palestine National Council (PNC) session in Algiers declaring an independent state of Palestine, its legitimacy based on UN Resolution 181 (1947) and with Jerusalem as its capital; PNC also voted to endorse UN Resolution 242 as basis for international Middle East peace conference (see 13 Dec. and DOCUMENTS).

16 In general election in Pakistan, Benazir Bhutto's Pakistan People's Party won 94 seats in National Assembly; its main rival, Islamic Democratic Alliance, won 54 seats (see 2 Dec.).

17 Mrs Thatcher on two-day visit to Washington for farewell meeting with President Reagan and talks with President-elect Bush.

18 President Gorbachev on three-day official visit to India.

In Yugoslavia, thousands of Albanians demonstrated in Pristina, Kosovo, following resignations of two of their leaders under Serbian pressure (see 6 Oct.).

21 General election in Canada was won by the ruling Progressive Conservative party led by PM Brian Mulroney.

22 In UK, state opening of Parliament; Queen's Speech foreshadowed Bills on water and electricity privatization and reform of Official Secrets Act.

US-Australian accord reached on continued US use of two controversial joint defence facilities in Australia.

In US, the B-2 'Stealth' bomber, the most expensive warplane ever built, made first public appearance.

23 In S. Africa, President Botha announced reprieve for the so-called 'Sharpeville Six' who had been sentenced to death for murder of black township official.

24 In Hungary, Miklos Nemeth appointed PM.

In USSR, Muslim Azerbaijanis were reported to be massacring Christian Armenians in renewed ethnic violence in Azerbaijan and Armenia.

Egypt and Algeria restored diplomatic relations, broken by the latter over the 1979 Egypt-Israel peace treaty; among Arab states, only Syria, Libya and Lebanon remained without formal ties with Cairo.

25 In Thailand, after four days of floods and mudslides over 400 people were reported dead.

26 US State Department announced refusal of visa to enable PLO leader Yassir Arafat to address UN General Assembly in New York; 30 Nov., Assembly deplored US action in 151–2 vote (see 13, 15 Dec.).

President Mitterrand of France in USSR for launch of Franco-Soviet space mission and talks with President Gorbachev.

28 In USSR, Central Committee of Communist Party approved controversial changes to the country's constitution and a new electoral law: these were passed into law by the Supreme Soviet on 29 Nov.

CHRONICLE OF EVENTS 615

In UK, Picasso's *Acrobate et Jeune Arlequin* sold at Christie's, London for record £20.9 million.

84th Opec ministerial meeting in Vienna concluded with first unanimous oil production agreement since 1986; covering the first half of 1989, it specified an aggregate ceiling of 18,500,000 bpd (including parity between Iran and Iraq) and a reference price of $18 per barrel.

29 In Bangladesh, more than 3,000 died when a tidal wave struck coastal areas.
30 In UK, Government published a Bill to replace 1911 Official Secrets Act.

DECEMBER

1 Carlos Salinas de Gortari inaugurated as President of Mexico (see 6 July).
2 Miss Benazir Bhutto sworn in as PM of Pakistan (see 16 Nov.).
 A two-day summit conference of EC Heads of Government opened in Rhodes.
 Five armed robbers hijacked Soviet plane and forced it to fly to Israel; the hijackers were returned to USSR by Israeli authorities.
4 In presidential election in Venezuela Carlos Andrés Pérez (ruling Democratic Action Party) defeated his Christian Democrat opponent by a wide margin.
 In Argentina, a mutiny by 500 army officers was put down by troops loyal to President Alfonsín.
5 In S. Korea, President Roh Tae Woo announced major Cabinet reshuffle, naming Kang Young Hoon PM.
7 President Gorbachev, addressing UN General Assembly in New York, announced plans to reduce Soviet armed forces by 500,000 and to cut conventional arms (see DOCUMENTS).
 In USSR, a devastating earthquake in Armenia killed an estimated 25,000 and made 500,000 homeless; an unprecedented international relief effort was mounted in subsequent days.
9 In Japan, Finance Minister Kiichi Miyazawa resigned over Recruit/Cosmos share-trading scandal.
11 In USSR, 78 died when a plane carrying relief supplies to earthquake victims crashed at Leninakhan; a Yugoslav relief plane crashed on 12 Dec. killing 7.
12 In UK, 34 died in a rail crash at Clapham, S. London, Britain's worst such accident for 20 years.
 In N. Korea, Yon Hyong Muk replaced Yi Kun Mo as PM.
13 PLO leader Yassir Arafat, addressing UN General Assembly in Geneva, pledged PLO support for 'a joint and lasting settlement' of the Palestinian problem, stressed his opposition to terrorism and proposed a new three-point plan for international conference on Middle East peace (see 15 Dec.).
14 In Spain, trade unionists staged 24-hour general strike, the first general strike in Spain for 50 years.
15 In UK, Conservatives held seat at Epping by-election with reduced majority.
 US announced resumption of contacts with PLO, ending 13-year boycott; 16 Dec. US ambassador in Tunis had talks with PLO representatives.
16 In UK, Mrs Edwina Currie, Under-Secretary of State for Health, resigned over a controversy about salmonella infection which had plunged British egg industry into crisis.
19 In Sri Lanka, Ranasinghe Premadasa narrowly defeated Mrs Sirima Bandaranaike in presidential election: many had died in pre-election violence.
 Rajiv Gandhi held summit talks in Beijing with Chinese leaders; he was the first Indian leader to visit China for 34 years.
21 In UK, a Pam Am Boeing 747 crashed at Lockerbie, Scotland, killing all 258 aboard and 11 people on the ground; it was Britain's worst-ever air disaster; 38 Dec. investigators confirmed crash was caused by terrorist bomb.

In Vanuatu, President Sokomanu arrested on orders of PM Fr Walter Lini on charge of inciting mutiny.
22 Namibian independence agreement formally signed at UN in New York by Angolan Cuban and South African Foreign Ministers, providing for implementation of UN Resolution 435 from 1 April 1989 and phased withdrawal of Cuban forces from Namibia (see DOCUMENTS).
29 Indian PM Rajiv Gandhi in Pakistan for talks with PM Bhutto and summit conference of SAARC.
30 Government of Yugoslavia, led by PM Branko Mikulic, resigned after Parliament blocked proposed economic reform package.

INDEX

AALTO, Alvar, 474
ABBADO, Claudio, 478
ABDIC, Fikret, 132
ABDUL-JABBAR, Kareem, 526
ABEYGUNASEKERA, Ossie, 320
ABRAHAMS, Gerald, death, 475
ABU IYAD, 204
ABU JIHAD (Khalil al Wazir), 204, 205, 212
ABU MUSA, 214
ABU NIDAL (Sabri al Banna), 204, 215
ABUBAKAR III, Alhaji Sir Sadiq, Sultan of Sokoto, death, 260; obit., 581
ACLAND, Janet, 527
ACQUIRED IMMUNE DEFICIENCY SYNDROME (AIDS), 56, 387, 442–3, 470
ADAMEC, Ladislav, 121, 612
ADAMI, Dr Eddie Fenech, Prime Minister of Malta, 188–9
ADAMS, John, 474, 477
ADDAMS, Charles, obit., 581
ADLER, Kurt Herbert, death, 475
AFEWERKI, Isayas, 247
AFGHANISTAN, 1, 60-1, 72, 218, 304, 305–7, 311; Geneva agreements (*text*), 563–7; Soviet troop withdrawal, 306–7, 315, 378–80, 563–7
AFRICAN CONFERENCES AND ORGANIZATIONS, 414–17
AFRICAN NATIONAL CONGRESS (ANC), 290, 293–4, 295, 296, 298, 300
AGA KHAN, Prince Sadruddin, 379, 605
AHERN, Mike, 364
AHMED, Moudud, 316
AIDS, *see* Acquired Immune Deficiency Syndrome
AITKEN, John, 31
AKHROMEYEV, Marshal, 434
AKIHITO, Crown Prince, of Japan, 356, 611
ALATAS, Ali, 337
ALBANIA, 135, 136–7, 191
ALBERY, Sir Donald, death, 482
ALBORETO, Michele, 524
ALDEN, David, 474
ALDRIDGE, John, 518
ALEBUA, Ezekiel, Prime Minister of Solomon Islands, 374
ALEKSANDROV, Chudomir, 129
ALESANA, Tofilau Eti, 374, 603
ALFONSÍN, Raúl, President of Argentina, 73, 598, 615
ALGABID, Hamid, 270
ALGERIA, 2, 197, 233, 239–42; foreign relations, 236–8, 243

ALLAIS, Maurice, 533
ALMEIDA, Maria, 479, 480
ALSTON, Richard, 480
ALVAREZ, Prof. Luis Walter, obit., 581
AMIN, Idi, 255
AMIRTHALINGAM, Appapillai, 318
AMIS, Kingsley, 508
AMNESTY INTERNATIONAL, 81, 98, 198, 248, 290
ANANIASHVILI, Nina, 479
ANDERSON, Bob, 527
ANDERTON, Jim, 369
ANDREEVA, Nina, 104
ANDREOTTI, Giulio, 154, 157
ANDREWES, Sir Christopher, obit., 581
ANGA, Colonel Pierre, 274
ANGELL, Norman, 1
ANGOLA, 1, 283–6; ceasefire, 285; Cuban forces in, 284–6, 297, 384, 577, 616; foreign relations, 277; peace negotiations, 84, 284–6; South African forces in 283–6; tripartite agreement, 286, 292–3, 577–8, 616; US mediation, 284–6
ANNIGONI, Pietro, obit., 581
ANTHEIL, George, 477
ANTIGUA AND BARBUDA, 100–1
ANYAGOLU, Anthony, 257
AOUITA, Said, 517
AOUN, General Michel, 213, 214, 611
AQUINO, Corazon, President of the Philippines, 334, 338, 339
ARAB MONETARY FUND, 221, 223
ARAB STATES OF THE GULF, 223–30
ARAB WORLD, 203–6
ARAFAT, Yassir, 42, 64, 201, 204, 205, 210, 212, 214, 221, 376, 382, 383, 397, 406, 603, 614, 615
ARCHITECTURE, 501–4
ARENS, Moshe, 199, 201
ARGENTINA, 72–4, 82, 424
ARGENTO, Dominick, 475
ARIAS MADRID, Dr Arnulfo, 89; obit., 581
ARIAS SÁNCHEZ, Oscar, President of Costa Rica, 88
ARIE, Raffaele, death, 475
ARMS CONTROL, 377–8, 427–34; ABM Treaty, 428; chemical weapons, 145; conventional forces, 62, 113, 432–4; Intermediate-range Nuclear Forces (INF) Treaty, 1, 61, 111, 427; space defence, US draft treaty, 60; strategic nuclear arms, 111, 427–8
ARMS TRADE, 423–7
ARMSTRONG, Henry, obit., 581
ART, 497–501

INDEX

ARUNDELL, Dennis, death, 475
ARUP, Sir Ove, death, 504; obit., 581
ASAD, Hafiz al-, President of Syria, 204, 211, 212
ASAMOAH, Dr Obed Y., 256
ASHBY, Hal, death, 492
ASHDOWN, Paddy, MP, 27, 35, 37, 608
ASHTON, Sir Frederick, 479, death, 475, 482; obit., 581–2
ASKOLDOV, Aleksandr, 491
ASYLMURATOVA, Altynai, 479, 481
ATHULATHMUDALI, Lalith, 319
ATTAS, Haidar Abu Bakr al-, President of South Yemen, 222
ATTENBOROUGH, Sir Richard, 489
AUGUST, Bille, 491
AUKEN, Svend, 167
AUNG GYI, 328, 329
AUSTRALIA, 360–4; Aboriginals, 360, 364; arts, 473, 475, 477; bicentenary, 360; corruption, 364; economy, 362–4; education, 363, 364; foreign relations with: Canada, 360, Indonesia, 337, Italy, 157, Japan, 354, 360, Mauritius, 325, New Zealand, 360, 370, Papua New Guinea, 366, UK, 41, 360, USA, 360; new Houses of Parliament, 360–1; political affairs, 361–2
AUSTRIA, 176–8, 474
AUTHUKORALE, Gamini, 319
AVRIL, General Prosper, 85, 610
AXEL, Gabriel, 491
AYARI, Mohamed Saleh, 235
AYAT, General Lakhad, 241
AYCKBOURN, Alan, 486
AYRES, Gillian, 500
AZCÁRRAGA, Luis, 183
AZCONA DEL HOYO, José, President of Honduras, 66, 87
AZIZ, Muhammad Abd al-, 237, 238
AZIZ, Tariq, 216, 381

BABANGIDA, General Ibrahim, Head of State of Nigeria, 257, 259, 261
BABBITT, Bruce, 49, 50
BABOO, Mohamad Khalit, 334
BACON, Francis, 498, 500
BADJIE, Amadou, 262
BADJOGOUMÉ, Lieut.-Colonel Hilaire, 271
BAHAMAS, 99
BAHRAIN, 225, 226, 228, 229
BAICHOO, Anil, 325
BAKA, Prof. Wladyslaw, 118
BAKER, James, 53, 530
BAKER, Kenneth, MP, 24–5, 579, 599
BAKKOUCHE, Hédi, 236, 243
BALAGUER, Joaquín, President of Dominican Republic, 84–5
BALANCHINE, Georges, 480
BALFOUR OF INCHRYE, Lord, obit., 582

BALKAN FOREIGN MINISTERS' CONFERENCE, 135, 137, 191, 197
BALLARD, Lucien, obit., 582
BALLESTEROS, Seve, 520–1
BANDA, Hastings Kamuzu, President of Malawi, 289
BANDARANAIKE, Sirima, 319, 320, 615
BANETH, Jean, 530
BANGEMANN, Martin, 149
BANGLADESH, 316–17
BANHAM, Peter Reyner, death, 504
BANNA, Sabri al, see Abu Nidal
BARBADOS, 96–7
BARCO, Virgilio, President of Colombia, 77, 78, 598
BARKER, George, 509
BARNES, John, 518
BARODA, former Maharajah of, obit., 582
BAROUAN, General Zézé, 268
BARR, Jean-Marc, 486
BARRE, Raymond, 141, 603
BARROW, Dame Nita, 377
BARSCHEL, Uwe, 148
BART, Graham, death, 482
BARTLETT, Debbie, 407
BARTLETT DIAZ, Manuel, 90
BARYLA, General Jozef, 120
BARYSHNIKOV, Mikhail, 479
BASU, Jyoti, 310
BATMÖNH, Jambyn, President of Mongolia, 138, 139
BATU, Inal, 191
BAVADRA, Dr Timoci, 372
BEARDSLEY, Peter, 518
BEASANT, Dave, 519
BECK, Chip, 521
BECKER, Boris, 522
BECKETT, Samuel, 488
BEHESHTI, Ali Mohammed, 224, 225
BEIN, Johanan, 382
BEITH, Alan, MP, 27
BELAU, 373–4, 386
BELGIUM, 41, 157–9, 183
BELHADJ, Ali, 240
BELHOUCHET, Maj.-Gen. Abdallah, 241
BELIZE, 97–8, 101
BELLISARIO, Marisa, obit., 582
BELSTEAD, Lord, 9, 579, 598
BEN ALI, General Zayn al-Abdin, President of Tunisia, 232, 235–7, 241, 242
BENFREHA, Ahmed, 239
BENIN, 271
BENN, Tony, MP, 27–8, 29, 511
BENOIS, Nicola, death, 475
BENTSEN, Lloyd, 51, 52
BERECZ, János, 124
BÉRÉGOVOY, Pierre, 143, 144
BERGER, Gerhard, 524
BERGHAUS, Ruth, 474

INDEX

BERGMAN, Ingmar, 490
BERGSMA, Deanne, 479
BERKOFF, Steven, 488
BERLINGUER, Enrico, 155
BERNSTEIN, Leonard, 477, 485
BERRADA, Mohamed, 244
BERRI, Nabih, 214
BERTIE, Andrew, 189
BERTOLUCCI, Bernardo, 488
BESSAIEH, Boualem, 241
BESTMAN, John, 264
BHATTACHARYA, Bhabani, obit., 582
BHUTAN, 311
BHUTTO, Benazir, Prime Minister of Pakistan, 312, 314–15, 417, 511, 614–16
BHUTTO, Zulfikar Ali, 314
BIEHL, John, 88
BIKANER, former Maharajah of, obit., 582
BILAK, Vasil, 121
BILDT, Carl, 413
BINGHAM, John, 512
BINTLEY, David, 480
BIONDI, Matt, 516
BIRD, Lester, 101, 421
BIRD, Vere, Prime Minister of Antigua and Barbuda, 100
BIRENDRA, HM King, of Nepal, 321, 322
BÎRLEA, Stefan, 127
BIRTWISTLE, Harrison, 478, 484
BISHOP, Alan, 510
BISHOP, Maurice, 98
BIYA, Paul, President of Cameroon, 272
BJELKE-PETERSEN, Sir Johannes, 364
BLACK, Sir James, 448
BLACKLEY, Alexander, 476
BLAISDELL, Thomas C., obit., 582
BLAIZE, Herbert, Prime Minister of Grenada, 98
BLAKEMORE, Michael, 486
BLANCO, Salvador Jorge, 84
BLESSING, Lee, 487
BOAHEN, Prof. Adu, 256
BOITO, Arrigo, 474
BOLIVIA, 74
BOLKIAH, Sir Hassanal, Sultan of Brunei, 334
BOMBERG, David, 500
BOND, Samantha, 484
BONGO, Omar, President of Gabon, 273
BOODHOO, Harish, 324
BOOLELL, Sir Satcam, 324
BORDER, Allan, 523
BORJA CEVALLOS, Dr Rodrigo, President of Ecuador, 79, 604, 609
BOSSANO, Joe, Chief Minister of Gibraltar, 187, 602
BOTCHWAY, Kwesi, 256
BOTHA, P. W., President of South Africa, 277, 283, 289, 292, 293, 295, 299, 610, 612, 614

BOTHA, R. F. (Pik), 294, 296, 578, 609, 610
BOTSWANA, 293–4
BOUCETTA, M'hamed, 243
BOULARES, Habib, 236
BOULEZ, Pierre, 477
BOURASSA, Robert, 69, 70–1
BOURGUIBA, Habib, 235, 237, 243
BOUSENA, Sadok, 241
BOUTERSE, Desi, 102
BOWEN, Otis R., 580
BOWNESS, Sir Alan, 500
BRADY, Nicholas, 53, 580
BRAKE, Brian, obit., 582
BRANAUGH, Kenneth, 484
BRANDT, Willy, 182
BRAZIL, 74–6, 82, 424
BRENAA, Hans, death, 482
BREWSTER, Kingman, obit., 582
BREZHNEV, Leonid, 105, 113
BRIGHTMAN, Lord, 555
BRITTAN, Leon, 36, 39
BRITTEN, Benjamin, 473, 474
BRÍZOLA, Leonel, 75
BROAD, Eli, 501
BROADBENT, Edward, 69
BROCKWAY, Lord, obit., 582
BROME, Vincent, 510
BRONFMAN, Edgar Miles, 116
BROWN, Gordon, MP, 18
BRUNDTLAND, Gro Harlem, Prime Minister of Norway, 170, 171, 455
BRUNEI, 333–4
BRUNO, Frank, 526
BRUNSWIJK, Ronny, 102
BRYANT, David, 527
BUCARAM ORTIZ, Abdalá, 79
BUCEARA, Abdala, 604
BUCHANAN, John, 71
BUCKLEY, Nigel, 528
BUDD, Zola, 604
BUGOYA, Pierre, President of Burundi, 252, 278
BUHARI, General Mohammadu, 259
BUKHARIN, Nikolai, 599
BULGARIA, 128–30, 137, 197
BULL, Steve, 519
BURKE, Brian, 362
BURKINA FASO, 269–70
BURMA, 2, 328–9, 331
BURMEISTER, Anneliese, death, 475
BURNLEY, James H., IV, 580
BURNS, Arnold, 59
BURUNDI, 1, 277–8
BUSH, George, 48, 49–53, 55, 59, 62, 63, 82, 429, 455, 535–6, 580, 613, 614
BUSSOTTI, Sylvano, 475, 477
BUTLER-SLOSS, Lord Justice, 607

CACERE, Carlos, 77
CAFIERO, Antonio, 73

CALCAVECCHIA, Mark, 520
CAMARA, Commander Kerfalla, 266
CAMDESSUS, Michael, 387
CAMEROON, 272
CAMILION, Oscar, 194
CANADA, 68–72; arts, 499; economy, 71–2; foreign relations with Albania, 137, Australia, 360, US (free trade agreement), 68; general election, campaign and results, 68–70; language controversy, 70–1; peacekeeping role in Afghanistan, 72; provincial elections, 71
CANEPA, Adolfo, 187
CANIN, Ethan, 508
CAPE VERDE, 279–80
CAPELLI, Ivan, 524
CAPOTE, Truman, 510
CAPUTO, Dante, 73, 377, 384
CÁRDENAS, Lázaro, 90
CAREY, Peter, 506–7
CARIBBEAN COMMUNITY (Caricom), 98, 99, 421–2
CARIBBEAN ORGANIZATIONS, 421–2
CARIDI, General José, 73
CARLING, Will, 520
CARLSSON, Bernt, 384; obit., 582–3
CARLSSON, Ebbe, 172
CARLSSON, Ingvar, Prime Minister of Sweden, 172, 173, 174, 413
CARLUCCI, Frank, 244, 425, 580, 601
CARPIO NICOLLE, Jorge, 421
CARR, Lord, 20
CARRINGTON, Lord, 148
CARRINGTON, Norman, 511
CARTER, Elliott, 476
CARTER, Jimmy, 55
CARVER, Raymond, 508
CASH, Pat, 522
CASSIN, René, 386
CASTELL, Andrew, 486
CASTILLO, Herberto, 90
CASTRO RUZ, Fidel, President of Cuba, 79, 84, 91, 284
CAUTHEN, Steve, 525
CAVACO SILVA, Anibal, Prime Minister of Portugal, 185
CAVASOS, Lauro, 580
CAYGILL, David, 368
CEAUŞESCU, Elena, 127
CEAUŞESCU, Nicolae, President of Romania, 126, 127, 128, 401, 504, 612
CECIL, Henry, 525
CENTRAL AFRICAN REPUBLIC, 273–4
CEREZO AREVALO, Vinicio, President of Guatemala, 86
CHAD, 233, 272–3
CHADLI, Bendjedid, President of Algeria, 233, 236, 238, 240–2, 612
CHADWICK, Fiona, 480
CHAILLY, Riccardo, 478
CHALKER, Lynda, MP, 294

CHANNON, Paul, MP, 33, 579
CHAOVALIT YONGCHAIYUT, General, 330, 331
CHARLES, Eugenia, Prime Minister of Dominica, 101
CHARLES, HRH Prince, of Wales, 23, 360, 478, 501–2, 511, 598, 601, 613
CHARLTON, Jack, 518
CHATICHAI CHOONHAVAN, Maj.-Gen., 330, 609
CHATWIN, Bruce, 507
CHAVAN, S. B., 308
CHÁVEZ MENA, Fidel, 87
CHELWOOD, Lord, 20
CHEVÈNEMENT, Jean-Pierre, 143, 146
CHIAM SEE TONG, 334
CHIANG CHING-KUO, 350, 598; death, 349; obit., 583
CHIANG KAI-SHEK, 349
CHIANG WEI-GO, 351
CHIDZERO, Dr Bernard, 291
CHIEPE, Dr G., 294
CHILE, 76–7
CHINA, PEOPLE'S REPUBLIC OF, 337, 343–9; arms trade, 424–5, 426; FOREIGN AFFAIRS: relations with Hong Kong, 352; India, 311; Japan, 348, 354; Kampuchea, 341; Laos, 343; Mongolia, 140; Morocco, 243; Nepal, 321–2; Palestine, 205; Qatar, 225; Saudi Arabia, 219; Seychelles, 324; Taiwan, 344, 348; USA, 348; USSR, 344, 348; Vietnam, 340, 348
HOME AFFAIRS: corruption, 344, 347; economy, 343, 345–7; elections, 344; hijack, 351; inflation, 346; political reform, 344–5; population growth, 348–9; student unrest, 344, 347–8
CHIRAC, Jacques, 141–2, 144–5, 146, 372, 603, 604
CHISSANO, Joaquim Alberto, President of Mozambique, 283, 610
CHŇOUPEK, Bohuslav, 122
CHOE KWANG, 359
CHOUCHOUNOVA, Elena, 517
CHOWDHURY, Humayun Rasheed, 316, 317
CHOWDHURY, Mizanur Rahman, 316
CHOYBALSAN, Marshal Horloogiyn, 138
CHRÉTIEN, Jean-Loup, 447
CHRISTIE, Linford, 516
CHUN DOO HWAN, 357, 358
CHUN KYUNG HWAN, 357
CHURBANOV, General Yury, 113, 610
CINEMA, 488–92
CISSE, Souleymane, 491
CLAES, Willy, 157
CLANMORRIS, Lord, death, 512
CLARK, Joe, 68
CLARKE, Gerald, 510
CLARKE, Kenneth, MP, 13–14, 579

INDEX

CLEESE, John, 490
CLEMENTS, Sir John, death, 491; obit., 583
CLERIDES, Glafkos, 194, 600
CLOUTHIER, Manuel, 90
CLOWES, Peter, 188
CLWYD, Ann, MP, 45
COCKFIELD, Lord, 39, 394
COE, Sebastian, 517
COHAN, Robert, 480
COHN, Nat, death, 491
COLLIER, Matthew, 10
COLLINS, William, publishers, 506
COLOMBIA, 77–8, 82
COMECON (Council for Mutual Economic Assistance), 122, 128, 400–4
COMMONWEALTH, THE, 388–90; Committee of Foreign Ministers, 388; Commonwealth of Learning, 389; Commonwealth Trust, 390; environment, 389–90; programme funding, 390; small states, 390; South African issue, 388; UK attitude towards, 389;
COMOROS, 326
COMPAORÉ, Captain Blaise, Head of State of Côte d'Ivoire, 270
COMPTON, John, Prime Minister of St Lucia, 101, 421
CONFERENCE ON SECURITY AND COOPERATION IN EUROPE (CSCE), 177, 562
CONGO, 274
CONNOLLY, Maureen, 522
CONNOR, Dennis, 527
CONRAD, Peter, 511
CONSTÂNCIO, Manuel Vitor, 186
CONTÉ, Brigadier-General Lansana, President of Guinea, 266
COOK ISLANDS, 374
COOPER, Charles, 59
COOPER, Malcolm, 517
COPE, Jonathan, 479, 480
CORCUERA, José Luis, 181
CÓRDOVEZ, Diego, 306, 378
COSSIGA, Francesco, President of Italy, 153, 154, 157
COSTA, Manuel Pinto da, President of São Tomé and Príncipe, 280
COSTA RICA, 87, 88
CÔTE D'IVOIRE, 257, 268–9
COUNCIL OF EUROPE, 175, 406–8
COUTTS, Sir Walter, obit., 583
COWAN, Sir Zelman, 390
CRAFT, Hugh, 390
CRAGG, Tony, 499
CRAM, Steve, 517
CRANKO, John, 480
CRAXI, Bettino, 153, 154, 155
CRICHTON, Charles, 489
CRISTIANI, Alfredo, 87
CROCKER, Dr Chester, 284, 285, 286, 293
CRUICKSHANK, Andrew, death, 492

CRUMB, George, 476
CUBA, 79, 84, 91, 297, 384
CULLINAN, Brian, 295
CUNHAL, Alvaro, 186
CUNNINGHAM, Dr John, MP, 37, 482
CURRIE, Edwina, MP, 38, 615
CURTIS, Jamie Lee, 490
CUTHBERTSON, Allan, death, 491
CYPRUS, 5, 193–5, 195, 383; Greek-Turkish talks, 194, 197, 383
CZECHOSLOVAKIA, 120–3; dissent, 121–3; economy, 120; foreign relations, 122, 137; human rights, 122; resistance to reform, 121

DAGLEY, Norman, 527
DAHAR, Michel, 213
DALAI LAMA, 439, 602
DALI, Salvador, 500
DALLI, John, 189
DANCE/BALLET, 479–82
DANIEL, Yuli, obit., 583
DARMAN, Richard, 53
DART, Prof. Raymond, obit., 583
DĂSCĂLESCU, Constantin, 127
DASUKI, Ibrahim, 260
DAVIES, Denzil, MP, 29, 45
DAVIES, George, 505
DAVIES, Jonathan, 519
DAVIES, Laura, 521
DAVIES, Siobhan, 480
DAVIES, Terence, 489
DAVIS, Jack, 486
DAVIS, Steve, 527
DE BEER, Dr Zach, 299
DE CLEENE, Trevor, 368
DE CLERCQ, Willy, 400, 411
DE KOONING, Willem, 498
DE MEL, Ronnie, 320
DE MELO, Enrico, 184
DE MITA, Ciriaco, Prime Minister of Italy, 154–7, 601, 612
DE MOJANA, Fra Angelo, death, 190
DE TAYA, Lorenzi, 521
DE VALOIS, Dame Ninette, 482
DE VILLA, Maj.-Gen. Renato, 338
DEACON, Richard, 499
DEBT PROBLEMS (see also International Monetary Fund, World Bank), 529–31; Africa, 255, 258, 264, 274, 275; France as creditor, 145; Latin America and Caribbean countries, 74, 75, 77–8, 79, 82, 83, 87, 88, 91, 92, 94, 98, 101, 102; others, 126, 129, 326, 337, 339
DEE, Ruby, 488
DEHAENE, Jean-Luc, 157
DEISENHOFER, Dr Johann, 449
DEL MONACO, Giancarlo, 474
DEL POMAR, Manuel Angel, 81
DELAMURAZ, Jean-Pascal, 180
DELLUMS, Ronald V., 276

DELORS, Jacques, 31, 33, 40, 391–2, 395, 462
DELVALLE, Eric Arturo, 65, 89, 420, 600
DEMJANJUK, John, 603
DENCH, Judi, 484
DENG XIAOPING, 345
DENKTASH, Rauf, President of Turkish area of Cyprus, 194, 197
DENMARK, 166–8, 457, 459
DIAMOND, I. A. L., death, 491
DIANA, HRH Princess, of Wales, 478, 598, 613
DIBNAH, Corinne, 521
DIOUF, Abdou, President of Senegal, 264, 265, 266, 408, 600
DIRO, Ted, 365
DISARMAMENT, see Arms Control
DISHY, Bob, 488
DISSANAYAKE, Gamini, 319
DJIBOUTI, 248–9
DLAMINI, Prince Mfanasibili, 296
DLAMINI, Sotsha, 296
DO MUOI, 341, 606
DOE, General Samuel K., President of Liberia, 263, 608
D'OFFAY, Anthony, 500
DOLE, Robert, 49, 50
DOMINICA, 101
DOMINICAN REPUBLIC, 84–5
DORATI, Antal, death, 479; obit., 583
DOS SANTOS, Alfonso, 280
DOS SANTOS, José Eduardo, President of Angola, 283
DOUGLAS, Roger, 367, 368
DOWELL, Anthony, 479, 480
DOWNIE, Prof. Allan, obit., 583
DOYNOV, Ognyan, 129
DREES, Dr Willem, obit., 583
DRUG-TRAFFICKING, Latin America and Caribbean countries, 65, 74, 77, 81, 85, 88, 99, 101, 421–2; others, 57–8, 215, 324, 343
DRUMMOND, John, 478
DU PONT, Pierre, 49
DUARTE, José Napoléon, President of El Salvador, 87
DUBA, Ali, 212
DUBA, Rifa'at, 212
DUBČEK, Alexander, 121, 122–3, 157
DUBERSTEIN, Kenneth, 580
DUE, Ole, 463
DUFF, Hugh, 527
DÜGERSÜREN, Mangalyn, 140
DUKAKIS, Michael, 49–53, 608, 613
DUMAS, Roland, 143
DUMBUTSHENA, Enoch, 291
DUNCAN, Maria-Theresa, death, 482
DUNWOODY, Richard, 525
DUPUIS, George Bonello, 189
DURHAM, Bishop of, see Jenkins, Dr David

DURRANT, Jennifer, 500
DUVAL, Sir Gäetan, 324
DZARDYHAN, Kinayatyn, 139

EBAN, Abba, 201, 202
ECKERT, Fred, 387
ECONOMIC AND SOCIAL AFFAIRS (see also Comecon, Council of Europe, Debt Problems, Oil, Organization for Economic Cooperation and Development), 529–39; economic summits, 353; international economy, 531–33; statistical data, 540–54
ECONOMIC COMMUNITY OF WEST AFRICAN STATES (Ecowas), 261, 262, 271, 416
ECUADOR, 78–9
EDBERG, Stefan, 522
EDDERY, Pat, 525
EDDINGTON, Paul, 485
EDMONDS, John, 31
EDWARDS, Eddie, 515
EGAR, Colin, 523
EGYPT, 206–8, 460; anti-Coptic violence, 207; arms trade, 425; debt, 207–8; economy, 207–8; foreign relations, 197, 206–7, 217, 221, 225–6, 233, 237; Islamic investment companies, 208
EKUEMME, Alex, 259
EL SALVADOR, 87
ELDRIDGE, Florence, obit., 583–4
ELIASSON, Jan, 380, 381
ELIOT, Valerie, 509
ELIZABETH II, HM Queen, 184, 360, 603, 607, 612
ELLIS, Prof. John, 448
ELSEWORTH, David, 525
ELWAY, John, 527
ENGLHOLM, Björn, 148
ENVIRONMENT, 454–7; Antarctica, 455; Armenian earthquake, 109 (map), 113, 198; Commonwealth on, 389–90; deforestation, 75–6, 387, 456; dolphins, 455–6; drought and famine, 136, 232, 246, 267, 343, 388; earthquakes, 321; floods 231–2, 317, 321, 388; 'greenhouse effect', 34, 49, 76, 454; hurricanes and cyclones, 88, 92, 101, 370; locusts, 267, 388; North Sea seals, 150, 455; ozone layer depletion, 34, 76, 454; poaching of ivory and rhino horn in Kenya, 251; pollution, 130, 150–1; Swedish policy on, 172; toxic wastes and emissions, 127, 156, 259, 274, 279, 455, 456; tree-planting, 279
EQUATORIAL GUINEA, 260, 274–5
ERSHAD, Hussain Mohammad, President of Bangladesh, 316, 317, 321, 440, 601
ERSKINE, Ralph, 502
ERUNDINA, Luiza, 75
ESCHEIKH, Abdelhamid, 236
ESPERT, Nuria, 473

ESPIELL, Hector Gros, 238, 383
ESQUIVEL, Manuel, Prime Minister of Belize, 97
ETHIOPIA, 1, 207, 230, 245–7, 248
ETPISON, Ngiratkel, 373, 613
ETXEBESTE, Eugenio, 182
EUROPEAN COMMUNITY (*see also* European Community Law), 39–41, 391–7
 EXTERNAL AFFAIRS: aid to Ethiopia, 246; anti-dumping proceedings, 462; GCC, 227; meeting with Efta, 410–11; membership applications: Morocco, 243, Turkey, 196; relations with: Austria, 177–8, Malta, 189, New Zealand, 370, Switzerland, 179, Trinidad and Tobago, 96, USA, 66–7, 396, 462, USSR and Eastern Europe, 396–7; trade relations, 395–6
 INTERNAL AFFAIRS: agriculture, 394–5; budget, 395; Delors address to TUC, 31; Delors package, 391–2; economic and monetary union, 395; European Monetary System (EMS), 39; 'set-aside' schemes, 457; Single European Market, 173–4, 179, 392–4
EUROPEAN COMMUNITY LAW, 461–5
EUROPEAN COURT OF JUSTICE, 457, 462–4
EUROPEAN FREE TRADE ASSOCIATION (Efta), 402, 410–12
EUROPEAN SPACE AGENCY, 453
EVANS, Dr Williams, obit., 584
EVANS, Gareth, 362
EVANS, Gertrude, 448
EVANS, Ray, 519
EVERT, Chris, 522
EVREN, Kenan, President of Turkey, 196, 197, 608, 612
EVTIMOV, Evtim, 130
EYRE, Ronald, 487
EYSKENS, Gaston, obit., 584

FADIKA, Lamine, 268
FAGEOL, Rev Suzanne, 437
FAHRAT, David, 263
FALCONE, Giovanni, 156
FALDO, Nick, 520–1
FALKLAND ISLANDS, 73
FAMINE, *see* Environment
FARRELL, Mairaed, 187
FASHION, 504–5
FAURE, Edgar, obit., 584
FEBRES CORDERO, León, President of Ecuador, 79
FELDSTEIN, Martin, 536
FELDT, Kjell-Olof, 173
FELFE, Werner, 116
FERNÁNDEZ, Eduardo, 83
FERNÁNDEZ, Matilde, 181
FERNÁNDEZ, Sergio, 77
FERNÁNDEZ ORDÓÑEZ, Francisco, 180

FERNANDO, Father Chandra, 318
FERRANTI, Basil de, obit., 584
FERRARI, Enzo, obit., 584
FEYNMAN, Prof. Richard, obit., 584
FIENNES, Ralph, 483
FIJI, 3, 5, 372–3
FILALI, Abdel Latif, 243
FILMON, Gary, 71
FINLAND, 174–6
FINNBOGADÓTTIR, Vigdis, 169, 607
FINNISSEY, Michael, 475
FISCHER, Oskar, 116
FISHER, Alison, 527
FISHMAN, Michael, 512
FITZGERALD, Penelope, 507
FLATT, Jane, 407
FLETCHER, Roger, 528
FOJTIK, Jan, 121
FONTEYN, Dame Margot, 479
FOOT, Michael, MP, 510
FORD, Gerald, 55
FORNASETTI, Piero, obit., 585
FORSTER, R. F., 512
FOWLER, Norman, MP, 579
FRANCE, 141–7
 ARTS AND ENTERTAINMENT: 473–5, 481–2, 499, 507–8
 EXTERNAL AFFAIRS AND DEFENCE: aid for Côte d'Ivoire, 269; arms trade, 426; defence and nuclear weapons, 145–6; foreign relations, 237, 238; hostages in Lebanon, 144–5; *Rainbow Warrior* affair, 145; relations with: Algeria, 242, Cameroon, 272, Djibouti, 249, East Germany, 114, 145, Iran, 144–5, Iraq, 145, Mauritius, 325, New Zealand, 145, 369–70, São Tomé and Príncipe, 280, Saudi Arabia, 219, Spain, 183, Turkey, 196, USSR, 112, 145, Vietnam, 340; space mission, 145
 HOME AFFAIRS: economy, 144; political developments, 141–3; presidential and parliamentary elections, 141–3; strikes, 143–4
 OVERSEAS DEPARTMENTS AND TERRITORIES: 145, 146–7, 371–2
FRANJIEH, Sulaiman, 213
FRANTSEVA, I., 400
FRENAY, Henri, obit., 585
FRENCH POLYNESIA, 372
FREUD, Lucian, 500
FRIEDRICH, Götz, 473
FRIEL, Brian, 486
FUCHS, Dr Klaus, obit., 585
FULLER, Peter, 501
FURSTENBERG, H. E. Cardinal, obit., 585

GABON, 270, 273, 280
GALIMULLIN, 481
GALTIERI, Leopoldo, 613
GAMBIA, THE, 262

GANDHI, Rajiv, Prime Minister of India, 306, 308, 312, 315, 327, 417, 615, 616
GARANG, Col. John, 231
GARCÍA MÁRQUEZ, Gabriel, 508
GARCÍA PÉREZ, Alan, President of Peru, 81
GASKILL, William, 511
GATTING, Mike, 523
GAYLARD, Max, 390
GAYOOM, Maumoun Abdul, President of Maldives, 327, 613
GBEDEMAH, Lieut.-Colonel Mensah, 256
GEAGEA, Samir, 213, 214
GELLI, Licio, 156
GEMAYEL, Amin, 213, 611
GENERAL AGREEMENT ON TARIFFS AND TRADE (Gatt), 396
GENSCHER, Hans-Dietrich, 149, 400, 401
GEPHARDT, Richard, 49, 50
GERARD, Father Joseph, 295
GERASIMOV, Gennady, 61
GERMAN DEMOCRATIC REPUBLIC (East Germany), 114–16; economy, 116; foreign relations, 114–15, 145; Olympic games success, 116; treatment of Jews, 115–16
GERMANY, FEDERAL REPUBLIC OF (West Germany), 147–52
EXTERNAL AFFAIRS AND DEFENCE: arms trade, 426; nuclear weapons, 151; relations with: Albania, 137, Cameroon, 272, Costa Rica, 88, East Germany, 115, Finland, 175, India, 311, Nigeria, 260, Romania, 127, São Tomé and Príncipe, 280, Turkey, 196, USSR, 112, 147
HOME AFFAIRS: air crashes, 151; economy, 151–2; influx of ethnic Germans 147–8; political developments, 148–50; pollution of rivers and North Sea, 150–1; sport, 152
GERSONY, Robert, 281
GHAFFER KHAN, Khan Abdul, obit., 585
GHANA, 255–7, 270
GHANI, Major Abdul Aziz Abdul, 220
GHÉDIRA, Mohamed, 235
GHISING, Subash, 310
GHOZALI, Sid-Ahmed, 241
GIBRALTAR, 46, 183–4, 187–8
GIELGUD, Sir John, 486
GILBERT, Martin, 511
GILMOUR, Sir Ian, MP, 11
GLASS, Philip, 473
GLASSER, Ralph, 512
GLOUCESTER, HRH Duke of, 188
GOFF OF CHIEVELY, Lord, 555
GOH CHOK TONG, 334
GOLDFINGER, Erno, 503
GOMBOSÜREN, Tserenpiliyn, 140
GÓMEZ HURTADO, Alvaro, 78
GONZÁLEZ, Felipe, Prime Minister of Spain, 180, 182, 183, 184, 243

GOOCH, Graham, 523
GOOSSENS, Léon, death, 479; obit., 585
GORBACHEV, Mikhail, President of USSR: and defence and arms control, 1, 42, 62, 111, 113, 378, 427, 432–4, 575–6, 605, 610, 615; foreign affairs, 60, 112, 120, 123, 128, 135, 140, 154–5, 157, 178, 284, 311, 379, 571–6, 598–9, 601–3, 614; home affairs, 103–8, 110, 115, 121, 400, 574–5, 600, 607, 612; UN address, 571–6
GORBACHEV, Raisa, 435
GORDEEVA, Ekaterina, 515
GORE, Albert, 49, 50
GORIA, Giovanni, 153
GORSHKOV, Admiral Sergei, obit., 585–6
GOSTEV, Boris, 108, 109
GOUBAYDULINA, Sofiya, 476
GOULDING, Marrack, 385
GOULED APTIDON, Hassan, Head of State of Djibouti, 249
GRAF, Steffi, 522
GRAHAM, Billy, 435
GRAHAM, Martha, 482
GRAHAM, Sheilah, obit., 586
GRAMAJO, General Héctor, 86
GRANDI, Count Dino, obit., 586
GREECE, 190–3; financial scandal, 192; foreign relations, 67, 135, 191; relations with Turkey, 190–1, 196–7; terrorism, 191–2
GREENBERG, Richard, 488
GREENE, Graham, 485, 508
GREENE, Justin, 486
'GREENHOUSE EFFECT', see Environment
GREENIDGE, Carl, 94
GREENSPAN, Alan, 55
GREENWOOD, Major Tom, 97
GREINER, Nick, 361
GRENADA, 98
GRETZKY, Wayne, 526–7
GRICE, Prof. Paul, obit., 586
GRIFFITH-JOYNER, Florence, 517
GRIFFITHS, Lord, 555
GRIMSHAW, Nicholas, 504
GRINKOV, Sergei, 515
GROMYKO, Andrei, 106, 107, 607, 611
GRÓSZ, Károly, General Secretary, Hungarian Socialist Workers' Party, 123–4, 128, 605
GUARE, John, 486
GUATEMALA, 86–7, 97
GUEDEN, Gladys, death, 475
GUÉRIN, Isabelle, 480
GUERRERO PAZ, General Manuel, 78
GUEYE, Tené Youssouf, death, 268
GUILLEM, Sylvie, 480
GUIMARÃES, Ulysses, 75
GUINEA, 266–7
GUINEA-BISSAU, 279

INDEX

GUINNESS, Sir Alec, 487
GULF COOPERATION COUNCIL (GCC), 211, 224, 227
GULF STATES, see Arab States of the Gulf
GULF WAR, 1, 205–6, 218, 223, 224–5, 302–4, 380–1; ceasefire, 215–17, 304, 375, 380–1; peace talks, 304, 380–1
GULLIT, Ruud, 518
GUNAWARDENE, Charles, 390
GURNEY, A. R., 487
GUTIÉRREZ, Antonio, 182
GUTTENBERG, Steve, 490
GUTTO, Shadrack, 290
GUYANA, 3, 93–4
GUZMÁN, Abimael, 80

HABGOOD, Most Rev Dr John, 437
HABRÉ, Hissène, President of Chad, 233, 273, 415, 605
HADLEE, Richard, 523
HADLEY, Adrian, 519
HAGEN, Carl I., 170
HAIG, General Alexander, 49
HAILSHAM, Lord, 20
HAITI, 2, 85, 421
HAITINK, Bernard, 473, 478
HAKIM, Albert, 58
HAKIM, Sayyid Mahdi al-, 231
HALL, Sir Peter, 474, 483, 486
HAMAD, Rashid, 253
HAMAD, Seif Shariff, 253
HAMADA, Takujiro, 137
HAMBURGER, Michael, 509
HAMENGKUBUWONO IX, Sultan, obit., 586
HAMID OMAR, Tan Sri Abdul, 332
HAMILTON, Sir Denis, obit., 586
HAMILTON, Hamish, obit., 586
HAMILTON, Ian, 510
HAMMOND, Eric, 30, 31
HAMPE, Michael, 474
HANCOCK, Sir Keith, obit., 586–7
HANCOCK, Tim, 528
HANNAH, Darryl, 490
HANNAH, Nicholas, 296
HANSEN, Dr James, 454, 518
HARE, David, 485
HARFORD, Ray, 519
HARMEL, Mohamed, 235
HARRIS, Rev Barbara, 437, 611
HARRIS, Rosemary, 486
HARRISON, Frank Ll., death, 479
HART, Gary, 49, 50
HARTMANN, Rudolf, death, 475
HARVEY, Cynthia, 479
HASSAN, Sir Joshua, 187
HASSAN II, HM King, of Morocco, 238, 239, 243, 244
HATTERSLEY, Roy, MP, 27, 28, 29, 32
HAU PEI-TSUN, 351
HAUGHEY, Charles, Prime Minister of Irish Republic, 41, 163–6

HAUK, Rick, 59
HAUSSMANN, Helmut, 149
HAWKE, Bob, Prime Minister of Australia, 361, 363, 364
HAWKING, Stephen, 512
HAYDEN, Bill, 361–2
HAYHOE, Sir Barney, MP, 19
HEALEY, Denis, MP, 28
HEANEY, Seamus, 510
HEATH, Edward, MP, 18, 19, 22, 23
HEFFER, Eric, MP, 28, 32
HEINLEIN, Robert, death, 512
HELMINEN, Major-General Rauli, 379
HENDRICKSE, Rev Allan, 299
HENDRICKSON, Mason, 335
HENG SAMRIN, 341, 418
HENSON, Nicky, 486
HENZE, Hans Werner, 477, 479
HERMANNSSON, Steingrimur, Prime Minister of Iceland, 169, 611
HERRINGTON, John, 447, 580
HERRMANN, Edward, 487
HERZOG, Chaim, President of Israel, 202, 604, 613
HESELTINE, Michael, MP, 19, 22, 33
HICK, Graeme, 523
HIGGINS, Lt.-Col. William, 600
HILAIRE, Laurent, 480
HILL, Graham, 524
HILLER, Dame Wendy, 486
HILLIER, Bevis, 510
HIROHITO, HM Emperor, of Japan, 356, 611
HITCHCOCK, Prof. Edward, 443
HITCHINS, George, 448
HNATSYSHYN, Ray, 70
HOCKNEY, David, 500
HODEL, Donald Paul, 580
HODGES, Sally, 528
HOFFMAN, Karel, 121
HOLDEN, Anthony, 511
HOLDGATE, Dr Martin, 390
HOKERI, Harri, 174
HOLLINGHURST, Alan, 508
HOLM, Richard, death, 475
HOLMES, Andy, 517
HOLMES, Larry, 526
HOLMES, Neil, 528
HOLMES, Prof. John Wendell, obit., 587
HOLROYD, Michael, 510
HONDURAS, 66, 87, 458
HONECKER, Erich, Head of State of East Germany, 114–16, 145, 598
HONEYGHAN, Lloyd, 526
HONG KONG, 351–2
HORNE, Alistair, 511
HOSS, Salim al-, 213, 611
HOUGHTON, Ray, 518
HOUNTOUNJI, Captain, death, 271
HOUPHOUËT-BOIGNY, Félix, President of Côte d'Ivoire, 268–9

626 INDEX

HOUSEHOLD, Geoffrey, death, 512; obit., 587
HOUSEMAN, John, death 492; obit., 587
HOWARD, Brian, 475
HOWARD, John, 361, 362
HOWARD, Trevor, death, 491; obit., 587
HOWE, Sir Geoffrey, MP, 14–15, 39, 42, 184, 188, 255, 259, 409, 579, 601
HOYTE, Desmond, President of Guyana, 94
HUBER, Prof. Robert, 449
HUGHES, Arwel, 475
HUGHES, Roy, MP, 45
HUGHES, Ted, 486
HULTON, Sir Edward, obit., 587
HUMAN RIGHTS (*see also* Amnesty International), 79, 81, 98, 111, 115, 122, 128, 130, 198, 247–8, 250, 259, 335, 386, 407, 460–1
HUMPHREY, John, 95
HUN SEN, 341
HUNGARY, 123–5; economy, 124; foreign relations, 127–8, 137, 178, 311; leadership change, 123
HUNT, General Sir Peter, obit., 587
HURD, Douglas, MP, 23, 494, 579
HUSAIN, HM King, of Jordan, 64, 201, 208, 209–10, 221, 608
HUSÁK, Gustáv, President of Czechoslovakia, 121
HUTCHINSON, Sir Joseph, obit., 587
HUXLEY, Sir Leonard, obit., 587
HWANG, David Henry, 487
HYTNER, Nicholas, 473

IACOVOU, George, 194
IANCU, Georghe, 480
IBÁÑEZ, Blanca, 83
ICELAND, 169
IDIAGBON, General Tunde, 259
IKEDA, Youson, obit., 587
ILETO, Rafael, 338
IMLACK, Mark, 509
INDIA, 1, 2, 5, 308–12; ballistic missile, 425; by-elections, 309; Defamation Bill, 309; economy, 310–11; foreign relations, 112, 205, 306, 311–12, 315, 321; Government reshuffle, 308; paratroopers in Maldives, 312, 327; surface-to-surface missile, 312; terrorism and unrest, 309–10
INDONESIA, 1, 336–7, 366
INDRA, Alois, 121
INSALCO, Giuseppe, death, 155
INTER-AMERICAN DEVELOPMENT BANK (IDB), 88
INTERNATIONAL COURT OF JUSTICE, 226, 259, 376, 458, 459
INTERNATIONAL LAW, 458–61
INTERNATIONAL MONETARY FUND (IMF), Africa, 244, 248, 251, 256, 264, 266, 271–2, 274–5, 287; Americas and Caribbean, 87,
79, 92, 96; Asia, 326, 331, 339; Berlin meeting, 17; meetings with other organizations, 387, 399
IRAN (*see also* Gulf War): 1, 197, 229, 302–5; civilian airliner shot down, 304; domestic politics, 305; economy, 305; foreign relations, 304–5; relations with: France, 144–5, Kuwait, 224, Lebanon, 214, Oman, 225, Saudi Arabia, 219, Syria, 211–12, Turkey, 197, UAE, 225, UK, 42, USA, 62–3
IRAQ (*see also* Gulf War), 1, 215–18; arms trade, 424; economy, 217–18; mediation between Chad and Libya, 273; oil, 229; relations with: Egypt, 217, France, 145, Lebanon, 217, Syria, 211, 217, Turkey, 197; President's son disgraced, 217
IRELAND, REPUBLIC OF, 162–6; Anglo-Irish relations: extradition problems, 46, 164, 165–6; Ryan affair, 165–6; other issues, 41, 164–6; economy, 162–3; European Community, 166; report on poverty, 163
ISAACS, Jeremy, 473
ISAYEV, Stanislav, 481
ISLAMIC CONFERENCE ORGANIZATION (ICO), 270
ISLAMIC DEVELOPMENT BANK (IDB), 223
ISRAEL, 199–202; arms trade, 424–5; attitude to PLO, 382–3; economy, 202; elections, 199–201; Middle East peace prospects, 204–5; relations with: Egypt, 206–7, 460, Saudi Arabia, 219, Singapore, 336, Syria, 211, US, 63–4, 425; uprising in occupied territories, 1, 201–2, 203; 'Who is a Jew?', 200
ISSIGONIS, Sir Alec, obit., 587–8
ITALY, 153–7, 474–5, 477; economy, 156; elections, 154–5; foreign relations, 157, 183, 198, 311; institutional reforms, 155; political developments, 153–5; pollution and waste, 156, 455; terrrorism and crime, 155–6;
IVORY COAST, *see* Côte d'Ivoire

JACKSON, Michael, 478
JACKSON, Rev Jesse, 6, 49–51
JACOBI, Derek, 484
JACOBS, Prof. Francis, 464
JACOBSEN, Svend, 167
JACOBSON, Lord, obit., 588
JAKEŠ, Miloš, 121
JAKOBOVITS, Lord, 438, 440
JALLOUD, Major Abdul Salem, 233, 234
JAMAICA, 91–3, 101
JAMALUDDIN, Awang Abdul Samad, 334
JAPAN, 227, 229, 352–7; Cabinet reshuffle, 356–7; Emperor's illness, 355, 356; foreign trade, 462; rail and sea disasters, 353; Recruit scandal, 355–6; relations

with: Albania, 137; Australia, 354, 360, China, 348, 354, India, 311, Laos, 343, New Zealand, 354, Philippines, 339, South Korea, 354, Turkey, 198, UK, 353, 356, USA, 353, USSR, 354–5, Vietnam, 340; tax problems, 355; technology, 449, 452, 453; transport and communications, 353
JARDIN, Alexandre, 508
JAROWINSKY, Werner, 115
JARRE, Jean-Michel, 479
JARUZELSKI, General Wojciech, Head of State of Poland, 118, 609
JASARI, Kacusa, 133
JASTRZEBSKI, Dominik, 119
JAUNCEY OF TULLICHETTLE, Lord, 555
JAWARA, Sir Dawda Kairaba, President of The Gambia, 262
JAYAWARDENE, Junius R., President of Sri Lanka, 318
JEFFERIES, Stephen, 479
JENKINS, Clive, 30
JENKINS, Dr David, Bishop of Durham, 24, 437
JENKINS, Lord, 19, 512
JENNINGER, Dr Philipp, 148, 614
JEWKES, Prof. John, obit., 588
JEYARETNAM, J. B., 335
JHA, Lakshmi, obit., 588
JOBS, Steve, 449–50
JOFFREY, Robert, death, 482; obit., 588
JOHANES, Jaromír, 122
JOHN, Brynmor, MP, death, 45
JOHN, Elton, 498
JOHN PAUL II, HH Pope, 80, 177, 282, 292, 295, 407, 436, 438, 600, 604, 606, 610
JOHNS, Jasper, 497, 498
JOHNSON, Ben, 515, 516, 527, 611
JOHNSON, Philip, 504
JONATHAN, Chief Leabua, 295
JONES, Barry, MP, 45
JONES, Bill T., 482
JONES, Rev Richard, 437
JONES, Rosie, 522
JONES, Roy, 516
JORDAN, 64, 208–11, 221, 311, 426; West Bank, 201, 208–9, 569–70
JORDAN, Bill, 31
JORDAN, Neil, 490
JOTTI, Nilde, 155
JOXE, Pierre, 143
JUAN CARLOS I, HM King, of Spain, 184, 370, 408
JUGNAUTH, Sir Aneerood, Prime Minister of Mauritius, 324
JUMA, Dr Omar Ali, 253
JUNEJO, Mohammad Khan, 313, 605

KÁDÁR, János, 123, 124, 125, 604
KAIPAYI, Joseph, 263
KAMPUCHEA, 1, 2, 337, 340, 341–2

KANG YOUNG HOON, 615
KANTHASAMY, K., 318
KAPOOR, Raj, death, 491
KARANJA, Dr Josephat, 249, 602
KARANJA, Peter, 250
KARGE, Manfred, 485
KARIKARI, Kwame, 256
KARSTENS, Gerda, death, 482
KAUNDA, Kenneth, President of Zambia, 237, 287–8, 414, 605, 613
KAWAWA, Sophia, 253
KEATING, Paul, 361, 363, 364
KEITH OF KINKEL, Lord, 36, 555
KEMP, Jack, 49, 50
KENGO WA DONDO, 277
KENNEDY, Anthony, 58
KENNEDY, Douglas, death, 482
KENNEDY, Edward, 276
KENNER, Ralph, 510
KENYA, 41, 249–51, 255
KENYON, John, 512
KERLY, Sean, 517
KERSEE-JOYNER, Jackie, 517
KHAMENE'I, Seyed Ali, President of Iran, 304
KHAN, Ghulam Ishaq, President of Pakistan, 313, 314, 609
KHAN, Sahabzada Yaqub, 314
KHAN, Zafrullah, 386
KHARCHEV, Konstantin, 435, 436
KHEDIRI, El-Hadi, 240
KHIEU SAMPHAN, 341
KHOMEINI, Ayatollah Ruhollah, 63, 144, 305, 608
KHURAFI, Jassim al-, 226
KIARO, General Ernest Mwita, 252
KIBAKI, Mwai, 249, 250
KIESINGER, Dr Kurt Georg, obit., 588
KIESLOWSKI, Krzyztof, 490
KIM YONG CHUL, 358
KIM IL SUNG, President of North Korea, 359
KING, Mackenzie, 69
KING, Tom, MP, 164, 579, 600
KINNOCK, Neil, MP, 10, 11, 24, 27–30, 32–33, 35–38, 292
KISEKKA, Dr Samson, 254
KISZCZAK, General Czeslaw, 118
KIVENGERE, Festo, Bishop of Kigezi, 255
KIVISTÖ, Kalevi, 174
KIWELU, Maj.-Gen. Tumainieli N., 252
KIYONGA, Dr Crispus, 254
KJELLIN, Alf, death, 491
KLEIN, Melanie, 485
KLEPPE, Per, 412
KLINE, Kevin, 490
KOERING, René, 475
KOHL, Helmut, Chancellor of West Germany, 40, 112, 115, 122, 147–9, 196, 392, 431–2, 598–9, 613
KOIVISTO, Mauno, President of Finland, 174, 176, 599

KONTAGORA, Brigadier Moman, 260
KONZELMANN, Gerhard, 475
KOPP, Elisabeth, 178
KOPP, Hans W., 178
KOREA, DEMOCRATIC PEOPLE'S REPUBLIC OF (North Korea), 247, 358–9
KOREA, REPUBLIC OF (South Korea), 354, 357–8, 358–9
KOSKOTAS, George, 192, 613
KOSSOFF, Leon, 500
KOSTOPOULOS, Sotiris, 191
KOUTSOGIORGAS, Agamemnon, 192
KOYAMI, Lieut.-Col. François, 271
KPOLLE, Gabriel, 263
KRIEHL, Marina, 515
KRISTIANSEN, Ingrid, 517
KROLIKOWSKI, Werner, 116
KRUNIC, Bosko, 133
KUDU, Sarkin, 260
KUMARANATUNGA, Vijaya, 319
KUPFER, Harry, 474, 475
KURDS, 5, 197–8, 216, 217
KURIA, Archbishop Manasses, 250
KUWAIT, 197, 224–7, 229–30, 304
KYPRIANOU, Spyros, 194, 600

LACROIX, Christian, 505
LAFLEUR, Jacques, 372
LAFONTAINE, Oskar, 149, 150
LAING, Hugh, death, 482
LAKWENA, Alice, 254
LALONDE, Danny, 526
LAMBSDORFF, Otto Graf, 149
L'AMOUR, Louis, death, 513
LAMPERT, Catherine, 500
LANGE, David, Prime Minister of New Zealand, 367, 368
LANGER, Bernhard, 521
LAOS, 331, 342–3
LARGO COX, Guillermo, 81
LASKI, Marghanita, death, 512; obit., 588
LASKY, Jess, Jr, death, 491
LAWRENCE, Laurie, 515
LAWSON, Nigel, MP, 10, 11, 12, 14–18, 34–5, 39, 538–9, 579
LE PEN, Jean-Marie, 141, 603
LEBANON, 1, 213–15; drugs, 215; foreign relations, 206, 217, 218, 304; hostages, 215; internal divisions, 213–14; Iranian involvement, 214; Syrian intervention, 211–12, 213–15;
LEDERMAN, Dr Leon, 449
LEE HYUN JAE, 351, 600
LEE KUAN YEW, Prime Minister of Singapore, 333, 334, 335, 610
LEE OF ASHERIDGE, Baroness, obit., 588
LEE SIEW CHOH, Dr, 334
LEE TENG-HUI, President of Taiwan, 349, 350
LEFÈBVRE, Archbishop Marcel, 438, 607

LEIBMAN, Ron, 488
LEICH, Bishop Werner, 115
LEIGHTON, Kenneth, death, 479
LEIJON, Anna-Greta, 172–3
LEIRIS, Louise, obit., 588
LEKHANYA, Maj.-Gen. Justin, Head of State of Lesotho, 295
LENDL, Ivan, 522
LENNON, John, 121
LEONARD, Dr Graham, 437
LEONARD, Ray, 526
LESOTHO, 295
LESSER, Anton, 483
LEVI, Peter, 509
LEVINE, James, 476
LEWIS, Carl, 516, 517
LI PENG, Premier of People's Repubic of China, 344, 345, 346
LI XIANNIAN, 322, 345
LIANI, Dimitra, 192
LIBERIA, 261, 263–4
LIBYA, 197, 232–4, 242, 276; arms trade, 424, 427; foreign relations, 189, 206–7, 233–4, 236, 238, 255, 272–3
LIEPA, Andris, 479
LIGACHEV, Yegor, 104, 611
LINDGREN, Astrid, 457
LINEKER, Gary, 518
LINI, Walter, Prime Minister of Vanuatu, 373, 616
LITERATURE, 505–14
LITTLE, William A., 478
LIVINGSTONE, Ken, MP, 32
LIVINGSTONE, Robert, death, 491
LLOYD WEBBER, Andrew, 487
LODGE, David, 507
LOEWE, Frederick, obit., 588–9
LOPEZ, Nancy, 522
LORGE, Rabbi Ernest, 116
LORING, Eugene, 481
LOSEV, Sergei, obit., 589
LOUDIÈRES, Monique, 480
LOUGANIS, Greg, 517
LUBBERS, Ruud, Prime Minister of the Netherlands, 160
LURIE, Alison, 508
LUSINCHI, Jaime, President of Venezuela, 82, 83
LUXEMBOURG, 161–2
LYLE, Sandy, 520
LYNG, Richard E., 580
LYUBIMOV, Yuri, 473

MCANALLY, Ray, 486
MCAVENNIE, Frank, 519
MACBRIDE, Sean, death, 166; obit., 589
MCCANN, Daniel, 187–8
MCCRACKEN, James, death, 475; obit., 589
MACDONALD, Flora, 70

INDEX

MACDONALD, Jim, 526
MACDONALD, Margo, 43
MACDOUGALL, Sir Donald, 18
MCEWAN, Geraldine, 484
MCFARLANE, Robert, 58
MACGREGOR, John, MP, 579
MCINTYRE, Mike, 517
MACKAY OF CLASHFERN, Lord, 42, 439, 579
MCKENNA, Frank, 71
MCKENZIE, Duke, 526
MACKENZIE STUART, Lord, 463
MACLENNAN, Robert, MP, 26
MCLAUGHLIN, Ann Dore, 580
MCMAHON, Sir William, obit., 589
MCMILLAN, Tom, 70
MACSHARRY, Ray, 163, 166
MCWILLIAM, Candia, 508
MADAGASCAR, 326
MAGNUS-ALLCROFT, Sir Philip, obit., 589
MAGHREB COMMISSION, 237, 242
MAGUIRE, Lieut., 73
MADHI, Sayyid Sadiq al-, Prime Minister of Sudan, 231
MAHER, Terry, 506
MAHFOUD, Shaikh, 240
MAHFOUZ, Naguib, 208, 440, 506
MAHLER, Dr Halfdan, 387
MAHMUD, Anisul Islam, 317
MAHATHIR MOHAMAD, Dr, Prime Minister of Malaysia, 332, 333
MAJOR, John, MP, 17, 579
MAKAROVA, Natalia, 479, 480
MALAKHOV, Vladimir, 481
MALAN, Dr D. F., 297
MALAN, General, 284
MALAWI, 288–9
MALAYSIA, 331–3, 335, 343
MALDIVES, 312, 327
MALE, James, 528
MALENKOV, Georgiy, obit., 589
MALI, 267
MALIK, Charles, 386
MALILE, Reis, 137
MALMIERCA PEOLI, Isidoro, 577, 578
MALTA, 188–90
MALUF, Paulo, 75
MAMBA, George, 296
MAMET, David, 487
MANAROV, Musa, 446
MANCHESTER, William, 511
MANCINI, Frederico, 464
MANDELA, Nelson, 300, 479, 608
MANGOPE, Lucas M., President of Bophuthatswana, 599
MANIGAT, Leslie, 85, 598, 606
MANLEY, Dexter, 527
MANLEY, Michael, 92
MANN, Charles, 527
MANSELL, Nigel, 524
MAQEKEZA, Mazizi Attwell, 295

MARA, Ratu Sir Kamisese, Prime Minister of Fiji, 373, 420
MARAJ, Dr James, 389
MARCHAND, Jean, obit., 589
MARJAI, József, 402
MARSHALL OF GORING, Lord, 38
MARSHALL, Sir John, obit., 589–90
MARSHALL, Sir Peter, 390
MARTENS, Dr Wilfried, Prime Minister of Belgium, 41, 158, 159, 604
MARTIN, Christopher, 502
MARTIN, Peter, 481–2
MASIRE, Quett, President of Botswana, 294, 609
MASLYUKOV, Yuri, 108
MASSIGLI, René, obit., 590
MASTROIANNI, Marcello, 490
MATES, Michael, MP, 19
MATTHEWS, Dennis, death, 479
MAUNG MAUNG, Dr, 329, 609, 611
MAURIN, Elisabeth, 480
MAURITANIA, 267–8
MAURITIUS, 323, 324–5
MAXIMOVNA, Ita, death, 475
MAXWELL, Robert, 495, 505
MAXWELL-DAVIES, Peter, 475
MAYHEW, Sir Patrick, MP, 164
MAYOTTE, Tim, 522
MBAYE, Kéba, 460
MEAD, Robert, death, 482
MECCANICO, Antonio, 154
MECIR, Miloslav, 522
MEDICINE (see also Acquired Immune Deficiency Syndrome, Sciences, Technology), 442–6
MEESE, Edwin, 58, 59, 607
MEHRI, Abdelhamid, 241
MEIER, Richard, 502
MEISNER, H. E. Cardinal Joachim, 438
MELEN, Ferit, obit., 590
MELLOR, David, MP. 409
MELTON, Richard, 66
MENDES, Francisco, 76
MENDEZ, Dr Aparicio, obit., 590
MENEM, Carlos, 73
MENGES, Chris, 489
MENGISTU HAILE-MARYAM, Lieut.-Colonel, President of Ethiopia, 245, 246, 247, 614
MERBAH, Kasdi, 239, 241, 613
MESSAADIA, Mohamed Cherif, 241
MESSIAEN, Olivier, 475, 477
MESSNER, Prof. Zbigniew, 118, 120, 611
MESTIRI, Ahmed, 235
MEXICO, 82, 89–91
MICHEL, Dr Hartmut, 449
MIKHAYLOV, Stoyan, 129
MIKI, Takedo, obit., 590
MIKULIC, Branko, 132, 616
MILLER, Ann, 487
MILLER, Jonathan, 484

MILNE, Alasdair, 511
MILNER, Ron, 488
MILOSEVIC, Slobodan, 133
MINAH, Francis, 261
MINIS, Dr Adultashiyn, 139
MIODOWICZ, Alfred, 119
MIRGHANI, Sayyid Muhammed Osman al-, 230
MITCHELL, Brian, 526
MITCHELL, John, obit., 590
MITCHELL, John, Prime Minister of St Vincent, 101–2
MITTERRAND, François, President of France, 112, 119, 122, 141–2, 145, 183, 196, 237, 598, 603–4, 614
MIYAZAWA, Kiichi, 356, 615
MKHATSHWA, Smangaliso, 439
MOBUTU SESE SEKO, President of Zaïre, 276, 277, 612
MOCK, Dr Alois, 177
MOHAMMED, Sheikh, 525
MOI, Daniel Arap, President of Kenya, 249, 250, 251, 602
MOLYNEAUX, James, 166
MOMOH, Joseph Saidu, President of Sierra Leone, 261
MONGOLIA, 138–40
MONK, Dr Marilyn, 445–6
MONTEIRO, Luis Otavio, 76
MOONEY, Sylvester, obit., 590
MOORE, Colleen, death, 491–2
MOORE, John, MP, 9, 13, 579
MOORE, Steven, 528
MOORHOUSE, Adrian, 517
MORGAN, General, 248
MORO, Aldo, 612
MOROCCO, 238, 242–4
MOROTE, Osman, 81
MORRIS, Mark, 482
MORRISON, Toni, 506
MOSCOW SUMMIT, 103, 111–12
MOSES, Ed, 517
MOSHOESHOE II, HM King, of Lesotho, 295
MOUSAVI, Mir Hussain, 305
MOZAMBIQUE, 252, 280–3; churches in, 282; foreign aid, 281–2; foreign relations, 282, 283; hydroelectric works, 283; movement from rigid marxism, 282; refugees leave, 289; war in, 280–2
MRAVINSKY, Yevgeny, death, 479; obit., 590
MSUYA, Cleopa, 251
MUBARAK, Husni, President of Egypt, 206–8, 221, 226, 599
MUGABE, Robert, President of Zimbabwe, 289, 290, 291, 406
MUHAMMAD, Ali Nasser, 221, 222
MUHAMMAD BIN ABDUL AZIZ, Prince, obit., 590–1
MULDER, Dr Connie, obit., 591

MÜLLER, Peter, 515
MULRONEY, Brian, Prime Minister of Canada, 68–9, 71–2, 455, 614
MUNAP, Abdul Hamid, 334
MUNGRA, Soebhas, 102
MUNTEANU, Petre, death, 475
MURDANI, General Benny, 336, 337
MURDOCH, Rupert, 494–5, 506
MURRAY, John, 165
MUSA HITAM, Datuk, 333
MUSEVENI, Yoweri, President of Uganda, 253, 254, 255
MUSGRAVE, Thea, 475
MUSIC (*see also* Opera), 475–9
MUZENDA, Simon, 289
MWINYI, Ali Hassan, President of Tanzania, 252

NABABSINGH, Prem, 325
NADARAJAH, S., 318
NAHAYYAN, Shaikh Zayad bin Sultan al-, 225
NAIR, Devan, 335
NAIR, Mira, 491
NAJIBULLAH, Mohammed, President of Afghanistan, 306, 311, 602
NAKAJIMA, Dr Hiroshi, 387
NAKASONE, Yasuhiro, 353, 354
NAMALIU, Rabbie, Prime Minister of Papua New Guinea, 365, 366
NAMIBIA, 1, 285, 286, 292–3, 383–4; tripartite agreement on, 292–3, 297, 578
NAMPHY, General Henri, 85, 421, 606, 610
NASIR, Ibrahim, 327
NATTA, Alessandro, 155
NAURU, 374
NAVARRA, Andre, death, 479
NAVRATILOVA, Martina, 522
NDIAYE, Babacar, 416
NE WIN, General, 328, 329, 608
NEIKRUG, Marc, 475, 477
NEIL, Andrew, 559
NELLIGAN, Kate, 488
NEMETH, Karoly, 607
NEMETH, Miklos, 614
NEPAL, 320–1
NETHERLANDS, 102, 159–61
NEUMANN, Rabbi Isaac, 116
NEW CALEDONIA, 1, 145, 146–7, 369, 371–2
NEW ZEALAND, 366–70; Antarctic minerals, 370; cyclone, 370; economy, 367, 368–9; Maoris, 369; political conflict, 367–8; privatization, 369; public and social policy, 368, 369; relations with: Australia, 360, 370, EEC, 370, France, 145, 369–70, Italy, 157, Japan, 354, Spain, 370
NEWLANDS, Peter, 528

NEWTON, Antony, MP, 579
NGUEMA, Macias, 274
NGUESSO, Denis Sassou, President of Congo, 274
NGUGI, John, 516
NGUYEN VAN LINH, 340, 341
NIANG, Babacar, 265
NICARAGUA, 66, 79, 88, 458
NICHOLAS, Alison, 521
NICHOLAS, Mike, 488
NICHOLSON, David, 525
NICKLAUS, Jack, 521
NIELSON, Denis, 481
NIGER, 270
NIGERIA, 257–60; economy, 258–9; foreign relations, 41, 261; preparations for return to civilian rule, 257–8; toxic wastes, 455
NIHILANI, Govind, 491
NKOMO, Joshua, 289
NOBEL PRIZES: economics, 533; literature, 208, 259; peace, 166, 177, 384–5; sciences, 448–9
NOBLE, Adrian, 483
NÓBREGA, Mailson Ferreira da, 75
NOGUCHI, Isamu, obit., 591
NON-ALIGNED MOVEMENT, 195, 404–6
NOORANI, Zain, 564, 566
NORDIC COUNCIL, 412–14
NORIEGA, General Manuel Antonio, Panamanian leader, 65, 88, 89, 420, 600, 601, 605
NORMAN, Geraldine, 497
NORMAN, Greg, 521
NORSTAD, General Lauris, obit., 591
NORTH, Lieut.-Col. Oliver, 58
NORTH ATLANTIC TREATY ORGANIZATION (Nato), 429–34, 560–2; Anglo-French cooperation, 431; burden sharing, 430; Denmark, 167; Franco-German cooperation, 431; short-range nuclear forces, 431–2; Spain, 180, 183–4; summit declaration (text), 560–2; Turkey, 196; West Germany, 151
NORTHCOTE, Anna, death, 482
NORTHERN IRELAND, see under United Kingdom
NORWAY, 170–1, 459
NOTT, Sir John, 8
NOVAK, Eva, death, 492
NUJOMA, Sam, 293
NUNN, Sam, 430
NUREYEV, Rudolf, 480
NWACHUKWU, Brigadier Ike, 260
NYERERE, Dr Julius, 252
NYERS, Rezsö, 124
NYKAENEN, Matti, 515

O GUK RYOL, General, 359
OBIMPEH, Commodore, 256
OBRESHKOV, Damyan, 130
OCCHETTO, Achille, 155
O'CONNOR, Justice, 472
ODINGA, Oginga, 250
ODINGA, Raila, 250
OFFIA, Martin, 520
OFORI-ATTA, William, obit., 591
OGI, Adolf, 179
OGUNKOYA, Michael, 259
O'HANA, Maurice, 475
OIL (see also Organization of Petroleum Exporting Countries), British Petroleum shares, 226, 230; joint Libya-Tunisian exploration, 232; Nigeria, 258; pipeline, 222; prices, 171, 218, 219, 305; revenue dispute, 337; Syria, 212
OKAMOTO, Ayako, 522
OKUM, Herbert, 376
OLAV V, HM King, of Norway, 603
OLAZABAL, José-Maria, 521
OLEKSIAK, Kazimierz, 119
OLMI, Ermanno, 491
OLYMPIC GAMES (see also Sport), 116, 152, 247, 354, 357, 359, 515–18
OMAN, 205, 222, 225–6, 228–9
ONASSIS, Christina, death, 193; obit., 591
O'NEILL, Sir Con, obit., 591
OPERA (see also Music), 473–5
ORGANIZATION FOR ECONOMIC CO-OPERATION AND DEVELOPMENT (OECD), 102, 397–400
ORGANIZATION OF AFRICAN UNITY (OAU), 237, 273, 279, 287, 414–16
ORGANIZATION OF AMERICAN STATES (OAS), 420–1
ORGANIZATION OF PETROLEUM EXPORTING COUNTRIES (Opec) (see also Oil), 83, 228–9
ORR, Robin, 475
ORSENNA, Erik, 507
ORTEGA SAAVEDRA, Daniel, President of Nicaragua, 66, 79, 88, 605
O'TOOLE, Peter, 490
OTTO, Kristin, 516
OUEDDEYE, Goukouni, 273
OUMAR, Acheikh Ibn, 233, 273
OUMAROU, Mamane, 270
OWEN, Dr David, MP, 26, 27
OWUSU, Colonel (rtd.) Osei, 256
ÖZAL, Turgut, Prime Minister of Turkey, 190, 191, 194–8, 599, 602, 606, 607
OZBEK, Rifat, 505

PAGANO, Mauro, death, 475
PAGE, Ashley, 480
PAKISTAN, 312–15; death of President Zia, 312–13, 597; economy, 315; elections, 313–14; foreign relations, 205, 306, 311, 315
PALESTINE LIBERATION ORGANIZATION (PLO), 42, 64–5, 203, 214, 237, 382–3,

458–9; declaration of independence (*text*), 567–9; intifada, 201, 203, 208–10, 568–70
PALESTINE NATIONAL COUNCIL (PNC), 204–5, 212, 567–70, 614
PALIN, Michael, 490
PALME, Olof, 172–3, 380
PÁLSSON, Thorsteinn, 169, 413
PANAMA, 65, 88–9
PANDAY, Basdeo, 95
PANEV, Ivan, 129
PAPANDREOU, Andreas, Prime Minister of Greece, 190–4, 196, 599, 606
PAPANDREOU, George, 192
PAPANDREOU, Margaret, 192
PAPUA NEW GUINEA, 337, 365–6
PARAGUAY, 80
PARIKIAN, Manoug, death, 479
PARKINSON, Cecil, MP, 33, 37, 579
PARR, Gladys, death, 475
PÄRT, Arvo, 476
PASKAI, H. E. Cardinal László, 436
PATON, Alan, death, 512; obit., 591
PAUL, Colonel Jean-Claude, 85
PAVAROTTI, Luciano, 476
PAWLEY, Howard, 71
PAWSON, John, 527
PAYE, Jean-Claude, 397–8
PAZ ESTENSSORO, Victor, President of Bolivia, 74
PEART, Lord, obit., 591
PECSI, Kalman, 402, 403
PEDERSEN, Niels Helveg, 168
PEDERZINI, Gianna, death, 475
PELLETREAU, Robert, 64
PELLI, Cesar, 502–3
PENDERECKI, Krzysztof, 474
PENNEY, Jennifer, 480
PERES, Shimon, 199, 201, 202, 204, 206
PÉREZ, Carlos Andrés, 83, 615
PÉREZ DE CUELLAR, Javier, UN Secretary-General, 23, 194, 243, 293, 375, 380, 383, 384
PERRIN, Sir Michael, obit., 591
PERU, 80–1, 82
PETERSON, Alec, obit., 592
PETERSON, David, 70
PETROVSKY, Vladimir, 383
PHAM HUNG, death, 341, 601, 606; obit., 592
PHILBY, H. A. R. (Kim), obit., 592
PHILIP, HRH Prince, Duke of Edinburgh, 603, 607
PHILIPPINES, 2, 67, 334, 338–9
PHILLIPS, Andre, 517
PICKARD, Tony, 522
PICKFORD, Errol, 479
PIDDINGTON, Kenneth, 456
PIENAAR, Louis, 292
PIERCE, Samuel R., Jr, 580
PIETALUGA, Joe, 187
PIMEN, Patriarch, 105, 435

PINDLING, Sir Lynden, Prime Minister of the Bahamas, 99, 422
PINOCHET UGARTE, General Augusto, President of Chile, 76–7, 612
PIPE, Martin, 525
PIZARELLO, Felix, 187
PLISETSKAYA, Maya, 479
PLJAKIC, Mustafa, 133
POCKLINGTON, Peter, 527
PODIER, Nicholas, 263
POINDEXTER, John, 58
POL POT, 341, 418
POLAND, 117–20; economy, 117, 118; foreign relations, 42, 112, 120; political developments, 118–20; Solidarity, 117, 118, 120; strikes, 117, 118; Walesa-Kiszczak talks, 118, 119; Walesa-Thatcher meeting, 42, 120
POLI, Afro, death, 475
POLLOCK, Jackson, 498
PONCE, Colonel René Emilio, 87
PONNELLE, Jean-Pierre, 474; obit., 592
PONS, Bernard, 146
PORTER, Dorothy, 512
PORTER, Roy, 512
PORTUGAL, 184–6; foreign relations, 280, 282, 283
POWELL, Colin, 580
POZDERAC, Hakija, 132
POZSGAY, Imre, 124
PRAWIRO, Radius, 336
PREBBLE, Richard, 367
PREM TINSULANONDA, General, 330, 331
PREMADASA, Ranasinghe, 320, 615
PRESCOTT, John, MP, 28, 29, 32
PRESSBURGER, Emeric, death, 492; obit., 592
PRESTHUS, Rolf, 170
PRESTWICH, Michael, 512
PREVEDI, Bruno, death, 475
PRICE, Nick, 521
PRIEUR, Dominique, 369, 604
PRODEV, Stefan, 130
PROETTA, Carmen, 188
PROFUMO, David, 508
PROST, Alain, 524, 525
PUTTNAM, David, 490
PYM, Lord, 20

QADAFI, Col. Muammar, Libyan leader, 207, 232–4, 236, 238, 241, 273, 415, 605, 610
QATAR, 225, 226, 228, 229
QIAN QICHEN, 348, 603
QIAO SHI, 321
QIN QWEI, 603
QUAINOO, Lieut.-Gen. Arnold, 256
QUAYLE, Dan, 51–2

RAB, Abdur A. S. M., 316
RABAH, Sadok, 236

INDEX

RABI, Dr Isidor, obit., 592
RABIN, Yitzhak, 199
RABUKA, Colonel Sitiveni, 372
RADIO, *see* Television and Radio
RAFALO, Dr Michael, 189
RAFINDADI, Ambassador, 259
RAFSANJANI, Hojatolislam Hashemi, 304, 305
RAHMAN, Mahbubur, 317
RAINES, Ella, death, 492
RAKOWSKI, Mieczyslaw, 118–19, 611, 613
RAMNATH, Kelvin, 95
RAMOS, General Fidel, 338
RAMPHAL, Shridath, 389
RAMSEY OF CANTERBURY, Lord, obit., 593
RANA, Shakoor, 523
RANSOME-KUTI, Prof., 260
RAO, N. T. Rama, 309
RAO, P. V. Narasimha, 308
RATSIRAKA, Didier, President of Madagascar, 326
RATTIGAN, Terence, 485
RATTLE, Simon, 478
RAU, Johannes, 150
RAUSCHENBERG, Robert, 497, 498
RAWLINGS, Flight-Lieut. Jerry, Head of State of Ghana, 256, 270
RAZALI HAMZAH, Tengku, 333
RAZUMOVSKY, Georgi, 129
REAGAN, Nancy, 61
REAGAN, Ronald, President of USA: arms control and USSR, 60–2, 111, 423, 425, 427–8, 605, 611; economy, 55–7, 535, 600; foreign affairs, 8, 63–7, 157, 176, 598, 599, 603, 607, 610, 614; home affairs, 48–9, 51, 59
REARDON, John, death, 475
REDGRAVE, Steven, 517
REDGRAVE, Vanessa, 486
REDONDO, Nicolás, 180, 181, 182
REES-MOGG, Lord, 37, 495
REGALA, General Williams, 85
REHFUS, Heinz, death, 475
REID, Dale, 521
REISCH, Georg, 412
REISE, Jay, 475
RELIGION, 435–41
  CHRISTIANITY: and other religions, 437; papal concerns, 80, 177, 282, 292, 295, 407, 436, 438–9, 600, 604, 606, 610; and politics, 437; Russian millennium, 435–6; women priests and bishops, 436–7;
  ISLAM, 440
  JUDAISM, 439–40
REMENGESAU, Thomas, 373, 609
RENÉ, France-Albert, President of Seychelles, 323
RENTOUL, John, 12

REVILLA, Emiliano, 182, 183
REY PRENDES, Adolfo, 87
RHYS WILLIAMS, Sir Brandon, MP, 9
RICH, Irene, death, 492
RICKS, Christopher, 509–10
RICO, Colonel Aldo, 72–3
RIDLEY, Nicholas, MP, 19, 20, 22, 25, 503, 579
RIFKIND, Malcolm, MP, 30, 43, 579
RINCHIN, Lodongiyn, 140
RISQUET, Jorge, 284
ROBERTS, Gwilym 444
ROBERTSON, Patsy, 390
ROBERTSON, Rev Pat, 49, 50
ROBINSON, Arthur Napoleon Raymond, Prime Minister of Trinidad and Tobago, 95, 96
ROBLES PLAZA, Luis, 79
ROBSON, Bobby, 518, 519
ROCARD, Michel, 142, 143–4, 147, 196, 372, 496, 604, 606, 607
RODIL PERALTA, Juan José, 86
RODRIGUEZ, Velasquez, 460
ROGERS, Richard, 504
ROGERS, Will, 63
ROGLIČEK, Rudolf, 400
ROH TAE WOO, President of South Korea, 354, 357, 358, 600, 615
ROLAND-BILLECART, Yves, 416
ROLFE, Christopher, 231
ROLÓN, Archbishop Ismael, 80
ROMANIA, 126–8, 135, 191, 504
ROONEY, Mickey, 487
ROSAS, Juan Manuel de, 73
ROSS OF MARNOCK, Lord, obit., 593
ROTHSCHILD, Baron Philippe, obit., 593
ROUIGHI, Mohamed, 239
ROZHDESTVENSKY, Gennady, 476
RUDA, José Maria 460
RUDINI, General, 336
RUFFILLI, Roberto, 603; death, 155
RUNCIE, Most Rev Dr Robert, Archbishop of Canterbury, 436
RUSH, Ian, 519
RUSHDIE, Salman, 440, 507
RUSSELL, John, 499
RÜST, Matthias, 608
RUZIMATOV, Faroukh, 479, 481
RWANDA, 277–8
RYAN, Father Patrick, 41, 165

SABAH, Shaikh Ali Khalifah as-, 226
SABAH, Shaikh Saad Abdullah al-Salem as-, 226
SABAH, Shaikh Subah al-Ahmed as-, 226
SABBATINI, Gabriela, 522
SACHS, Albie, 298
SADAT, Mohamed Anwar el-, 207
SADDAM HUSAIN, President of Iraq, 217
SADDAM HUSAIN, Uday, 217

INDEX

SAHNOUN, Shaikh, 240
SAIBOU, Colonel Ali, President of Niger, 270
ST JOHN OF FAWSLEY, Lord, 503
ST KITTS AND NEVIS, 100
ST LAURENT, Louis, 69
SAINT LAURENT, Yves, 505
ST LUCIA, 101
ST VINCENT AND THE GRENADINES, 101–2
SAITOTI, Prof. George, 250
SAKHAROV, Andrei, 605, 613
SAKS, Gene, 488
SALEH, Ali Abdullah, President of North Yemen, 220, 221, 607
SALEM, General Mamdouh, obit., 593
SALII, Lazarus, death, 373, 609
SALINAS, Abel, 81
SALINAS DE GORTARI, Carlos, President of Mexico, 89, 90, 607, 615
SALLAH ABAS, Tun Mohamad, 332
SALMOND, Alex, MP, 10
SALONGA, Jovito, 338
SALVATORE, Renato, death, 492
SAMARANCH, Juan Antonio, 516
SAMBWA PIDA, 277
SAMPSON, Colin, 164
SAN YU, 329
SANCHEZ, Laurie, 519
SANDIFORD, Erskine, Prime Minister of Barbados, 97, 421
SANKARA, Captain Thomas, 270
SANKARA, Mariam, 270
SANNEH, Musah, 262
SANSOM, Bruce, 480
SANYANG, Kukoi Samba, 262
SÃO TOMÉ AND PRÍNCIPE, 280
SAOUMA, Edouard, 388
SARAGAT, Giuseppe, obit., 593
SARDINIAS, Eligio, obit., 593
SARNEY, José, President of Brazil, 75, 455
SAUD, Muhammad, 220
SAUDI ARABIA, 218–20; arms trade, 424, 426–7; defence deals, 219; economy, 219–20, 227; foreign relations, 177, 197, 218–19, 221, 224, 229, 237; pilgrims to Mecca, 219, 304
SAUVÉ, Jeanne, 68
SAVAGE, Sean, 187
SAVANÉ, Landing, 265
SAVIMBI, Jonas, 284, 285
SAW MAUNG, General, 329, 611
SAYED, Bechir Mustapha, 238, 243
SCARGILL, Arthur, 31, 32
SCARMAN, Lord, 36
SCHENK, Otto, 474
SCHLÜTER, Poul, Prime Minister of Denmark, 166–7, 168, 413, 604
SCHMÄLING, Admiral Elmar, 151
SCHNITTKE, Alfred, 476
SCHORLEMMER, Friedrich, 436

SCHREKER, Franz, 473
SCHROEDER, Patricia, 430
SCHWARTZ, Dr Melvin, 449
SCIENCES, 442–57
SCORZA, Carlo, obit., 593
SCOTLAND, see under United Kingdom
SCOTT, Sheila, obit., 593–4
SCUDAMORE, Peter, 525
SCULTHORPE, Peter, 477
SCUPHAM, Peter, 509
SEAGA, Edward, Prime Minister of Jamaica, 92, 421
SECHIOTIS, Tassos, 192
SECORD, Richard, 58
SEEFRIED, Irmgard, death, 475; obit., 594
SEIN LWIN, General, 329
SELLARS, Peter, 474
SEMBENE, Ousmane, 491
SEMOGERERE, Paul, 254
SENEGAL, 264–6
SENNA, Ayrton, 524
SEONG, Patrick, 335
SEOW, Francis, 334, 335
SEPTEMBER, Dulcie, 298
SEQAT, Mohamed, 243
SERENGI, General Liber, 82
SEROTA, Nicholas, 500
SERRA, Narcís, 180
SEYCHELLES, 322–4
SEYMOUR, Lynn, 480
SHAGARI, Shehu, 259
SHAH, Bindeswari, 321
SHAH, Mahboob, 523
SHAH, Zahir, 307
SHAHER, Abdy, 528
SHAHRIR ABDUL SAMAD, Datuk, 333
SHAMIR, Yitzhak, Prime Minister of Israel, 64, 199–201, 204, 603, 613
SHAMUYARIRA, Nathan, 290
SHANKAR, Ramsewak, President of Suriname, 102, 598
SHANKARANAND, B., 308
SHANKLY, Bill, 516
SHARIF, Bassam Abu, 204, 205
SHARIF, Nawaz, 313
SHARON, Ariel, 199
SHAW, Robert, 477
SHEEHAN, Patty, 521
SHEPHERD, John, 59
SHERRIFF, R. C., 486
SHEVARDNADZE, Eduard, 61, 112, 307, 354, 432, 455, 565, 566, 603
SHRESTHA, Marich Man Singh, Prime Minister of Nepal, 321
SHULTZ, George, 60, 62, 64, 65, 79, 203, 204, 205, 209, 211, 376, 565, 566, 580, 600, 603
SIBLEY, Antoinette, 480
SIBOMANA, Adrien, 278
SICA, Dr Domenico, 156

SIDDHI SAVETSILA, 331
SIEGHART, Paul, obit., 594
SIERRA LEONE, 260–1
SIHANOUK, Prince Norodom, 341, 418
SILIVAS, Daniela, 517
SILKIN OF DULWICH, Lord, obit., 594
SILLARS, Jim, MP, 43–4
SILVA, Luis Inácio da, 75
SILVA TUESTA, General Victor Raúl, 81
SIMON, Dr Ernst, obit., 594
SIMON, Neil, 487
SIMON, Paul, 49, 50
SINDELAR, Joey, 521
SINGAPORE, 325, 333, 334–6
SINGH, Buka, 310
SINGH, Karpal, 333
SINGH, Dr Nagendra, death, 460; obit., 594
SINGH, Sohan, 440
SINGH, Vir Bahadur, 308
SINGH, V. P., 309, 606
SINOWATZ, Dr Fred, 177
SISAY, Sherif, 262
SITWELL, Sir Sacheverell, death, 512; obit., 594
SIYAD BARRE, General Maslah, 248
SIYAD BARRE, Mohammed, President of Somalia, 247, 248
SLANEY, Mary, 517
SLYNN, Sir Gordon, 463–4
SMITH, John, MP, 11, 18
SMITH, Timmy, 527
SMITHSON, Alison, 503
SMITHSON, Peter, 503
SOKOMANU, George, President of Vanuatu, 373, 616
SOLANKI, Madhavisan, 308
SOLCHAGA, Carlos, 181
SOLER, Michael, 189
SOLH, Taki Eddine, obit., 594
SOLIS PALMA, Manuel, 89
SOLOMON, death, 479; obit., 594
SOLOMON ISLANDS, 374
SOMALIA, 1, 246–7, 247–8
SOMARE, Michael, 365, 366
SOPE, Barak, 373
SOPHIA, HM Queen, of Spain, 184
SOUTH AFRICA, REPUBLIC OF, 3, 84, 297–301; ANC sabotage campaign, 298; arms trade, 424, 427; elections, 299, 300; Namibian independence agreements, 292–3, 297, 383–4, 577–8; relations with black African states, 277, 289, 290, 293, 295, 296, with UK 41; security/political trials, 299; tricameral constitutional system, 299–300; US sanctions 279; White Wolves, 300–1
SOUTH ASIAN ASSOCIATION FOR REGIONAL COOPERATION (SAARC), 312, 315, 321, 417–18
SOUTH PACIFIC, 371–4, 419–20
SOUTH-EAST ASIAN ORGANIZATIONS, 418–19
SOUTHWARK, Bishop of, 24
SOYINKA, Wole, 259
SPACE, 446–7, 453
SPAIN, 180–4; Basques, 5; defence: 180, 183–4, and Nato 180, 183–4, US bases 429–30; economy, 181–2; ETA terrorist activity, 182–3; new train system, 183; relations with: Belgium, 103, East Germany, 114, France, 183, India, 311, Italy, 183, Morocco and Western Sahara, 238, 243, Mozambique, 282, New Zealand, 370, Portugal, 186, Romania, 127, UK (Gibraltar question), 183–4, USA, 184, 429–30; strikes, 181–2
SPALDING, Frances, 510
SPARK, Muriel, 508
SPÄTH, Lothar, 149
SPENDER, Sir Stephen, 509
SPINKS, Michael, 526
SPORT (see also Olympic Games), 515–28; American scene, 526–7; association football, 518–19; boxing, 526; cricket, 523–4; golf, 520–2; motor racing, 524–5; rugby football, 519–20; tennis, 152, 522; turf, 525–6; weight-lifting, 198; world champions, 527–8
SPRINKEL, Beryl W., 580
SRI LANKA, 1, 2, 318–20; elections, 319–20; Indian troops in, 318, 319; JVP violence in, 319; Tamil violence in, 318–19
STALKER, John, 164
STASSINOPOULOS HUFFINGTON, Arianna, 511
STASZAK, General Czeslaw, 118
STEEL, David, MP, 26
STEIN, Peter, 474
STEINBERGER, Dr Jack, 449
STEINITZ, Paul, death, 479
ŠTĚPHÁN, Miroslav, 121
STEPHEN, Sir Ninian, 362
STEPTOE, Dr Patrick, obit., 594–5
STEVENS, Dr Siaka, death, 261; obit., 595
STEVENS, Tim, 528
STICH, Otto, 179
STOCKHAUSEN, Karl-Heinz, 475, 477
STONE, Carl, 92
STONEHOUSE, John, obit., 595
STOYANOV, Dimitar, 129
STRANGE, Curtis, 521
STRATOU, Dora, death, 482
STRAUB, Bruno Ferenc, 607
STRAUSS, Franz Josef, death, 148; obit., 595
STRICKLAND, Hon. Mabel, obit., 595
STROESSNER, General Alfredo, President of Paraguay, 80, 600
STROLZ, Hubert, 515
ŠTROUGAL, Lubomír, 121, 403, 612

SUÁREZ GÓMEZ, Roberto, 74
SUBTROTO, Dr, 606
SUDAMA, Trevor, 95
SUDAN, 207, 230–2, 251, 255, 273
SUDHARMONO, Lieut.-General, 336
SUDOMO, Admiral, 337
SUGAR, Alan, 495
SUHARTO, General T. N. J., President of Indonesia, 336, 601
SÜLEYMANOGLU, Naim, 198, 516
SUNUNU, John, 53
SURINAME, 101, 102
SÜSSMUTH, Rita, 148
SUTRISNO, General Try, 336–7
SWAGGART, Rev Jimmy, 439
SWAZILAND, 296
SWEDEN, 127, 172–4, 282, 457
SWITZERLAND, 178–80, 473–4, 499
SYCHEV, Vyacheslav, 400
SYDOW, Max von, 484
SYMINGTON, Stuart, obit., 595
SYRIA, 211–13; arms trade, 425; foreign relations, 204–6, 211–12, 217, 304, 311; intervention in Lebanon, 211–12, 213–15; oil, 212
SYSE, Jan P. 170
SZERYNG, Henryk, death, 479; obit., 595

TAIB, Abdul Rahman, 334
TAIF, Ammar al-, 234
TAIWAN, 344, 348, 349–51, 425
TAKESHITA, Noboru, Prime Minister of Japan, 348, 353–6, 598, 604, 609
TALABANI, Jallal, 212
TALYZIN, Nikolai, 108
TANZANIA, 251–3, 282, 325
TAYA, Col. Moaouia Ould Sidi, Head of State of Mauritania, 267
TAYLOR, Paul, 482
TEBBIT, Norman, MP, 9, 12, 511
TECHNOLOGY, 449–53
TEKERE, Edgar, 291
TELEVISION AND RADIO, 492–7
TEMBO, General Christon, 288
TERENTYEV, Igor, 481
TERRORIST ATTACKS: bus hijack in Lesotho, 295; Chinese hijack, 351; ETA, 182–3; Greece, 191–2; hijack of Kuwaiti airliner, 242, 304; India, 309–10; Italy, 155–6; Lockerbie air disaster, 38, 233; Middle East, 205, 215, 220, 226–7
TERRY, Quinlan, 502
THAILAND, 330–1, 342, 343
THAMRONG NAVASAWAT, Luang, obit., 595–6
THANI, Shaikh Khalifah bin Hamad al-, 225
THATCHER, Margaret, MP, Prime Minister of United Kingdom; and defence, 431, 601; European Community, 39–41, 391, 461, 611; foreign affairs, 37, 39–41, 62, 66, 120, 157, 164–5, 183–4, 196, 206, 209, 251, 259, 333, 373, 437, 602, 605, 608, 613, 614; home affairs, 8–9, 12–21, 23–4, 27, 33–5, 454, 492, 496, 539, 579, 598
THEATRE, 482–8
THEOTOKIS, Spyros, obit., 596
THERESA, Mother, of Calcutta, 301
THIREAUT, Commander, 372
THOMAS, Isaiah, 526
THOMAS, Jeremy, 489, 490
THOMAS, Michael Tilson, 478
THOMAS, Prof. Clive, 94
THOMPSON, Curl, 97
THOMPSON, Daley, 517
THOMPSON, Lieut.-Colonel, 256
THOMSON, Lord, 494
THORBURN, Paul, 519
THORNBURGH, Richard, 59, 580
THORSTENSDOTTIR, Sigrun, 169
THWAITE, Anthony, 509
THYSSEN, Baroness, 498
TINBERGEN, Prof. Nikolaas, obit., 596
TIPPETT, Sir Michael, 473, 474
TITOV, Vladimir, 446
TJIBAOU, Jean-Marie, 372
TODD, Mark, 517
TODD, Ron, 32, 33
TODOROV, Stanko, 129
TOGO, 271
TOMASEK, Cardinal Frantisek, 436
TOMBA, Alberto, 515
TONYPANDY, Viscount, 20
TOOLEY, Sir John, 473
TOWER, Joan, 476
TRAORÉ, Moussa, President of Mali, 605
TRENCH, Sir David, obit., 596
TREVIS, Di, 483
TRINIDAD AND TOBAGO, 95–6
TRUDEAU, Pierre, 68, 69, 71
TRUONG CHINH, obit., 596
TSEDENBAL, Yumjaagiyn, 138, 139
TSHISEKEDI WA MALUMBA, 276
TUBBS, Tony, 526
TUBMAN, William, 263
TUNISIA, 232, 235–7, 243; foreign relations, 236–7, 241
TURABI, Dr Hasan al-, 231
TURKEY, 195–8; Bosphorus bridge, 198; Cyprus problem, 197; economy, 198; European Community, membership application, 196; foreign relations, 130, 179, 196–7, 198, 205, 311; human rights, 198; Kurds, 197–8; role in Middle East, 197–8
TURNAGE, Mark-Anthony, 475
TURNER, John, 69, 70
TURNER, Sherrl, 521
TUTIN, Dorothy, 485
TUTU, Most Rev Desmond, Archbishop of Cape Town, 300, 439, 600
TYSON, Mike, 526

INDEX

U SEIN LWIN, 608, 609
UGANDA, 253–5
UHRY, Alfred, 487
ULANHU, 345, obit., 596
UNION OF SOVIET SOCIALIST REPUBLICS (USSR), 103–14
DEFENCE AND FOREIGN AFFAIRS (*see also* Arms Control; Moscow Summit; Warsaw Pact); Afghanistan, withdrawal of forces, 60–1, 112, 306–7, 315, 378–80, 563–7; arms trade, 426; conventional forces in Europe, 1, 62, 113; Gorbachev addresses United Nations, 103, 112–13, 571–6; relations with: Africa, 243, 247, 248, 282, China, 348, Cuba, 84, East European bloc, 112, 115, 120, 122, 128, 135, 140, Finland, 175, India, 112, 311, Japan, 354–5, Middle East, 205, 211, 218, 219, 222, 225, USA, 60–2, 103, 111, 112, Vietnam, 340, Western Europe, 42, 112, 145, 157, 177–8, 197; and United Nations 378, 379–80, 573–4
HOME AFFAIRS: 19th Party conference, 103, 104–6; Armenia-Azerbaijan conflict, 1, 5, 109–10; Armenian earthquake, 109 (*map*), 113; Baltic states, unrest, 2, 110–11; Christian millennium, 105, 435–6; constitution reforms, 107, 111; corruption, 113–14; economy, 107–9; electoral law, 106–7; *perestroika*, 104–6, 574–5
UNITED ARAB EMIRATES, 224–5, 226, 227, 228, 229
UNITED KINGDOM, 8–47
ARTS AND ENTERTAINMENT: 473–5, 477–87, 489–90, 492–6, 497–512
CRIME AND VIOLENCE: 22–3; political violence, 45–6
DEFENCE AND SECURITY: arms trade, 426–7; Falkland Islands, 73; General Communications Headquarters (GCHQ), 36–7; Gibraltar shootings affair, 46, 187–8, 496; Official Secrets legislation, 36, 465–6; *Spycatcher* affair, 36, 465, 555–560
DISASTERS: 37, 38
ECONOMY: Budget, 10–12; consumer credit, 11–12, 14, 17; costs and prices, 537–8; exchange rate, 14–15, 18–19; external trade, 538; growth, 16–18, 536; house price boom, 14, 17; income distribution 12; industry, 17; inflation, 17; infrastructure, 17; monetary policy, 14–16, 18, 538–9; output and employment, 537; privatization, 37–8, 457; taxation, 10–11, 12, 19–20, 44; trade balance, 16, 17; unemployment, 14, 16–18
ENVIRONMENT: 34, 37
FOREIGN AND COMMONWEALTH AFFAIRS: aid for Mozambique, 282; Commonwealth, 41, 389; European Community, 31–2, 39–41, 391, 392, 395; Gibraltar, 183–4, 187–8; Hong Kong, 351–2; relations with: Algeria, 242, Argentina, 73, Australia, 41, 360, Belgium, 41, Botswana, 293, 294, Denmark, 167, Dominica, 101, Fiji, 373, Iran, 42, Israel, 42, Italy, 157, Jamaica, 93, Japan, 353, 356, Jordan, 209, Kenya, 251, Malaysia, 333, Malta, 189, Middle and Far East, 41–2, Nigeria, 41, 259–60, Palestine, 205, 206, Poland, 42, 120, Republic of Ireland, 41, Romania, 127, Saudi Arabia, 219, Spain, 183–4, Trinidad and Tobago 96, Turkey, 196, Uganda, 255, USA, 62, 66, USSR, 42; South Africa and sanctions, 41
GOVERNMENT AND POLITICS: Cabinet lists, 579, moral issues, 23–4, parliamentary by-elections, 35–6, 43–4
LAW AND LEGISLATION: 19–20, 24–5, 36, 37–8, 465–70
NORTHERN IRELAND: 5, 45–7; economy, 46, 47; educational system, 46; European Convention of Human Rights, 47; extradition from Republic of Ireland, 46; political violence, 45–6; 'shoot-to-kill' policy, 46
POLITICAL PARTIES: Conservative Party, conference, 33–4; in Scotland, 42–3; Labour Party, defence of NHS, 9, defence policy, 29, 32, leadership contest, 28, 32–3, policy review, 28–9, in Scotland, 35, 43–4, Shadow Cabinet, 18; Scottish National Party, 35, 43–4; Social Democratic Party, 27; Social and Liberal Democratic Party (SLDP), formed from alliance parties, 26, leadership election, 26–7
PRESS AND BROADCASTING MEDIA: 12, 27, 492–7
SCOTLAND: by-election, 43–4; community charge, 44; devolution and Conservative unpopularity, 42–3; economy, 43; Elders' take-over bid, 44; Scottish National Party, 35, 43–4
SOCIAL POLICY: control of local government spending, 25, 466; education, 24–5; egg controversy, 38; family law, 469; Green Belt deregulation, 22; housing, 466–7; National Health Service, 9–10, 12–14, 21, 34; sex and race discrimination, 468; social security system, 9, 21, 34–5; student loans, 36
TRADE UNIONS: banned at GCHQ, 36–7; conference, 31–3; decline in membership, 31; inter-union dispute, 29–31; single union deals, 30, 31
WALES: arson campaign, 44–5; devolution, 45; economy, 22, 45; language, 44–5
UNITED NATIONS, 375–88; and Afghanistan, 112, 306, 378–80, 566–7;

Cyprus, 383; Development Programme, 323, 399; disarmament, 62, 377–8; economic and social matters, 385–6; founding principle, 4, 6–7; General Assembly, 73, 205; Gulf War, 1, 216, 217, 223, 380–1; human rights, 84, 351, 386, 460; Middle East, 203–5, 214, 381–2, 382–3; Namibia, 285, 292–3, 297, 383–4, 577–8; Nobel Peace Prize, 384–5; Paraguay, 80, PLO, 375–7, 458–9; refugees in Yemen, 221; report on Kampuchea, 342; trusteeship, 386; US contribution paid, 67; Western Sahara, 237–8, 243, 383

AGENCIES AND OTHER BODIES (*see also* International Court of Justice; International Monetary Fund; World Bank): Disengagement Observer Force (UNDOF), 382; Economic Commission for Africa, 416–17; Environment Programme, 455, 456; Food and Agriculture Organization (FAO), 387–8; Fund for Drug Abuse, 343; Good Offices Commission in Afghanistan and Pakistan (UNGOMAP), 379; High Commissioner for Refugees (UNHCR), 318; High Commission on Human Rights (UNHCHR), 84, 351; Interim Forces in Lebanon (UNIFIL), 382; Iran-Iraq Military Observer Group (UNIIMOG), 224, 380; Military Observer Group in the Gulf, 304; Peacekeeping Forces, 177, 384–5; Transition Assistance Group (UNTAG), 384; Truce Supervision Organization (UNTSO), 382; World Health Organization (WHO), 387, 456

UNITED STATES OF AMERICA (USA), 48–67

ARTS AND ENTERTAINMENT: 473–6, 479, 487–9, 496, 499, 508, 510

DEFENCE: arms trade, 426; military bases, 67, 324, 429–30; SDI, 429; space programme, 59–60, 446–7; technology exports, 425–6

ECONOMIC AFFAIRS: Budget, 55–6; Dow Jones index, 55–6; electoral formula, 53–4; exchange rate, 55; external trade, 227, 462, 535–6; growth, 56; inflation, 56; monetary and fiscal factors, 534–5; omnibus Trade Bill, 56–7; output and employment, 534; trade deficit, 55, 56; unemployment, 56

ELECTIONS: candidates, 49; Democratic convention, 50–1; presidential elections, 48, 53; primaries, 49–50; Republican campaign, 51–2; television debates, 52

FOREIGN AFFAIRS: dependencies, 374; foreign aid: Mozambique, 282, Zaïre, 276–7; Gulf War, 62–3, 216, 217, 303–4; mediation in Angola, 293; relations with: Algeria, 242, Australia, 360, Bahamas, 99, Bolivia, 74, Botswana, 293, Canada, 68, 70, China, 348, Costa Rica, 88, Cuba, 84, Denmark, 167, Dominica, 101, Ecuador, 79, EEC, 66–7, Egypt, 207, El Salvador, 87, Ethiopia, 247, Finland, 176, Greece, 67, Haiti, 85, Honduras, 66, 87, Iran, 62–3, Israel, 63–4, 425, Italy, 157, Japan, 353, Jordan, 64, 208–9, Laos, 343, Libya, 233–4, Mauritius, 324, 325, Mexico, 91, Morocco, 244, Nicaragua, 66, 88, Panama, 65, 88–9, Philippines, 67, 339, PLO, 64–5, 458–9, Romania, 127, São Tomé and Príncipe, 280, Singapore, 335, South Africa, 279, South Korea, 358, Spain, 184, Syria, 211, Tunisia, 237, Turkey, 196, UK, 62, 66, United Nations, 67, 375–7, Uruguay, 82, USSR, 60–2, Vietnam, 340

HOME AFFAIRS: Administration appointments, 53; Cabinet list, 580; civil rights, 6, 57, 58; climate, 48–9; corruption investigation, 58–9; elections, *see above*; Iran-Contra affair, 58–9; legislation, 470–2; medical developments 445; war against drug abuse, 57–8; welfare reform, 57

UNO, Sosuko, 354
UNWIN, Peter, 390
UPADHYA, S. K., 321
UPDIKE, John, 508
URQUHART, Sir Brian, 385
URUGUAY, 82

VACCA, Jorge, 526
VĂDUVA, Ilie, 127
VAILE, Bryn, 517
VAN BASTEN, Marco, 518
VAN DEN BROEK, Hans, 160
VAN DER MERWE, Stoffel, 293
VAN-DÚNEM (MBINDA), Afonso, 577, 578
VAN EEKELEN, Wim, 160
VAN EYCK, Aldo, 502
VAN GENNIP, Yvonne, 515
VANUATU, 373
VANUNU, Mordechai, 602
VASSILIOU, Georgios, President of Cyprus, 193–5, 197, 600
VÄYRYNEN, Paavo, 174
VENEZUELA, 77, 79, 82–3
VERITY, C. William, Jr, 580
VERSTER, Victor, 300
VIETNAM, 331, 339–4, 341, 343, 348
VILLANUEVA DEL CAMPO, Armando, 81
VLACHOS, Helen, 192
VLADIMIR, Metropolitan, 436
VLASI, Azem, 133
VOGEL, Bernhard, 148
VOGEL, Hans-Jochen, 150
VOLK, H. E. Cardinal, obit., 596
VORONTSOV, Yuri, 307
VRANITZKY, Dr Franz, Chancellor of Austria, 122, 176, 177

WADE, Abdoulaye, 262, 264–5, 600
WADE, Sir William, 20
WAGONER, Dan, 480
WAIN, John, 508
WAKEHAM, John, MP, 579, 598
WAKIL, Idris Abdul, 252, 253, 564, 566
WALDHEIM, Kurt, President of Austria, 176, 177, 599
WALES, *see under* United Kingdom
WALESA, Lech, 42, 117–18, 119, 120, 610, 613
WALKER, Colleen, 522
WALKER, Peter, MP, 18, 22, 45, 579
WALLACH, Eli, 488
WALLER, Fats, 488
WALSH, Lawrence, 58
WALSH, Thomas, death, 475
WALTER, Jessica, 488
WALTERS, Sir Alan, 15–16
WALTERS, General Vernon, 383, 580
WANG BINGQIAN, 346
WANG ZHEN, 345
WANKEL, Felix, obit., 596
WARDHANA, Ali, 336
WARHOL, Andy, 497, 498
WARIOBA, Joseph, Prime Minister of Tanzania, 252
WARNER, Marina, 507
WARREN, Kim, MP, 22
WARSAW PACT (*see also* Arms Control), 432–4
WASHINGTON, Denzel, 488
WASIR, Khalil, *see* Abu Jihad
WATSON, John, 524
WATT, Sir Alan, obit., 596
WEBB, James, 600
WEBSTER, William H., 580
WEINBERGER, Caspar, 599
WEIZSÄCKER, Richard von, President of West Germany, 260
WELCH, Racquel, 471
WELD, William, 59
WELLER, Michael, 488
WELLES, Orson, 497
WENDERS, Wim, 490
WERTENBAKER, Timberlake, 485
WESTERN EUROPEAN UNION (WEU), 183, 186, 409–10, 432
WESTERN SAHARA, 1, 237–9, 242–3, 383
WESTERN SAMOA, 374
WHELAN, Ronnie, 518
WHITELAW, Viscount, 8–9, 20, 37, 598
WHITEMORE, Hugh, 486
WIJEWEERA, Rohan, 319
WILANDER, Mats, 522
WILCZEK, Mieczyslaw, 119
WILLEBRANDS, H. E. Cardinal, 435
WILLIAMS, Alan, MP, 45
WILLIAMS, Clifford, 484
WILLIAMS, Doug, 527
WILLIAMS, Heathcote, 509
WILLIAMS, Kenneth, death, 492
WILLIAMS, Raymond, death, 512; obit., 596
WILLIAMS, Tennessee, 486
WILLIS, Norman, 30
WILSON, A. N., 510
WILSON, Lois, death, 492
WILSON, Michael, 71–2
WINDLESHAM, Lord, 496
WINGTI, Paias, 365, 366
WINTER, Dr Greg, 445
WITT, Katerina, 515
WOLFE, Tom, 508
WOLLENBERGER, Vera, 436
WOLSKA, Hélène, death, 482
WONG KANG SEN, 335
WOODWARD, Bob, 101
WOOSNAM, Ian, 521
WOOTON OF ABINGER, Baroness, obit., 596–7
WORLD BANK (IBRD), 17, 76, 96, 102, 207, 246, 258, 266, 272, 274, 287, 326, 339, 387, 399, 456
WÖRNER, General Manfred, 148, 507
WORRAL, Dr Dennis, 299
WORTHY, James, 526
WRIGHT, Joseph R., Jr, 580
WRIGHT, Kit, 509
WRIGHT, Nicholas, 485
WRIGHT, Peter (ex-MI5), 555–60, 605, 612
WRIGHT, Peter (ballet director), 480

YAKOVLEV, Aleksandr, 122
YANG SHANGKUN, President of People's Republic of China, 345, 602
YELTSIN, Boris, 106
YEMEN, PEOPLE'S DEMOCRATIC REPUBLIC OF (South Yemen), 222–3, 226
YEMEN ARAB REPUBLIC (North Yemen), 220–1
YEUTTER, Clayton, 67, 580
YONDON, Daramyn, 140
YORK, Duke and Duchess of, 360
YOUNG OF GRAFFHAM, Lord, 33, 579
YOUNGER, George, MP, 579
YU KUO-HUA, 351
YUGOSLAVIA, 1, 131–5; economy, 131–2; ethnic unrest, 133, 135; foreign relations, 112, 135–6, 311

ZAÏRE, 276–7
ZAMBIA, 277, 287–8
ZANE, Arnie, death, 482
ZEFFIRELLI, Franco, 476
ZHAO XIYANG, General Secretary of Chinese CP, 344
ZHIVKOV, Todor, Head of State of Bulgaria, 129

ZIA-UL-HAQ, General Mohammad, 312–314, 417, 605, 609; obit., 597
ZIMBABWE, 282, 289–92, 325; corruption, 290–1; economy, 291–2
ZIMMERMAN, Bernd-Alois, 475
ZMERLI, Saadadine, 236
ZURBRIGGEN, Pirmin, 515
ZWEIG, Dr Ferdynand, obit., 597

REF D 2 .A7 1988